Carnage and Culture

Also by Victor Davis Hanson

Victor Davis Hanson

Carnage and Culture

Landmark Battles in the Rise of Western Power

DOUBLEDAY

New York   London   Toronto

Sydney   Auckland

PUBLISHED BY DOUBLEDAY
a division of Random House, Inc.
1540 Broadway, New York, New York 10036

DOUBLEDAY and the portrayal of an anchor with a dolphin are
trademarks of Doubleday, a division of Random House, Inc.

Library of Congress Cataloging-in-Publication Data

Hanson, Victor Davis.
Carnage and culture: landmark battles in the rise of Western power
Victor Davis Hanson.—1st ed.
p. cm.
Includes bibliographical references and index.
Contents: Salamis, Sept. 28, 480 B.C.—Gaugamela, Oct. 1, 331 B.C.—Cannae, Aug. 2,
216 B.C.—Poitiers, Oct. 11, 732—Tenochtitlán, June 24, 1520–Aug. 13, 1521—
Lepanto, Oct. 7, 1571—Rorke's Drift, Jan. 22–23, 1879—Midway, June 4–8, 1942—
Tet, Jan. 31–Apr. 6, 1968—Western warfare: past and future.
1. Battles. 2. History, Military. I. Title.
D25.5 .H25 2001
904'.7—dc21
00-065582

Book design by Paul Randall Mize
Maps by Jeffrey L. Ward after maps by M. C. Drake

ISBN 0-385-50052-1

1   3   5   7   9   10   8   6   4   2

For Donald Kagan and Steven Ozment

Contents

Picture Credits for Insert

List of Maps

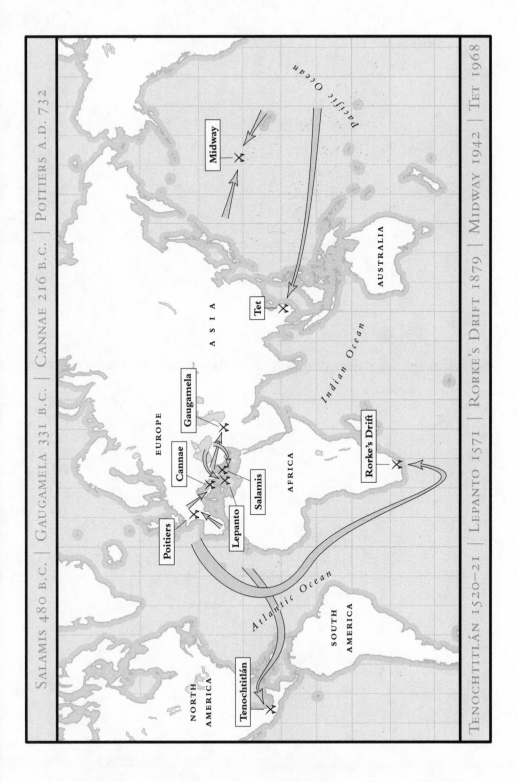

NORTH
AMERICA

Tenochtitlán

SOUTH
AMERICA

Atlantic Ocean

EUROPE

Cannae

Poitiers

Lepanto

Salamis

Gaugamela

A S I A

AFRICA

Rorke's Drift

Indian Ocean

Tet

AUSTRALIA

Pacific Ocean

Midway

Preface

THROUGHOUT THIS BOOK I use the term "Western" to refer to the culture of classical antiquity that arose in Greece and Rome; survived the collapse of the Roman Empire; spread to western and northern Europe; then during the great periods of exploration and colonization of the fifteenth through nineteenth centuries expanded to the Americas, Australia, and areas of Asia and Africa; and now exercises global political, economic, cultural, and military power far greater than the size of its territory or population might otherwise suggest. While the chapter titles reflect key elements of this common Western cultural tradition, they should not imply that all European states always shared exactly the same values, or that these core institutions and practices were unchanging over some 2,500 years of history. While I grant that critics would disagree on a variety of fronts over the reasons for European military dynamism and the nature of Western civilization itself, I have no interest in entering such contemporary cultural debates, since my interests are in the military power, not the morality, of the West.

Consequently, I have deliberately concentrated on those West-East fault lines that emphasize the singular lethality of Western culture at war in comparison to other traditions that grew up in Asia, Africa, and the Americas. These valid generalizations should not imply that at times there were not real differences among particular European states themselves or that Western and non-Western cultures were either monolithic or always at odds with each other. And while I discuss larger issues of government, religion, and economy, my primary aim is to explain Western military power, not the general nature and evolution of Western civilization at large.

This is not a book, then, written for academic specialists. Instead, I have tried to offer a synthesis of Western society at war for the general reader across some 2,500 years of history that concentrates on general trends, rather than an original work of primary research within a defined historical period. I have used formal scholarly citations in parentheses in the text only for the longer direct quotations—although detailed information concerning factual material is derived from primary sources and secondary books and articles discussed at the conclusion of the book.

I have many to thank. Sabina Robinson and Karin Lee of CSU Fresno's Honors Program were effective proofreaders. Katherine Becker, a doctoral student in Ohio State University's military history program, helped with editing and bibliographical duties. Once more my colleague in classics at CSU Fresno, Professor Bruce Thornton, read the entire manuscript and saved me from numerous errors. Dr. Luis Costa, dean of the School of Arts and Humanities at CSU Fresno, provided a timely research grant that allowed me to visit a number of libraries and to see the manuscript through final submission. I owe him once more a debt of gratitude.

I have also learned a great deal about Western warfare from the works of Geoffrey Parker, John Keegan, and Barry Strauss, and from conversations and correspondence with Josiah Bunting III, Allan Millett, Geoffrey Parker, John Lynn, and Robert Cowley. I wish to thank Charles Garrigus, Donald Kagan, John Heath, Steven Ozment, and Bruce Thornton for their continued friendship. Donald Kagan and Steven Ozment have taught me much about Western civilization in the past decade; both have served as model custodians of our cultural heritage in often scary and depressing times. Correspondence with Rita Atwood, Nick Germanicos, Debbie Kazazis, Michelle McKenna, and Rebecca Sinos was of great help during the writing of the manuscript.

Ms. M. C. Drake, professor of theater arts and design at CSU Fresno, drew the original version of the maps. I owe her a great deal of thanks. My literary agents, Glen Hartley and Lynn Chu, have been friends for more than a decade and have given me advice and support that I could not have found elsewhere. They have been my lifeline from a rather isolated farm south of Fresno to the complex and often baffling world of New York. By the same token, I owe my editor at Doubleday, Adam Bellow, appreciation, for the present book and for others in the past.

My wife, Cara, proofread the final typeset manuscript; once more I thank her for her continual support—and for the maintenance of sanity in a household of three teenagers, six dogs, seven cats, a bird, one rabbit, a creaking 120-year-old farmhouse, and sixty acres of money-losing trees and vines. My three children, Susannah, William, and Pauline, once more took up many of my responsibilities on our farm and in our household that helped to allow me to finish this book.

V.D.H.
Selma, California
September 2000

Carnage and Culture

ONE

Why the West Has Won

When the trumpet sounded, the soldiers took up their arms and went out. As they charged faster and faster, they gave a loud cry, and on their own broke into a run toward the camp. But a great fear took hold of the barbarian hosts; the Cilician queen fled outright in her carriage, and those in the market threw down their wares and also took to flight. At that point, the Greeks in great laughter approached the camp. And the Cilician queen was filled with admiration at the brilliant spectacle and order of the phalanx; and Cyrus was delighted to see the abject terror of the barbarians when they saw the Greeks.

—XENOPHON, *Anabasis* (1.2.16–18)

ENLIGHTENED THUGS

EVEN THE PLIGHT of enterprising killers can tell us something. In the summer of 401 B.C., 10,700 Greek hoplite soldiers—infantrymen heavily armed with spear, shield, and body armor—were hired by Cyrus the Younger to help press his claim to the Persian throne. The recruits were in large part battle-hardened veterans of the prior twenty-seven-year Peloponnesian War (431–404 B.C.). As mercenaries, they were mustered from throughout the Greek-speaking world. Many were murderous renegades and exiles. Both near adolescents and the still hale in late middle age enlisted for pay. Large numbers were unemployed and desperate at any cost for lucrative work as killers in the exhausted aftermath of the internecine war that had nearly ruined the Greek world. Yet there were also a few privileged students of philosophy and oratory in the ranks, who would march into Asia side by side these destitute mercenaries—aristocrats like Xenophon, student of Socrates, and Proxenus, the Boeotian general, as well as physicians, professional officers, would-be colonists, and wealthy Greek friends of Prince Cyrus.

After a successful eastward march of more than 1,500 miles that scattered all opposition, the Greeks smashed through the royal Persian line at the battle of Cunaxa, north of Babylon. The price for destroying an entire wing of the Persian army was a single Greek hoplite wounded by an arrow. The victory of the Ten Thousand in the climactic showdown for the Persian throne, however, was wasted when their employer, Cyrus, rashly pursued his brother, Artaxerxes, across the battle line and was cut down by the Persian imperial guard.

Suddenly confronted by a host of enemies and hostile former allies, stranded far from home without money, guides, provisions, or the would-be king, and without ample cavalry or missile troops, the orphaned Greek expeditionary infantrymen nevertheless voted not to surrender to the Persian monarchy. Instead, they prepared to fight their way back to the Greek world. That brutal trek northward through Asia to the shores of the Black Sea forms the centerpiece of Xenophon's *Anabasis* ("The March Up-Country"), the author himself one of the leaders of the retreating Ten Thousand.

Though surrounded by thousands of enemies, their original generals captured and beheaded, forced to traverse through the contested lands of more than twenty different peoples, caught in snowdrifts, high mountain passes, and waterless steppes, suffering frostbite, malnutrition, and frequent sickness, as well as fighting various savage tribesmen, the Greeks reached the safety of the Black Sea largely intact—less than a year and a half after leaving home. They had routed every hostile Asian force in their way. Five out of six made it out alive, the majority of the dead lost not in battle, but in the high snows of Armenia.

During their ordeal, the Ten Thousand were dumbfounded by the Taochians, whose women and children jumped off the high cliffs of their village in a ritual mass suicide. They found the barbaric white-skinned Mossynoecians, who engaged in sexual intercourse openly in public, equally baffling. The Chalybians traveled with the heads of their slain opponents. Even the royal army of Persia appeared strange; its pursuing infantry, sometimes whipped on by their officers, fled at the first onslaught of the Greek phalanx. What ultimately strikes the reader of the *Anabasis* is not merely the courage, skill, and brutality of the Greek army—which after all had no business in Asia other than killing and money—but the vast cultural divide between the Ten Thousand and the brave tribes they fought.

Where else in the Mediterranean would philosophers and students of rhetoric march in file alongside cutthroats to crash headlong into enemy flesh? Where else would every man under arms feel equal to anyone else in the army—or at least see himself as free and in control of his own destiny? What other army of the ancient world elected its own leaders? And how could such a small force by elected committee navigate its way thousands of miles home amid thousands of hostile enemies?

Once the Ten Thousand, as much a "marching democracy" as a hired army, left the battlefield of Cunaxa, the soldiers routinely held assemblies in which they voted on the proposals of their elected leaders. In times of crises, they formed ad hoc boards to ensure that there were sufficient archers, cavalry, and medical corpsmen. When faced with a variety of unexpected challenges both natural and human—impassable rivers, a dearth of food, and unfamiliar tribal enemies—councils were held to debate and discuss new tactics, craft new weapons, and adopt modifications in organization. The elected generals marched and fought alongside their men—and were careful to provide a fiscal account of their expenditures.

The soldiers in the ranks sought face-to-face shock battle with their enemies. All accepted the need for strict discipline and fought shoulder-to-shoulder whenever practicable. Despite their own critical shortage of mounted troops, they nevertheless felt only disdain for the cavalry of the Great King. "No one ever died in battle from the bite or kick of a horse," Xenophon reminded his beleaguered foot soldiers (*Anabasis* 3.2.19). Upon reaching the coast of the Black Sea, the Ten Thousand conducted judicial inquiries and audits of its leadership's performance during the past year, while disgruntled individuals freely voted to split apart and make their own way back home. A lowly Arcadian shepherd had the same vote as the aristocratic Xenophon, student of Socrates, soon-to-be author of treatises ranging from moral philosophy to the income potential of ancient Athens.

To envision the equivalent of a Persian Ten Thousand is impossible. Imagine the likelihood of the Persian king's elite force of heavy infantry—the so-called Immortals, or *Amrtaka,* who likewise numbered 10,000—outnumbered ten to one, cut off and abandoned in Greece, marching from the Peloponnese to Thessaly, defeating the numerically superior phalanxes of every Greek city-state they invaded, as they reached the safety of the Hellespont. History offers a more tragic and real-life parallel:

the Persian general Mardonius's huge invasion army of 479 B.C. that was defeated by the numerically inferior Greeks at the battle of Plataea and then forced to retire home three hundred miles northward through Thessaly and Thrace. Despite the army's enormous size and the absence of any organized pursuit, few of the Persians ever returned home. They were clearly no Ten Thousand. Their king had long ago abandoned them; after his defeat at Salamis, Xerxes had marched back to the safety of his court the prior autumn.

Technological superiority does not in itself explain the miraculous Greek achievement, although Xenophon at various places suggests that the Ten Thousand's heavy bronze, wood, and iron panoply was unmatched by anything found in Asia. There is no evidence either that the Greeks were by nature "different" from King Artaxerxes' men. The later pseudoscientific notion that the Europeans were racially superior to the Persians was entertained by *no* Greeks of the time. Although they were mercenary veterans and bent on booty and theft, the Ten Thousand were no more savage or warlike than other raiders and plunderers of the time; much less were they kinder or more moral people than the tribes they met in Asia. Greek religion did not put a high premium on turning the other cheek or on a belief that war per se was either abnormal or amoral. Climate, geography, and natural resources tell us as little. In fact, Xenophon's men could only envy the inhabitants of Asia Minor, whose arable land and natural wealth were in dire contrast to their poor soil back in Greece. Indeed, they warned their men that any Greeks who migrated eastward might become lethargic "Lotus-Eaters" in such a far wealthier natural landscape.

The *Anabasis* makes it clear, however, that the Greeks fought much differently than their adversaries and that such unique Hellenic characteristics of battle—a sense of personal freedom, superior discipline, matchless weapons, egalitarian camaraderie, individual initiative, constant tactical adaptation and flexibility, preference for shock battle of heavy infantry—were themselves the murderous dividends of Hellenic culture at large. The peculiar way Greeks killed grew out of consensual government, equality among the middling classes, civilian audit of military affairs, and politics apart from religion, freedom and individualism, and rationalism. The ordeal of the Ten Thousand, when stranded and near extinction, brought out the polis that was innate in all Greek soldiers, who then conducted themselves on campaign precisely as civilians in their respective city-states.

In some form or another, the Ten Thousand would be followed by equally brutal European intruders: Agesilaus and his Spartans, Chares the mercenary captain, Alexander the Great, Julius Caesar and centuries of legionary dominance, the Crusaders, Hernán Cortés, Portuguese explorers in Asiatic seas, British redcoats in India and Africa, and scores of other thieves, buccaneers, colonists, mercenaries, imperialists, and explorers. Most subsequent Western expeditionary forces were outnumbered and often deployed far from home. Nevertheless, they outfought their numerically superior enemies and in varying degrees drew on elements of Western culture to slaughter mercilessly their opponents.

In the long history of European military practice, it is almost a truism that the chief military worry of a Western army for the past 2,500 years was another Western army. Few Greeks were killed at Marathon (490 B.C.). Thousands died at the later collisions at Nemea and Coronea (394 B.C.), where Greek fought Greek. The latter Persian Wars (480–479 B.C.) saw relatively few Greek deaths. The Peloponnesian War (431–404 B.C.) between Greek states was an abject bloodbath. Alexander himself killed more Europeans in Asia than did the hundreds of thousands of Persians under Darius III. The Roman Civil Wars nearly ruined the republic in a way that even Hannibal had not. Waterloo, the Somme, and Omaha Beach only confirm the holocaust that occurs when Westerner meets Westerner.

This book attempts to explain why that is all so, why Westerners have been so adept at using their civilization to kill others—at warring so brutally, so often without being killed. Past, present, and future, the story of military dynamism in the world is ultimately an investigation into the prowess of Western arms. Scholars of war may resent such a broad generalization. Academics in the university will find that assertion chauvinistic or worse—and thus cite every exception from Thermopylae to Little Big Horn in refutation. The general public itself is mostly unaware of their culture's own singular and continuous lethality in arms. Yet for the past 2,500 years—even in the Dark Ages, well before the "Military Revolution," and not simply as a result of the Renaissance, the European discovery of the Americas, or the Industrial Revolution—there has been a peculiar practice of Western warfare, a common foundation and continual way of fighting, that has made Europeans the most deadly soldiers in the history of civilization.

THE PRIMACY OF BATTLE

War as Culture

I am not interested here in whether European military culture is morally
superior to, or far more wretched than, that of the non-West. The conquistadors, who put an end to human sacrifice and torture on the Great
Pyramid in Mexico City, sailed from a society reeling from the Grand
Inquisition and the ferocious *Reconquista,* and left a diseased and nearly
ruined New World in their wake. I am also less concerned in ascertaining
the righteousness of particular wars—whether a murderous Pizarro in
Peru (who calmly announced, "The time of the Inca is over") was better
or worse than his murdering Inca enemies, whether India suffered enormously or benefited modestly from English colonization, or whether the
Japanese had good cause to bomb Pearl Harbor or the Americans to incinerate Tokyo. My curiosity is not with Western man's heart of darkness,
but with his ability to fight—specifically how his military prowess reflects
larger social, economic, political, and cultural practices that themselves
seemingly have little to do with war.

That connection between values and battle is not original, but has an
ancient pedigree. The Greek historians, whose narratives are centered on
war, nearly always sought to draw cultural lessons. In Thucydides' history
of the Peloponnesian War, nearly 2,500 years ago the Spartan general
Brasidas dismissed the military prowess of the tribes of Illyria and
Macedonia, who confronted his Spartan hoplites. These men, Brasidas
says of his savage opponents, have no discipline and so cannot endure
shock battle. "As all mobs do," they changed their fearsome demeanor to
cries of fright when they faced the cold iron of disciplined men in rank.
Why so? Because, as Brasidas goes on to tell his soldiers, such tribes are
the product of cultures "in which the many do not rule the few, but rather
the few the many" (Thucydides 4.126).

In contrast to these enormous armies of screaming "barbarians"
without consensual governments and written constitutions—"formidable
in outward bulk, with unbearable loud yelling and the frightful appearance of weapons brandished in the air"—"citizens of states like yours,"
Brasidas assures his men, "stand their ground." Notice that Brasidas says
nothing about skin color, race, or religion. Instead, he simplistically con-
nects military discipline, fighting in rank, and the preference for shock
battle with the existence of popular and consensual government, which
gave the average infantryman in the phalanx a sense of equality and a su-

perior spirit to his enemies. Whether or not we wish to dismiss Brasidas's self-serving portrait of frenzied tribesmen as a chauvinistic Western "construct" or "fiction," or debate whether his own Spartan oligarchy was a broad-based government, or carp that European infantrymen were often ambushed and bushwhacked by more nimble guerrillas, it is indisputable that there was a tradition of disciplined heavy infantrymen among the constitutionally governed Greek city-states, and not such a thing among tribal peoples to the north.

In an analysis of culture and conflict why should we concentrate on a few hours of battle and the fighting experience of the average soldier—and not the epic sweep of wars, with their cargo of grand strategy, tactical maneuver, and vast theater operations that so much better lend themselves to careful social and cultural exegesis? Military history must never stray from the tragic story of killing, which is ultimately found only in battle. The culture in which militaries fight determines whether thousands of mostly innocent young men are alive or rotting after their appointed hour of battle. Abstractions like capitalism or civic militarism are hardly abstract at all when it comes to battle, but rather concrete realities that ultimately determined whether at Lepanto twenty-year-old Turkish peasants survived or were harpooned in the thousands, whether Athenian cobblers and tanners could return home in safety after doing their butchery at Salamis or were to wash up in chunks on the shores of Attica.

There is an inherent truth in battle. It is hard to disguise the verdict of the battlefield, and nearly impossible to explain away the dead, or to suggest that abject defeat is somehow victory. Wars are the sum of battles, battles the tally of individual human beings killing and dying. As observers as diverse as Aldous Huxley and John Keegan have pointed out, to write of conflict is not to describe merely the superior rifles of imperial troops or the matchless edge of the Roman *gladius,* but ultimately the collision of a machine-gun bullet with the brow of an adolescent, or the carving and ripping of artery and organ in the belly of an anonymous Gaul. To speak of war in any other fashion brings with it a sort of immorality: the idea that when hit, soldiers simply go to sleep, rather than are shredded, that generals order impersonal battalions and companies of automatons into the heat of battle, rather than screaming nineteen-year-olds into clouds of gas and sheets of lead bullets, or that a putrid corpse has little to do with larger approaches to science and culture.

Euphemism in battle narrative or the omission of graphic killing altogether is a near criminal offense of the military historian. It is no accident that gifted writers of war—from Homer, Thucydides, Caesar, Victor

Hugo, and Leo Tolstoy to Stephen Runciman, James Jones, and Stephen Ambrose—equate tactics with blood, and strategy with corpses. How can we write of larger cultural issues that surround war without describing the way in which young men kill and die, without remembering how many thousands are robbed of their youth, their robust physiques turned into goo in a few minutes on the battlefield?

We owe it to the dead to discover at all costs how the practice of government, science, law, and religion instantaneously determines the fate of thousands on the battlefield—and why. During the Gulf War (1990–91) the designer of an American smart bomb, the assembler in its plant of fabrication, the logistician who ordered, received, stockpiled, and loaded it onto a jet, all functioned in a manner unlike their Iraqi opposites—if there were such exact counterparts—and so ensured that an innocent conscript in Saddam Hussein's army would find himself blown to pieces with little chance to escape the attack, display heroism in his demise, or kill the pilot who killed him. Why Iraqi adolescents were targets in the flashing video consoles of sophisticated American helicopters, and not vice versa, or why GIs from icy Minnesota were better equipped to fight in the desert than recruits from nearby sweltering Baghdad, is mostly a result of cultural heritage, not military courage, much less an accident of geography or genes. War is ultimately killing. Its story becomes absurd when the wages of death are ignored by the historian.

The "Great Battles"

The idea of studying arbitrary "decisive battles" has fallen into disrepute—classic studies like Sir Edward Creasy's *The Fifteen Decisive Battles of the World*, Thomas Knox's *Decisive Battles Since Waterloo*, or J. F. C. Fuller's *Decisive Battles of the World: From Salamis to Madrid*. Such compendiums once sought to show how the course of civilization rested on a successful charge or two in a given landmark battle—those acts of individual cowardice, bravery, and luck that Creasy called "human probabilities," which warred with larger "causes and effects" or the determinist currents that he called "fatalism."

The Great Battles were also selected as worthwhile objects of moral and ethical study. "There is," Creasy admitted in his preface, "undeniable greatness in the disciplined courage, and in the love of honor, which makes the combatants confront agony and destruction" (vii). Battles bring out the coward or hero in all of us. The nineteenth-century logic was that there is no better way to form our character than through reading of the heroism and cowardice inherent in fighting of the past. At first glance, it is hard to argue with either of Creasy's premises that single battles change history and offer timeless moral instruction. Had Themistocles not been present at Salamis, the Greeks in the vulnerable infancy of Western civilization may well have been defeated and then subjugated as the westernmost satrapy of Persia, with catastrophic results for the subsequent history of Europe. Likewise, we can learn the lessons of martial audacity by reading of the frightening charge of Alexander's phalangites at Gaugamela, or the price of folly in Livy's account of the Roman command at Cannae. Yet I wish to take up again this nineteenth-century genre of the Great Battles for an entirely different purpose from either uncovering pivotal hours in history or posturing about the gallantry of war. There is also a cultural crystallization in battle, in which the insidious and more subtle institutions that heretofore or were murky and undefined became stark and unforgiving in the finality of organized killing.

No other culture but the West could have brought such discipline, morale, and sheer technological expertise to the art of killing than did the Europeans at the insanity of Verdun—a sustained industrial approach to slaughter unlike even the most horrific tribal massacre. No American Indian tribe or Zulu *impi* could have marshaled, supplied, armed—and have killed and replaced—hundreds of thousands of men for months on end for a rather abstract political cause of a nation-state. The most gallant Apaches—murderously brave in raiding and skirmishing on the Great Plains—would have gone home after the first hour of Gettysburg.

By the same token, there was little chance that the American government in the darkest days of December 1941—Britain on the ropes, the Nazis outside Moscow, the Japanese in the air over Hawaii—would have ordered thousands of its own naval pilots to crash themselves into Admiral Yamamoto's vast carrier fleet or commanded B-17s to plunge into German oil refineries. After Hasdrubal's catastrophic setback at the Metaurus, there was no likelihood that the Carthaginian Assembly, as Rome had done after the far worse slaughter at Cannae, would have ordered a general muster of *all* its able-bodied citizenry—a real nation-in-arms arising to crush the hated resurgent legions. In battle alone we receive a glimpse of the larger reasons precisely why and how men kill and die that are hard to disguise and harder still to ignore.

About a century ago, Creasy wrote of Alexander's victory at Gaugamela that it "not only overthrew an Oriental dynasty, but established European rulers in its stead. It broke the monotony of the Eastern world by the impression of Western energy and superior civilization, even as England's present mission is to break up the mental and moral stagnation of India and Cathay by pouring upon and through them the impulsive current of Anglo-Saxon commerce and conquest" (E. Creasy, *The Fifteen Decisive Battles of the World*, 63). Nearly everything in that statement is false—except for one indisputable phrase: "Western energy." England was in India, India not in England. Alexander's brigands were hardly emissaries of culture, and went east to loot and plunder, not to "civilize." But they killed without dying because of a military tradition that for centuries prior had proved unlike any other in the ancient world, itself the product of a different social, economic, and political culture from Achaemenid Persia.

The nine engagements chosen for this book were not selected solely because the fate of civilizations has hinged on their outcomes—although in the instance of Salamis, Gaugamela, and the siege at Mexico City that surely was the case. Nor have I chosen these battles because of their unusual heroism and gallantry—ethical instruction in which we are supposed to appreciate or dismiss people's moral fiber or national character itself as well. Although an army's organization, discipline, and arms can surely magnify or whittle down the martial spirit of a man, bravery nonetheless is a more universal human characteristic, and so tells us little about the singular lethality of a particular people's military or its culture at large. Europeans were intrinsically no smarter or braver than the Africans, Asians, and Native Americans whom they usually butchered. The Aztec warriors who were blown to bits by Cortés's cannon or the Zulus who were shattered by British Martini-Henry rifles at Rorke's Drift may have been the most courageous fighters in the history of warfare. The brave American pilots who blew up the *Kaga* at Midway were no more gallant than the brave Japanese who were engulfed in its flames below.

I am also unable to offer universal military "lessons"; there are no anatomies here of tactical blunders that doomed an entire army—unwise battles like Kursk that ruined the German Panzers in Russia, or Varus's ill-thought expedition into Germany that resulted in thousands slaughtered and essentially ended the chance that Germany might be incorporated into the Roman Empire. True, there is something to this idea of a timeless "art of warfare" that transcends the centuries and continents, and so is innate to man in battle, rather than specific to culture: concentration of force, the proper use of surprise, or the necessity of safe lines of supply and so on. Yet most such books on battle knowledge have already been written. In most of their efforts at universal truths of how wars are won and lost, they often fail to appreciate the cultural baggage with which an army enters the battlefield.

Instead, I have selected these collisions for what they tell us about culture, specifically the core elements of Western civilization. They are "landmark" for what they reveal about how a society fights, not necessarily because of their historical importance. The battles are snapshots of a cultural tradition of war making, not progressive chapters in a comprehensive history of Western warfare. Not all are European victories. Cannae, for example, was a horrific Roman defeat, Tet an American political embarrassment. Nor are all these engagements clear-cut clashes between Western and non-Western forces. We can learn just as much about the phenomenon of Westernization from militaries like Carthage, imperial Japan, and the North Vietnamese, which all adopted in some part elements of Western battle practice and weaponry that accordingly gave them advantages on the battlefield unmatched by their African and Asian neighbors—and that eventually resulted in their ability to kill thousands of Westerners themselves. In this regard, there must be some common strand that explains why Darius III had Greeks in his employment, why the Ottomans transferred their capital city to the newly conquered European Constantinople, why Zulus used Martini-Henry rifles at Rorke's Drift, why the *Soryu* looked something like the *Enterprise* at Midway, and why an AK-47 and M-16 appear almost identical. The opposite was not true: Alexander did not hire the Immortals; the Crusaders did not transfer the capital of France or England to a conquered Tyre or Jerusalem; the British did not outfit regiments with assegais; and the American navy did not institute samurai sword training.

In an effort to identify common and recurring themes, I have sought diversity in the broadest sense: battle at sea, in the air, and on land; battle in the New World, on the Mediterranean and the Pacific, and in Europe, Asia, and Africa; battles that were both relatively small and also huge; battles like Midway that were pivotal and others like Rorke's Drift that were ultimately irrelevant; battles between colonists and aborigines, or states against empires, or religion against religion. I have also attempted to illustrate Western characteristics of war in their most *unlikely* occurrence: the value of civic militarism at Cannae when a mercenary army demolished the militia of Rome; the supremacy of landed infantry during the so-called Dark Ages of purported Western impotence when the mounted knight alone was thought to rule the battlefield; the singularity of Western technology and research among the conquistadors, who were products of the Inquisition and the *Reconquista;* the superiority of Western discipline against the Zulus, Africa's most disciplined and well organized indigenous army; and the value of dissent and self-critique during the Tet Offensive, when clear military victory on the battlefield was turned into defeat by a sometimes overzealous opposition. It is easy to see that civic militarism or landed infantry saved the West at Plataea, that the militaries of England, France, and Germany embodied the excellence of Western technologies, and that colonial armies were better disciplined than Pacific islanders. Yet we can learn more of the resilience of Europe and its culture from these worst-case scenarios in which the Western way of war at first glance seems hardly dynamic at all, if at times counterproductive to the struggle for victory itself.

The only other constant besides the fault line of mostly non-West versus West conflict is a vague sense of chronology, beginning with the ancient world and ending in the modern age, starting with spears and concluding with jets. This emphasis on classical antiquity is deliberate: while most historians admit of a European dominance in arms from the sixteenth to twentieth centuries, fewer profess that since its creation the West has enjoyed martial advantages over its adversaries—or that such dominance is based not merely on superior weaponry but on cultural dynamism itself. The landmark battles do not reflect radical evolutionary changes in war making through the centuries. While Western warfare grew more sophisticated and deadly over time, its main tenets were well established during classical antiquity. Consequently, all our examples reflect a commonality in military practice: freedom of expression, for instance, was integral to the Greek cause at our first battle, Salamis, and characteristic of the American army at our last example, Tet, some 2,500 years later. I shall argue that what led to the present Western superiority in arms ("Part Three: Control") was not fundamental alteration and improvement in the classical military paradigm ("Part One: Creation") but rather its gradual spread throughout Europe and the Western hemisphere ("Part Two: Continuity"). This issue of cultural heritage is a controversial but critical historical point, with fundamental consequences for the future, because it suggests that Western lethality shall continue, despite even the proliferation of advanced technology into the non-West.

Critics might seek more examples of Western reverses. Yet even horrific individual disasters like Carrhae (53 B.C.) did not affect the ultimate superiority of Western forces. Parthia is beyond the Euphrates, and the legions who died there thousands of miles from home comprised only a fifth of Rome's available military manpower. Adrianople (378) and

Manzikert (1071) were horrendous Western defeats; but the Romans and Byzantines who were slaughtered there were for the most part vastly outnumbered, far from home, poorly led, and reluctant emissaries of crumbling empires. Some might ask, "Where is Dien Bien Phu?," forgetting that the Vietminh defeated the French in Vietnam, not in France, with Western-designed artillery, rockets, and automatic weapons, not arms indigenous to Southeast Asia—and as patriots with ample Chinese aid defending their fatherland, not as colonial troops without clear support from home. In Oran, Afghanistan, Algiers, Morocco, and India, outnumbered Spanish, French, and British troops were sometimes annihilated—usually surrounded, without logistical support, and opposed by numerically superior opponents making use of European firearms.

For every Isandhlwana, where vastly outnumbered and poorly commanded Westerners were surprised and slaughtered by indigenous troops, there is a Rorke's Drift, where 139 British soldiers held off 4,000 Zulus. Can we envision the opposite—a handful of Zulus butchering thousands of rifle-carrying redcoats? In any case, both the slaughter of British troops and the killing of Zulus do not in any way nullify a general truth that European armies fought Africans with superior weapons, logistics, organization, and discipline, and thereby overcame the vast numerical advantages and remarkable courage of their enemies. All such wars against the Zulus were fought in Africa—it was surely impossible that the latter could even contemplate an invasion of England. When the Zulu king Cetshwayo wished to go to London, it was as a defeated curiosity, dressed in suit and tie, to delight and shock Victorian society.

IDEAS OF THE WEST

Western Preeminence?

Behind the economic and political hegemony of the West has stood the peculiar force of Western arms, past and present. Militarily, the uniforms of the world's armies on both sides of the modern battle line are now almost identical—Western khaki, camouflage, and boots are worn when Iraqis fight Iranians or Somalians battle Ethiopians. Companies, brigades, and divisions—the successors to Roman military practice—are the global standards of military organization. Chinese tanks look European; African machine guns have not evolved beyond American models; and Asian jets have not incorporated new propulsion systems with a radically novel Korean or Cambodian way of producing thrust. If a Third World autocrat buys weapons from China, India, or Brazil, he does so only because these countries can copy and provide Western-designed weapons more cheaply than the West itself. Indigenous armies in Vietnam and Central America have had success against Europeans—but largely to the degree that they were supplied with automatic weapons, high explosives, and ammunition produced on Western specifications.

A small school, it is true, has argued that non-European forces were in no way inferior to Western armies. But examination of such case studies of European setbacks—in the Pacific, Africa, Asia, and the Americas—reveals consistent and recurring themes. Europeans were more often outnumbered and fighting *outside* Europe. If defeated, their victors were usually employing some type of European weaponry; and rarely did Western battle defeats lead to capitulation and armistice. Only a few places in Africa and Asia—Nepal, Tibet, Afghanistan, and Ethiopia—resisted European entry. Others that did—Japan most notably—emulated Western military practice almost entirely. After Thermopylae, and with the exception of the Moors in Spain and Mongols in eastern Europe, there is virtually no example of a non-Western military defeating Europeans in Europe *with non-European weapons.* That European colonial armies sometimes found themselves vastly outnumbered, often opposed by courageous indigenous warriors equipped with Western firearms, and then were annihilated tells us little about Western military weakness.

Sometimes critics of the idea of Western military predominance point to the easy transference of technology in arguing that, say, American natives became better shots than European settlers or that Moroccans quickly mastered Portuguese artillery. Such arguments have the paradoxical effect of proving the opposite of what is intended: Englishmen were in the New World and selling guns to natives, not vice versa. Moroccans were not in Lisbon teaching Portuguese the arts of indigenous Islamic heavy gunnery. Here the human quality of utilizing, mastering, and improving a tool is confused with the cultural question of providing an intellectual, political, and social context for scientific discovery, popular dissemination of knowledge, practical application, and the art of mass fabrication.

As we shall see with Carthage and Japan, the very controversial question of Westernization has a reductionist and sometimes absurd quality about it: there is no military concept of "Easternization" within the armed forces of the West, at least in which entire Western cultures adopt whole-sale the military practices and technology of the non-West. Meditation, religion, and philosophy are not the same as industrial production, scientific research, and technological innovation. It matters little where a weapon was first discovered, but a great deal how it was mass-produced, constantly improved, and employed by soldiers. Few scholars, however, can disconnect the question of morality from energy. Thus, any investigation of why the military of the West has exercised such power is far too often suspect of cultural chauvinism.

Nature Over Culture?

Is Western hegemony a product of luck, geography, natural resources, or itself a late phenomenon due largely to the discovery and subsequent conquest of the New World (1492–1700) or to the Industrial Revolution (1750–1900)? Many cite the West's natural and geographical benefaction. In this line of thinking—made most popular by Fernand Braudel and most recently by Jared Diamond—the West's apparent "proximate" advantages in technology like firearms and steel are due largely to more "ultimate" causes that are largely accidental. For example, the Eurasian axis favored a long crop season, a different sort of animal husbandry, and species diversity. The resulting rise in urban population and animal domestication created a lethal brew of germs that would decimate outsiders without long-standing exposure and ensuing biological immunity. European topography both prevented easy access by hostile nomads and promoted rival cultures, whose competition and warring led to constant innovation and response. Europe was blessed with abundant ores that made iron and steel production possible, and so on.

Natural determinists are to be congratulated in their efforts for the most part to dismiss genes. Europeans were not by any means naturally smarter than Asians, Africans, or the natives of the New World. They were *not* genetically dumber either—as Jared Diamond, the purportedly natural determinist, has unfortunately hinted at. In an especially disturbing reference to racial intelligence, Diamond argues for the genetic inferiority of Western brains:

> New Guineans . . . impressed me as being on the average more intelligent, more alert, more expressive, and more interested in things and people than the average European or American. At some tasks that one might reason-

ably suppose to reflect aspects of brain function, such as the ability to form a mental map of unfamiliar surroundings, they appear considerably more adept than Westerners. (J. Diamond, *Guns, Germs, and Steel*, 20)

One wonders what would have been the response of critics had Diamond juxtaposed the words "New Guineans" and "Europeans." Are we to believe that Columbus lacked the brain function to make a "mental map" of unfamiliar surroundings in an empty ocean?

The efforts of those who seek to reduce history to biology and geography deprecate the power and mystery of culture, and so often turn desperate. While Chinese civilization did give the world gunpowder and printing, it never developed the prerequisite receptive cultural environment that would allow those discoveries to be shared by the populace at large and thus freely to be altered and constantly improved by enterprising individuals to meet changing conditions. This rigidity was not because of "China's chronic unity," or a result of a "smooth coastline" and the absence of islands, but because a complex set of conditions favored imperial autocracy that became entrenched in a natural landscape not at all that different from the Mediterranean.

In contrast, Rome, whose continuous rule was comparable in duration to many of the dynasties of imperial China, was an especially innovative empire, which drew strength from its unity and nearly four centuries of tranquillity. Despite the general anti-utilitarian nature of classical science, the Romans developed and then dispersed among millions of people sophisticated building techniques with cement and arches, screw presses and pumps, and factories to produce bulk supplies of everything from arms and armor to dyes, woolen cloth, glass, and furniture, as the government had little control over the dissemination or use of knowledge. The Greeks likewise found even greater power vis-à-vis other cultures during the Hellenistic period, when their national armies devastated the East. Hellenistic applied science under the Successor dynasties made practical strides unknown during the classical period when Greece was composed of over a thousand squabbling and autonomous polities. Political unity outside of China has brought other cultures advantages as well as atrophy. Neither the geography nor the political history of China alone accounts for its culture.

We must remember also that farmland in America is as rich as Europe's—and gave many New World palatial dynasties prosperity. China, India, and Africa are especially blessed in natural ores, and enjoy growing seasons superior to those of northern Europe. True, Rome and

Greece are situated in the central Mediterranean and thus were a nexus of sorts for traders arriving from Europe, western Asia, and northern Africa—but so was Carthage, whose location was as fortunate as Rome's. The fact is we shall *never* know the precise reasons why Western civilization in Greece and Rome developed so radically on a diverse path from its neighbors to the north, south, and east, especially when the climate and geography of Greece and Italy were not especially different from those of ancient Spain, southern France, western Persia, Phoenicia, or North Africa.

In this most recent sort of biological determinism, natural advantages like irrigated arable land in the Fertile Crescent or expansive plains in Persia and China encourage political unity, which is a "bad" thing, while climatological and geographical adversity lead to war and fighting, which is ultimately good. Yet the East possesses no uniform geography—who indeed can sort out the differing characteristics of a small isolated valley in Greece from its nearly identical counterpart in Persia or China? Modern biologists have unknowingly returned to the Greeks' crude historical determinism, the theories of Hippocrates, Herodotus, and Plato that asserted the harsh Greek mainland made Hellenes tough, even as the bounty of Persia enervated its population.

Few ancient societies, in fact, were situated in a more *disadvantageous* position than Greece, neighbor to a hostile Achaemenid empire of 70 million, directly north of the warring states of the Near East, with less than half its land arable, without a single large navigable river, cursed with almost no abundance of natural resources other than a few deposits of gold, metals, and timber, its coastline vulnerable to the Persian fleet, its northern plains open to migrating nomads from Europe and southern Asia, its tiny and vulnerable island polities closer to Asia than Europe. Are we then to blame its mountains, which discouraged vast hydraulic farming and contained few riches, or commend the rocky terrain for ensuring political fragmentation that led to innovation? The old Victorian idea that Greece wore itself out with internecine killing is now to be replaced by the popular biological notion that such natural diversity led to "rivalry" that gave the West the advantages of embracing innovation.

Grain harvests in Ptolemaic Egypt (305–31 B.C.) reached astounding levels of production. Far from an exhausted Nile valley ending the power of the Egyptian dynasties, it bloomed as never before under Greek and Roman agricultural practice. If the pharaohs were doomed because of the disadvantages of nature and an exhausted soil, the Ptolemies who walked their identical ancient ground most assuredly were not—Alexandria, in a way Karnak could not be, for nearly five hundred years was the cultural and economic hub of the entire Mediterranean. How was that possible when thousands of prior harvests should have exhausted the Nile basin for Greek colonialists? Why did not the pharaohs utilize the great delta of Alexandria to create an emporium on the Mediterranean to facilitate trade between Asia, Europe, and Africa? Clearly, culture in Egypt—not geography, not weather, and not resources—had changed from 1200 to 300 B.C.

Vast cultural changes could also occur not only in the same place but among the same people. Mycenaean Linear B of the thirteenth century B.C. was a clumsy, largely pictographic script used by a small cadre to record royal inventories; the Greek language of the seventh century B.C. was widely disseminated and facilitated philosophy, science, literature, and poetry. Obviously, the climate, geography, and animals of central Greece did not mutate all that much in five hundred years. What allowed a written language in mainland Greece to evolve so differently from others elsewhere in the Mediterranean and from past Hellenic civilization was a radical revolution in social, political, and economic organization. Mycenaeans and polis Greeks lived in exactly the same place and spoke roughly the same language, but their respective values and ideas were a world apart. The biology and the environment of Greece may explain why both cultures farmed olive trees, herded sheep, relied on stone, mud brick, and tiles for construction materials, and even had the same words for mountains, cow, and sea, but it does not explain the vast difference between Mycenaean state agriculture and the family farms of the polis—much less why classical Greek militaries were far more dynamic than those of the earlier palaces.

No one denies the great role that geography, climate, and natural history play in history—Scandinavians obviously developed ideas of time, travel, and war different from the natives of Java. The absence of horses ensured that the Incas and Aztecs would lack the mobility of their Spanish adversaries. Yet the fact is that the ancient civilizations of the Near East, India, China, and Asia often encompassed for long periods of time areas of similar latitude, climate, and terrain as the West, with more or less the same advantages and disadvantages in resources and location. Land, climate, weather, natural resources, fate, luck, a few rare individuals of brilliance, natural disaster, and more—all these play their role in the formation of a distinct culture, but it is impossible to determine exactly whether man, nature, or chance is the initial catalyst for the origins of Western civilization. What is clear, however, is that once developed, the

West, ancient and modern, placed far fewer religious, cultural, and political impediments to natural inquiry, capital formation, and individual expression than did other societies, which often were theocracies, centralized palatial dynasties, or tribal unions.

A Late Ascendancy?

Others have argued that the rise of Western military power is relatively late and a quirk of either the spread of gunpowder (1300–1600), the discovery of the New World (1492–1600), or the Industrial Revolution (1750–1900), dismissing the possibility of cultural continuity from Greece and Rome that might explain *why* there was a military or industrial revolution in Europe and *not* in Egypt, China, or Brazil. As is true of any civilization, there have been wide swings in the influence of the West, from a Dark Ages from A.D. 500 to 800, to a relatively isolated and somewhat backward era between 800 and 1000, when Europeans fought off the invasions of northern and eastern nomads and Muslims. Yet two points need to be stressed about the notion of a rather late Western military dominance in arms that is characterized largely by technological superiority. First, for nearly a thousand years (479 B.C. to A.D. 500) the military dominance of the West was unquestioned, as the relatively tiny states in Greece and Italy exercised military supremacy over their far larger and more populous neighbors. The scientific, technological, political, and cultural foundations of classical culture were not entirely lost, but passed directly from the Roman Empire to European kingdoms or were rediscovered during the Carolingian period and later the Italian Renaissance.

The critical point about firearms and explosives is not that they suddenly gave Western armies hegemony, but that such weapons were produced in quality and great numbers in Western rather than in non-European countries—a fact that is ultimately explained by a long-standing Western cultural stance toward rationalism, free inquiry, and the dissemination of knowledge that has its roots in classical antiquity and is not specific to any particular period of European history. There is also something radically democratic about firearms that explains their singularly explosive growth in the West. Guns destroy the hierarchy of the battlefield, marginalizing the wealthy mailed knight and rendering even the carefully trained bowman ultimately irrelevant. It is no accident that feudal Japan eventually found firearms revolutionary and dangerous. The Islamic world never developed the proper tactics of shooting in massed volleys to accompany weapons that were so antithetical to the idea of personal bravery of the mounted warrior. The effective use of guns requires the marriage of rationalism and capitalism to ensure steady improvement in design, fabrication, and production, but in addition an egalitarian tradition that welcomes rather than fears the entrance of lethal newcomers on the battlefield.

Even after the fall of the Roman Empire, the West, purportedly now backward and far inferior to the cultures of China and the Islamic world, was militarily strong far beyond what its population and territory would otherwise indicate. During the so-called Dark Ages, the Byzantines mastered the use of "Greek fire" that allowed their fleets to overcome the numerical superiority of Islamic armadas—as, for example, the victory of Leo III in 717 over the far larger Islamic fleet of the caliph Sulaymān. The European discovery of the crossbow (ca. 850)—it could be fabricated more rapidly and at cheaper cost than more deadly composite bows—allowed thousands of relatively untrained soldiers the ready use of lethal weapons. From the sixth to the eleventh centuries the Byzantines maintained European influence in Asia, and no Islamic army after the early tenth century again ventured into western Europe. The *Reconquista* was slow, but steady and incremental. The fall of Rome in some sense meant the spread of the West much farther to the north as Germanic tribes became settled, Christianized, and more Western than ever before.

The dramatic European expansion of the sixteenth century may well have been energized by Western excellence in firearms and capital ships, but those discoveries were themselves the product of a long-standing Western approach to applied capitalism, science, and rationalism not found in other cultures. Thus, the sixteenth-century military renaissance was a reawakening of Western dynamism. It is better to call it a "transformation" in the manifestation of European battlefield superiority that had existed in the classical world for a millennium and was never entirely lost even during the darkest days of the Dark Ages. The "Military Revolution," then, was no accident, but logical given the Hellenic origins of European civilization.

We should not expect to see precisely in Greek freedom, American liberty; in Greek democracy, English parliamentary government; or in the agora, Wall Street. The freedom that was won at Salamis is not entirely the same as what was ensured at Midway, much less as what was at stake at Lepanto or Tenochtitlán. All ideas are in part captives of their time and space, and much of ancient Greece today would seem foreign if not nasty to most Westerners. The polis would never have crafted a Bill of Rights; in the same manner, we would not turn our courts over to majority vote of mass juries without the right of appeal to a higher judiciary. Socrates would have been read his Miranda rights, had free counsel, never have testified in person on his own behalf, been advised to plea-bargain, and when convicted would have been free on bail during years of appeal. His message, which seemed radical to his Athenian peers, would strike us as reactionary in the extreme. The key is not to look to the past and expect to see the present, but to identify in history the seeds of change and of the possible across time and space. In that sense, Wall Street *is* much closer to the agora than to the palace at Persepolis, and the Athenian court akin to us in a way pharaoh's and the sultan's law is not.

THE WESTERN WAY OF WAR

The West has achieved military dominance in a variety of ways that transcend mere superiority in weapons and has nothing to do with morality or genes. The Western way of war is so lethal precisely because it is so amoral—shackled rarely by concerns of ritual, tradition, religion, or ethics, by anything other than military necessity. We should not be held captive by technological determinism, as if the tools of war appear in a vacuum and magically transform warfare, without much thought of either how or why they were created or how or why they were used. Even the monopoly of superior Western technology and science has not always been true—Themistocles' triremes at Salamis were no better than Xerxes', and Admiral Nagumo's carriers at Midway had better planes than the Americans did. The status of freedom, individualism, and civic militarism at those battles, however, was vastly different among the opposing forces. As these encounters reveal on nearly every occasion, it was not merely the superior weapons of European soldiers but a host of other factors, including organization, discipline, morale, initiative, flexibility, and command, that led to Western advantages.

Western armies often fight with and for a sense of legal freedom. They are frequently products of civic militarism or constitutional governments and thus are overseen by those outside religion and the military itself. The rare word "citizen" exists in the European vocabularies. Heavy infantry is also a particularly Western strength—not surprising when Western societies put a high premium on property, and land is often held by a wide stratum of society. Because free inquiry and rationalism are Western trademarks, European armies have marched to war with weapons either superior or equal to their adversaries, and have often been supplied far more lavishly through the Western marriage of capitalism, finance, and sophisticated logistics. By the same token, Europeans have been quick to alter tactics, steal foreign breakthroughs, and borrow inventions when in the marketplace of ideas their own traditional tactics and arms have been found wanting. Western capitalists and scientists alike have been singularly pragmatic and utilitarian, with little to fear from religious fundamentalists, state censors, or stern cultural conservatives.

Western warring is often an extension of the idea of state politics, rather than a mere effort to obtain territory, personal status, wealth, or revenge. Western militaries put a high premium on individualism, and they are often subject to criticism and civilian complaint that may improve rather than erode their war-making ability. The idea of annihilation, of head-to-head battle that destroys the enemy, seems a particularly Western concept largely unfamiliar to the ritualistic fighting and emphasis on deception and attrition found outside Europe. There has never been anything like the samurai, Maoris, or "flower wars" in the West since the earliest erosion of the protocols of ancient Greek hoplite battle. Westerners, in short, long ago saw war as a method of doing what politics cannot, and thus are willing to obliterate rather than check or humiliate any who stand in their way.

At various periods in Western history the above menu has not always been found in its entirety. Ideas from consensual government to religious tolerance are often ideal rather than modal values. Throughout most of Western civilization there have been countless compromises, as what was attained proved less than what Western culture professed as the most desirable. The Crusaders were religious zealots; many early European armies were monarchical with only occasional oversight by deliberative bodies. It is hard to see in Cortés's small band religion and politics as entirely separate. Not a phalangite in Alexander's army voted him general, much less king. During the sixth to ninth centuries A.D. there is little evidence that Western forces always enjoyed absolute technological superiority over their foes. German tribesmen were ostensibly as individualistic as Roman legionaries.

Yet, abstract ideas must often be seen in the context of their times: while Alexander's Macedonians were revolutionaries who had destroyed Greek liberty, there was no escaping their ties with the Hellenic tradition. That shared heritage explains why soldiers in the phalanx, commanders in the fields, and generals at Alexander's table all voiced their ideas with a freedom unknown in the Achaemenid court. While the Inquisition was an episode of Western fanaticism and at times unrestrained by political audit, the tally of its entire bloody course never matched the Aztec score of corpses in a mere four days at the Great Temple to Huitzilopochtli in 1487. Even on the most controversial of issues like freedom, consensual government, and dissent, we must judge Western failings not through the lenses of utopian perfectionism of the present, but in the context of the global landscape of the times. Western values are absolute, but they are also evolutionary, being perfect at neither their birth nor their adolescence.

In any discussion of military prowess, we should also be clear about the thorny divide between determinism and free will. Throughout this study, we are *not* suggesting that the intrinsic characteristics of Western civilization predetermined European success on every occasion. Rather, Western civilization gave a spectrum of advantages to European militaries that allowed them a much greater margin of error and tactical disadvantage—battlefield inexperience, soldierly cowardice, insufficient numbers, terrible generalship—than their adversaries. Luck, individual initiative and courage, the brilliance of a Hannibal or Saladin, the sheer numbers of Zulu or Inca warriors—all on occasions could nullify Western inherent military superiority.

Over time, however, the resiliency of the Western system of war prevailed, allowing horrible disasters like Thermopylae (480 B.C.), Lake Trasimene (217 B.C.), *la Noche Triste* (1520), Isandhlwana (1879), and Little Big Horn (1876) not to affect the larger course of the conflict or to lead to an overall Western collapse. Western armies often owed their prowess to brilliant and savage individuals like Alexander the Great, Scipio Africanus, Julius Caesar, Charlemagne, Richard the Lion-Hearted, and Hernán Cortés, as well as to now nameless gallant individuals: the right wing of Spartans at Plataea (479 B.C.), the veterans of Caesar's Tenth Legion in Gaul (59–51 B.C.), or the heavy knights at Arsouf (1191), whose battlefield conduct, along with chance and enemy blunders, often changed the course of the battle.

Yet much of what courageous Westerners accomplished must be seen in an overall cultural landscape that afforded them inherent military advantages not usually shared by their adversaries. We must be careful not to judge the record of Western military skill in absolute terms, but always in a relative context vis-à-vis the conditions of the times: scholars can argue over the effectiveness of Western arms, the impressive power of Chinese and Indian armies, the occasional slaughter of European colonial forces, but in all such debate they must keep in mind that non-European forces did not with any frequency and for long duration navigate the globe, borrowed rather than imparted military technology, did not colonize three new continents, and usually fought Europeans at home rather than in Europe. Although important exceptions should always be noted, generalization—so long avoided by academics out of either fear or ignorance—is indispensable in the writing of history.

As examination of these battles shall show, throughout the long evolution of Western warfare there has existed a more or less common core of practices that reappears generation after generation, sometimes piecemeal, at other times in a nearly holistic fashion, which explains why the history of warfare is so often the brutal history of Western victory—and why today deadly Western armies have little to fear from any force other than themselves.

PART ONE

Creation

TWO

Freedom—or "To Live as You Please"

Salamis, September 28, 480 B.C.

"O sons of Greece, go forward! Free your native soil. Free your children, your wives, the images of your fathers' gods, and the tombs of your ancestors! Now the fight is for all that."
—Aeschylus, *The Persians* (401–4)

THE DROWNED

IT MUST BE a terrible thing to drown at sea—arms thrashing the waves, lungs filling with brine, the body slowly growing heavy and numb, the brain crackling and sparking as its last molecules of oxygen are exhausted, the final conscious sight of the dim and fading, unreachable sunlight far above the rippling surface. By day's end in late September 480 B.C., a third of the sailors of the Persian fleet were now precisely in those awful last moments of their existence. A few miles from the burned Athenian acropolis as many as 40,000 of Xerxes' imperial subjects were bobbing in the depths and on the waves—the dead, the dying, and the desperate amid the wrecks of more than two hundred triremes. All were doomed far from Asia in the warm coastal waters of the Aegean, all destined for the bottom of the Saronic Gulf. Their last sight on earth was a Greek sunset over the mountains of Salamis—or their grim king perched far away on Mount Aigaleos watching them sink beneath the waves. Unlike battle on terra firma, where lethality is so often predicated on the technology of death, and not the landscape of battle itself, war at sea is a primordial killer of men, in which the ocean itself can wipe out thousands without the aid of either man or his weapons. At Salamis most died from water in their lungs, not steel in their bodies.

Originally either a Phoenician or an Egyptian invention, an ancient trireme in battle was a rowing, not a sailing, ship. Usually, 170 sailors powered the vessel. An additional crew of thirty or so marines, archers, and helmsmen crowded above on the decks. Unlike the oarsmen in later European galleys, rowers sat in groups of three, one on top of another, each one pulling a single oar of a standard length. The great strength of the trireme's design was its extraordinary ratio between weight, speed, and propulsion. The sleekness of the ship and the intricate arrangement of the oarsmen made it possible for two hundred men in a few seconds to reach speeds of nearly nine knots. That quickness and agility ensured that its chief weapon—a two-pronged bronze ram fitted at the waterline of the prow—could smash right through any ship on the seas. So complex was the ancient design of vessel, oar, and sail that in the sixteenth century when Venetian shipwrights attempted to duplicate the Athenian method of oarage, the result was mostly unseaworthy galleys. Modern engineers have still not mastered the ancient design, despite the use of advanced computer technology and some 2,500 years of nautical expertise.

The trireme was also a fragile and vulnerable heavily laden craft that put two hundred men out in the open water with little margin of safety— the oar ports of its bottom bank of rowers were a mere few feet above the waterline. Unlike modern naval warfare, ancient ships offered scarcely any time for the crew to evacuate. Most capsized almost instantaneously when rammed in battle, since even a glancing blow could send water rushing into the ship and quickly toss the crew into the sea. The sailors' only hope was to make for land or to grab on to any debris that remained floating from the wreckage. For rowers and marines who could not swim—and such unfortunates were numerous in the ancient world and nearly without exception in the Persian fleet—death by drowning would come in seconds. It mattered little that most crews were not shackled like sixteenth-century galley slaves, since triremes could turn over or fill with water without much warning. The long robes of the Persians only made things worse. The playwright Aeschylus, who was probably a veteran of Salamis, eight years later wrote of their helplessness in the water: "The corpses of the Persian loved ones, soaked with saltwater, were often submerged and tossed about lifeless in their long robes" *(Persians* 274–76).

Their burial water between the island of Salamis and the Attic mainland was a small strait, not much more than a mile wide. Like most great sea battles of the preindustrial age, the respective fleets fought in sight of land. The battle, involving more than 1,000 triremes, took place in only about a square mile of sea, ensuring that the dead littered the ocean surface and washed up on the surrounding coast. Aeschylus recalls that "the shores of Salamis and all the neighboring coast are full of the bodies of men who perished by a wretched fate" *(Persians* 272–73).

Thousands of Egyptians, Phoenicians, Cilicians, and assorted Asians were washed up on the shores of Salamis and Attica, a few marooned on the wrecks of what was left of two hundred ships. Greek sailors finished off the dying at sea with javelins and arrows. At the same time, heavy hoplite infantrymen scoured the beaches of Salamis harpooning the few stranded survivors. Despite Aeschylus's claim that "the entire armada has perished," hundreds of fleeing Persian ships managed to row past the carnage to safety, too terrified of the ordered lines of pursuing Greek triremes to pick up their kindred. The Athenian architect of the victory, the admiral Themistocles, after the battle purportedly walked along the shore viewing the remains, and invited his men to plunder the gold and silver from the Persian corpses. According to Aeschylus, the bodies were lacerated by the surf and grotesquely gnawed by marine scavengers.

Salamis—the name is still synonymous with abstract ideals of freedom and "the rise of the West"—is not associated with a bloodbath. Although no battle better deserves such an association, references to the battle disasters during the Persian Wars evoke images of the final Spartan contingent at Thermopylae (480 B.C.), which was wiped out to the man, King Leonidas, the leader of the famous 299 Spartans, decapitated and his head impaled on a stake—or the Persians at Plataea (479 B.C.), who were butchered mercilessly by Spartan hoplites and sent fleeing into the croplands of Boeotia. Yet at least two hundred imperial ships were rammed and sunk at Salamis. Most went down with their entire crews of two hundred rowers and auxiliaries, ensuring that at least 40,000 sailors drowned and countless others were captured or killed as they washed up onshore. Because the strait of Salamis is so narrow and the Persian armada was so large—somewhere between 600 and 1,200 ships—the dead were unduly conspicuous and made a ghastly impression on the Persian king, Xerxes, who viewed the battle from the nearby Attic heights.

Because the frenzied Greeks were determined to annihilate the occupiers of their homeland, and since, as Herodotus points out, "the greater part of the Barbarians drowned at sea because they did not know how to swim," Salamis remains one of the most deadly battles in the entire history of naval warfare. More perished in the tiny strait than at Lepanto (ca. 40,000–50,000), all the dead of the Spanish Armada (20,000–30,000), the Spanish and French together at Trafalgar (14,000), the British at Jutland (6,784), or the Japanese at Midway (2,155). In contrast, only forty Greek triremes were lost, and we should imagine that the majority of those 8,000 Greeks who abandoned their ships were saved. Herodotus says only a "few" of the Greeks drowned, the majority swimming across the strait to safety. Rarely in the history of warfare has there occurred such a one-sided catastrophe—and rarely in the age before gunpowder have so many been slaughtered in a few hours.

The Greco-Persian Wars, which until the battle of Mycale were fought exclusively in Europe, witnessed terrible butchery—none more awful than the thousands who drowned off the Attic coast. Drowning, in the Greek mind, was considered the worst of deaths—the soul wandering as a shade, unable to enter Hades should his body not be found and given a final proper commemoration. Almost eighty years later the Athenian court would execute its own successful generals after the sea victory at Arginusae (406 B.C.), precisely for their failure to pick up survivors bobbing in the water—and the idea that hundreds of Athenian husbands, fathers, and brothers were decomposing in the depths without proper burial.

Who were Xerxes' 40,000 sailors thrashing about in the strait of Salamis? Almost all of them are lost to the historical record. We know only a few names of the elite and well connected, and then only from Greek sources. Herodotus singles out only King Xerxes' brother and admiral, Ariabignes, who went down with his ship. Aeschylus has a roll call of dead generals and admirals: Artembares "dashed against the cruel shore of Silenia"; Dadaces "speared as he jumped from his vessel"; the remains of the Bactrian lord Tenagon "lapping about the island of Ajax"; and so on. He goes on to name more than a dozen other leaders whose corpses were floating in the channel. In a particularly gruesome passage, presented on the Athenian stage a mere eight years after the battle, the playwright has a Persian messenger describe the human mess:

> The hulls of our ships rolled over, and it was no longer possible to glimpse the sea, strewn as it was with the wrecks of warships and the debris of what had been men. The shores and the reefs were full of our dead, and every

ship that had once been part of the fleet now tried to row its way to safety through flight. But just as if our men were tunny-fish or some sort of netted catch, the enemy kept pounding them and hacking them with broken oars and the flotsam from the wrecked ships. And so shrieks together with sobbing echoed over the open sea until the face of black night at last covered the scene. (*Persians* 419–29)

Many of these unfortunates were not Persians but conscripted Bactrians, Phoenicians, Egyptians, Cypriots, Carians, Cilicians, and men from other tributary states of the vast empire—including Ionian Greeks—who had voyaged to Salamis under coercion as part of Xerxes' grand muster. The majority who rowed had little say about the conditions of their own participation, and even less desire for fighting in the strait of Salamis. Both Herodotus and Aeschylus relate that any hesitation on their part to row out on the morning of September 28 meant summary execution. One of the most gruesome passages in all of classical literature is Herodotus's account of Pythius the Lydian, who asked the Great King that one of his five sons be allowed to remain behind to tend the old man when the imperial forces left Asia for Greece. In answer, Xerxes had Pythius's favorite boy dismembered—his torso on one side of the roadway, legs on the other—so that the vast conscripted army who trudged between the mutilated and decaying parts for hours on end might learn the wages of disobedience. One of the ironies of Salamis is that the heroic Greek resistance, waged to thwart Persian aggression and preserve Greek freedom, actually resulted in the slaughter of thousands of reluctant allied Asian sailors. Under penalty of death, they fought as Xerxes watched the sea battle from his throne on Mount Aigaleos above—his secretary nearby to record his subjects' gallantry and cowardice for rewards and punishments to follow.

A decade earlier, 6,400 Persians died at Marathon during Darius's ill-fated initial invasion. Just weeks before Salamis, more than 10,000 imperial troops were sacrificed in the Persians' "victory" at Thermopylae to break the Hellenic resistance and open the pass into Greece. And at Artemisium near the pass, a storm may have sunk more than two hundred Persian ships, resulting in nearly as many drowned as at Salamis. In the following autumn another 50,000 subjects of Xerxes would die at Plataea, and yet 100,000 more during the last retreat out of Greece. A quarter million of the king's troops were thus to perish in a vain attempt to take away the freedom of a tiny Balkan country of less than 50,000 square miles.

The end of the Persian Wars signaled not merely a setback for Persia but a catastrophic loss of imperial manpower as well. "Divine Salamis," as the Greeks commemorated the sea victory, was fought for "the freedom of the Greeks." The price of that liberation was the mass slaughter of a host of peoples who had come under the whip, not out of religious, ethnic, or cultural hatred of Hellenic culture. Because none of Xerxes' dead were free citizens in a free society, we understandably know almost nothing about them. There is no Persian play devoted to their memory. No Persian historian, as Herodotus had done at Thermopylae, Salamis, and Plataea, wrote down the names of the brave. Xerxes issued no civic decree from Persepolis offering commemoration for their sacrifice. Neither public cenotaph nor mournful elegy recorded their loss. We owe it to those anonymous and largely innocent dead to keep in mind that the story of Salamis is mostly the daylong saga of 40,000 men thrashing, shrieking, and sobbing as they slowly sank to the bottom off the Attic coast. As Lord Byron dryly wrote of the unnamed "they":

> A king sate on the rocky brow
>   Which looks o'er sea-born Salamis
> And ships, by thousands, lay below,
>   And men in nations;—all were his!
> He counted them at break of day—
>   And when the sun set where were they?
> (*Don Juan*, 86.4)

THE ACHAEMENIDS AND FREEDOM

The Persian Empire at the time of the battle of Salamis was huge—1 million square miles of territory, with nearly 70 million inhabitants—at that point the largest single hegemony in the history of the civilized world. In contrast, Greek-speakers on the mainland numbered less than 2 million and occupied about 50,000 square miles. Persia was also a relatively young sovereignty, less than a hundred years old, robust in its period of greatest power—and largely the product of the genius of its legendary king Cyrus the Great. In a period of not more than thirty years (ca. 560–530 B.C.), Cyrus had transformed the rather small and isolated Persian monarchy (Parsua in what is now Iran and Kurdistan) into a world government. He finally presided over the conquered peoples of most of Asia—ranging from the Aegean Sea to the Indus River, and covering most of the territory between the Persian Gulf and Red Sea in the south and the Caspian and Aral Seas to the north.

After the subsequent loss of the Ionian Greek states on the shores of the Aegean, the mainland Greeks grew familiar with this huge and sophisticated empire now expanding near its eastern borders. What the Greeks learned of Persia—as would be the later European experience with the Ottomans—both fascinated and frightened them. Later an entire series of gifted politicians and renegade intriguers such as Demaratus, Themistocles, and Alcibiades would aid the Persians against their own Greek kin, and yet at the same time loathe their hosts for appealing nakedly to their personal greed. In a similar manner Italian admirals, ship designers, and tacticians would later seek lucrative employment with the Ottomans. Greek moralists, in relating culture and ethics, had long equated Hellenic poverty with liberty and excellence, Eastern affluence with slavery and decadence. So the poet Phocylides wrote, "The law-biding polis, though small and set on a high rock, outranks senseless Nineveh" (frg. 4).

By the time of the reign of Darius I (521–486 B.C.) Persia was a relatively stable empire, governed by the so-called Achaemenid monarchy that oversaw a sophisticated provincial administration of some twenty satrapies. Persian governors collected taxes, provided musters for national campaigns, built and maintained national roads and an efficient royal postal service, and in general left local conquered peoples the freedom to worship their own gods and devise their own means for meeting targeted levels of imperial taxation. To the Greeks, who could never unify properly their own vastly smaller mainland, the Achaemenids' confederation of an entire continent raised the specter of a force of men and resources beyond their comprehension.

What mystified Westerners most—we can pass over their prejudicial view of Easterners as soft, weak, and effeminate—was the Persian Empire's almost total cultural antithesis to everything Hellenic, from politics and military practice to economic and social life. Only a few miles of sea separated Asia Minor from the Greek islands in the Aegean, but despite a similar climate and centuries of interaction, the two cultures were a world apart. This foreign system had resulted not in weakness and decadence, as the Greeks sometimes proclaimed, but ostensibly in relatively efficient imperial administration and vast wealth: Xerxes was on the Athenian acropolis, the Greeks (not yet) in Persepolis. An awe-inspiring impression of Persian power was what Greeks gleaned from itinerant traders, their own imported Eastern chattel slaves, communication from their Ionian brethren, the thousands of Greek-speakers who found employment in the Persian bureaucracy, and random tales from returning mercenaries. The success of the Achaemenid dynasty suggested that there were peoples in the world—and in increasing proximity to Greece—who did things far differently, and in the process became far more wealthy and prosperous than the Greeks.

The absolute rule of millions was in the hands of a very few. The king and his small court of relatives and advisers (their Persian titles variously translate as "bow carrier," "spear bearer," "king's friends," "the king's bene-factor," "the eyes and ears of the king," etc.) oversaw the bureaucracy and priesthood, which thrived from the collection of provincial taxes and ownership of vast estates, while a cadre of Persian elites and Achaemenid kin ran the huge multicultural army. There was apparently no abstract or legal concept of freedom in Achaemenid Persia. Even satraps were re-ferred to as slaves in imperial correspondence: "The King of Kings, Darius son of Hystapes, says these things to his slave Gadatas: 'I learn that you are not obeying my commands in all respects . . .' " (R. Meiggs and D. Lewis, eds., *Greek Historical Inscriptions*, #12, 1–5). The Achaemenid monarch was absolute and, though not divine himself, the regent of the god Ahura Mazda on earth. The practice of *proskynēsis*—kneeling before the Great King—was required of all subjects and foreigners. Aristotle later saw this custom of worshiping men as gods as proof of the wide difference be-tween Eastern and Hellenic notions of individualism, politics, and reli-gion. Whereas the victorious Greek generals of the Persian Wars—the regent Pausanias in Sparta, Miltiades and Themistocles at Athens—were severely criticized for identifying their persons with the Greek triumph, Xerxes, when attempting to cross a choppy Hellespont, had the sea whipped and "branded" for "disobeying" his orders.

Legal codes exist in every civilization. Under the Persians, local judi-ciaries were left in place at Lydia, Egypt, Babylonia, and Ionia—with the proviso that Achaemenid law superseded all statutes, and was established and amended as the Great King himself saw fit. Every man bobbing in the water on September 28 had no legal entity other than as a *bandaka*, or "slave," of Xerxes—a concept taken from the earlier Babylonian idea that the individual was an *ardu*, a "chattel," of the monarch.

Contrarily, in Greece by the fifth century almost all political leaders in the city-states were selected by lot, elected, or subject to annual review by an elected council. No archon claimed divine status; execution by fiat was tantamount to murder; and the greatest vigilance was devoted to pre-venting the resurgence of tyrants, who had plagued a number of the most prosperous and commercial Greek states in the immediate past. Even personal slaves and servants in Greek city-states were often protected from arbitrary torture and murder. These were not alternative approaches to state rule, but fundamental differences in the idea of personal freedom that would help determine who lived and died at Salamis.

The Persian imperial army was huge and commanded at the top by relatives and elites under oath to the king. At its core were professional Persian infantrymen—the so-called Immortals were the most famous—and various contingents of subsidiary heavy and light infantry, supported by vast forces of cavalry, charioteers, and missile troops. In battle the army depended on its speed and numbers. In place of a heavily armed shock force of pikemen that could shatter horsemen and ground troops, Persian infantrymen were often conscripted from hundreds of different regions, spoke dozens of languages, and were armed with swords, daggers, short spears, picks, war axes, and javelins, and protected by wicker shields, leather jerkins, and occasionally chain-mail shirts. Drill, strict adherence to rank and file, and coordinated group advance and retreat were largely unknown. The Greeks' dismissive view about the quality of Persian heavy infantry was largely accurate. Some years later, in the early fourth century, Antiochos, a Greek ambassador from Arcadia, said there was not a man fit in Persia for battle against Greeks. There was no need during the creation of the Persian Empire on the steppes of Asia to field phalanxes of citizen hoplites outfitted in seventy-pound panoplies.

The Achaemenid king was not always perched on a throne overlooking the killing ground—like Xerxes at Thermopylae and Salamis—but more regularly fought in a great chariot, surrounded by bodyguards, in the middle of the Persian battle line: both the safest and most logical position whence to issue orders. Greek historians made much of the obvious dissimilarity: Persian monarchs fled ahead of their armies in defeat, while there is not a single major Greek battle—Thermopylae, Delium, Mantinea, Leuctra—in which Hellenic generals survived the rout of their troops. Military catastrophe brought no reproach upon the Achaemenid king himself; subordinates like the Phoenicians at Salamis were scapegoated and executed. In contrast, there was also not one great Greek general in the entire history of the city-state—Themistocles, Miltiades, Pericles, Alcibiades, Brasidas, Lysander, Pelopidas, Epaminondas—who was not at some time either fined, exiled, or demoted, or killed alongside his troops. Some of the most successful and gifted commanders after their greatest victories—the Athenian admirals who won at Arginusae (406 B.C.), or Epaminondas on his return from liberating the Messenian helots

(369 B.C.)—stood trial for their lives, not so much on charges of cowardice or incompetence as for inattention to the welfare of their men or the lack of communication with their civilian overseers.

In such a vast domain as Persia, there were in theory thousands of individual landholders and private businessmen, but the economic and cultural contrast with fifth-century Greece was again telling. In classical Athens we do not know of a single farm larger than one hundred acres, whereas in Asia—both under the Achaemenids and later during the Hellenistic dynasties—estates exceeded thousands of acres in size. One of Xerxes' relatives might own more property than every rower in the Persian fleet combined. Most of the best land in the empire was under direct control of priests, who sharecropped their domains to serfs, and absentee Persian lords, who often owned entire villages. The Persian king himself, in theory, had title to all the land in the empire and could either exercise rights of confiscation of any estate he wished or execute its owner by fiat.

Greece itself had plenty of its own hierarchies concerning property owning, but the difference lay in the posture of a consensual government toward the entire question of land tenure. Public or religiously held estates were of limited size and relatively rare—comprising not more than 5 percent of the aggregate land surrounding a polis. Property was rather equitably held. Public auctions of repossessed farmland were standard, and prices at public sales low and uniform. Lands in new colonies were surveyed and distributed by lot or public sale, never handed over to a few elites. The so-called hoplite infantry class typically owned farms of about ten acres. In most city-states they made up about a third to half of the citizen population and controlled about two-thirds of all the existing arable land—a pattern of landholding far more egalitarian than, say, in present-day California, where 5 percent of the landowners own 95 percent of all agricultural property.

No Greek citizen could be arbitrarily executed without a trial. His property was not liable to confiscation except by vote of a council, whether that be a landed boule in broadly based oligarchies or a popular ekklēsia under democracy. In the Greek mind the ability to hold property freely—have legal title to it, improve it, and pass it on—was the foundation of freedom. While such classical agrarian traditions would erode during the later Roman Empire and the early Dark Ages, with the creation of vast absentee estates and ecclesiastical fiefdoms, the ideal would not be abandoned, but rather still provided the basis for revolution and rural reform in the West from the Renaissance to the present day.

While there were vast state mints in Persia, our sources for Achaemenid imperial administration—borne out by the later arrival of the looters and plunderers in Alexander the Great's army—suggest that tons of stored bullion remained uncoined and that there was a chronic stagnation in the Persian economy. With metals on deposit in imperial treasuries, provincial taxes were more often paid in kind as "gifts"—food, livestock, metals, slaves, property—rather than in specie, illustrative of high taxes and an undeveloped moneyed economy. One of the reasons for the initial rampant expansion and inflation of the later Hellenistic world (323–31 B.C.) was the sudden conversion of precious metals stored in the Achaemenid vaults into readily coined money by the Macedonian Successor kings, who, in transforming a command economy to a more capitalist one, hired out thousands of builders, shippers, and mercenaries.

Persian literature—a corpus of drama, philosophy, or poetry apart from religious or political stricture—did not exist. True, Zoroastrianism was a fascinating metaphysical inquiry, but its reason to be was religious, and thus the parameters of its thought were one with all holy treatises, embedded as it was with a zeal that precluded unlimited speculation and true free expression. History—the Greeks' idea of free inquiry, in which the records and sources of the past are continually subject to questioning and evaluation as part of an effort to provide a timeless narrative of explication—was also unknown among the Persians, at least in any widely disseminated form. The nearest approximation was the public inscriptions of the Achaemenids themselves, in which a Darius I or Xerxes published his own res gestae:

> A great god is Ahura Mazda, who created this earth, who created man, who created peace for man, who made Xerxes king, one king of many, one lord of many. I am Xerxes, the great king, king of kings, king of lands containing many men, king in this great earth far and wide, son of Darius the king, an Achaemenid, a Persian, so of a Persian, an Aryan, of Aryan seed. (A. Olmstead, *History of the Persian Empire,* 231)

The emperor Augustus issued similar proclamations in imperial Rome, but there were still a Suetonius, Plutarch, and Tacitus eventually to set the record straight. Just as the Ottomans would later bar printing presses throughout their empire in fear of free expression, the idea of public criticism of the Achaemenids through written documents was literally unknown.

All Persian texts—whether public inscriptions, palace inventories, or sacred tracts—concern the king, his priests, and bureaucrats at large, and confine themselves to government and religion. Even if other avenues of public expression had existed, the Persian victory at Thermopylae could not have been portrayed onstage or remembered in poetry without the approval of Xerxes—and not without Xerxes as chief protagonist in the triumph. The commemoration of the Persian victory in Bactria proves that well enough: "Says Xerxes the king: When I became king, there was within these lands which are written above one which was restless. Afterward Ahura Mazda brought me help. By the favor of Ahura Mazda I smote that land and put it in its place" (A. Olmstead, *History of the Persian Empire,* 231).

Persian religion was not as absolutist as that in Egypt, inasmuch as the Achaemenids were agents of Ahura Mazda, not divinities per se. Nevertheless, royal power was predicated on divine right, imperial edict was considered a holy act. So the constant refrain of all the Achaemenid kings: "Of me is Ahura Mazda, of Ahura Mazda am I." When Alexander the Great learned to say the same thing, even his most loyal Macedonian lords began to plot either an assassination, a coup, or a return to Greece. Conquered peoples of the Persian Empire like the Babylonians and Jews, however, at the local level were left to worship their own gods. Because *no* culture in the conquered East had any tradition of religion apart from politics, or even embraced the ideal of religious diversity, most Persian subjects considered the Achaemenid religious-political relationship not any different from their own—and if anything more tolerant.

That being said, there were numerous castes of holy men who not only enjoyed political power as agents of the king but also sought vast acreages to support their work. The official white-robed magi were employed by the monarchy as religious auditors in public ceremony and to ensure the piety of the imperial subjects. Mathematics and astronomy were advanced, but ultimately they were subject to religious scrutiny and used to promote in a religious context the arts of divination and prophesy. A humanist such as Protagoras ("Man is the measure of all things") or an atheist rationalist like Anaxagoras ("Whatever has life, both the greater and smaller, Mind *[nous]* controls them all . . . whatsoever things are now and will be, Mind arranged them all") could not have prospered under the Achaemenids. Such freethinking in Persia might arise only through imperial laxity; and if discovered, was subject to immediate imperial censure. The classical Greeks were as pious as the Persians, but when conservative citizens rallied to rid their cities of atheistic provocateurs, they first sought a majority decree of the people or at least the semblance of an open jury trial.

If in the past Western historians have relied on Greek authors such as Aeschylus, Herodotus, Xenophon, Euripides, Isocrates, and Plato to form stereotypes of the Persians as decadent, effete, corrupt, and under the spell of eunuchs and harems, the careful examination of imperial archives and inscriptions of the Achaemenids should warn us of going too far in the other direction. The Persian army at Salamis was not decadent or effeminate, but it did constitute a complete alternate universe to almost everything Greek. All things considered, there was no polis to the east. Achaemenid Persia—like Ottoman Turkey or Montezuma's Aztecs—was a vast two-tiered society in which millions were ruled by autocrats, audited by theocrats, and coerced by generals.

THE PERSIAN WARS AND THE STRATEGY OF SALAMIS

Salamis was the central battle in the clash of two entirely different cultures, one enormous, wealthy, and imperial, the other small, poor, and decentralized. The former drew its enormous strength from the taxes, manpower, and obedience that a centralized palatial culture can so well command; the latter from the spontaneity, innovation, and initiative that arise exclusively in small, autonomous, and free communities of lifelong peers. Contemporary Greeks themselves believed that the course of the war hinged mostly on a question of absolute values. Indeed, they felt that it centered on their own strange idea of freedom, or *eleutheria*—theirs to keep, Xerxes' to take away. The war, in their eyes, would hinge on how much freedom was worth and to what degree it might trump the king's enormous advantages in numbers, material wealth, and military experience. The Athenian infantry's triumph at Marathon ten years earlier had stopped cold a local punitive incursion of Darius, a day's battle that saw Athens and Plataea alone of the Greeks take the field. That initial Persian expeditionary force of 490 B.C. was not large by later standards—at most, 30,000 invading troops were pitted against a little more than 10,000 Greeks. Xerxes' subsequent muster, however, was a different army altogether.

Thermopylae, fought a decade after Marathon, was a terrible defeat— for all its gallantry and talk of Greek freedom perhaps the greatest loss in the entire history of Panhellenic operations, and one of the few times in history that an Asian army would defeat a Western force inside Europe.

The nearly simultaneous sea battle at Artemesium was at best a strategic Greek withdrawal. Hence in any analysis of why the Greeks won the Persian Wars, we are left to consider just two pivotal victories of the conflict: Salamis and the subsequent infantry battle of Plataea.

Mycale (August 479 B.C.), fought off the coast of Ionia in Asia Minor at or near the same time as Plataea, inaugurates a period of Greek expansion into the Aegean Sea, rather than a defense of the Greek mainland per se. Yet Mycale was made possible only by the previous victory at Salamis. Plataea, fought in a small valley about ten miles south of Thebes almost a year after the Greeks' mastery at Salamis, was a magnificent Greek triumph, resulting in the destruction of the remaining Persian infantry in the field and marking the final expulsion of the king's infantry forces from Greece. Yet that landmark battle—where the Persian general Mardonius was killed and most of the remaining Persians slaughtered or scattered—is understood only in the context of the tactical, strategic, and spiritual success of Salamis the September before, which energized the Greeks to press on with the war. The Persians subsequently at Plataea fought *without* King Xerxes, his battered armada, and some of his best Persian troops that had either drowned at Salamis or fled to Persian territory nearly a year earlier after their naval defeat at Salamis. There was to be no supporting Persian fleet for Mardonius's infantry off the coast of eastern Boeotia—it was either on the bottom of the channel off Salamis or long ago dispersed to the East. In addition, there may have been more Greek infantry at Plataea—60,000 to 70,000 hoplites and even more light-armed soldiers—than would ever marshal in one army again in Greek history. Herodotus believed that more than 110,000 combined Hellenic troops were present. Thus, the Persians fought at Plataea in summer 479 B.C. as a recently defeated force, without the overwhelming numerical superiority they enjoyed at Salamis and without their king and his enormous fleet. At Plataea the invaders could not be reinforced by sea or land. The confident Greeks, in contrast, poured into the small Boeotian plain, convinced that their Persian enemies were retreating from Attica, demoralized from their defeat at Salamis, and abandoned by their political and military leadership.

How different things were a year earlier at Salamis—and how difficult it is for the historian to fathom how the Greeks could actually win! After evacuating its countryside and city, Athens—its recently constructed fleet of two hundred ships composed two-thirds of the Greek contingent—was unwilling to fight one yard farther south. Nearly all the Athenian citizenry had been evacuated to Salamis proper, Aegina, and Troezen in the Argolid.

Thus, by September 480 B.C., for the Greeks to sail a league southward from the Saronic Gulf was to abandon the civilian refugees of Attica to Xerxes' troops—and essentially to end the idea of Athens itself, which, with the loss of Salamis, would now not possess a single inch of native soil. "If you do not do these things [fight at Salamis]," Themistocles warned his Peloponnesian allies, "then we quite directly shall take up our households and sail over to Siris in Italy, a place which has been ours from ancient times, and at which the oracles inform us that we should plant a colony. And the rest of you, bereft of allies such as ourselves, will have reason to remember my words" (Herodotus 8.62.). Greeks fought for freedom in the Persian Wars, but there were astute statesmen in the Peloponnese who wished to postpone their final reckoning with Xerxes until there was no other alternative and all the other city-states had first committed their final reserves in this war of Armageddon.

At Salamis most Greeks conceded that the further participation of the refugee Athenians, still the greatest sea power of the Panhellenic alliance, hinged on two prerequisites: a sea battle had to be fought immediately after the evacuation of Attica; and it had to be waged in a buffer area between the Persians and the Athenians' own vulnerable civilian population. A September fight off Salamis was thus the only alternative to retain Athenian participation, the foundation of the alliance. All other northern Greeks, with minor exceptions, had not only ceased resistance once their homeland was overwhelmed, but actually supplied troops to Xerxes' cause. The Athenians' threat to sail westward was no mere boast: they really did mean to abandon the cause should the southern Greeks not make a last effort of resistance at Salamis.

The Athenians had evacuated Athens because their 10,000 or so heavy hoplite infantrymen were no match for the Persian horde. After the slaughter at Thermopylae, no Panhellenic hoplite force was eager to marshal in the Attic plain to defend the city against a victorious enemy that was now swelled by the medizing Greeks of Thessaly and Boeotia. True, most Greeks still preferred decisive battle, preferably on land and by heavy infantry. Yet until Xerxes' source of naval support, transport, and allied help were ruined, any such spectacular last stand would result in little more than Greek slaughter. One heroic catastrophe at Thermopylae for the time was enough, as most realized that the existence of an enormous Persian enemy fleet meant that any Greek land defense might be outflanked from the rear through naval landings, while the loss of Boeotia had eliminated a pool of some of the best hoplites on the Greek mainland.

There are no large islands immediately off the Hellenic coast to the

south between Salamis and the Isthmus of Corinth or along the northeastern shore of the Argolid peninsula, no narrows and inlets that might
have offered the outnumbered and "heavier" Greek fleet a confined channel in which to offset the numerical advantage of the Persian armada.
Even if the Athenians could have been convinced to fight to the south of
Salamis, transporting those refugees on Aegina and Salamis southward to
join those already on Troezen, there were only two alternatives of defense:
a sea battle in the open waters to the south or a suicidal land defense behind the fortifications of the isthmus itself. Neither offered hope of victory.

Herodotus reports a pre-battle speech of Themistocles to his fellow
Greek generals in which he rejected such a naval engagement off Corinth:
"If you engage the enemy at the Isthmus, you will fight in open waters,
where it is to our worst advantage, inasmuch as our ships are heavier and
less in number. In addition, you will forfeit Salamis, Megara, and Aegina
even if we should win a victory there" (8.60). In contrast, Themistocles
added, a fight at Salamis would ensure that the Peloponnesians might
keep their enemies from approaching the isthmus and thus far distant
from their own territory. Victory at Salamis might save Athens and the
Peloponnese. Even success at the isthmus was too late for the salvation of
Attica. The key for the Greek defense was to keep its two greatest powers,
Athens and Sparta, free and committed to the spirit of Panhellenic defense.

Mnesiphilius, an Athenian, earlier warned Themistocles that, should
the Greeks not fight at Salamis, there was little chance that the Panhellenic
armada would again assemble as one fleet, even at the isthmus.
"Everyone," Mnesiphilius predicted, "will withdraw to their own city-
states, and neither Eurybiades nor any other man will be able to hold
them together, but rather the armada will break apart" (8.57). For that
reason, Herodotus makes Queen Artemisia, one of Xerxes' admirals, although fearing for her life, advise the Persians to avoid Salamis, wait, and
gradually head south by land to the isthmus. She argued that a sea battle
at Salamis would be the only chance of the squabbling Greeks to unite
against the Persian onslaught.

The Peloponnesian Greeks in Herodotus's account clung stubbornly
to the idea of a land defense and hurriedly fortified the isthmus while
their admirals debated at Salamis. Not only would the Athenian fleet have
been reluctant to participate in such an effort of the Peloponnesian states
when Athens's entire population was enslaved—its ships would have been
of little value anyway in a fight behind fortifications—but there is good

reason, as Herodotus foresaw, that it would have failed. An intact Persian fleet could easily have landed troops to the rear of the Greek army all along the coast of the Peloponnese.

The last hope of Hellenic civilization to defeat an empire twenty times larger than its own was to force a battle at Salamis. The slim chance of victory lay largely with the strategic and tactical genius of Themistocles and the courage and audacity of the sailors of the Panhellenic fleet, who were fighting for their freedom and the survival of their families. The problem, however, was that throughout 480 B.C. free Greeks continued to bicker, vote, and threaten each other, all the while unfree Persians annexed even more of their native soil. This freedom to explore different strategies, debate tactics, and listen to complaints of the sailors was raucous and not pretty, but when the battle itself got under way, the Greeks, not the Persians, had at last discovered the best way to fight in the strait of Salamis.

THE BATTLE

Had the 40,000 who drowned and their surviving comrades succeeded, there would have been no autonomous Greece, and Western civilization itself would have been aborted in its two-century infancy. Salamis was in some sense the last chance of the fragile Greek coalition to thwart Xerxes before his forces occupied the nearby Peloponnese and so completed his final conquest of mainland Greece. The Athenian refugees were huddled in makeshift quarters on the nearby islands of Salamis and Aegina and on the coast of the Argolid, their very culture on the verge of extinction. We must remember that when Salamis was fought, the Athenians had already lost their homeland. The battle was an effort not to save, but to reclaim, their ancestral ground.

Unfortunately, our ancient sources—the historian Herodotus and the playwright Aeschylus, along with much later accounts from the Roman period by Plutarch, Diodorus, and Nepos—tell us almost nothing about the battle itself, but do suggest that the reconstituted Greek fleet was outnumbered by at least two to one and perhaps by as much as three or even four to one. We are not sure how many ships were present at the battle on either side—given prior losses at the first sea battle at Artemesium weeks earlier and subsequent reinforcements—but there must have been somewhere between 300 and 370 Greek vessels arrayed against a Persian armada of well over 600 warships. Both Aeschylus and Herodotus, however, were certain that the Persian armada was even larger, numbering more than 1,000 ships and 200,000 seamen. If they are correct, Salamis involved the greatest number of combatants in any one engagement in the entire history of naval warfare.

Most ancient observers also remark that the sailors of the Greek fleet were less experienced than those of the imperial Persian flotilla, who were veteran rowers from Phoenicia, Egypt, Asia Minor, Cyprus, and Greece itself. The Athenian armada was scarcely three years old, its more than two hundred ships built suddenly on the advice of Themistocles, who presciently feared fellow Greek—or Persian—naval aggrandizement. With far fewer ships and less seaworthy craft, the Panhellenic armada's only hope, as Themistocles saw, was to draw the Persian fleet into the narrows between the island and the mainland. There the invaders would not have room to maneuver fully, and thus would lose their advantage in manpower and maritime experience, as spirited Greek rowers repeatedly rammed their triremes into the multicultural armada. Herodotus also speaks of the Greek ships as "heavier" (baruteras). This does not necessarily mean that the Hellenic triremes were better designed and more seaworthy. Some scholars suggest that Herodotus meant that the Greek vessels were either waterlogged, built of unseasoned timber, or larger and less elegant—both less maneuverable and more difficult to sink—than the Persians'. Whatever the case, it was clearly in the Greeks' interest *not* to go out to sea, where they would be not only outnumbered but outmaneuvered.

The Persians, perhaps fooled by a ruse of Themistocles, believed that the Athenians were retreating southward via the Bay of Eleusis through the strait of Megara. In response, they split and thus weakened their forces by sending ships to block the passages off both the northern and the western shores of Salamis as well. The king's fleet attacked just before dawn, rowing forward in three lines against the Greeks' two. Very quickly, the armada became disorganized due to the Greek ramming and the confusion of having too many ships in such confined waters. The uniformity of the Greek crews, their superior discipline and greater morale help explain why they were able to strike the enemy ships repeatedly without being boarded by the numerically superior enemy. The experienced Egyptian contingent did not fight at all, but waited in vain far to the north for an expected Greek retreat off Megara.

Themistocles led the Panhellenic attack in his own trireme. His sheer magnetism and threats had kept the Greeks together after the Persian occupation of everything north of the isthmus; and his secret but false promises to the Persian king of a surrender on the eve of the battle had

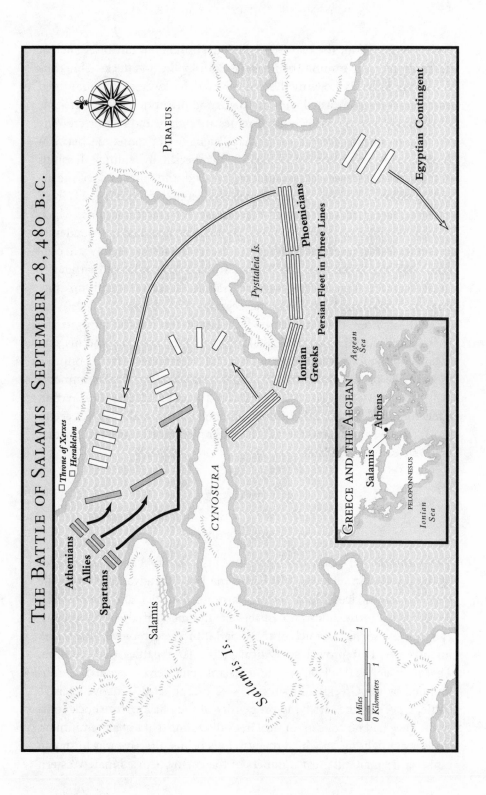

THE BATTLE OF SALAMIS SEPTEMBER 28, 480 B.C.

PIRAEUS

Egyptian Contingent

□ Throne of Xerxes
□ Herakleion

Athenians

Allies

Spartans

Phoenicians

Persian Fleet in Three Lines

Pystaleia Is.

Ionian Greeks

CYNOSURA

Salamis

Salamis Is.

0 Miles   1
0 Kilometers   1

GREECE AND THE AEGEAN

Aegean Sea

Salamis   Athens

PELOPONNESUS

Ionian Sea

fooled Xerxes about the real Greek intent. Throughout our brief ancient descriptions, the common theme is Greek discipline in attack—ships advancing in order, as crews methodically rowed, backwatered, and rammed on command—contrasted with the chaos and disruption of the Persians, who vainly tried to board Greek triremes at random and kill the crews.

The battle was fought for perhaps eight hours sometime between September 20 and 30, but most likely September 28. By nightfall the ships of the Persian fleet were either sunk or scattered, and the morale of the invading sailors lost. Most enemy vessels were sunk by ramming, as Greek triremes darted in and out of the clumsy Persian formations, which quickly became dispersed as national contingents operated independently and in their own interests. Although in theory the fleeing enemy still outnumbered the Greek fleet, the Persian armada was no longer battleworthy, with more than 100,000 imperial sailors killed, wounded, missing, dispersed, or sailing back across the Aegean.

Within a few days Xerxes himself began the march home to the Hellespont, accompanied by 60,000 infantry and leaving behind his surrogate commander, Mardonius, with a still enormous force to continue the struggle on the Greek mainland the next year. The Greeks immediately declared victory. The Athenians would soon reoccupy Attica. Within a few months Hellenic infantrymen streamed in from all over Greece to finish off the Persian land forces, who had retired northward into Boeotia and were camped at Plataea.

ELEUTHERIA

Free Seamen at Salamis

The outnumbered, poor, and beleaguered Greeks of 480 B.C., as is the lot of the invaded in all wars, still had some intrinsic advantages over the Persians: knowledge of local terrain, favorable logistics, and the possibility of using fortifications to offset the numbers of their opponents. Herodotus also makes much of the superior bronze panoply of the Greek infantrymen that proved so critical at the land battles of Marathon, Thermopylae, and Plataea. The Persians themselves seemed dumbfounded by the Greek willingness to seek out an all-destructive decisive battle, especially the terrifying propensity of the phalanx for shock collisions. They had no concept of the Greek discipline that put a premium on close-order fighting, in which the warrior's prime directive was to stay in rank, rather than kill great numbers of the enemy. Those innate Western military characteristics would resurface in the next century, and they help to explain why a European Xenophon, Agesilaus, and Alexander, with a mere few thousand troops, could do in Asia what Xerxes with hundreds of thousands could not in Europe.

All that being said, the Greeks who rammed the enemy head-on at Salamis believed that freedom *(eleutheria)* had proved to be the real key to their victory. Freedom, they believed, had made their warriors qualitatively better fighters than the Persians—or any other unfree tribe, people, or state to the west as well as east—breeding in them a superior morale and greater incentive to kill the enemy. Aeschylus and Herodotus are clear on this. While we are not so interested in their respective descriptions of Persian customs and motivations, which are often secondhand and can be biased, both authors are believable in reflecting what the Greeks believed was at stake at Salamis.

The moral drawn by Herodotus, for example, is unmistakable: free citizens are better warriors, since they fight for themselves, their families and property, not for kings, aristocrats, or priests. They accept a greater degree of discipline than either coerced or hired soldiers. After Marathon (490 B.C.), Herodotus makes the point that the Athenians fought much better under their newly won democracy than during the long reign of the Peisistratid tyrants: "As long as the Athenians were ruled by a despotic government, they had no better success at war than any of their neighbors. Once the yoke was flung off, they proved the finest fighters in the world." Herodotus explains why this is so: in the past "they battled less than their best because they were working for a master; but as free men each individual person wanted to achieve something for himself" (5.78).

When asked why the Greeks did not come to terms with Persia at the outset, the Spartan envoys tell Hydarnes, the military commander of the Western provinces, that the reason is freedom:

> Hydarnes, the advice you give us does not arise from a full knowledge of our situation. You are knowledgeable about only one half of what is involved; the other half is a blank to you. The reason is that you understand well enough what slavery is, but freedom you have never experienced, so you do not know if it tastes sweet or not. If you ever did come to experience it, you would advise us to fight for it not with spears only, but with axes too. (Herodotus 7.135)

Aeschylus, as the chapter epigraph indicates, suggested that the Greeks went to battle at Salamis exhorting each other to "Free your native soil. Free your children, your wives, the images of your fathers' gods, and the tombs of your ancestors!" (*Persians* 402–5). After the victory at Salamis the Athenians turned down all offers of mediation with a curt dismissal: "We ourselves know well the power of the Persian is many times that of our own; it is not necessary to taunt us on that account. Nevertheless, out of our zeal for our freedom, we shall defend ourselves in any way that we are able" (Herodotus 8.143). To the Greeks freedom was almost religious in nature. The Athenians worshiped the abstractions of "Democracy" and "Freedom," the latter as part of the cult of Zeus Eleutherios ("Zeus the Freedom-Giver")—deities that did more for the average Athenian than Ahura Mazda had ever done for a Persian subject.

Herodotus himself editorialized of the victory at Salamis, "Greece was saved by the Athenians . . . who, having chosen that Greece should live and preserve her freedom, roused to battle the other Greek states which had not yet submitted" (7.139). Almost a year later at the battle of Plataea, the Hellenic alliance required each soldier before the battle to swear an oath beginning, "I shall fight to the death, and I shall not count my life more valuable than freedom" (Diodorus 11.29.3). After the conclusion of the war, the Greeks dedicated a monument of their victory at the sanctuary at Delphi with the inscription "The saviors of wide Greece set up this monument, having delivered their city-states from a loathsome slavery" (Diodorus 11.33.2).

Not only did ancient observers believe that Salamis and the other battles of the Persian Wars were fought on behalf of freedom against a "loathsome slavery," but in an abstract sense they agreed that being free was the foundation for the battle morale that would overcome the superior numbers and wealth of any potential enemy. Greek authors repeatedly associated battle proficiency with a free militia; freedom in itself did not ensure victory but gave an army an advantage that might on any occasion cancel out the superior generalship, numbers, or equipment of an enemy. Aristotle, who lived in an age of increasing use of mercenary troops, nevertheless had no doubt about this relationship between freedom and military excellence. Of the free city-state, he wrote: "Infantrymen of the polis think it is a disgraceful thing to run away, and they choose death over safety through flight. On the other hand, professional soldiers, who rely from the outset on superior strength, flee as soon as they find out they are outnumbered, fearing death more than dishonor" (*Nicomachean Ethics* 3.1116b16–23).

There was always the obvious contrast of free Greeks with the largely multicultural army of serfs who were routinely mustered by imperial

Persia. Xenophon, for example, makes Cyrus the Younger explain to his Greek mercenaries before the battle of Cunaxa (401 B.C.) why he has hired them to fight his own people:

> Men of Greece, it is not because I do not have enough barbarian troops that I have led you here to fight on my behalf. But rather I brought you here because I thought you were braver and stronger than many barbarian soldiers. Therefore make sure that you will be worthy of the freedom *[eleutherias]* that you possess and for which I greatly admire you. For you know well that freedom *[eleutherian]* is one trait that I would choose before everything else that I have and much more besides. (*Anabasis* 1.7.3–4)

This passage reflects all the traditional stereotypes of a Greek author. Still, we should not forget three salient facts. One, Xenophon himself was a veteran of campaigns in which Greeks defeated Asian troops on every occasion. Two, Darius, Xerxes, Cyrus, and Artaxerxes (and Darius III to come) all hired large numbers of Greek mercenaries, while almost *no* Greek poleis—and many had capital to employ troops from almost everywhere in the Mediterranean world—ever sought out Persian infantry. Three, Cyrus acknowledges that the priceless freedom he alone enjoys by virtue of being an autocrat in Persia is extended on the other side of the Aegean Sea to the common man. Seventy years later at Cunaxa, not far from where the Ten Thousand had routed their Persian adversaries, Alexander the Great, who had done as much as anyone to destroy Greek freedom, nevertheless reminded his Macedonians on the eve of the battle of Gaugamela (331 B.C.) that they would win easily. They were, the king boasted, still *free* men fighting against the slave subjects of Persia.

Throughout Greek literature the singularity of Greek freedom is made clear, a strange idea that seems in its abstract sense not to have existed in any other culture of the time, but emerged in the seventh and sixth centuries among Greek-speakers in the small, relatively isolated farming valleys of the mainland, the Aegean islands, and the western Greek coast of Asia Minor. The word "freedom" or its equivalent—like the equally odd "citizen" (*politēs*), "consensual government" (*politeia*), and "democracy" (*dēmokratia, isēgoria*)—seems not to be found in the lexicon of contemporary ancient languages other than Latin (e.g., *libertas;* cf. *civis, res publica*). Neither tribal Gauls to the north nor sophisticated Egyptians south of the Mediterranean entertained such preposterous ideas.

The freedom of the Greek city-states was not the de facto freedom of tribal nomads who seek only to roam unchecked. The historian Diodorus, for example, admitted that even wild animals fight for their "freedom." Nor was it the unbridled latitude that the elite rulers in a ranked society such as Persia or Egypt enjoyed. Rather, the Greeks' discovery of *eleutheria* turned out to be a concept that could transcend the vagaries of time and space—urban and rural, a dense or a sparse landscape, consensual government that was narrowly defined as in oligarchies, or broadly practiced as in democracies. It ensured the individual citizen freedom of association, freedom to elect representatives, freedom to own property and acquire wealth without fear of confiscation, and freedom from arbitrary punishment and coercion.

Within the more than 1,000 city-states not everyone was free. In the four-century history of the autonomous polis (700–300 B.C.) there were gradations in which property qualifications were high, moderate, and nonexistent, and office-holding was variously open to the few, many, and all. In many cases there were nominal citizens who could not vote or voice their opinions so freely and publicly—though even the most oligarchic states never attempted to establish a theocracy that might control the social, cultural, and economic behavior of its subjects. Western autocracies in general that did arise never succeeded to the degree of Eastern despots in controlling the lives of their subjects. Still, none of the city-states from the Black Sea to southern Italy extended political equality to women, slaves, and foreigners. Such laudable concepts were confined to utopian thinkers and comic poets like Aristophanes, the pre-Socratics, Plato, and the Stoic philosophers.

In regard to such Greek political discrimination, we might keep in mind two considerations. First, by and large, the sins of the Greeks—slavery, sexism, economic exploitation, ethnic chauvinism—are largely the sins of man common to *all* cultures at *all* times. The "others" in the Greek world—foreigners, slaves, women—were also "others" in *all* other societies of the time (and sometimes continue to be "marginalized" in non-Western cultures today, if the continuance of slavery in Africa, the caste system in India, and the mutilation of women is any indication). Second, freedom is an evolving idea, a miraculous and dangerous concept that has no logical restrictions on its ultimate development once it is hatched. The early poleis of the seventh and sixth centuries insisted on property qualifications, which were dropped by Athens and other democracies in the fifth. By the Macedonian conquest of the fourth century, in literature, on the stage, in philosophical debate and oratory, Greeks were calling for a freedom and equality that might extend to others besides the native-born male citizen. We must be careful not to expect perfection from the first two centuries of freedom's existence; we should instead appreciate how peculiar it was to have appeared so early in any form at all.

The Meaning of Freedom

If we were to ask a Greek sailor at Salamis, "What is this freedom you row for?," he might provide a four-part answer. First, freedom to speak what he pleased. The Greeks, in fact, had not one, but two, words for free speech: *isēgoria,* equality in the right to speak publicly in the Assembly, and *parrhēsia,* the right to say what one wished. As Sophocles put it, "Free men have free tongues" (frg. 927a)—and we see just such unfettered expression not only on the Athenian stage but throughout the campaign at Salamis. Councils were called constantly. The Athenians debated on whether to evacuate Attica, the Peloponnesians whether to fight at the Isthmus of Corinth, and all the Greeks whether to stake all at Salamis—and then, when and how. Statesmen such as Eurybiades, Themistocles, Adeimantus, and the other generals shouted and screamed at each other in heated open disputation. These nearly constant deliberations Herodotus characterized as "wars of words" or "a great pushing match of words." Before the battle, men in the streets freely offered their opinions—what the historian Diodorus called the "unrest of the masses"—and generals in consequence fanned out to monitor the public pulse. Later the Athenians even had their triremes named *Dēmokratia, Eleutheria,* and *Parrhēsia*—nomenclature that would have gotten their captains decapitated in the Persian armada. The idea that a Persian ship would be called *Free Speech* is inconceivable.

Such license was not present on the Persian side. The result was inferior strategy, a high command removed from the realities of the fleet, and no sense that any Persian admiral had any hand in the plan of attack. Aeschylus makes a chorus of Persian elders lament that the defeat at Salamis boded ill: "No longer will men keep a curb on their tongues; for now people are free to express their thoughts as they pleased once the yoke of imperial power has been broken" (*Persians* 591–92). The Spartan turncoat Demaratus advises Dicaeus not to voice his fears for the Persian fleet before his king, Xerxes: "Keep your silence and speak to no other person. If your words were reported to the king, you will lose your head" (Herodotus 8.65). After the battle the Phoenician admirals came to Xerxes to complain that they had been betrayed by the Ionian Greeks, who had deserted the Persian cause. Their criticism displeased Xerxes, and so he had them all decapitated. As Greek rowers closed on their enemy, they pulled with the assurance that they could air their concerns about the fighting, whereas Persian sailors realized that to do so might mean their own immediate execution.

Second, the Greek rowers at Salamis also fought with the belief that their governments at Athens, Corinth, Aegina, Sparta, and the other states of the Panhellenic alliance were based on the consent of the citizenry. Men like Themistocles and Eurybiades were either elected directly by the people or appointed by popular representatives. At Salamis Greek rowers rammed their opponents' ships on the assurance that the battle was of their own choosing; the invaders who drowned accepted the stark truth that they were in the channel solely because of the fancy of the Persian king. Over the long haul, men fight better when they know that they have had the freedom to choose the occasion of their own deaths.

In the aftermath of Salamis the Greek veterans of the battle voted awards for heroism and commendation. In contrast, imperial scribes brought their lists down from Xerxes' perch to mete out punishment for the Persian disaster. Earlier at the battle of Thermopylae, Persian soldiers, as was routine, were whipped by their officers to charge the Greeks, while the Spartans willingly decided to sacrifice themselves to the man for the cause of Greek freedom. Hitting a Greek hoplite while on campaign might prompt a public audit of a general's conduct. Lashing Persian infantry was seen as essential in maintaining the morale of the Persian army. Themistocles, rebuked by his own sailors, pilloried in the Athenian Assembly, and attacked in the Panhellenic council, rowed to victory beside his own men, while Xerxes sat on an ornate stool far above the channel— with every one of his impressed sailors below terrified that the eye of the Great King was upon him. Coercion and fear of execution can be wonderful incentives to fight, but the Greeks were right that freedom in the long run is a far better motive still.

Third, the Greeks at Salamis freely had the right to buy and sell property, pass it on, and to improve or neglect it as they saw fit, immune from political or religious coercion or confiscation. Even the landless sailor at Athens, in theory, could open a shop, trade his leather goods for a small vineyard, or hire himself out as a teamster, in the hopes of eventually obtaining some capital and land for his children. Most of those who drowned at Salamis worked vast estates owned by kings, satraps, gods, or aristocrats. Men fight better when they believe that war will preserve their own property and not that of someone else. When the Persians vacated Greece, stories abounded of the vast hordes of precious metals and bullion left behind—understandable when we realize there were no banks or other mechanisms in the East to protect private wealth from confiscation or arbitrary taxation.

Later Eastern armies brought along their money into battle, while their Western counterparts left it at home, trusting in the law to protect the private capital of the free citizen. At Lepanto Ali Pasha hid a treasure on his flagship, *Sultana,* while Don Juan had none of his personal fortune on the *Reale.* Had the Greeks lost at Salamis, Attica would immediately have become the private domain of the Great King, who in turn would have distributed it to favored elites and relatives, who further would have sharecropped it to ex-soldiers under less-than-favorable conditions. Freedom is the glue of capitalism, that amoral wisdom of the markets that most efficiently allots goods and services to a citizenry.

Finally, the Greeks at Salamis entertained a freedom of action. Some stubborn Athenians, for example, chose to stay in the city and thus die on the acropolis. Other Peloponnesians remained at home to fortify the isthmus. Throughout the campaign refugees, soldiers, and onlookers came and went, some to Aegina, others to Troezen and Salamis as they saw fit. When Pythius the Lydian dared act individually, King Xerxes had his son cut in two. No Athenian contemplated slicing to pieces any of his fellow citizens who preferred not to follow the general decree of the Assembly to evacuate Attica. Aristotle notes of freedom that the key principle is "a man should live as he pleases. This, they say, is the mark of liberty, since, on the other hand, not to live as a man wishes is the mark of a slave" (*Politics* 6.1317b10–13). This idea of freedom as the unfettered ability to choose is championed in Pericles' majestic funeral speech, recorded in the second book of Thucydides' history: "The freedom which we enjoy in our government extends also to our ordinary life. There, far from exercising a jealous surveillance over each other, we do not feel called upon to be angry with our neighbor for doing what he likes." At Athens, he adds a little later, "we live exactly as we please" (2.37, 39). In the Persian army such freedom was restricted to the Achaemenid elite. If it existed for a few rowers in the fleet, it was a result of laxity in control, or through kinship or favor with the king, to be revoked at his whim—not as an innate, legal, and abstract privilege for all citizens.

A Persian sailor who preferred to stay behind in occupied Attica, who argued with his satrap or walked on Xerxes' beach without permission, was as likely to be punished as his counterpart across the strait on Salamis was to be left alone. Western armies, it is true, are often unruly. At Salamis it was a miracle that there was any unity in attack or even a rough agreement on an operational plan among so many diverse and independent entities—such pre-battle squabbling between freemen would also nearly wreck the Christian effort in the hours before Lepanto. Nevertheless, freedom of action again pays dividends in battle. Soldiers and sailors improvise and act spontaneously if they are assured they will not be whipped or beheaded. Their energies are not diverted to hiding failure in fear of execution. Free men fight openly with the trust that later audit and inquiry by their peers will sort out the cowards from the brave.

Themistocles on his own accord sent a secret deceptive message to the Persians before the battle. The Greeks marshaled for one last general assembly in the minutes before rowing out. Greek triremes singly and in groups joined at the last moment from the nearby islands and defected from the Persian armada itself. The Athenian conservative Aristides on his own initiative landed on the island of Pysttaleia to expel the Persian garrison. All were individual and free acts done by those who themselves were used "to do as they pleased." Freedom of speech draws on collective wisdom and is thus critical among high command. In the heated debate over the defense of Salamis, Plutarch relates that Themistocles snarled to his rival Eurybiades, who was in charge of the Peloponnesian fleet and had expressed little inclination to fight for the Athenians at Salamis, "Strike me, but at least hear me out!" (*Themistocles* 11.3). And he did— and the Greeks won.

Freedom in Battle

Western ideas of freedom, originating from the early Hellenic concept of politics as consensual government *(politeia)* and from an open economy that gave the individual opportunity to profit *(kerdos)*, protected his land *(klēros)*, and offered some independence *(autonomia)* and escape from coercion and drudgery, were to play a role at nearly every engagement in which Western soldiers fought. Freedom, along with other elements of the Western paradigm, would help to nullify customary European weakness in manpower, immobility, and vulnerable supply lines.

It is easy to identify the role of freedom among the ranks of Europeans at Salamis, less so at Mexico City, Lepanto—or among the intramural Western fights such as Agincourt, Waterloo, and the Somme. Yet whatever differences there were between the French and English of the Middle Ages, the French and English at the beginning of the nineteenth century, or Germans and the Allies in World War I, their shared measure of freedom on both sides of the battle line was not even remotely present in armies outside of Europe.

Even when constitutional government was retarded and lost, and the classical legacy almost forgotten, the Western tradition of economic and cultural liberality nevertheless survived enough to lend a European king's subjects more freedom than a conscript in an imperial Chinese army, a Janissary of the sultan, or one of Montezuma's flower warriors, who were subject to a degree of social, economic, and thought control unknown in most of Europe. What frightened Cortés's men about Aztecs, aside from the continual sacrificial slaughter on the Great Pyramid, is what frightened the Greeks about Xerxes, the Venetians about the Ottomans, the British about the Zulus, and the Americans about the Japanese: the subservience of the individual to the state, or the notion that a subject, without rights, might be summarily executed for speaking or even keeping silent in a way that displeased a monarch, emperor, or priest.

While strict obedience fueled by unquestioned devotion brings strengths to the battlefield, nevertheless when the central nerve center of such a regimented society is severed—a Montezuma kidnapped, a Xerxes or Darius III riding away from battle in open flight, a Zulu Cetshwayo hunted down, a Japanese admiral committing suicide—the will of the coerced serf or imperial subject often vanishes with him, leaving either fatalism or panic in its wake. Japan surrendered only when its emperor conceded; America fought when President Roosevelt's declaration of war was passed by an elective legislature, and ceased when the same body ratified the peace proposals of President Truman.

Freedom turns out to be a military asset. It enhances the morale of the army as a whole; it gives confidence to even the lowliest of soldiers; and it draws on the consensus of officers rather than a single commander. Freedom is more than mere autonomy, or the idea that men always fight well on their home soil to repel the invader. The Persians who were defeated at Mycale (479 B.C.), and those years later who were annihilated by Alexander the Great (334–323 B.C.), fought as defensive troops to repel foreign aggression from their homeland. But they were defeated as serfs in service to the sovereignty and home soil of Achaemenid Asia, not as freemen for the ideal of freedom.

THE LEGACY OF SALAMIS

The interest of the world's history hung trembling in the balance. Oriental despotism, a world united under one lord and sovereign, on the one side, and separate states, insignificant in extent and resources, but animated by free individuality, on the other side, stood front to front in array of battle.

Never in history has the superiority of spiritual power over material bulk,
and that of no contemptible amount, been made so gloriously manifest.

So wrote Georg Hegel of Salamis in his *Philosophy of History* (2.2.3)—
a melodramatic judgment at odds with Arnold Toynbee, who in one of his
more foolish asides suggested that a Greek loss to Xerxes might have been
good for Hellenic civilization: the omnipresent despot at least bringing
them relief from their own internecine rivalry. Toynbee should have examined carefully the fate of sixth-century Ionia and the demise of its preeminence in philosophy, free government, and unfettered expression
under a century of Eastern rule.

A Greek defeat at Salamis would have ensured the end of Western civilization and its peculiar institution of freedom altogether. Ionia, the islands, and the Greek mainland would have all been occupied as a Western
satrapy of Persia. Those few Greeks surviving as autonomous states in
Italy or Sicily would have succumbed to Persian attack, or remained in-
consequential backwaters in an eastern Mediterranean that was already
essentially a Persian and Carthaginian lake. Without a free Greek mainland, the unique culture of the polis would have been lost, and with that
ruin the values of a nascent Western civilization itself. In 480 B.C. democracy itself was only twenty-seven years old, and the idea of freedom a
mere two-centuries-old concept shared by only a few hundred thousand
rustics in a backwater of the eastern Mediterranean. What allowed Rome
later to dominate Greece and Carthage was its deadly army, its ability to
marshal manpower through levies of free citizens, its resilient constitution in which civilians oversaw military operations, and its dynamic scientific tradition which produced everything from catapults to advanced
siegecraft and superb arms and armor. Yet most of these practices were either directly borrowed from the Greeks or Greek-inspired.

After Salamis the free Greeks would never fear any other foreign
power until they met the free Romans of the republic. No Persian king
would ever again set foot in Greece. For the next 2,000 years no Easterner
would claim Greece as his own until the Ottoman conquest of the Balkans
in the fifteenth century overran an impoverished, unaided, and largely
forgotten Byzantine Hellas. Before Salamis Athens was a rather eccentric
city-state whose experiment with a radical democracy was in its twenty-
seven-year-old infancy, and the verdict on its success was still out. After
Salamis an imperial democratic culture arose at Athens that ruled the
Aegean and gave us Aeschylus, Sophocles, the Parthenon, Pericles,
Socrates, and Thucydides. Salamis proved that free peoples fought better

than unfree, and that the most free of the free—the Athenians—fought the best of all.

For the next three and a half centuries after Salamis, murderous Hellenic-inspired armies—the Ten Thousand, the Macedonians under Alexander the Great, and the mercenaries of Pyrrhus—possessed of superior technology and shock tactics, would run wild from southern Italy to the Indus River. The unmatched architecture of Greece, from the temple of Zeus at Olympia to the Parthenon at Athens; the timeless literature of Greece, from Attic tragedy, comedy, and oratory to Greek history itself; the rise of red-figure vase painting, mastery of realism and idealism in sculpture, and the expansion of the idea of democracy—all of this proceeded from the Persian Wars, prompting literary and artistic historians properly to mark the Greek victory as the fault line between the Archaic and classical ages.

There is one final irony about Salamis and the idea of freedom. The Greek victory not merely saved the West by ensuring that Hellenism would survive after a mere two centuries of polis culture. Just as important, it was also a catalyst for the entire Athenian democratic renaissance, which radically altered the evolution of the city-state by giving free people even more freedom—beyond the imagination of any agrarian hoplite soldier of the seventh century B.C. As Aristotle saw more than a century and a half later, what had been a rather ordinary Greek polis, in the midst of a recent experiment of allowing the native-born poor to vote—the soon-to-be heroes of Salamis—would suddenly inherit the cultural leadership of Greece.

Before Salamis most Greek city-states enforced a strict property qualification that limited full citizenship to about a third of the resident-born population, worried about the volatility and license of the uneducated, impoverished, and transient. Because Salamis was a victory of the poorer "naval crowd," not an infantry triumph of the small landowner, in the next century the influence of Athenian landless oarsmen would increase substantially. The humble and indigent would demand political representation commensurate with their prowess on the all-important seas. In the West those who fight demand political recognition. This newly empowered naval class refashioned Athenian democracy into a particularly unpredictable and aggressive imperial power of free citizens who could decide to do pretty much as they pleased on any given day through a majority vote of the Assembly. The will of the people would soon build the temples on the acropolis, subsidize the tragedians, send triremes throughout the Aegean—but also exterminate the Melians and execute Socrates.

Marathon had created the myth of Athenian infantry; with Salamis the navy had now superseded it.

Plato argued that while Marathon had started the string of Greek successes and Plataea had finished it, Salamis "made the Greeks worse as a people." Democracy was to Plato a degenerate form of government, and its rabble-rousing citizens little more than "bald-headed tinkers" who demanded rights that they had not earned, an equality of result rather than of opportunity, and majority vote in place of the rule of law. Before Salamis, Greek city-states embraced an entire array of constitutional prohibitions that limited the extension of this radical, new, and peculiar idea of freedom—property qualifications to vote, wars fought exclusively by those landowners whose capital and income gave them privilege, and a complete absence of taxes, navies, and imperialism. Those protocols of the traditional free agrarian city-state had defined freedom and equality in terms of a minority of the population who had ample capital, education, and land. Before Salamis the essence of the polis was not so much equality for all, but the search for moral virtue for all, guided by a consensus of properly qualified, gifted, and free men.

Plato, Aristotle, and most other Greek thinkers from Thucydides to Xenophon, who were wary of what had transpired in the aftermath of Salamis, were not just elitists. Rather, they saw inherent dangers in the latitude and affluence that snowballed from a radically democratic government, state entitlement, election by lot, subsidy for civic participation, free expression, and free markets. Without innate checks and balances, in this more reactionary view, a freedom-mad polis would inevitably turn out a highly individualistic but self-absorbed citizen whose unlimited freedoms and rights would preclude communal sacrifices or moral virtue. Prominent Western philosophers after Plato and Aristotle—Hobbes, Hegel, Nietzsche, and dozens of others—would express nearly identical reservations about this singular idea of democracy that gave unlimited political freedom to citizens on the basis of an inalienable right—that men in general are born and should die as freemen.

Better, the conservatives felt, that government policy should hinge on a majority vote of only those educated and informed citizens with some financial solvency. War—like the battles at Marathon and Plataea—should be for the defense of real property, on land, and require martial courage, not mere technology, public warships, or numbers. Citizens should own their own farms, provide their own weapons, be free from taxes and centralized government, and be responsible for their own economic security—not seek wage labor, public employment, or government

entitlement. The courageous oarsmen of Salamis and their publicly constructed and owned ships changed all that in an afternoon. Once unleashed, radical political freedom was a virus that even the most
autocratic of Western strongmen would have trouble extinguishing.

With the Aegean wide open after the retreat of the Persian fleet at
Salamis, and Athens now at the vanguard of the Greek resistance, radical
democracy and its refutation of the static old polis were at hand. The
philosophers may have hated Salamis—Plato's thoughts on the battle
were near treasonous—but Themistocles' and his rowers' victory at
Salamis had not only saved Greece and the West but irrevocably energized
Western forces and expanded the idea of freedom itself. Forty thousand
drowned imperial subjects in the strait of Salamis could attest well
enough to the power of an idea.

Salamis was not a reprieve, but proved to be the beginning of something entirely unseen in the eastern Mediterranean: the Western way of
war was unleashed beyond the borders of Greece. In a mere century and
a half, the military practices that had saved the Greek fleet a few thousand
yards off the Athenian coast would put Alexander the Great 3,000 miles
eastward on the Indus River.

THREE

Decisive Battle

Gaugamela, October 1, 331 B.C.

The Greeks, as I have learned, are accustomed to wage wars in the most stupid fashion due to their silliness and folly. For once they have declared war against each other, they search out the finest and most level plain and there fight it out. The result is that even the victors come away with great losses; and of the defeated, I say only that they are utterly annihilated.

—HERODOTUS, *The Histories* (7.9.2)

ANGLES OF VISION

The Old Man

POOR PARMENIO! Once more he was to be left behind as the divine Alexander, far away to the right, charged headlong into the Persian horde. Almost the entire battle line of the Macedonian army followed their king. The Companion Cavalry with Parmenio's own son Philotas in charge, the royal phalanx of pikemen, assorted mercenaries, and the veteran shield-bearing infantrymen, or hypaspists—everyone on foot and horse, it seemed, but Parmenio was heading to the right and to the kill. Once again the old man was to stay fast; there was to be no glory for Parmenio other than in anchoring the left wing. He was left only with a few hundred of his battle-hardened Macedonian horsemen, supported by companies of pikemen left behind under the commanders Craterus and Simmias, some Greek cavalry led by Erigyius, and the 2,000 redoubtable Thessalian horsemen under Philip.

Earlier at the Granicus River (334 B.C.) and Issus (333 B.C.), it had also been up to Parmenio to protect the left horn of the Macedonian army—his wing being "refused," in tactical parlance—while the mobile Alexander broke through a hole between the Persian center and left, drove behind the enemy, and routed their king. Alexander's way had always been to collapse the imperial army before Parmenio himself was buried by the mounted hordes of Persia. Parmenio holds; Alexander attacks—such was the traditional formula that made Alexander responsible for victory, and Parmenio alone for defeat.

At Gaugamela the Macedonian left under Parmenio almost did implode—it was "thrown back and in distress," the ancient biographer Plutarch dryly notes in his life of Alexander (*Alexander* 23.9–11). In fact, Parmenio's men were vastly outnumbered—perhaps by three to one—and for a brief moment, facing annihilation. Our ancient sources suggest that the numerical disparity at Gaugamela was greatest on the left wing, where the Macedonians were almost broken during the first onslaught. Parmenio's Macedonian mounted lords faced excellent enemy cavalrymen: Armenian and Cappadocian horsemen, some fifty scythed chariots, along with a mixed force of Persian infantrymen and imperial horsemen under the satrap of Syria, Mazaeus himself. A wave of 15,000 mounted killers was breaking against Parmenio's island of 5,000 foot and horse.

These cavalrymen were not to be underestimated. Persian horses were somewhat larger than Macedonian. Both rider and mount in great numbers at Gaugamela wore heavy frontal armor. From the Eastern provinces of the empire arose a rather different tradition of horsemanship that would come to resemble the later cataphracts, or heavy mailed cavalrymen on stout warhorses that could break fluid lines of light infantry and horsemen. While Persian cavalrymen were not so accomplished at brutal hand-to-hand fighting—their short javelins and swords were no match for the lance and broad slashing sword of Alexander's Companions—the size of their mounts, plentiful armor, sheer numbers, and the momentum of attack resulted in a brutal crash against Parmenio's stationary men.

Darius's marshals had learned what Macedonian heavy cavalry could do against Eastern horsemen and infantry, and thus at Gaugamela they were determined for once to field better-protected and more numerous mounted forces than their Greek adversaries—as if war might yet be won through manpower and matériel rather than by tactics and spirit. The historian Curtius records that at first the Macedonians were shocked at the appearance of these novel Bactrian and Scythian nomadic warriors because of their "shaggy faces and uncut hair, in addition to the sheer enormous size of their bodies" (*History of Alexander* 4.13.6).

Parmenio was among the first Europeans in Alexander's entourage to have invaded Asia, and later the rock of the king's line at the battles of Granicus, Issus, and now at Gaugamela. Parmenio had already lost a son in Alexander's cause, and his last surviving two were to die within the year. The seventy-year-old veteran had less than a year to live. His last son, Philotas, now charging with the Companions at the side of Alexander himself, would soon be tortured by his king and stoned to death before the assembled troops on the false charge of conspiracy. Poor Parmenio, one of the last of Philip's original Companions who had built Alexander's army before the king was even born. A marshal whom hundreds of Persian enemies could never kill in battle—the historian Curtius said he was "the most skilled of Alexander's generals in the art of war" (*History of Alexander* 4.13.4)—Parmenio would be decapitated ignominiously in peacetime, on the orders of the king he had saved so many times.

After his first battle in Asia at the Granicus River, the king had dedicated statues to the fallen Companions, visited the wounded, and released the families of the dead from taxes back home. Now three years later, Alexander was evolving into a different sort of monarch—increasingly suspicious of his officers, soon to be enlisting Persians into the army, enamored with the pomp and arrogance of an Eastern theocrat, intent to accomplish something megalomaniac well beyond the thuggery of looting and destroying the western satrapies of the Persian Empire. The king's paranoia would lead him to butcher the one man who had helped invent his army, who years earlier had cleared away the rival aristocratic opposition for Alexander's own succession, who had taught the young king how to keep the unruly Macedonian lowland princes in check, off and on the battlefield—and who would one more time stay put and so save the army at Gaugamela. One of the great ironies of Alexander's later military career was his systematic destruction of the very officer class which had guaranteed all his major victories—a calculated purge that would transpire only *after* these old marshals had ensured the destruction of the Achaemenid army.

Parmenio's demise—unexpectedly stabbed by Alexander's courtiers, his body further pierced after death, his head sliced off and sent to the king—was eleven months still in the future, in the far-off Persian provincial capital of Ecbatana. Now the loyal Parmenio had more immediate problems. He was surrounded. Blinded by the dust kicked up by thousands of horses on all sides, he was not yet defeated, despite what Diodorus called the "weight and sheer numbers" of Mazaeus's contingent (17.60.6). Not yet at least, and so he rallied his old guard of Macedonian horse lords to get in close with the Persians and hack and stab at their horses and faces. Along with his reliable Thessalians—the best light cavalry in the ancient world—he would beat off the waves of assault, ensuring that the Macedonian army at large was protected on its left and rear. If just one more time Parmenio stopped the Persians' predictable outflanking movement, protected the Macedonian rear, and drew off half the Persian army, Alexander—Alexandros Megas, king of Asia, divine son of Zeus-Ammon, conqueror of Darius III, and soon-to-be emperor of Persia and architect of the most brilliant victory in the history of East-West confrontation—might still ride on to triumph and finish the destruction of the Achaemenid dynasty itself.

Parmenio had two critical problems. By Darius's careful intent, there were neither mountains nor sea at the battlefield of Gaugamela—not even a river or gully nearby to protect the Macedonians' wings from the far longer enemy line. Soon the Persian horsemen to his left were piling up and outflanking Parmenio by hundreds of yards, forcing the thinning line of his own outnumbered troops to bend horseshoelike as they sloughed off the encircling Persians before they got to the rear. His Thessalians on the immediate right likewise beat back a wave of scythed chariots and even a few Greek mercenaries, holding firm so that the enemy would have to go around rather than through Parmenio. Farther to the right, about a quarter mile beyond the Thessalians, there was a growing gap in the Macedonian line that threatened to wipe out the whole middle of the army. Alexander's own charge to the right would prove deadly to the enemy, but for the time being his dash had taken most of the right center of the Macedonian army along with him. All that remained of a tactical reserve were two companies of phalangites and a few irregulars to protect Parmenio's right flank.

Hundreds of veteran Persian and Indian horsemen poured through this tear and were already charging to the rear of Alexander's army, into the Macedonian camp itself, plundering supplies, killing the guards, and freeing the Persian prisoners. At any moment they might turn on Parmenio's isolated left wing, meet up with Mezaeus's flanking Persians, and attack from both sides, encircling and annihilating the septuagenarian and his beleaguered horsemen. Arrian relates that Parmenio at this point was "struck from both sides" (*Anabasis* 3.15.1). If the Macedonian left could now be cracked, the Persian horsemen could finish the slaughter by riding down Alexander himself from the rear, before the galloping Companions could crack the Persians at their own front. Parmenio could either protect the Macedonian left wing from being outflanked or maintain the integrity of the center, but he could not do both.

The enemy's greed for plunder probably saved Parmenio, since the Persians and Indians in the gap first paused to slaughter the unarmed camp guards. Booty and easy killing apparently seemed preferable to charging into grim Macedonian horsemen. Realizing his danger, Parmenio immediately sent a messenger toward the rising dust cloud far across the battlefield—always a good indication of Alexander's position—to find the rambunctious king and get help. In the meantime he ordered the reserve pikemen still on his wing to turn about and begin spearing the plundering Persians. Then Parmenio readied his own horsemen for a final thrust through the circle, hoping to break out and meet Alexander halfway in no-man's-land, crushing the Persian right wing between two mounted pincers. Rumors that Darius III far across the battlefield was fleeing to the rear, and that even the successful Persian contingents in front were tottering, gave Parmenio some hope that the worst was over. He might yet get out alive. For the time being, the veteran general stayed where he was, as he broke the crest of the galloping Persian horsemen, readying himself for the final charge of his life to meet his king.

Alexander's Pique

Parmenio be damned, Alexander must have thought. The panicked messenger had somehow found him in the cloud—resplendent in a shiny iron and gem-encrusted helmet, puffed up in magnificent war belt and breastplate, bestride the venerable Bucephalas—just as he prepared to follow the fleeing King Darius himself. The latter's imperial guard and the entire middle of the Persian army were collapsing and retreating to the north. Dust, screams, and bodies dulled the senses of sight, hearing, and touch as Alexander was lost in the confusion and scarcely able to make out the chariot of the panicked Darius. Arrian says his horsemen "were striking the faces of their enemies with spears," as the phalanx "bristling with pikes" followed and slammed into the enemy, yelling the old Macedonian war cry "*alala, alala*" (*Anabasis* 3.14.2–3). If this new and sudden report from Parmenio was true—that more than a mile away to his left and rear his old marshal was about to be annihilated—then there could be no pursuit of the Achaemenid king, no further anything until his own army behind was secure.

It was bothersome for the triumphant Alexander to turn around 180 degrees and ride back into the swarm of interlocked horsemen to save his senior general. The historian Curtius says that Alexander "gnashed his teeth in rage" at the very thought of breaking off his pursuit (*History of Alexander* 4.16.3). After waiting for his moment of advance, Alexander was to retreat—not through his own failure, but because of the success that his own lieutenants apparently could not match. While Alexander had lost absolute control of the battle once he plunged into the Persian lines, Parmenio and his generals should have known their king's agenda: hold firm and pivot on the left. Alexander on the right would soon enough prevent the Persian outflanking movement while the Companions crashed through the inevitable enemy gap to come.

Well before his rescue, Alexander was growing more and more tired of the old man and his circle of reactionary barons from the Macedonian lowlands. "Sluggish and complacent," Plutarch says, the aged captain had become at Gaugamela, "his age undermining his courage" (*Alexander* 33.10–11). All the old horse lords were becoming a bothersome—and suspicious—lot: the farther the army marched eastward, the more these cavalry commanders grew nostalgic for home. The more Persians he defeated, the more Parmenio and his clique worried that they might still lose. The more he talked of empire and a world civilization to come under his own godhead, the more his parochial rustics talked of petty looting and a retirement of leisure and affluence back in Europe. Age and homesickness had gotten the best of them all.

Three years earlier at the Granicus River, Parmenio had warned Alexander that it was too late in the day to ford the river and start the attack. He had tried to beg off the onslaught since even the waters at the ford reached waist-high, prompting the king to scoff that he would feel ashamed of fearing an enemy across "a tiny stream" after he had just crossed the Hellespont (Arrian *Anabasis* 1.13.7)! Parmenio was overruled and the battle won directly. The next year at Issus, the sixty-eight-year-old Parmenio needlessly fretted that Alexander might be poisoned before the battle. During the next few months Parmenio had wished to commit to a sea battle in lieu of sacking the strongholds of Phoenicia! Here at Gaugamela before the battle even began, once more a jittery Parmenio and his old guard, numbed by the sight of Darius's vast horde, had advised a night attack. At that Alexander had finally snapped, "I shall not steal my victory" (Plutarch *Alexander* 31.12), insisting on a head-on confrontation. Parmenio had even (wisely) convinced his king to reconnoiter the battlefield in the days before the showdown, to ensure there were no hidden traps on the plain that might derail Alexander's planned mounted thrust to the right.

Alexander's sycophantic entourage ridiculed the caution of the old man. The philosopher Callisthenes (soon to be executed himself) is the most likely source of these pejorative morality tales, which culminated in the story of Parmenio's advice to cease entirely the advance eastward. Before the campaign of Gaugamela, he had purportedly urged acceptance of Darius's eleventh-hour offer of a Western Persian Empire for Alexander under the aegis of a general truce. "I would accept if I were you," he told his king. "And I too if I were Parmenio," Alexander barked back (Plutarch *Alexander* 29.8–9).

In the heat of battle, with Darius almost in his grasp, Alexander scoffed that Parmenio fretted more about the loss of the Macedonian camp and its valuables than the course of the battle itself. Nevertheless, he sent back the rider with the promise that Alexander and his Companions would reverse their course, though not without the insulting admonition to Parmenio that the victorious add the baggage of their enemies to their own, while the defeated must not worry about money or their slaves, but only how to fight bravely and die with honor. Parmenio was not worried about his own baggage, nor even about getting his hands on the rich camp of the enemy, but was terrified about the very survival of his entire wing, and with it the fate of a Macedonian army thousands of miles from the Aegean. That same specter struck Napoleon centuries later, when he remarked that Gaugamela was a great victory but too risky, since defeat would have stranded Alexander "nine hundred leagues from Macedonia." Parmenio knew that the gallant dash of his king, brilliantly timed to crack the weakened Persian left and middle, was nevertheless a tremendous gamble: a chasm opened in the Macedonian lines the moment the Companions took off. If Alexander was right that the Macedonians were a victory away from inheriting the entire Persian Empire, Parmenio was equally correct that they were also a defeat away from total annihilation—50,000 Europeans 1,500 miles from home in a sea of millions of enemies.

Up until Parmenio's messenger arrived, the battle had been a perfect day. Plutarch says that Alexander's chief problem when he slammed into the Persian line was the sheer mass of enemy dead and wounded who obstructed the pursuit "by grabbing on and entwining themselves around both riders and horses" (*Alexander* 33.7). Arrian adds that horsemen were

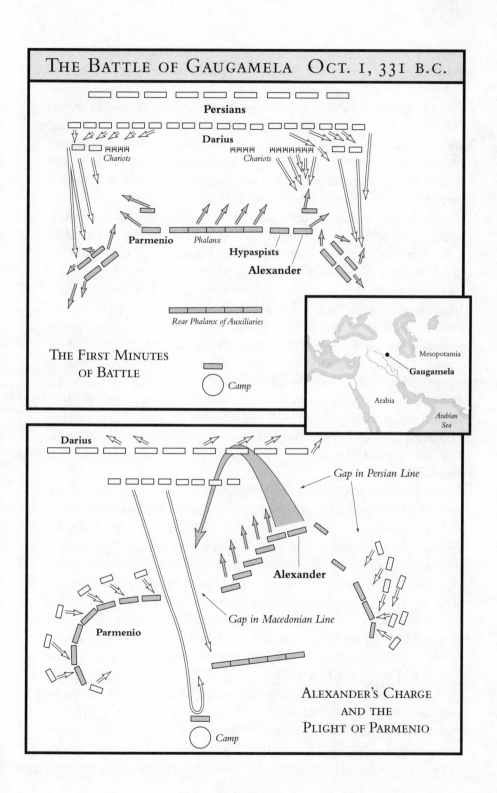

THE BATTLE OF GAUGAMELA OCT. 1, 331 B.C.

Persians

Darius

Chariots *Chariots*

Parmenio *Phalanx*

Hypaspists

Alexander

Rear Phalanx of Auxiliaries

THE FIRST MINUTES
OF BATTLE

Camp

Mesopotamia
Gaugamela

Arabia

*Arabian
Sea*

Darius

Gap in Persian Line

Alexander

Gap in Macedonian Line

Parmenio

ALEXANDER'S CHARGE
AND THE
PLIGHT OF PARMENIO

Camp

literally "shoving" the Persians before the phalanx came on with their bristling spears (*Anabasis* 3.14.2–3). Alexander's tactical plan was simple but typically brilliant: as Parmenio pivoted on the left, tying down the Persian right and securing the safety of the army's rear, he would have the entire Macedonian line drift slowly rightward, toward the rough ground where Darius's scythed chariots would be useless. In response, the Persian king would be forced to send his left wing to surround Alexander's right and block the Macedonian drift—and thereby deplete his own middle companies in an effort to herd Alexander back.

Alexander would continue to send rightward successive contingents—light-armed, horse, and infantry—to force the Persian flanking contingents into an ever-widening hook. Meanwhile, Alexander himself would sit tight with his veterans until he spotted a gap at the heart of the weakened enemy middle. For just such a moment, Alexander was holding back his grand punch—a wedge of his Companions, hypaspists, and the phalanx. With these veterans—the best fighting men the ancient world would produce—he would charge through the hole, into the heart of the Persian line and right at Darius himself. True, the Persian army was far larger and in theory might outflank both his wings. But as long as his horsemen and reserves channeled the flanking assaults outward, the base of the Persian attack at some point surely must thin and weaken. In every outflanking attack, troops must be transferred from somewhere; that somewhere Alexander was confident he could spot and exploit before it was too late.

The key for Alexander was organization, tactics, and timing. Novel mobile contingents of light skirmishers and horsemen must be placed independently on the wings—backed by a reserve line of 6,700 heavy infantrymen—while the best of the Macedonian cavalry and phalangites were to be kept out of the preliminary fighting, ready as a razor-sharp blade for the decisive blow against the Persian center. Alexander must strike before his two wings were overwhelmed—and yet not *too* soon lest he hit the massive wall of the Persian middle that had not yet become weakened. When the long-expected gap in the Persian line for a moment opened up, there rode Alexander into the imperial guard, directly after Darius and the prize of the empire itself.

With Alexander's recall the Achaemenid king escaped—only to be murdered nine months later by one of his satraps, Bessus. A disgruntled Alexander reined in Bucephalas and turned back out of the dusty cloud of dying men and horses to ride in the opposite direction, into the retreating Persians who had almost killed Parmenio. But the old baron no longer seemed to be in danger; in fact, Alexander spotted Parmenio's fleeing attackers and deliberately rode head-on into them. If he were not to slaughter Darius's fleeing entourage, he might as well wipe out the best horsemen of Scythia and Bactria in this secondary engagement.

All extant ancient sources emphasize that this final collision of horsemen was the most deadly moment of the entire battle. More than sixty Companions fell; hundreds of horses on both sides were slaughtered; and the Persian cavalry was nearly annihilated. Arrian adds that there was "no more javelin throwing or maneuvering of horses" (*Anabasis* 3.15.2), but rather a war of continual blows. More than sixty years earlier at the infantry battle of Coronea, the old Spartan king Agesilaus had likewise deliberately charged his victorious Spartan phalanx back into a retreating column of Theban hoplites and was nearly wiped out for his efforts. A battle like "none other of our time," the eyewitness Xenophon wrote of that dreadful collision between heavy shock troops. In the Hellenic tradition an enemy on the horizon was not to be avoided, bypassed, or ignored, if there was even a slight chance that he could be struck head-on, face-to-face, and en masse.

Lord of Asia

Alexander would come to Gaugamela, Darius thought. He was sure of that much. So the king had prepared for the Macedonian's arrival, seeking out a flat plain without obstacles for his scythed chariots, clear ground for his elephants, thousands of horsemen, and his much longer battle line— even Alexander could not overcome such advantages of terrain and numbers. At last, Darius thought, a cavalry battle in an open plain, precisely the type of mobile warfare his nomadic horsemen excelled at, and exactly the scenario dreaded by the phalangites of the West. Alexander, Darius also knew, would ride to battle at Gaugamela, just as he had charged across the river Granicus and up the high banks into the Persian mass, just as he had once ordered his men to advance through the stream, stockade, and embankment at Issus, just as he had insisted on storming the nearly impregnable Tyre and massive walls of Gaza, just as he had always come to destroy any obstacle, army, or citadel—flesh or stone—in his path. He would come to Gaugamela, river or no river, unfavorable ground or not, mused Darius. Alexander would come onto the chosen ground of King Darius III and thus once more be forced to battle according to His Majesty's plans.

And why not? These "most foolish" Greeks had always done just that.

At Marathon, Thermopylae, Salamis, and Plataea they had forced decisive battles against Persians, despite being outnumbered. Seventy-seven years ago not too far from this spot, the trapped Greek hoplites of the Ten Thousand had refused the terms of Darius's ancestor, Artaxerxes II, preferring to fight their way out of Persia. Even after their generals had been lured into a parley near Gaugamela itself, then tortured and executed, the leaderless Ten Thousand had still chosen to fight. They had battled the entire year, killing their way to the Black Sea and safety. Then in sight of Europe, many of them had stayed on, joined the Spartan army in Asia Minor, and fought Persians again. Yes, Darius thought, this crazed Macedonian youth would come up the Tigris River, hunt him down, and force a final battle for the empire of his forefathers.

This time Darius had picked his ground well. There were few hills. Alexander could use neither river nor sea to protect his flanks. Darius's subjects had cleared the plain for the easy onslaught of his scythed chariots. Traps and spikes had been hidden where it was most likely Alexander would ride in. Had the Macedonians, the king thought, ever encountered elephants in battle?

The only worry? Long gone were most of his Greek mercenary hoplites, who had fought so well in the two prior pitched battles against Alexander. The original phalanx of hired Hellenic killers had been surrounded, and exterminated or captured at Granicus. Their replacements—more than 20,000 strong—were destroyed or scattered at Issus. Nowhere in Persia were there any such comparable infantrymen left who welcomed shock battle, men who could stand up to Alexander's pikemen—surely neither the old Immortals of Persian legend nor the gaudy "Apple Bearers" with their famed sphere-butted spears. King Darius had only 2,000 Greek hoplites remaining, and thus no men in an empire of 70 million who were willing to charge the wall of Macedonian pikes. Alexander won at Gaugamela and elsewhere in Asia for the same reasons Greek infantry won overseas: theirs was a culture of face-to-face battle of rank-and-file columns, not a contest of mobility, numerical superiority, or ambush. It was no accident that Alexander's veterans aimed their pikes and swords at the faces of the aristocratic mounted Persian elite, lords who had no experience with an enemy who sought to crash into them, push them down, and spear or slice them to pieces.

Could not Darius's legendary scythed chariots—more than two hundred were assembled on the battlefield—mow down the clumsy phalanx if they could burst out unexpectedly from his line, race over the flat ground, and trap the phalangites before they were mobile? Could not elephants—he had obtained fifteen from India—also be useful if the Indians could bring them up safely through his lines and lead them head-on against Alexander's Companions? Darius knew he had no real quality heavy infantry, but thousands of cavalrymen to surfeit, and so he determined that Gaugamela would be a vast war of horses, the greatest cavalry battle in Asia since the legendary battle of Kadesh between Egyptians and Hittites nearly a millennium earlier. Darius may have had nearly 50,000 mounted troops against fewer than 8,000 cavalry of Alexander. If the king could sweep the flanks of the Macedonian army, send his prized Bactrians and Scythian cataphracts around the enemy right, and simultaneously his trusted Mazaeus behind their left, then Alexander's terrible phalanx would be not so terrible after all—surprised from the rear by mounted killers who could race around and cut the clumsy pikemen from behind. At Gaugamela, for the first time in the war for the Persian Empire, there were fearsome veterans from the steppes of the Eastern empire, men Alexander himself had never encountered before in the western satrapies, men of the caliber that could outflank and herd the Macedonians onto Darius's massive advancing Persian center.

The Empire's Last Battle

On October 1, 331, an aerial view of the battlefield of Gaugamela in the first few minutes would have revealed an enormous three-sided box of embattled Macedonians, as Alexander's two wings bent backward, in their struggle to keep their encircling enemies to their sides rather than allowing them to their rear. Within the hour, however, Gaugamela was a radically different picture, more a race between desperate horsemen of both sides who had penetrated their respective enemies' lines. Could Alexander and his Companions ride through the gap and shatter the Persians before the horsemen of Darius burst through a similar rip in his own lines? The answer was clearly yes. In singular fashion, Alexander wished to kill Darius, destroy his army, and annihilate every enemy soldier on the battlefield. He would pursue and slaughter his fleeing enemies unmercifully until they ceased to exist as a military force. For all that, he rode into the Persian mass: to stab the faces of the enemy with pikes, to throw them off their horses bare-handed, to crash their own mounts into the bigger horses of Darius. For all that and more, the dutiful Companions followed their king into the horde of enemy horsemen.

In contrast, the Persians and Indians who breached the Macedonian line headed directly for the cache of booty, more intent on the king's adulation in freeing the Achaemenid royal prisoners than on the hard work of finishing off Parmenio. Alexander in a sea of Persians went about slaughtering an army, while amid Macedonians the Persians butchered camp followers. To Persian horsemen of the plains, loot, the rare chance to kill the unarmed, the frenzy of riding and raiding among tents and wagons, were the stuff of nomadic warfare: better to get your hands on plunder than lose it to some rival band of rapacious interlopers. To Macedonians and Greeks, however, charging, killing, and still more killing face-to-face were the essence of three centuries of the Western way of war.

Gaugamela ("the camel's house") was Alexander's third, final, and greatest battle against the Achaemenid empire, more a slaughter than a real set piece per se, since a numerically superior force rapidly disintegrated through panic, fear, and the brilliant tactics of its adversaries. For hours until dusk Gaugamela was a story of thousands of imperial subjects—50,000 is a reasonable estimate—speared and ridden down from the rear as they sought safety along the plains of the upper Tigris valley. Scholars are unsure how many fought on October 1 and find unanimity only in rejecting the fantastic claims of our ancient sources that more than a million Persians were assembled. Most likely, Darius III had collected well over 100,000 horse and infantry, pitted against 47,000 Macedonians, some 7,500 to 8,000 of them horsemen—the largest European army that Alexander had hitherto mustered. Alexander may have had more Greeks in his army at Gaugamela than during his prior two battles, as Hellenic mercenaries—Thracians, Thessalians, and stout infantrymen from the Peloponnese—increasingly discovered that service with Macedon meant life and booty, while work for the Achaemenid king more likely ended in a lonely death in a far land.

Mesopotamia was a good enough place to fight. Both armies had ample provisions and plenty of water. The weather was dry and mild in early fall; and there was enough flat ground to accommodate thousands of killers. Babylon, with its promise for the victors of rest, feast, loot, and women, was a relatively easy three-week march downstream.

After tearing off the western portions of the empire and Egypt, Alexander in late summer 331 B.C. drove on toward Babylon in hopes of capturing the ancient city and forcing a showdown with the final military reserves of the Persian Empire. After having witnessed his own Achaemenid armies routed at Granicus (334) and again at Issus (333), as well as losing the key strongholds at Tyre and Gaza, in addition to the rich provinces of Ionia, Phoenicia, Egypt, and Cilicia, Darius understood that he must finally stay put and fight for the survival of the remaining, eastern half of his empire. He chose a small plain, more than three hundred miles north of Babylon on a small branch of the Tigris River, the Bumelus, about seventy-five miles from the town of Arbela.

Because Alexander's tactics were well known, Darius had a good idea what to expect. The king, always on the enemy right wing, would seek a gap or some flanking entry around his own left, pour through with 2,000 to 3,000 heavy horsemen, and head straight for the Persian high command, all in hopes of creating a breach through the mass, as his shield-bearing spearmen and dreaded pikemen followed. Meanwhile, Parmenio on the left would stay steadfast and pivot if need be, until the morale of the imperial army was shattered as the ruling Achaemenid clique fled for their lives. All that Darius knew, but was helpless to stop, and so the day's slaughter followed the script Darius feared and Alexander planned.

The Macedonians parted on cue for the scythed chariots—Gaugamela seems to be the only time these much-feared but rather impractical weapons were actually used en masse in any battle—and stabbed the drivers as they sped past. Darius's elephants apparently panicked or were let through the phalanx—or never even made it to the front. Both chariots and elephants were found largely unscathed after the battle and taken as trophies. The latter after their maiden appearance at Gaugamela became a mainstay of Hellenistic warfare; the former became little more than the rhetoric of Greek romances and the sketch-pad doodles of Western engineers until the age of Leonardo da Vinci. The Persian flanking columns never quite surrounded their enemies; and the decisive charge of Indians and Persians that slammed into the Macedonian left and center now went after plunder, not Parmenio.

The consequence was that when the dust cleared on the morning of October 2, the plain of Gaugamela was an ungodly mess—Diodorus says that "the complete area of the battlefield was full of corpses" (17.50.61). Fifty thousand Persians were dead or dying—we need not believe some ancient reports of 300,000 killed—among a general detritus of wandering camp followers, crippled horses, and booty scavengers. Thousands of wounded crawled to the tiny streams and mudholes of the surrounding alluvial plains. Alexander himself returned to the battlefield to bury his dead. He collected little more than a hundred men from under the carcasses of well over a thousand Macedonian horses. Five hundred Persians had fallen at Gaugamela for every Macedonian—such were the disparities when a polyglot, multicultural force of panicked men fled on level ground before heavily armed veteran killers with pikes and seasoned cavalry, whose one worry was not to turn fainthearted in front of lifelong companions-in-arms. The myriad corpses of his enemy were left to decompose in the autumn sun. Alexander, worried only about the rot and smell, quickly moved his army away from the stink and headed south to Babylon and the kingship of the Achaemenids. "The battle," Plutarch remarks, "resulted in the utter termination of the Persian Empire" (*Alexander* 34.1).

THE MACEDONIAN MILITARY MACHINE

There was irony in the Macedonian conquest of Greece and Persia. After spending two decades creating the army that had pacified Greece, Alexander's father, Philip II, was gutted by a young aristocrat and embittered hanger-on, Pausanias, perhaps as part of a broken homosexual affair, but more likely on orders of Alexander and his mother, Olympias, to ensure the young prince's succession. If Philip was assassinated at the moment when his murderous twenty years of command had at last borne fruit to create the unified kingdom of Macedon and Greece, so Alexander, after reaching the Indus, would die in Babylon at thirty-three, without enjoying the empire for which he had also fought so long and killed so many.

The royal army of Macedon was Philip's, not Alexander's. It had been formed and led for more than twenty years by Philip, while Alexander was at its head for little more than half that period. It was King Philip who crafted a grand new army; Philip who supplied it, led it, and organized it differently from anything in past Greek practice—in order to kill other Greeks. As it turned out, Alexander found his inheritance even more useful for killing Persians.

The equipment and tactics of his Macedonian phalanx in theory did not differ all that radically from that of the traditional hoplite spearmen of the Greek city-states, though the phalangites were mercenary and handpicked as the "tallest and strongest" of Philip's recruits. The thrusting spear was retained, but lengthened from eight to between sixteen and eighteen feet and fitted with a heavier iron point and stouter bronze butt spike. Thus, it became a true pike—weighing nearly fifteen pounds, more than six times heavier than the old hoplite spear—and required both hands for adequate control and handling. Such *sarissai* were held six feet from the butt, and so extended twelve feet in front of the phalangites, giving the Macedonian pikeman an advantage in reach of eight to ten feet more than the traditional hoplite spearmen. The old hoplite round shield of some three feet was discarded, and in its place a tiny disk was hung from the neck or shoulder; greaves, heavy bronze breastplates, and headgear were also replaced, with either leather or composite materials, or abandoned altogether. In the bargain, the first four or five rows, not three, were thrusting, giving 40 percent more spearheads in the killing zone. Such a hedgehoglike front also provided an unusual degree of offensive might as well as defensive protection for the lighter-clad initial ranks.

In ideological terms the traditional Greek hoplites' large shields, heavy breastplates and helmets, and spears of moderate size had reflected the old civic and defensive values of the militiamen of a free city-state—precisely the opposite mentality of pike-wielding, lightly protected, and aggressive Macedonian phalangites. The latter were hired and rootless men without a polis, often with no farm of their own, who added numerous feet to the hoplite's spear but reduced the shield's area by two-thirds: killing and the advance, rather than personal protection and holding ground, were prized. To this phalanx of grim, professional "foot companions" *(pezetairoi)*, Philip added the Companion Cavalry *(hetairoi)*, an elite body of aristocratic horsemen, heavily armored on strong mounts. Horse raising had always been frowned upon to the south in Greek city-state culture; it was an inefficient use of scarce land, privileged an elite who often agitated for autocracy, and was of little value against a wall of yeoman spearmen. Not so in Macedon, a society of two, not three, classes, of masters and serfs, in a land as broad and wide as Thessaly. The Companion Cavalry, we should remember, was ultimately to end up fighting lighter-armed Eastern, not Western, spear-carrying infantry.

Another contingent of infantry, with more armor and shorter spears, the "shield bearers" (hypaspists), also occupied the center of the Macedonian line, beside the phalanx. The hypaspists were the first infantry forces to follow behind the Companion Cavalry's initial onslaught, thereby providing a crucial link between the mounted attack and the subsequent follow-up by the phalanx proper. Professional corps of light infantry, slingers, archers, and javelineers rounded out the composite army group, supplying both preliminary bombardment and crucial reserve support. The latter at Gaugamela—along with the tough Agrianians—held off the flanking movements of the Persian left, while Alexander and the *hetairoi* rode in, the hypaspists following, with the *pezetairoi* lumbering behind, clearing and widening the gap with their pikes.

The old Hellenic phalanx had been reinvented by Philip and had therein gained fresh importance. It was to evolve even further from the dependence on rural protocol and ritual that made Greek armies operate close to home, and without the ability to be supplied for extended marches. Philip's intention was to craft a new national army that might outmaneuver a Greek phalanx, and yet still easily crash through the Persian Immortals. He wanted an army like the phalanx of the Ten Thousand that had cleared the field of Persian infantry at Cunaxa (401 B.C.), but one that also might outflank such heavily armed and far more deadly Greek hoplites.

The Greeks' central idea of fighting en masse through shock battle remained predominant at Macedon. Integrated with, and protected by, such variegated forces, Philip's phalanx of true pikemen was more lethal and more versatile than the traditional hoplite columns. "Nothing," the historian Polybius concluded nearly two centuries later, "can stand up to the phalanx. The Roman by himself with his sword can neither slash down nor break through the ten spears that all at once press against him" (18.30.9–10). Surely, Polybius was correct: the idea that men could stand firm when three, four, five, and more iron spearheads plunged into their limbs, heads, necks, torsos, and legs is improbable. Since the first five ranks of the Macedonian phalanx would present a staggered wall of points—with the first row's pikes extending ten feet into the killing zone—an enemy would have to fight his way through "a storm of spears," which protruded at every angle, before he could even reach the initial rank of the phalanx.

The Macedonian phalangites turned their full attention to thrusting their dreadful spears, without the cumbersome weight of the old hoplite panoply—or the need to protect with an enormous shield their immediate comrades on the right. Offensive movement, leveled pikes, and constant motion forward meant everything; defense, large shields, and worry over covering neighbors were of little consequence. Once a phalanx achieved momentum, and its pikes were rambling forward, nothing could withstand the terrifying force of oncoming Greek iron. Imagine the Persian unfortunates shredded by repeated stabbing: the chief problem for their victorious Macedonian executioners was to keep spearheads free of ruined enemy equipment and the weight of mutilated corpses. From literary sources we receive the impression that in this horrendous world of phalanx-killing, it was not sleek youth or elegant muscle that the infantry commander sought out, but stout, grubby old veterans, with the nerve and experience not to flinch in the task at hand and thus stay in rank during the charge and collision to follow.

Used with greater precision and power, the new Macedonian phalanx delivered a knockout blow once the target had been sighted and left vulnerable by the work of cavalry and ancillary contingents. Hammerlike, the Macedonian cavalry charges concentrated on a set spot on the enemy line, broke through, and eventually battered the enemy back onto the clumsy anvil of the spear-bristling phalanx. This coordination between infantry and horsemen was an entirely new development in the history of Western warfare, and was designed to make numbers superfluous. Philip's battles were not to be huge shoving matches between phalanxes, but sudden Napoleonic blasts to particular spots, which when exploited would collapse and thereby ruin the morale of the others. Unlike the prior evenly matched battles inside Greece, the Macedonian army in Asia had to assume it would be outnumbered by three to one.

Alexander's Successors in the decades after his death were often criticized for abandoning his mastery of mounted and infantry coordination in favor of sheer bulk: lengthening pikes to twenty feet and more and bringing in elephants and torsion artillery in place of skilled, seasoned cavalry. In their defense, captains like Antigonus, Seleucus, Eumenes, and Ptolemy were not, like Alexander, fighting Persians but other Macedonian and Greek armies against which mounted charges had little effect. To break apart a phalanx of pikemen in a decisive battle required elephants or another phalanx. Consequently, Alexander's fluidity and mastery of cavalry battle were not so much forgotten by his successors as deemed irrelevant in the new wars that saw armies of Greek and Macedonian pikemen, led by tough European veterans who would have frightened Alexander's horsemen.

Philip brought to Western warfare an enhanced notion of decisive war. True, the Macedonians' face-to-face, stand-up fighting was reminiscent of the shock assaults of the Greek phalanxes of the past. The running collisions of massed infantry, the spear tip to the face of the enemy, were still the preferred Hellenic creed of any Macedonian phalangite. But no longer were Macedonians killing merely over territorial borders. Battle was designed predominantly as an instrument of ambitious state policy. Philip's destructive mechanism for conquest and annexation was a radical source of social unrest and cultural upheaval, not a conservative Greek institution to preserve the existing agrarian community. Decisive face-to-face battle, once embedded in Greek cultural protocol—notification of intent, limited pursuit, exchange of prisoners, agreement to accept the victory of the battlefield scrum—had become the centerpiece of a new total war of brutal annihilation which the world had not yet seen. Small Greek armies of the seventh and sixth centuries B.C. had met on small plains to collide together, push, stab, and force their adversaries off the battlefield, an hour or so of battle often deciding an entire war. The Macedonians saw no reason to stop fighting at the collapse of their enemy on the battlefield when he could be demolished in toto, and his house and land looted, destroyed, or annexed.

Philip's men, too, were a completely different breed from the Greek hoplites of the city-state. In his lost comedy *Philip,* the playwright Mnesimachus (ca. 350 B.C.) makes his characteristic Macedonian phalangites brag:

> Do you know against what type of men you'll have to fight?
> We who dine on sharpened swords,
> and drink down blazing torches as our wine.
> Then for dessert they bring us broken Cretan darts
> and splintered pike shafts. Our pillows are shields
> and breastplates, and beside our feet lie bows and slings.
> We crown ourselves with catapult wreaths.
> (Mnesimachus frg. 7 [cf. Athenaeus 10.421b])

In the conservative fourth-century-B.C. oratory of the Greek polis, Philip himself appeared as a limping, one-eyed monster, a terrible man who would fight at any time, in any manner. Demosthenes warned the Athenians:

> You hear of Philip marching unchecked, not because he leads a phalanx of hoplites, but rather because he is accompanied by skirmishers, cavalry, archers, mercenaries, and similar troops. When relying on these forces, he attacks a people that is at odds with itself, and when through distrust no one goes forth to fight for his country, he next brings up his artillery and lays siege. I need hardly tell you that Philip makes no difference between summer and winter, and has no season set apart for inaction.
> (Demosthenes 9, *Third Philippic* 49–51)

After the assassination of Philip (336 B.C.), and Alexander's subsequent subjugation of the Greek states following the destruction of Thebes, the twenty-year-old king inaugurated his deceased father's planned Persian invasion with a victory at the Granicus River near the Hellespont (334). In his first savage onslaught at the Granicus, Alexander established a pattern of battle in which we can distinguish a rough sequence of events that appears at all three of his subsequent major triumphs at Issus (333), Gaugamela (331), and the Hydaspes River (326): brilliant adaptation to often unfavorable terrain (all his battles were on plains chosen by his adversaries); generalship by frightful example of personal—and always near fatal—courage at the head of the Companion Cavalry; stunning cavalry blows focused on a concentrated spot in the enemy line, horsemen from the rear turning the dazed enemy onto the spears of the advancing phalanx; subsequent pursuit of enemy forces in the field, reflecting Alexander's impulse to eliminate, not merely to defeat, hostile armies. In all such cases, the overriding agenda was to find the enemy, charge him, and annihilate him in open battle—victory going not to the larger force, but to the one who could maintain rank and break the enemy as a cohesive whole.

Alexander never led an army larger than 50,000 men—by necessity more than by intent: he was forced to leave at least 40,000 Macedonians back in Greece to keep the peace. In his first battles (e.g., Granicus and Issus) there were more Greeks fighting against him than for him. Given the fact that garrisoning and constabulary forces were also needed to secure his conquest, it is a wonder—given the limited manpower reserves of Macedonia—that he had any army left at all. Such practical manpower considerations are critical in any assessment of his later "humanitarian" efforts at including Persians and other Asians in his army. Remember also that for the first four years of his invasion (334–331), there were thousands of Greeks who made their way to Persia to fight Alexander the "liberator"—and almost no Persians who fought for him.

To Alexander, as was true of Napoleon, the size of the opponent mattered little, since he would concentrate on only a small segment of the enemy line, while his father's old marshals would hold the enemy fast elsewhere. Reserves would help to ensure that the enemy did not reach his own rear. Alexander himself would wait, seek his opening, and send his wedge of horsemen and heavy pikemen to blast apart the enemy, his charge sending ripples of fear through thousands of less disciplined imperial subjects. Who of the enemy—themselves of differing speech and custom—would be the first to stay and die against the crazed Macedonian so that others in the Great King's army could follow their sacrifice and swarm Alexander?

KILLING SPREE

Was Alexander Greek? Linguistically not in the pure sense, for few in the central and southern Greek world could understand much Macedonian, a distant Hellenic dialect less akin to proper Dorian or Ionic Greek than an Arkansas twang is to Oxford English. To the Greeks, the problem with Macedon was not its harsh and mostly incomprehensible language, much less matters of race, but its culture. Specifically, there were no true city-states north of the Greek border with Thessaly, just hamlets and villages of the poor, juxtaposed to the few vast estates of the horse-breeding rich—all overseen by a conglomeration of warring and often petty monarchs whose palaces and tombs today constitute most of the archaeological record of ancient Macedonia. Philip had united these lords into a real kingdom, and he had brought Hellenic artists, philosophers, and men of science to Macedon, subsidizing the Greek influx of talent with booty and stolen gold.

Thousands of hired Greek scientists and craftsmen eventually accompanied Alexander and his Macedonians eastward to ensure technological and organizational superiority over the Achaemenid armies: Diades, the Thessalian siege engineer who "took Tyre," with his colleague Charias, and the other designers, Phillipus and Poseidonius; Gorgias, the hydraulic engineer, and Deinocrates, the town planner who laid out Alexandria; Baeton, Diongnetos, and Philonides, who systematically organized camps and surveyed routes; the naval experts Nearchus and Onesicritus; Eumenes, the head of the secretarial service; the natural philosopher and historian Callisthenes and his assistants; and Aristobolus, architect and engineer. The Macedonians had also hired thousands of southern Greeks in their army, from mercenaries to scientists, all seeking a steady wage and the patronage of the royal house. Whereas the Peloponnesian War (431–404 B.C.), fought for principle and leadership of Greece, had nearly wrecked the old Greek city-states, Alexander's nakedly predatory rampage in the East had the opposite effect of creating, not consuming, capital for the Western world.

Where Philip and Alexander drew the line on the imported Hellenic tradition was, like the later Japanese, politics—*ta politika* ("matters of the polis"). From Greece—Philip had been a young hostage at Thebes (369–368 B.C.) during the heyday of the brilliant Theban general Epaminondas—the king welcomed the phalanx, and with it the tradition of large infantry musters, decisive head-on assault, disciplined ranks, and the beginning of real tactical maneuver. From Greece Philip embraced the rationalist tradition and the disinterested pursuit of science and natural inquiry apart from religion and government—only that way might he build elaborate siege engines and torsion catapults. From Greece he adopted the traditions of individual initiative, coupled with iron-clad military discipline that put more emphasis on group solidarity than the number of enemy killed by heroic warriors. In that manner, he might recruit and train spirited phalangites who would charge into a wall of spear tips on his orders.

Before the battle at Gaugamela Alexander reminded his hired mercenaries that they were nonetheless "free" men—in contrast to the Persians, who were felt to be mere slaves. While not a single man had voted for Alexander as their king, there was nevertheless some truth to what he said. The legacy of Hellenic freedom was not to be defined entirely in political terms, but, as Aristotle noted, as "doing as one pleased." Alexander's phalangites, like the hired Ten Thousand earlier, enjoyed a liberality of association, as they held spirited and boisterous assemblies, voted on proposals when it was convenient to Alexander, and at royal banquets and sports enjoyed a familiarity with their betters unknown at the Persian court. It would turn out that even hired killers who were not citizens eventually became disgusted with the growing orientalism of Alexander—and the revolting custom of *proskynēsis*, or a free man's kowtowing to another as if he were a living god.

Philip, however, had no interest in civic militarism, civilian control over his military, or abstract political freedom for his soldiers—the entire baggage of the weak and squabbling city-states. That distrust he taught Alexander—and he added one brilliant piece of propaganda as well: the Great Idea of a Panhellenic crusade into Persia, a final Götterdämmerung that would pay back the Achaemenids for the burning of the Athenian acropolis, revenge their enslavement of Hellenic Ionia and a century of meddling in Greek affairs, empty the Persian treasuries to enrich the Balkans beyond imagination, and provide a final unification of all Greek-speaking peoples, a real nationhood of men-in-arms at last. Only this way, Philip knew, could he leave a secure Greece to his rear as he headed eastward. True, there would always be patriots and firebrands like Demosthenes and Hyperides who would intrigue and revolt, always Greek hoplites eager to fight him in Asia for the Great King's pay. Under his phony "League of Corinth," Philip could say he was killing "for Greece," not himself. In this first European "Crusade" Philip offered to a squabbling Greece the unification necessary to ransack a unified and despotic East.

Consequently, Alexander's entire relationship with Hellenism, with Western culture itself, is paradoxical. No single man did more to spread the art, literature, philosophy, science, architecture, and military practice of Hellenic culture eastward beyond the borders of mainland Greece than Alexander the Great—and no foreigner did more to destroy three hundred years of liberty and freedom of the Greeks inside Greece than did Philip and his son. Alexander the Great mustered more Greek-speaking soldiers to kill more non-Greeks than any other Greek in history—and himself engineered the death of more Greeks at Chaeronea, at Thebes, at the Granicus, and at Issus than any Greek general in history. Alexander's original intention was to rob and loot an aging Achaemenid kleptocracy. In the process he unleashed the stored tribute of centuries, whose newly coined money fueled a cultural renaissance unimagined under Persian rule, as thousands of Greek profiteers, engineers, and itinerant craftsmen followed him into Persia. Alexander went eastward, he said, to spread Hellenism. Yet no philosopher, king, or holy man did more to Orientalize Greeks than Alexander, who weakened secular Greek city-states in order to embrace Asian theocracy, leaving as his legacy the three-century-old Hellenistic practice of a plutocratic god-king, ensconced and isolated from his subjects in an imperial capital.

Alexander's expropriation of the Hellenic military tradition, without the bridle of parochial local government and the logistical constraints of amateur hoplites, meant that the Greeks for the first time in their history might find the natural limits of their military power at the distant Indus River. By the same token, Alexander's rejection of constitutional government, of civic militarism, and of municipal autonomy ensured that his conquests would never result in a stable Hellenic civilization in Asia, or even liberty in Greece—but simply the Successors' kingdoms (323–31 B.C.) of his like-minded marshals who followed. For three centuries theocrats—Macedonians, Epiriots, Seleucids, Ptolemies, Attalids—would rule, fight, plunder, and live in splendor amid a Hellenic veneer of court elites and professionals in Asia and Africa until at last they were subdued by the legions of republican Rome. The latter, unlike the Hellenistic Greeks, really would combine the ideas of Hellenic politics, civic militarism, and decisive battle, to forge vast and deadly forces of voting citizens, whose government created the army, rather than the army the government.

What were the political and cultural results of decisive battle in the hands of Alexander the Great? Ancient historians of the Roman age, their sources traceable in a convoluted trail back to contemporaries of Alexander himself, present both a "good" and a "bad" Alexander—either Homer's Achilles come alive whose youthful exuberance and piety brought Hellenism to its proper florescence, or a megalomaniac, drunken, and self-indulgent thug, who butchered most in his path before turning on his father's friends and compatriots, the men whose loyalty and genius created him in the first place. That debate continues today. The majority of contemporary Greeks despised Alexander for robbing them of their freedom and butchering them from Thebes to the Granicus. If we put aside later romance about Alexander—his supposed efforts to achieve the "brotherhood of mankind" or to bring "civilization" to the barbarians—we can agree that his real genius is mostly military and political, not humanitarian or philosophical: a brilliant innovation of Hellenic warfare, with the savvy needed to use such power to liquidate and bribe rivals who wished to do the same to him.

Alexander brilliantly employed decisive battle in terrifying ways that its long-conquered Hellenic inventors had never imagined—and in a stroke of real genius he proclaimed that he had killed for the idea of brotherly love. Cortés, a similar military prodigy, would likewise slice through the ranks of the Mexicas, slaughtering them in decisive battle that was largely outside their cultural experience, claiming that he did it for the Spanish crown, the glory of Christ, and the march of Western civilization. To Alexander the strategy of war meant not the defeat of the enemy, the return of the dead, the construction of a trophy, and the settlement of existing disputes, but, as his father had taught him, the annihilation of all combatants and the destruction of the culture itself that had dared to field such opposition to his imperial rule. Thus, Alexander's revolutionary practice of total pursuit and destruction of the defeated enemy ensured battle casualties unimaginable just a few decades earlier.

At the Granicus River (May 334 B.C.) Alexander destroyed outright the Persian army, surrounded the trapped Greek mercenaries, and massacred nearly all of them—except 2,000 whom he sent back as slaves to Macedon. Our sources disagree over the precise casualty figures; Alexander may have exterminated between 15,000 and 18,000 Greeks after the battle was essentially won. He killed more Hellenes in a single day than the entire number that had fallen to the Medes at the battles of Marathon, Thermopylae, Salamis, and Plataea combined! As many as 20,000 Persians fell as well at Granicus—far more than in any single hoplite battle in two centuries of warfare on the mainland. Granicus proved two points: Alexander would have to kill like no other Westerner before him to achieve his political ends, and he would be forced to eliminate thousands of Greeks, who for either greed or principle were willing to fight him in service of the Persian king.

The next year at Issus (333 B.C.), against the grand army of Darius III himself, the fatalities reached new magnitudes never before seen in battle involving either a Greek or a Macedonian army. Another 20,000 Greek mercenaries fell, and anywhere from 50,000 to 100,000 Persian recruits were dead by the end of the day—a formidable challenge of time and space to butcher more than 300 men every minute for eight hours. This was extermination taken to new heights, evidence of what the Western way of war might evolve into when shock battle was used to annihilate the enemy rather than settle parochial border disputes. The Macedonian phalanx did not push men off the battlefield as much as slaughter them from the rear for hours on end after the battle was already decided.

After Gaugamela, at his fourth and last victory over the Indian prince Porus at the Hydaspes River (326), Alexander killed around 20,000 of the enemy. Very conservative figures suggest that in the space of just eight years Alexander the Great had slain well over 200,000 men through decisive battle alone—at the cost of a few hundred of his own Macedonians. Only the Greek mercenary hoplites at Granicus and Issus had caused him real problems, and finally they were outnumbered, surrounded, and almost annihilated—nearly 40,000 at the two battles, enough to ensure that there were scarcely any available at Gaugamela. Only Caesar in Gaul and Cortés in Mexico would rival Alexander's record of battlefield dead and subsequent civilian losses during years of pacification. Clearly, the Western approach to war—shock and frontal collision by walls of highly trained and disciplined professional foot soldiers—had created a one-sidedness in casualties heretofore unforeseen in Asia.

In between these formal battles, Alexander also stormed a host of Greek and Persian cities, displaying the truth that the Western way of war was no longer a technique of infantry battle, but an ideology of brutal frontal assault against any obstacle in its way. Alexander systematically captured and enslaved nearly all cities in his path, beginning in Asia Minor, proceeding to the Syrian coast, then into the eastern satrapies of Persia and ending with the carnage of Indian communities in the Punjab. We hear little from any sources about the precise number of those killed in Alexander's capture of Miletus (334), Halicarnassus (334), Sagalassus (333), Pisidia (333), Celanae (333), Soli (333), the massacre of the Branchideae (329), the various fortresses of Syr-Darya (329), the stronghold of Ariamazes (328), the Indian cities of Massaga (327), Aornus (327), and Sangala (326). Most of these strongholds were larger than Thebes, his inaugural siege, which saw 6,000 Greeks butchered in the streets. Arrian suggested 80,000 were cut down in the storming of the southern Punjabi cities around Sindimana, and 17,000 Indians killed and 70,000 captured at Sangala. A conservative estimate would assume a quarter million urban residents were killed outright between 334 and 324 B.C., most of them civilian defenders who lived in the path of Alexander's trek east.

The most well documented carnage was in Phoenicia at Tyre and Gaza. After months of heroic defense, Tyre fell on July 29, 332. We have no exact record of how many were lost in the city's defense, but on the city's final day of existence 7,000 to 8,000 residents were slain in the chaos. Two thousand surviving males were crucified as a lesson in the futility of resistance. Anywhere from 20,000 to 30,000 women and children were enslaved. Tyre, like Thebes before, ceased to exist as a community. Gaza, farther south on the Syrian coast, was next. After a two-month siege Alexander let his troops murder the city's inhabitants at will. All Syrian males were exterminated. Nearly 10,000 Persians and Arabs died. All captured women and children, numbering in the untold thousands, were sold into slavery. Alexander bound Batis, the governor of Gaza, pierced his ankles with thongs, and dragged him around the city, Achilles-style, until the tortured victim expired.

For most of his decade in Asia, Alexander was unable to draw his enemies out to pitched battle, and so brought battle to them, marching in obscurity to the East, systematically burning villages, murdering local elites, and razing strongholds in dirty wars of retaliation, in which nomadic Eastern traditions of skirmishing, ambushes, and hit-and-run attacks wreaked havoc on his army. The list of decimated peoples in what is now Afghanistan, Iran, and the Punjab is nearly endless, but a small sampling can give some idea of the sheer number of tribes that were either pacified or exterminated through Alexander's Western propensity to advance ruthlessly against the main loci of enemy settlement. To the south of Susa, the mountain villages of the Uxiis of the Zagros Mountains were systematically sacked. Most of the inhabitants were killed or displaced. At the Susian Gates, in western Iran, during his approach to Persepolis, Alexander wiped out the forces of the satrap Ariobarzanes; only a handful of survivors escaped down the mountain. It took Alexander only five days to hunt down and conquer the Mardis of eastern Iran, who were incorporated in Alexander's empire and forced to provide men, horses, and hostages (331).

In Bactria Alexander began to cleanse in earnest when faced with local revolts and secessions. An expatriate community of Greeks, the so-called Branchideae, were said to have been wiped out to the man. The Sacans of Sogdiana—fierce veterans of Gaugamela—were extinguished and their territory ravaged. Convinced that the rich villages of the Zervashan valley to the south had aided the rebellions in Sogdiana,

Alexander stormed their fortresses too. He executed all the defenders whom he found alive; 8,000 alone were killed in the capture of Cyrupolis. The revolts in Bactria and Sogdiana (329–328) were little more than two years of uninterrupted fighting, looting, and executing. Alexander followed the same pattern of total war in India (327–326). He massacred all the defenders along the Choes River in Bajaur. After promising the surrounded Assacenis their lives upon capitulation, he executed all their hired soldiers who surrendered. Their other strongholds at Ora and Aornus were likewise stormed. The garrisons were probably slaughtered. Most of the villages of the Mallis of the lower Punjab were razed. The civilian refugees were butchered in the flight into the desert. Most agree that tens of thousands were killed.

The East had never experienced anything like Alexander's army, which offered the enemy the choice of submission or death, and had the will and power to accomplish both. None of these tribes had a prayer against the Macedonians in pitched battle. Their only chance was to wage desultory wars in the mountains, in hopes of slowing down and frustrating Alexander's progress, rather than defeating him outright. On his passage through the Gedrosian desert in 325 B.C., when his own men were not dying, Alexander attacked the Oreitae. Alexander's lieutenant Leonnatus killed 6,000 of them in one engagement. Between famine and military conquest the Oreitae had their territory depopulated. Any figure for the human costs for the subjugation of Bactria, Iran, and India is impossible, but many villages and provincial strongholds were the homes of thousands. After the arrival of Alexander, their communities were destroyed and their male defenders killed, enslaved, or recruited.

For what purpose was all the killing? Alexander's desires are not known, although pacification of a new empire from the bones of Achaemenid rule are the most likely explanations for his continuous rampage through Asia. Sometimes the Macedonians killed in transit or in general quarters; so lethal had Alexander's war machine become that it was a danger even to itself. After the Persian capital of Persepolis was handed over in submission, Alexander had allowed his Macedonians an entire day of plunder and gratuitous butchery. The frenzied Macedonians pillaged the houses even of the common people, carried off the women, and sold into slavery any who survived the day of random killing. Plutarch remarks that there was also much slaughter of the prisoners. Curtius adds that many residents preferred to jump from the walls with their wives and children or torch their own households and families rather than be gutted in the streets. Mass suicide is rare among European populations, but more common among the victims of Western arms: non-Western peoples when confronted with the hopelessness of resisting Western arms, from Xenophon's Ten Thousand to Roman legions in the Holy Land to Americans on Okinawa, have often preferred voluntary group death.

After a respite of a few months, all the imperial treasury was carted off—few precious metals were ever found in Persepolis by modern excavators—and the royal palace torched amid a mass orgy of drunken debauchery. Fires probably spread beyond the palace and for a time left the capital uninhabitable. Documentary sources chronicle the immense loot gathered—120,000 talents by most accounts, the material bounty requiring 10,000 pairs of mules and 5,000 camels to carry away—but do not calculate the human cost. If Persepolis was capital of an empire of millions, and its population was in the hundreds of thousands, thousands died during the initial killing, subsequent enslavement, and final deportations and dispersals.

In an empire of 70 million there was no native constabulary force that could prevent 30,000 veterans from the West from doing whatever they pleased. The result was that hundreds of thousands died literally from being in Alexander's way. Macedonians and indigenous tribes were killed on Alexander's ill-fated crossing of the Gedrosian desert in late summer 325 along the northern coast of the Indian Ocean, from the Indus River delta to the Persian Gulf. Ancient sources give lurid accounts of the suffering and death on the march of some 460 miles over sixty days. Alexander embarked with an army of at least 30,000 combatants, followed by a lengthy train of thousands more women and children. Arrian, Diodorus, Plutarch, and Strabo speak of unending losses to thirst, exhaustion, and sickness, and mention tens of thousands left dead. In three months Alexander was responsible for more deaths among his own troops than in a decade of losses to Persian soldiers. The real threat to Macedonian phalangites was not a Persian or Indian renegade, but their own murderous general.

Unlike the prior practice of the Greek city-states, there were no shared commands by a board of generals in the Macedonian army—no civilian audits, no ostracism through voting or court trials to oversee the high leadership of the Macedonian army and its king. Alexander as absolute ruler reacted to suspicions of disloyalty with instant sentences of death. An entire generation of Macedonian noblemen was executed by the king they served. The murders increased with the paranoia and dementia of his last years—and with the realization that their services in pitched battle were no longer needed after the collapse of the Achaemenid royal army and the extermination and enslavement of the dangerous Greek mercenaries.

The mock trial and subsequent torture and stoning of his general Philotas (330) are well known. Far from being a conspirator, Philotas, who had shared command of the Macedonian cavalry and fought heroically in all of Alexander's major campaigns—he led the charge of the Companions through the Persian line at Gaugamela—was guilty of little more than arrogance and failure to pass on gossip about possible dissension against the king. With Philotas's gruesome death, his father, Parmenio (no charges were ever brought against him) was murdered as well. Various other Macedonian nobles disappeared or were killed outright as the army moved farther east from Babylon. The so-called Black Cleitus, who had saved Alexander at the Granicus, was speared to death at a drunken banquet by the intoxicated king himself. After a number of young Macedonian pages were stoned to death for suspicion of sedition (327 B.C.), Alexander executed the philosopher Callisthenes, nephew of Aristotle, who had objected to the king's practice of *proskynēsis.*

After emerging from the Gedrosian desert, Alexander went on a seven-day binge of drink and revelry, culminating in a series of further execution decrees. The generals Cleander and Sitacles, and later Agathon and Heracon, and six hundred of their troops were killed without warning or legal trial. Purportedly, they were guilty of either malfeasance or insubordination. More likely, they were cut down because of their past involvement in carrying out Alexander's order to execute the popular Parmenio—a blunder that had not gone down well with the rank-and-file veterans and required some ceremonial show of expiation.

Alexander literally decimated an entire corps of 6,000 men—the first clear evidence in Western warfare of that practice of lining up and executing one out of every ten soldiers. Alexander had introduced to the West from the East and South the twin ideas of decimation and crucifixion. In turn, his own original contribution to Western warfare was the carnage of decisive battle when completely divorced from moral restraint and civic audit. Alexander unleashed the idea of shock battle as the annihilation of the enemy. The Greek world had never seen anything quite like him.

Alexander the Great was not a well-meaning emissary of Hellenism. He was an energetic, savvy adolescent and an authentic military genius, who was naturally curious and saw propaganda value in being surrounded by men of letters. He inherited from his father a frighteningly murderous army and was wise enough to secure the loyalty of a cadre of shrewd and experienced battle administrators—at least until the Persian army was defeated. Alexander understood how to modify the Hellenic tradition of decisive battle for murderous new ends, baffling his opponents in the East, who believed that ambush, ruse, negotiation, raiding, and plundering were all preferable to a head-on collision of shock troops.

The Hellenistic age (323–31 B.C.) began with Alexander's final destruction of Greek freedom and political autonomy. His introduction of Greek military culture beyond the Aegean and the economic stimulus of flooding the Greek world with the stored and previously untapped gold and silver of the imperial Persian treasuries fueled political oppression and economic disparity—even as it drew writers and artists to the new courts of the age. He left exploiting monarchies in place of Greek autonomous polities—which nevertheless drew on the Western traditions of rationalism and disinterested learning to create cities, great art, and sophisticated agriculture and commerce. There was no room in Alexander's world for patriots and politicians, but far more opportunity and money for artists and academics than in the past.

For all his professed devotion to Greek culture, Alexander died a man closer at heart to Xerxes than to Themistocles. Under the subsequent Hellenistic dynasts, militiamen gave way to paid mercenaries, and war consumed budgets and manpower at astronomical rates. Free markets, military research, and sophisticated logistics combined to form deadly Western armies unimaginable a few decades earlier. The Eastern notion of a divinity enthroned became the norm in the Hellenistic Successor states—with all the accustomed megalomania, gratuitous slaughter, and oppression that we associate with theocracies. Scholars sometimes compare Alexander to Caesar, Hannibal, or Napoleon, who likewise by sheer will and innate military genius sought empire far beyond what their own native resources might otherwise allow. There are affinities with each; but an even better match would be Adolf Hitler—a sickening comparison that will no doubt shock and disturb most classicists and philhellenes.

Hitler similarly engineered a brilliant but brutal march eastward during the summer and fall of 1941. Both he and Alexander were singular military geniuses of the West, who realized that their highly mobile corps of shock troops were like none the world had seen. Both were self-acclaimed mystics, intent on loot and plunder under the guise of emissaries bringing Western "culture" to the East and "freeing" oppressed peoples from a corrupt, centralized Asian empire. Both were kind to animals, showed deference to (but were not really interested in) women, talked of their own destiny and divinity, and could be especially courteous to subordinates even as they planned the destruction of hundreds of thousands, and ultimately murdered many of their closest associates and greatest field marshals. Both were half-educated pop philosophers who sprinkled their orders of mass destruction with allusions to literature and poetry. For every promise of a "brotherhood of man," there was a "thousand-year Reich"; for every house of Pindar saved among the rubble of Thebes, there were visions of a new Rome in Berlin; for every gutted Parmenio, there was a murdered Rommel; for every desolate Tyre, Gaza, or Sogdiana, there was a ransacked Warsaw or Kiev; and for every Gedrosian desert, a suicidal Stalingrad.

Just as Alexander understood that European individualism and the know-how of Hellenism could forge highly spirited troops and thereby serve for a time autocracy, so Hitler drew on the rich legacy of Germany and its once-free citizenry to create an equally dynamic and frightening blitzkrieg. History calls Alexander an emissary of world government and a visionary, while it rightly sees Hitler as a deranged and deadly monster. Had Alexander died at the Granicus on his entry into Asia (his head was almost cleaved in two by an enemy cavalryman) and had Hitler's Panzers not stalled a few miles outside Moscow in December 1941, a few historians might consider the Macedonian merely an unbalanced megalomaniac whose insane ambitions ended in a muddy stream near the Hellespont, and the latter a savage but omnipotent conqueror who through brilliant decisive battles vanquished Stalin's brutal communist empire.

The failure of these ancient and modern autocrats—Alexander's empire disintegrated into squabbling fiefdoms before being annexed by Rome, while Hitler's thousand-year Reich lasted thirteen years—reminds us that decisive battle, superior technology, capitalism, and unmatched discipline give Western armies only ephemeral victories if they lack the corresponding foundation of Western freedom, individualism, civic audit, and constitutional government. Given the complexity and origins of Western military practice, it is more effective when confined within the parameters of its birth. The ancient world produced no man more personally courageous, militarily brilliant, and abjectly murderous than Alexander the anti-Hellene, truly the first European conquistador in a long train to follow.

DECISIVE BATTLE AND WESTERN WARFARE

Ultimately, wars are best decided by men who approach each other face-to-face, stab, strike, or shoot at close range, and physically drive the enemy from the battlefield. Missile weapons can aid infantry battle but in themselves—whether blow darts, slings, or howitzers—cannot send an enemy into defeat and decide a war:

> Fire and fire only is hopeless if the enemy ever makes contact. Weapons of shock are the crushers and pincers which are held in the hands of the assailant. Shock weapons are the military instruments par excellence. They are not only employed by courageous fighters anxious to close with the enemy, deliver him a blow, and win a decision, but they are truly the deadly one. They win battles. (H. Turney-High, *Primitive War: Its Practice and Concepts,* 12)

At the Granicus, Issus, and Gaugamela, the Persian army was stationary, waiting for Alexander's arrival, intent on selecting superior terrain for a defense against the invaders. Stockades, riverbanks, caltrops, scythed chariots, and elephants were to stop what their men-at-arms could not. Alexander's famous retort that he would fight Darius III openly by day rather than stealthily at night is one of the many anecdotes that illustrate the Hellenic desire for open, direct, and deadly confrontation. Curtius relates that Alexander also scoffed at the idea of a war of attrition, much less extended negotiations with Darius III: "To fight a war with captives and women is not my way; he must be armed for battle whom I hate" (*History of Alexander* 4.11.18).

Before Gaugamela, Curtius recorded that Alexander worried only that Darius might not fight. When Parmenio woke him from a sound sleep on the morning of the battle, he arose in confidence and said, "When Darius was torching the countryside, burning villages, and destroying the food supply, I was beside myself. But now, what do I have to worry about since he is preparing to fight it out in open battle? By God, he has satisfied my every wish" (4.13.23). Plutarch adds that Alexander also explained on the morning of Gaugamela, "What is the matter? Don't you think that now we already appear to have won, since no longer do we have to wander about in a vast and denuded country in pursuit of a Darius who avoids pitched battle?" (*Alexander* 32.3–4). That same morning Alexander went on to goad his troops that their vast enemies—"on their side more men are standing, on ours more will fight"—were not shock troops like themselves, scarred and maimed from hand-to-hand collisions. Persians, he told his men, were but "a mixed mob of barbarians, in which some threw javelins, others stones, and only a few used real *[iusta]* weapons" (Curtius *History of Alexander* 4.14.5). "Real weapons" in the Western mind meant pikes and swords that were to be used face-to-face at close quarters. During the battle itself the outnumbered Macedonians alone charged en masse to break the enemy line. When safely through the horde, they ignored the Persian camp and went directly for Darius's chariot. Where the king fled, there Alexander's men followed, nearly riding their horses to death as they sought to kill everyone on the battlefield and catch a fleeing king.

Whence did this peculiar Western notion of decisive battle derive? Where did the idea arise that men would seek their enemy face-to-face, in a daylight collision of armies, without ruse or ambush, with the clear intent to destroy utterly the army across the plain or die honorably in the process? Decisive battle evolved in early-eighth-century Greece and was *not* found earlier or elsewhere. The earlier great crashes of Egyptian and Near Eastern armies of the second millennium B.C. were not shock collisions of heavily armed foot soldiers, but vast battles of maneuver between horsemen, charioteers, and bowmen. The circumstances of the birth of decisive battle—wars of small property-owning citizens, who voted for and then fought their own battles—account for its terrifying lethality. Only freemen who voted and enjoyed liberty were willing to endure such terrific infantry collisions, since shock alone proved an economical method of battle that allowed conflicts to be brief, clear-cut—and occasionally deadly.

In the seventh and sixth centuries B.C. if a small Greek community was self-supporting and governed by its surrounding private landowners, then hoplite warfare, far better than fortification or garrisoning passes, made perfect sense: muster the largest, best-armed group of farmers to protect land in the quickest, cheapest, and most decisive way possible. It was far easier and more economical for farmers to defend farmland on farmland than to tax and hire landless others to guard passes—the sheer ubiquity of which in mountainous Greece ensured that they could be turned by enterprising invaders anyway. Raiding, ambush, and plundering were still common—such activities seem innate to the human species—but the choice of military response to win or protect territory was a civic matter, an issue to be voted on by free landowning infantrymen themselves. In that regard, other means of conflict resolution seemed unending, costly, and often indecisive.

Hoplite fighting through shock collision in the tiny valleys of early Greece marks the true beginning of Western warfare, a formal idea fraught with legal, ethical, and political implications. Almost all these wars of a day between impatient yeomen of the seventh and sixth centuries B.C. were infantry encounters over land, usually disputed border strips signifying agrarian prestige more than prized fertility. Customarily, the army of one city-state, an Argos, Thebes, or Sparta, met its adversary in daylight in formal columnar formation—the word "phalanx" means rows or stacks of men—according to a recognized sequence of events, which allowed battle to be brutal, but not necessarily so deadly.

There arose an entire vocabulary for horrific moments of fighting that is ubiquitous in Greek literature, reflecting the centrality of shock battle to Greek culture in a way not true of other methods of fighting elsewhere. Hoplite engagements themselves were known as "drawn-ups" *(parataxeis)*, "battles by agreement" *(machai ex homologou)*, "battles in the plain" *(machai en to pediō)*, or battles that were "just and open" *(machai ek tou dikaiaou kai phanerou)*. Stations and areas of the battlefield—the front ranks *(prōtostatai* or *promachoi)*, no-man's land *(metaixmion)*, the close-in fighting *(sustadon)*—were carefully delineated. Clear stages—the initial run *(dromō)*, the clash and breaking of the line *(pararrēxis)*, spear thrusting *(doratismos)*, hand-to-hand *(en chersi)*, push *(ōthismos)*, encirclement *(kuklōsis)*, and rout *(egklima* or *trophē)*—were also formally recognized. Such nomenclature suggests that the mechanics of hoplite battle itself entered into the popular culture in a way unknown of mounted or light-infantry warfare.

The Greeks of the city-state acknowledged that decisive land warfare of their age was different from earlier practice. For example, the historian Thucydides begins his history with the recognition that the earlier Greeks did not fight as they did in his own time, and he presents a picture of the close tie between agrarian societies and land warfare. Capital, stationary agrarian populations on the mainland, and permanent crops, in Thucydides' description, led to the predominance of decisive land warfare. Aristotle much more concretely mapped out the evolution of Greek warfare, and likewise put great emphasis on the later emergence of infantry battle in general and hoplite infantrymen in particular. Early Greek states that evolved after monarchies, he said, were primarily run by aristocratic horsemen. Thus, their war lay with cavalry, since hoplites were not yet effective troops, possessing neither "orderly formation" nor the "experience and knowledge of troop deployment." Later, hoplites became stronger, which led to social transformation and the rise of constitutional governments (*Politics* 4.1297b16–24).

Aristotle implies that early Greek warfare was once primarily fought by mounted troops, but at the dawn of the city-state evolved into battles between heavily armed infantry. The rise of such soldiers, and presumably the manner in which they fought, gave the hoplites political preeminence in their poleis, leading to the spread of constitutional governments. Whereas mass collisions were a part of Mediterranean warfare at every age and locale, in Greece they became the exclusive domain of heavily armed infantrymen, who fought in file and rank, charged and crashed together in a truly shock fashion. Moreover, the militias of the polis Greeks were subject to a general set of protocols that had political and cultural implications beyond the battlefield: set battles might decide entire wars, even when the war-making potential of the loser was not exhausted by defeat.

As we have seen, Philip put a final end to hoplite battle as arbitrarily resolving conflict itself. In the process he took the Greek discovery of shock infantry battle and applied it to a new Western concept of total war. At the twilight of the free city-state and in the shadow of Philip II, the orator Demosthenes, in his *Third Philippic* (48–52), composed sometime around 341 B.C., lamented on how decisive battle had transmogrified into something terrifying: "whereas all the arts have made great advances, and nothing is the same as it was in the past, I believe that nothing has been more altered and improved than matters of war." He goes on to remind his audience that in the past "the Lacedaemonians, like all the others, used to spend four or five months—the summer season—invading and ravaging the territory of their enemy with hoplites and civic armies and retire home again." Finally, Demosthenes points out that hoplite armies were "so bound by tradition or rather such good citizens of the polis that they did not use money to seek advantage, but rather their war was by rules and out in the open."

In contrast to this evolving Greco-Macedonian tradition, Darius drew on a distinguished but very different heritage, one that went back to Cyrus the Great and was enriched by fighting Scythian and Bactrian heavy horsemen, the chariot armies of Egypt, and tribal contingents to the east and mountainous north. The Persian army relied on mobility, speed, and ruse, and was thus especially strong in horsemen and archers—and weak in heavy infantrymen, as was befitting a nomadic people of the steppes, who had no agrarian city-state traditions and never a history of consensual government. The warrior ethos in Asia was not that of the yeoman farmer. No Mede, Scythian, or Bactrian trudged into the Assembly, voted to muster, pulled his armor off the wall, joined in his local regiment, and with his "general" at his side, marched off to challenge his opposing phalanx to a brutal collision—and then hurried back home to defend his own property and to conduct a public audit of the battle performance of the army and its generals.

Persians, Medes, Bactrians, Armenians, Cilicians, and Lydians, who either enjoyed tribal rule or were subject to imperial governments, relied on superior manpower, aerial bombardment by missile troops and archers, and vast encircling movements of hordes of horsemen and chariots. If a Western army—the later Romans at Carrhae (53 B.C.) are a good example—was foolish enough to fight in the sweeping plains of Asia without adequate mounted support, it might well be surrounded and overwhelmed by such forces. Usually, the superiority of Western infantry and its preference for shock battle meant that if the army was led properly—by a Pausanias at Plataea (479 B.C.), Caesar in Gaul (59–50 B.C.), or Alexander at Gaugamela—there were no forces in the world that could stand its onslaught.

The Hellenistic autocrats who followed Alexander the Great had found their phalanxes unconquerable against Asiatic troops, and were adequate enough against one another. They were eventually to learn that Rome brought to each battle a haughty new bellicosity and bureaucracy of war that were the material and spiritual dividends of a united and politically stable Italy and a revived idea of civic militarism that had helped the Greeks win at Salamis so long ago. Unlike Hellenistic battle practice, Roman decisive warfare was always presented as a legal necessity *(ius ad bellum),* a purportedly defensive undertaking that was forced by belligerents upon the rural folk of Italy. Whereas their generals may have killed for *laus* and *gloria,* the republican legionaries themselves felt confident that they fought to preserve the traditions of their ancestors *(mos maiorum)* and in accordance with the constitutional decrees of an elected government. Roman armies continued to win because they added their own novel contributions of regularization to decisive war. As we shall see with the unrivaled slaughter at Cannae, Roman militarism was based on mass confrontation in pitched battles, and on applying the entire engine of Hellenic-inspired science, economic practice, and political structure to exploit such battlefield aggressiveness in annihilating the enemy in a single day if possible—or being nearly consumed in the process.

The Greek way of war was not dead with the rise and passing of the Hellenistic kingdoms (323–31 B.C.) that followed the division of Alexander's empire. Far from it. For the next two millennia in Europe, battle would be energized as never before by those who were not Greeks, but who inherited their peculiarly Western dilemma of being able to do what they knew they sometimes should not. Alexander the Great for a time created a deadly army by separating decisive battle from civic militarism; the Romans crafted an even deadlier military by returning the notion of shock battle to its original womb of constitutional government in ways far beyond even the Hellenic imagination.

This Western propensity for shock battle survived Rome as well, in the Byzantines' century-long wars against nomadic and Islamic horsemen, and the deadly internecine struggles between the Franks and then against the Muslims. The Teutonic Knights of the Middle Ages adapted the idea of face-to-face fighting to mass heavy-cavalry charges, which had served their outnumbered forces well during the Crusades in the Middle East. Phalanxes—unique to Europe—were to reappear in fourteenth- and fifteenth-century Switzerland, Germany, Spain, and Italy. Renaissance abstract thinkers sought to apply ancient discussions of *stratēgia* ("generalship") and *taktika* (the arrangement of troops) to improving the crash of contemporary pikemen. Pragmatists as diverse as Machiavelli, Lipsius, and Grotius also envisioned such armies in constitutional service to the state, realizing that heavy infantrymen, mustered from yeomen free citizens, were the most effective shock troops when engaged in mass collision. These small armies of central Europe followed in the classical tradition of shock land battles. By the sixteenth century the West was convulsed in an era of shock battles as professional armies sought to destroy one another's ability to resist, in a manner not found in China, Africa, or the Americas. Between 1500 and 1900 thousands more infantry collisions took place inside Europe than in the rest of the world.

The Aztecs, who tried to pull Cortés and his men off their warhorses and bind his conquistadors as sacrificial offerings on the Great Pyramid, were of an entirely different heritage, one that did not see battle as the occasion to meet the enemy and settle the dispute instantaneously through the destruction of its ability to resist. In contrast, when Cortés at last took Mexico City, he advanced by destroying the city block by block, intent on annihilating all Aztec adversaries until they capitulated or were no more. The Zulus thought that after their sole victory at Isandhlwana, the British would retreat, having been defeated in open battle. They had no conception that the Western way of war meant a series of such battles until the will—or culture—of the adversary was crushed. The Ottoman Janissaries, who learned and mastered the European art of firearms, never embraced the corresponding Western idea of fighting as shock troops in disciplined columns, in which individual heroism was subjugated to the larger goal of achieving mass firepower and collision which alone might obliterate the enemy. The Marings on New Guinea, the Maoris of New Zealand, the mythical Homeric heroes of the pre-polis Greek past, and most other tribal peoples sought from war social recognition, religious salvation, or cultural status—anything other than the dismemberment of the enemy on the battlefield by the collective effort of shock encounter.

The idea of decisive battle continues in the West. The classical notion that pitched, shock confrontation is the only way to resolve wars in part explains why Americans consider it honorable and effective to bomb the Libyans when they have committed a terrorist act in Europe; or to rain down enormous battleship projectiles upon Palestinian villages openly and "fairly" from offshore when a few of their residents are alleged to have bombed in a "cowardly" fashion American marines asleep in their barracks. As long as Westerners engaged the enemy in an open contest of firepower, the ensuing carnage was seen as relatively immaterial: terrorists who shamelessly killed a few women and children, or states that surprised us on Sunday morning in a bombing attack on our fleet, usually found mechanized murderous armies of retaliation on their soil and daylight fleets of bombers over their skies.

Due to our Hellenic traditions, we in the West call the few casualties we suffer from terrorism and surprise "cowardly," the frightful losses we inflict through open and direct assault "fair." The real atrocity for the Westerner is not the number of corpses, but the manner in which soldiers died and the protocols under which they were killed. We can comprehend the insanity of a Verdun or Omaha Beach, but never accept the logic of far fewer killed through ambush, terrorism, or the execution of prisoners and noncombatants. Incinerating thousands of Japanese civilians on March 11, 1945, is seen by Westerners as not nearly so gruesome an act as beheading on capture parachuting B-29 fliers.

Will such a paradox always be true? Between the hoplite battlefields of classical antiquity and the present age lie the trenches of World War I, the carpet bombing and death camps of World War II, and the apocalyptic threat of World War III. Modern Western man finds himself in a military dilemma of sorts. His excellence at frontal assault and decisive battle—expanded to theaters above the earth's atmosphere and below the sea—could end all that he holds dear despite the nobility of his cause and the moral nature of his war making. We in the West may have to fight as non-Westerners—in jungles, stealthily at night, and as counterterrorists—to combat enemies who dare not face us in shock battle. In consequence, we may not always fully draw on our great Hellenic traditions of superior technology and the discipline and ardor of our free citizen soldiers in shock battle—unless we are to face another Western power in a murderous collision of like armies. Alexander the Great, remember, fought mostly non-Greeks in short, decisive battles in which he suffered little. When he did meet other Westerners—whether in the pitched battle of Chaeronea or against the Greek mercenaries in Asia Minor—the result was frightful carnage.

I leave the reader with the dilemma of the modern age: the Western manner of fighting bequeathed to us from the Greeks and enhanced by Alexander is so destructive and so lethal that we have essentially reached an impasse. Few non-Westerners wish to meet our armies in battle. The only successful response to encountering a Western army seems to be to marshal another Western army. The state of technology and escalation is such that any intra-Western conflict would have the opposite result of its original Hellenic intent: abject slaughter on both sides would result, rather than quick resolution. Whereas the polis Greeks discovered shock battle as a glorious method of saving lives and confining conflict to an hour's worth of heroics between armored infantry, Alexander the Great and the Europeans who followed sought to unleash the entire power of their culture to destroy their enemies in a horrendous moment of shock battle. That moment is now what haunts us.

FOUR

Citizen Soldiers

Cannae, August 2, 216 B.C.

Infantrymen of the polis think it is a disgraceful thing to run away, and they choose death over safety through flight. On the other hand, hired soldiers, who rely from the outset on superior strength, flee as soon as they find out they are outnumbered, fearing death more than dishonor.

—ARISTOTLE, *Nicomachean Ethics* (3.1116b16–23)

A SUMMER SLAUGHTER

BY LATE IN THE AFTERNOON of August 2, 216 B.C., no room remained to fight and little more in which to die. Given the crashing press of their exhausted fellow soldiers, the Roman legionaries could not retreat, advance, or even find much area to wield their swords. Frenzied Iberians in white tunics and half-naked Gauls were in their faces. Veteran African mercenaries suddenly appeared at the flanks. From their rear arose cries that Celtic, Iberian, and Numidian horsemen had cut off any hope of escape. Thousands of Hannibal's hired men—a who's who of the old tribal enemies of Rome—were everywhere. Nowhere were there enough Roman cavalry and reinforcements. A vast mass of 70,000 brave souls was encircled in a small plain in southwestern Italy by a poorly organized but brilliantly led invading army half its size.

Confusion and terror only grew greater as dusk neared, as each Roman pushed blindly and was shoved into the enemy at all sides. Stacked in rows to the depth of thirty-five and more, the size of the unwieldy mass began to ensure its destruction. A marvelous army designed for fluidity and flexibility was unaccustomedly caught fast in an immovable column. The men of Rome had never before marched out to a single battle in Italy in such huge numbers—and would never do so again. And not until a similar disaster at Adrianople (A.D. 378) six centuries later did the Roman army deploy itself to such an unwieldy depth, making it an easy target for missiles and preventing the great majority of its soldiers from ever reaching the enemy.

The sight of the mass fighting must have been as spectacular as it was soon sickening. Unlike the Romans, Hannibal's men were a heterogeneous-looking bunch. In the center the backpedaling Celts and Gauls, as was their custom, fought stripped to the waist ("naked," Polybius says), probably armed only with heavy wooden shields and clumsy swords that were virtually pointless and were only effective in sweeping, slashing blows that left the attacker wide open to quick counterjabs. A few may have had javelins or spears. Their white, muscular physiques and great size were favorite topics of Roman historians, who were quick to imply that smaller tanned Italian legionaries used training, order, and discipline to butcher such wild tribesmen in the thousands. For the next two centuries commanders like Marius and Caesar would wipe out entire armies of just such brave and physically superior warriors. We think of French slaughter in terms of Agincourt or Verdun, but the true holocaust occurred in the mostly unknown battles of the two-century encounter with the Romans, who cut down more Gauls than at any time before or after. Roman steel, not disease or hunger, doomed an autonomous ancient France, whose manhood was systematically destroyed in battle as no other people would be in the entire history of Western colonial subjugation. Caesar's final annexation of Gaul made the nineteenth-century American fighting on the frontier look like child's play—a million killed, a million enslaved, Plutarch recorded, in the last decades alone of that brutal two-century conquest.

Hannibal may have put these brave Gauls in the center to incur the Romans' fury and thus draw them farther into the encirclement. Livy remarks that they were the most terrifying of all Hannibal's troops to look upon. In the classical world the stereotype of utter uncivilized savagery was a white skin, long greasy blond—or worse, red—hair, and a flowing unkempt beard. Four thousand of them were sliced to pieces by the methodical Italians. Alongside them at the vortex marched hired Spaniards—ostentatious infantrymen with iron helmets, heavy javelins, and dazzling white cloaks bordered with crimson, which, like the nakedness of their pale Gallic allies, would soon only highlight the bloodletting. Unlike the Gauls, the Spanish also wielded the short double-edge sword—copied and improved upon by the Romans as the *gladius*—lethal as a slashing and stabbing weapon. Stationed next to the Gauls, they were cut down mercilessly—though Polybius says hundreds, not thousands, of these better-armed and protected warriors fell.

At the front of the oncoming Roman mass, the fighting soon degenerated into swordplay and hand-to-hand pushing, biting, and clawing. Only the steady feigned withdrawal of the Gauls and Spanish and the impending encirclement at the flanks saved these sacrificial tribal contingents from utter annihilation. Livy and Polybius both focus on the doom of the surrounded Roman legions, but more than 5,000 Spaniards and Gauls must have suffered ghastly wounds before being trampled to death by the legionary steamroller. How Hannibal and his brother Mago survived the slaughter we are not told; but both stood gallantly among the Gallic and Spanish front ranks, ensuring that their retreating pawns not break before the trap was set.

Hannibal's best were his African mercenaries stationed on the flanks and ordered to turn about and hit the legionaries as they rushed by, heedless in their bloodlust. These were grim professional soldiers who had battled a score of North African tribes, fought Europeans during their march from Spain, and on occasion turned on their own Carthaginian masters when pay was not forthcoming. Centuries later their legendary toughness impressed the novelist Gustave Flaubert, whose novel *Salammbô* has as its backdrop one of their numerous bloody revolts. At Cannae they probably first pelted the outer ranks of the legions with javelins and then cut their way in through the Roman flanks, since legionaries could scarcely turn sideways on the run to meet this new and unexpected threat.

Although they were not used to the Roman equipment—the Africans more often fought Macedonian-style as phalangites with two-handed pikes—they were veteran killers, and far more experienced than the adolescents who filled the Roman ranks, which were depleted by the thousands butchered earlier at Trebia and Lake Trasimene. Moreover, the African heavy infantrymen on the flanks were stationary and fresh, the oncoming Romans exhausted from killing and pressing the Gauls and Spaniards. The former were staring intently on their prey, the latter oblivious to their danger. Within seconds the killers became the killed, and it is

a wonder that even 1,000 Africans were lost during the entire afternoon—
a mere fiftieth of the Roman total. The collision of African infantry with
the Roman flanks must have been horrendous, as dense files of shuffling
legionaries were suddenly hacked and ripped apart on their vulnerable
sides, without opportunity or room to halt and face their attackers.
Roman infantrymen were superbly protected at their front, and ade-
quately from their rear; but their sides were relatively bare—exposed arms
behind the shield, less body armor below the shoulder, and the ears, neck,
and portions of the side of the head without cover.

Who could distinguish friend from foe, as Africans and Italians sliced
away at each other, wearing similar breastplates, crested helmets, and oblong Roman shields? Polybius claimed that when the Africans hit the
Romans broadside, order was lost for good and the mass rent beyond repair. The rear flanks and base of the Roman column were still unenclosed,
and here the other great failure of the Roman army became manifest: besides its poor generalship, there were far too few Roman horsemen. Most
of the mounted troops present were vastly inferior to the some 2,000
Numidian light cavalry on the right flank, men who had been on their
horses since childhood, who could throw javelins with deadly accuracy at
a gallop and slash away with swords and battle-axes at close quarters as
easily mounted as on foot. On the Carthaginian left wing a horde of 8,000
Spanish and Gallic horsemen—with spears, swords, and heavy wooden
shields—likewise tore apart the Roman cavalry. Hannibal had arrayed
10,000 skilled horsemen on the two wings against 6,000 poorly trained
mounted Italians. After driving off the enemy cavalry, the Numidian and
European horsemen turned to slaughtering the enclosed infantry from
the rear.

The presence of some 10,000 fresh horsemen at the base of the
Roman column, and 20,000 Africans on the flanks, with the dust in the
Romans' faces, the screaming of dying Gauls and Spaniards, and the sheer
difficulty of distinguishing friend from foe, made the tiny summer battlefield a confused slaughterhouse. Three hours earlier the Roman army had
marched out as a foreboding mass of iron, bronze, and wood, rank after
rank of crested helmets, huge shields, and deadly javelins in a solemn pro-
cession of undisguised pride against Hannibal's motley and outnumbered
mercenaries. Now there was little left but a heap of broken weapons, ooz-
ing bodies, severed limbs, and thousands of the crawling half-dead.

The terror of battle seems not the mere killing of humankind, but the
awful metamorphosis that turns on a massive scale flesh to pulp, clean to

foul, the courageous to the weeping and defecating, in a matter of minutes. Just as Admiral Nagumo's beautiful four carriers at Midway had been a showcase of power, grace, and undefeated energy at 10:22 A.M. on June 4, 1942, and six minutes later blazing infernos of charred bodies and melting steel, so the thousands of plumed swordsmen in perfect order were transformed nearly instantaneously from a majestic almost living organism into a gigantic lifeless mess of blood, entrails, crumpled bronze, bent iron, and cracked wood. Men and matériel that were the products of weeks of training and months at the forge were reduced in moments to flotsam and jetsam by the genius of a single man. Brilliant generalship in itself is a frightening thing—the very idea that the thought processes of a single brain of a Hannibal or Scipio can play themselves out in the destruction of thousands of young men in an afternoon.

For the next 2,000 years armchair tacticians would squabble over the mechanics of the slaughter at Cannae—seduced by the idea that a numerically inferior invader in a few hours could exterminate its enemy through simple encirclement. Clausewitz ("Concentric activity against the enemy is not appropriate for the weaker side") and Napoleon both felt Hannibal's trap too risky and the product more of luck than genius. For the Prussian strategist Count Alfred von Schlieffen, Cannae was not the chance butchery of thousands, but a tactician's dream come true that was "most wonderfully fought" and planned to the last detail—the essence of what military erudition combined with fighting spirit might accomplish. Schlieffen, who in his own time foresaw a Germany besieged by more numerous enemies, found it reassuring that the intellect of one man could nullify the training, expertise, and sheer numerical superiority of thousands. Indeed, Schlieffen would write an entire book, aptly entitled *Cannae*, on the Prussian army's bold and repeated attempts to achieve Hannibalic encirclement on a massive scale. The great German invasion that ended at the Marne (September 1914) and the battle of Tannenberg (August 1914) were both efforts to entrap and surround entire armies, and thus invoked the mythical idea of Cannae—without real appreciation that tactical encirclement, ancient and modern, need not lead to strategic victory. Yet rarely does any great captain encounter an enemy deployed so absurdly as the legions in August 216 B.C. The Romans, who might have outflanked Hannibal's outnumbered line by two miles, instead presented a front that was roughly the same size—and far more inflexible.

Many wounded had been hamstrung by marauding small bands, their writhing bodies left to be finished off by looters, the August sun, and

Carthaginian cleanup crews the next day. Two centuries later Livy wrote that thousands of Romans were still alive on the morning of August 3, awakened from their sleep and agony by the morning cold, only to be "quickly finished off" by Hannibal's plunderers. Roman corpses "were discovered with their heads buried in the earth. Apparently they had dug holes for themselves and then, by smothering their mouths in the dirt, had choked themselves to death" (22.51). A few thousand crawled about like crippled insects, baring their throats and begging to be put out of their misery. Livy goes on to record examples of extraordinary Roman courage discernible only through autopsy of the battlefield: a Numidian who had been brought alive out of the pile from beneath a dead Roman legionary, his ears and nose gnawed away by the raging Roman infantryman who had lost the use of everything but his teeth. The Italians, it seemed, fought desperately even when they knew their cause was hopeless—a realization that must have sunk in among most after the first minutes of battle.

Hannibal, in the ancient tradition of victorious military commanders, grandly inspected the battlefield dead. He was said to have been shocked at the carnage—even as he gave his surviving troops free rein to loot the corpses and execute the wounded. The August heat made it imperative to strip promptly the bloated bodies and torch the stinking flesh—a feat of logistics in itself just to hack away the armor from the torsos and haul away thousands of putrid corpses. No grave site near the battlefield has as yet been uncovered, nor any traces of the bones of the dead, so the bodies were probably left to rot.

The destruction of some 50,000 snared Italians in a single afternoon—more than 200 men were probably killed or wounded each minute—was in itself a vast physical challenge of slicing thousands with muscular power and iron in the age before the bullet and gas canister. Livy (22.49) remarks of the legionaries' "refusal to budge," and emphasizes their willingness "to die where they stood," which only further "incensed the enemy." There must have been at least 30,000 gallons of blood spilled on the battlefield alone; even three centuries later the satirist Juvenal dubbed Cannae the scene of "rivers of spilt blood." The sea "turned red at Lepanto" from the blood of 30,000 butchered Turks, but the tide cleansed the site within minutes. The horrible carnage of some 50,000 to 100,000 at the final siege of Tenochtitlán was beside a lake, whose waters eventually might mitigate the stench. Given the deep columns of the Romans and Hannibal's tactics of encirclement, Cannae became an unusually tiny battlefield, one of the smallest killing fields to have hosted such large numbers in the entire history of infantry battle. For the rest of the summer of 216 B.C. the plain of Cannae was a miasma of decaying entrails and putrid flesh and blood.

From our written sources—the Greek and Roman historians Appian, Plutarch, Polybius, and Livy—we know that the late afternoon of August 2 was one of the few ancient battles in which an entire army was destroyed after hitting the enemy head-on. In general, the complete slaughter of hoplites, phalangites, and legionaries was somewhat rare and accomplished only by flank attack, lengthy pursuit by cavalry, or ambush. At Cannae the entire Roman army advanced frontally as one unit and at the same time in unobstructed terrain, ensuring a magnificent collision of arms that would lead to either spectacular victory or horrendous defeat. Polybius called the daylight encirclement at Cannae a "murder." Livy also thought it a slaughter, not a battle, and the ill-famed nature of the fighting explains why Cannae is one of the better-recorded battles—three detailed accounts survive—of the ancient world.

Never in the five-century history of Rome had so many infantrymen and their elected leaders been trapped on the battlefield with no certainty of escape. After the battle the thirty-one-year-old Hannibal would collect the gold rings of more than eighty consuls, ex-consuls, quaestors, tribunes, and scores of the equestrian class in a bushel. Military historians have praised Hannibal's genius and blamed the Roman catastrophe on Rome's bureaucratic system of electing and training its generals. In their eyes Cannae is a result of singular tactical brilliance pitted against institutionalized mediocrity. That analysis is scarcely half-true: if the Roman system of tactical leadership, with its commitment to civilian oversight and nonprofessional high command on the battlefield, was responsible for producing a succession of amateurish generals who would lose a string of battles during the Second Punic War (219–202 B.C.), it also deserves credit for ensuring that Cannae and the previous disasters at the Ticinus and Trebia Rivers and Lake Trasimene were not fatal to the Roman war effort. Cannae, like so many of these landmark battles, is the exception that proves the rule: even when Roman armies were poorly led, foolishly arranged, squabbling before battle over their proper deployment, and arrayed against a rare genius, the catastrophic outcome was not fatal to their conduct of the war. The reason for such astonishing Roman resilience— emblematic of Western armies throughout history—is the subject of this chapter.

HANNIBAL'S JAWS

The defeat of August 216 B.C. is usually attributed to three factors: the
Romans were poorly commanded and deployed; they faced a military genius in Hannibal; and they were demoralized from a string of three defeats in the past twenty-four months that had cost them thousands of
their fathers, sons, and brothers. All three explanations have merit. The
Roman plan of battle at Cannae was poorly thought out. It made no sense
for legions to mass on narrow, flat terrain where they might be trapped
and squeezed between flanking enemy infantry pincers and rapidly moving mounted troops at their rear. In these natural or man-made valleys
and canyons, infantry companies had no chance to flow independently
but were prone to conglomerate and could thus be hacked at from all
sides. With no room to maneuver to the side, individual legionaries lost
open space and the crucial ability to use their swords with advantage. Like
underpowered phalangites—who had wielded massive pikes, not short
swords—they were to be funneled against columns of Hannibal's heavily
armed swordsmen and spearmen. Legionaries in dozens of columns to
the rear were waiting in line, as it were, helpless to prevent their own predictable annihilation to come. The Roman army would go on in the next
century to smash through columns at the battles at Cynoscephalae,
Magnesia, and Pydna by outflanking and outmaneuvering far more
clumsy Greek phalanxes. They would learn that the way to beat foreign
armies of the Mediterranean was to fight in a manner *opposite* from their
charge at Cannae.

Due to Hannibal's string of unbroken successes during his descent
through northern Italy (218–216 B.C.), the Senate had transferred command of the legions from its brilliant general Fabius Maximus—given pro
tempore dictatorial powers in the field—back into the hands of its annually elected consuls, who for the year 216 B.C. were the aristocratic and
careful L. Aemilius Paulus and the more adventuresome Terentius Varro,
the latter purportedly a popular leader of the masses. Scholars have criticized Varro's decision to march the army on the morning of August 2
across the Aufidus River into the flat, treeless plain of Cannae (command
rotated between the consuls on alternating days). In fact, the Roman general had reason to initiate battle, since Hannibal's mounted patrols were
raiding his lines, devastating the surrounding countryside, and making it
ever more difficult to keep such a huge force well supplied. The specter of
such a huge army gave his men confidence that at last they could catch
Hannibal in an open plain. Their superior numbers and organization

might annihilate his mercenaries, who would have no chance for ambush or cover by darkness or fog. A year earlier Roman weight had almost crushed the Carthaginians at Lake Trasimene before being entrapped and outflanked in the mist. At Cannae the plain was relatively flat, the weather windy but reasonably good, and the Carthaginians seemingly deployed only in front of the legions, making the resort to deception unlikely.

Varro's real mistake lay in committing most of his forces at once—only 10,000 Roman reserves were left behind far from the battlefield in two camps on either side of the river—without keeping a third line ready to exploit success or prevent collapse. In any case, because Varro either worried about the quality of his new replacement recruits or desired to ensure that his army was not strung out too far, he reduced his battle line to about a mile. Out of an army of between 70,000 and 80,000, not more than 2,000 could engage the enemy at the front in the initial attack. The depth of the Roman mass in some places along the long line was well beyond thirty-five men, and as great as fifty—the deepest formation in the history of classical warfare since the great mass of the Theban army had obliterated the Spartans at Leuctra (371 B.C.). But at that earlier battle, the Theban column met few cavalry and a timid king, and was led by the gifted tactician Epaminondas.

There may have been only 40,000 Carthaginian infantrymen facing an army almost twice that size. Surely, most other enemies who faced such a huge force would have crumbled before the legionary onslaught. The difference was in large part due to the tactical genius of Hannibal, who adapted his battle plans precisely to facilitate the impatience of Roman tactics. As we have seen, Hannibal and his brother Mago stationed themselves with the less dependable Gauls and Spaniards right at the acme of the Roman attack, convinced that their presence could steady their unreliable troops long enough to conduct a gradual withdrawal, to backpedal slowly, sucking in the oncoming Roman weight. The Punic center was bowed out toward the Romans—Polybius called the curious formation a *mēnoeides kurtōma*, "a crescent-moon-shaped convexity"—both to hide somewhat the African pikemen on the wings and to give the impression that the line was deeper than it actually was. The bulge allowed a margin of retreat: the greater the distance the center backpedaled without collapse, the easier the wings might envelop the narrower Roman formations.

The key for Hannibal and his European allies was to survive until North African infantry on the wings—the elite of Hannibal's army—and cavalry streaking to the rear and sides could enclose the enormous legionary mass, thereby deflating its forward pressure before it smashed the core of the Punic army. Livy noted in his history of Rome that the Punic center was far too thinly deployed "to withstand the pressure" (22.47). The problem was that there were not more than 2,000 to 3,000 legionaries at the front of the huge column who were actually fighting with drawn weapons; the others, more than 70,000, were pushing blindly ahead on the assumption that the cutting edge of their army was mowing down the enemy in front. The least trained were probably on the wings—and thus the first to confront the closing jaws of Hannibal's superb African infantry. Whatever the estimation of our ancient sources concerning the Gauls and Spaniards, they fought bravely and in some sense saved the battle for the Carthaginians.

Just in time, the charges of African horsemen at the flanks and at the back, the ubiquitous barrage of missiles, and the sheer confusion of seeing enemies in all directions stalled the Roman advance. Hannibal, in broad daylight and without cover, had created an ambush by the sheer deployment and maneuver of his men—and he had done so while battling at the apex of the Roman assault, convinced that his physical presence in the maelstrom would allow his outnumbered and exhausted hired Iberians and Gauls to backpedal without collapsing. The envelopment was soon completed. A thin wall of Punic and European irregulars held tight a surging throng of Roman infantry. Had each legionary killed one man before dying, the battle would have been a decisive Roman victory. Had they known that their adversaries were only two or three ranks deep, the legions might have broken out. The wind, dust, noise, and panic brought on by rumors that the enemy was everywhere only added to the chaos. Because of the enormous losses during the prior two years at Trebia and Trasimene, the Romans at Cannae were fresh recruits without many veterans to calm their fears, and thus immediately became demoralized at the realization that for a third time an enormous Roman army was being led into a Punic trap from which few might escape alive. Many must have been adolescents and so have frantically thrown down their weapons the second they realized they were trapped. The great strategist Ardent du Picq believed that Hannibal had guessed right that the "terror" and "surprise" resulting from his encirclement would outweigh "the courage of despair in the masses." In short, panic killed the legionaries at Cannae. Still, for a time the prominence of so many Roman luminaries on the field of battle—like the presence of doctors, lawyers, and other elites at the gates of Auschwitz—must have given some the false reassurance that total destruction was impossible. The army at Cannae was larger than

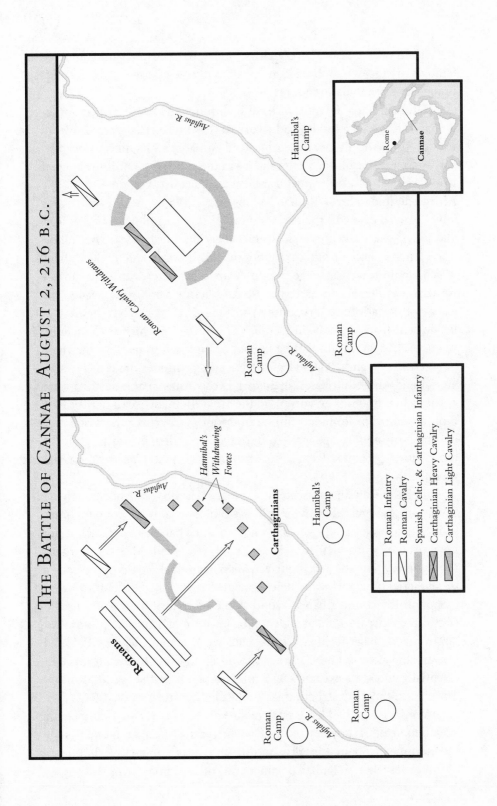

The Battle of Cannae August 2, 216 B.C.

Legend:
- Roman Infantry
- Roman Cavalry
- Spanish, Celtic, & Carthaginian Infantry
- Carthaginian Heavy Cavalry
- Carthaginian Light Cavalry

Rome
Cannae

Romans
Carthaginians
Hannibal's Camp
Roman Camp
Aufidus R.

Roman Cavalry Withdraws
Hannibal's Withdrawing Forces

the citizen population of every city in Italy except Rome, and contained enough aristocrats to have run most of the legislative and executive branches of the Italian republic.

Hannibal Barca ("Grace of Ba'al Lightning") had little respect for legionary repute. At nine he had sworn an oath of eternal hatred toward Rome—dramatically portrayed in Jacob Amigoni's magnificent oil canvas—and was one of the few foreigners in the entire history of the ancient world who actually welcomed frontal assault against Western armies. The African desired to break Roman legions outright in the field, as part of his larger plan to discredit the entire notion of Roman military invincibility, and so systematically uncouple Rome's allies in central and southern Italy.

Shattered and disgraced legions meant a weak and divided Italy, which would leave Carthage free to arrange its mercantile affairs in the western Mediterranean as it saw fit, and at the same time avenge the shame of defeat of the First Punic War (264–241 B.C.). From the time of his descent from the Alps in October 218 to the slaughter at Cannae on August 2, 216 B.C., Hannibal had killed or captured in battle somewhere between 80,000 and 100,000 legionaries, along with hundreds of the senatorial and knightly classes, including two consuls at the head of their armies and numerous ex-consuls in the ranks. In the space of twenty-four months a third of Rome's frontline troops of more than a third of a million men of military age were to be killed, wounded, or captured in the bloodbaths at Ticinus, Trebia, Trasimene, and Cannae. Cannae, then, was no fluke.

After the Roman massacre at Cannae, Hannibal did not march on Rome—to the great dismay of military pundits, from his contemporary subordinate Maharbal ("you know how to win a battle, Hannibal, but not how to use your victory" [Livy 22.51]) to Field Marshal Bernard Montgomery. For the next fourteen years Hannibal would experience a seesaw series of victories and defeats inside Italy that had little strategic effect upon the course of the Second Punic War, until he was recalled to Carthage to save his homeland from the invasion of Scipio Africanus. Not far from Carthage itself at Zama (202 B.C.), Scipio's legions defeated Hannibal's veterans, and Carthage submitted to harsh Roman terms that essentially ended its existence as a military power in the Mediterranean. The city's ultimate destruction was only a half century away (146 B.C.).

Hannibal, who had left Carthage for Europe in 219, had unknowingly been on a fruitless odyssey of some twenty years, a vast circuit across the Mediterranean, Spain, the Alps, and Italy that came to a close thousands of dead later where it had all begun—and with a Roman army once again free to march on Carthage itself. As the historian Polybius concluded of the Roman recovery after Cannae and its effect on the Carthaginians: "Hannibal's pleasure in his victory in the battle was not so great as his dejection, once he saw with amazement how steady and great-souled were the Romans in their deliberations" (6.58.13).

CARTHAGE AND THE WEST

What is remarkable about Cannae is not that thousands of Romans were so easily massacred in battle, but that they were massacred to such little strategic effect. Within a year after the battle the Romans could field legions nearly as good as those who fell in August—themselves fresh replacements for the previous thousands killed at Trebia and Trasimene—but now to be led by Senate-appointed commanders who had learned the lessons of past tactical imbecility. Scholars attribute this resilience of Rome to its government's remarkable ability to reorganize its legions, mobilize its citizenry, and do so in legal, constitutional fashion that guaranteed the support of even the lowliest farmer. Hannibal would come to learn in Italy that the Roman army was not so much better equipped, better organized, more disciplined, and more spirited than his mercenary forces as far more insidious. It could be cloned and replicated at will even after the most abject of disasters, as recruits and their officers still willingly joined the army, mastered a hard course of training, and thus became linked to both their fathers, who were rotting in the soil at Cannae, and their sons to come, who would soon kill thousands of Africans outside Carthage itself.

Victory brought Hannibal few new troops, whereas defeat created entire new legions for Rome. A legionary in his fifties who was sliced to pieces at Cannae no doubt went to his death believing that his infant grandson, like himself a Roman citizen, would someday wear the same type of armor, undergo similar training—and in a battle to come avenge his fall and Rome's disgrace in Africa, not Italy. And he would be right. The army that would massacre Hannibal's mercenaries at Zama (202 B.C.) represented less than a tenth of the available infantry and naval manpower that Rome had at its disposal at the time. Throughout the entire nightmare of the Second Punic War, the Romans, as Livy pointed out, "breathed not a word of peace" (22.61). Hannibal's success at Cannae resembled the Japanese surprise at Pearl Harbor—a brilliant tactical victory that had no strategic aftermath and tended to galvanize rather than unnerve the manpower of the defeated. The assemblies of Romans and

Americans mobilized vast new armies after their embarrassments; the confident forces of the imperial war states of Carthage and Japan basked in their battle success and hardly grew.

It is difficult to attribute Rome's success at making good such catastrophic losses entirely to their singular idea of a constitutional form of government, inasmuch as the Carthaginians themselves had also evolved beyond both monarchy and tyranny. Given their common Hellenic source, there is some superficial similarity between the constitutions of Carthage and Rome. In addition, Carthage's Phoenician mother language had been the prototype of the Greek alphabet, while Punic literature— *libri Punici*—which was written in Punic and Greek, was well respected by Roman writers. That communality was natural given Carthage's similar integration for the past century in the Hellenistic economy of the eastern Mediterranean, its sophisticated practice of viticulture and arboriculture, and its own prior three centuries of contact with the free Greek city-states through constant warring and colonization in Sicily.

The Carthaginian coast was closer to the ancestral Hellenic cultures in Sicily and southern Italy than was Rome. Many Greeks by the fourth and third centuries would be more knowledgeable of the coastal North Africans than of Italians in the hills of central Italy. Despite lurid stories of child sacrifice at the sacred burial ground (the *tophet*)—a practice that seemed to flourish the more wealthy and urban Carthage became—the huge bureaucracy of priests and diviners of the bloodthirsty god Ba'al, and the brutal record of the Magonid dynasty (whose kings were priests and supreme commanders in the field), the Carthaginians fielded armies not that different from other mercenaries of the eastern and largely Hellenic Mediterranean.

Carthage, like the Hellenistic monarchies of the era, recruited phalanxes of pikemen, incorporated elephants into its ranks, and employed professional Greek tacticians and generals to train and advise its paid soldiers. Though outnumbered, Hannibal's men were not in the same predicament as the Aztecs or Zulus, who suffered from vast technological inferiority against their outnumbered Western enemies. In the military sense Carthage had also become a quasi-Western state through fighting Greek hoplite armies and hiring phalangite mercenaries since the era of its early-fifth-century invasions of Sicily. The Spartan mercenary Xanthippus was brought in to reorganize the entire Carthaginian army during the First Punic War. Our ancient sources also credit him with engineering the pivotal victory over Regulus's Roman army that perished outside Carthage in 255 B.C. The Greek historian Sosylus accompanied

Hannibal on his campaigns and served as a direct conduit of Hellenic military expertise and *exempla*. Hannibal himself sought to forge ties with King Philip V in Macedon in hopes that phalangites from the Greek mainland might land on the eastern coast of Italy to coordinate joint Punic-Macedonian attacks on Rome.

While its government was more aristocratic than the Roman constitution, Carthage by the time of the Second Punic War was also governed by two annually elected magistrates *(suffetes)*, who worked in tandem with a deliberative body of thirty elders *(gerousia)* and a high court of 104 judges, all of whose decisions were ratified by a popular Assembly of a few thousand nobles. The historians Polybius and Livy were able to use, if clumsily so, Greek and Latin political nomenclature—*ekklēsia, boulē, senatus, consul*—to approximate Carthaginian offices and institutions in their descriptions of Hannibal's civilian overseers. Even Aristotle in his *Politics* includes frequent mention of Carthaginian constitutional practice in a discussion of earlier forms of lawful oligarchies, praising its mixed government, which separated powers among judicial, executive, and legislative branches.

Carthage may have been a Phoenician colony founded in North Africa at the end of the ninth century B.C. by the mythical Elissa-Dido. In language, religion, and culture it was a Semitic people who had emigrated from its mother city of Tyre. Nevertheless, by the third century B.C. its political structure was quasi-Western in nature, and its economy was fully tied to the northern shore of the western Mediterranean.

Where Rome most fundamentally differed from its Punic neighbor to the south—besides in matters religious and linguistic—was in the notion of citizenship and the responsibilities and rights inherent in being a *civis Romanus*, a political idea that far transcended the legalistic aspects of a deliberative body merely following constitutional precepts. The early Western notion of consensual rule that arose in the eighth century B.C. in rural Greece was at its inception rife with contradictions, since the original discovery of politics meant not much more than a minority population of middling property banding together to decide on community policy. The radical concept that citizens should craft their own government raised an immediate paradox: who were to be the citizens and why?

If civic participation in early, broadly oligarchic Greek city-states originally marked a revolutionary invention of consent by the governed, such governments nevertheless often represented less than a fourth of the total resident population. Yet, as Plato lamented, there was a constant evolutionary trend toward egalitarianism and inclusion in the city-state. By the fifth century, especially in Boeotia and some states in the Peloponnese, the qualification for voting and office-holding was as small as a ten-acre farm or the cash equivalent.

The eventual result was that the clear majority of free adult male residents of the surrounding territory by the fifth century B.C. could participate fully in Hellenic government. At imperial Athens and among its democratic satellites every free male born to a male citizen, regardless of wealth or lineage, was eligible for full citizenship, giving rise to an enormous navy of free citizen rowers. Even more startling, the spread of Western democratic ideology evolved far beyond formal matters of voting, but lent an egalitarian aura to every aspect of the Greek city-state, from familiarity in speech and dress to a sameness in public appearance and behavior—a liberality in private life that would survive even under periods of monarchy and autocracy in the later West. Conservatives like the anonymous so-called Old Oligarch (ca. 440 B.C.) scoffed that slaves and the poor were treated no differently from men of substance at Athens. Plato felt that the logical evolution of democracy had no end: all hierarchies of merit would disappear as even deckhands would see themselves as captains, with a birthright to take their turn at the rudder whether or not they knew anything about seamanship. Even the animals at Athens, he jested, would eventually question why they, too, were not equal under an ideology whose aim was to lower all to a common level.

Although many of these Hellenic traditions of autonomy and freedom were eroded by the rise of the dynasts Philip and Alexander (359–323 B.C.) and their imperial Successors (323–31 B.C.) in the Hellenistic world, the ideals of the city-state were not entirely forgotten, but incorporated by states outside Greece itself. Italians, for example, learned more about constitutional rule from the old Greek colonies of southern Italy than from the contemporary Hellenistic kings across the Adriatic. So it was one of the great ironies of the Roman-Greek conflicts of the third and second centuries B.C. that the legions were more Hellenic than the Greek-speaking mercenaries they slaughtered at the battles at Cynoscephalae (197 B.C.) and Pydna (168 B.C.) inside Greece.

Unfortunately for purposes of mustering quality military manpower, Carthage, unlike Rome, had not evolved beyond the first phase of Hellenic-inspired consensual rule. Its government remained in the hands of a select body of aristocrats and landed executives, themselves chosen from that same elite cadre. Carthage was a vast empire run by a small deliberative clique of noble merchants and traders. In contrast, Rome borrowed and improved upon the Greek ideal of civic government through its unique idea of nationhood *(natio)* and its attendant corollary of allowing autonomy for its Latin-speaking allies, with both full *(optimo iure)* and partial citizenship *(sine suffragio)* to residents of other Italian communities—and in the centuries to come full citizenship to those of *any* race and language that might accept Roman law and pay taxes. What at its inception had nominally been a government of Latin-speaking aristocrats in Rome proper would logically evolve into a pluralistic state, in which local assemblies would weigh in against the Senate, and popular leaders would veto oligarchic legislation. Even consuls like Flaminius and Varro—the former killed at Trasimene, the latter in large part responsible for the catastrophe at Cannae—were purportedly "men of the people" voicing the poor's desire for precipitate military action in opposition to aristocrats like Fabius Maximus, who favored patience and delay. They had no popular counterparts at Carthage.

LEGIONS OF ROME

The Roman army, especially when deployed in strength on Italian soil, was not expected to lose, much less to be annihilated. Already by the late third century B.C. Roman legionaries had become the world's most deadly infantry precisely because of their mobility, superb equipment, singular discipline, and ingenious organization. The Epirote king and general Pyrrhus (280–275 B.C.), the Carthaginian commanders of the First Punic War (264–241 B.C.), and the northern tribes in Gaul (222 B.C.) could attest to the slaughter when their best troops tried to confront the Roman way of war. The Romans had developed a mobile and flexible method of fighting that could hunt down and smash through loosely organized tribal forces in Gaul and Spain, yet could also disrupt columns of highly disciplined phalangites from the East in pitched battles through encirclement or the manipulation of terrain. The history of the Roman third and second centuries is a story of bloody legion deployment throughout the Mediterranean, first to the west and south against the Iberians and Africans (270–200 B.C.), then against the Hellenistic kingdoms in Greece and to the east (202–146 B.C.).

To indicate the scope of Roman campaigning and the wide-ranging experiences of the legionaries, Livy reports in his history of Rome the often quoted example of the Roman citizen soldier Spurius Ligustinus. In his thirty-two-year career in the army (200–168 B.C.) the fifty-year-old soldier, father of eight, fought against the phalanx of Philip V in Greece, battled in Spain, returned to Greece to fight Antiochus III and the

Aetolians, then was back on duty in Italy, then off again to Spain. "Four times," Spurius claimed in Livy's highly rhetorical account, "within a few years I was chief centurion. Thirty-four times I was commended for bravery by my commanders; I received six civic crowns [for saving the life of a fellow soldier]" (42.34). Spurius might have added that he had collided against the pikes of Macedonian phalangites, faced the elephants of Hellenistic dynasts, and fought dirty wars against tribal skirmishers across the Pyrenees. Roman genius lay in finding a way to take an Italian farmer like Spurius and to make him fight more effectively than any mercenary soldier in the Mediterranean.

Comprising anywhere from 4,000 to 6,000 infantrymen, the legion was, by the end of the third century B.C., in reality a loose conglomeration of thirty companies called maniples ("fingers"), each composed of two smaller "centuries" of between sixty and one hundred soldiers, each led by a professional, battle-toughened centurion who mastered the Roman system of advance and assault in unison. When a Roman legion marched out to the battlefield, its sixty centuries did so in three vast lines, each wave itself able to coalesce into a mass or disperse into smaller contingents depending on the terrain and the nature of the enemy. The entire tactical design of the Roman army was intended precisely *not* to enter into clumsy, massed collisions with hostile columns, where it might either fall prey to encirclement or be broken apart by the greater depth of enemy formations.

Unlike the Greek phalanx from which it had evolved, Roman legionaries advanced in a fluid formation, as neat lines of soldiers cast their javelins, or *pila,* and ran to meet the enemy head-on with their deadly short sword, the infamous double-edged *gladius* forged of Spanish steel—a far more lethal and versatile weapon than the Macedonian pike. Rectangular shields often themselves served as offensive weapons, as legionaries banged their metal bosses against the flesh of the enemy. In their combined use of javelin, massive shield, and double-bladed sword, the Romans had solved the age-old dilemma of choosing between missile and hand-to-hand attack, and fluidity versus shock, by combining the advantages of both. Legionaries hurling their javelins matched the offensive punch of Asiatic missile troops; yet with their large body shields and razor-sharp swords might also serve as a shock corps in the manner of Greek phalangites. Unlike the phalanx, however, the three lines of successive advance allowed both for reserves and for concentration of force upon particular weak spots in the enemy line.

Against a Macedonian phalanx, Roman missile attacks might stun and wound pikemen, even as individual maniples rushed ahead for face-to-face battle at weak points in the enemy's tattered columns. Similarly, when facing northern European tribesmen, the legions might advance wall-like to present a disciplined solid front of shield and sword that would plow through the poorly organized skirmishers of tribal armies who had little chance against disciplined shock troops. Against both such adversaries two lines of maniples to the rear (the *principes* and *triari*) watched the initial engagement of the front lines (the *hastati*), eager to exploit success or prevent collapse.

What was it like to face the three lines of an oncoming Roman army? Most classical historians of Roman battle—Caesar, Livy, Plutarch, and Tacitus especially—view the collision through Roman eyes. Their ethnocentric and lurid accounts portray shaggy six-foot Germans making queer sounds, deep resonating war cries (the *barritus*), and beating their equipment; screaming half-naked Gauls with their hair greased and piled high to increase their apparent height; or robed and painted Asians in vast droves, whose chatter and garishness give way to the disciplined advance of grim professionals—intelligence and civilization offsetting greater numbers, barbarism, and brute strength every time. War paint, tattoos, bare-breasted women, ululation, and an assortment of iron collars, chains, spiked hair, and occasional human heads and body parts hanging from the war belt are the usual requisites in any Western description, from Roman legions to the Spanish conquistadors, of fighting the Other.

Yet it was not the "barbarian" advance but the Roman that was truly inhuman and chilling. The legions, as the Christians did at Lepanto and the British at Rorke's Drift, fought in silence; they walked until the last thirty yards of no-man's-land. At a predetermined distance the first line threw their seven-foot *pila*, for the first time yelling in cadence as they unleashed the volley. Immediately and without warning, hundreds of the enemy were impaled, or their shields rendered useless by the rain of projectiles. Now with the lethal short swords unsheathed, the first rank crashed into the stunned enemy mass. The oblong shields had iron bosses in the centers, and the Romans used them as battering rams to shock the enemy, as the well-protected legionaries hacked off arms, legs, and heads during the confusion. Individual soldiers pushed in to exploit gaps where the dead and wounded had fallen. Almost immediately, an entire second army, the succeeding line of *principi*, surged in to widen the tears in the enemy line, hurling their *pila* over their friends' heads in the melee, the entire process of charging, casting, and slicing now beginning anew—with yet a third wave ready at the rear.

The terror of war does not lie in the entirely human reaction of tribal cultures to bloodletting—screaming and madness in giving and receiving death, fury of the hunt in pursuit of the defeated, near hysterical fear in flight—but rather in the studied coolness of the Roman advance, the predictability of the javelin cast, and the learned art of swordsmanship, the synchronization of maniple with maniple in carefully monitored assaults. The real horror is the entire business of unpredictable human passion and terror turned into a predictability of business, a cold science of killing as many humans as possible, given the limitations of muscular power and handheld steel. The Jewish historian Josephus later captured that professionalism in his chilling summation of legionary prowess: "One would not be wrong in saying that their training maneuvers are battles without bloodshed, and their battles maneuvers with bloodshed" (*Jewish War* 3.102–7).

The utter hatred for this manner of such studied Roman fighting surely explains why, when Roman legions were on occasion caught vastly outnumbered, poorly led, and ill deployed in Parthia, the forests of Germany, or the hills of Gaul, their victors not only killed these professionals but continued their rage against their corpses—beheading, mutilating, and parading the remains of an enemy who so often in the past could kill without dying. The Aztecs also mutilated the Spanish—and often ate the captives and corpses; and while this was purportedly to satisfy the bloodlust of their hungry gods, much of the barbarity derived from their rage at the mailed conquistadors, with their Toledo blades, cannon, crossbows, and disciplined ranks, who had systematically and coolly butchered thousands of the defenders of Tenochtitlán. In the aftermath of the British defeat at Isandhlwana, the Zulus decapitated many of the British and arranged their heads in a semicircle, in part because so many of their own kinsmen had minutes earlier been blown apart by the steady firing of Martini-Henry rifles.

The Roman republican army was not merely a machine. Its real strength lay in the natural élan of the tough yeoman infantry of Italy, the hard-nosed rustics who voted in the local assemblies of the towns and demes of Italy and were every bit as ferocious as the more threatening-looking and larger Europeans to the north. In the tradition of constitutional governance—the Greek Polybius marveled at the Roman Republic, whose separation of powers, he felt, had improved upon the more popular consensual rule of the Hellenic city-state—the Romans had marshaled a nation of free citizens-in-arms.

Like most of the Greeks at Salamis, Roman yeomen in vast numbers had voluntarily imposed civic musters, voted through their local assemblies for war, and marched to Cannae under elected generals, determined to rid Carthaginian invaders from Italian soil. Like the phalangites of Alexander the Great, and influenced by the earlier Greek tradition of decisive warfare, the Romans put little faith in ruse or ambush, let alone archers, horsemen, or skirmishers. Would that they had listened to the warnings of Fabius Maximus and continued to wage a war of attrition, not annihilation, against a brilliant opponent like Hannibal.

Better yet, would that Roman armies had developed, as Philip and Alexander had, a shock force of heavy cavalry that could have been integrated with the advance of the maniples and thus nullified the superb mobility and dash of Hannibal's horsemen. The tactics of delay and scorched earth, along with the culture of the mounted grandee, went against the Roman tradition of frontal infantry shock assault. For a variety of cultural, military, and political reasons, the horseman was rarely the mainstay of classical armies—either in his incarnation as a mounted and gaudy seignior or as an impoverished nomadic raider. The use of cavalry by Philip and Alexander was exceptional rather than representative of Greek and Roman military practice, and Greco-Roman armies would pay in blood on numerous occasions for that critical shortcoming.

Despite the simplicity of Roman advance and the occasional inexperience of the recruits, the discipline of the legions was unmatched, and the strength and courage of Italian infantry unquestioned. The Roman Senate, like the earlier Greek Assembly and the caucuses of the royal Macedonian elite, was nurtured in a tradition that sought to send its armies against the enemy head-on, and thus through the hammerblows of decisive infantry battle destroy him in a matter of hours. Few Roman commanders were ever prosecuted in the wake of defeat for their incompetence—only for cowardice in failing to engage the enemy in decisive battle. When Varro, the surviving consul at Cannae, returned to Rome after the debacle, he was greeted with enthusiasm: apparently his tactical blunders that resulted in thousands killed were overshadowed by his proven desire to lead inexperienced young Roman yeomen headlong to their deaths against Hannibal.

The infantrymen who marched into the death trap at Cannae were probably better armed and equipped than their enemies: their shields, breastplates, helmets, and swords were the fruits of a scientific tradition that incorporated and improved upon the military practice found elsewhere. The West, unlike most other cultures, has always freely borrowed and incorporated from others, without worries over either national chauvinism or renunciation of native customs and traditions. When married with a rational tradition of scientific inquiry and research, this flexibility has guaranteed superior weapons in the hands of Europeans. Thus, most of Hannibal's European and African mercenaries had reequipped themselves with superior Roman arms and armor plundered from the booty of the previous Italian disasters at Trebia and Trasimene. Nearly all of Rome's enemies stripped its dead for weapons, whereas few legionaries sought to wear the equipment of dead Gauls or Africans.

The Roman army at Cannae marked the zenith of the Western military tradition in the late third century B.C. Yet it was slaughtered by a Carthaginian army that enjoyed none of Rome's cultural advantages. Hannibal's men made use of inferior weapons and technology. They were a mercenary rather than a citizen militia. Much less did the Punic state recruit from a free citizenry of patriotic small farmers. Carthaginians lacked any abstract concept of individual political freedom or civic militarism. Aristotle tells us that they gave rewards to their warriors for individual kills—far different from classical armies that stressed staying in rank and keeping formation, avoidance of flight, and the protection of one's comrade. Spurius Ligustinus was decorated with civic crowns for saving his comrades, not for piling up kills or collecting scalps. Cannae was an abject reversal of the usual military paradigm of the ancient world: a Western army that outnumbered its foe, fought at home, and relied on an unintelligently deployed but savage power was defeated by an enemy seeking victory for its outnumbered expeditionary forces through the coordination of its contingents and the organizational brilliance of its generals.

THE IDEA OF A NATION-IN-ARMS

Individual Greek city-states in the past had occasionally enrolled new citizens, but such grants were honorific and rare. Much of the commerce of the Hellenic polis remained in the hands of noncitizen resident aliens, the brilliant and industrious metics who might own more capital than any citizen but nevertheless lacked the ability to vote in Assembly. The Greeks were too jealous of their autonomy and freedom and too chauvinistic about their surrounding countryside to grant on any wide scale foreigners and immigrants—or even Greeks from different city-states—the same citizenship rights as hardy farmers who worked their ancestral plots.

Although a few Greek thinkers as diverse as Herodotus and Isocrates came to envision Greekness, *to Hellenikon,* as an ideal rather than a prerequisite of language or race—open to any foreigners who might share the culture and political premises of the polis—the rise of Macedonian monarchy cut short the evolution of the consensual and independent city-state. Military manpower was always the chief bane of classical Greek armies—a shortage of infantrymen brought about by the blinkered prerequisite that all soldiers should be citizens, but not all residents should be citizens. Even the poor who rowed for their freedom at Salamis were matched in number by slaves and foreigners who had—and would have—no say in the government of Athens. This narrow conception of citizenship would soon doom the independent Greek city-state.

In contrast, the culture that Hannibal fought in Italy was in the midst of a revolutionary transformation in the idea of what Rome was. The irony of the Second Punic War was that Hannibal, the sworn enemy of Rome, did much to make Rome's social and military foundations even stronger by incorporating the once "outsider" into the Roman commonwealth. By his invasion, he helped accelerate a second evolution in the history of Western republican government that would go well beyond the parochial constitutions of the Greek city-states. The creation of a true nation-state would have military ramifications that would shake the entire Mediterranean world to its core—and help explain much of the frightening military dynamism of the West today. In the crisis after Cannae, the property qualification for infantry service—itself a borrowed idea from the Greeks' concept of the hoplite census—was halved, and thereafter continually further lowered throughout the second century until ended altogether by Marius.

The population of Italy—Samnites, Etrurians, and the Greek-speakers of the south—was allied in varying degrees to Rome. Even the distrust of things Roman by Italian confederates was the result not so much of fear and hatred of foreign domination as of envy and resentment to the degree that they had not yet become Roman citizens with full rights to hold office and vote. The Other in the ancient world often migrated to Hellenic and Italian cities to find economic opportunity and greater freedom. Under the Greeks they found on occasion tolerance, indifference, or prosperity; among the Romans eventually citizenship. The Italian musters to oppose Hannibal's presence were, in short, further catalysts in an ongoing evolution toward parity between Rome and Italy.

Already by the third century there were many visionaries in Rome calling for Italian-wide full citizenship—the matter would not be resolved until the Social Wars of the early first century B.C.—or recognition that whole communities akin in ideology and material circumstances to Rome should be in theory eventually incorporated into the Roman common-wealth. By the time of Hannibal's invasion, Italian communities that were not Latin-speaking were nevertheless often comprised of Roman citizens, who were protected under Roman law even if they were not full voting members of the republic. The need to galvanize Italian support, man the legions, and prevent defections to Hannibal accelerated concessions from Rome to its allies. Under the late republic and empire to follow, freed slaves and non-Italian Mediterranean peoples would find themselves nearly as equal under the law as Roman blue bloods.

This revolutionary idea of Western citizenship—replete with ever more rights and responsibilities—would provide superb manpower for the growing legions and a legal framework that would guarantee that the men who fought felt that they themselves in a formal and contractual sense had ratified the conditions of their own battle service. The ancient Western world would soon come to define itself by culture rather than by race, skin color, or language. That idea alone would eventually bring enor-mous advantages to its armies on the battlefield. In the centuries of em-pire to follow, the legionaries of a frontier garrison in northern England or northern Africa would look and speak differently from the men who died at Cannae. They would on occasion experience cultural prejudice from native Italians; nevertheless, they would also be equipped and or-ganized in the same fashion as traditional Roman soldiers, and as citizens they would see their military service as a contractual agreement rather than ad hoc impressment.

Even as early as the Punic Wars slaves in real numbers were on occa-sion freed and, depending on their military contributions, given Roman citizenship. The aftermath of Cannae would see their military participa-tion and emancipation in the thousands. The Romans, in short, had taken the idea of a polis and turned it into the concept of *natio:* Romanness would soon not be defined concretely and forever by race, geography, or even free birth. Rather, citizenship in theory could be acquired someday by those who did not speak Latin, who were born even into servitude, and who lived outside Italy—if they could convince the relevant deliberative bodies that they were Roman in spirit and possessed a willingness to take on Roman military service and pay taxes in exchange for the protection of Roman law and security brought on by a free and mercantile economy.

Juvenal three centuries after Cannae would ridicule the "hungry Greeklings" that bustled about Rome, but such men ran the commercial life of Rome and would prove to be, along with thousands of other foreigners like them, as good citizen legionaries as any Italians. Rome, not classical Greece, created the modern expansive idea of Western citizenship and the notion of plutocratic values that thrive in a growing and free economy. Money, not necessarily birth, ancestry, or occupation, would soon bring a Roman status. The ex-slave Trimalchio and his *nouveau riche* freedmen dinner guests, lounging in splendor in Petronius's first-century-A.D. novel, the *Satyricon,* were the logical fruition of the entire Roman evolution in civic inclusiveness—social, economic, and cultural—that went on even as political liberty at the national level was further extinguished under the empire. It is no accident that some of the most Roman and chauvinistic of Latin authors—Terence, Horace, Publius Syrus, Polybius, and Josephus—were themselves the children of freedmen, ex-slaves, Africans, Asians, Greeks, or Jews. By the second century A.D. it was not common to find a Roman emperor who had been born at Rome. What effect did this vast difference in the respective ideas of citizenship of the antagonists have on the fighting in August 216 B.C.? Quite a lot—very few trained mercenary replacements available to Hannibal in the exuberance of victory, a multitude of raw militiamen recruits for Rome in the dejection of defeat.

The earlier Greeks had invented the idea of civic militarism, the notion that those who vote must also fight to protect the commonwealth, which in the exchange had granted them rights. The result was that the classical city-states came to field infantries made up of almost half their male resident population. At the battle of Plataea (479 B.C.) perhaps 70,000 free Greek citizens annihilated a Persian army of 250,000 forced conscripts. This was a good start in mobilizing the manpower reserves of the tiny Hellenic landed republics well beyond the old aristocratic elite. Nevertheless, the potential of civic militarism was never fully appreciated by the classical Greeks due to their jealously guarded notion of citizenship that was not extended to all residents of the polis. The Greeks had kept Hellas free from Persian occupation in part through the revolutionary idea that all the citizens must serve in the battle, but by the same token lost their autonomy a century and a half later to the Macedonians through a shortage of just those citizen warriors.

The consequence of this blinkered vision of war making was the rise of the royal army of Philip and Alexander, who cared little which men fought, only whether they fought well and in service to their paymasters. The Macedonians and their Successors were not democrats. Yet their readiness to welcome all Macedonians and Greeks alike into their multicultural professional armies with a common wage—the desperate united by a shared desire for loot and glory, rather than divided by language, locale, and ethnic pride—was in some ways perversely egalitarian in a fashion undreamed of by the classical city-states. This rise of huge Greek-inspired mercenary armies in the Hellenistic period (323–31 B.C.) for a time solved the traditional problem of manpower, but it did so in a manner that often forfeited the past civic élan of the city-state. That dilemma earlier had bothered Xenophon, Plato, and Aristotle, who saw their ideal of large armies of citizen soldiers vanishing in their own lifetimes. Greeks could field either sizable armies or patriotic and dutiful ones, but no longer any that were both sufficiently large and spirited. Every Greek who died at the battle of Chaeronea (338 B.C.) in a failed effort to preserve his liberty had voted to do so. Not a single one of Philip II's Macedonians who killed them had a direct say in where, how, or why he fought. That the former—poorly led, less well equipped, and haphazardly organized—nearly beat back Philip's immense royal army is a tribute to the spirit of civic government.

The solution to this classical paradox was to field spirited citizen armies that were nevertheless huge, combining the classical Greek discovery of civic militarism with the Hellenistic dynasts' willingness to recruit infantrymen from all segments of society. The Roman nation and its radical idea of an expansive citizenship would eventually do both brilliantly—in the process ensuring that its armies were larger than those of the classical Greeks and yet far more patriotic than the mercenaries who enrolled in the thousands in service to the Hellenistic monarchs.

This idea of a vast nation-in-arms—by the outbreak of the war in 218 B.C. there were more than 325,000 adult male Roman citizens scattered throughout Italy, nearly a quarter million of them eligible for frontline military service—was incomprehensible to the Carthaginians, who restricted citizenship to a small group of Punic-speakers in and around Carthage. Worse still in a military sense, citizenship to Carthaginians never fully embraced the Hellenic tradition of civic levies—citizens who enjoy rights are required to fight for their maintenance. Carthage also had no concept of the Roman idea of nationhood transcending locale, race, and language. Local nearby African tribes, and even Carthage's own mercenaries, were as likely to fight the Punic state as were the Romans. Aside from the veneer of a few elite representatives, upon examination there was little Western at all in Carthage's approach to politics and war. Unlike the Greeks, Carthage failed to insist that its own citizens fight their own battles. Unlike the Romans, it lacked any mechanism of incorporating North African or western European allies, conquered peoples, or serfs into rough political equality with native-born Carthaginians—hence the constant and often barbarous wars with its own rebellious mercenary armies. Nor was there even the pretense that the Carthaginian Assembly voiced the wishes of a nonelite. Carthage seems to have been a society mostly of two, not three, classes—a commercial and aristocratic privileged few served by a disenfranchised body of serfs and laborers.

The Roman Senate was probably as aristocratic as the Carthaginian, but there were no corresponding Punic assemblies that could check aristocratic power, and little tradition of a popular reformer—a Licinius, Hortensius, or Gracchus—who sought to broaden the franchise, allow the middling classes and "new men" to obtain high office, and agitate for agrarian reform and a redistribution of land. In a military sense the result was chronic shortages of Punic soldiers and a complete reliance on mercenary recruitment. Both phenomena would mean that however brilliantly led Carthaginian armies were, and despite their battle experience acquired from nonstop warring, they would find it nearly impossible for long to field troops as numerous or as patriotic as the legions. Centuries after Cannae, Romans continued to create enormous armies even during the darkest hours of the Civil Wars; in the seventeen years of fighting after Caesar crossed the Rubicon (49–32 B.C.) 420,000 Italians alone were conscripted into the military.

In contrast, for Hannibal to succeed, he had to do far more than defeat the Romans at Cannae; he needed to win four or five such battles in succession that would eliminate a pool of well over a quarter million farmers throughout Italy, men between the ages of seventeen and sixty who fought for either the retention or the promise of Roman citizenship. Hannibal had to accomplish such slaughter with an army that probably did not contain a single voting Carthaginian citizen, but was made up of African mercenaries and European tribesmen. Both groups fought not for the expectation of Carthaginian citizenship, or for the freedom to govern their own affairs, but mostly either out of hatred for Rome or for the money and plunder that their strong leader might continue to provide—strong incentives both, but in the end no match for farmers who had voted to replace their fallen comrades at Cannae and press on to the bitter end to ensure the safety of the *populus Romanus,* the preservation of the res publica, and the honor of their ancestral culture, *mos maiorum.* Most Italian farmers rightly surmised that their children would have a better future under Roman republicanism than allied to an aristocratic, foreign, and mercantile state like Carthage.

"RULERS OF THE ENTIRE WORLD"— THE LEGACY OF CIVIC MILITARISM

The Manpower of Rome

Non-Romans and Greeks of the ancient world could always mobilize enormous numbers of warriors—Gauls, Spaniards, Persians, Africans, and others—but in no sense did these tribal musterings and mercenary armies constitute a nation of arms. Not a single one of Rome's formidable adversaries in the centuries to come would ever grasp this Western dual idea of free citizen/soldier. Jugurtha's impressive Numidians (112–104 B.C.), the hundreds of thousands of Germans under Ariovistus (58 B.C.), the quarter million who joined the Gallic tribal leader Vercingetorix (52 B.C.), and the multitude of Goths who crossed the Danube to kill thousands of Romans at Adrianople (A.D. 378) were formidable fighters and they were often multitudinous. Many of such adversaries enjoyed a rich tribal history and crafted complicated methods of military organization. Nevertheless, they remained at heart armies of a season—migratory and ad hoc musters whose conditions of service depended solely on pay, plunder, and the magnetism and skill of a particular battle commander or regime. When such forces were satiated, they receded; when defeated, they disbanded; and when victorious, they were often effective for no more than another battlefield victory.

The advantages of the republican system were immediately apparent in the days after the disaster at Cannae. The government and culture of Rome were shaken to their foundations. Livy confessed in his description of Cannae's aftermath that "never, except when Rome itself had once been captured, was there so much terror and confusion within the walls. I shall therefore confess that I am unequal to the task of narration, and will not attempt to provide a full description, which would only fall short of the truth" (22.54). Much of southern Italy began to defect or for a time stopped sending men and matériel to Rome. The rich city of Capua went over to Hannibal. Others in Campania and Apulia followed. A Roman army in Spain, under the leadership of Postumius, consul-elect for 215 B.C., was annihilated and the consul killed; Livy says that more than 20,000 legionaries died and that Postumius's skull was hollowed out to be used as a Gallic drinking cup. The Carthaginian fleet was off the coast of

Sicily, raiding at will. Half of the consuls elected between 218 and 215 had been killed in battle—Flaminius, Servilius, Paulus, and Postumius. The others were disgraced.

Rome's reaction to these national catastrophes? After calm was restored in the streets and panic averted, the Senate met and systematically issued a series of decrees, reminiscent of the far-reaching decisions made by the Athenians after the catastrophe at Thermopylae, the Byzantines in the sixth century A.D. following the collapse of the Western Empire, the Venetians after the fall of Cyprus in 1571, and the Americans after Pearl Harbor. Marcellus was to be dispatched to Sicily to restore the situation. The bridges and roads to Rome were to be garrisoned. Every able-bodied man in the city was to be drafted into the home militia to defend the walls. Marcus Junius was appointed dictator, with formal directives to raise armies in any manner possible. He did so magnificently. More than 20,000 were recruited into four new legions. Some legionaries were not yet seventeen. Eight thousand slaves were purchased at public expense and given arms, with a proviso that courage in battle for Rome might lead to freedom. Junius himself freed 6,000 prisoners and took direct command of this novel legion of felons. Demands were made upon the Italian allies to muster an additional 80,000 troops within the year. For the duration of the war, the equivalent of nearly two legions was created each year to ensure a steady replacement for battle losses. Weapons were in short supply: Hannibal's men now possessed most of the abandoned arms that had been fabricated in Italy during the previous decade. For new equipment to be manufactured, temples and public buildings were to be stripped of their ancestral military votives.

Within a year after the defeat, the Roman navy was on the offensive in Sicily, all the losses of Cannae had been replaced, and the thrice-defeated legions were twice the size of Hannibal's victorious force lounging in winter quarters in southern Italy. The contrast with Hannibal's army is striking: while Rome drafted emergency legislation to raise new legions, Hannibal's veterans spent days scavenging the battlefield as their ingenious commander pleaded with his wary aristocratic overseers in Carthage to send more men.

The Continuity of Citizen Soldiers

In the next five centuries Roman armies would be confronted by an array of tactical geniuses, more Pyrrhuses and Hannibals, whose brilliance led to the annihilation of poorly led Roman armies: the one-eyed Sertorius and his tough Roman-Iberian renegades, the brave Spartacus and his enormous throng of seasoned gladiators, the canny Jugurtha of Numidia, the astute Mithridates of Pontus, Vercingetorix at the head of an enormous horde of Celts and Gauls, and the Parthians who exterminated the triumvir Crassus and most of his army. Together, these enemies of Rome slaughtered nearly a half million legionaries on the battlefield. In the end, all that glorious fighting was for naught. Nearly all of these would-be conquerors ended up dead or in chains, their armies butchered, enslaved, crucified, or in retreat. They were, after all, fighting a frightening system and an idea, not a mere army. The most stunning victories of these enemies of Rome meant yet another Roman army on the horizon, while their own armies melted away with a single defeat.

With the transition to empire and Rome's subsequent collapse (31 B.C.–A.D. 476), republicanism for a time would all but disappear from Europe. Western armies would at times become every bit as mercenary as their adversaries and often in some areas as tribal. Nevertheless, the idea of a voting citizen as warrior and the tradition of an entire culture freely taking the field of battle under constitutional directive with elected generals were too entrenched to be entirely forgotten. In the dark days of the late empire and the chaos that followed, there remained the ideal that men who fought should be citizens, with legal—and sometimes extralegal—rights and responsibilities to their community.

Even with the apparent end of civic militarism, the so-called professional soldiers of imperial Rome, like their republican counterparts of centuries past, still found in the army of the empire a continuance of five centuries of codified law. That meant to the average recruit freedom from arbitrary conscription, steady wages, contractual protections concerning service, and a fixed retirement—not press-gangs, ad hoc musters, and arbitrary punishments. If anything, the rights of the individual soldier expanded under the empire, to such a degree that his self-interested demands for greater pay and freedom tended to make provincial generals more receptive to his complaints than had been the elected republican leaders of the past. Just as the thriving empire and its Mediterranean economy benefited ex-slaves, the poor, and foreigners to a degree unimagined under the more democratic agrarian republic of central Italy, so, too, thousands of professional legionaries on the frontier found imperial bureaucrats more attuned to their needs even as their ability to vote for state officials was eroded and lost.

Civic militarism would be kept alive even when republicanism was on the wane, in a direct line of transmission from classical antiquity by elites in government and religion, as well as in popular folk traditions among the people. It was an entirely Western phenomenon. The warrior as citizen, and the army as assembly of warriors with legal rights and civic responsibilities, were ideas found in no other culture outside of Europe. Asia, Africa, and the Americas shared no intellectual or cultural heritage with Rome and Greece and thus possessed no source from which to adopt fully the peculiar Roman republican notion of voting assemblies and formal citizen soldiers.

Even during the so-called Dark Ages in "barbaric" Europe (A.D. 500–1000), civic armies like the Merovingians in western Europe, the Visigoths in Spain, and the Lombards in Italy would, like the Byzantines to the east, adopt Roman military nomenclature and organization to defend their *civitates* through the use of levies of citizen soldiers. Northern European skill at fortifications, road-building, and military science that kept Islam at bay was handed down directly from the old Roman imperial administration; *exercitus, legio, regnum, imperium,* and other Latin military and political terminology—or in the East their Greek counterparts—continued to be the language of war from the fifth century A.D. on into the medieval period. The stratagems of Frontinus and Valerius Maximus concerning the use of civic armies would be carefully studied in the late Middle Ages. The patristic writers of the late empire, Dark Ages, and medieval Christendom—from Ambrose and Augustine to Gratian in his *Decretum* (1140) and Thomas Aquinas in the *Summa Theologiae*—outlined the conditions under which the Christian commonwealth could wage a just and legal war *(ius in bello),* one that would be attuned to the values of a mobilized citizenry.

During the Renaissance the military precepts of thinkers as diverse as Xenophon and Vegetius—the most widely cited Latin author of the ancient world between the fifth and seventeenth centuries A.D.—would be adopted by Italians like Leonardo Brunni and Machiavelli. Pocket-sized manuscripts of Vegetius, translated into English, French, German, Italian, Portuguese, and Spanish, were published in book form to be used by medieval generals in the field. Even the conquistadors of Charles V's autocratic reign were imbued with the notion that they were a tiny nation-in-arms as they marched on Tenochtitlán, each soldier enjoying particular rights and protections as a Spanish subject that were unknown among their Mexica adversaries.

Constitutional government itself would eventually reappear and expand among the pikemen of Switzerland during the Middle Ages, again in fifteenth-century Italy, and in a manner of sorts never forgotten even in monarchial Byzantine Greece, before becoming firmly entrenched with the rise of the modern nation-state in Europe, the Americas, and Australia. In all such instances the best exemplar for those like Montesquieu, Rousseau, and Guibert who called for a return to "a nation-in-arms" was the classical state, and the authors of emulation Sallust, Cicero, Livy, and Plutarch, with their stories of the great levies of the Roman Republic.

Citizens as Killers

Civic militarism itself would not always ensure numerical superiority for Western armies—the manpower pool of Europe and its colonies would often turn out to be inferior to that of Asia, Africa, and the Americas. Nor would a nation-in-arms always be guaranteed victory through greater morale. At times Christianity would prove that the Sermon on the Mount is a less effective incentive for warriors than jihad. Moreover, Western armies that ventured abroad and across the sea would often be small, professional, and on occasion mercenary. Nevertheless, the ideal of a collective defense by its free citizenry—the musters of the Franks, the pikes of Switzerland, sailors of Venice, or yeomen of England and France—would help to ensure that for most of the time post-Roman Europe itself was safe from invasion, and its overseas expeditionary troops trained, organized, and led with a zeal that emanated from beyond a narrow aristocratic caste—and were thereby more than a match for the numbers and the skill of their non-Western adversaries.

Again, the latter were sometimes braver men. On occasion they fought for a better cause than the Westerners who invaded their country, ruthlessly enslaved their people, slaughtered women and children, and looted their treasure. The study of military dynamism is not necessarily an investigation into morality—armies of the caliber of Rome's were often able to do what they should not have. Civic militarism ensured large and spirited armies, not necessarily forces that would respect the cultural and national aspirations of others and the sanctity of human life in general. In that narrow regard of military efficacy, no other people on a single occasion—not Persians, Chinese, Carthaginians, Indians, Turks, Arabs, Africans, or Native Americans—would ever march as free citizens with abstract conceptions of civic rights, and at the formal direction of an elected assembly, but were more commonly paid, frightened, or mesmerized into service to a chief, sultan, emperor, or god. In the end, that fact in and of itself often proved a disadvantage on the battlefield. Sadly, the Western method of creating public armies and legal terms of service was not necessarily a question of good or evil, fairness or injustice, right versus wrong, but one of military skill.

The significance of Cannae? The worst single-day defeat in the history of any Western military force altered not at all the final course of the war. Sheer stupidity in the form of incompetent generals and bad tactics had thrown away the intrinsic advantage of Western armies: superior discipline, excellence in and preference for shock engagement, technology, and the readiness to turn out en masse for decisive battle. Poor planning had also nullified the natural advantages that accrued to the embattled Romans: fighting at home, in greater numbers, and on the defensive. Bad luck (fighting a military genius in his prime) and inexperienced soldiers (fresh recruits pitted against a veteran mercenary army) had guaranteed the Romans untold problems. In the end, all that made little difference at all.

The real lessons of Cannae are not the arts of encirclement or Hannibal's secret of tactical genius, and so they have for too long been ignored by military historians. Students of war must never be content to learn merely how men fight a battle, but must always ask why soldiers fight as they do, and what ultimately their battle is for. The tragic paradox of warfare is that so often courage, audacity, and heroism on the battlefield—what brave warriors can do, see, hear, and feel in the heat of killing—are overshadowed by elements far larger, abstract, and often insidious. Technology, capital, the nature of government, how men are mustered and paid, not merely muscular strength and the multitude of flesh, are the great levelers in conflicts between disparate cultures, and so far more often determine which side wins and which loses—and which men are to die and which to live on.

Naïve Hannibal—who led thousands of tough warriors into Italy in the belief that his genius was to be matched against other generals and warriors similar to his own, rather than pitted against the faceless and anonymous institutions of republicanism and civic militarism itself. Naïve Hannibal—who believed that this war could be decided by his men's ephemeral heroism and cunning at Cannae rather than by the lasting power of an idea. Citizens, it turns out, are history's deadliest killers.

Contemporary scholars and general students often display a natural empathy toward Hannibal. It is easy to champion an underdog as courageous as Hannibal, and easier still for us moderns to find Roman aggression and imperialism of the third through first centuries B.C. loathsome—their tally of slaughtered Spaniards, Gauls, Greeks, Africans, and Asians finally overwhelms the moral sense. But if we ask what are the military wages of constitutional government and the resulting battle dividends of citizenship, the answer is not found with a Juvenal's "one-eyed commander perched on his monstrous beast," but with the nameless and silent men who were gutted and left to rot under the August sun of Cannae.

Polybius, who witnessed firsthand the later barbaric destruction of Carthage in 146 B.C. and wrote of Cannae seventy years after the Roman defeat, rightly attributed Rome's resurgence after the catastrophe to its constitution and the rare harmony between civilian and military affairs under consensual government. The aftermath of the slaughter on August 2, 216 B.C., affected the Greek historian as no other event in Roman history. He used the occasion to present a long analysis of the Roman constitution and the legions—nearly all of book 6 in his history—which remains the clearest and most concise account of those institutions to this day. Polybius ended his excursus about Rome's remarkable constitutional and military system with a final thought on the aftermath of Cannae:

> For although the Romans had clearly been defeated in the field, and their reputation in arms ruined, yet because of the singularity of their constitution, and by wisdom of their deliberative counsel, they not only reclaimed the sovereignty of Italy, and went on to conquer the Carthaginians, but in just a few years themselves became rulers of the entire world. (3.118.7–9)

PART TWO

Continuity

FIVE

Landed Infantry

Poitiers, October 11, 732

But once the city-states grew and those with infantrymen in heavy armor became stronger, more people shared in government.
—Aristotle, *Politics* (4.1297b16–24, 28)

HORSE VERSUS FOOT

THE BATTLEFIELD CONFRONTATION between foot soldier and horseman is universal, age-old, and brutal. Cavalrymen have always mercilessly ridden down, trampled, and slain with impunity fleeing infantrymen or unfortunate pockets of poor disorganized skirmishers. Cowardly, in a sense, is this mounted knight's slaughter of the isolated or terrified foot soldier, whether Pedro de Alvarado's shameless lancing of unarmed Aztecs, the British 17th Lancers' butchery of terrified Zulus at Ulundi, or sweeps of Mongol slashers in the villages of Asia Minor. At Omdurman (1896) a young Winston Churchill wrote glowingly about the last charge of the British lancers, but his story is mostly about the systematic spearing of the already defeated and fleeing.

There is also a class bias in war between horse and foot soldier, in which the aristocratic disdain of the peacetime noble is instantaneously realized in the murderous downward stroke of his lance or saber. Or perhaps the natural insolence of the knight derives not entirely from the past cargo of his birth and wealth, but is created at the moment he mounts, and therein realizes a freedom of movement, relative impunity, and the need for a coterie of retainers unlike his brethren below. The same is true of the modern fighter pilot, whose command of the air, speed, and possession of a complex machine make his rocketing and strafing of soldiers seem almost effortless and in a macabre sense therefore nearly deserved—a different task from shooting face-to-face men who are charging into his foxhole.

In defeat, the swift horseman can beat death through flight—those few British who survived the Zulu slaughter at Islandhlwana were almost all mounted. In victory, fresh and clean knights (the war world of the horseman is not the muddy universe of the infantrymen) often appear from nowhere to kill—but only after the tough hand-to-hand of their inferiors on the ground is over. The Locrian cavalry who nearly ran down a fleeing Socrates at the battle of Delium (424 B.C.) did so only after their tough Theban hoplite allies had shattered the Athenian phalanx. More often, horsemen at the onset of battle fear lines of grim infantrymen. Mounted warriors the world over, whether they are born or invited into the cosmos of the horse, have always hated crossbow bolts, a wall of spears, a line of shields, or a spray of bullets—anything that allowed the man without a mount to destroy in seconds the capital, training, equipment, and pride of his mounted superior.

Just as in peace the middling and poor are always more plentiful than the elite, so in Western battle horsemen are rarely as numerous as foot soldiers. Whereas away from the chaotic killing of the battlefield, the wealthy man has the predictable structures of society on his side, in the melee such protocols of class and tradition mean nothing. War, as the antebellum failures Grant and Sherman both learned, is democratic in a way: the carnage of battle is one of the few arenas in which ingenuity, muscle, and courage can still trump privilege, protocols, and prejudices.

No horse will charge a wall of serried pikes. Even the most heavily mailed mounted warrior will be thrown or pulled down from his mount and killed on his back should he try. In a crowded throng of swords and bobbing spear points, where the horseman cannot use his speed to attack or to retreat, even the advantage of his height and the power of the downward angle of his blows are no guarantees of success. Consequently, armies value disciplined heavy infantrymen because when properly organized and deployed they can kill horsemen. Foot soldiers are more nimble. They can dart easily behind the rider, who turns to his rear only with difficulty. The infantryman's sharp pike or sword blows to the animal's flanks, rear, legs, and eyes can send the poor horse rearing in milliseconds, throwing his master several feet up into the air, often with a lethal landing for a man in heavy armor. Horses are large targets and, when wounded, can become the enemies, not the servants, of their riders. Foot soldiers have two hands free for fighting, not one on the reins.

Riding a horse is also a dangerous thing in itself and has killed thousands in peacetime. Xenophon reminded his horseless Ten Thousand that they enjoyed intrinsic advantages over mounted Persians: "We are on much surer footing than horsemen; they hang on their horses' backs, afraid not only of us, but also of falling off" (*Anabasis* 3.2.19). The masterful equestrian George S. Patton was nearly crippled while galloping at his leisure and at home, only to come through unscathed amid German bullets and shells. Throughout the worst of the fighting in the Civil War, Grant was also immobilized not by enemy guns, but by the bucking of his own mount. Whereas horsemen attack far more quickly, kill with a flick of the lance or saber, and vanish in minutes, infantrymen have the advantage when the killing zone is at last clogged and the fighting face-to-face. It has been unwise, whether at Gaugamela, Agincourt, or Waterloo, for even the best cavalry to charge formations of tough foot soldiers—and Europeans, more than any other culture in the history of civilization, produced infantrymen who wished to meet the enemy shoulder-to-shoulder at close quarters, mounted or not.

THE WALL

At Poitiers the Islamic throng of mounted Berbers and Arabs, generally known by Europeans as Saracens, from the original homeland of Syrian tribesmen in the Middle East, swept against the line of Frankish infantrymen. Charles Martel and his assorted army—spearmen, light infantry, and aristocratic nobles who had ridden to battle—formed up on foot to hold firm for hours until nightfall. The Arabs shot arrows from their mounts and flayed the Franks with sword blows and spear thrusts while wheeling at their flanks and sides; but they neither killed nor dislodged the Europeans.

The meager accounts of the battle of Poitiers that survive are in agreement on one key point: the Islamic invaders rushed repeatedly against the Franks, who were static and arrayed in a protective square of foot soldiers.

The defending infantrymen who were blocking the road to Tours methodically beat back the assaults until the attackers withdrew to their camp. The chronicle of the continuator of Isidore relates that the Franks (or rather "the men of Europe") were "an immovable sea" (104–5). They "stood one close to another" and stiffened like a "wall." "As a mass of ice, they stood firm together." Then "with great blows of their swords," they beat down the Arabs. The image from the contemporary chronicle is clearly one of near motionless foot soldiers, standing shoulder-to-shoulder using their spears and swords to repel repeated charges of horsemen. The Franks' surprising strength lay in the collective weight of their bodies and their skill in hand-to-hand fighting. In the fourth book of the continuum of the *Chronicle of Fredegar,* we learn further that Charles Martel "boldly drew his battle line" before the Arabs. Then he "came down upon them like a great man of battle." Charles routed them, overran their camp, killed their general, Abd ar-Rahman, and "scattered them like stubble." Clearly, a "wall" of some sort had saved France. Abd ar-Rahman had been stopped by the "many spears" of the Franks.

What was it like in the confused fighting at Poitiers? The Franks were large and physically formidable, well protected with chain-mail shirts or leather jerkins covered with metal scales. Their round shields, like those of the old Greek hoplite, were nearly three feet in diameter, curved, made of heavy hardwood, stoutly constructed with iron fittings, and covered with leather. If a man was strong and skilled enough to handle such a monstrosity, there was little chance that either an arrow or a javelin could penetrate its nearly one-inch thickness. A small conical iron helmet protected the head, ideal for warding off downward strokes from horsemen. Each Frankish infantryman lumbered into battle with nearly seventy pounds of arms and armor, making him as helpless in open skirmishing as he was invulnerable in dense formation.

In past battles with the Romans, lightly clad Germanic tribesmen had either thrown their feared axes from fifteen yards distant or cast their light spears before closing with large double-edged broadswords—weapons that required plenty of room to slash and hack. Battle on the frontier had quickly evolved into a confused affair of individual duels and weapon prowess before successive attacks of Roman cohorts broke barbarian resistance. By the eighth century, however, Frankish infantrymen were less inclined to use their traditional javelins or axes and shunning individual combat for the more classical Roman technique of fighting in unison. At Poitiers the heavily protected Franks were more likely to have used stouter spears for thrusting and short swords that could be stabbed upward while maintaining shields chest-high along a continuous line.

When the sources speak of "a wall," "a mass of ice," and "immovable lines" of infantrymen, we should imagine a literal human rampart, nearly invulnerable with locked shields in front of armored bodies, weapons extended to catch the underbellies of any Islamic horsemen foolish enough to hit the Franks at a gallop. Unable to penetrate the Frankish lines, most Arabs would wheel around in confusion to shoot arrows, cast javelins, or slash with their long swords. There was no attempt of Islamic cavalrymen to hit the European lines head-on in efforts to blast through the phalanx. Penetration through shock alone was impossible. Instead, the Muslims would ride up in large bodies, slash at the clumsier Franks, shoot arrows, and then ride away as the enemy line advanced, hoping that their own attacks and the irregular movement of the enemy would result in gaps for successive horsemen to exploit.

In response, each Frankish soldier, with shield upraised, would lodge his spear into either the horsemen's legs or the face and flanks of his mount, then slash and stab with his sword to cut the rider down, all the while smashing his shield—the heavy iron boss in the center was a formidable weapon in itself—against exposed flesh. Gradually advancing en masse, the Franks would then continue to trample and stab fallen riders at their feet—careful to keep close contact with each other at all times. In the dust and confusion of battle, it was not so critical for lines of foot soldiers to see their enemy as to stay in rank while slowly walking and striking out at anything ahead. In contrast, men on horses and fighting as individuals needed clear sight to search for gaps in the enemy line or to target those wounded and disoriented soldiers that might provide a rare inroad to the enemy mass.

It was exhausting for heavy-armed foot soldiers to pound their shields and stab spears against mobile mounted targets. There were also other critical factors in the battle beyond mere questions of endurance. A foot soldier presented a far less inviting target than a mounted warrior at close range: his conical helmet, armored limbs and shoulders, and upraised shield made him nearly invulnerable. Not so the mounted Arabs. Once their horses were wounded or their shins sliced, they might easily fall, and then find themselves on the ground and helpless. The chroniclers leave the impression that Abd ar-Rahman never anticipated that his fast-moving pack of raiders would find themselves opposed by a large mass of heavily armed foot soldiers in a confined valley. Under such conditions the ingredients that made his army a thing of terror in the streets of Poitiers—isolated, galloping horsemen riding down unprotected groups of twos and threes—ensured their slaughter by a waiting line of armored spearmen.

Charles's men were the first generation of such heavy-armored foot soldiers of western Europe to face Islamic armies. Poitiers would thus inaugurate a near thousand-year struggle between the discipline, strength, and heavy armament of western Europeans and the mobility, numbers, and individual skill of their Islamic enemies. As long as the Franks stayed in rank—and miraculously they seem to have maintained order even in the aftermath of battle rather than pursue the withdrawing Arabs—it was impossible for them to be broken or ridden down. Although contemporary accounts wrongly suggest that little more than a thousand Frankish fell, while killing hundreds of thousands of Arabs, it may well be true that Charles lost only a fraction of his men in repelling an enemy unusually large for the times. Poitiers was, as all cavalry battles, a gory mess, strewn with thousands of wounded and dying horses, abandoned plunder, and dead and wounded Arabs. Few of the wounded were taken prisoner— given their previous record of murder and pillage in Poitiers.

The word *Europenses*, used by the continuator of Isidore, makes one of its first appearances in historical narrative as a generic noun for Westerners. While the chronicler perhaps meant that Charles's army was an amalgam of a number of Germanic tribes and Gauls, he may have also intended "Europeans" to emphasize an emerging cultural fault line: men above the Pyrenees still fought in the Roman tradition of heavy infantry, and, for all their internecine killing, were more alike than disparate when facing Islamic armies.

After the day's fighting, the respective armies, who had already eyed each other for a week before the battle, returned to their camps. The Franks made ready to renew battle at dawn, hoping for more reinforcements and expecting another wave of Arab horsemen to attack their positions. Instead, when they returned to the battlefield at daylight, the entire Arab army had vanished, leaving behind empty tents and booty— and their dead on the battlefield. Dead also was their emir and leader of the invasion, Abd ar-Rahman himself. Plans for the Islamic sack and occupation of nearby Tours—they had looted the Church of St. Hilary at Poitiers in the days before the battle—were abandoned.

Poitiers was only the beginning of a gradual expulsion of Muslims from southern France. Frankish lords in the decade to follow would beat back other raids from Islamic Spain, Charles himself soon defeating

Saracen armies at Avignon (737) and Corbière (738). Yet Poitiers signaled the high-water mark of Islamic advance into Europe: Muslim armies never again reached so far north. With the near simultaneous repulse of the Arabs from the harbors of Constantinople in 717, the Islamic wave of the prior century was at last checked on the periphery of Europe.

THE HAMMER

We do not know the precise date of the battle—probably a Saturday in October 732. Some historians continue to call the engagement the battle at Tours, since the actual battle took place somewhere on the old Roman road between there and Poitiers. Later Christian hostility against Charles Martel because of his confiscation of ecclesiastical property encouraged medieval chroniclers to ignore or downplay his achievement; and the greater glory of the subsequent Crusades naturally overshadowed this initial confrontation between Muslim and western European armies. Most of the contemporary and modern mythology that surrounds the battle can easily be dispensed with. The Muslims did not invade with hundreds of thousands of troops—300,000 of which, according to one source, were killed. Just as likely, both forces were about the same size—somewhere between 20,000 and 30,000. Given the Franks' success in calling out thousands of rural folk to protect their farms and estates, the Europeans may well have outnumbered the invaders. Although Arab losses were much higher than the number of Frankish dead, the attackers were hardly wiped out. Somewhere around 10,000 Arabs were killed at Poitiers.

The near contemporaneous spread of early feudalism probably does not explain the Frankish victory either. Charles's expropriation of ecclesiastical lands to be distributed to his lords and retainers occurred mostly after the battle. Nor was Charles's achievement, as sometimes claimed, the result of newly adopted stirrups by his European cavalry. Stirrups, in fact, had appeared in the West decades earlier, but there seems to have been only haphazard appreciation of their true value in western Europe—and then not until much later, between 800 and 1000. In their emphasis on Frankish technological dynamism and sudden organizational innovations to explain the Muslim defeat, most scholars have misunderstood two universal tenets of ancient battle: that good heavy infantry, if it maintained rank and found a defensible position, usually defeated good cavalry; and that an army of horsemen far from home needed a sophisticated logistical system if it was to be anything more than a throng of raiders, in constant search of forage and booty.

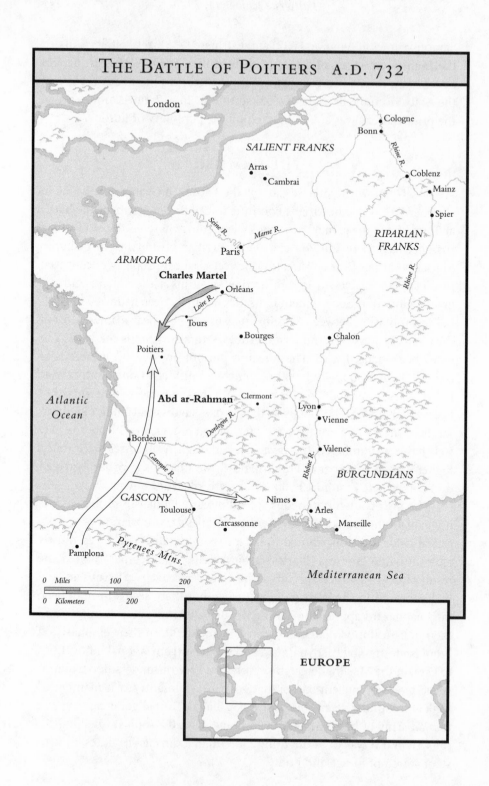

THE BATTLE OF POITIERS A.D. 732

London

SALIENT FRANKS

Cologne
Bonn
Rhine R.
Coblenz
Mainz
Spier

Arras
Cambrai

RIPARIAN
FRANKS

Seine R.
Marne R.
Paris

ARMORICA

Rhine R.

Charles Martel

Orléans
Loire R.
Tours
Bourges
Chalon

Poitiers

Atlantic
Ocean

Abd ar-Rahman Clermont

Lyon
Vienne

Dordogne R.

Bordeaux

Valence

Garonne R.

Rhine R.

BURGUNDIANS

GASCONY

Toulouse

Nîmes

Carcassonne

Arles
Marseille

Pyrenees Mtns.

Pamplona

Mediterranean Sea

0   Miles   100   200
0   Kilometers   200

EUROPE

Abd ar-Rahman's invasion of 732 was not in itself a systematic attempt to conquer France and to establish Islamic rule north of the Pyrenees. Contemporary chroniclers made much of the prominent role of booty in their accounts of the battle: the Arabs plundered every church and monastery in their path to Poitiers, were burdened before the battle with spoils, and left tents full of loot in the middle of the night to ensure their escape. Both the morale and mobility of the Muslims were probably diminished by the time they arrived at Poitiers, laden as they were with baggage and captives. Had the Muslims won—Poitiers is not much more than two hundred miles from Paris—such raiding would have been continuous and perhaps have led eventually to an Islamic enclave such as had been established two decades earlier in southern Spain.

Permanent Islamic possession of the entirety of France, however, was unlikely, chiefly because the Franks under Charles possessed a well-armed and spirited army of some 30,000 infantrymen, aided by a few thousand heavy cavalrymen. Arabs and their Berber subjects also for much of the latter eighth century in Spain were fighting each other as frequently as they were Europeans, as Syrian tribes with difficulty imposed Islamic culture far to the west on native North Africans. By 915 the Muslims were expelled entirely from the southern border of France. For most of the ninth century, the Franks were more likely to raid Islamic settlements across the Pyrenees than Muslims were to invade France.

Charles won at Poitiers for a variety of reasons. His troops were fighting for their homes, not for plunder far from their bases of operations. The armies were evenly matched, and rough numerical parity is an advantage for the defender. While both sides had chain mail and steel swords adopted from earlier standard Roman designs, the Franks probably used heavier armor and weapons. The Carolingians were careful to prohibit the export of their mail and offensive arms, suggesting a superiority in design and quantity. Charles had found a naturally strong position at Poitiers, in which his phalanx of infantrymen could not be outflanked or surrounded. He kept his ranks together and was apparently determined to fight entirely on the defensive. For his surprising resistance of the mounted charges at Poitiers, Charles became known as "the Hammer" (Martellus)—an allusion to the biblical hammerer, Judas Maccabaeus, whose Israelite armies through divine intervention had smashed the Syrians.

For much of the seventh century the Muslims, with relatively small mounted forces, had swept aside a variety of weak enemies—the Sassanid Persians and overextended Byzantines in Asia, and Visigoths in North

Africa and Spain. When Abd ar-Rahman crossed the Pyrenees, however, he encountered an entirely new force in the Franks. French scholars of the battle were largely correct when they pointed out that the Arabs had been successful against similarly nomadic interlopers like the Visigoths and Vandals, who had themselves migrated into North Africa and Spain, but hit a wall against the Frankish rustics who were indigenous to Europe. In their eyes, the battle of Poitiers was a referendum of looters versus soldiers *"sédentarisés,"* who stayed in one place, owned property, and considered battle more than a raid.

The Franks, descendants of the *Germani* described by Tacitus in the first century A.D., originally lived in what is now Holland and in eastern Germany around the lower Rhine. They seemed to have migrated in large numbers into nearby Gaul by the fifth century. Scholars do not agree on the origin of the word "Franks"; most associate it with either their famed throwing ax, the *francisca,* or the old Germanic word *freh/frec,* meaning "brave" or "wild." In any case, under Clovis (A.D. 481–511) the Frankish tribes united in the old Roman province of Gaul in what came to be known as the Merovingian monarchy, named after the legendary Frankish chieftain Merovech (Merovaeus), grandfather of Clovis, who had fought against the Huns at Châlons (A.D. 451).

After Clovis's death a series of dynastic wars among his offspring led to independent kingdoms: Burgundy to the southeast in the valleys of the upper Seine, Rhône, and Loire Rivers; Austrasia to the east across the Meuse, Moselle, and Rhine Rivers; and Neustria in the west along the large plains bordering the Atlantic coast. By 700 Gaul was a petty kingdom of warring states until the reign of Charles Martel; nevertheless, the Franks increasingly saw themselves more as a nation than a tribe, more in the classical than in the Germanic tradition. Indeed, the Merovingians sought to trace their Frankish ancestry not back to the dark forests of Germany, but to migrations of mythical Trojans after the conquest of Troy.

Charles Martel was not in direct line of succession to the Merovingian throne, but the bastard son of King Pippin. Despite the absence of a legal claim on the Frankish kingdom—Charles was mayor of the palace, equivalent to being a duke of the Austrasian Franks—he engaged in a lifelong effort to unite these kingdoms. His eventual victories provided the foundation of the much larger, stronger Carolingian dynasty, which under his grandson Charlemagne saw the reunification of central Europe. In eighteen years of uninterrupted civil war, from 714 to 732, Charles consolidated the old tripartite realm of Clovis and then quickly expanded his rule throughout Gaul. Almost every year of the reign of Charles until his death in 741 was spent in warring to unite Gaul or to rid Europe of Islam. In 734 he fought in Burgundy; the next year he furthered his consolidation of Aquitaine. The years 736–41 saw war once more in Burgundy, in Provence, and against the Saxons. This yearly fighting eventually allowed his son Pippin (751–680) to rule over a united Francia officially as the first Carolingian king. It is often forgotten in accounts of Poitiers that when Charles brought his infantrymen to the battlefield, they were hardened veterans from nearly twenty years of constant combat against a variety of Frankish, German, and Islamic enemies.

Besides his stunning victory over Abd ar-Rahman at Poitiers, contemporaries record three great accomplishments of Charles, which reflect the continuity of classical approaches to religion and government. The first was to reestablish political control over the church, by allotting more ecclesiastical lands to private landowners, who would in turn serve in Charles's national army. Second, he attempted to bring more secularization to the church hierarchy through appointments of his own servants and generals to Christian offices. Third, Charles extended Frankish control over most of the old province of Gaul, and was able to tie local lords and barons together into a national army, which systematically defeated Islamic incursions until Gaul was mostly free for a generation from Muslim attackers.

Every free household in Charles's realm was to provide an adult warrior for a national army, most commonly a heavily armed infantryman who was to fight with similarly armed foot soldiers, with large wooden shields, reinforced leather or chain-mail jerkins, conical metal helmets, broadswords, and either spears, javelins, axes, or combinations of such arms. Strong classical antecedents explain the preponderance of heavily armed foot soldiers in Merovingian armies:

> The Merovingian military was greatly influenced by the Roman empire and its institutions, and it owed comparatively little to the Franks, who were only a minority of the population and a small part of the fighting forces. As with many aspects of Merovingian life, the military organization recalls *Romania* and not *Germania*. (B. Bachrach, *Merovingian Military Organization*, 128)

Charles Martel's most important legacy, besides creating a unified Western state strong enough to withstand the onset of Islam's advance into southern Europe, was the continuance of the classical tradition of mustering free men into a large infantry force, in which citizens, not slaves or impressed serfs, formed the corps of the army. Charles reestablished the principle that the Frankish monarchy and the church were separate entities, and that ultimately church property and offices were dependent on a central monarch. All this was in antithesis to his adversaries at Poitiers. In theory, for the next thousand years of warring, all Muslim political states were theocracies subservient to the laws of the Koran, while their mostly mounted armies would be built around a corps of servile soldiers. The thousand-year-old cultural fault lines characteristic of the past Greco-Roman wars against the Achaemenids and Sassanids reappeared in the Christian struggle against Islam.

ISLAM ASCENDANT

The prophet Muhammad died exactly one hundred years before the battle of Poitiers. In that century between 632 and 732, a small and rather impotent Arab people arose to conquer the Sassanid Persian Empire, wrest the entire Middle East and much of Asia Minor from the Byzantines, and establish a theocratic rule across North Africa. In the past the Romans had built a wall to protect their province of Syria from the warring tribes of Arabia, thinking that there was little danger from an impoverished and nomadic people of the desert, who had no real settlements, a tiny population, and no systematic logistical capability. Yet by the mid-eighth century, the suddenly ascendant kingdom of the Arabs controlled three continents and an area larger than the old Roman Empire itself.

The Arab conquests were a result of two phenomena: prior contact with Byzantines, from whom they borrowed, looted, and then adapted arms, armor, and some of their military organization; and the weakness of the Persian Sassanids and the barbarian Visigoth successors in the old Roman provinces of Asia and North Africa. It is often forgotten that Islamic dynamism between the eighth and tenth centuries represented a *reconquista* of territory that had been ruled largely by others from Persia or Europe. Despite nearly seven hundred years of Greek and Roman power in northern Africa, local populations still maintained indigenous religious, linguistic, and cultural practices, and vastly outnumbered Europeans and their own educated Westernized elites. All these Islam swept away. Once the old Asian and African provinces returned to a religion and government of the East, only Europe proper of the old Roman Empire remained uninvaded from the Islamic south and east. Yet conquest of central Europe—"the Great Land" to the Arab chroniclers—was a different matter altogether. It was understandable that Islam—without a tradition of heavy infantry, shock battle, and civic militarism, or the ability to create sophisticated lines of supply and transport—stalled in its attack against the West until the rise of the Ottomans in the fifteenth century.

The weakness of other empires, the borrowing of arms and organization from the Byzantines, and the natural role of an Asiatic kingdom in Asia proper still do not entirely explain the miraculous Islamic conquests. Arab armies also won because of the peculiar nature of their newfound religion, which offered the nomad singular incentives to fight. There was to be a novel connection between war and faith, creating a divine culture that might reward with paradise the slaying of the infidel and the looting of Christian cities. Killing and pillaging were now in the proper context, acts of piety.

Second, the onslaught of the Muslims into the Persian, Byzantine, and European realms was considered a natural—or fated—act. The world was no longer bound by national borders or ethnic spheres, but was properly the sole domain of Muhammad—if only his followers were courageous enough to fulfill the Prophet's visions. Islam was not a static or reflective religion, but a dynamic creed that saw conquest and conversion as prerequisites to world harmony. Islam came at an opportune time for conquest, as the eroding urban centers of the seventh-century Persian and Byzantine Empires were especially vulnerable to large mounted attacks of spirited warriors.

Finally, race, class, and status themselves were secondary to faith. The slave, the poor, and both the darker- and the lighter-skinned foreigner were all welcomed into the army of Muhammad—once they professed fealty to Islam. Abd ar-Rahman's army that swept into Poitiers was probably composed mostly of Berber converts, supervised by Syrian Arabs, and replete with conquered and converted Spanish Visigoths and Jews. The Arabs were a relatively small tribe, so the mechanics of pacification and control of their newly acquired Islamic domains was impossible without the active participation of conquered peoples themselves.

The contrasts between the lightning-quick rise of Islam and the gradual spread of Christianity are often glossed over, but nevertheless striking. As Edward Gibbon most famously argued, in strictly military terms the thousand-year rise of Christianity after the fall of the Western Roman Empire (500–1500) had weakened Western armies. European military atrophy came not merely from evolving religious schisms and dynastic rivalries, or even from the loss of a uniform Latin language and Roman culture, but in part from the very nature of Christian dogma.

The worship of the rather mystical Jesus, who was not a man of this world—not a soldier, trader, or politician—the message of the Sermon on the Mount, and the call to "render unto Caesar what was Caesar's" would for a time turn out to be poor incentives for achieving European political unity, religious orthodoxy, and military power. The pacifist traditions of Christianity in the short term stood in stark contrast to Islam, which in theory professed that Muslims should not fight fellow believers, but kill all others until "there is no god but Allah." As late as the twelfth century, church fathers attempted to deny a proper Christian burial to any knight who had been killed in a joust or tournament; their aim was not merely to save Europeans for the struggle against Islam but also to curb the bloody and barbaric spectacle from the daily experience of Christian society. Turning the other cheek, repugnance for bloody combat, and preparing for the next world in the present one were antithetical to most traditional classical notions of civic militarism, patriotism, and the zeal for martial recognition from the state. The message of the New Testament was much different from the *Iliad, Aeneid*—or Koran.

The army of the Arabs was never designed to engage in a systematic collision of heavy infantry, followed by possession of territory and the installation of permanent garrisons, in the manner of Western imperialism of Macedonian, Roman, and Byzantine militaries. The Islamic army—itself largely mounted—counted on swiftness, mobility, and terror, with the assurance that ideology rather than ramparts would ensure lasting victories. Mounted sorties and ambushes, not decisive battle between phalanxes of heavy infantry, marked the Muslim way of war:

> The make-up of Islamic armies was very different from those of the West. Horsemen of all kinds were predominant and infantry played a limited role. . . . There was much reliance on ambush, partly because this was an obvious tactic for light cavalry. But the really great contrast between East and West was in the approach to battle. Everywhere, close-quarter confrontation was decisive and the Western tradition was to bring that about as quickly as possible. In the East, light cavalry could outflank and unhinge formations by rapid movements. (J. France, *Western Warfare in the Age of the Crusades*, 212–13)

As long as the Arabs faced either dying empires like the Sassanids or the tribal Visigoths in northern Africa and Spain, success was guaranteed. None of those powers could provide large enough numbers of heavily armed infantrymen to bring the Muslims to close quarters; after the disastrous battle of Manzikert (1071), even the Byzantines were to learn that they no longer had the manpower or the logistical support to defeat Islam in Asia.

The breakneck spread of Islam was astounding. By 634, a mere two years after Muhammad's death, Muslim armies were well engaged in the conquest of Persia. Syria fell in 636; Jerusalem was captured in 638. Alexandria was stormed in 641, opening the entire Visigothic realm to the west. Forty years later Muslims were at the gates of Constantinople itself, and from 673 to 677 nearly succeeded in capturing the city. By 681 the Arabs neared the Atlantic, formalizing Islam's incorporation of the old kingdoms of the Berbers. Carthage was taken for good in 698 and their last queen, Kahina, captured, her head sent to the caliph at Damascus. Only seventeen miles now separated Islam from Europe proper. By 715 the Visigoths had been conquered in Spain, and periodic forays into southern France were commonplace. In 718 Arabs had crossed the Pyrenees in large numbers and occupied Narbonne, killing all the adult male inhabitants and selling the women and children into slavery. By 720 they were freely raiding in Aquitane. The large expedition of 732, led by Abd ar-Rahman, the governor of Moorish Spain, had already captured Poitiers and was advancing to sack Tours when it was intercepted by Charles Martel between the villages of Vieux-Poitiers and Moussais-la-Bataille on the road to Orléans.

For the rest of the ninth through the tenth centuries, the war between East and West would break out in northern Spain, southern Italy, Sicily, and the other larger islands of the Mediterranean, as the old *mare nostrum* of the Roman Empire became the new line of battle between two entirely antithetical cultures. The presence of Muslim ships on the Mediterranean and near constant wars with the Byzantines in the Adriatic and Aegean meant that western and eastern Europe were to be permanently separated. The idea of a unification of the old empire was abandoned for good, leaving a growing rivalry in Europe between a monolithic, imperial, and Orthodox Christian East and the fragmented and warring states of the Roman Catholic West.

Yet war by horsemen had only so many advantages. Mounted armies were difficult to transport by sea; they required enormous amounts of forage and grazing land and were hard to bring over mountain passes in great numbers. When Muslims reached the valleys of Spain and eastern Europe, the landscape was not that of the steppes or desert, and so did not favor large sweeps of flanking cavalry. In addition, Middle Eastern forces were never numerous enough to create the foundations of a national

army; instead, they would become dependent on slave soldiers—
Mameluks in the Middle East and later Janissaries among the Ottomans.
Once the Islamic tide lapped on the shore of western Europe and the
Byzantine Empire, its advance began to be halted. A static line of defense
was established, as civilization in the West—in Spain, the Balkans, and the
eastern Mediterranean—slowly returned to the offensive with infantry of
mostly freemen.

DARK AGES?

With the collapse of the Western Roman Empire in the latter fifth century
A.D. the rule of empire vanished in northern Europe, and with it for a time
an integrated market economy in the Mediterranean, North Africa, and
Asia. The absence of the legions to provide security in the countryside
against brigands and invaders at first led to ever greater disruption of
farmland, while massive fortifications, not the courage of soldiers in open
battle, were seen as the more reliable defense of the cities. The lack of central taxation meant that aqueducts, terraces, bridges, and irrigation canals
were not properly maintained and often abandoned, leading not merely
to the loss of potable water in the cities but also to a decline in agricultural productivity as valleys silted up and terraced land eroded.

The erosion of central imperial government and the collapse of urban
culture also meant an end to large standing armies. Italy, Spain, Gaul, and
Britain, in the absence of authority from Rome, were convulsed by a series of invasions and migrations by Vandals, Goths, Lombards, Huns,
Franks, and Germans. Yet the victorious newcomers by the sixth and seventh centuries were no longer nomadic, but often had settled permanently in Roman territory, gradually converted to Christianity, learned
some Latin, and carved out petty kingdoms guided loosely by the old
Roman bureaucratic and legal tradition. If the new armies of western
Europe were tiny and fragmented in comparison to Rome and often ensconced in fortified castles and towns, they nonetheless continued to rely
on levies of heavy infantrymen fighting in columns, not tribal swarming,
when it became necessary to engage in decisive battles.

The final collapse of Rome also brought a population decline in western Europe; and economic activity was lethargic for much of the so-called
Dark Ages between 500 and 800. Christianity began to encroach on public and private lands, requiring enormous acreages to support monaster-
ies, churches, and nunneries, whose clergy in the strict economic sense
were not especially productive. If the estates of the old Roman patricians

were sometimes unwisely expropriated for horse raising by the aristocracy of Franks and Lombards, then similarly the church also used the harvests from scarce and precious farmland to support a vast bureaucracy and an ambitious building program. By the end of the fifth century A.D., no single kingdom from Lombard Italy to Visigoth Spain could muster an army the size of the Roman force that had been annihilated at Cannae seven hundred years earlier.

Yet the fall of Rome often spread, rather than destroyed outright, classical civilization, as the fragments of empire slowly recovered and kept alive the cultural core of the old West. Writing continued. Even literature and scientific investigation were never completely lost. Latin remained the universal script of government, religion, and law from Italy to the North Sea. The Dark Ages (the term originally referred to the dearth of written knowledge that survived about the era) were characterized not so much by the chaos of an empire fallen as by the new diffusion of much of classical culture—language, architecture, military practices, religion, and economic expertise—into northern Europe, especially Germany, France, England, Ireland, and Scandinavia.

Islam had spread in the south and east by the creation of an entirely new theocratic state; in contrast, the remnants of classical culture, fused with Christianity, advanced throughout western and northern Europe due to the collapse of the Roman Empire. "Despite the resulting turmoil and destruction," Henry Pirenne pointed out in regard to the supposed end of Roman civilization in northern Europe during the fifth century A.D., "no new principles made their appearance either in the economic or social order, nor in the linguistic situation, nor in the existing institutions. What civilization survived was Mediterranean" (*Mohammed and Charlemagne*, 284).

The sixth and seventh centuries actually saw improvements. Throughout the latter decades of the Roman Empire, there had been a gradual displacement of agrarians, concentrations of huge amounts of wealth, and constant class strife in the cities. The continuance of classical culture in ancient Gaul in the sixth through eight centuries, even under radically different and troubled material conditions, often meant that local government was more responsive to rural problems than had been Rome in its last two centuries. Under the Merovingians and Carolingians there nowhere reappeared the vast numbers of slaves that had characterized Roman civilization (by the fourth century A.D. in certain parts of the empire nearly a quarter of the population had been servile). Though Roman wealth and nationhood were gone for a time from the West, the deadly military tradition of classical antiquity was nevertheless kept alive. Most of the great military discoveries in both weaponry and tactics to come in the next millennium would originate in Europe—the continuing dividends of the Western approach to the dissemination of empirical data, the scientific method, and free inquiry.

"Greek fire" emerged at Byzantium somewhere around 675. Although the exact ingredients and their ratios of mixture remain unknown to this day, the torrent of flame that was shot out of Byzantine galleys was apparently a potent fusion of naphtha, sulfur, petroleum, and quicklime that could not be extinguished by water—a nearly unquenchable toxic spume that could incinerate enemy ships in seconds. Equally ingenious as the chemistry of Greek fire was its method of delivery, which involved a keen knowledge of pumps, pressurization, and mechanical engineering. A sealed container was heated from below with fuel and bellows and injected with forced air from a pump. Then the compressed mixture was forced out another outlet into a long bronze tube. The jellied mass was ignited at the end of the barrel, resulting in a sea of continuous flame spurting out from this ancient flamethrower. Ships with such fiery contraptions allowed the small Byzantine navy mastery of the eastern Mediterranean and saved Constantinople itself on occasion—none more dramatic than Leo III's incineration of the Islamic armada of the caliph Sulaymān in 717 in waters surrounding the capital.

Controversy surrounds the exact origins of the stirrup—it may have been originally of Asian design—but by A.D. 1000 most Western cavalrymen were employing new saddles equipped with stirrups, even if they learned of their use via the Arabs, who had copied the original designs either from the Byzantines or by trading with the Orient in the early seventh century. Under the western European kingdoms, the stirrup was envisioned not merely as an aid to horse mastery but as integral to the emergence of a new lance-bearing knight, who could for the first time absorb the shock of spearing a fixed target on the gallop without being thrown from his mount. While such lancers could never break true infantry, small corps could easily ride down isolated groups of foot soldiers during both attack and retreat. The stirrup meant not that western European militaries were dominated by heavy lancers, but that their mostly infantry armies, at key moments in the battle—when gaps appeared in enemy lines or during the rout—could send out small corps of deadly horsemen to slaughter with impunity light infantrymen and poorly organized foot soldiers.

The crossbow—in use throughout Europe by 850—was a smaller-sized derivative of the classical "belly-bow," through substitution of a handheld crank for large torsion cables and sprockets. Scholars cite the crossbow's deficiencies in comparison with either the later English long-bow or the Eastern composite bow, both of which had greater range and rates of fire. The crossbow, however, required far less training to use than either, did not tire the archer to the same degree as hand-pulled bows, and its smaller all-metal bolts had greater penetrating power at short ranges. Crossbow bolts alone were able to slice through the heavy chain mail of the knight, and meant that a relatively poor man without much training could kill both an aristocratic horseman and his armored mount in seconds for the cost of a tiny metal projectile. Consequently, the church often issued edicts against its use—a doomed prospect of technological repression with no heritage in the West—and finally retreated to the position that crossbows should be outlawed in all intramural wars between Christians.

Siege engines underwent constant improvement. After 1180, vast catapults were powered by counterbalances rather than torsion alone. Such trebuchets often had ten-ton counterweights and could throw stones of three hundred pounds well over one hundred yards, exceeding the delivery weight of the old Roman traction catapults fivefold, while maintaining nearly the same range. In turn, fortifications were built entirely of stone and to heights unimagined by classical engineers, replete with intricate towers, crenellations, and interior keeps. It was not merely that European castles and walls were larger and stouter than those in Africa and the Near East, they were more numerous as well, due to improvements in the cutting, transportation, and lifting of stone. Plate armor, common by 1250, was also a European specialty, ensuring that most European knights and infantrymen were far better protected than their Islamic opponents. When gunpowder was introduced from the Chinese in the fourteenth century, Europe alone was able to craft dependable and heavy cannon—Constantinople fell in 1453 through the efforts of Western-fabricated artillery—and handheld matchlock weapons in any great number. So, too, fully rigged, multisailed ships were common in European waters by 1430, and were superior to any vessels in either the Ottoman or the Chinese navies.

Key to this continuing Western ability to craft good weapons, along with fluid and innovative tactical doctrine, was the embrace of published military research, which married theory with field experience to offer pragmatic advice to commanders in the field. The late Roman handbooks of Frontinus, and to a greater extent Vegetius, were copied even throughout the Dark Ages and became a bible of sorts to many western European warlords. Rabanus Maurus, the ninth-century archbishop of Mainz, published an annotated *De re militari* specifically to improve Frankish warfare. For the next four hundred years, adaptations and translations of Vegetius appeared throughout Europe by Alfonso X (1252–84), Bono Gimaboni (1250), and Jean de Meung (1284).

European siegecraft itself was unmatched, precisely because it followed in the past tradition of classical *poliorkētika* (the arts of "polis enclosing"). Manuals such as the *Mappae Clavicula* instructed besiegers in the use of engines and incendiary devices. The emperors Maurice *(Ars militaris)* and Leo VI *(Tactica)* outlined Byzantine infantry and naval tactics in preparing manuals for their generals and admirals to keep the Mediterranean Sea and its harbors free from Arab fleets. In contrast, Islamic writing on war was rarely abstract or theoretical—or even practical—but more holistic and philosophical, and largely concerned itself with the proper rules and conduct of the jihad.

Among the early Franks this need to write about war and to publish manuals about its practice were in direct emulation of Roman and Greek thinkers. Military practice did not operate in a vacuum, but was closely connected to the presence of an educated elite familiar with classical ideas of military organization and weaponry. Under the Carolingians, a systematic approach was undertaken to the preservation of classical manuscripts, along with efforts to assure education in the Greco-Roman tradition:

> Though defined by religion, Europe was also a community of scholars who read and wrote the same Latin language and who rescued a great part of the legacy of antiquity from irretrievable loss. In the ninth and tenth centuries, schoolmasters devised a new curriculum of studies based in part on the classics that they had rediscovered. In doing so they laid the foundations of educational practices for centuries. (P. Riché, *The Carolingians,* 361)

In addition, the historiographic tradition of Greece and Rome continued in the Christian East and West, especially the Hellenic and Roman propensities of Herodotus, Thucydides, Livy, and Tacitus to see history largely as the story of war and politics. Thus, Gregory of Tours (534–94, *History of the Franks),* Procopius (born ca. 500, *History of the Wars of Justinian),* Isidore of Seville (*History of the Goths,* written 624), and Venerable Bede (672–735, *Ecclesiastical History of England)* all provided anthropological detail about various tribes as part of larger exegeses of intercultural conquests and defeats. The works of hundreds of other lesser-known chroniclers and compilers circulated throughout Europe, the sheer number of titles unmatched by anything published elsewhere.

There were numerous early Islamic historians, many of whom were candid and remarkably critical, but few saw history as really existing before the era of the Prophet (thus the maxim "Islam cancels all that was before it"). And the parameters of inquiry were limited by the Koran, whose literary and historical primacy tolerated no competition from mere mortals. Contrary to classical historiography—there seems to be little evidence of any early Arabic translation of the major Greek historians—lapses in morality, not tactical blunders or structural flaws, were cited as reasons for Islamic defeats. After Poitiers, Arab chroniclers, as would be true of Ottoman observers in the aftermath of Lepanto, attributed the Muslim slaughter to their own wickedness and impiety that had brought on the wrath of Allah.

The horse-drawn, iron-tipped plow first emerged in Europe, allowing farmland to be broken up more quickly and deeply than with the old wooden blades drawn by oxen. The ability to farm more efficiently gave Westerners greater food and opportunity than their counterparts to the south and east. By the end of the twelfth century, windmills, which were unlike anything in the Near East or Asia, appeared in England and northern Europe. With a rotating horizontal axis and a system of gears, such machines could mill wheat at rates unimagined either in classical antiquity or the contemporary non-West. Improved water wheels—more than 5,000 in eleventh-century England alone—were used not only to grind grain but to manufacture paper, cloth, and metal. The result was that Western armies were able to campaign farther from home—both because they could take greater amounts of supplies with them and because farmers could go on campaigns for longer periods. Historians often remark on the unruliness of Crusader armies, constant bickering in command, horrendous camp conditions, and the occasional imbecility of their tactics, forgetting that the transportation and supply of thousands of soldiers to the other side of the Mediterranean was a feat of logistical genius unmatched by Islamic armies of the day.

Science and technology alone did not save the smaller and more fragmented western European armies from their adversaries. The classical traditions of infantry organization and landed musters were kept alive as well. Military command and discipline followed Roman tradition, and so naturally nomenclature remained Greek and Latin. Byzantine emperors, in the manner of Macedonian lords, addressed their soldiers as *systratiō-tai*—"comrades-in-arms." Generals, as in classical Greece, remained *stratēgoi* and soldiers *stratiōtai*, while in the West free soldiers were *milites*, both *pedites* (foot soldiers) and *equites* (knights). Citizens continued to be recruited under legal and published codes of conduct—the so-called "capitularies"—with explicit rights and responsibilities.

Charles Martel's army was not as disciplined or as large as a Roman consular army, but the manner in which its heavily armed spearmen and swordsmen were mustered, attacked on foot, and kept in rank was consistent with the classical tradition. Campaigns required the approval of assemblies, and rulers were subject to audit after battle.

By the end of the eighth century two seemingly insurmountable obstacles that had once weakened the old Roman imperial levies of the fifth and sixth centuries A.D.—the failure of Roman citizens to serve in their own armies, and the religious strictures against civic militarism and wars of conquest by the early Christian church—were beginning to erode. Augustine had composed his *City of God* after the sack of Rome in A.D. 410 to associate divine punishment with the sins of Romans. Even earlier, a few Christian emperors, like Gratian, had dismantled public statues and commemoration of military victory as somehow antithetical to Christ's message of peace and forgiveness. Yet by early medieval times the earlier pacifism of the Roman church fathers like Tertullian *(Ad martyres, De corona militis)*, Origen *(Exhortatio ad martyrium, De Principiis)*, and Lactantius *(De mortibus persecutorum)* was often ignored, as the creed of the Old Testament and its idea of wars against the unbelievers regained primacy over the message of the Gospels. Thomas Aquinas, for example, could outline the conditions of "just" Christian wars, in which the cause of the conflict could make war a moral Christian enterprise. Christianity would never exhibit the martial fervor of Islam, but during the Dark Ages it more or less curbed its early pacifist pretenses and its distance from the affairs of worldly politicians. The military of Joshua and Samson, not the loving remonstrations of Jesus, was invoked to keep Islam at bay.

Franks, Lombards, Goths, and Vandals may have been tribal, and their armies were poorly organized; yet such "barbarians" nevertheless shared a general idea that as freemen of their community they were obligated to fight—and free to profit from the booty of their enemies. In that sense of civic militarism, they were more reminiscent of the old classical armies of a republican past than had been the hired imperial legionaries on Rome's defensive frontier:

The massive reliance on citizen-soldiers in the West lowered the demands on the central government for expenditures to support the military.... Indeed, the flexibility of the West in building on developments that took place during the later Roman Empire resulted in immense military strengths, which, for example, proved their worth in the success for two centuries of the crusader states against overwhelming odds. (B. Bachrach, "Early Medieval Europe," in K. Raaflaub and N. Rosenstein, eds., *War and Society in the Ancient and Medieval Worlds,* 294)

The legions had crumbled not because of organizational weaknesses, technological backwardness, or even problems of command and discipline, but because of the dearth of free citizens who were willing to fight for their own freedom and the values of their civilization. Such spirited warriors the barbarians had, and when they absorbed the blueprint of Roman militarism, a number of effective local Western armies arose—as the Muslims learned at Poitiers.

INFANTRY, PROPERTY, AND CITIZENSHIP

A Mounted Monopoly?

Charles Martel and his Carolingian successors—son Pippin III and grandson Charlemagne—would craft the foundations of the medieval feudal state, with which by A.D. 1000 we traditionally associate knights, chivalry, and huge mailed warhorses. The usual view is that between the final collapse of Rome (A.D. 500) and the widespread use of gunpowder (1400), the mounted knight came to dominate the battlefields of Europe. In fact, in most of the larger battles during this millennium, infantrymen continued to outnumber cavalry by at least five to one.

Even in the latter Middle Ages at the three greatest battles of the Hundred Years War—Crécy (1346), the second great battle at Poitiers (1356), and Agincourt (1415)—most of the mounted combatants, who were a minority of both the English and the French armies, dismounted and fought on foot. Cortés's fearsome knights, who tore apart the mass of swarming Aztecs, accounted for less than 10 percent of the conquistadors in Mexico. The infantry wall of Charles Martel at Poitiers was no aberration—Frankish, Swiss, and Byzantine infantrymen all made up the unheralded core of their respective medieval armies.

While it is true that medieval art glorified the horseman as an aristocratic knight, that the church sought to implant in him a sense of moral responsibility for the preservation of Christian society, and that most monarchies drew their natural support from landowning mounted elites, horsemen were never numerous, economical, or versatile enough in Europe to ensure success in major engagements—especially in battles that might involve up to 20,000 or 30,000 combatants. There is not a single major Carolingian engagement in which infantrymen were not the dominant force on the battlefield. The role of feudalism and the romance of the early mounted warrior must be put in a proper cultural perspective:

> Carolingian feudalism, despite the emphasis it laid on horse-owning, should not be equated with the military system of the nomads. The cultivated lands of western Europe could support a horse population of no large size, and the feudal armies that answered the summons to arms resembled a horse people's horde in no way at all. The difference derived in great measure from the distinctive military culture of the Teutonic tribes, which encouraged face-to-face fighting with edged weapons, a tradition reinforced by their encounters with the Roman armies before they had lost their legionary training. This culture had been preserved when the Western warriors took it horseback, and it was reinforced by the potentialities of the equipment they wore and the weapons they used from the saddle. (J. Keegan, *History of Warfare*, 285)

Charles Martel's army at the battle at Poitiers was the continuation of a 1,400-year Western tradition beginning in Greece and Rome that put a premium on landed infantry. The reasons for this original Western chauvinism concerning heavily armed and well-protected foot soldiers again were unique to Europe and arose largely from Western economic, political, social, and military realities that had been established centuries earlier in Greece and survived the collapse of Rome. To field effective infantry—meaning the ability to stand in the face of mounted assaults and to charge and overrun lines of archers and missile troops—there were three prerequisites in the ancient and medieval worlds. First, landscape: the best infantrymen were rooted country folk and the product of a geography largely composed of valleys and lowlands situated between mountain ranges that favored intensive farming. In contrast, mountainous terrain is the haunt of herdsmen, who with slings, bows, and javelins master the arts of ambush and guarding routes of transit—the various hill tribes, for example, of central Asia Minor who attacked Xenophon's Ten Thousand on their retreat to the Black Sea. On the other hand, steppes or uninterrupted plains favor nomadic and tribal horsemen, ensuring plentiful grazing lands and, more important, the room for vast cavalry sweeps that might outflank and envelop columns of foot soldiers—as the Romans, for example, learned in Parthia. Europe, however, from the Balkans to the British Isles, was largely a continent of good farmland and valleys, cut off by mountains and rivers, that was ideal for the operations of heavy infantrymen: flat ground for decisive charges of cumbersome foot soldiers, with nearby hills and mountains to prevent mounted flank attack.

Second, the best infantrymen of the preindustrial age were often a product of centralized rather than tribal government. City-states and republics had the power to muster the great majority of the population, instill some training in marching in time and staying in rank, and eliminate or at least unify private barons and elite clans. True, the end of the Roman Empire destroyed for centuries the classical idea of a vast nation-in-arms and a strong central political authority enrolling, training, paying, and retiring 250,000 uniformly armed legionaries throughout the Mediterranean world. Nevertheless, on a vastly reduced scale, local communities in the West and an isolated Byzantium attempted to keep alive the old classical traditions of organizing tenants and small landowners through large-scale levies to unite in organized defense of their homeland.

Third, to produce a potent and numerous infantry arm, there also had to be the pretense of egalitarianism, if not consensual government— or at least the absence of widespread serfdom. Successful infantrymen needed enough capital to provide adequate weapons. They required some sort of political voice, or a reciprocal relationship with the more wealthy, to ensure a sense of limited autonomy. Ideally, the best foot soldiers either owned or enjoyed the use of farmland, and thus fought with a sense of territorial chauvinism—the idea that they battled shoulder-to-shoulder in protection of real property that they felt was their own.

In the Dark and Middle Ages the landscape of Europe did not change from classical times. While the central control of Rome had vanished and the population of autonomous yeomen had been largely lost as early as the third century A.D., nonetheless western Europe maintained a considerable population of viable rural folk, who found in their local lord and regional king a semblance of the old system of mustering and fighting with like kind. If they are sometimes called the "dependent free," the foot soldiers of Europe between A.D. 600 and 1000 were not servile and were far better off in a political sense than Eastern serfs. All duties and obligations were predicated on certain rights and privileges. In contrast, the great Byzantine general Belisarius (A.D. 500–65) was not far off the mark when he described Eastern infantry in Persia as undisciplined rustics who were forced into the army solely to undermine walls, plunder corpses, and wait on real soldiers. There was nothing like either the Mameluks or Janissaries in western Europe.

The Origins of Heavy Infantry

Whence arose this Western tradition of infantry supremacy that survived even the collapse of Rome? In Greece and not earlier. As we have seen earlier in discussion of their invention of shock battle, the creation of the Hellenic polis (800–600 B.C.) came as a result of a new class of small, free property owners, who as hoplite heavily armed infantrymen formed up in the phalanx and engaged in shock battles over property disputes. Their emergence marked the decline of aristocratic knights who had enjoyed privilege for centuries. The emergence of infantrymen was a revolutionary development unseen either in the Greeks' own Mycenaean past or in the contemporary world of the eastern Mediterranean.

As cultivated ground began to be more equitably distributed and farmed more intensively, grazing land for horses was in short supply. Even when forage was found, horses made no sense economically. Ten acres devoted to grain, trees, and vines could feed a family of five or six, rather than provide a mount for a single wealthy man. By the time of Charles Martel a horse cost as much as twenty cattle. For the amount of forage consumed, oxen were also more efficient behind the plow; and, of course, cattle provided beef. In contrast, many Europeans had cultural taboos about the eating of horseflesh. In Greek mythology horses like Arion, Pegasus, and the talking steeds in the *Iliad* were venerated and near human in their loyalty, courage, and intelligence. It made no farming or cultural sense to raise horses in the settled plains and small communities of early Greece.

Once citizenship was extended to middling farmers in Greece of the eighth through sixth centuries B.C., the defense of the community rested in the hands of property owners, who voted when and where to fight—usually brief, decisive battles of colliding heavy infantrymen to ensure clear results and allow the farmer combatants to return home quickly to their harvests. Among yeomen hoplites, horsemanship brought no prestige, but rather suspicion of political intrigue by wealthy rightists who might overthrow popular government. Men with horses were felt to have somehow diverted resources from the community for their own indulgence. Militarily, the spears of the serried ranks of the phalanxes made the charges of horsemen—without stirrups and on small ponies—impotent.

Just as it was cheaper to "grow" a family rather than a horse on a small plot of ground, so it was more economical for a state to train a farmer with a spear to stay in rank than a mounted grandee to remain on his horse while fighting.

The result was that until Alexander the Great, four centuries of Hellenic culture pilloried cavalrymen. At Sparta Xenophon claimed that only the "weakest in strength and the least eager for glory" mounted horses (*Hellenica* 6.4.11). That dismissive view of cavalry was commonplace throughout classical Greece; the orator Lysias, for example, bragged to the assembly that his client, the wealthy aristocratic Mantitheos, at a battle at the Haliartos River (395 B.C.) chose to face danger as a hoplite, rather than serve "in safety" as a horseman (16.13). Alexander realized that this landed monopoly of the Greek city-states made no military sense when war evolved beyond the small valleys of the mainland and involved a variety of Asian enemies—archers, light-armed troops, and variously armed horsemen—in the large plains and hill country of the East. He also had antipathy, not allegiance, to agrarianism. His aristocratic Macedonian Companions, like the Thessalian light cavalrymen who accompanied him, were horse lords, living on vast estates on the expansive plains of northern Greece. All were the products of monarchy, not consensual government.

There is an entire corpus of passages in ancient literature that reflects this ideal that small farms grew good infantrymen, while vast estates produced only a few elite horsemen: the proper role of farmland is to nurture families of infantry, not to lie idle or to rear horses. Aristotle lamented that by his own time in the latter fourth century B.C., the territory around Sparta was no longer inhabited by male Spartiate hoplite households—although, he says, that country might have supported "thirty thousand hoplites" (*Politics* 2.1270a31). In his own era at the end of the first century A.D., the biographer Plutarch deplored the wide-scale depopulation of the Greek countryside, noting that the entire country could scarcely field "three thousand hoplites," roughly the size of the contingent Megara alone fielded at the battle of Plataea (*Moralia* 414A). Similarly, the historian Theopompus, in commenting on the elite nature of a squadron of Philip's Companion Cavalry, remarked that although only eight hundred in number, they possessed the equivalent income of "not less than ten-thousand Greek owners of the best and most productive land" (*Fragments of Greek History* 115, 225). Theopompus's point is that intensively worked farmland resulted in an abundance of hoplite infantry, and that this was a political, cultural, and military ideal—in contrast to vast estates to the north that supported horsemen, not yeomen soldiers, and so nurtured autocracy.

Despite the mastery of the mounted Companions, Philip and Alexander learned more from the Greeks than they from him, since the core of the royal army of Macedonia lay with the spears of phalangites and hypaspists—no more than 20 percent of Alexander's military was mounted. Alexander conquered Persia through the combination of horse and pikeman; but that legacy was either quickly forgotten by the Successors or felt to be irrelevant in subsequent wars against other Macedonian dynasts. Between 323 and 31 B.C. the Hellenistic East was convulsed by near constant war, which was usually decided by the collision of professionally trained pikemen, who alone could break other infantrymen and rid the battlefield of the enemy. Alexander himself, who shredded the ranks of Persian infantry, might have had far less success charging head-on into the phalangites of his own Successor generals.

Rome for nearly a thousand years put its faith in infantry, a tradition that grew up among the Italian yeomen of the fourth and third centuries B.C. who protected republican government through their own service in the legions. Small numbers of horsemen were recruited into the Roman military as auxiliaries from northern European tribes and North African nomadic peoples. Such infantry traditions were enduring. The accompanying failure to develop a highly trained heavy cavalry contingent of the caliber of Alexander's Companions cost Rome on a number of occasions, from Crassus's slaughter in Parthia (53 B.C.) to the triumph of the Goths over Valerian at Adrianople (A.D. 378). Yet again the history of Greece and Rome remains the story of a millennium of military superiority over their enemies, a dominance that was the result of a primacy in landed infantry.

Classical Continuity in the Dark and Middle Ages

Did the fall of Rome mean a return to the conditions of the first European Dark Ages (1100–800 B.C.) before the polis when local barons, stock raising, and mounted warriors ruled in a larger chaotic and depopulated Greek landscape? Not entirely, for the traditions of Rome, as we have seen, were not forgotten, and the second European Dark Ages between A.D. 500 and 1000 were never so dim as after the collapse of the Mycenaean kingdoms in Greece. In the disruption of the fifth and sixth centuries A.D., infantry remained the mainstay of the Byzantines—who fought with a ratio of four men on foot to every one on horseback—even when they eventually developed shock mailed cavalrymen on larger horses with stirrups.

The Franks, Normans, and Byzantines all took pride in the fearsome charges of their elite and rather small contingents of heavy-mailed knights, which in some sense represented the Western idea of armored, pike-bearing foot soldiers transferred to horseback. Western cavalrymen, rider for rider, in general were better armed, heavier, and more deadly lancers than their more nimble and mobile Islamic counterparts, and reflected just this European preference for decisive shock battles. Yet during the larger battles in Europe and among the Crusader armies in the Holy Land, such fearsome cavalry charges spelled disaster, unless there was a much larger contingent of infantrymen to close with the enemy. Usually, infantry, not horsemen, determined the outcome of Carolingian conflict.

Even with the adoption of stirrups in western Europe sometime between A.D. 800 and 1000, most heavily armed knights could not charge well-trained infantry who stood firm with locked shields and spears. Moreover, not all knights were vastly wealthy. Often cadres of horsemen from more modest landed properties were used to dismount and fight as foot soldiers. Horses per se did not always equate to true shock cavalry, but served as taxis of sorts that transported heavy infantrymen to the fighting. The point is not that Europe fielded few good cavalrymen, but that mounted troops were always outnumbered by infantry. The glamour and mythology of the Dark and Middle Ages were with mounted knights. In small battles and raids, mailed horsemen held an enormous advantage over unprotected peasants. While Europe never possessed the requisite grazing land to produce a true horse culture—nomadic horsemen might string along five to ten ponies per mounted warrior—its rich estates were often sufficient to raise enough animals to create a small cadre of mounted knights, who as petty lords helped to create the system of vassalage and with it early medieval feudalism. The absence of a central state also meant that systematic and uniform drill and training were often difficult for foot soldiers. Contemporary folk wisdom suggested that in battle one hundred well-trained armored knights could be worth one thousand poorly organized peasant foot soldiers.

Yet around the atolls of aristocratic knights, there remained a sea of rustics who made up the majority of all European armies in times of great crisis. Most were small landholders, who either as vassals gave percentages of their harvest to wealthy lords for protection or themselves enjoyed grants of property and thus were given the use of land by aristocrats in exchange for military service. While the foot soldiers of Charles Martel's army lacked the full concept of citizenship found in classical Greece and republican Rome, such middling farmers were nevertheless recognized as freemen, with rights and responsibilities protected by local aristocrats. They were not of the same status as the mercenaries, herdsmen, serfs, or outright slaves who constituted a great part of the later Berber, Mongol, Arab, and Ottoman armies that invaded Europe. Such men (the *landwehr*) were the backbone of early Carolingian armed forces, especially during the decline of cities and commerce after the disintegration of the Roman Empire:

> As the economic structure became predominantly agrarian, military service tended to be closely associated with landowning. Each free household owed the service of a man with complete arms and equipment, and this military obligation became hereditary. The Frankish army thus became a levy of free men serving at the king's will, under the command of his local representative. (J. Beeler, *Warfare in Feudal Europe, 730–1200,* 9)

The increasing use of the stirrup, which allowed horsemen to charge scattered and poorly trained foot soldiers, and the need to combat Islamic mobile cavalry, led to the greater role of aristocratic knights by the tenth century. Yet even then, the idea of entire armies of heavy horsemen sweeping all before them is once again largely a myth.

The Value of Infantrymen

Is it legitimate to value one branch of the military over another? Who can ascertain whether archers, cavalry, artillery, or marines are greater assets on the battlefield, given the vagaries of landscape, weather, and strategic goals? In every great army—Alexander's, Napoleon's, Wellington's— horsemen, infantrymen, and missile troops acted in concert; without such symmetry in battle, all great captains would have found success illusory. Cavalry could always charge and retreat at greater speeds than infantry, and imparted an element of psychological terror lacking among even the fiercest infantrymen. Because the vast majority of Western adversaries were mounted and extremely mobile, it was critical that Europeans developed counterforces of good horse soldiers. Victories were often left incomplete without dogged pursuit by mounted warriors.

That being said, permanent victory in war, ancient and modern, is impossible without crack foot soldiers, who alone can approach the enemy face-to-face, cut him down or blast him apart, occupy the battlefield, and take physical possession of the land under dispute. Their ancient weapons—swords and spears—are cheap and more deadly than missiles.

Foot soldiers, not horsemen, were critical to conducting sieges and defending walls—far more likely the locus of medieval warring than the open battlefield. Infantry, in addition, was far more versatile in difficult terrain, whether areas of dense woods or high hills, or in those areas without fertile croplands that offered little pastureland and forage.

Horsemen and archers—like modern brigades of mobile armor, artillery, and airpower—could aid, but in themselves not replace infantry troops. Ultimately, war is a question of economics, in which the options of all states are confined by their ability to produce goods and services; thus every armed force calibrates the greatest military power for the least cost. Armies in the Dark Ages and medieval era, like their classical predecessors, were not immune from such constraints, and so learned quickly that man for man, infantry could be provided for at a tenth of the expense of mounted troops.

With the onset of gunpowder and handheld firearms between the fourteenth and sixteenth centuries, infantry entered an especially deadly phase; shooters, not just pikemen, could decimate the ranks of mounted lancers as horses became increasingly vulnerable. Yet the spread of firearms throughout the globe did not everywhere automatically result in the creation of disciplined corps of gun-toting soldiers. The Ottomans never mastered the art of volley firing while in rank. The Janissaries shot as they stabbed—as heroic individuals in individual combat. In similar fashion, mounted warriors of North Africa shot muskets largely from horses and camels in swift raids and plundering expeditions. Natives in Africa and the New World saw firearms as improved javelins or arrows and were also ignorant of the possibility of volley firing and sequential shooting. Nor did the introduction of handheld firearms create effective armies in China and Japan.

Only in Europe was the art of loading, firing, and reloading in unison mastered; and only in England, Germany, Spain, Italy, and the other central states of the West was there a prior infantry tradition of the Dark and Middle Ages that had survived from classical antiquity and molded the prior shock tactics of the Germanic tribes into ordered face-to-face confrontations. The gunpowder age saw an ascendant Europe precisely because firearms—mass-produced and easy to use by individuals—were best employed by preexisting disciplined columns and lines of infantrymen. In the age before the repeating and automatic rifle, shooters with harquebuses and muskets in rank with feet on the ground offered more concentrated, accurate, and rapid fire than those who used their weapons while either mounted or acting solitarily and as skirmishers. In some sense, Renaissance guns in Europe were seen as the natural successors to medieval pikes.

POITIERS AND BEYOND

A victorious line of march had been prolonged above a thousand miles from the rock of Gibraltar to the banks of the Loire; the repetition of an equal space would have carried the Saracens to the confines of Poland and the Highlands of Scotland: the Rhine is no more impassable than the Nile or Euphrates, and the Arabian fleet might have sailed without a naval combat into the mouth of the Thames. Perhaps the interpretation of the Koran would now be taught in the schools of Oxford, and her pupils might demonstrate to a circumcised people the sanctity and truth of the revelation of Mahomet. (E. Gibbon, *The Decline and Fall of the Roman Empire,* vol. 7)

So wrote Edward Gibbon—perhaps somewhat tongue in cheek, or at least intrigued with the possibility of a non-Christian Oxford—of the possible consequences of a Frankish defeat at Poitiers. Most of the renowned historians of the eighteenth and nineteenth centuries, like Gibbon, saw Poitiers as a landmark battle that marked the high tide of the Muslim advance into Europe. Leopold von Ranke felt that Poitiers was the turning point of "one of the most important epochs in the history of the world, the commencement of the eighth century, when on the one side Mohammedanism threatened to overspread Italy and Gaul" (*History of the Reformation,* vol. 1, 5). Edward Creasy included Poitiers in his select group of "decisive battles of the world" and likewise felt that it marked the salvation of Europe: "The progress of civilization, and the development of the nationalities and governments of modern Europe, from that time forth went forward in a not uninterrupted, but ultimately certain career" (The *Fifteen Decisive Battles of the World,* 167). Hans Delbrück, the great German military historian, said of Poitiers that there was "no more important battle in world history" (*The Barbarian Invasions,* 441).

More skeptical observers like Sir Charles Oman and J. F. C. Fuller were not so convinced that Western civilization had been saved outright at Poitiers, but they were impressed that the battle marked the emergence of a new consensus that would later on save Europe: spirited Frankish infantrymen of a new Carolingian culture, flanked by their mounted lords, at last might offer a bulwark in the West against both Muslim and Viking raiders. As Oman put it, "For the future we hear of Frankish invasions of Spain, not of Saracen invasions of Gaul" (*The Dark Ages, 476–918,* 299).

Recent scholars have suggested either that Poitiers—so poorly recorded in contemporary sources—was a mere raid and thus a "construct" of Western mythmaking or that a Muslim victory might have been preferable to continued Frankish dominance. What is clear is that Poitiers marked a general continuance of the successful Western defense of Europe. Flush from the victory at Poitiers, Charles Martel went on to clear southern France from Islamic attackers for decades, unify the warring kingdoms into the foundations of the Carolingian empire, and ensure ready and reliable troops from local estates.

The spread of direct Roman political control of Asia and northern Africa (100 B.C. to A.D. 400) had been a five-hundred-year aberration—the imposition of Roman law, custom, language, and political organization of millions on conquered peoples to the south and east, while simultaneously conducting a slow assimilation of millions more barbarian peoples to the north. With the inevitable retrenchment of the empire in the fifth century A.D., it was clear that classicism was not dead after all, that it had been remarkably successful in conquering the minds of its own purported conquerors: the core of Europe would retain Roman and Christian precedents and thus once more begin to extend its influence beyond its own borders:

> Not only did the conversion of Poland, Hungary and the Scandinavian kingdoms enlarge the zone of influence of Latin Christendom to the north and east, but Islam fell back in Spain, through the progress of the *Reconquista,* and in the Mediterranean, with the annexation of Sicily and the establishment of Latin states in the Middle East. At the same time, in the wake of a movement that was not only military but also economic and demographic, a new Germany was created beyond the Elbe. Facing their enemies, neighbours or rivals, the warriors of the West marked up a string of successes. This expansion is all the more remarkable because it occurred at a time of increasing fragmentation of power. (P. Contamine, *War in the Middle Ages,* 30)

The story of Byzantium is a thousand-year resistance to Persian and Islamic encroachment. The fall of Constantinople was seen as a horrific event in Christendom, but for centuries Byzantine ingenuity and discipline had destroyed a succession of much larger Islamic armies. The capital fell a thousand years after Rome's collapse—and only after it was largely isolated from and abandoned by the West. The reign of Charlemagne (768–814) saw the final expulsion of most Muslims from France and Italy and the creation of a central European state that spread its influence throughout France, Germany, and Scandinavia and into northern Spain.

By 1096 a fragmented western Europe was strong enough to send thousands of soldiers across the sea to the Middle East. In a series of three great Crusades between 1096 and 1189, Europeans occupied Jerusalem and carved out Western enclaves in the heart of Islam. Throughout the Middle Ages it was Europe, not the Middle East, that was more secure from foreign assault. It was impossible for any Muslim army, unlike the Crusaders, to transport large armies by sea to storm the heartland of Europe. Arab armadas had long ago learned in the seventh and eighth centuries at the height of Islamic power that it was unfeasible to take nearby Constantinople.

Such European resiliency offers the proper explanation for the great advance of Western power in the New World, Asia, and Africa after 1500. Europe's renewed strength against the Other in the age of gunpowder was facilitated by the gold of the New World, the mass employment of firearms, and new designs of military architecture. Yet the proper task of the historian is not simply to chart the course for this amazing upsurge in European influence, but to ask *why* the "Military Revolution" took place in Europe and not elsewhere. The answer is that throughout the Dark and Middle Ages, European military traditions founded in classical antiquity were kept alive and improved upon in a variety of bloody wars against Islamic armies, Viking raiders, Mongols, and northern barbarian tribes. The main components of the Western military tradition of freedom, decisive battle, civic militarism, rationalism, vibrant markets, discipline, dissent, and free critique were not wiped out by the fall of Rome. Instead, they formed the basis of a succession of Merovingian, Carolingian, French, Italian, Dutch, Swiss, German, English, and Spanish militaries that continued the military tradition of classical antiquity.

Key to this indefatigability was the ancient and medieval emphasis on foot soldiers, and especially the idea of free property owners, rather than slaves or serfs, serving as heavily armed infantrymen. Once firearms came on the scene, Europe far more easily than other cultures was able to convert ranks of spearmen and pikemen to harquebusiers, who fired as they had stabbed—in unison, on command, shoulder-to-shoulder, and in rank. Cortés in Mexico City and the Christians at Lepanto were successful largely because they were not the products of a nomadic horse people, tribal society, or even theocratic autocracy, but drew their heritage from tough foot soldiers of settled small valleys and rural communities—the type of men who formed a veritable wall of ice at Poitiers and so beat Abd ar-Rahman back.

SIX

Technology and the
Wages of Reason

Tenochtitlán, June 24, 1520–August 13, 1521

> A cunning fellow is man. His tools
> make him master of beasts of the field
> and those that move in the mountains . . .
> He has a way against everything,
> and he faces nothing that is to come without contrivance . . .
> With some sort of cunning, inventive
> Beyond all expectation
> He reaches sometimes evil,
> And, sometimes good.
> —SOPHOCLES, *Antigone* (347–67)

THE BATTLES FOR MEXICO CITY

Besieged—June 24–30, 1520

CLOUDS OF JAVELINS, stones from slings, and arrows wounded forty-six conquistadors. Twelve were killed outright. In the narrow passageways around Cortés's headquarters, the Spanish were hemmed in on all sides. "But I declare," wrote the eyewitness Bernal Díaz del Castillo of the Spaniards' suddenly desperate plight in Tenochtitlán, "that I do not know how to describe it, for neither cannon nor muskets nor crossbows availed, nor hand-to-hand fighting, nor killing thirty or forty of them every time we charged, for they still fought on in as close ranks and with more energy than in the beginning" (*The Discovery and Conquest of Mexico*, 302).

The odds were now dramatically against the vastly outnumbered

Castilians, who foolishly had brought their entire tiny force inside the island city of Tenochtitlán. During this awful week the Spaniards gave up their grandiose ideas that had taken root over their prior eight-month occupation of Mexico City. The thought of ruling the city as European lords now seemed utter folly. Soon the notion of either a truce or an Aztec surrender became equally ludicrous. Finally, Cortés's men began to have doubts that they could even come out of the infernal city with their lives, much less with their trove of looted gold.*

Only repeated fire from their harquebusiers and crossbowmen, and occasional volleys from the cannon—thirty or so Mexica attackers often fell with each shot—allowed the stalwart Diego de Ordaz to return to the Castilians' bunker and report to his caudillo that he had failed in his breakout attempt: the streets were all blocked and full of their enraged hosts. Still, Ordaz's men hacked away entire limbs of the unarmored Mexicas with their Toledo swords. The iron lances of the mounted mailed knights killed even more with single thrusts. Grapeshot from the cannon shredded wave after wave of Mexicas. A few horses trampled dozens of unprotected Aztecs. The ugly Spanish mastiffs tore at the legs and arms of the shrieking attackers. Volleys of crossbow bolts and lead balls from the harquebuses mowed natives at distances of one hundred yards and more.

The density of metropolitan warfare and the sheer number of enraged and courageous native warriors were new experiences for the undefeated conquistadors. Their commanders, veterans of Spain's wars against the Italians and Ottomans, had never seen such audacity or bravery in all the fighting in the Mediterranean. Ordaz was soon to learn that his excellence in technology and tactics might not any longer be able to nullify the numerically superior enemy if the Spanish were continually forced to fight in the back alleys and narrow corridors of Tenochtitlán, where they could be thronged and pelted from the rooftops by men often as brave as themselves. The more desperate Aztecs were beginning to kill a few of his soldiers, not merely wrestling them to the ground to bind them as captives for their hungry gods.

The rout of this trial sally of Ordaz's four hundred conquistadors—including almost all the Spanish crossbowmen and harquebusiers that Cortés had left—was proof enough that there was no way out of the

---

*I have used the terms "Mexicas" and "Aztecs" (from the Nahuatl "Aztlan") interchangeably, although Montezuma and his subjects probably called themselves "Mexicas." The use of "Aztecs" came into common use by European chroniclers after the seventeenth century. Most of Cortés's Spanish soldiers were Castilians, and so I employ both words to describe his conquistadors.

fortress city. Or so it seemed. The neighboring allies in Tlacopán (mod-ern-day Tacuba) on the shore had wisely warned Cortés the day before *not* to reenter the dreaded Tenochtitlán, but to remain with them on the coast of Lake Texcoco. "Lord," they pleaded with Cortés, "stay here in Tacuba, or in Coyoacán, or in Texcoco . . . because here on the mainland, in these meadows, if the Mexica rise against you, you would defend yourself bet-ter than in the city" (H. Thomas, *Conquest*, 395).

Excellent advice, but back in the Mexica capital of Tenochtitlán were the carefully guarded captured Aztec treasure, the hostage emperor, Montezuma, and the beleaguered Pedro de Alvarado with fewer than one hundred of the expedition's best conquistadors. These had stayed behind while Cortés marched back to the coast to put down a rival Spanish chal-lenge to his campaign. Besides, with this new contingent of Pánfilo de Narváez's Cuban army, who had "joined" Cortés in Vera Cruz in the af-termath of their commander's failed attempt to subvert the conquest of Tenochtitlán, Cortés had more than a thousand soldiers. The city had been all but his anyway for almost the last eight months. After his brief ex-cursion to Vera Cruz, he had far more arms and supplies than when his men had first dismantled their ships and marched inland in July 1519, reaching Montezuma's capital on November 8 of that year. Why should he worry now?

What tribe in all of Mexico had shown they could stop such a force? In the prior twelve months the Mayas, Totonacs, Tlaxcalans, Otomis, and Cholulas had all learned the futility of opposing mounted lancers, gun-powder weapons, crossbows, fierce war dogs, and Spanish steel—not to mention the classical battle tactics of massed infantry and the generalship of Cortés himself, who sought to annihilate, not capture, his enemies through disciplined squares, carefully timed mounted attacks, and mass volleys of gunfire. Surely if Cortés had initially marched into Tenochtitlán in November 1519 with 500 conquistadors, could he not just as easily now march out in June 1520 with more than 1,200?

He proudly announced to the anxious residents of Tlacopán that, in fact, his Castilians would go back across the causeways into the capital city of his New-Spain-to-be—Cortés's gift to the adolescent king, Charles V. They would make a show of force, throw down some more idols, threaten a few Aztec lords, reenter the imperial palace, collect their booty, rescue Alvarado, and then order Montezuma to cease the futile resistance of his subjects.

But after Cortés rode into Tenochtitlán and rejoined Alvarado's men, the entire reunited contingent was soon cut off in the Palace of Axayácatl and the temple of Tezcatlipoca. The once-friendly Mexicas were blocking all three causeways leading out of their great island capital. More than 1,000 Spaniards, with a small contingent of their gallant Tlaxcalan allies— some 2,000 indigenous enemies of the Aztecs—were completely surrounded in a tiny compound by well over 200,000 enraged Mexicas and a growing number of their tributary allies from the surrounding lakeside communities. Once it was clear that the captive Montezuma no longer had control of his subjects, and that Ordaz had failed to find a way out, the Castilians packed their gold, hunkered down, and began planning their escape before they were utterly annihilated.

Had not the diabolical Narváez—now half-blind and in shackles in Cortés's jail—interrupted his plans, Cortés and his fanatics would have thrown down all the Aztec stone idols, fumigated the pyramids in the Valley of Mexico from the stench of their human offal, tossed the Mexica priests with their odious capes of human skin down from the heights, eradicated the horrific sacrifices, banned cannibalism and sodomy, introduced the love of the Savior, and then usurped Montezuma as lord and master of an empire of a million Christian subjects and ensconced Cortés himself in the former's palace as doge of this Venice of New Spain! And what works such an enormous force of laborers might accomplish for their European overseers under Cortés's megalomaniac tutelage! What subterranean gold treasures such a throng of miners might uncover! Upon entry to Tenochtitlán the awed Mexicas for a while thought Cortés's soldiers of fortune were white-skinned gods, their horses supernatural centaurs who talked to men, their cannon murderous thunder weapons from the heavens. And their enormous sharp-fanged mastiffs? Surely a far cry from the local tiny lapdogs that were castrated and eaten; more like some devilish fanged creatures of myth. Such were the Castilian fantasies dashed by the thousands of enraged Aztecs now outside the Spanish compound.

Despite Cortés's defeat of Narváez's army, the incorporation into his own force of the latter's troops, and his successful return across the causeways back into the island city, everything had suddenly gone terribly wrong in the capital. In his absence, the maniacal Pedro de Alvarado had massacred thousands of the Mexica nobles and instigated hostilities against their unarmed women and children. The crazy Castilian had murdered festivalgoers on the pretext that they were plotting insurrection. Or was it their purported resurrection of the now forbidden human sacrifice, or Alvarado's own paranoia, his greed at the sight of so much gold and jewels on the ceremonial dress of the Aztec nobles, or finally perhaps the sheer sadistic delight of the mounted aristocrat in hacking to pieces hundreds of the defenseless but hated Mexicas? How Alvarado and his tiny coterie of fewer than a hundred conquistadors had managed to slaughter more than 8,000 of them, albeit initially surprised and unarmed in a confined place, was still not altogether clear. Evil could only serve a man like Alvarado so far.

In any case, Cortés was not gone for more than two months before his jittery lieutenants had sparked a murderous revolt of his once-pacified hosts. "You have done badly," Cortés lectured the hothead on his return. "You have been false to your trust. Your conduct has been that of a madman" (W. Prescott, *History of the Conquest of Mexico*, 407–8). Or perhaps a psychopath—Aztec witnesses a few years after the slaughter reported the effect of steel swords and iron lances upon unprotected flesh:

> They attacked all the celebrants, stabbing them, spearing them from behind, and these fell instantly to the ground with their entrails hanging out. Others they beheaded: they cut off their heads, or split their heads to pieces. They struck others in the shoulders, and their arms were torn from their bodies. They wounded some in the thigh and some in the calf. They slashed others in the abdomen, and their entrails all spilled to the ground. Some attempted to run away, but their intestines dragged as they ran; they seemed to tangle their feet in their own entrails. (M. Leon-Portilla, ed., *The Broken Spears*, 76)

Now a little more than a month later, the Spaniards themselves could find no escape. For a week they sortied out of their headquarters, probing the Aztec resistance in vain attempts to find an exit to the elevated causeways across Lake Texcoco. At night, Cortés's men saw through the windows of their headquarters the heads of their slain comrades bobbing on sticks; groaning and making wild gestures as if the rotting corpses were some sort of talking dead, the Aztecs used them as puppets of sorts to terrorize the beleaguered Spaniards. Despite the mounting casualties in these battles to the death around the Spanish compound, it was still likely that any Castilian who stumbled in the fighting might be bound and taken captive, to mark resumption of the sacrifices atop the Great Pyramid. The Spaniards' supplies of fresh water and food were cut off, as they were blockaded and then continuously bombarded with missiles from the surrounding roofs.

After a week of this mayhem, Cortés was desperate, and in the immediate crisis would survive only through his reliance on his impromptu machines and his own military acumen. All the while, the cannon fired grapeshot that slaughtered the Aztec swarms, killing hundreds and breaking up their efforts to storm his temple redoubt. His men dug a well to find brackish water. They somehow constructed from roof timber and beams in the Aztec temples vast *manteletes,* or mobile wooden tanks, that could protect up to twenty-five men, as they shot and stabbed in safety from the engines' apertures. His engineers thereby hoped to clear the area around the Palace of Axayácatl and halt the nightly missile attacks.

Cortés at last dragged the discredited Montezuma himself onto the roof of the temple to order his subjects below to desist. Instead, the fired-up Mexicas jeered the shackled emperor and pelted their once-divine ruler with stones. Soon the Spaniards pulled the dazed emperor back inside, only to find Montezuma mortally wounded—their last chance of parley extinguished. Later rival accounts suggested that the Castilians murdered the emperor in their anger—and on rumors that Montezuma had earlier sent heralds to the Spanish usurper Narváez on the coast to join forces with him against Cortés.

Cortés next stormed the nearby temple of Yopico. The newly constructed siege engines shielded himself and forty men who climbed the pyramid, cast down idols, threw the priests off their sanctuary, destroyed the stores of ceremonial flayed skins, and generally cleared the rival tower of archers and slingers who had rained death down on the Spaniards. The desperate killing was driven by religion and tactics: sorties against the immediate military challenge of enemy missiles, coupled with the continual Christian crusade to obliterate all traces of the Mexicas' machinery of sacrifice. Whereas at first the religious war was seen by some conquistadors as an impediment, the Spaniards were learning that the destruction of Aztec idols and priests brought benefits to the battlefield as well—in steadily sapping enemy morale and cohesion, as the Aztecs despaired of seeing their gods, whom they fought to feed, unable to prevent their own destruction.

In the struggle for Yopico, Cortés reinjured his wounded hand and was almost cast off the pyramid in the terrible melee. The contemporary encomiast Bernal Díaz del Castillo wrote of the Spaniards' mad climb up Yopico: "Oh! What a fight and what a fierce battle it was that took place; it was a memorable thing to see us all streaming with blood and covered with wounds and others slain" (*The Discovery and Conquest of Mexico,* 306). At least another twenty conquistadors were killed in this desperate second sortie; despite the cannon, horses, and siege engines, there were too many Aztecs in such a confined place to make any headway. Now powder was growing short and shot scarce (should the gold and silver be melted into cannonballs? Cortés wondered). His wounded were hungry and without medical treatment. The mud-brick walls themselves of the temple fortress were eroding from the impact of thousands of missiles and stones. As one Aztec herald pointed out to them, the Mexicas and their allies could lose 250 for every one Spaniard and still annihilate the trapped guests.

At the end of this last week of June 1520, Cortés was at a crossroads. The choice, as his lieutenants put it to him, was apparently clear-cut: either flee empty-handed or stay and die with the gold in his supposed new tributary city. Characteristically, the caudillo chose neither option. He would instead attempt a night escape across the causeway despite the rain and fog, and carry out under the noses of the Aztecs the cumbersome bars of looted gold and bags of precious jewels. The Castilians would muffle the horses' hooves. Cortés would order them to bring along a newly constructed movable bridge to span the breaks in the causeways. They would load the golden bars on horses and let the soldiers take out the rest—each man deciding how much gold he would carry under his tunic or breastplate, the choice being to march wealthy and cumbersome for the fighting to come or to be nimble and poor—and perhaps stay alive. As Francisco López de Gómara, the contemporary chronicler put it, "Among our men, those who were most encumbered with clothing, gold, and jewels were the first to die, and those who were saved carried the least and forged fearlessly ahead. So those who died, died rich, and their gold killed them" (*Cortés*, 222).

For the next two decades the survivors of that awful night of sorrows would engage in mutual recriminations, lawsuits, and slander to determine exactly how much gold was carried out and how much saved. Most was clearly lost, and yet the accusations went on. Cortés would confiscate anyway what precious metal the lucky had brought out on their persons. But all that was years and hundreds of dead in the future. For the moment Cortés's 1,300 conquistadors had to find a way out of this island maze that had so suddenly been transformed from their paradise to their execution yard.

Noche Triste—June 30–July 1, 1520

It was pitch-black and raining. Still, the Castilians had nearly made it, miraculously crossing three canals—the Tecpantzinco, Tacuba, and Atenchicalco—that bisected the causeway of escape leading to the shore town of Tlacopán. They were mostly out of Tenochtitlán proper and strung in a long column on the levee above Lake Texcoco. Their wondrous portable bridge was successful so far in spanning the gaps in their path of escape. But as they began to make their way over the fourth canal, the Mixocoatechialtitlan, a woman who was fetching water spotted the clumsy band and sounded the alarm: "Mexica, come quickly, our enemies are leaving." The priest of Huitzilopochtli heard her screams and ran wildly to muster the warriors: "Mexican chiefs, your enemies are escaping! Run to your canoes of war" (H. Thomas, *Conquest*, 410).

Within minutes hundreds of canoes dotted Lake Texcoco, embarking their crews at various places along the narrow causeway to ambush the column. Others docked beside the army and smothered the Castilians with missiles. The portable bridge quickly gave way under the weight of the frantic fugitives. From now on, the only way out was to trample over the baggage horses and the bodies of those in the vanguard who fell into the canal—and had the macabre effect of providing enough flotsam and jetsam to offer footing for their terrified comrades. Hordes from Tenochtitlán left the city and attacked the retreating conquistadors from the rear, while a new Aztec muster blocked the advance. The Spaniards' four sloops—control of Lake Texcoco was critical for any successful fighting on the causeways—had long since burned. Help by water was impossible.

What followed in the next six hours was the greatest European defeat in the New World since its discovery by Columbus, as the heavily armed Spaniards, far too many laden with gold tucked up in their armor, struggled to bring up their cannon, to keep the horses calm, to organize their harquebusiers and crossbowmen, and somehow while under constant aerial attack to fill in with rubble the chasm that blocked their escape. Contemporary Mexica witnesses later recounted the confused scene as the Spaniards realized their highway of escape was breached, the bridge down, and an open canal blocking their advance:

> When the Spaniards reached the Canal of the Toltecs, the Tlatecayohuacan, they hurled themselves headlong into the water, as if they were jumping from a cliff. The Tlaxcaltecas, the allies from Tliliuhquitepec, the Spanish foot soldiers and horsemen, the few women who accompanied the army— all came to the brink and plunged over it. The canal was soon choked with the bodies of men and horses; they filled the gap in the causeway with their own drowned bodies. Those who followed crossed to the other side by walking on the corpses. (M. Leon-Portilla, ed., *The Broken Spears*, 85–86)

Those luckily at the fore of the column made it to shore, followed closely by Cortés himself and the second division—but no others. Rounding up five of his best horsemen who had reached safety—Ávila, Gonzalo, Morla, Olid, and the redoubtable Sandoval—Cortés plunged back among thousands to carve out a pocket through which the few still alive of his army might yet be saved. Too late.

At least half his Castilians were swarmed by Mexicas, while dozens of others were knocked off the causeway and into the water, some being clobbered to death with obsidian blades by warriors in canoes, others captured, bound, and dragged off by those in Lake Texcoco. Many Mexica warriors were excellent swimmers and far more mobile in the water than the heavily laden and often mailed conquistadors. Cortés himself was hit, stunned, and nearly cuffed before being pulled back to safety by his companions Olea and Quiñones. It would not be the last time that the Aztec obsession for capturing Malinche for their gods, rather than killing him outright, saved Cortés from being hacked to pieces.

By early morning even the murderous Alvarado was at last overwhelmed and lost control of the rear guard. Unhorsed and wounded, he staggered to the shore alone, after leaping his way over the breach. His co-commander, Juan Velázquez de Léon, was never heard from again, presumably either slain, drowned, or dragged off alive to be sacrificed and eaten. Although the Spaniards had marched out in the rainy and foggy night as an ordered army of four divisions, the escape march had quickly become every man for himself, as the confused Europeans were surrounded and mostly pushed into the lake along the mile and a quarter of causeway over Lake Texcoco.

Seeing the human detritus ahead, some of Alvarado's men at the rear turned around and fled back to the compound inside Tenochtitlán. They apparently preferred a glorious last stand on dry land to being clubbed to death at night in the muck of the causeway. Once there, this doomed band of stragglers purportedly met a few other terrified Castilians who had been left behind in confusion—presumably barricaded in the nearby temple of Tezcatlipoca—or who had not been willing to risk the sortie across Lake Texcoco. As many as two hundred Castilians never made it back out of Tenochtitlán. Later Aztec accounts related that after a few days of stout resistance they were killed or captured and sacrificed.

Fewer than half the Castilians and Tlaxcalans finally stumbled onto shore. What saved them from seeming annihilation was the near maniac determination of Cortés himself. Far from panicking, Cortés quickly organized in Tlacopán what was left of his little army and then set out the next day on the long way back to the Tlaxcalan capital, nearly 150 miles away, much of it through hostile and rugged terrain. For all the Aztec slaughter, the best of his men had survived. Alvarado—under dubious circumstances—had made it across the causeways, though he lost nearly all the men he was entrusted to lead. The other great knights—Ávila, Grado, Olid, Ordaz, Rangel, Sandoval, and Tapia—were yet alive. So was the irrepressible and deadly María de Estrada, who had once so terrified the Mexicas as some sort of supernatural Christian she-god.

The survival of these skilled killers ensured that the Spaniards would retain a core of mounted warriors. These trusty few had had long experience in coolly charging through Indian swarms, lancing and hacking away with near impunity—in sharp contrast with the caliber of the later recruits from Narváez's failed expedition. For the most part, the newcomers took far too much gold, were far more terrified of the Mexicas, and felt little affinity with Cortés and his original, battle-hardened cohort that had landed in fall 1519.

Cortés also noted that the loyal and invaluable translator Doña Marina, La Malinche herself, was safe. Even more important, his brilliant shipwright, Martín López, had sliced his way through along the levee. Though badly wounded, he, too, survived. The caudillo remarked to his shattered and demoralized troops, "Well, let's go, we lack nothing." At the moment of his greatest defeat, Cortés realized he still had the services of the one man who could craft new ships, which would allow him victory in his inevitable and deadly return to come. The contrast with the Mexicas was startling: after expelling the Spaniards, thousands of the courageous victors rejoiced and for critical hours ceased pursuit of a few hundred fugitives—who themselves on the brink of obliteration were already determined somehow to return to wipe out their tormentors.

Flight—July 2–9, 1520

When light broke after the *Noche Triste*, nearly eight hundred Europeans were dead or missing. More than half the Castilians who had entered Tenochtitlán during the prior month were gone, either rotting in the lake or about to have their chests ritually cut open. Nine months of the Spaniards' constant campaigning and careful alliance-building among dozens of Indian cities were for naught. The half year of conniving inside Tenochtitlán itself to gain the city peaceably, characterized by alternate threats to and reconciliation with Montezuma, was likewise apparently wasted. In some six hours of slaughter on the dikes Cortés had literally lost the army that had taken nearly a year to create. Stalwarts like Alonso de Escobar and Velázquez de Léon were missing—and logically presumed to have been dragged atop the Great Temple to Huitzilopochtli to have their hearts ripped out during the Mexica victory parade. The Mexica priests were already preparing trophies of Castilian heads to send around to the surrounding villages on the lakeshore and beyond as proof of the mortality of the newcomers—with accompanying threats not to aid the desperate fugitives, who bled and fled like men, not gods.

Contemporary Aztec accounts record the immediate aftermath at Tenochtitlán of the Castilians' "Melancholy Night":

> But they laid out the corpses of the Spaniards apart from the others; they lined them up in rows in a separate place. Their bodies were as white as the new buds of the canestalk, as white as the buds of the maguey. They removed the dead "stags" [horses] that had carried the "gods" on their shoulders. Then they gathered up everything the Spaniards had abandoned in their terror. When a man saw something he wanted, he took it, it became his property; he hefted it onto his shoulders and carried it home. They also collected all the weapons that had been left behind or had fallen into the canal—the cannons, arquebuses, swords, spears, bows and arrows—along with all the steel helmets, coats of mail and breastplates, and the shields of metal, wood, and hide. (M. Leon-Portilla, ed., *The Broken Spears*, 89)

Nearly all the Spanish survivors were wounded or sick. Given weeks of marching and inhaling summer dust, poor food and wounds incurred in the compound in Tenochtitlán, the sudden rain and cold water of the lake, and the constant need to wear their heavy metal breastplates, many developed bronchial ailments—most likely pneumonia—and dozens expired along the route of escape. Despite the wretched condition of his men, Cortés nevertheless had to leave Tlacopán and the lake's shore as quickly as possible while the Mexicas for a time celebrated and regrouped. Most of the stolen gold was gone. The cannon were at the bottom of Lake Texcoco. The harquebuses and crossbows were almost all lost. The few weapons remaining were without powder and bolts. In theory, the Mexicas, with the captured arms that they had stripped from the dead on the causeway and the doomed Spaniards back in the compound, had at their disposal better missile weapons than the Castilians.

No exact record exists of the number of Tlaxcalans killed or captured—no doubt their dead were more than a thousand. Further allied Indian reinforcements were miles away. The tiny Spanish garrison at Vera

Cruz was incommunicado. All in all, Cortés figured that he had lost 70 percent of his horses and 65 percent of his men. Worse still, he was more than 150 miles from the first friendly town of Tlaxcala. Had he any allies at all left? For the moment he was at the shore of the seemingly still neutral city of Tlacopán. But in hours thousands of Mexicas would be at his heels, with bribes and incentives for any confederates who could bind and deliver the pitiful starving Castilians. The trick was getting out of the valley alive, since the entire plain was full of former allies increasingly hostile, and eager to ride the wave of Aztec victory.

Whether or not Cortés knew it at the time, his fortunes were about to change dramatically. First, he was not quite surrounded, at least not yet. Apparently, the Aztecs were not completely familiar with this new type of European battle, which, unlike their accustomed "flower wars," campaigns aimed at submission, had nothing to do with rules or rituals, much less captives, but hinged on the science of killing the enemy outright, pursuing the defeated, ending his will to resist, and thus gaining through slaughter what negotiations and politics had failed to deliver. Under the tenets of European wars of annihilation, letting a man like Cortés—or an Alexander the Great, Julius Caesar, Richard the Lion-Hearted, Napoleon, or Lord Chelmsford—escape with his army after defeat was no victory, but only an assurance that the next round would be bloodier still, when an angrier, more experienced, and wiser force would return to settle the issue once and for all.

Cortés, for his part, had inflicted great damage on the Mexicas. Alvarado's foolish and cowardly but deadly massacre a few weeks earlier at the festival of Toxcatl had robbed the unsuspecting Mexicas of the best of their military leadership—one almost wonders if Alvarado's diabolical massacre had the implicit approval of the absent Cortés, since it did irreparable harm to the Aztec cause. Thousands more of the warrior nobles were dead or severely wounded from the week of fighting in late June. The Mexicas' most powerful emperor was shamefully killed when (or immediately after) addressing his subjects. Vital tribute was permanently interrupted. Hundreds of houses inside Tenochtitlán had been burned, and dozens of shrines looted and desecrated.

In the battle's aftermath the shell-shocked Mexicas were busy back in Tenochtitlán, as if the danger was at last past, cleaning up the mess in their streets, glad to be rid of these murderous interlopers and their terrible propensity to destroy almost everything they touched. More important than the considerable Mexica losses was a series of seven separate squadrons of Spanish ships on the seas headed for Vera Cruz, in transit with more powder, crossbows, horses, and cannon from Cuba and Spain, filled with desperate men sniffing profit and ready to join in on the rumored goldfest.

Cortés knew that the slaughter of so many Spanish kinsmen, and the subsequent rumors of human sacrifice and the eating of flesh, would enrage the proud Castilians and call forth each man's sense of honor to return and bring fire and ruin to these cannibalistic infidels. Cortés had sized up the Aztec way of war: their emphasis was on capturing rather than on killing; their weapons could stun but rarely kill without repeated blows. Aztec warriors preferred individual sword- and clubplay, rather than mass tactics of shock assault in disciplined ranks and files. Their brigades centered around gaudy, feather-clad, banner-carrying lieutenants whose death might send their regional musters fleeing in terror. The commander in chief was remote and mostly apart from his men in battle. The Aztec army was even more hated by other natives than were the Castilians.

Cortés was now on dry land, away from the infernal causeways and the canoes, with room for his horses and phalanxes of swordsmen. In his fear and depression after the *Noche Triste* he did not yet realize amid the slaughter of his Castilians and Tlaxcalans that there were still thousands of Indians—Tepanecs, Totonacs, Chalcans, and fresh Tlaxcalans—who were not yet ready to join the Aztecs, but wavering still. Many were secretly eager for the Castilians to return to Tenochtitlán.

To Cortés the *Noche Triste* had been a great defeat. But for the most stalwart of the Aztecs' native enemies, who provided food for the tables of the Aztec elite and their own bodies for the infernal Aztec gods, the thought that the caudillo's army had pranced its way into the fortress city, kidnapped the hated emperor, and slaughtered thousands of Aztecs on their retreat was cause for wonder, not contempt. The tales that flew across the Valley of Mexico were not all of Aztec triumph over the Castilians; they also emphasized that the audacious and lethal white men had slashed their way out to safety along the frightful causeways. The reports stressed the butchery of the thousands of Aztecs, not merely the hundreds of Castilians killed. The new Aztec emperor, Cuitláhuac, might claim that his display cases of flayed skins and skulls were those of Cortés, Sandoval, and Alvarado, but the truth soon emerged that all three legendary killers were alive and determined to return. Even the Aztec ambassadors' confident tales that some forty-five Castilians left behind in Tlaxcala had been waylaid and slaughtered en route to the coast made little impression. As the wavering tribes of Mexico weighed the odds and nursed their grievances over the yearly human tribute demanded by the Aztecs, a great many would prefer Castilian to Aztec brutality—and perhaps the strange Jesus Christ of the white killers they did not know to the bloodthirsty Huitzilopochtli they were only too familiar with.

Finally, it was rumored that a recent European arrival on the coast—purportedly an African slave from Narváez's contingent—was ailing from smallpox. The Castilians, on the verge of extinction in summer 1520, had thus gained a new and unforeseen ally: a lethal bacillus amid a population without much immunity. New germs among people who slept in group huts, who were largely urban rather than rural dwellers, who communally ate and washed together, and who had neither biological nor cultural experience with European epidemics would soon wipe out hundreds of thousands—friendly, neutral, and hostile alike—killing far more Aztec warriors than the Toledo blades of the Castilians. On the morning of July 2, wet, wounded, and facing annihilation, little did Cortés and his pathetic band at Tlacopán know that in a few months his men would not only regain their reputation as the dreaded strangers with steel blades and thundering weapons but once again take on the appearance of supermen whom alone this terrible new curse of angry gods did not infect.

So Cortés on this July 2, 1520, gathered his men together and for the next few days lumbered out under constant harassment. Finally, about halfway back to the safety of the Tlaxcalans, at the small village of Otumba, the new Mexica emperor, Cuitláhuac, and his vast army caught up with the Castilians. The Spanish annals later claimed that 40,000 were assembled, a plausible number given the change of heart among the surrounding villages in the immediate vicinity of Tenochtitlán. The Mexicas quickly surrounded Cortés's men and for the next six hours gradually beat them down, inasmuch as there were fewer than twenty horses left, all were wounded, and they were without cannon or harquebuses. Even skeptics concede that Cortés's Spaniards may have been outnumbered on the Plain of Otumba by as much as a hundred to one.

As the Spaniards were nearing obliteration, Cortés spotted the commander of the Aztec line, the *cihuacoatl*, and his subordinates decked out in bright colors and gaudy feathers, the leader himself carrying the Aztec plumed standard on his back. Díaz del Castillo notes that Cortés was unimpressed by the terrible insignia, but instead selected Sandoval, Olid, Ávila, Alvarado, and Juan de Salamanca—the most deadly lancers of the age—and rode with them into the throng. "When Cortés saw him with many other Mexican chieftains all wearing great plumes, he said to our Captains: 'Now, Señores, let us break through them and leave none of them unwounded' " (B. Díaz del Castillo, *The Discovery and Conquest of Mexico*, 320). Despite vast numerical superiority and the recent victory on the causeways, the Aztecs were defenseless against mounted attacks on the plains and dense ranks of swordsmen—and the Plain of Otumba was tailor-made for Spanish horsemen. None of the Mexicas had ever encountered a mounted enemy that charged directly at their *cihuacoatl*. With their leader torn apart by the lancers, and the Aztec war banner in Spanish hands, thousands fled back to Tenochtitlán.

The battle at Otumba, coming as it did just eight days after the *Noche Triste*, was in many ways Cortés's greatest victory. In a famous passage William Prescott noted the role of discipline, military science, and the personal leadership of Hernán Cortés in the sudden reversal of Aztec fortune (Cuitláhuac, as Montezuma before, kept out of the fighting):

> The Indians were in all their strength, while the Christians were wasted by disease, famine, and long protracted sufferings; without cannon or firearms, and deficient in the military apparatus which had so often struck terror into their barbarian foe,—deficient even in the terrors of a victorious name. But they had discipline on their side, desperate resolve, and implicit confidence in their commander. (*History of the Conquest of Mexico*, 465)

When at last Cortés fought his way to safety at Tlaxcala, many of his men, especially the few surviving late-comers who had joined him after defecting from his archenemy Narváez, were spent and tired of Mexico. Most were ready to march to Vera Cruz to find passage back to Cuba. Others were furious that Juan Páez, left behind in Tlaxcala when Cortés entered Tenochtitlán, had stayed put—although he had a force of thousands of Tlaxcalans who were eager to march to the relief of the beleaguered conquistadors when they learned that they and their kinsmen were trapped in the Aztec capital. In addition, news reached the exhausted army of the ambush and slaughter of an auxiliary of forty-five Spaniards who had attempted to reach Vera Cruz.

Then Cortés only made things worse: he announced that he would confiscate all the gold carried out of the city to pay for provisions. He also forbade any of the survivors to march to the coast to find a ship home. Francisco López de Gómara wrote of their grumbling:

> What does Cortés think he is doing? Why does he want to keep us here to die the evil death? What has he got against us that he won't let us go? Our

heads are broken, our bodies are rotting and covered with wounds and sores, bloodless, weak, and naked. We are in a strange land, poor, sick, surrounded by enemies, and without hope of rising from the spot where we fall. We would be fools and idiots if we should let ourselves in for another risk like the past one. Unlike him, we do not wish to die a fool's death, for he, in his insatiable thirst for glory and authority, thinks nothing of dying himself, and still less of our death. He does not consider the fact that he is without men, guns, arms, and horses (which bear the brunt of war), and has no provisions, which is the worst lack of all. (*Cortés*, 228)

No one could envision that in a mere thirteen months Hernán Cortés would return to Tenochtitlán, kill thousands, and then end the Aztec nation forever.

The Destruction of Tenochtitlán—April 28–August 13, 1521

Once the Castilians reached safety at the Tlaxcalan town of Hueyotlipan on July 9, 1520, their plight improved incrementally during the rest of the year. In July the Tlaxcalans agreed to a perpetual alliance—they had the wherewithal to muster nearly 50,000 warriors from their allied domains—in exchange for a share of the booty from Tenochtitlán, perpetual relief from tribute, and a fortified presence inside the city once the Aztec capital was conquered. During August Cortés re-formed his army and at the head of thousands of Tlaxcalans stormed the fortress of Tepeaca and began systematically to overrun its surrounding villages. In September the brilliant Martín López was given the best craftsmen in the army, thousands of Tlaxcalan workers, and the salvaged hardware from the destroyed ships in Vera Cruz, and told to build fourteen brigantines that could be dismantled, carried over the mountains to Tenochtitlán, reassembled, and then launched on Lake Texcoco.

By the end of that month the virulent smallpox epidemic had made its way from Vera Cruz to Tenochtitlán. Thousands of Mexicas began dying from what they at first thought was a mysterious skin ailment. Years later Mexica survivors related to Bernardino de Sahagún the terrible symptoms; he in turn recorded their accounts in near Thucydidean fashion:

Sores erupted on our faces, our breasts, our bellies; we were covered with agonizing sores from head to foot. The illness was so dreadful that no one could walk or move. The sick were so utterly helpless that they could only

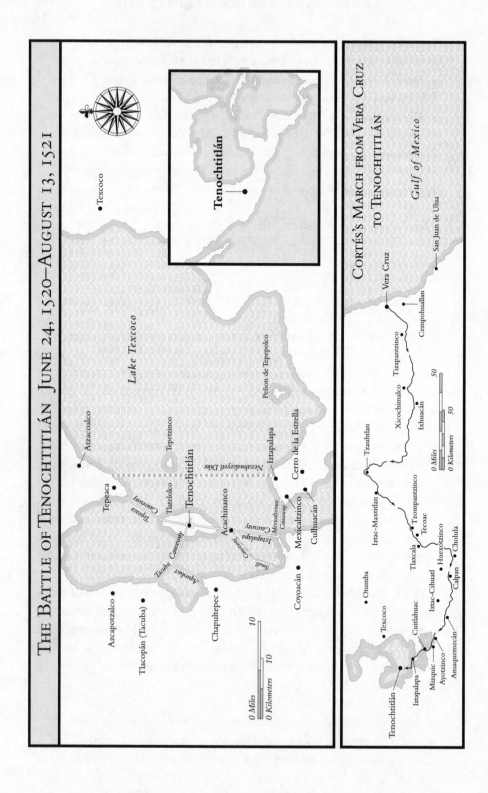

THE BATTLE OF TENOCHTITLÁN JUNE 24, 1520–AUGUST 13, 1521

Texcoco

Lake Texcoco

Tenochtitlán

Atzacoalco

Tepetzinco

Tlatelolco

Tepeaca

Tepeaca Causeway

Tacuba Causeway

Small Causeway

Iztapalapa Causeway

Aqueduct

Acachinanco

Mexicalzinco Causeway

Peñón de Tepepolco

Nezahualcoyotl Dike

Iztapalapa

Cerro de la Estrella

Mexicalzinco

Culhuacán

Coyoacán

Chapultepec

Azcapotzalco

Tlacopán (Tacuba)

0 Miles   10

0 Kilometers   10

Tenochtitlán

CORTÉS'S MARCH FROM VERA CRUZ TO TENOCHTITLÁN

Gulf of Mexico

San Juan de Ulua

Vera Cruz

Cempohuallan

Tizapantzinco

Xicochimalco

Ishuacán

Tzauhtlan

Iztac-Maxtitlan

Tzompantzinco

Tecoac

Tlaxala

Huexotzinco

Cholula

Calpan

Otumba

Texcoco

Cuitlahuac

Iztac-Cihuatl

Amaquemecán

Ayotzinco

Mizquic

Iztapalapa

Tenochtitlán

0 Miles   50

0 Kilometers   50

lie on their beds like corpses, unable to move their limbs or even their heads. They could not lie face down or roll from one side to the other. If they did move their bodies, they screamed with pain. A great many died from this plague and many others of hunger. They could not get up to search for food, and everyone else was too sick to care for them, so they starved to death in their beds. Some people came down with a milder form of the disease; they suffered less than the others and made a good recovery. But they could not escape entirely. Their looks were ravaged, for wherever a sore broke out, it gouged an ugly pockmark in the skin. And a few of the survivors were left completely blind. (M. León-Portilla, ed., *The Broken Spears*, 85–86)

Montezuma's successor, Cuitláhuac, who had attacked Cortés at Otumba, fell to the disease and was replaced by the younger and more audacious Cuauhtémoc. The latter would eventually surrender a destroyed Tenochtitlán—the third Aztec emperor in less than a year to deal with Hernán Cortés.

This strange sequence of events that gradually turned Cortés's ruined army into a terrible force of vengeance against the Aztecs continued unabated. In the late fall of 1520 seven squadrons of ships docked in Vera Cruz, adding another two hundred men to Cortés's remnant of four hundred to five hundred conquistadors. For the first time in six months, there were fresh horses and plenty of powder, cannon, harquebuses, and crossbows. Cortés, in addition, sent ships to Hispaniola and Jamaica for even more horses and arms. Meanwhile, for much of December 1520 while he was putting down the Tepeacans, the ever-dependable Sandoval had conquered all the tribes between Tlaxcala and the coast, and thus ensured safe transit of supplies from Vera Cruz to the conquistadors' headquarters in Tlaxcala. If the huge city of Tenochtitlán was amply supplied by water transport, the Spanish had the entire Atlantic to draw in supplies in safety at Vera Cruz. But whereas Cortés could build a fleet to cut off the canoes of Tenochtitlán, no Aztec warrior had a clue how to prevent the "floating mountains" from docking at Vera Cruz with even more of the infernal whiteskins and their thunderous weapons.

By new year 1521, Cortés had pacified most of the hostile tribes between Vera Cruz and Tenochtitlán and had gained plentiful supplies and additional soldiers. He was in the midst of an enormous shipbuilding program to ensure naval protection when his infantry and cavalry returned to the causeways on the lake. Cortés may have started his march back to Tenochtitlán with some 550 Spanish infantrymen—still only half as many Castilians who had fled the city the prior June—including 80 harquebusiers and crossbowmen, along with at least forty fresh horses and nine new cannon. In addition, he selected 10,000 of the best Tlaxcalan warriors, as preparations were made for the march on the satellite cities that surrounded Tenochtitlán. By early April 1521 the new army was on the outskirts of the Mexica capital, the ships were readied for launching, and roving parties had systematically begun to cut off food and water supplies to the city. This second offensive had none of the pretense of conciliation and alliance of the first "visit." After the *Noche Triste* Cortés was intent on either obtaining the unconditional surrender of the new emperor, Cuauhtémoc, and his people or defeating the Aztec army in battle. Should the Aztecs not capitulate, the Castilians would destroy Tenochtitlán block by block and turn it over to the Tlaxcalans to loot—reminiscent of the manner in which Alexander had leveled Thebes and then allowed the surrounding Boeotians to rob, enslave, and kill the survivors with impunity.

In late April, after six months of constant campaigning in the surrounding countryside to amputate the Aztec tributary empire, Cortés's reconstituted army was back on the causeways and blockading Tenochtitlán. Most of the cities on the lakeshore and in the Valley of Mexico were subdued or had joined Cortés. A year earlier it may have been unwise for the Spanish to enter an island fortress city, but now Cortés was eager to prove it was even more foolish for the Mexicas to stay in it, as the Castilians' former besiegers would become the besieged. By April 28, 1521, Martín López's flat-bottomed brigantines—masted, oared, decked with cannon, and bristling with crossbowmen and harquebusiers—were over the mountains, reassembled, and launched on Lake Texcoco, ensuring that the Aztec canoes could no longer attack the Castilians on the causeways. In a world without horses or oxen—or even the wheel—an enormous city of a quarter million like Tenochtitlán could only be supplied by water. Indeed, its daily survival depended on tons of maize, fish, fruits, and vegetables shipped over the lake by thousands of canoes. The destruction of that fleet would not only cripple Aztec military power but starve the city into submission.

With shouts of "Castilla, Castilla, Tlaxcala, Tlaxcala!" Cortés led his Spanish-Indian army toward Tenochtitlán itself. While contemporary observers put the coalition's size at nearly half a million, the invading army more likely numbered around 50,000 to 75,000. With last-minute reinforcements from Vera Cruz, it was spearheaded by some 700 to 800 Castilian foot soldiers, 90 horsemen, 120 crossbowmen and harquebusiers, and three large cannon, as well as smaller falconets and the fire-power of the fourteen brigantines. Many Castilians also had new steel helmets, swords, occasional breastplates, and shields, in addition to spare parts for their firearms.

Cortés's plan was simple. His three veteran knights—Alvardo, Olid, and Sandoval—would each lead a quarter of the army along the three main levees into the city. The causeway to Tlacopán would for a while be left open but guarded, to allow fugitives to flee the siege. Cortés himself would take the fourth component and embark on the brigantines, with some three hundred Castilians, about twenty-five men to a ship. In addition, thousands of Texcocans and Tlaxcalans would follow in boats—Ixtlilxochitl, the leader of the Texcocans, would later claim his people manned 16,000 canoes in Cortés's armada. The combined fleet would aid the three land assaults, enforce the blockade, and destroy the enemy vessels.

By June 1, 1521, Cortés had cut entirely the city's supply of fresh water and stormed the island fortress of Tepepolco, which the Mexicas used to coordinate their attacks on the multipronged Castilian invasions. The Spaniards deemed that the siege had officially begun on May 30, when they had blockaded the city's sources of supply—later memorializing the destruction of Tenochtitlán as "the seventy-five days" between May 30 and August 13, 1521. But progress remained difficult for the rest of the summer as the Aztecs still vastly outnumbered the invaders. They placed sharp sticks in the mud of the lake to tear up the brigantines and swarmed all over the flagship, the *Capitana*. Had it not been for the courageous Martín López—in some ways the most impressive of Cortés's men—and a small group of swordsmen, who rallied to expel the Aztec boarders and slaughter those who would bind and drag off the caudillo, both the *Capitana* and its captain would have been captured.

The Castilians were also learning that they not only had to defeat the Aztec army but had to storm the city and raze it to the ground if they were to crush all resistance. The four-pronged Spanish attack would slowly advance along the causeways, enter the suburbs, and then retreat back to safety during the evening. Success was determined by the degree to which Cortés could fill in breaches in the dikes and keep the causeways intact. That way, the Spaniards could move freely, as they began to dismantle the city blocks of Tenochtitlán, tearing down temples, walls, and houses. Gradually, the horsemen, crossbowmen, and harquebusiers gained room to operate and found clear lines of fire, while eliminating the source of ambushes in corners and narrow streets. Cortés drew on 2,000 years of

European siegecraft—the ancient Hellenic science of poliorcetics ("fenc-ing in the polis")—that addressed the target city's supply of water, food, and sanitation, as artillery, sorties, and missile attack were concentrated on weak places in the Aztec defenses to augment nature's assault of hunger and plague.

If the Spanish proceeded too far inside Tenochtitlán proper—where they could be ambushed and swarmed, while their levees of retreat were breached—they faced annihilation. But if the brigantines kept the cause-ways passable, then each day the attackers could cross into the city, destroy another block or two, kill hundreds more Aztecs, and then retreat during the night to their fortified compounds. Usually, foot soldiers advanced, supported by the fire of cannon, harquebuses, and crossbows, slashing away at the unarmored Aztecs with their Toledo blades. At key moments, dozens of mounted mailed lancers would charge concentrations of the enemy or ambush the Mexicas when at dusk they rashly pursued the re-treating foot soldiers. By late June the emperor, Cuauhtémoc, had seen the futility of Aztec tactics and radically revised his defenses by removing most of the surviving population of Tenochtitlán proper—warriors, civil-ians, and even the idols and effigies of the gods from the Great Temple—to the adjoining northern island suburb of Tlatelolco. This was a wise move: the change of defense drew in the Spaniards, who wrongly believed the Aztecs were defeated and fleeing. In addition, the Castilians were un-aware that Tlatelolco was a far more crowded precinct, far more suitable for urban warfare than the broad avenues of the mostly destroyed Tenochtitlán.

The key to the entire struggle was to deny the Spaniards room for their horses to charge, space for their infantry to form into ranks, and clear lines of vision for their artillery and firearms. Now as the battle shifted to Tlatelolco, the Tlatelolcons joined the Aztecs in swarming the Castilians in the winding and narrow streets and cutting the causeways to the mainland. Cortés himself was unhorsed and for the third time nearly dragged off; Cristóbal de Olea and an unnamed Tlaxcalan hacked away at the enraged Mexicas, severing their hands and thus saving their caudillo. In the initial ambush at Tlatelolco, more than fifty Spaniards were bound and dragged off and twenty more killed, as thousands of Tlaxcalans paid for the Castilians' impetuosity by being killed or captured. One brigantine was sunk and another precious cannon lost.

The Mexicas immediately beheaded some of their captives, waving them in front of the retreating Spaniards, claiming them to be Cortés and his officers: "So we shall kill you, as we have killed Malinche and

Sandoval." Once the Spaniards reached safety, the sound of drums was heard. Bernal Díaz del Castillo recalls what followed:

> When they got them up to a small square in front of the oratory, where their accursed idols are kept, we saw them place plumes on the heads of many of them and with things like fans in their hands they forced them to dance before Huichilobos, and after they had danced they immediately placed them on their backs on some rather narrow stones which had been prepared as places for sacrifice, and with stone knives they sawed open their chests and drew out their palpitating hearts and offered them to the idols that were there, and they kicked the bodies down the steps, and Indian butchers who were waiting below cut off the arms and feet and flayed the skin off the faces, and prepared it afterwards like glove leather with the beards on, and kept those for the festivals when they celebrated drunken orgies, and the flesh they ate in chilmole. (*The Discovery and Conquest of Mexico*, 436)

The Spanish feared a repeat of the *Noche Triste*. The Mexicas yelled at the Tlaxcalans, throwing them roasted legs of their captured brethren and pieces of the Castilians. "Eat of the flesh of these Teules [Castilians] and of your brothers, for we are already glutted with it, and you can stuff yourselves with this" (*The Discovery and Conquest of Mexico*, 437). When news spread throughout Cortés's Indian alliance that the Aztecs were eating Spanish flesh, and dozens of bound conquistadors were feathered and marched up the steps of the pyramid to their deaths, nearly the entire Indian alliance suddenly collapsed. Most indigenous leaders feared the return of the Aztec terror, realizing that the Europeans themselves were as vulnerable before the hungry Aztec gods as they themselves had been before the Spanish arrival. Meanwhile, Cortés and his men nursed their wounds and regrouped as Cuauhtémoc rallied his allies, sought new support, and sent the body parts of captured Castilians and their horses among the villages around Lake Texcoco as proof of the Spaniards' failure. But then an odd thing happened—or perhaps a predictable occurrence, given the earlier Mexica failure to follow up immediately on the morning after the *Noche Triste*. The Aztecs for most of July did not storm the beleaguered Spanish compounds. Hunger, disease, the great destruction of their city, and thousands of battle casualties had decimated their army. Once again, it was almost as if the Aztecs were dispirited after their dramatic victory. Killing and sacrificing Castilians did not stop the invaders, even as Cortés grew more confident after a setback.

By the latter part of July the wearied Aztecs could no longer cut the dikes, thereby ensuring the Castilians free access in and out of Tenochtitlán and Tlatelolco. Supplies from Vera Cruz reached Cortés uninterrupted. His men fabricated additional gunpowder by lowering themselves into Mount Popocatépetl to fetch the critical ingredient of sulfur. Aztec deserters confirmed that Tenochtitlán was starving and the eighteen-year-old emperor increasingly unable to marshal an effective resistance. Cortés in his famous third letter to Charles V described the desperate plight of the Aztecs:

> The people of the city had to walk upon their dead while others swam or drowned in the waters of that wide lake where they had their canoes; indeed, so great was their suffering that it was beyond our understanding how they could endure it. Countless numbers of men, women, and children came toward us, and in their eagerness to escape many were pushed into the water where they drowned amid the multitude of corpses; and it seemed that more than fifty thousand had perished from the salt water they had drunk, their hunger and the vile stench. So that we should not discover the plight in which they were in, they dared neither throw these bodies into the water where the brigantines might find them nor throw them beyond their boundaries where the soldiers might see them, and so in those streets where they were we came across such piles of the dead that we were forced to walk upon them. (*Letters from Mexico*, 263–64)

Castilian horsemen roamed the dikes at will and slaughtered hundreds who emerged from their hovels in Tlatelolco searching for food. The Tlaxcalans became increasingly hard to rein in; they roamed the city butchering—and occasionally eating—any of the Mexicas they found. On August 13 Sandoval and García Holguín caught Cuauhtémoc fleeing in a canoe. Both fought over honors for the prize of his capture, prompting Cortés to intervene, in the manner, he mused, that Marius and Sulla had fought over the shackled Numidian king Jugurtha. Fernando de Alva Ixtlilxochitl, a descendant of the allied prince of Texcoco, Ixtlilxochitl, who wrote a history from the allied Indian side decades after the conquest, related Cuauhtémoc's surrender speech.

> Ah Captain, I have already done everything in my power to defend my kingdom and free it from your hands. And since my fortune has not been favorable, take my life, which would be very just. And with this you will put

an end to the Mexican Kingdom, since you have destroyed my kingdom and vassals. (*Ally of Cortés*, 52)

Cortés would spare the young emperor, then drag him along during his disastrous expedition to Honduras—only shamelessly to hang him in transit in 1523 on trumped-up charges that he was inciting revolt among the Indian allies.

Since the city had been cut off in late May, more than 100,000 Aztecs had fallen in the fighting, along with at least a hundred Castilians and 20,000 Indian allies. But that was a small percentage of the actual losses in the two-year struggle for Mexico City. Disease, hunger, and constant fighting had essentially wiped out the population of Tenochtitlán. The final tally of the dead would eventually reach more than 1 million of the peoples surrounding Lake Texcoco. In the entire two-year campaign since Cortés had marched in from Vera Cruz, Spanish losses were no more than 1,000 out of some 1,600 who had at various times fought for Tenochtitlán.

The eventual carnage was to be even more appalling. In the ensuing decades smallpox was followed by measles, bubonic plague, then flu, whooping cough, and mumps, reducing the population of central Mexico from more than 8 million when Cortés landed to well below a million a half century later. In less than two years Cortés and his tiny army had inaugurated a chain of events that changed the face of an entire subcontinent and destroyed a civilization.

AZTEC WAR

Misconceptions and stereotypes abound concerning the Aztecs at war. Too often Mesoamericans are seen as little more than bizarre savages who fought in hordes solely to facilitate human sacrifice on a vast scale, captive-takers whose queer rules of engagement preempted real killing on the battlefield. More recently, apologists have reinvented them as New World Greeks whose impressive architecture symbolized an enlightened and progressive civilization that did not really sacrifice or eat fellow humans, and saw no reason to craft military technology they did not need. In fact, the Aztecs were neither Greeks nor savages, but shrewd theocratic imperialists who had ruthlessly created a loosely knit political empire based on the perception of terror, backed up by a deadly army, and fueled by a vast system of tribute.

What differentiated Aztec from European warfare were its far greater cultural and geographical constraints. Without horses or oxen, or even the wheel, the operational range of Aztec armies was limited by the amount of food and supplies their human porters could carry along. As Tenochtitlán expanded its influence in Mesoamerica, as the size of the city grew, and as war became even more predictable, the political organization of the entire Mexican subcontinent grew more vulnerable to attack: Europeans might topple the entire imperial structure by decapitating a tiny elite on an island city, which needed thousands of tons of food shipped in daily for its very survival.

Wars ceased for brief periods between October and April—precisely the time Cortés entered Tenochtitlán in November 1519—to allow agricultural laborers to work the harvests. Fighting was rare altogether in the rainy period between May and September, while battle at night was also discouraged. In contrast, the Spaniards, as a maritime people in a temperate climate, and as veterans of the murderous wars in Europe and on the Mediterranean, were willing and able to fight year round, day or night, at home and abroad, on land and sea, with few natural or human restrictions.

Many confrontations between the Aztecs and their neighbors began as "flower wars" (xochiyaoyotl). These staged contests, without much killing between elite warriors of either side, revealed Aztec superiority—through the greater training, zeal, and battle experience of its warriors—hence the futility of real armed insurrection. Should the enemy persist in resistance, flower wars might escalate into full-fledged battles of conquest designed to defeat an enemy outright and annex its territory. In that regard, we should assume that the creation of the Aztec empire had resulted in hundreds of thousands of Mesoamericans killed in wars during the fifteenth century alone.

Whereas Mesoamerican warriors were adept at handling weapons, there were two further factors that inhibited their ability to slay enemy soldiers in vast numbers outright. In all wars the taking of captives for human sacrifices was important proof of individual battle excellence and social status and was deemed critical to the religious health of the community at large. More often still, sacrifices were shrewd occasions for nightmarish intimidation, spectacles of bloodletting to warn potential adversaries of the consequences of resistance. For example, the Aztec king Ahuitzotl purportedly organized the butchery of 80,400 prisoners during a four-day blood sacrifice at the 1487 inauguration of the Great Temple to Huitzilopochtli in Tenochtitlán—an enormous challenge in industrialized murder in its own right. Ahuitzotl's killing rate of fourteen victims a minute over the ninety-six-hour bloodbath far exceeded the daily murder record at either Auschwitz or Dachau. The presence of four convex killing tables—so arranged that the victims could be easily kicked down the pyramid—turned human sacrifice into an assembly-line process. Companies of fresh executioners periodically replaced those exhausted from the repeated obsidian-blade strokes, to ensure that the entire train of victims could be dispatched during the festival. We do not know the number of victims otherwise sacrificed under normal conditions, but surely it was in the thousands. Ixtlilxochitl believed that one of every five children of Mexica tributaries was killed each year, though Bishop Don Carlos Zumárraga's lower estimate of 20,000 a year is more plausible. Oddly, few scholars have ever likened the Aztec propensity to wipe out thousands of their neighbors through carefully organized killing to the Nazi extermination of Jews, Gypsies, and other eastern Europeans.

Although under dire circumstances Aztecs could fight to the death, the warrior's training in the methods of stunning, binding, and passing back captives through the ranks would prove an impediment against the Spanish. Scholars who argue that the Aztecs quickly dropped their notions of ritual fighting against Cortés are correct, but they must concede that years of such military training were hard for many warriors to discard in a few months—especially when pitted against Spanish swordsmen and pikemen who had drilled since adolescence in the art of killing with a single stroke.

To what degree such rituals were predicated on technological constraints we cannot be sure, but the tools of Aztec warfare—oak, stone, flint, obsidian, hide, and cotton—were incapable in themselves of killing warriors in any great numbers. Broadswords *(machuahuitl)* and spears *(tepoztopilli)* were wooden, with flakes of obsidian embedded along their double cutting edges. Both could match the sharpness of metal, but only for a few strokes before chipping or losing their edge. Aztec swords were without points, while the stone heads of lances likewise made them poor thrusting weapons.

Since the aristocratic infantry arm of the Aztec military was singularly inefficient against Spanish foot soldiers and cavalry, native commanders depended upon an array of missile weapons that might penetrate the unprotected arms, legs, necks, and faces of Cortés's men. A peculiar type of spear-thrower *(atlatl)* was made from a wooden stick about two feet in length, with grooves and hook at one end in which to place the projectile. Fire-hardened darts *(tlacochti)* were occasionally flint-tipped; when used with the *atlatl* these missiles could achieve accurate ranges of 150 feet. But they were essentially useless against metal armor and at great distances incapable of tearing even through layered cotton. The Aztecs used simple, rather than composite, bows *(tlahuitolli)*. While they could achieve a rapid rate of fire with more than twenty arrows *(yaomitl)* per quiver, such weapons lacked the penetrating power and distance of European models that since classical antiquity had been fabricated from glued horn, hide, and wood.

Many accounts testify to the danger of Aztec stone missiles; and while native slingers were without metal bullets and sophisticated slings, nevertheless they were able to wound unprotected flesh at ranges approaching a hundred yards. The Aztecs' wood, hide, and feathered shields, like cotton war suits, might ward off Mesoamerican stone blades but were of no value against Toledo steel, metal crossbow bolts, or harquebus shot. It is an accurate generalization that Montezuma's arms were of an inferior caliber to the artillery, missile weapons, body armor, and offensive armament of Alexander the Great's army some eighteen centuries prior.

Mexico had all the natural resources necessary for a sophisticated arms industry. There was no shortage of plentiful iron ores at Taxco. Copper was in abundance in Michoacán. The volcano Popocatépetl furnished supplies of sulfur. Indeed, within a year of the conquest Cortés himself, against the edicts of the crown, was producing gunpowder and casting muskets and even large cannon in the former domains of the Aztecs. Why amid such a cornucopia of ingredients for munitions did the Mexicas produce only clubs, blades of obsidian chips, and javelins and bows and arrows? The most popular explanations suggest need. Because Aztec warfare was designed largely to capture rather than kill, stone blades were sufficient against similarly armed Mesoamericans. The implication is that the Aztecs *could* have fabricated weapons comparable to the Europeans', but saw no need for such additional expense in their brand of ritually crafted warfare whose aim was to stun rather than cause death. Yet such claims of latent technological know-how are preposterous for a culture without a sophisticated rational tradition of natural inquiry. The opposite is more likely to be true: the Aztecs had no ability to craft metals or firearms and so were forced to fight ritual wars with weapons that would largely wound and not easily kill. Against a large and fierce army such as the Tlaxcalans, it is hard to envision how the Aztecs, despite vast numerical superiority, might have waged a war of annihilation with nonmetallic weapons—explaining why Tlaxcala was largely autonomous, and settled its disputes with the Aztecs through quasi-ceremonial flower wars.

Aztec battle, like Zulu fighting or the attacks of Germanic tribes, was one of envelopment. Swarms of warriors systematically attempted to surround the enemy, the front lines mobbing and stunning their adversaries, before passing them through the rear ranks to be bound and led off. The ensuing need to march prisoners back with the army also contributed to the Aztecs' inability to campaign at large distances, since the combined throng of victors and defeated only increased logistical requirements. While there was a national Aztec army, in fact local contingents thronged around their own captains and might exit the field altogether should their leaders or standards go down. Francisco de Aguilar relates the desperate fighting at Otumba, after the *Noche Triste:*

> As Cortés battled his way among the Indians, performing marvels in singling out and killing their captains who were distinguishable by their gold shields, and disregarding the common warriors, he was able to reach their captain general and kill him with a thrust of a lance. . . . While this was going on, we foot soldiers under Diego de Ordaz were completely surrounded by Indians, who almost had their hands on us, but when Captain Hernándo Cortés killed their captain general they began to retreat and give way to us, so that few of them pursued us. (P. de Fuentes, *Conquistadors,* 156)

Relays of soldiers might enter the fray every fifteen minutes or so, as there was no concept of decisive shock battle in which heavily armed foot soldiers sought to collide head-on with the enemy at the first encounter. Ranks and files were nonexistent; warriors failed to charge and retreat in step or on command; missiles and arrows were not launched in volleys. Nor were missile troops used in concert with infantry charges. Without horses, Aztec battle doctrine was largely a one-dimensional affair, in which the greater training and numbers of the emperor's warriors, together with the pomp and circumstance of feathered warriors and standards, were enough to collapse or scare off resistance.

Finally, Aztec society was far more ranked than even aristocratic sixteenth-century Spain. The weapons, training, armor, and position in battle of most Mexica warriors were predicated on birth and status. In a cyclical pattern of cause and effect, such greater innate advantages gave aristocrats predominance on the battlefield in taking captives, which in turn provided proof of their martial excellence—and then led again to even more privilege. The Spanish were a class-bound society as well, but during the invasion, a variety of lowly conquistadors mounted horses as the military situation demanded. Harquebuses, crossbows, and steel blades were distributed freely throughout the army. The fuel that drove Cortés's army was not so much aristocratic privilege as a desperate desire by both hidalgos and the impoverished to acquire enough money and fame to advance upward in Castilian society. On the battlefield itself, the result was that in matters of weapons, tactics, recruitment, and leadership the Spanish army operated on meritocratic principles of sheer killing: men and tools were trained and designed to dismember people first and provide social advancement, prestige, and religious rewards second. Killing was more likely to result in status than status was in killing.

THE MIND OF THE CONQUISTADORS

The brutal conquistadors ("the conquerors") who followed Hernán Cortés into the valley of Tenochtitlán seem at first glance a poor representation of the Western rationalist tradition. Many of the most notorious were fanatical Castilian Christians who lived in a Manichean world of absolute good versus evil. Sixteenth-century Spain under Charles V was in the midst of the Inquisition (begun officially in 1481), and witch burning, torture, and secret tribunals terrorized the countryside. Jews, Moors, and Protestants were fair game, in addition to Catholics of dubious faith who were accused of anything from bathing daily to reading imported literature. Unwavering adherence to a beleaguered orthodox Catholicism was expected of all in royal service, and was the ideology of almost every conquistador who sailed westward—sometimes to the detriment of military and political logic.

Cortés and his followers, when surrounded by an enemy of some 200,000 Mexicas in the middle of Tenochtitlán, insanely demanded of Montezuma that he cast down Aztec idols so that his subjects might convert en masse to Christianity. Catholic priests were ubiquitous in the New World; various Dominicans, Franciscans, and Jeronymite friars were given imperial powers of audit to ensure that the Indians were converted to Christianity, rather than gratuitously slaughtered. What they saw—the tearing out of beating hearts from sacrificial victims, rooms smeared with human blood, racks of skulls, priests with flayed human skins on their backs—terrified the Spanish priests. They were convinced that the Aztecs and their neighbors were satanic, their rites of human sacrifice and cannibalism the work of the Antichrist. An anonymous conquistador summed up the Spanish revulsion:

All the people of this province of New Spain, and even those of the neigh-boring provinces, eat human flesh and value it more highly than any other food in the world; so much so, that they often go off to war and risk their lives just to kill people to eat. The majority of them, as I have said, are sodomites and they drink to excess. (P. de Fuentes, *The Conquistadors*, 181)

To protect the tiny forces of Christendom from the contamination of these purported legions of darkness, mass, confession, and absolution were prerequisites of the Spanish before battle. Throughout the vicious two-year campaigning the conquistadors were convinced that a series of supernatural beings hovered in protection over their heads. Shrines soon dotted the Mexican landscape to thank the Virgin and various saints for victories and salvation from Aztec infidels. The conquest was as much to convert souls as to gain gold and ground, the church's de facto attitude of-ten being that the conquistadors' killing was wrong and counterproduc-tive, but that Mexicas were better off dead than as live practicing agents of the devil.

Martin Luther was excommunicated in the year Cortés first occupied Tenochtitlán, yet nascent Protestantism and its accompanying debate about religious doctrine would find no receptive audience back in con-temporary Castile. A mere three decades before Cortés set foot in Mexico Ferdinand and Isabella had at last finished the four-century-long *Reconquista,* by uniting Aragon and Castile and expelling the Moors from Granada in 1492, establishing in the struggle the modern nation-state of Spain. For much of the subsequent century the crown was busy putting down insurrection in southern Spain among the Moriscos, who agitated for a return of Islamic rule. Moreover, due to its presence near Italy and North Africa, Spain also found itself a frontline state in the European re-sistance to the Ottoman onslaught, as well as bogged down in its periodic fighting against the Italian city-states and the rebellious Dutch. Thus, the grim veterans who landed at Vera Cruz were a world away from the farm-ers and religious exiles who landed off Plymouth Rock.

Christian fanaticism and strict Catholicism were the bedrock defenses of southern Mediterranean cultures besieged by Islamic enemies to the south and east, and the newer Protestant adversaries of northern Europe. Protestant Europeans were far from the front lines of Islamic attack; and, without the strong traditions of adherence to a centralized autocrat in Rome, they might find religious reform an indulgence that beleaguered Italians, Spaniards, and Greeks could not afford. In the era of the conquest of Mexico, Spain increasingly felt itself besieged on all sides. Powerful Jews, through economic might and commercial influence, might exploit and dominate the Catholic peasantry; Protestant fanatics might scour the Spanish countryside, undermining local churches and papal estates; Moors and Ottomans might conspire to return Spain to the Islamic world and thereby overturn the new national creation of Ferdinand and Isabella. In the paranoid Spanish mind the Inquisition and the *Reconquista* alone had saved Spain, yet the new nation's continued survival depended on a class of knights who might spread Catholicism to the New World before it, too, was colonized by northern Europeans and its treasures used to further religious strife in the Old World.

With real and perceived enemies such as these, no wonder that as the sixteenth century wore on, Spain would become even more repressive— foreign study sometimes discouraged, northern European scholarship often ignored, and research increasingly nonsecular. As Cortés set out for the New World, the old Mediterranean cosmos of the Roman Empire was soon to embrace a vast revolutionary shift. The exploitation of Atlantic trade routes, North American exploration, Protestantism, and radical economic changes would insidiously transfer economic power away from the Mediterranean world to the northern European Atlantic nations of England, Holland, France, and the German states.

Before the Castilians set foot in the New World there was already established a sense of missionary zeal and military audacity unknown to the same degree in the rest of Europe. Spain saw itself as the continuance of the Holy Roman Empire. The Hapsburg Charles V was not merely the emperor of the new nation of Spain but the proper inheritor of the domains of the old Roman imperators. The most gifted of the latter—Trajan and Hadrian come first to mind—had been born in Iberia. The courage of the ancient Iberians was legendary, both before and after the Roman conquest. Hannibal's slaughter at Cannae, for example, would have been impossible without the audacity of his Iberian mercenaries. No more deadly and romantic figure exists in Roman literature than the renegade Sertorius and his army of Iberian rebels, which devoured Roman legions for nearly a decade in their Spanish redoubt (83–73 B.C.). Thus, it was particularly unfortunate for the indigenous peoples of Mexico that they experienced not merely European interlopers or religious pilgrims per se, but the most audacious, deadly, and zealous warriors of the sixteenth-century European world, the most vicious men Spain had to offer in its greatest century of imperial grandeur.

What drove on Cortés and his men were the quest for status back in Spain and the hope of material betterment in the New World: free land and vast estates in Mexico, of course, and, for the more idealistic, the spiritual rewards of converting millions to Christianity. But, above all, gold beckoned. Gold was the first topic of interrogation with the natives. Worthless trinkets, iron knives, and glass were traded for gold. Only gold, not the precious feathers, intricate cotton clothes, or even the elaborate silver plate of the Mexicas, satisfied the Castilians. Gold might make a man a noble in Spain; gold might ensure the bankrupt Spanish crown that it could keep up with the more efficient economies in England and Holland, and so maintain the Hapsburg empire in Europe. Eventually, a quarter of all imperial Spanish revenues would be bullion from Mexico and Peru: 180 tons of gold and 16,000 tons of silver were to reach Spanish shores from the New World between 1500 and 1650.

Mexica and Peruvian gold might fuel the galleys to keep the Turk at bay and pay the armies in Holland. Gold in the hand meant not beauty, but power, money, status—and so intricate Mexica golden lizards, ducks, and fishes, the products of hundreds of hours of careful New World craftsmanship, were melted down into portable golden bars that represented the purchasing power of both goods and services. To the Spaniard the shiny metal was an abstract and distant rather than an immediate and concrete pleasure; hours of native dexterity were of no value when compared to the goods, status, and security that such metal might buy. When Cortés saw the intricate goldwork of his hosts, his first thoughts were not merely of his own personal wealth to come, or even tribute to the Spanish crown, but of the stored capital to purchase more horses, gunpowder, harquebuses, cannon, and crossbows from ships arriving from Cuba and Spain. So bewildered were they by the conquistadors' incessant demands for gold that the Indians of Mexico at first believed the Castilians' ruse that they needed the metal as medicine for "their hearts"; some more thoughtful Aztecs believed that the Spanish even ate the silly gold dust!

The conquistador in the New World in the century after Columbus's discovery was a law unto himself; there was little imperial oversight in the underpopulated and vast American domains. Foreigners were excluded from Central and South America—the French and English especially were not welcome. Governors arrived, became embroiled in petty local politics, typically were recalled, killed, died of disease—or looted the province under their care. The Spanish monarchy was nearly a five-week voyage away, and its bureaucracy transient, hard to locate, and notorious for inaction.

One such audit looking into the retirement of the viceroy of Peru took thirteen years and 50,000 sheets of paper and even then did not conclude until 1603, long after the ex-viceroy had passed away.

There was a known propensity for the government to grant post facto sanction to any audacious explorers who might find new land and bullion for the crown. The way to beat a *residencia,* or royal inquiry into a provincial governor's malfeasance, was to draw it out, to lead an expedition, colonize new territory for the crown, claim widespread baptism of the natives, and then send back the king's fifth of all gold, silver, and jewels that could be looted from the Indians. Gold might trump insubordination; gold might mitigate the priests' worries about decimating rather than converting the Indians of the Americas; gold might make a Castilian renegade or an Andalusian thug the equal of a viceroy in the eyes of the king's ministers—earning him an imperial pension or at least a coat of arms in his old age. With the opening of the New World, Spanish society began to evolve more from a landed aristocracy to a plutocracy, allowing an entire sort of previously poor and middling adventurers to advance through the acquisition of a fortune in the Americas.

Few Castilian adventurers brought their families. Even fewer sought a new life through the drudgery of yeoman farming. The desideratum was not to plow a homestead, and thereby through self-sufficiency raise a family free and immune from Europe's religious persecution and political oppression, but to become an absentee owner of a vast ranch, on which hundreds of Indians might tend cattle, mine, and raise luxury goods like coffee or sugar to guarantee the caudillo a steady income. Very few conquistadors had any doubts about the primacy of either the crown or the pope. Unlike the settlers of North America, the early Spanish came to the New World as emissaries of, rather than fugitives from, the church and state of their homeland. Some Castilian leaders in the Caribbean were battle-hardened veterans from the campaigns in Italy and continual wars against the Moriscos in Spain and the Ottomans on the Mediterranean. A few, like Cortés, were hidalgos of middling means but aristocratic pretensions, whose families enjoyed some relief from various imperial taxes. Most were young men in their twenties, keen to return to Spain by forty with rank, money, and vast estates—something impossible for most if they stayed in the homeland. The result was that Mexico was seen not as a place to start the world anew as in Puritan New England, but as a helpful source of Spanish vigilance against the forces of darkness.

Economic life was depressed in early-sixteenth-century Castile. Agriculture especially was on the wane, as petty lords and bishops presided over vast estates of cattle and sheep. The expulsion of the Jews and Moriscos—a quarter million of the latter in the fifteenth century—had decimated the economy of the Spanish countryside; immigration to the New World further robbed the Iberian Peninsula of hundreds of thousands of its most energetic citizens. While lucrative for a while, the Atlantic trade routes were perilous, given the weather, northern European raiders, and freelancing pirates. The exchange of New World bullion for Old World luxury goods—paintings, furniture, clothes, books—would eventually disrupt the economies of both Spain and Mexico, as each fell further behind northern Europe and North America, which were developing yeomen farmers and entrepreneurial capitalists. Simple mining and the crafting of luxury items were no substitute for large manufacturing production and market-oriented agriculture, as the gold of the New World hid for nearly a century structural deficiencies in the Spanish economy. There was a plethora of noble families and titles among the Castilian conquistadors, but little actual money and almost no opportunity back in Spain for upward mobility. No wonder nearly a million Castilians left for the New World in the two centuries after Columbus.

By 1500 printed books had spread through Spain, and an entire generation of aristocrats had versed themselves not only in religious tracts and military science but also in poems, ballads, and fantastic romances replete with Amazons, sea monsters, the fountain of youth, and legendary cities of gold. Bankrupt, would-be grandees sailed westward—more than two hundred Spanish ships voyaged to the Indies alone between 1506 and 1518—not only to escape poverty in Spain, not merely to enrich themselves and the Spanish crown, and not entirely to convert millions to Catholicism in the religious wars to come. The conquistadors also put to sea because the New World, with its bizarre flora, fauna, and indigenous peoples was seen as a fountainhead of popular myth, wonder, and sheer adventure—a suitable challenge for a young knight of courage and piety. Atlantis (the Antilles), Amazons (the Amazon River), and California (the island in the romance *Las Sergas de Esplandián*) really did exist after all.

All the conquistadors shared a clear-cut agenda to crush indigenous opposition, loot the countryside for gold, convert heathens to Christianity, enjoy the local women, father mestizo children—Cortés seems to have had several—and then establish local estates and baronies in which landed Spanish magníficos might oversee vast gangs of Indian laborers in exporting New World foods and bullion. In his early twenties Cortés announced in his first year in the New World that he would either "dine to the sound of trumpets or die on the scaffold," and then spent much of his twenties and early thirties amassing a fortune from gold mining and ranching on Cuba—capital to help finance an expedition to the new lands of Mexico that might bring in even more fortune.

Given free rein to explore and conquer an unknown Caribbean world between 1492 and 1540, within fifty years the conquistadors were anachronistic curiosities, if not nuisances altogether. Witness the decline in the fortunes of Cortés and his caballeros within a decade of the conquest of 1521. The great critic of Spanish imperialism in the New World, the Dominican friar Bartolomé de Las Casas, railed against the "forty years" (1502–42) in which a handful of his countrymen, through military conquest, disease, and economic exploitation, had wiped out the population of the Caribbean basin. By 1550 Spanish America was a world of bureaucrats, miners, and priests, with no room for impoverished Castilian loose cannon, who wished to intrigue without supervision in the affairs of the crown and pope and thereby ruin others' more careful work of extracting souls and gold from the people and soil of the Americas. King and church alike were coming to understand that men like Cortés had a disturbing tendency to flay, rather than shear, the sheep of the New World, and they spared no effort in ensuring that the era of the conquistador was over just a few years after its inception.

This first generation who settled and exploited the Caribbean basin were tough men like Diego Velázquez, governor of Cuba, seasoned from Columbus's second voyage and the final battles to free Granada; Francisco de Garay, ruler of newfound Jamaica, another veteran of the Columbus explorations and in-law to the famous explorer; and Pedro Arias Dávila, caudillo of Panama, battle-hardened survivor of the Spanish civil wars, and at seventy-eight, the most ruthless of the Spanish governors. Hernán Cortés himself was a native of Medellín, the son of a legendary soldier with fifty years of military service for the crown.

The conquistadors were a world apart from the priests and men of the quill who followed to solidify and bureaucratize what these far more brutal men had won by the sword, men who shared what to us now seems an uneven morality: slaughtering unarmed Indians in battle brought no odium, nor did turning an entire conquered population into gangs of indentured serfs. In contrast, human sacrifice, cannibalism, transvestitism, and sodomy provoked moral indignation and outrage, as did the absence of clothes, private property, monogamy, and steady physical labor. Much of the Castilian ethical world was predicated on professed status, manners, and the presumption of civilization, not fundamental questions of life and death:

The member of a civilized polity, then, as conceived by the sixteenth-century Spaniard, was a town-dweller who was dressed in doublet and hose, and wore his hair short. His house was not overrun with fleas and ticks. He ate his meals at a table and not on the ground. He did not indulge in unnatural vice, and if he committed adultery he was punished for it. His wife—who was his only wife and not one among several—did not carry her children on her back like a monkey, and he expected his son and not his nephew to succeed to his inheritance. He did not spend his time getting drunk; and he had a proper sense of respect for property—his own and other people's. . . . (J. Elliott, *Spain and Its World*, 55–56)

SPANISH RATIONALISM

The legacy of Cortés's men and of men like them was brilliant military conquest—and the decimation of the indigenous population of the Caribbean and Mexico in a mere thirty years through military conquest, the destruction of native agricultural practice, and the inadvertent importation of smallpox, measles, and influenza. Like the "Hellene" Alexander the Great, the "Christian" Cortés slaughtered thousands, looted imperial treasuries, destroyed and founded cities, tortured and murdered—and claimed he had done it all for the betterment of mankind. His letters to Charles V proclaiming interest in establishing a brotherhood among all natives and Spaniards read a great deal like Alexander's oath at Opis (324 B.C.), in which he proclaimed a new world embracing all races and religions. In both cases the body count told a different tale.

The conquistadors were far from ignorant fanatics. For all their religious devoutness, they did not live in the mythic world of the Mexicas— Montezuma sent an array of wizards and necromancers to hex and bewitch the approaching Castilians—but in a romantic cosmos that, ultimately despite its wild tales and improbable rumors, ceded to sensory perception and hard data. The Spaniards, for all their bluster, did not believe that the Mexicas were superhuman agents of the devil, but sophisticated indigenous tribes, who could be met, thwarted, and conquered through a combination of political intrigue and Castilian arms. The Mexicas were as unfamiliar to the Spaniards as the Spaniards were to the Mexicas, but the difference—besides the obvious fact that the Spaniards, not the Mexicas, had sailed halfway around the world to conquer an unknown people—was that Cortés's men drew on a 2,000-year-old tradition that might account for strange phenomena without resorting to religious exegesis. Through sense perception, reliance on a prior body of abstract knowledge, and inductive reasoning, the Castilians quickly sized up the political organization of Tenochtitlán, the military capability of its army, and the general religion of the Mexica nation.

They had never seen anything like the Mexica priests with their matted hair, caked blood, and cloaks of human skins, nor mass sacrifices or the rites of tearing bleeding hearts from drugged victims. But they soon surmised that these Indian holy men were no gods. For all the rhetoric of the Catholic church, they were not even devils, but humans, conducting some sort of bizarre religious rites which might logically incur the hatred of their subjugated allies. Christianity told them the Aztec religion was evil; but the European intellectual tradition gave them the tools to investigate it, probe its weakness, and eventually destroy it. In contrast, the Aztecs for weeks after the entry of the Castilians were still baffled as to whether they were up against men or demigods, centaurs or horses, ships or floating mountains, foreign or domestic deities, thunder or guns, emissaries or enemies.

Cortés himself was half-educated, and for a time worked as a notary, studied Latin, and read Caesar's *Gallic Wars,* Livy, and other classical military histories. At least some of his success in the darkest hours of the Mexica wars was due to his mesmerizing oratory, laced with classical allusions to Cicero and Aristotle and punctuated with Latin phrases from the Roman historians and playwrights. Spain, we must remember, in the first century B.C. during the latter days of the Roman Republic and early years of the Principate, was the intellectual center of Europe, producing moral philosophers such as the elder and younger Senecas, the poet Martial, and the agronomist Columella.

Although the Inquisition and religious intolerance that were sweeping Spain would soon isolate the Iberian Peninsula from the main centers of learning in northern Europe, leading to clear decline by 1650, in the sixteenth century the Spanish military was still at the cutting edge of military technology and abstract tactical science. Many of the men who marched with Cortés were not merely notaries, bankrupt hidalgos, and priests acquainted with Latin literature but avid readers of contemporary Spanish political and scientific tracts. More important, they were trained as bureaucrats and lawyers in the inductive method of adducing evidence, prior precedent, and law to prove a point before an audience of supposedly disinterested peers.

Cortés's conquistadors may not have been intellectuals, but they were equipped with the finest weapons of sixteenth-century Europe and buttressed by past experience of fighting the Moor, Italian, and Turk. The fundamentals of some two millennia of abstract Western military science, from fortification, siegecraft, battle tactics, ballistics, and cavalry maneuver to logistics, pike and sword fighting, and medical treatment in the field ensured that it would take literally hundreds of Mexicas to kill each Castilian. When rushed and swarmed, the Spaniards fell in rank and file, fought in unison with unquestioning discipline, and fired group volleys. In the myriad sudden and unexpected crises that arose each week, Cortés and his close advisers—the brilliant Martín López, the courageous and steady Sandoval, and the mercurial Alvarado—did not merely pray but coolly met, argued, and worked out a tactical or mechanical solution to salvage their blunder of marching into an island fortress of thousands. Cortés also worried that his actions would be recorded, criticized, audited, and made known to thousands back in Spain.

Spanish individualism was evident throughout. The most unlikely came forward with ideas—some half-baked, like the veteran of the Italian wars who, as powder grew short, convinced Cortés that he could build a vast catapult (it would prove an utter failure). There was a familiarity between soldiers and general that was unknown among the Mexicas: no Aztec warrior might dare approach Montezuma or his successor Cuauhtémoc to propose a new approach to ship construction, tactics, and logistics. Just as Alexander's "Companions" enjoyed a level of intimacy with their king unimaginable between Darius and his Immortals, so Cortés ate, slept, and was rebuked by his caballeros in a manner unthinkable among the Mexicas.

Westerners had ventured in non-Western lands to travel, write, and record since the emergence of the Ionian logographers of the sixth century B.C. Periegetics such as Cadmus, Dionysius, Charon, Damastes, and Hecataeus—ultimately to be followed in Asia and Egypt by explorers and conquerors like the Athenian imperialists, Xenophon's Ten Thousand, and Alexander the Great—had written didactic treatises on Persia (*Persica*) and voyages outside Greece (*Periploi*). In contrast, during Xerxes' great invasion of Greece (480 B.C.), the king apparently had little, if any, information about the nature of the Hellenic city-states.

This rich Hellenic tradition of natural inquiry was continued by Roman merchants, explorers, conquerors, and scientists whose canvas widened to include the entire Mediterranean, northern Africa, and Europe. Unlike the Aztec emperors, Cortés had the benefit of an anthropological tradition of written literature describing foreign phenomena and peoples, cataloging and evaluating them, and making sense of their natural environment that went back to Herodotus, Hippocrates, Aristotle, and Pliny—the age-old and arrogant Western idea that nothing is inexplicable to the god Reason, if only the investigator has enough empirical data and the proper inductive method. Montezuma either feared or worshiped the novelty that he could not explain; Cortés sought to explain the novelty that he neither feared nor worshiped. In the end that is one reason why Tenochtitlán and not Vera Cruz—let alone Seville—would lie in ruins.

WHY DID THE CASTILIANS WIN?

The Inexplicable

Nearly a quarter million people lived in the twin island cities of Tenochtitlán and Tlatelolco. More than a million more Nahuatl-speaking Mexicas surrounding the lake were tributary subjects of the Aztec empire. Even more people outside the Valley of Mexico gave Tenochtitlán their obeisance. The great marketplace of Tenochtitlán could hold 60,000 people. The city itself was larger than most of the major urban centers of Europe—Seville, the largest city in Spain, had fewer than 100,000 inhabitants. Ingeniously crafted causeways with numerous drawbridges, a huge stone aqueduct, pyramid temples larger (in volume) than those in Egypt, and fleets of thousands of canoes on an engineered lake made the island fortress impregnable and an architectural marvel.

Floating gardens, zoos of exotic tropical animals, and an enormous privileged religious and political elite, bedecked in gold, jewels, and exotic feathers, intrigued Cortés's men enough to swear in contemporary accounts that no city in Europe could rival Tenochtitlán in wealth, power, beauty, and size. Yet within two years a tiny Castilian force—without sure supply lines, unfamiliar with local territory and custom, initially attacked by every native group they encountered, suffering from tropical diseases and an unfamiliar diet, opposed by their own superiors in Cuba, and later confronted by another Castilian force sent to arrest Cortés—defeated the Aztec empire, inaugurating a series of events that would wipe out most of its population and ruin the majestic capital of Tenochtitlán.

The Spanish themselves incorrectly attributed their amazing success to innate virtue, superior intelligence, and the Christian religion. For nearly five hundred years both Mexican and European critics have offered a variety of contradictory explanations for this seemingly impossible feat, explanations that range from the role of the Tlaxcalan allies and disease to the genius of Cortés himself and cultural impediments in time-reckoning and systematic communication. Few have sought answers in the wider context of a long lethal Western military tradition.

Native Allies?

Did Cortés play off native against native, in a cynical alliance that saw a civil war in Mexico destroy its own culture, with Cortés the sole and ultimate beneficiary? To understand the conquest of Mexico as essentially due to internal disputes between Mexica nations, three propositions would have to be true. First, Mesoamerican tribes *could* have accomplished the obliteration of Tenochtitlán sometime earlier on their own without Spanish aid. Yet contemporary accounts prove that all the neighboring tribes had failed to overthrow the Mexicas prior to the Spanish arrival, and afterward were ineffective in fighting the Aztecs without European support. Second, after the destruction of Mexico City, the natives of Mexico *could* have turned on the Spanish, renewed their assaults on the Europeans as they had during the arrival of Cortés, and then annihilated the Castilian presence altogether, ensuring their own perpetual autonomy from both Aztec and European oppressors. The opposite took place: the destruction of Tenochtitlán marked the end of *all* Mexica autonomy. Neither could an indigenous tribe before the Spanish arrival defeat the Aztecs, nor after the conquest could any natives overthrow the Spanish. Third, squabbling and fractious Mesoamerican peoples were co-opted by a united and cohesive European force, suggesting that native infighting, not Spanish military superiority, prevented an eventual Indian victory. The Europeans, however, had nearly as much dissension in their ranks as the natives of Mexico. Cortés himself barely escaped arrest in Cuba and became the target of several assassination plots. He was officially branded a renegade by authorities in Hispaniola and was forced to steal and expropriate supplies at gunpoint. In the midst of delicate negotiations with Montezuma, he was obliged to abandon Tenochtitlán. Leaving only a small force under Alvarado, his men marched the difficult and dangerous 250-mile route back to Vera Cruz and then faced and defeated a Castilian armada under Narváez larger than their own—the entire time under attack by various Mesoamerican peoples who sought to capitalize on just such signs of weakness.

In short, an embattled Cortés, without official sanction and suffering from near outlaw status among his Caribbean superiors, turned a preexisting native world of tension and constant battle into an entirely new war of utter annihilation against the most powerful people in the history of

Mexico—something impossible without superior technology, horses, and tactics. Upon conclusion of that campaign, within a few years he pacified all of Mexico under Spanish authority, a condition that, aside from occasional revolts, would characterize Mexican history from the fall of Tenochtitlán in 1521 to the nineteenth-century Mexican war of independence.

In all discussions of the Mexican conquest numbers tell us little. The discipline, tactics, and technology of the invaders, not the unwieldy size of the Aztec army or the corresponding huge musters of their native enemies, explain why the Aztec empire vanished in less than two years after the arrival of Cortés. Routine native conflicts were turned into a final war of annihilation by the Spanish, who then ended the autonomy of every tribe in Mexico. After the disastrous *Noche Triste* of July 1, 1520, Cortés lost most of his Tlaxcalan allies and was surrounded by thousands of warriors from hostile tribes. Tlaxcala itself was miles distant and deliberating whether to continue its alliance. Yet the Spaniards, aided for the most part by just a few surviving Tlaxcalans, fought their way out from Lake Texcoco, slaughtered thousands of natives on their march, and coerced others back into their federation. Additionally, in early July 1521—almost a year to the day after the *Noche Triste*—after being ambushed in Tlatelolco, most of Cortés's allies suddenly and without warning vanished as dozens of Castilian captives in a gruesome public festival were herded up the Great Pyramid to their slaughter. Native accounts of the spectacle that followed explain why Cortés's coalition suddenly evaporated:

> One by one they were forced to climb to the temple platform, where they were sacrificed by the priests. The Spaniards went first, then their allies, all were put to death. As soon as the sacrifices were finished, the Aztecs ranged the Spaniards' heads in rows on pikes. They also lined up their horses' heads. They placed the horses' heads at the bottom and the heads of the Spaniards above, and arranged them all so that the faces were toward the sun. (M. León-Portilla, ed., *The Broken Spears*, 107)

Contemporary sources emphasize that from the once-vast native army that Cortés had mustered from the villages on the lake, fewer than a hundred Mesoamerican natives at this point remained. The more distant peoples of Malinalco and Tula revolted outright, causing Cortés to send punitive expeditions against them to secure the confidence of the wavering lords of Cuernavaca and Otomí.

In all such engagements, the numerical disparities are staggering, as the Castilians were outnumbered on the battlefield by well over one hundred to one—a far greater disparity even than the British experienced during most of the engagements of the Zulu wars in 1879. In the midst of such revolts and the dissolution of his army, Cortés nevertheless maintained the siege of Tenochtitlán, conquered the rebellious allies, and restored the skeptical Mesoamericans to his army. Apparently, the besieged Aztecs could not conquer the isolated Castilians; nor did the other peoples of Mexico feel confident on their own to destroy Tenochtitlán without Spanish assistance—and yet themselves did not march on the causeways to kill the weakened Cortés.

Perhaps it is hard for modern deskbound scholars to understand the utter dread that existed in the minds of those who were routinely sliced to pieces by Toledo steel, shredded by grapeshot, trampled by mailed knights, ripped to pieces by mastiffs, and had their limbs lacerated with impunity by musket balls and crossbow bolts—not to mention those thousands who were summarily executed without warning by Cortés and Alvarado in Cholula and at the temple of Tlacochcalco. Throughout contemporary oral Nahuatl and written Spanish accounts, there are dozens of grisly scenes of the dismemberment and disemboweling of Mesoamericans by Spanish steel and shot, accompanied by descriptions of the sheer terror that such mayhem invoked in indigenous populations. We of the twentieth century who have witnessed millions of Jews gassed by just hundreds of Nazi guards, or hundreds of thousands of Cambodians murdered by a few thousand deranged and cowardly Khmer Rouge, should not be surprised that the horror and the fright incurred by sophisticated tools of death so often and so easily trump sheer numbers.

The distinguished Aztec scholar Ross Hassig has rightly pointed out that most narratives of the conquest underplay the Mesoamerican contribution to the Spanish victory. So let us be clear: Cortés could not have conquered Tenochtitlán within a mere two years without vast support of native allies (initially the Totonacs and later the Tlaxcalans); nor could the surrounding Indians, who had fought the Aztecs in vain for decades prior to the European arrival, have destroyed the Aztec capital without the support of Cortés. The answer in assessing the critical role of the native involvement is one of degree, and involves the question of time and cost.

The tens of thousands of Indians who, as warriors, porters, and construction workers, aided, fought alongside, and fed Cortés were indispensable to the Castilians' effort. Without their assistance Cortés would have required thousands of Spanish reinforcements and lost hundreds more men in an effort that might have taken a decade or more. Nevertheless, he would have accomplished his conquest even had he battled a united Mexico without native assistance. The Spanish conquest of Mexico—against populations without horses, the wheel, steel or iron weapons, oceangoing ships, gunpowder weapons, and a long tradition of scientific siegecraft—is emblematic of a systematic pattern of brutal conquest of the New World that elsewhere did not necessarily demand native complicity.

The Mesoamericans fought the Aztecs not because they were enamored of the Spanish—indeed for much of 1519 and early 1520 they tried to exterminate Cortés—but because they met an unexpected and powerful enemy who could be unleashed on their even greater adversary, Tenochtitlán, which had systematically butchered their own women and children in a most gruesome and hideous fashion. The near constant wars of the past century with the Aztecs had left most Mesoamerican peoples between the interior and the coast—the Tlaxcalans especially—under either an oppressive subjugation that stripped their fields and often their population for material and human tribute, or a state of siege for as much as six months out of the year to ward off Aztec depredations.

The appearance of the Spanish convinced most of the subjects of the Aztec empire that here was a people whom they could not defeat, yet who could annihilate their archenemies, the Mexicas, and possessed such technological and material advantages—as the prescient Aztec defenders reminded the Tlaxcalans during the last bitter days of the siege—as to be able to establish a lasting hegemony over *all* the natives of Mexico. We should see the indigenous contribution as the fuel that fed the fire that consumed the Aztecs, but concede the spark and flame to be all Spanish. Without the Spaniard presence even the brave Tlaxcalans would not have freed—and heretofore had never freed—themselves from Aztec oppression. Given the Western ability to produce deadly weapons, its propensity to create cheap, plentiful goods, and its tradition of seeing war in pragmatic rather than ritual terms as a mechanism to advance political ends, it is no surprise that Mesoamericans, African tribes, and native North Americans all joined European forces to help kill off Aztecs, Zulus, and Lakotas.

The key to dismantling the Aztec empire, which centralized its communications, bureaucracy, and military in an island fortress, was the destruction of Tenochtitlán—a task that no Mesoamerican tribe could carry out, much less even envision. It is true that native peoples sought to use Cortés as a tactical asset in their ongoing war against the Mexicas. But they failed utterly to understand the Spaniards' larger strategic goals of destroying the Aztec empire as prerequisite to annexing Mexico as a tributary of the Spanish empire—and therefore unwittingly became pawns in the age-old European tradition of strategic thinking that was mostly alien to their own idea of what war was for.

Neither the Tlaxcalans nor the Mexicas had any abstract notion that war is the ultimate and final arbiter of politics, a uniquely Western idea that goes back to Aristotle's amoral observation in the first book of his *Politics* that the purpose of war is always "acquisition" and thus a logical phenomenon that takes place when one state is far stronger than the other and therefore "naturally" seeks the political subjugation of its inferior rival through any means possible. Such views are later thematic in Polybius's *Histories,* omnipresent in Caesar's *Gallic Wars,* and once again amplified and discussed in abstract terms by Western thinkers as diverse as Machiavelli, Hobbes, and Clausewitz. Plato in his *Laws* assumed that every state would, when its resources were strained, seek to annex or incorporate land that was not its own, as a logical result of its own ambition and self-interest.

Disease?

No precise figures exist on the final tally of Aztecs who died of sickness during 1519–21. It is a highly charged subject that involves not merely numbers but questions of deliberate intent and European culpability. For most of the sixteenth century Mexico was beset by a succession of European diseases—smallpox, flu, plague, mumps, whooping cough, and measles—that reduced its indigenous population by some 75 to 95 percent of its pre-invasion total. In one of the great tragedies of the entire European subjugation of the Americas, a Mexican subcontinent that may have supported nearly 25 million people before the Spanish conquest was within a century inhabited by only a million or two.

For our strictly military purposes, however, we are concerned here with the more narrow and largely amoral issue of sheer military efficacy. To what degree did the smallpox outbreak of 1520 per se account for the Spanish conquest of Tenochtitlán in August 1521? Native observers, who described the pox in excruciating detail to the later Spanish believed that the epidemic wiped out almost one out of fifteen inside Tenochtitlán itself. Modern scholars have estimated that somewhere between 20 and 40 percent of all the population of central Mexico—Aztecs and their enemies alike—perished from this first wave of the outbreak. Perhaps as many as 20,000 or 30,000 Aztecs died from the disease during the two years in which Cortés was engaged in the conquest of Mexico, a staggering number of fatalities that surely helped to weaken the power of the Mexicas.

As horrible as those figures are, it is not clear that smallpox had a great deal to do with the final destruction of Tenochtitlán, although the subsequent creation of the province of New Spain was brought about by the millions who died in the century following Cortés's victory, especially during the typhus epidemics of 1545–48 and 1576–81. According to the *Florentine Codex,* the first outbreak of the disease had a definite and limited course, spreading among the population from early September to late November 1520. Then it was largely gone by the time of the final siege (April to August 1521). By the time Cortés approached Tenochtitlán for his second campaign in April 1521, the city had been largely free of the disease for nearly six months. Smallpox also killed thousands of Cortés's allies in even greater numbers than the Aztecs, since the Totonacs, Chalcans, and Tlaxcalans were in closer contact with the succession of European arrivals at Vera Cruz, where the outbreak originated. Furthermore, the disease seems to have been most virulent on the coast, near the base of Spanish operations and in the midst of those tribes allied to Cortés. To a limited degree the island isolation of Tenochtitlán, its elevation, and the no-man's-land of the battlefield provided an initial barrier, feeble as it would ultimately prove, to ready sources of the infection.

The disease argument cuts both ways: there was a variety of tropical illnesses with which the Europeans had almost no experience or immunity against. Most contemporary accounts mention constant bronchial ailments and fevers that severely weakened and sometimes killed Cortés's soldiers. New World malarias and dysenteries were far more virulent than similar outbreaks in Spain. Some also suffered from syphilis-like cankers, an especially unpleasant experience for armored men in the tropics. Moreover, not all of Cortés's men had been exposed to smallpox and gained immunity against a disease that still wiped out thousands in the major urban areas of Europe. Given the small numbers in his army, even a few dozen Spaniards with the disease could have had as great an effect on the relative military efficacy of the conquistadors as did the thousands of infected natives in an Aztec empire of more than a million. In Cortés's own letters and the annals of contemporary Spanish observers, smallpox, though mentioned, is never characterized as a predominant factor on either side of the struggle. This was because the Castilians, themselves beset by a host of diseases and unable to detect any sudden weakness in the resistance of Tenochtitlán, never fully appreciated the degree to which the outbreak had become pandemic among their enemies.

What prevented the Europeans from being wiped out by these new fevers and old illnesses is explained as much by demographics and culture as by biological causes. As a largely heterogeneous group of younger male warriors with varying backgrounds and travel experience, the Castilians were rarely cooped up in small urban quarters in constant contact with women, children, and the aged. They also had almost no responsibility or need to care for the civilian infected. Besides some biological immunity to smallpox, there was among the Spanish arrivals a long empirical tradition of combating disease outbreaks—Seville would lose half its population to plague in 1600, yet recover without being destroyed by either the disease or opportunistic foreign invasion.

Throughout the fighting, the conquistadors applied wool and cotton bandages to wounds, and found, in a gruesome manner, that the fat from freshly slain Indians worked as an excellent salve and healing cream. While scientific knowledge of viruses and bacilli was, of course, absent in sixteenth-century Europe, and indeed the entire mechanism of infectious agents unknown, the Spaniards did draw on a long empirical tradition that went back to classical medical writers like Hippocrates and Galen, who drew on firsthand observations of epidemics in Greek and Italian cities and had thus helped establish Western traditions emphasizing the importance of proper quarantine, medicinal diets, sleep, and the careful burning of the dead.

As a consequence of that long legacy, the Spaniards realized that close contact with the ill spread infection, that the dead had to be immediately disposed of, that the course of diseases was predictable by acute observation of symptoms, and that the process of empirical observation, diagnosis, and prognosis was superior to mere incantation and sacrifice. Catholic priests may have argued that one became ill as God's punishment for prior sins and offered prayer as healing, but most Spaniards realized that once the infection set in, there was a predictable course of illness to follow, one that to some degree could be ameliorated by medicines, careful nursing, diet, and isolation.

In contrast, the native people of Mexico, like the ancient Egyptians and many Catholic priests, believed that internal diseases were a result of gods or evil adversaries, who wished to punish or take possession of the afflicted—and could thus be thwarted by charms and incantations. Aztec fortune-tellers consulted the pattern of beans thrown on cotton fabrics to determine the etiology of the disease. Various sacrifices, human and animal, would surely appease the angry Macuilxochitl or Tezcatlipoca—or was it Xipa? The idea that communal sleeping and bathing, group sweat-houses, eating on the floor, wearing of human skin, cannibalism, or the lack of immediate burial and disposal of the dead had anything to do with the spread of diseases was poorly known even among the Mesoamerican herbalists.

The real advantage of the smallpox epidemic to Cortés was not the reductions in Aztec numbers per se but its cultural and political consequences. Because the Spaniards did not die at the same rate as the Indians, there spread the notion—mostly forgotten for a time after the *Noche Triste*—that the Europeans were more than mortal. As smallpox swept through the Mesoamerican population and wiped out its leadership, the Castilians were careful to support and assist only those new leaders who were favorable to their cause. Smallpox enhanced the Spanish reputation for superhuman strength and solidified their support among native allies, despite the fact that the disease killed as many supporters as enemies—and thus had no real effect on the numerical parity between attackers and besieged.

Cultural Confusion?

A recent popular explanation of the Spanish miracle is the notion of cultural confusion. Either a semiotic exegesis is adduced that the Aztecs conceived and expressed reality in radically different ways than the Spanish, and were thus bewildered to the point of impotence by the European arrival, or the more logical argument that their culture did not practice a type of warfare that could thwart such a radically different foe. It is true that the Aztecs at first were unaware of the danger that the Spaniards and their superior military technology and tactics posed. They may have believed that the conquistadors were some sort of divine beings—the long-prophesied return of the light-skinned god Quetzalcoatl and his retinue from across the sea. Many Mexicas believed that Spanish firearms were thunder weapons, their oceangoing ships floating mountains, horses some sort of divine centaurlike beasts, rider and beast being the same creature. Many scholars argue that the absence of a syllabic script, the highly ritualized nature of Aztec formal speech, and the foreign ideas of the Spanish made the Aztecs confused by European directness and vulnerable to their cause-and-effect method of state politics and warfare.

Montezuma, well before the arrival of the Spaniards at Vera Cruz, seems to have associated rumors of their presence in the Caribbean with the fated return of Quetzalcoatl and the overthrow of the Aztec empire. The combination of religious authority and absolute political power in the hands of a single ruler, coupled with Montezuma's mythic worldview, in part explains the fatal decision of the Aztec hierarchy to admit Cortés into Tenochtitlán in November 1519. Soon they sized up the Spaniards as no gods at all, but their initial hesitancy and fear had given Cortés a critical edge in the campaign. Others have emphasized the ubiquity of religious ritual in Aztec life, especially the degree to which Aztec warfare was scripted and conventional, with its overriding emphasis on taking captives as sacrificial victims for their gods, rather than killing the enemy outright. In this view, hundreds of times Spanish conquistadors (Cortés among them) could have been easily killed, but escaped due to the failed efforts of the Aztecs to capture them alive.

As in the case of the smallpox outbreak, the argument is one of degree. The Mexicas may have believed that Cortés and his men were divinities and either let down their guard or feared to attack such "gods" when they were surrounded and vulnerable inside Tenochtitlán in late 1519. The Aztecs did not immediately attempt to kill the Spaniards in battle and thus lost countless opportunities to exterminate their vastly outnumbered enemy. But by the time of the *Noche Triste* the Spaniards had been in Tenochtitlán for nearly eight months. The Aztecs had the opportunity to examine the Spaniards firsthand—their propensity to eat, sleep, defecate, seek out sex with native women, and exhibit greed for gold. From reports that had long ago reached Montezuma they knew that in the prior Spanish wars with the Otomis and Tlaxcalans (April to November 1519), the Spaniards had bled like men. In fact, a few of them had been killed in battle, making it abundantly clear that their physical bodies were similar to any in Mexico. Before they entered Tenochtitlán, horses had also been brought down, sliced to pieces, and sacrificed: on arrival it was clear to all in the Valley of Mexico that these beasts were large deerlike creatures without any divine propensities.

At the first real military engagement on the causeways on July 1, 1520, the Aztecs surrounded Cortés with the clear idea of exterminating men, not gods. Under the conditions of these nocturnal mass attacks on the narrow dikes, it was nearly impossible to capture the Castilians, and it is no accident that the vast majority of the six hundred to eight hundred or so Spaniards lost that night were deliberately killed outright or left to drown.

In the subsequent fighting during the Spanish flight to Tlaxcala, and again at the final siege of Tenochtitlán, the Mexicas employed captured Toledo blades. They may even have attempted to coerce captured conquistadors to show them the intricacies of crossbows. The Mexicas often changed their tactics, learning to avoid swarming attacks in the plains, and during the great siege showed ingenuity in confining their fighting to narrow corridors of the city, where ambushes and missile attack might nullify the Spaniards' horses and cannon. The Aztecs eventually guessed that the Spanish were intent on their slaughter, and so logically distrusted all affirmations of Spanish mediation. They taunted their Tlaxcalan enemies with prescient boasts that after their own demise, they, too, would end up as slaves to the Spanish.

If the Aztecs fought with any disadvantage, it was one of training and custom that had taught them to capture and bind rather than slice apart an adversary—habits that would prove hard to shake even against killers like the Spanish, who gave no quarter. Still, we must remember that the notion that soldiers should seek to capture rather than kill their enemy is a most un-Western one, and only reaffirms our general thesis that the entire menu of Western warfare—its tactics of annihilation, mass assault, disciplined files and ranks, and superior technology—was largely responsible for the conquest of Mexico.

Besides the overriding problem of inferior weaponry and tactics, the greatest cultural disadvantage of the Aztecs has often gone unnoticed: that of the age-old problem of systems collapse that threatens all palatial dynasties in which political power is concentrated among a tiny elite— another non-European phenomenon that has given Western armies enormous advantages in cross-cultural collisions. The abrupt destruction of the Mycenaean palaces (ca. 1200 B.C.), the sudden disintegration of the Persian Empire with Darius III's flight at Gaugamela, the end of the Incas, and the rapid collapse of the Soviet Union all attest that the way of palatial dynasties is one of extreme precariousness to outside stimuli. Anytime a narrow elite seeks to control all economic and political activity from a fortified citadel, island redoubt, grand palace, or walled Kremlin, the unraveling of empire shortly follows the demise, flight, or discrediting of such imperial grandees—again in contrast to more decentralized, less stratified, and locally controlled Western political and economic entities. Cortés himself sensed that vulnerability and thus kidnapped Montezuma within a week of arrival. With the final flight of the successor emperor Cuauhtémoc in August 1521 the final resistance of the Aztecs came abruptly to an end.

Malinche

The great narratives of William Prescott and Hugh Thomas suggest that the abrupt collapse of the Mexicas at little Spanish cost would have been impossible without the singular genius and criminal audacity of Hernán Cortés—whom the natives dubbed "Malinche," a derivative from the Nahuatl name, Mainulli or Malinali, of his constant companion and Mayan interpreter, the brilliant and irrepressible Doña Marina. The implication is prevalent in almost all modern European accounts of the conquest that other conquistadors—even intrepid men such as Governor Velázquez of Cuba, Narváez, who was sent to arrest Cortés, or Cortés's own capable henchmen, the brave Sandoval and the reckless Alvarado—could not have replicated Cortés's achievement.

One does not have to be a believer in the "great man" theory of history to realize that on a number of key occasions—the initial dismantling of the ships and march inland, the war against and then brilliant alliance with Tlaxcala, the kidnapping of Montezuma, the defeat of Narváez and miraculous appropriation of his troops at almost no cost in lives, the heroic trek after the *Noche Triste,* the return march and launching of the brigantines, and the recovery after the final setback at Tlatelolco—the bravery, oratory, and political savvy of Cortés alone saved the expedition. A mere seven years after the conquest of 1521, Pánfilo Narváez, who had failed to stop Cortés and lost an eye for the trouble, led an expedition into Florida, comparable in size to Cortés's initial force in Mexico, replete with five hundred men and one hundred horses. Apparently, only four conquistadors survived. They took years to be rescued—illustrating the abject catastrophe that might befall even well-supplied Spanish forces in the New World when led by men without ability and courage.

Manuel Orozco y Berra paints a near Machiavellian figure of Cortés beyond good and evil, but clearly one unlike any of his generation:

> Consider his ingratitude to Diego Velázquez, his double and deceitful dealings with the tribes, his treachery toward Montezuma. Put to his account the useless massacre of Cholula, the murder of the Aztec monarch, his insatiable desire for gold and for pleasures. Do not forget that he killed his first wife, Catalina Juárez, that in torturing Cuauhtémoc he committed a base deed, that he ruined his rival, Garay, that by retaining command he made himself suspected of the death of Luis Ponce and Marcos de Aguilar. Even accuse him of everything else which history records as proven. But then allow him the plea he was a sagacious politician and a valiant and able

captain; that he concluded successfully one of the most astounding feats of modern times. (Ixtlilxochitl, *Ally of Cortés,* xxvi)

Cortés was indeed a warrior, ruthless intriguer, and politician of superhuman energy and talent unmatched even among his gifted rivals of the sixteenth-century Spanish exploration of the New World. He was deathly ill from tropical viruses numerous times and had contracted a serious case of malaria even before he set sail from Spain. In the battles for Mexico City he suffered a near concussion and wounds to the hand, foot, and leg. On three occasions he was nearly captured and dragged off to be sacrificed on the Great Pyramid at Tenochtitlán. He put down numerous attempts on his own life by native and Castilian cabals and neutralized rivals in the far-distant court of Charles V. Cortés fathered several children by various women and was accused of murdering his first wife, Catalina. Almost wiped out during the *Noche Triste,* suffering from wounds himself, his army surrounded by enemies, Cortés—because of religious fanaticism, Castilian honor, Spanish patriotism, sheer greed, or personal repute, or a mixture of all that and more—refused to retreat to the safety of Vera Cruz:

> I remembered that Fortune always favors the bold, and furthermore that we were Christians who trusted in the great goodness of God, who would not let us perish utterly nor allow us to lose so great and noble a land which had been, or was to be, subject to Your Majesty; nor could I abandon so great a service as continuing the war whereby we would once more subdue the land as it had been before. I determined, therefore, that on no account would I go across the mountains to the coast. On the contrary, disregarding all the dangers and toil that might befall us, I told them that I would not abandon this land, for, apart from being shameful to myself and dangerous for all, it would be great treason to Your Majesty; rather I resolved to fall on our enemies wherever I could and oppose them in every possible way. (H. Cortés, *Letters from Mexico,* 145)

Cortés saw well over half his men—some 1,000 out of 1,600—killed or captured in a two-year period. On three occasions his sick and wounded survivors were ready to revolt. He kidnapped Montezuma, waged war against the Aztec emperor's brother and nephew, at various times fought and repulsed his allied Tlaxcalans, and defeated and then won over a Spanish relief force sent to bring him back in chains. He sailed to Spain to plead his cause, took an enormous force to Guatemala, and claimed he still could lead a voyage to China if given ships and men. All this from a small man of five feet four inches and about 150 pounds, who arrived in Hispaniola penniless at the age of twenty in 1504.

All that being said, without horses, firearms, steel weapons, armor, ships, dogs, and crossbows, not to mention the military acumen of his lieutenants who between them possessed expertise ranging from shipbuilding to gunpowder fabrication to the use of integrated cavalry and infantry tactics, even Cortés would have failed. The disparity—far more marked than in the Roman-Carthaginian or Macedonian-Persian encounters—was too great for either a brilliant Aztec leader or an inept Spanish conquistador to alter the eventual outcome. Had an Alvarado or Sandoval led the Castilians into Mexico City in November 1520, and had they met a fiery Cuauhtémoc rather than a cautious and confused Montezuma, the entire expedition might have floundered. But just as seven successive fleets reached Mexican shores during Cortés's rebound in 1521, there would have been larger expeditions to replace the losses of an initial setback, some of them led by better generals, with even more men—30,000 Spaniards were in the immediate Caribbean settlements. Cortés himself after the disaster of the *Noche Triste* claimed that his life was worth little, since there were now thousands of Castilians in the New World who would take his place and subdue the Aztecs.

The conquest of Mexico was one of the few times in history in which technology—Europe in the midst of a military renaissance pitted against foes that had neither horses nor the wheel, much less metals and gunpowder—in itself trumped the variables of individual human genius and achievement. The subjugation of western North America was accomplished in four decades of concerted warfare without a European conqueror as skilled as Cortés or a centralized and vulnerable nerve center like the island city of Tenochtitlán. The battle for the American frontier was marked by a number of incompetent English-speaking generals who lost their command and lives in idiotic assaults against brave and ingenious Indian tribes armed with Western weaponry and horses in a vast landscape—all without much effect on the continual encroachment on Indian lands and the systematic defeat of native war parties. We also should keep in mind that the Norse explorers of the northwestern coast of North America—the first European aggressors in the New World—during the tenth and eleventh centuries had little permanent success against native tribes because of their lack of firearms, horses, and sophisticated tactics and their inability to arrive in sufficient numbers on successive flotillas of large oceangoing ships. Neither Norse brilliance in navigation and seamanship nor legendary prowess in arms was enough to ensure conquest or colonization without an easy and continual supply of manpower and matériel.

Spanish Weapons and Tactics

Modern scholars who attribute the Castilians' astounding success to cultural confusion, disease, native allies, and a host of other subsidiary causes are reluctant to admit to the critical role of Western technological and military superiority. Perhaps they fear that such conclusions might imply Eurocentrism, or suggest Western mental or moral preeminence. But the enormous gulf between the equipment and tactics of the Mexica and Spanish armies is a question not of virtue or genes, but of culture and history.

In all categories of arms and armor the Spanish were vastly superior to every native tribe they met. Their steel swords were sharper and lighter than the Mexicas' obsidian-tipped clubs and held an edge far longer. When used by skilled swordsmen as both a thrusting and a cleaving blade, such weapons—as written sources and Mexica artwork attest—could lop off entire limbs and dispatch an unarmored opponent in a single blow. The conquistador sword was a direct descendant of the shorter Roman *gladius,* it, too, originally a Spanish blade that gave the Roman legionary the greatest degree of penetrating power of any weapon in the ancient Mediterranean. All 1,600 Castilians who fought at various times in Mexico were equipped with such lethal swords, which in large part accounts for Spanish victories even when their shot and bolts were depleted.

Many soldiers bore long pikes of ashwood. Most were twelve to fifteen feet in length, tipped with heavy sharp metal heads. Like the Macedonian *sarissai,* which inspired these weapons, Spanish pikes when wielded by dense bodies of men—the Castilian *tercio* became for a time the deadliest infantry force in sixteenth-century Spain—created an impenetrable wall. In Spanish parlance it was an "iron cornfield" that could not be entered. When the pike was used as a lance by an armored horseman riding down stragglers, a single blow could take a man's head right off. Finally, there were also hundreds of lighter, steel-tipped javelins, the *jabalinas,* which like the Roman *pila* were deadly when thrown by swordsmen closing in for the kill.

Nearly all the Spaniards wore steel helmets that also protected parts of the face and could not be penetrated by either arrow or stone. A great many donned steel breastplates and carried steel-reinforced shields, which explains why few were killed by Aztec club or sword blows. Instead, those killed were swarmed and pulled down, as dozens of Mexica warriors tried to trip or knock down the heavily laden Castilians. Nor had any tribe in the New World ever experienced the European idea of shock infantry collision—a tradition originating with the phalanx of the seventh century B.C. on the killing fields of ancient Greece, and rarely found outside of Europe.

The chief problem for the Europeans in many infantry battles with the Tlaxcalans and the Aztecs was one of exhaustion. The mailed Spaniards, nearly invulnerable from sword and missile attacks, soon tired after constant slashing and stabbing with heavy blades and lances, and at last were often forced to retreat behind the curtain of cannon and small-arms fire:

> They surrounded them [the Spanish] on all sides, the Spanish started to strike at them, killing them like flies. No sooner were some slain than they were replaced with fresh ones. The Spaniards were like an islet in the sea, beaten by waves on all sides. This terrible conflict lasted over four hours. During this many Mexicans died, and nearly all the Spaniards' allies and some of the Spaniards themselves. When it came noon, with the intolerable exertion of battle, the Spaniards began to lag. (B. Sahagún, *The Conquest of Mexico*, 96)

Each Castilian butchered dozens of the enemy, and in some cases hundreds, to ensure his own survival, an enormous effort of muscular strength and endurance for such relatively small men encased in mail. Their chief worry was either stumbling or being tripped and dragged off. Our sources report that over the course of the two-year fighting, hundreds of Castilians were wounded, but nearly all such cuts and contusions were to the limbs and rarely fatal. The way to kill a man is to penetrate his chest or face with thrusting metal blades, and that was nearly impossible for Aztec warriors pitted against mailed foot soldiers.

Scholars who dismiss the importance of Spanish steel must explain why, after the *Noche Triste* and the ambush at Tlatelolco, the Aztecs quickly employed the precious few Castilian swords and lances they captured. Why did the Tlaxcalans welcome the Spanish infantry as a cutting edge in all infantry engagements against the Aztecs, on the premise that only Castilians could hack their way through Aztec lines? During the humid season many conquistadors felt that lighter and more comfortable local quilted cotton fabrics offered enough protection from native stone-edged missiles and blades. On occasion they jettisoned their mail—dramatic proof that they feared little from Aztec weapons, despite being wielded by some of the most ferocious fighters in the history of warfare.

Superior metal arms were only part of the Spanish advantage. Harquebuses and crossbows were more accurate and had greater range and far more penetrating power than any native sling or arrow. The Spanish crossbow could send a bolt in an arc over two hundred yards and was deadly accurate in direct fire at nearly a hundred. Little skill was required in its use, and bolts and replacement parts were easily fabricated from indigenous materials. The chief drawback was the weight of the machine (fifteen pounds) and the relatively slow rate of fire (one bolt per minute). Although Aztec archers could shoot five or six arrows in a minute, they could rarely reach targets at two hundred yards, and at even close ranges their flint-tipped arrows could not penetrate the vital organs of the armored Spanish. Native arrows were also far less accurate than crossbow bolts. Moreover, archery took years of training to master, while a Castilian could reemploy the bow of a fallen or wounded crossbowman in minutes.

Harquebuses (early muskets with a matchlock firing device) had much the same advantages and drawbacks as the crossbow—enormous penetrating power, little required training, good accuracy, and great range, versus slow rates of fire and clumsiness—but were even deadlier in stopping numerous unarmored warriors with single shots. They were also easier to fabricate and repair. The real advantage of firearms lay not in their ease of use—they were awkward and hard to load—but in their greater accuracy and deadliness. A good shooter could kill with some assurance at 150 yards. His enormous projectiles—some lead balls might weigh up to six ounces—at closer ranges could often go right through the flesh of a number of unarmored Aztecs. Cortés had nearly eighty harquebusiers and crossbowmen when he returned to Tenochtitlán in spring 1521. In serried ranks with bowmen shooting over the heads of the gunners, his men were capable of putting down a sequential carpet of about ten or fifteen projectiles every ten seconds. For short periods of ten or fifteen minutes, against dense masses of Mexicas where misses were few, the Castilians were capable of killing hundreds, especially when placed behind pikemen, on boats, or atop fortifications.

In contemporary European warfare there was an ongoing renaissance in tactics and armament, as harquebusiers were blasting apart even the most disciplined ranks of well-armed Swiss and Spanish pikemen at Marignano (1519), La Bicocca (1522), and Pavia (1525). If the new muskets, fired in careful volleys, could tear apart columns of fast-moving and well-disciplined European pikemen, there was little doubt of their effectiveness against larger but less well organized and poorly protected swarms of Aztec warriors. Even if the Aztecs had captured and mastered the use of harquebuses, such technology, without a supporting framework of scientific research, would have soon stagnated: harquebuses were a mere phase in the continual evolution of European firearms that would soon see flints, better-cast barrels, rifling, and improved powder.

On the plains the Spanish had nearly a century of battle experience in integrating pikemen with harquebusiers—the latter walked out, shot, retreated behind a wall of spears to reload, then again came forward to shoot—to stave off the charges of European aristocratic cavalry. Against the near naked Mexica foot soldiers, these tried-and-tested Castilian squares were nearly invulnerable. Skeptics of European gunpowder superiority must remember that the swarming tactics of indigenous armies— the Zulus are an excellent example—made Western guns especially lethal well before the age of repeating rifles.

Spanish discipline was legendary. Cannon, musket, and crossbow were shot on orders, achieving a murderous symphony against charging masses. Rarely would a harquebusier or swordsman flee should his immediate superior go down. In contrast, regional contingents of the Aztecs were prone to disintegrate once the revered *cuachpantli*—the gaudy standards mounted on bamboo frames and worn on the backs of illustrious warriors—fell or were seized. Personal bravery and prowess in arms are not always synonymous with military discipline, which in the West is largely defined as staying in formation and fighting shoulder-to-shoulder.

What terrified the Aztecs most, however, were the Spanish cannon, some wheeled or fitted on carts, with at least a few of the more rapid-firing breech-loading models. Sources disagree about the actual number and types employed by Cortés's men over the two-year campaign (many were lost during the *Noche Triste*), but the Spaniards brought along ten to fifteen, ranging from small falconets to larger lombards. When properly used against the Aztec mobs, they were absolutely deadly weapons, firing both grapeshot—canisters of smaller iron projectiles—and large cannonballs and stones up to ten pounds. The smaller breech-loading falconets could fire almost a round each minute and a half, point-blank at five hundred yards or with arced shots reaching nearly a half mile. When aimed at the charging Mexicas, each volley tore off limbs, heads, and torsos, as shots went through dozens of warriors.

Spanish chronicles make much of Cortés's horses—forty were present at the final siege of Tenochtitlán—and the complete terror they brought to the Aztecs. The Mexicas at first considered them strange half-human centaurs or divine creatures who could talk with their riders, and only later realized they were large grazing beasts like some sort of gigantic deer. Besides the obvious advantages that horses brought to the fighting—terror, reconnaissance, transport, and mobility—they were unstoppable when ridden by mailed lancers, prompting Bernal Díaz del Castillo to label them the Spaniards' "one hope of survival."

Historically, the only way to defeat cavalry was to fight en masse, as the Franks had done at Poitiers, or with extended pikes in the manner of Swiss phalanxes, or, like the French, to put down a carpet of musket fire into the approach of a mounted charge. The Aztecs could do none of these, lacking a tradition of landed infantry, shock warfare, and firearms of any sort. If they tried to mass in great numbers to clog the lanes of charging horsemen, they soon became vulnerable to cannon volleys. Thus, in concert with artillery, the Spanish horsemen proved deadly in either riding down and spearing individual Aztecs or causing the enemy to seek protection in bunches and thus offering better targets for Cortés's cannon.

Unlike the horses of antiquity, Cortés's mounts were no ponies, but Andalusian Barb-Arabs, bred from larger Arabian horses brought to Spain by the Moors. English observers later exclaimed that the horses of the West Indies were the finest they had ever seen. Their great size and the expertise of their riders—Spanish aristocrats like Sandoval and Alvarado had ridden since childhood and were masters of the mounted lance thrust—made a terrifying spectacle:

> It is extraordinary what havoc a baker's dozen of horsemen could inflict on a vast horde of Indians: and indeed it seems as if the horsemen did not do the damage directly, but that the sudden appearance of these "centaurs" (to use Díaz del Castillo's word) caused so much demoralization that the Indians faltered and enabled the Spanish infantrymen to dash at them with renewed force. . . . The Indians had no idea how to deal with this supernatural beast, half animal and half man, and simply stood paralysed while the pounding hoofs and flashing swords cut them down. (J. White, *Cortés and the Downfall of the Aztec Empire*, 169)

Not all the weapons that would prove so deadly were objects brought from Spain. Some of the most lethal were in the minds of the conquistadors themselves, latent mental blueprints of killing machines that sprang from their heads to became real only under the exigencies of the fighting. The Spanish quickly recognized that among the vast wealth of Mexico were untold—and untapped—raw materials for European-style weapons, ranging from fine lumber for ships and siege machines to metal ores for blades and ingredients for gunpowder.

It is popular to suggest that natural resources alone determine cultural or military dynamism. If true, we should remember that the Aztecs were sitting atop a war merchant's bonanza—an entire subcontinent replete with the ingredients of gunpowder, iron, bronze, and steel. In truth, it was the absence of a systematic approach to abstract learning and science, not the dearth of ores or minerals, that doomed the Aztecs. They lacked wagon wheels perhaps because of the absence of horses; but they were also entirely without other wheel-based instruments of war and commerce—wheelbarrows, rickshaws, water wheels, mill wheels, pulleys and gears—because there was neither a rational tradition of science nor a climate of disinterested research.

Nowhere was the rational Spanish approach more apparent than in their ad hoc construction of battle machinery, which followed siege and ship designs dating back to classical antiquity. During the bitter fighting on the eve of the *Noche Triste* the Spanish within a few hours constructed three *manteletes*, portable wooden towers that protected harquebusiers and crossbowmen who fired over the heads of the infantrymen. When Cortés next discovered that the causeways were breached, he ordered movable bridges built—a European specialty that dated back to Caesar's campaigns in Gaul and Germany. After the flight from Tenochtitlán, gunpowder was fabricated, sulfur being drawn from the nearby "smoky mountain" (Mount Popocatépetl, 17,888 feet above sea level). Native metalsmiths were given Spanish designs and instructions to assist in the making of more than 100,000 copper arrowheads for their own bows, and another 50,000 metal bolts for the Spanish crossbows. In an effort to save powder, during the final siege a gigantic catapult was even fabricated—the mechanics of its winch, armature, and springs apparently being misdesigned by amateurs, since it proved ineffective.

The most impressive project was Martín López's brilliant launching of thirteen prefabricated brigantines. These were enormous galleylike boats more than forty feet long and nine feet at the beam, powered with sails and paddles, and yet with flat bottoms that drew only two feet of water and were thus especially designed for the shallow and swampy waters of Lake Texcoco. Each held twenty-five men and could carry a number of horses, as well as a large cannon. To craft such ships, the Spaniards drafted thousands of Tlaxcalans to haul lumber and the iron hardware salvaged from their beached ships at Vera Cruz. Then López had his carefully organized native work gangs entirely dismantle the brigantines and transport them over the mountains in a large column of some 50,000 porters and warriors to Lake Texcoco. When they arrived in the dry season at Tenochtitlán, López engineered a canal twelve feet wide and about the same depth, through which to navigate the ships from the marshes into deeper waters of the lake: 40,000 Tlaxcalans were involved in the latter project for seven weeks.

The brigantines proved the deciding factor in the entire war, as they were manned by a third of the Spanish manpower and were allotted nearly 75 percent of the cannon, harquebuses, and crossbows. The ships kept the causeways free, ensured that the Spanish camps were secure in the evening, landed infantry at weak points in the enemy lines, enforced a crippling blockade of the city, systematically blew apart hundreds of Aztec canoes, and transported critical food and supplies to the various isolated Spanish contingents. They turned Lake Texcoco from the Spaniards' chief vulnerability to their greatest asset. Their high decks prevented boarding and gave ample cover for the harquebusiers and crossbowmen to fire and reload—characteristic of traditional Western skill in combined infantry and naval tactics:

> However, in the final analysis, Tenochtitlán had an importance that cannot be assigned to Salamis: Tenochtitlán was synonymous with final victory, the conclusion of a war; Salamis was not. At Salamis a civilization was challenged; at Tenochtitlán a civilization was crushed. Possibly in all history there is no similar victorious naval engagement that concluded a war and ended a civilization. (C. Gardiner, *Naval Power in the Conquest of Mexico*, 188)

The brigantines, despite being fabricated more than a hundred miles from Lake Texcoco, proved to be far more ingeniously engineered for fighting on the Aztecs' native waters than any boat constructed in Mexico during the entire history of its civilization—a feat possible only through a systematic approach to science and reason that had been ubiquitous in the West for two millennia.

Almost all elements of the Western military tradition played their respective roles in assuring a Spanish victory, trumping problems of numerical inferiority, logistics, and unknown geography. The hundreds of thousands of pages of postbellum Spanish lawsuits, formal inquiries, and judicial writs among the conquistadors attest to the strong sense of freedom and entitlement each warrior possessed: a sense of civic militarism of individuals with rights and privileges that neither Cortés nor the Spanish crown could infringe upon without constitutional support. While on the road to meet Narváez, some of Cortés's men caught Alonzo de Mata, an emissary with legal papers and summons for their leader's recall. What ensued next was a legalistic debate about the official status of de Mata, ending when the latter could not produce documentation to prove that he was a genuine king's notary and therefore had no authority to vouch for the authenticity of his own decrees.

In fact, throughout the sixteenth century there was a strong sense of political freedom in Spain, perhaps best epitomized in Juan de Costa's (1549–95) treatise *Govierno del ciudadano,* on the proper rights and behavior of the citizen in a constitutional commonwealth. About the same time, Jerónimo de Blancas, a biographer of Cortés, wrote *Aragonesium rerum comentarii* (1588), on the contractual nature of the Aragonese monarchy and its relationship with legislative and judicial branches of government.

The Castilians' drive for decisive horrific engagements—in the streets of Tenochtitlán, on the causeways, in the Plain of Otumba, on Lake Texcoco—was not shared by the Mexicas, who preferred daylight spectacle, in which status, ritual, and captive-taking were sometimes integral to battle. Throughout the fighting, eager traders and entrepreneurs from the New World and Spain docked at Vera Cruz to supply Cortés with shot, food, weapons, and horses. Near extinction, Cortés nevertheless confiscated gold from enemy and friend alike to pay for his supplies, assured in a society of free markets that if there was profit to be made in Vera Cruz, there would eventually be European rascals replete with fresh powder, arms, and men in Tenochtitlán.

The conquistadors, whether led at times by Sandoval, Ordaz, Olid, or Alvarado, owed their lives to an abstract system of command and obedience, not just to a magnetic leader like Cortés. Throughout the conquest individual initiative gave Cortés innumerable advantages. Even the constant complaints of his outspoken men and the threat of formal audit and inquiry from Spanish authorities forced Cortés to consult on strategy with his top lieutenants and to craft tactics with every expectation that there were scores of critics who would appear should he fail. All these components of the Western military tradition gave the Spanish an enormous edge. But in the last analysis a tradition of rationalism, some two millennia old, guaranteed that Hernán Cortés's tools of battle could kill thousands more than those of his enemies.

REASON AND WAR

People from the Stone Age onward have always engaged in some form of scientific activity designed to enhance organized warfare. But beginning with the Greeks, Western culture has shown a singular propensity to think abstractly, to debate knowledge freely apart from religion and politics, and to devise ways of adapting theoretical breakthroughs for practical use, through the marriage of freedom and capitalism. The result has been a constant increase in the technical ability of Western armies to kill their adversaries. Is it not odd that Greek hoplites, Roman legionaries, medieval knights, Byzantine fleets, Renaissance foot soldiers, Mediterranean galleys, and Western harquebusiers were usually equipped with greater destructive power than their adversaries? Even the capture or purchase of Western arms is no guarantee of technological parity—as the Ottomans, Indians, and Chinese learned—inasmuch as European weaponry is an evolving phenomenon, ensuring obsolescence almost simultaneously with the creation of new arms. Creativity has never been a European monopoly, much less intellectual brilliance. Rather, the West's willingness to craft superior weapons is just as often predicated on its unmatched ability to borrow, adopt, and steal ideas without regard to the social, religious, or political changes that new technology often brings—as the incorporation of and improvement on the trireme, Roman *gladius*, astrolabe, and gunpowder attest.

Scholars are correct to point out that Europeans neither invented firearms nor enjoyed a monopoly in their use. But they must acknowledge that the ability to fabricate and distribute firearms on a wide scale and to improve their lethality was unique to Europe. From the introduction of gunpowder in the fourteenth century to the present day, all major improvements in firearms—the matchlock, flintlock, percussion cap, smokeless powder, rifle barrel, minié ball, repeating rifle, and machine gun—have taken place in the West or under Western auspices. As a general rule, Europeans did not employ or import Ottoman or Chinese guns, and they did not pattern their technique of munitions production on Asian or African designs.

This idea of continual innovation and improvement in the use of technology is embodied in Aristotle's dictum in his *Metaphysics* that prior philosophers' theories contribute to a sort of ongoing aggregate of Greek knowledge. In the *Physics* (204B) he admits, "In the case of all discoveries, the results of previous labors that have been handed down from others have been advanced bit by bit by those who have taken them on." Western technological development is largely an outgrowth of empirical research, the acquisition of knowledge through sense perception, the observation and testing of phenomena, and the recording of such data so that factual information itself is timeless, increasing and becoming more accurate through the collective criticism and modification of the ages. That there were an Aristotle, Xenophon, and Aeneas Tacticus at the beginning of Western culture and not anything comparable in the New World explains why centuries later a Cortés could fabricate cannon and gunpowder in the New World, while the Aztecs could not use the Spanish artillery they captured, why for centuries the lethal potential of the land around Tenochtitlán was untapped, but was mined for its gunpowder and ores within months after the Spanish arrival.

Western technological superiority is not merely a result of the military renaissance of the sixteenth century or an accident of history, much less the result of natural resources, but predicated on an age-old *method* of investigation, a peculiar mentality that dates back to the Greeks and not earlier. Although the theoretical mathematician Archimedes purportedly snapped that "the whole trade of engineering was sordid and ignoble, and every sort of art that lends itself to mere use and profit," his machines—cranes and a purported huge reflective glass heat ray—delayed the capture of Syracuse for two years. The Roman navy in the First Punic War not only copied Greek and Carthaginian designs but went on to ensure their victories by the use of innovative improvements such as the *corvus,* a sort of derrick that lifted enemy ships right out of the water. Long before American B-29s dropped napalm over Tokyo, the Byzantines sprayed through brass tubes compressed blasts of Greek fire, a secret concoction of naphtha, sulfur, and quicklime that like its modern counterpart kept burning even when doused with water.

Military knowledge was also abstract and published, not just empirical. Western military manuals from Aelian *(Taktike theoria)* and Vegetius *(Epitoma rei militaris)* to the great handbooks on ballistics and tactics of the sixteenth century (e.g., Luigi Collado's *Practica manual de artiglierra* [1586] or Justus Lipsius's *De militia Romana* [1595–96]) incorporate first-hand knowledge and abstract theoretical investigation into practical advice. In contrast, the most brilliant of Chinese and Islamic military works are far more ambitious and holistic texts, and thus less pragmatic as actual blueprints for killing, embedded with religion, politics, or philosophy and replete with illusions and axioms from Allah to the yin and the yang, hot and cold, one and many.

Courage on the battlefield is a human characteristic. But the ability to craft weapons through mass production to offset such bravery is a cultural phenomenon. Cortés, like Alexander the Great, Julius Caesar, Don Juan of Austria, and other Western captains, often annihilated without mercy their numerically superior foes, not because their own soldiers were necessarily better in war, but because their traditions of free inquiry, rationalism, and science most surely were.

SEVEN

The Market—or Capitalism Kills

Lepanto, October 7, 1571

Accumulated capital, not forced exactions, is what sustains wars.
—THUCYDIDES, *The Peloponnesian War* (1.141.5)

GALLEY WAR

No Quarter

WERE THEY MERCHANT BARGES? The Ottoman admiral, Müez-zinzade Ali Pasha, had never seen anything like the six bizarre ships float-ing a few hundred yards in front of his attacking galleys. Perhaps they were some sort of supply vessels? Clearly, they were both new and huge—and drifting right toward his flagship, the *Sultana*! In truth, the six colos-sal oddities were recently constructed Venetian galleasses. Each carried nearly fifty heavy guns—bristling from starboard and port, shooting over the bow and from the poop deck, guns it seemed booming everywhere. Each of these novel monstrosities could deliver more than six times as much shot as the largest oared ships in Europe—and in terms of fire-power alone were worth a dozen of the sultan's standard galleys.

On such calm seas they were mobile too and with sails and oars could maneuver and turn to fire in every direction. Now four of the six bobbing behemoths methodically began to blast apart Ali Pasha's galleys—"*tanta horribile et perpetua tempesta*," a contemporary account recorded. Grapeshot and five-pound balls tore through the Turkish decks. The rarer thirty- or even sixty-pound iron projectiles blew apart entire sections of the Turkish ships at the waterline—men, planking, and oars obliterated altogether.

"Big ships, big ships with big cannon," the Turkish crews reportedly screamed of the murderous incoming fire. Two of the galleasses' commanders, Antonio and Ambrogio Bragadino, had just heard of the ghastly torture and murder of their brother, Marcantonio, on Cyprus a few weeks earlier. Now the brothers urged hundreds of their gunners to fire continuously, determined this Sunday morning to take no prisoners in revenge.

If Ali's ships could not get past the galleasses to close quickly with the Christian armada, the entire Ottoman fleet, despite its far greater size, would be systematically torn apart at sea:

> The sea was wholly covered with men, yardarms, oars, casks, barrels, and various kinds of armaments, an incredible thing that only six galleasses should have caused such great destruction, for they had not hitherto been tried in the forefront of a naval battle. (K. M. Setton, *The Papacy and the Levant*, 1056)

Most of the Christian observers believed that a third of the Ottoman armada was scattered, disabled, or sunk before the battle proper between galleys had even commenced. As many as 10,000 Turkish seamen were thrown into the sea when their galleys were obliterated in thirty minutes of firing from just four European ships—two of the six galleasses on the right wing drifted out of position and saw little action. Ali Pasha had seen in these strange galleasses some glimpses of the future of naval warfare, and it rested not with rams, boarders, or rowers, but with mass-produced iron cannon, high decks, and large vessels.

Nevertheless, a portion of the center of the Ottoman fleet, ninety-six galleys and escorts led by Ali Pasha's *Sultana*, headed through and finally around the blistering gunfire toward Don Juan's *La Reale*—an enormous galley in its own right, launched from the dockyards of Seville and adorned by the artistic hand of Juan Bautista Vázquez himself. The prince's gaudy embroidered banner of the Crucifixion and the combined arms of Spain, Venice, and the Holy See marked for all to see the center of the Christian line, where Don Juan was flanked by the papal captain Marcantonio Colonna—to die bravely in the battle to come—and the Venetian septuagenarian Sebastian Veniero. Thanks to Don Juan's singular genius and magnanimity, the shaky confederation fleet was under the shared tactical command of a Genoese, Venetian, and Spaniard.

As the battered Turkish ships approached the armada of the Holy League, priests scurried across the decks, blessing the crews in the final seconds before the collision of galleys; many of them were armed and had every intention of offering material as well as spiritual comfort to their flocks. "My children," Don Juan had told his men in the minutes before the collision, "we are here to conquer or to die as Heaven may determine." Crucifixes adorned every ship in the fleet at Lepanto. The Christians, not the supposed "fanatical" Muslims, would fight like men possessed. All were enraged over rumors of the most recent Ottoman atrocities on Cyprus and Corfu, and convinced this was the best and last chance that they might have to engage the Turkish fleet in a decisive battle and thus seek retribution for decades of Islamic raiding of their shores.

Soon eight hundred Christian and Turkish soldiers mixed it up on the *Sultana,* itself an ornate galley with decks of polished black walnut. But for all its beauty, the *Sultana* lacked the protective boarding nets of the *Reale* and thus became the central slaughter place of the two lines, a veritable floating battlefield between cross and crescent. The Christians, most of whom wore steel breastplates and fired harquebuses, twice nearly forced their way to the center of Ali Pasha's ship before swarms of Turks fought them back. Smaller Ottoman galliots that had survived the galleasses' initial broadsides docked constantly beside the two locked flagships and unloaded reinforcements, in hopes that the sheer manpower and skill of the Janissaries might cancel out the superior firearms, armor, and group cohesion of the Spanish and Italian infantry. More Christian ships were also pulling up beside the *Sultana* and unloading fresh harquebusiers to join the fight for Ali Pasha's ship.

Many of the European galleys, particularly the Spanish vessels, were larger than their Ottoman counterparts. Their higher decks allowed boarding parties to jump down into the Turkish ships, while hundreds more of the Christian gunners remaining on board poured shot downward with impunity on the beleaguered enemy archers. The Christians—

the Spanish especially—were also comfortable with mass charges, in which discipline, cohesion, and sheer weight might overwhelm the individual bravery and martial skill of the Janissaries.

At last a final rush led by Don Juan himself, brandishing battle-ax and broadsword, overwhelmed the *Sultana*'s crew. Ali Pasha, shooting arrows from his small bow, fell with a harquebus bullet in his brain. Soon his head was on a pike and posted on the *Reale*'s quarterdeck, as his treasured gilded and green flag from Mecca was ripped from the mast, the papal pennant raised in its place. Panic engulfed what was left of the ninety-six ships at the center of the Ottoman fleet once their crews saw that their admiral was decapitated and the sultan's flagship now the property of Don Juan himself. The Spaniards pulled their vessels away from the death ship and sought out additional prey to their beleaguered right.

Meanwhile, the Christian left wing under Agostino Barbarigo—a few days after the battle he would perish from a ghastly wound to the eye— was outflanked and being driven onto the Aetolian mainland by the longer Ottoman right under the wily Mehmed Siroco ("Suluk"). Indeed, the three wings of Don Juan's fleet constituted a battle line of only some 7,500 yards; the admirals of the Holy League were thus rightly worried that the longer Ottoman front might circumvent their wings and sweep them from the rear. But in a brilliant feat of seamanship Barbarigo back-watered, kept most of the enemy ships in front of his own line, and then began driving them onto the shore as he raked their decks with gunfire and awaited the inevitable boarding by the numerically superior Turkish galleys. Barbarigo had under his command the best galleys from the Arsenal at Venice—among them *Christ Raised*, *Fortune*, and *Sea Horse*— and both his outnumbered ships and crews were qualitatively superior to their Ottoman counterparts.

Once the Turkish soldiers had exhausted their supply of arrows— many of them poison-tipped—the struggle between Siroco and Barbarigo became another land battle of sorts between infantry. The frenzied Christians, wearing armor, equipped with firearms, and advancing over the decks in dense lines and columns, found they could systematically slaughter the Turkish peasants, most of whom soon ran out of arrows and were without metal body protection, harquebuses, or the succor of the Janissaries. At close ranges on the decks of the galleys, fire from the harquebuses tore right through the unarmored Turks, killing and wounding with almost every shot. Mehmed Siroco would also soon lose his head, his truncated corpse thrown ignominiously overboard. The Christians sank or captured most of his fifty-six ships, killed the crews, and spared neither

Salamis (above) was one of the largest, most confused—and deadliest—engagements in naval history. European artists reinvented it as a struggle between high-prowed Mediterranean galleys, but they at least capture the congestion of a quarter-million sailors in hundreds of triremes, rowing, boarding, killing, and drowning—all within a few thousand square yards of sea. Themistocles (below left) created the Athenian fleet, engineered the Persian defeat, and laid the foundations of Athenian imperialism before being ostracized and sentenced to death in absentia by the very citizenry he had saved. On this relief from Persepolis (below right), Darius and Xerxes, who would both invade Greece and be defeated, appear as near divinities—stiff and unapproachable, with none of the realism of classical Greek sculpture.

East meets West (above) in a Roman floor mosaic from Pompeii. In Alexander's rush toward Darius III, their antithesis is striking: Darius is frightened although perched on his imperial chariot amid bodyguards, while a solitary Alexander strives to plunge into the melee. Sometimes associated with the Battle of Issus (333 B.C.), the scene seems to be a mélange, incorporating moments from all four of his great fights. At left, a Hellenistic bust reflects the Olympian divinity of Alexander, emphasizing his youth, beauty, and farseeing gaze.

In the majestic canvas above by Charles Le Brun (1619–90), Alexander's men mop up a battlefield full of captives and booty at Gaugamela. The reality was far worse: Over 50,000 corpses were left to rot in the October sun. Persian reliefs like the one below were meant to suggest the uniformity and anonymity of imperial soldiers. Notice the absence of metal body armor, helmets, and heavy shields.

Classical sculptors and authors alike were fascinated with Hannibal Barca (left). While he was imbued with all the stereotypical traits of non-Western enemies—perfidy, arrogance, and cruelty—there was also a grudging admiration for his skill, courage, and tenacity in a hopeless cause. It is notable that all surviving art and literature surrounding Hannibal—much of it sympathetic and romantic—derive from the very culture that destroyed his country, family, and himself. An illustrated manuscript of the late fifteenth century (below) attempts to capture the sheer magnitude and hand-to-hand fighting of Cannae. Yet the rather tame nature of Renaissance warfare paled in comparison; even the most imaginative illustrators had no conception of battles involving well over 100,000 combatants, in which hundreds might be killed every minute.

Carl von Steuben's romantic painting of the Battle of Poitiers (above) suggests the power of the Frankish "mass of ice," the wall of tough mailed spearmen who broke the repeated mounted attacks of Islamic horsemen. The battle was viewed as a major event in the preservation of Christianity, in which faith trumped numbers— hence the prominent religious iconography. Often seen as a battle of horsemen, as below in *The Pursuit of the Defeated*, in reality most Frankish knights probably dismounted during the fight. While the artist has typically represented the Franks as mounted, the density and position of their spears suggest the onset of a classical phalanx.

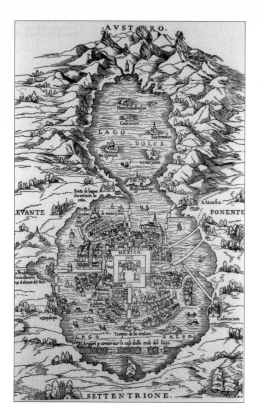

This map of Mexico City (above), often attributed to Cortés himself, suggests its size and wealth. The enormous population—estimated at over 200,000—was fed by a vast fleet of lake-borne canoes. Hernan Cortés (above right) was often portrayed as a triumphant knight of a grateful monarchy; in fact, he died poor, disillusioned, and ignored by those he had enriched. While this Spanish woodcut (right) presents Montezuma in warrior dress, he took no part in the fighting and was killed months before the destruction of his imperial city.

Later Mexican drawings stressed the deadly effect of Spanish steel on unprotected flesh. At the festival of Toxcatl (above), 120 Spaniards massacred over 3,000 unarmed Aztec nobles at the cost of a few wounded. This image of the subsequent siege of the Spanish (below) shows them superbly armed, arrayed in dense formation, and vastly outnumbered, as more numerous lighter-clad Aztecs attempt to storm their redoubt. All contemporary Spanish and Mexican observers felt that European weapons were the key to the conquistadors' victory.

To sixteenth-century Europeans, the sudden muster and vast size of the Christian fleet at Lepanto were proof of the power of Christ to resist the Muslim onslaught. In this haunting canvas of Giorgio Vasari (1511–74), the supernatural forces of good and evil watch as the six enormous galleasses lead out the Holy League's massive armada. The dense formation of his galleys conveys an accurate impression that the fighting resembled more a land than a sea battle, as hundreds of ships quickly became interlocked in the confused fighting.

The last minutes of thousands of Ottoman sailors at Lepanto were a favorite topic of European illustrators. Eyewitness accounts provided lurid descriptions of robed survivors clinging to the flotsam of wrecked galleys before sinking beneath the waves or being harpooned by Christian pikemen. Most Ottoman fatalities occurred after the actual fighting was over; and we should assume the majority of the 30,000 lost either drowned or were executed at sea.

Rorke's Drift (above) had almost no defensive advantages; yet within a few hours the British crafted a redoubt of bags and boxes that proved unassailable. The chief mistake of King Cetshwayo (below left) was underestimating the strength of his enemies; only later when he visited London himself did he appreciate England's enormous resources. The three-pronged attack on Zulu power centers conceived by Lord Chelmsford (below right) resulted in the complete destruction of a vast kingdom in less than a year.

Nearly the entire 24th Regiment was wiped out at Isandhlwana, but B company was assigned to "easy duty" at Rorke's Drift. Above, fifty survivors of B company a few days after their harrowing ordeal. Lieutenant Bromhead is at lower right. The Zulu warriors below were the terror of southern Africa, but proved incapable of breaking even small numbers of British riflemen in squares or behind fortifications.

In Griffin Baily Coale's watercolor of Midway, both the *Kagi* and the *Akagi* are set afire by the first wave of American dive bombers. Japanese Zeros plunge into the sea, gunned down by the surprise appearance of high-flying Wildcat fighters far above. The gassed and armed planes on the wooden Japanese decks ensured that even a few American bomb hits could envelop the carriers in flames. Pilots later reported that the rising suns painted on the Japanese decks made natural targets.

Wounded by Japanese dive and torpedo bombers, the *Yorktown* (above) was finally doomed by torpedoes from a Japanese submarine. Earlier, the miraculous repair of the *Yorktown*—severely damaged at the Battle of Coral Sea—at Pearl Harbor (below) ensured that there were three, not two, American carriers at Midway. Had the Japanese shown similar ingenuity, they would have had six carriers, an overwhelming force.

By 1942, American SBD and TBD bombers were both obsolete. Yet at Midway the screeching dives of the SBDs (above) proved lethal and went unopposed—due to the unplanned and tragic sacrifice of the TBD torpedo planes far below. Rear Admiral Tamon Yamaguchi was probably the most capable leader in the imperial fleet. He is shown below, thanking his staff as he prepares to go down with his flagship, the *Hiryu*.

None of the pilots in Torpedo Squadron 8 of the *Hornet* (above) had flown a combat mission before Midway. All were killed in the first minutes of fighting except Ensign George Gay (front row, fourth from left), who was shot down and watched the battle from a small raft on the water. Of the eighty-two TBD Devastator crewmen who took off from the three American carriers, only thirteen survived, and not a single torpedo hit a target. The torpedo planes approached the fleeing enemy carriers at no more than seventy miles an hour and were riddled by Zero fighters diving from above at speeds of over 300 miles an hour.

Fighting under close media scrutiny in dense urban centers, unable to distinguish the enemy from neutral civilians, American soldiers like those at left nevertheless crushed local communist resistance during the Tet Offensive of 1968. Keys to the American success were devastating armor and artillery attacks, constant air support, and the discipline and ferocity of small companies of marines. Above, marines hold a tower position in the stone fortress of Hué.

the surrendering nor the wounded. Later they claimed that not a single galley or its crew escaped.

Barbarigo's troops made it a point to butcher every dumbfounded and by now mostly defenseless Ottoman sailor and soldier they found, as they freed thousands of shackled Christian galley slaves—15,000 in all were eventually liberated at Lepanto. Italian and Spanish accounts repeatedly glorify the salvation of the European slaves, yet only in passing acknowledge that most of the Turkish dead at Lepanto were probably killed in cold blood as they begged for mercy on deck or floated helpless among the debris on the water. Still, the cost of preserving Don Juan's left wing was high. Most of the cream of the Venetian naval leadership—Marino Contarini, Vincenzo Querini, and Andrea Barbarigo, nephew of Agostino—were shot down in the ordeal.

Only on the right wing, under the veteran Genoese Gian Andrea Dorea, were the Christians still in any danger. As he drifted far to the right, Dorea appeared dilatory and sluggish in maintaining the Christian front intact. The Holy League's admirals would swear that Dorea was heading laterally, more away from Don Juan's center than forward toward the Turkish fleet. Was the crafty Venetian, as was later alleged, hoping to save his own ships from possible destruction? In any case, the Christian galleys that had just engaged Ali Pasha's center were alarmed that if Dorea kept rowing to the right to prevent his national contingent from being outflanked and attacked by the legendary and dreaded corsair Uluj Ali, their own flanks would soon be exposed.

Within minutes their worst fears were realized. A gap opened in the Christian front between the right and center. Uluj Ali and a dozen Ottoman galleys, reminiscent of Alexander at Gaugamela, immediately streamed into the chasm and headed for the flanks and backs of the exhausted Christian center. Here occurred most of the Christian losses in the battle. The surprised galleys were hit broadside without opportunity to turn and fire. Uluj's corsairs greedily began to tow away his prizes; the decks of the outnumbered Venetian and Spanish galleys—among them three manned by the Knights of Malta under the command of the legendary Pietro Giustiniani—were littered with killed and wounded. But unfortunately for the Ottomans, Uluj's last-ditch effort was governed by greed as he paused to tow prizes rather than press on to ram and blast apart more enemy galleys.

Two of the League's bravest admirals—Juan de Cardona and Alvarode Bazán, the marquess of Santa Cruz, leading the uncommitted Christian reserve of over forty galleys—were ready for just such a contingency. With

The Battle of Lepanto October 7, 1571

To
Corfu

OXIA

Point Scropha

GALLEASS

GALLEASS

TURKISH Right, Led by
Mehmed Siroco (Suluk)
56 GALLEYS

CHRISTIAN Left,
Led by Agostino Barbarigo
63 GALLEYS

To Lepanto

Adriatic Sea

Lepanto

Mediterranean Sea

GALLEASS

CHRISTIAN Center,
Led by Don Juan of Austria
63 GALLEYS

CHRISTIAN Reserve,
Led by Don Álvaro de Bazán
35 GALLEYS

GALLEASS

CHRISTIAN Reserve,
Led by Don Juan de Cardona
8 GALLEYS

GALLEASS

TURKISH Reserve
128 SHIPS

TURKISH Center,
Led by Müezzinzade Ali Pasha
96 GALLEYS

Gulf of Lepanto

GALLEASS

CHRISTIAN Right,
Led by Gian Andrea Dorea
64 GALLEYS

TURKISH Left,
Led by Uluj Ali
93 GALLEYS

help from the victorious galleys in the Christian center, the reserve ships began firing away at Uluj. Within minutes the Christian cannon drove the corsair off. Had he not cut his towlines and fled, his contingent would have been blown apart. Still, Dorea's timidity cost the Christians dearly. The escape of Uluj was more grievous still: he was the last veteran Turkish admiral in the Mediterranean still alive, and would supervise the rebuilding of the sultan's fleet the next year and oversee the successful capture of Tunis in 1574.

Center, right, and left—the Christians now achieved success across the battle line. The victory was partly because of the opening murderous barrages of the galleasses that were posted nearly a mile in front of the fleet, and partly because of the superior quality and number of cannon on the individual European galleys that shot right over their truncated prows into the waterlines of the Turkish ships. The return fire was aimed too high, slower, and finally nonexistent. In almost every case, Christian ships literally destroyed their enemies in exchanges of gunfire. Once the galleys were locked, and it was a question of infantry fighting on deck, the Europeans—especially the 27,800-man Spanish contingent, of which 7,300 were German mercenaries—proved superior to Turkish foot soldiers. The harquebuses of the Spaniards weighed fifteen to twenty pounds and could shoot a two-ounce ball four hundred to five hundred yards, shredding all flesh in its path. The Ottomans found success only when they could swarm isolated Christian galleys, bury them under a sea of arrows, and overwhelm the wounded defenders. They had little experience with the shock warfare of heavy infantry in a confined setting, where group solidarity and discipline, not personal heroism or maneuver, brought victory.

By 3:30 Sunday afternoon, a little more than four hours after the galleasses opened fire, the battle was over. More than 150 Muslims and Christians had been killed every minute of the fighting, ranking Lepanto's combined 40,000 dead—thousands more were wounded or missing—with Salamis, Cannae, and the Somme as one of the bloodiest single-day slaughters on land or sea in the history of warfare. When it was over, two-thirds of all the galleys in the great Mediterranean fleet of the Ottoman Empire were either floating junk or in tow behind Christian galleys headed westward.

Floating Sewers

Nearly 180,000 men were present at Lepanto, rowing, firing, and stabbing each other under conditions that modern soldiers can scarcely imagine. War galleys on both sides were filthy, ghastly ships, as dirty on inspection as they were elegant at a distance. Once they were locked in mortal combat, they became little more than grisly floating platforms of death, no longer the sleek boats of ancient fable that glided through the whitecaps of the Mediterranean. The radical changes of the last two millennia in naval combat were not so much due to advances in technology or nautical design. Classical Greek triremes and Venetian galleys were not that dissimilar in size, construction, and propulsion. Rather, there were alterations in the conditions of the later ships' service or operation, specifically the forced labor of chained rowers, the larger contingents of on-board marines, and voyages of much greater distances on the open sea.

Whereas the Athenians' invasion fleet of 415 B.C. had beached their much lighter craft each night onshore in their circuitous and weeks-long voyage from the Piraeus to Sicily, by the sixteenth century galleys could on occasion cut directly across the Mediterranean. Such ships in theory could have on board twenty days' supply of water—and thus sail overnight without adequate shelter for their servile oarsmen. In addition, cross-Mediterranean voyages between Asia Minor and Spain and France—practically unheard-of in antiquity—were commonplace by 1571 and often lasted for days on end without nightly stops at safe ports.

The great Venetian war galleys at Lepanto were often 160 feet and more in length and as much as 30 feet wide at the beam. From twenty to forty banks of oars pulled from each side of the ship, five men handling together an enormous forty-foot "sweep," resulting in crews that were twice and three times the size of those of classical antiquity. Sails were raised only during transit to and from battle—or for brief periods during combat when a sudden onslaught might be enhanced by a tailing wind. As many marines, bowmen, and harquebusiers as possible crammed onto the decks, sometimes nearly sinking the galley under the combined weight of four hundred to five hundred rowers and soldiers. Besides the firepower of the boarding parties—nearly two hundred independent infantrymen per ship—each galley attacked its prey with a ten- to twenty-foot iron beak and up to twenty cannon: larger ones in the poop and prow, more numerous three- to four-pounders arranged haphazardly along the decks to issue broadsides. The main gun of many galleys was a vast bronze 175-millimeter cannon of several tons that could hurl a sixty-pound ball well over a mile.

If the galley was a rather frail ship, vulnerable to capsizing in even small storms (the Christian states lost nearly forty a year to bad weather on the Mediterranean in the late sixteenth century), it was an easy vessel to construct. The sleek standardized designs resulted in a galley achieving twenty-minute bursts of speed of eight knots and more, its low sides allowing marines to scurry throughout the ship and leap onto a captured vessel. The overcrowding of the rowing crews and the proximity of man to sea, however, made the ships wretched in transit and a charnel house in battle. Galleys and their crews were rammed, peppered with cannonballs and grapeshot, torched by fire grenades, and raked by small-arms fire and arrows. The absence of high decks, armor, and heavy roofing guaranteed terrible fatalities with almost every barrage.

The contemporary historian Gianpiertro Contarini said the waters around Lepanto were *"tutto il mare sanguinoso"*—a sea of blood—as thousands of Christians and Turks bled to death in the water. Thousands more of the wounded clung to the junk of battle among the bobbing corpses. Eye witnesses record that the trapped Janissaries—easy targets due to their size, gaudy clothing, and bobbing plumes—were huddling and seeking shelter under the rowing benches as the Turkish galleys were smashed apart by cannon fire and raked by harquebuses from the higher Christian decks. Finally, out of ammunition, the Janissaries resorted to throwing anything they found on deck, including lemons and oranges, at the murderous Christian gunners.

So many combatants were confined within such a small space—often as many as four hundred rowers and soldiers occupying 3,000 square feet—that few shots could miss, whether powered by muscle or powder. Whereas in ancient trireme ramming, most fatalities were due to drowning, in sixteenth-century sea fights men just as often died from arrows and cannon fire, if not frequently butchered by boarding parties as they rowed chained and immovable. Galleys were ingeniously designed for relatively calm waters—there is essentially little tide in the Mediterranean—and their firepower and speed made them terrible predators of merchant ships. But once galley met galley, their assets were often neutralized, and the resulting battle more resembled a confused free-for-all on land than a contest of seamanship.

The maximum range of most smaller galley cannon was not more than five hundred yards. Given the slow rates of fire—especially in the

Ottoman fleet—most ships could shoot off only one volley before their target had closed the distance and was either ramming or boarding as the attackers desperately reloaded. A real European advantage at Lepanto lay in having more numerous and heavier cannon throughout the fleet— Venetian artillery was the most finely crafted in the world—that could concentrate their fusillades on the Ottoman galleys as they approached to board, ensuring that a single volley from dozens of heavy guns could annihilate the entire first wave of skirmishers.

The advent of cannon, harquebusiers, and shackled slave rowers brought to the ancient idea of oared warships unprecedented death and suffering at Lepanto, torment unimagined by the crews at Salamis two millennia earlier, despite the greater aggregate losses at the ancient battle. Often the crews of whole ships—rowers and skirmishers in the hundreds—were slaughtered when hooked, boarded, and raked at point-blank range with antipersonnel cannon and musket fire. Gianpietro Contarini says that at Lepanto there was an enormous confusion of swords, scimitars, iron maces, knives, arrows, harquebuses, and fire grenades on every ship. One Spanish source mentions a galley on the right wing on which after the battle every single man was found dead or wounded. It was a truism that European navies in the Mediterranean— the Venetians especially—were without the manpower of the Ottoman fleet and therefore increasingly counted on gunpowder to do what muscle could not. Galley warfare also left the combatants far more vulnerable than on land: on the overloaded boats there was scarcely enough room to turn around, and the surrounding sea cut off all avenues of retreat. The armor of the Christians and the robes and purses of the Ottomans ensured that there was little chance to keep afloat once a soldier was thrown or fell into the water. Most decks were deliberately waxed and oiled to undermine footing and topple intruders.

Ramming was still frequently employed by the Ottomans, as well as boarding by swordsmen and archers. But the introduction of cannon that could hurl iron or stone projectiles of thirty and more pounds right through the side of a low-lying galley also meant that the onrushing seas could swallow chained rowers in a few minutes. Many Turkish galleys were sunk or abandoned at Lepanto, not hauled away as prizes, since cannon fire, not boarding parties, had brought on their demise. The classical protocols of attacking in unison with beaks outward, ship by ship, to prevent enemy inroads was not so important when the new European ships were bristling with cannon on all sides and could fire in any direction. To save powder and lead, the Christians in small boats used long pikes to spear any Turks they found still alive in the sea.

Ramming was eventually doomed by the advent of relatively plentiful bronze-cast cannon: the mounting of each 5,000-pound gun meant that additional oarsmen were necessary to recover an overburdened galley's original speed. But the increase in rowers added more weight to the ship, required ever more deck space, and ultimately revealed that the laws of physics limited how large and heavy a galley might grow and still find it-self seaworthy—quite apart from questions of how to feed and support four hundred rowers, crew, and gunners.

Larger, three-masted galleons, not even the novel and well-armed gal-leasses, were the answer. The former had no oars; but with higher decks and broad sails, galleons alone possessed the requisite on-ship surface area, smaller crews, and locomotive power to support an ever-increasing number of heavy cannon and tons of stored shot and powder. Larger ships could also navigate the rough Atlantic and Pacific and stay at sea for weeks, unlike the Mediterranean galley. In contrast to Spain and France, the Ottomans had no ports on the Atlantic and so by the seventeenth cen-tury lacked transoceanic navigational experience and the sheer techno-logical know-how to build topflight galleons. It was more common to see European warships than Ottoman galleys in the Islamic waters of the Persian Gulf and the Red Sea.

The name of Lepanto conjures up clean images of gaudy Renaissance banners, vast oil canvases of the European masters, and a variety of fasci-nating Christian spiritual and material commemoratives. Yet life aboard a sixteenth-century Mediterranean galley was nearly unbearable. Most ships in continual service rotted and were unseaworthy within five years. Unlike the ancient trireme, which was less often powered by servile row-ers and allowed more space for each oarsman, the galley slave was usually chained to his rowing bench alongside four others. He urinated, defe-cated, and in rough seas often vomited where he was bound. Clothed in a brief loincloth, he had no protection from seawater, rain, or frost—or the scorching heat of the Mediterranean summer that constituted the greater portion of the sailing season. The sixteenth-century rower was also not free, like his ancient counterpart was, to forage onshore. Nor did his ship seek shelter on land at nightfall—so that on occasion he worked, slept, and ate at his bench for days on end. Dry biscuits and a cup of wine were standard, not the cakes and adequate provisions characteristic of the ra-tions for freemen in the ancient Athenian navy. When a fleet of a hundred such ships pulled into port, a veritable floating city of 40,000 hungry mouths quickly exhausted the local municipal food reserves, as the noisome cargo of tons of raw sewage spread disease and a lingering miasma throughout the port.

Contemporary accounts also relate a number of bizarre details that only confirm the horror. Sailors, marines, and rowers all wore scented scarves—purportedly the origin of the Mediterranean male's propensity to use strong perfumes—to mask the stench and prevent vomiting. When flies, roaches, lice, fleas, and rats had overrun a galley, and its four-inch-thick boards became inundated with offal, captains—particularly the more fastidious Knights of Malta—sometimes temporarily sank the boats right offshore, in hopes that a few hours of total submersion in seawater might rid them of their cargo of vermin. Plagues—most often cholera and typhus—could wipe out entire flotillas, and understandably so, when four or five men were chained day and night alongside each other, stewing in each other's lice, fleas, excrement, urine, and sweat. Such were the conditions of service for the nearly 200,000 desperate seamen who collided on October 7, 1571.

Culture and Military Innovation at Lepanto

Lepanto, situated off the western coast of Greece, was a likely place for a sea battle between Europe and its enemies, being on the general fault line between the Ottoman-held Balkans and the Christian western Mediterranean. Whenever East met West in the Mediterranean, the waters off the Gulf of Corinth made a logical nexus of battle, as the two great sea fights nearby at Actium (31 B.C.) and Prevesa (1538) attest. Salamis itself lay not more than two hundred miles to the east across the isthmus at Corinth. The Ottoman fleet, after a successful season of conquest on Cyprus, was planning to winter in the small bay of the present-day tourist community of Naupactus, on the northwestern shore inside the gulf. Once the spring weather came and his crews were rested and refitted, Ali Pasha, the Sultan's admiral, looked forward to a season of raiding far from Istanbul—and perhaps an invasion itself of European shores to cap off the capture of Cyprus the prior August.

In response to the attack on Malta (1565), the Turkish massacre of Christians at Famagusta in August 1571, and the subsequent appearance of Ottoman raiders off European coastlines, the confederation of Venice, Spain, and the Papal States had at last formed a grand, if somewhat shaky, alliance. By early fall 1571 the combined fleet of the newly christened

Holy League had made its way across the Adriatic from Sicily. The Christians were desperately searching for the Ottoman armada before the winter season set in and the Mediterranean turned too rough for a decisive battle between oared ships. The alliance's fear was that such a large Ottoman fleet wintering close to western Europe would race throughout the Adriatic, plundering, kidnapping, and killing at will among Italian coastal communities, even sacking Venice itself.

Rather than be caught and defeated in small flotillas by the sultan's enormous predatory navy, Pope Pius V had at last convinced Philip II of Spain and the Venetian Senate to stake their combined fleets in a do-or-die gamble to rid once and for all the western Mediterranean of the Turkish menace. If they did not find the Ottomans this autumn, the pope warned, there was every likelihood that the rare unanimity of action would be lost. Each Christian state would be forced once more to resist by itself or make terms with the sultan on its own. Word had reached the Holy League's fleet in Corfu as early as the evening of September 28 that the Turkish armada was anchored not far away on the non-Western shores of the Gulf of Corinth. Once his fleet arrived off the coast of Aetolia a week later, Don Juan convinced his squabbling admirals to attack the Turks the next day, the Sunday morning of October 7. He cut off debate with a terse "Gentlemen, the time for counsel is past and the time for fighting has come." As at Salamis, squabbling Europeans met a unified though autocratic Asiatic command.

What the Holy League lacked in manpower and ships (the Ottomans enjoyed a numerical advantage of at least thirty galleys, even more lighter ships, and more than 20,000 soldiers) was more than made up by superior Christian tactical leadership and numerous subtle advantages in nautical technology. The confederates' admiral, Don Juan of Austria, the illegitimate son of Charles V of Spain and half brother to the reigning king, Philip II, was one of the more remarkable and gifted captains of a sixteenth-century Mediterranean world characterized by an array of brilliant and headstrong Venetian and Genoese sailors and generals: Sebastian Veniero, governor of Crete and future doge of Venice, Pietro Giustiniani, prior of Messenia, Marcantonio Colonna, commander of the papal contingent, and Agostino Barbarigo, admiral of the left wing at Lepanto.

Contemporary accounts remark on Don Juan's selflessness and his single-minded zeal in uniting the disparate nations of southern Europe to deny the Turks any further inroads in the West, especially along the coastal cities on the western Mediterranean. We need not believe all the romance about the twenty-six-year-old prince—tales of his pet marmoset, his tame lion, his dancing a jig on the deck of his flagship, *Reale,* moments before the fighting—to acknowledge that few men of the time could have held together such an ill-sorted coalition of rivals. Commercially minded Venetians fought their former Ottoman trading partners reluctantly and only when threatened with annihilation. Imperial Spaniards were as ready to battle the Italians, Dutch, English, and French as the Turks. The Papal States' shrill warnings about the Mediterranean becoming an Islamic lake were seldom taken seriously, especially given the popes' intrigue in the dynastic wars of European succession. In any case, for the first time in decades Christendom found at its helm a magnanimous leader—one more interested in checking the spread of Islam than enriching himself or even gaining advantage for his native state at the general expense of Europe. (Don Juan turned over his one-tenth share of the prize money from Lepanto to the impoverished and wounded in the fleet, as well as a gift of 30,000 gold ducats from the grateful city of Messina.)

The Christians approached the seas off Lepanto with nearly 300 Venetian, Spanish, Genoese, and other assorted European ships of all sizes: 208 galleys, 6 galleasses, 26 galleons (which were late and played no role in the actual fighting), and another 76 smaller craft, all comprising an armada of more than 50,000 rowers and 30,000 soldiers—a pan-Christian force in size not seen since the Crusades. Still, this force was smaller than the nearly 100,000-man fleet of 230 major warships of the sultan, with another 80 assorted gunships. But the quality of the Christian galleys, not the superior number of Ottomans, would prove the critical factor at Lepanto. Venetian galleys were the best-designed and most stable craft on the Mediterranean, serving as models for the Turkish fleet itself. The Spanish vessels, too, were better built and stouter than those of the Ottomans. Don Juan, in consultation with his Venetian admirals, had provided the allied galleys with innovations unknown to the Ottoman fleet, which had ironically confirmed that at the greatest galley battle since Actium, the age of the oared ship was already over. Lepanto would be the last large galley fight in naval history.

First, the Christians had sawed off the beaks of their galleys, surmising that the age of ramming was past and that their ships could be better supplied with additional cannon. Rams also obstructed cannon placed on the forecastles, and caused the gunners to shoot high to clear their own prows. But with a clear view and more room for additional artillery, the Christian galleys could fire directly in the path of their own advance. At

Lepanto their blasts tore through the sides of the Ottoman galleys, while most of the enemy's volleys were high, harmlessly striking the outrigging and masts of the Christians. Credit Don Juan and his admirals with realizing that cannon fire, not a galley's bronze beak, could sink more Ottoman ships.

The Arsenal at Venice and the expertise of Spanish craftsmen had also ensured that the Christian galleys were far better armed. Not only were there more cannon per galley—1,815 total guns on the ships of the Holy League against 750 in the much larger Ottoman armada—but each weapon was better cast and maintained than its Ottoman counterpart. After the battle the Venetians found hundreds of captured Turkish cannon to be unsafe and worthless—a judgment borne out by modern metallurgical analysis of extant Ottoman guns. The only uses the victorious Europeans had for them were as trophies or scrap for recycling; under a free market such inferior weapons had no real value other than as raw material. They might as well have been anchors or ballast for all the profit their sale would bring in a competitive European market, replete with cannon crafted from the latest designs of Italian, English, German, and Spanish workshops.

The Christians also had a far greater number of smaller swivel cannon that could pepper Ottoman galleys and clear them of boarders. European soldiers on deck wore heavy breastplates, making thousands of them nearly invulnerable against Turkish arrows. Far more Christian infantrymen were armed with harquebuses, clumsy weapons but deadly at ranges of up to three hundred to five hundred yards when fired into masses of confined soldiers. For that reason, the Turkish vice-admiral Pertau Pasha had cautioned his commanders to avoid battle altogether; his men were feudal conscripts without firearms and were not up to battling mailed harquebusiers. While primitive muskets were scarcely accurate in the modern sense, they could be rested on deck and aimed into the mass of the Turkish crews as the Christian gunners were safe behind boarding nets. Given the crowded conditions of galleys and the crashing and locking together of ships, it was hard for a harquebusier to miss his target.

European troops had longer experience with and better training in the use of firearms, and so could shoot their more reliably manufactured cannon and muskets with more dependable gunpowder at rates three times faster than their much fewer Ottoman counterparts. True, the composite recurved bow of the Ottomans was a deadly weapon—possessing greater range, accuracy, and rates of fire than the crossbow—but it required months of training, exhausted the bowman after a few dozen shots, and could not be fabricated as quickly or plentifully as either cross-bows or firearms. The European emphasis was typically to put as many deadly weapons into as many hands as quickly as possible, worrying little about the social position of the shooter or the degree of status and train-ing necessary to employ a weapon effectively.

In Europe the social ramifications of military technology were far less important than its simple efficacy; the sultan, however, was careful that weapons in and of themselves—like printing presses—should not prove to be sources of social and cultural unrest. Even when the Janissaries and less well trained Ottoman troops adopted European firearms, they often failed to embrace the appropriate tactics of mass infantry warfare, which went against the heroic code of the Muslim warrior and the elite status of that professional corps. "Instead of using musketry *en masse,* as was de-veloping in the West, or massed pikemen acting in unison, the Ottomans looked upon each musketeer or sharpshooter as a warrior risking his life for a place in paradise" (A. Wheatcroft, *The Ottomans,* 67).

At Lepanto heavier and more plentiful firearms, greater rates of fire, more reliable ammunition, and better-trained gunners added up to enor-mous European advantages—if the captains would not panic but sail di-rectly into the heart of the dreaded Turkish fleet. Since European seamen had for decades been caught in small groups on the Mediterranean by Islamic corsairs and had their seaside villages often devastated by sudden onslaught of the Ottoman galleys, it was Don Juan's singular achievement to convince his admirals that for the first time in memory the advantages were all with the Europeans. The Ottomans were trapped and forced to fight in daylight and head-on against the combined might of the best of European military seamanship, which at last could bring its overwhelm-ing firepower to the collision.

North African and Turkish ships were more numerous, lighter, and less well armed than their European counterparts, and relied on numbers, quickness, surprise, and agility to raid coastal waters and outmaneuver enemy flotillas. They were designed to guard merchant ships, engage in amphibious operations, and support sieges—*not* to square off in cannon duels with Europeans. Unfortunately, Ali Pasha forgot those innate strengths and waged a decisive naval shoot-out against massive Christian firepower, a set battle that no fleet in the world—except one comprised of English galleons and gunners—could have won. Yet in a sense Ali had no choice, for history was on the side of neither galleys in general nor the Ottoman military in particular: within twenty years after Lepanto two or three British galleons alone might mount as many iron cannon as the entire Turkish fleet in the Mediterranean.

In addition to the presence of the six galleasses, themselves originating from the abstract studies of ship design dating back to Hellenistic Greece, and the greater number of cannon and firearms, the Christians had rigged up steel boarding nets designed to protect their own galleys, as gunners targeted the enemy. Don Juan later claimed that thanks to his nets not a single Christian ship was boarded by the Ottomans—an astounding declaration, if true. The oarsmen of the respective fleets were also qualitatively different. Much of the sixteenth-century naval policy at Venice had been characterized by a great debate over the composition of the republican fleet's crews. For decades the Venetians were slow to accept the idea that to match the size of the Ottoman armada, their own fleet required thousands of additional rowers of all kinds—far more oarsmen than available among the republic's free citizenry. At first the Venetians hired foreign oarsmen, then turned to their own destitute, finally to convicts—and on rare occasions to captives and slaves as well. The same exigencies were true of the other Italian states and Spain, which all came to the use of slave rowers rather late and with real reluctance. While there were servile crews on both sides at Lepanto, the oarsmen of the Holy League still included free rowers, and the coalition was more likely to free those slaves it did employ. In contrast, the Christian slaves on Turkish galleys were threatened with death before the battle should they raise their heads, and there is some indication that at least on a few ships they mutinied in the midst of the battle.

In effect, there was not a single free fighter in the Turkish fleet—not the shackled oarsmen, not the Janissaries, not those peasants mustered under feudal service, not the renegade admirals and seamen, and not even Ali Pasha himself. Across the water, the Christian admirals at the battle were free aristocrats; many of them were not even professional military men—civilians like seventy-six-year-old Sebastian Veniero, the Venetian lawyer who shared command of the center with Don Juan, or the Italian noble and landowner Marcantonio Colonna, who commanded the papal contingent. None of these proud and often headstrong individuals could be arbitrarily executed by the pope, the doge at Venice, or King Philip II for simple failure to win at Lepanto. In contrast, Ali Pasha and his commanders knew that an embarrassing defeat required a sufficient number of heads for the sultan.

LEGENDS OF LEPANTO

More than 15,000 Christian slaves were freed at Lepanto and more than two hundred galleys and nearly one hundred lesser craft were mostly destroyed or lost to the sultan. Italy itself was saved from Ottoman maritime invasion. In the battle's aftermath Europe flirted with the idea of sailing right up the Golden Horn or freeing the Greek-speaking populations of the Morea, Cyprus, and Rhodes. The Christian fleet—the largest European armada in the Mediterranean until modern times—lost around 8,000 to 10,000 killed, 21,000 wounded, and ten galleys. In contrast, there were 30,000 Ottomans slain at Lepanto, many of them skilled bowmen who would not be replaced for years. Thousands were simply executed when their galleys were taken in tow, and even more were left to drown or to be finished off by scavengers. In the battle's aftermath Christians in small boats shot and speared any Ottomans still alive in the water; plunderers hunted for private purses, clothes, and jewelry of the defeated Turkish elite. Christian annals report that only 3,458 Turkish prisoners were taken, an astoundingly low figure given the almost 100,000 of the enemy present before the battle. Most of the 6,000 Janissary shock troops also perished; the historian Gianpietro Contarini believed thousands of that elite corps had been killed. There are no records of the thousands of Ottoman wounded, many of whom must have suffered horrific gunshot wounds. One hundred eighty ships of all types—most of them later found to be beyond repair—were towed to Corfu. Dozens more washed up on the shores of Aetolia. A mere handful returned to Lepanto.

The losses were doubly grievous for the sultan, since unlike the Europeans he had neither the capacity to fabricate thousands of new harquebuses nor the ability to draft a new army of conscripts. Rowers—not to mention munitions fabricators and designers—had to be brought in as mercenaries, renegades, or slaves from European shores. Most quality-manufactured guns would need to be imported, given this singular European propensity to fabricate cheap, plentiful, and easily used firearms:

> The main impact of the development of efficient small arms upon warfare at sea came not, as we would suppose, directly through an increase in fire power, but indirectly through a sharp reduction in training requirements. This gave the nations which depended upon the arquebus greater resilience in the face of heavy manpower losses than those which depended upon the composite recurved bow. While it was fairly easy to turn Spanish villagers

into musketeers, it was virtually impossible to turn Anatolian peasants into masters of the composite recurved bow. (J. Guilmartin, *Gunpowder and Galleys*, 254)

The loss of 34 Ottoman admirals and 120 galley commanders ensured that even the sultan's massive replacement program—150 ships of green timber and shoddily fabricated cannon built within the next twelve months—would be short of experienced seamen, archers, and seasoned galleys.

Non-Westerners rightly complain about Europe's monopoly of commemoration, and its hold on the art of history itself. Nowhere was this imbalance more true than in the aftermath of Lepanto, a Western "victory" soon known as such to millions, through published histories, commissioned art, and popular literature. In none of those genres was there any consideration of the battle from the Ottomans' point of view. Instead, we hear only of the sultan's postbellum threats to execute Christians in Istanbul, the grand vizier's scoff that the Ottoman's beard "was only shaved," not cut, and various accounts of lamentation among the families of the lost. The few Turkish accounts of the battle were not literary and not widely published, but dry, government-sanctioned, and rigidly formal accounts that had little or no likelihood of appealing to any readership other than a tiny screened government elite in Istanbul. The parameters of inquiry in such court chronicles of Selânki, Ālī, Lokman, and Zeyrek were carefully delineated—if the scribe was not to be exiled or executed. Ottoman sources attributed the Turkish loss to the wrath of Allah and the need for punishment for the sins of wayward Muslims. Vague charges of general impiety and laxity only enhanced the government's anger at its own people; there was to be little exegesis and analysis concerning the shortcomings in the sultan's equipment, command, and naval organization.

In contrast, dozens of highly emotive firsthand narratives in Italian and Spanish—often at odds with each other in a factual and an analytical sense—spread throughout the Mediterranean. We know as little of the Turkish experience at Lepanto as we do of the plight of Abd ar-Rahman at Poitiers or the Mexicas at Tenochtitlán. What we do learn of the non-West in battle is secondhand, and most often a result of European investigation and publication. Thus, nearly all of the names of the soldiers of Xerxes, Darius III, Hannibal, Abd ar-Rahman, Montezuma, Selim II, and the Zulu king Cetshwayo are lost to the historical record. The few that are known survive largely to the efforts of an Aeschylus, Herodotus, Arrian,

Plutarch, Polybius, Livy, Isidore, Díaz, Rosell, Contarini, Bishop Colenso, or Colonel Hartford, who wrote in an intellectual and political tradition unknown among the Persians, Africans, Aztecs, Ottomans, and Zulus.

Things have changed little today in terms of the exclusive Western monopoly of military history. Six billion people on the planet are more likely to read, hear, or see accounts of the Gulf War (1990) from the American and European vantage points than from the Iraqi. The story of the Vietnam War is largely Western; even the sharpest critics of America's involvement put little credence in the official communiqués and histories that emanate from communist Vietnam. In the so-called Dark Ages of Europe, more independent histories were still published between A.D. 500 and 1000 than during the entire reigns of the Persian or Ottoman Empire. Whether it is history under Xerxes, the sultan, the Koran, or the Politburo at Hanoi, it is not really history—at least in the Western sense of writing what can offend, embarrass, and blaspheme.

Such is the nature of societies that allow dissenting voices and free expression. Even when European and American citizens openly attack the military conduct of their own governments, candor often has the ironic result only of enhancing Western credibility and furthering its dominance of the dissemination of knowledge. So it was at Lepanto: most readers in Europe, the Americas, Africa, and even throughout Asia are more likely to know of the battle through an account in English, Spanish, French, or Italian—or an allusion in Cervantes, Byron, or Shakespeare—than a sympathetic Ottoman chronicle written in Turkish.

Christendom had never seen such a celebration as the aftermath of Lepanto. Crowds all over Italy and Spain sang *Te Deum Laudamus,* the church's traditional hymn of praise and thanks to God. A special October Devotion of the Rosary was inaugurated by the Vatican, still celebrated today in a few churches of Italy. For most of the subsequent winter, captured Turkish rugs, banners, arms, and turbans lined the streets and shops of Venice, Rome, and Genoa. Special commemorative coins were struck with the inscription "In the year of the great naval victory by the grace of God against the Turks." Hundreds of thousand of woodcuts, engravings, and medals circulated even in Protestant northern Europe. The winged lion of St. Mark appeared on victory monuments throughout Venice. The great Venetian painters Veronese, Vicentino, and Tintoretto produced vast canvases of Lepanto; the latter's stunning depiction focused on the taking of Ali Pasha's flagship and the mortal wounding of Barbarigo. A remarkable fresco of the battle by Vasari still adorns the Vatican. Dozens of other monuments and paintings in the pope's palace celebrate the astounding victory. Titian painted a commemorative portrait for Philip II, in which the monarch is seen kneeling at an altar holding up to heaven his son Don Fernando as Victory descends from the clouds; a captive Turk is in the foreground, a burning fleet in the distance.

At Messenia Andrea Calamech sculpted a grandiose statue of Don Juan—still impressive today—in appreciation of the prince's salvation of the city from the Turkish fleet. Fernando de Herrera's *Canción de Lepanto* remains today a selection of modern anthologies of Western literature. Miguel Cervantes, a veteran of the battle who lost the use of his hand, years later immortalized Lepanto in his *Don Quixote*: "Those Christians who died there were even happier than those who remained alive and victorious." The boy prince who would be King James I of England composed 11,000 lines of an epic in commemoration of Lepanto. At Stratford the young Shakespeare was also apparently deeply affected: in his later plays his duke is called Prospero after notable Italian nobles at the battle, and his Othello is made to serve with the Venetians at Cyprus to defend the island against Turkish attack.

Most of the paintings and popular songs attributed the remarkable Christian victory to divine intervention. But even more secular contemporary historians who sought tactical exegeses were not sure how the Holy League had halted centuries of Turkish aggression in a few hours. Why, in fact, did the Europeans win, when they were outnumbered, discordant, and fractious until the moments before the battle, in unfamiliar enemy waters, far from their home bases, their governments in mortal hatred of one another? Was it luck—the sudden change in winds that gave Don Juan's galleys added speed as they sailed into the Ottoman center or the gentle breezes that blew their cannon smoke into the enemy's eyes? Or was it the relatively calm seas and absence of rain that ensured the plodding galleasses could easily maneuver and take aim right before the Turkish fleet—and that thousands of Christian harquebuses had dry firelocks? Surely critical to the outcome was the Ottoman foolhardiness in accepting a challenge of decisive battle with heavier and better-armed Christian ships. Once the galleasses unleashed their opening salvos and were seen to approach firing from all sides, contemporaries on both sides noted that even the indomitable Turks "became afraid." All narratives attribute much of the Christian success to the six floating fortresses and their initial shelling of the Ottoman front lines.

Or perhaps the edge was spiritual? Lepanto was fought on a Sunday morning, and the crews were given mass by priests on deck even as they prepared to kill. A few days earlier on Corfu the Christians had received the gruesome news of the fall of Cyprus, and the Ottoman perfidy in slaughtering all the hostages and prisoners of Famagusta. The most repeated tale among the crews of Lepanto was the horrific account of the torture and disfigurement of Marcantonio Bragadino, leader of the brave garrison there, who was flayed alive and stuffed after being promised safe passage on capitulation. Don Juan's crews had seen the Ottomans' most recent sacrilege on Corfu—Christian graves desecrated, priests tortured, civilians kidnapped, and churches defiled. All contemporary sources remark that once Christian infantrymen boarded the Turkish galleys, they fought with an almost inhuman savagery.

Or was the verdict at Lepanto due to the brilliant battlefield leadership of Don Juan, who had mixed the Italian, Spanish, and Venetian galleys throughout the armada to maintain harmony? No less important was the rare statesmanship of both the pope and Philip II. Yet what most nullified Ottoman courage and numbers was the presence of so many topflight European ships, equipped with superior firepower and better-armed soldiers—a testament to the Western manner of designing, producing, and distributing armaments that operated only within the confines of capitalist economies. The abundance of cannon, harquebuses, crossbows, and finely crafted ships trumped Ottoman numbers, the reputation of the dreaded Turkish soldier, and the convenience of home waters in a single stroke, and so gave the Holy League a good chance of victory—if its cohesion, generalship, and tactics were competent—when victory was unforeseen.

EUROPE AND THE OTTOMANS

A Fragmented Continent

Sixteenth-century middle and eastern Europe, as had been true since the sixth century A.D., felt itself besieged by the East. Whereas northern Africa and Asia Minor had become unified by Islam, and were for the most part provinces or protectorates of a vast Ottoman hegemony, Europe was ever more wracked by religious strife. Christendom, split asunder by Roman Catholicism and Eastern Orthodoxy, was by the sixteenth century to fragment further with the schism of Protestantism and the growth of nation-states in England, France, Holland, Italy, and Spain, founded on principles of ethnic, cultural, and linguistic affinity, not monolithic allegiance to the Vatican.

France, having rid itself of the last Islamic attackers in the early tenth century, was more or less in alliance with the Ottomans for much of the sixteenth century. The friendship was not always passive: the French had used Ottoman help to take Corsica from Genoa in 1532 and had allowed the Turkish admiral Barbarossa to winter his galley fleet—manned by Christian slaves, no less—in French ports (1543–44). No wonder that on the morning of the battle, the Ottoman admiral Hassan Ali confidently urged the Turks to leave the harbor and row out to battle outside the Gulf of Corinth, since the Christians were "of different nations and had different religious rites."

As the Ottomans increasingly looked westward, not merely for additional slaves and plunder but also for European weaponry and manufactured goods, the West itself turned farther to the west and south. The newly discovered Americas and the trade routes along coastal Africa offered riches without struggle with the Turks or the stiff tariff charges of the long caravan routes through Ottoman-occupied Asia. By the sixteenth century a disunited western Europe was not merely beset by a hegemonic East but had itself grown powerful at a variety of new mercantile centers—Madrid, Paris, London, and Antwerp—which had increasingly little interest in the backwaters of the eastern Mediterranean.

The Balkans and the islands of the eastern Mediterranean were considered costly sideshows not worth confrontation with the Turkish fleet, given the general stagnation of the Ottoman Empire in comparison to newer avenues of trade and commerce elsewhere. Most enslaved Christians were Orthodox anyway, and western Europeans had feuded with the Byzantines well before the fall of Constantinople. The absolute fault lines of Christian versus Muslim, or East against West, were also eroding. England and France sometimes ignored and at other times aided the sultan, while Venice became increasingly dependent on trade along the Turkish coast. Lepanto would be one of the last great battles in history in which a few Western powers united solely on the basis of shared culture and religion against Islam.

Still, the Ottomans in particular, and Islam in general, were in theory more powerful in terms of population, natural resources, and territory occupied than any one Mediterranean Christian state. But by the same token, Islamic power was clearly inferior to southern Europe as a whole should it ever unite for a grand expedition. On the rare occasions of even partial alliances—the great First Crusade (1096–99) during the Middle Ages is the best example—Western success even far from Europe was not uncommon well before the Reformation, gunpowder, and Atlantic exploration. European military dynamism was a continuum from classical antiquity, not a later fluke of the gunpowder age and the discovery of the New World. The First Crusade had ended with Franks in occupation of the Holy Land and revealed a singular ability to move and feed armies by land and sea not matched in the Islamic world. In rare cases of foreign attacks inside Europe—Xerxes, the Moors, Arabs, Mongols, and Ottomans—foreign dynasts found themselves at the heads of unified imperial or religious armies, their Western opponents isolated, divided, and often squabbling among themselves. But Christendom's rare collective efforts soon waned, and by 1300 the Crusades were not to be followed by any comparable pan-European expedition across the Mediterranean. Yet even in a state of religious and political fragmentation Europe was relatively safe from Islamic invasion, since such invasions required logistical expertise and heavy infantry beyond even the sultan's resources. The fifteenth-century Ottoman unification of much of Asia, the Balkans, and northern Africa, and the general acceptance of one god who put a high value on the advancement of religion by the sword, placed a divided Europe at an enormous disadvantage. As in the eighth century at the dawn of Islamic conquest, once again many small warring Christian and Western states were to be attacked continuously and individually by a vast religious and political unity.

Ottoman intellectuals and mullahs did not see war as innately wrong. Nor were there objections by the intelligentsia to the idea of a jihad—nothing at all comparable to a growing Western interest in pacifism or even "just war" theory. No Islamic tract was similar to the idea promulgated by Erasmus and others that war itself was somehow intrinsically evil and might be waged only under the narrowest moral circumstances. Europe's citizens might have inherited a notion of personal freedom from classical antiquity and of spiritual brotherhood from Christ, but the survival of the West lay in how well they ignored the idea that killing was always sinful.

So Europe combined the earlier Western traditions of decisive battle to annihilate the enemy, of capitalism to craft plentiful and effective weapons, and of civic militarism to bring out the population en masse to resist the Ottomans. Fortunately, there was little in Christianity as it evolved in the Middle Ages that was antithetical to private profit or capitalism in general. If for a time priests worried about the taking of life, they had no compunction in allowing their brethren to profit while they could.

By the time of the battle of Lepanto, long gone from European control were the old Roman provinces of northern Africa, the Near East, Asia Minor, and most of the Balkans as well as the coastal waters of the eastern

Mediterranean, which had become firmly Muslim and were increasingly under the control of Istanbul. For the expansion of an enormous multicultural empire, the Ottomans found useful a unifying religion that advocated aggressive war against nonbelievers—presenting non-Westerners with enemies of moral and religious fervor not seen earlier even in the deadly onslaughts of the Carthaginians, Persians, and Huns, who all likewise had invaded Europe and for a time threatened to annex Greece and Rome into their domains.

The discordant Christians, however, still retained enormous advantages over the sultan's armies. Despite the erosion of hegemonic Western military power with Rome's fall, most states in Europe proper for more than a thousand years had managed to retain in latent form the cultural traditions of classical antiquity—rationalism, civic militarism, forms of capitalism, ideas of freedom, individualism, reliance on heavy infantry and decisive battle—which allowed them greater military power than their individual populations, resources, or territory would otherwise suggest. The chief problem for Europe was no longer a prevailing pacifism, but near continuous war: the absence of central political control in the Middle Ages after the end of Charlemagne's kingdom had allowed Western warfare to be used suicidally, in constant internecine and extremely bloody fights between European princes.

The technology of galley construction was far more advanced in the republican city-states of Italy and imperial Spain than in Asia, and far more flexible and likely to evolve to meet new challenges at sea. The entire organization and even terminology of the Turkish fleet was copied from either Venetian or Genoese models, in the same manner as earlier medieval Islamic fleets had emulated Byzantine nautical engineering and naval administration. Both sides rowed ships that were strikingly similar—and exclusively of Italian design. All military innovation—from the cutting off of the galley rams to the creation of the galleasses and the use of boarding nets—was on the European side. Military science—the rebirth of abstract notions of strategy and tactics in the new age of gunpowder—was a Western domain; it was thus no accident that the leading captains of both fleets were European. The sultan himself preferred renegade Italian admirals who were acquainted with European customs and language and therefore far more likely to adapt his galleys to the latest innovations of the enemy.

The soldiers in the Christian fleet were not all free voting citizens—only Venice and a few Italian states were republican. Yet the crews of the Holy League were not exclusively servile either, as was true of the

Ottoman armada, in which elite Janissaries and galley slaves alike were political nonentities. A Turkish galley slave was more likely to flee than a Christian, and European common soldiers were free persons and not the property of an imperial autocrat:

> Throughout the fleet the Christian slaves had their fetters knocked off and were furnished with arms, which they were encouraged to use valiantly by promises of freedom and rewards. Of the Muslim slaves, on the contrary, the chains which secured them to their places were carefully examined and their rivets secured; and they were, besides, fitted with handcuffs, to disable them from using their hands for any purpose but tugging at the oar. (W. Stirling-Maxwell, *Don Juan of Austria,* vol. 1, 404)

In addition, the Christians, plagued by constant raiding from North African corsairs and Turkish galleys, deliberately sought decisive battle. It was the armada of the Holy League that wished to collide head-on with the sultan's fleet and kill every Ottoman on the water. The latter army was docked in its winter quarters and somewhat reluctant to fight. Moreover, in the Christian fleet, a variety of individual minds and personalities was at work. Spanish, Italian, French, English, and German adventurers— Knights of Malta, nobles of various other religious orders, even Protestants and at least one woman under arms—argued and bickered until seconds before the first fusillade, ultimately bestowing upon the armada the advantages of diverse opinion and the free reign of commanders to react as they felt best to the changing conditions of battle. Even the autocracy of Christian monarchy in Spain—operating as it did in a labyrinth of civic and judicial oversight and audits—usually did not hamstring the liberty of the individual to the same degree as the totalitarianism of the sultan's rule.

Yet what gave the much smaller states of the Christian federation a fighting chance for victory was their remarkable ability—given their limited populations and territory—to create capital, and thereby to fabricate excellent vessels, mass-produce advanced firearms, and hire skilled crews. Although Europe was represented in force by only three real Mediterranean powers at Lepanto—the pope, Spain, and Venice—their aggregate economies were far larger than the national product of the entire Ottoman Empire. Before the fleet had even sailed, papal ministers had calculated the entire cost of manning two hundred galleys, with crews and provisions, for a year—and had raised the necessary funds in advance.

A Most Remarkable City-State

A good example of the vast differences in economic life between the adversaries is that of the Venetian republic—its output of goods and services far smaller than that of the French, Spanish, or English economy. At the time of Lepanto the population of Venice itself was less than 200,000. Its territory was confined to a small circuit of a few hundred square miles in northern Italy and some commercial outposts in the eastern Mediterranean, Greece, Crete, and the Adriatic coast. In contrast, the sultan ruled a population a hundredfold greater than Venice, with far more reserves of wood, ores, agricultural products, and precious metals. He also controlled a territory literally thousands of times larger that served as a lucrative mercantile nexus between East and West. Yet in terms of military assets, trade, commerce, and influence on the Mediterranean, Venice by itself throughout the sixteenth century was the near rival of the Ottomans.

Ostensibly, Venetian power lay in its uncanny ability to craft weapons of war according to modern principles of specialization and capitalist production—500,000 ducats of the annual 7 million in revenue were reserved to finance the operations of the great Arsenal, where thousands of muskets, harquebuses, and cannon, plus supplies of dry timber, were fabricated and then kept in a constant strategic reserve. Besides dozens of small private shipwrights, there was also a public council that ensured ready-made ships in time of crisis—not unlike the American War Production Board of World War II that marshaled industry and labor under the auspices of private enterprise to create near instantaneous lines of weapons production. Three years after Lepanto, Henry III, the French monarch, was entertained in Venice by a firsthand inspection of the Arsenal, which purportedly assembled, launched, and outfitted a galley in the space of an hour! Even under normal conditions the Arsenal was able to launch an entire fleet of galleys within a few days, utilizing principles of ship construction, financing, and mass production not really rivaled until the twentieth century:

> Under the order of the Council of Ten, twenty-five of the galleys were to be kept in the basins armed and equipped to sail. The rest were to be kept on land complete in hull and superstructure, ready to be launched as soon as the caulkers should have filled their seams with tow and pitch. Both the docks on which they were stored and water in front were to be kept cleared so they could be quickly launched. Each galley was to be numbered, and its rigging and other furnishings were to be marked with the same number, so

that they might be assembled as quickly as possible. (F. Lane, *Venetian Ships and Shipbuilders of the Renaissance,* 142)

The Arsenal itself was copied by the sultan with a facsimile near the Golden Horn, where shipwrights from Naples and Venice were hired to duplicate the Venetian success (with mixed results: foreign visitors saw scores of artillery pieces lying randomly about, for the most part stolen and plundered from Christian forces rather than fabricated on the premises). But if the Turkish ability to build a modern galley fleet was predicated on its efforts to import or steal Western products and expertise—in that manner it would nearly replace its losses at Lepanto within two years—Venetian power was an independent outgrowth of a larger intellectual, political, and cultural prowess not found to the east and *not* predicated on population, natural resources, territory, or even the ability to acquire plunder, forced taxes, or foreign talent.

The Arsenal was a natural expression of Venetian capitalism and constitutional government that operated in a way unimaginable at Istanbul. Venice was ruled as a republic with an elected chief executive (the doge) and a Senate of largely aristocratic merchants who allowed capital from commerce to go relatively untaxed and to be legally immune from confiscation. In addition, corporations in Venice were allowed legal protection that made them abstract, meritocratic entities, businesses that might transcend any one individual and find success or failure on the basis of profit. A Venetian corporation was not dependent on the life, health, or status of any particular person or clan, but solely on its efficiency to operate on abstract business principles such as investment and return, with the corollary financial instruments of stock, dividends, insurance, and maritime loans. Since the state undertook the expensive investments of producing merchant ships and providing naval protection, small traders with little capital could compete with larger corporations in bidding on the rights to the use of ships and commercial routes under the aegis of public auctions. By the time of Lepanto more than eight hundred commercial voyages a year were arriving at and departing from Venice's port—more than two new ships docking in its harbor every day.

When such state-sanctioned capitalism operated in a rather free society overseen by the elected public councils of the republic, the talented of all classes found a hospitable business climate like none other in the Mediterranean. Added to the mix of consensual government, free markets and investment was a devotion to rationalism and disinterested inquiry that explains why the Venetian galleys were the best designed and armed on the Mediterranean. There was nothing in Asia like the European marketplace of ideas devoted to the pursuit of ever more deadly weapons—the published empirical research on bronze and iron cannon effectiveness, for example, found in Vannoccio Biringuccio's *Pirotechnia* (Venice, 1540), Niccolò Tartaglia's *La nova scientia* (Venice, 1558), and Luigi Collado's *Practica manual de artiglierra* (Venice, 1586 [Italian]; Milan, 1592 [Spanish]). Such formal treatises were often supplemented by annual published reports by commissions and boards in Venice and Genoa and more informal tracts from master shipwrights themselves, like Theodoro's 1546 report on galley construction at the Arsenal. The freedom to exchange ideas and the classical heritage of rationalism—evident in Don García de Toledo's treatise on seamanship, ship propulsion, and armament (Madrid, ca. 1560) or in Pedro de Medina's *Regimento de navegación* (Seville, 1563)—meant that Europeans were incorporating firsthand experience with abstract theory to advance the science of nautical construction and navigation. Military research was part of higher learning at Venice centered at the nearby University of Padua, where scientific and medical training, under the direction of the renowned Gabriello Falloppio (1523–62) and Fabricus Aquapendente (1537–1610), was unrivaled. In painting, Tintoretto, Giorgione, and Titian kept alive the Hellenic-inspired excellence of the Italian Renaissance, while printers like Aldus Manutius (1450–1515) soon established the greatest publishing center in Europe, focusing on its famous Aldine editions of Greek and Roman classics.

In contrast, printing presses were not introduced at Istanbul until the late fifteenth century, and even then for a long time were forbidden due to fears that information harmful to the state would be distributed. Islam itself would never come to terms with unfettered printing and the idea of free mass dissemination of knowledge. Most well-known Ottoman art and literature were court-inspired, subject to imperial and religious censorship far beyond anything found in the West. Rationalism was felt to be at odds with the political primacy of the Koran, which lay at the heart of the sultan's power. Knowledge gained from galley warfare was thus found only from hands-on training and the oral tradition that circulated among Mediterranean seamen, since there were no real Ottoman universities, publishing houses, or widespread readership to facilitate abstract speculation.

Venice's strength vis-à-vis the Turks lay not so much in geography, natural resources, religious zealotry, or a commitment to continual warring and raiding as in its system of capitalism, consensual government, and devotion to disinterested research. Only that way could skilled nautical engineers, pilots, and trained admirals trump enormous Ottoman advantages in territory, tribute, a cultural tradition of warrior nomadism, and sheer manpower. The sultan sought out European traders, ship designers, seamen, and imported firearms—even portrait painters—while almost no Turks found their services required in Europe.

Ottomanism

Perhaps the most marked example at Lepanto of the difference in the economies of the belligerents was the 150,000 gold sequins found in the captured flagship of Ali Pasha. Treasures nearly as large were also discovered in the galleys of the other Ottoman admirals. Without a system of banking, fearful of confiscation should he displease the sultan, and always careful to keep his assets hidden from the tax collectors, Ali Pasha toted his huge personal fortune to Lepanto. There it was plundered after the battle when the admiral was killed at sea and his ship sunk. If a member of the highest echelons of Ottoman society—he was brother-in-law to the sultan, and on a great jihad for his ruler—could neither safely invest nor hide his capital in Istanbul, then thousands of less fortunate subjects could scarcely hope to.

Wealthy Ottoman traders and merchants often stealthily invested money in Europe and chose to import costly European luxury items; or they hid or buried their savings rather than risk seizure of their stored coined money in the future. The result was a chronic shortage of investment capital in the Ottoman Empire for education, public works, and military expenditure. Perhaps Adam Smith had Ali Pasha in mind when he wrote that "in those unfortunate countries, indeed, where men are continually afraid of the violence of their superiors, they frequently bury and conceal a great part of their common stock, a common practice in Turkey, in Indostan, and I believe, in most other governments of Asia" (The Wealth of Nations). In any case, the thousands of Venetians and other Italians and Greeks who lived in Istanbul facilitated, along with Jews and Armenians, a vast East-West trade network. Value-added products such as European firearms, manufactured goods, and textiles were commonly exchanged for raw Asian cotton, silk, spices, and agricultural produce. In contrast, Venice saw no need to welcome an elite trading and banking cadre of Turkish specialists to enhance its own economy.

The political and religious organization of the Ottomans behind their rather closed economy was at once both enlightened and horrific, efficient and static, logical and backward—and in most every way antithetical to market capitalism. Traditional portraits of a corrupt, inept bureaucratic Ottoman government are as misleading as recent revisionist attempts to portray the empire as little different from, if not more progressive than, its European counterparts. At the time of Lepanto, Ottoman political, economic, and military practice could not have been more different from European custom. First, the bureaucracy of the army and government was staffed by slaves—to the number of 80,000 or more—either bought from slave traders, conquered in war or raids, or collected as forced "taxes" under the *devshirme*, the inspection every four years of the conquered Christian provinces to select suitable Christian youths for forced conversion to Islam. The best of the young Christian captives were educated in the language and religion of the Ottomans, given high posts in government and the military, and became the lifelong loyal and prized slaves of the sultan himself.

The result was a continual revolving governmental and military elite. It was not readily open to native-born Muslims and not replicated through hereditary or dynastic succession. The children of the *devshirme* were not promoted on criteria of birth or wealth. Thus arose a meritocracy of sorts—a nightmarish version of the model proposed by Plato in his *Republic*—under which youths would be separated from their parents, publicly educated, advanced on merit, and thereby motivated to serve the state. The *devshirme* ensured the sultan a loyal cadre of followers, who had no parents and no vision of upward mobility for their own children: the latter were born Muslims and thus ineligible to follow as government interns or Janissary recruits. While the theft of Christian youth was bitterly resented by most conquered subjects in the Balkans, the parents of the kidnapped could on occasion confess that imperial service in the sultan's government might give their children a better future than the impoverishment of their own local serfdom.

The use of former Christians removed some of the threat of native-born Turks' acquiring power and threatening insurrection, while it provided proof throughout the empire of the dynamism of Islam in its ability to transmogrify the best of Christian youth into the most loyal and devout of the sultan's Muslim subjects. Millions of Christians were captured and converted during the centuries of the empire. At Lepanto most of the military command, the bureaucrats who handled the logistics of the fleet, the Janissaries, and the chained galley slave rowers were former Christians, who were forced slave converts to Islam.

The *devshirme* also illustrated the degree to which religion permeated all aspects of Ottoman life. The greatest admirals in the sixteenth-century Ottoman fleet—Khaireddin Barbarossa, Uluj Ali ("Occhiali"), and Turghud Ali Pasha ("Dragut")—had all been born European Christians. The sultan's mother herself, Hürrem Sultan, wife of Süleyman the Magnificent, was a Ukrainian Christian, daughter of a priest. The grand vizier, or chief minister of state, of the empire during the battle of Lepanto, Mehmet Sokullu, was a Slav from the Balkans. Part of the secret of the Ottomans' martial success was its ambivalent relationship to Europe, which it both courted and hated, robbed and traded with—all the time as it welcomed in Western traders, kidnapped European adolescents, and hired renegade criminals. That the capital of the Ottomans was the venerated European city of Constantinople, and no longer in the East, was itself acknowledgment of the financial advantages inherent in proximity to the West.

The empire, as in the case of the earlier Achaemenid rulers of Asia Minor, was completely in the hands of the sultan, in theory himself a slave by virtue of his birth to a member of his father's servile harem and also as a servant of Allah. Reminiscent of a Darius or Xerxes, in 1538 Süleyman the Magnificent had inscribed at Bender the following:

I am God's slave and sultan of this world. By the grace of God I am head of the Muhammad's community. God's might and Muhammad's miracles are my companions. I am Süleyman, in whose name the *hutbe* is read in Mecca and Medina. In Bagdad I am the shah, in Byzantine realms the Caesar, and in Egypt the sultan; who sends his fleets to the seas of Europe, the Maghrib and India. I am the sultan who took the crown and throne of Hungary and granted them to a humble slave. The Voivoda Petru raised his head in revolt, but my horse's hoofs ground him into the dust, and I conquered the land of Moldavia. (H. Inalcik, *The Ottoman Empire*, 41)

Succession passed to the most ambitious of a ruler's many sons, aided by the degree to which mothers in the harem and full siblings might eliminate rival claimants who could number in the dozens. Most male offspring of the sultan's daughters were killed at birth. Court intrigue, poisonings, and gratuitous execution proved every bit as macabre as anything in Suetonius's account of the twelve Caesars. Autocracy, Eastern or Western, is bad enough, but it could prove ruinous when combined with a succession ritual of bloodletting among the elite to determine the new strongman. Consequently, the two fleets at Lepanto represented opposite poles of political and religious organization—the Ottoman navy, an entire cadre of slaves of the sultan; the Christian fleet an alliance of autonomous states, a few of which were ruled by elected governments.

The spectacular growth of the Ottomans in the fifteenth century had hinged on two phenomena: the ability of nomadic peoples to unite and ride west and southward to capture and plunder the older and more settled wealthy states in its environs—Byzantines, Christian fiefdoms in the northern Balkans, Mamluks in Egypt, and Islamic regimes in eastern Anatolia and Iran—and their skill in taxing and transporting the wealth of the Orient such as cotton, spices, silk, and agricultural produce to Europe in exchange for weapons, ships, and manufactured goods. As long as Ottoman armies could acquire fresh lands and new plunder, find new sources of slaves, and monopolize the trade routes from East to West, the empire could spread and prosper, despite intrinsic inefficiencies in its economy and political instability in its imperial administration.

In principle the sultan owned all the land in the empire; in actual practice the best estates were allotted to military and government grandees. All property was subject to sharp taxes. There was no large land-holding class of voting citizens. Local appointments went solely to the aristocracy who collected tribute or owned estates, while national offices, including the viziers, were mostly staffed by Christian slaves brought in through the *devshirme*. The majority of Ottoman military manpower came not from the Janissaries, but from the *timar* system under which a military lord was given conquered land and near absolute control of its environs. After collecting imperial taxes, the timariot kept what remaining profit he could exact from his indentured peasants and then promised to muster his retainers in time of war. If the Janissaries were foreign-born slave soldiers, the rest of the Ottoman military was primarily an army and navy of serf farmers, beholden to their local lord. Such a system of unfree labor was in sharp contrast to the European militaries, which either conscripted many of their fighting men and oarsmen from their own populace (as in the case of Venice) or hired soldiers on the open market with clear and understood contractual obligations. At first glance the Ottoman system of military conscription had the advantage of being "cost-free" and predicated on local trust and comradeship rather than wages. But on closer examination the entire *timar* method of mustering depended on a continual supply of new land, wise battle leadership of an autocratic timariot, relatively brief campaigns to prevent disruptions in agricultural production, and constant victories to provide plunder for what was essentially a coerced soldiery.

All despotic rule is subject to some checks on power either through religious stricture or as a result of the rise of a necessary commercial or intellectual class. Under the Ottomans, however, the political power of the state was never separate from Islamic control. This general ubiquity of Muslim ideology had the effect of placing most commercial and intellectual life ostensibly under the auspices of the Koran. While Muslim scholars were able to create centers of religious teaching and exegesis revolving around the Koran, no real research in universities that might lead to military innovation, technological progress, or an economic renaissance was possible:

> Ottoman scholarship was bounded by traditional Islamic concepts which saw religious learning as the only true science, whose sole aim was the understanding of God's word. The Koran and the traditions of the Prophet formed the basis of this learning; reason was only an auxiliary in the service of religion. The method of the religious sciences was to seek proof for an argument first in the Koran, then in the traditions of the Prophet, then in recorded precedent, and only as a last resort in personal reasoning. (H. Inalcik, *The Ottoman Empire,* 173)

Despite the efforts of recent revisionist scholars to deny the nineteenth-century view of a "stagnant" Ottoman economy, there is little doubt that Islam had a far more deleterious effect on free market activity than did Renaissance Christianity on European capitalism. First, there was never a real system of supply and demand or profit and loss, much less interest under the empire: "Islam categorically disapproves of the existence of interest in all economic transactions. The Quranic concept of *riba* is not limited to loan interest. Literally, *riba* means over and above a thing, be it in money terms or in physical units of good" (M. Choudhury, *Contributions to Islamic Economic Theory,* 15).

True banking was nonexistent. European investors, in fact, founded the first Ottoman bank in 1856. Personal fortunes in coinage were more likely buried or sequestered than put on deposit or invested. Prices were regulated by government decree and fiercely watched by guilds. Private property was not protected by constitutional stricture, but subject to imperial confiscation. Taxes were arbitrarily set—high, and capricious in their enforcement. Landowners could never guess when and how frequently the tax collectors might arrive—or how much they would demand. The huge Ottoman bureaucracy and military devoured the budget and absorbed available capital. Literacy was low; not more than 10 percent of the population could read. There were no real secular universities to educate a financial or diplomatic class. Estates owned by mullahs were large and tax-exempt, and Islam itself was often able to curtail lending and borrowing as usurious and against the tenets of the Koran.

Consequently, when radical shifts in the world economy transpired, such as the wholesale importation of bullion from the New World and the opening of alternative trade routes to the East by western European galleons, the Ottomans found themselves relatively powerless to adjust. Any individual, smaller European state—a Venice, Spain, England, France, or the Netherlands—could produce a fleet the size of the sultan's without the huge territory and manpower of the Ottoman Empire. In short, a disastrous but logical sequence of events overtook the Ottomans right around the time of Lepanto, once the empire reached its maximum point of easy growth:

> With military expansion brought to a halt, the state came under severe stress. Revenues sank and the army and navy could not be properly maintained, which in turn reduced the military options. The system turned to prey on itself with a quite indecent haste. Taxes were raised so high as to depopulate. The road to personal wealth for officials and military officers was quickly perceived as the purchase and exploitation of public posts. The rot began to set in as early as the mid-sixteenth century when Süleyman permitted the sale of offices and the accumulation of private fortunes by Turkish élite within the imperial bureaucracy, the members of the so-called Ruling Institution. (E. Jones, *The European Miracle*, 186)

The Meaning of Lepanto

Scholars tend to see Lepanto as a tactical victory that led to strategic stalemate. After the crushing defeat of the Turkish fleet—for nearly a year there were few Ottoman warships on the Mediterranean—the Holy League failed to press home its advantage. Cyprus was not retaken, Greece not freed. In but two years Venice, struggling under lost revenues due to the cutoff of its Asian trade, had made peace with the sultan. The Ottoman advance in the next two centuries would overwhelm Crete, sweep into Hungary, and end at the gates of Vienna. Within a year the sultan's shipyards, copied from the Arsenal at Venice and manned by European engineers, built an entirely new fleet, albeit one of questionable quality.

Lepanto, like Poitiers, was nevertheless a watershed event in the history of East-West relations. The western Mediterranean was to be secure, and the galleys of Islam would rarely venture across the Adriatic—in the same manner that the Muslims in Spain after Poitiers would offer no more threat to northern Europe. Once the Ottomans were stopped at Lepanto, the continued long-term autonomy of the western Mediterranean would never again be in doubt. Lepanto ensured that the growing Atlantic trade with the Americas would continue, as Europeans not only became enriched by New World treasure but found the Ottoman Empire increasingly irrelevant to their growing commercial interests in the Orient via routes around the Horn of Africa. In 1580 Emir Mehmet ibn-Emir es-Su'udi wrote, "The Europeans have discovered the secret of oceanic travel. They are Lords of the new world and of the gates to India. . . . The people of Islam are without the latest information in the science of geography and do not understand the menace of the capture of the sea trade by the Europeans" (W. Allen, *Problems of Turkish Power in the Sixteenth Century*, 30).

Lepanto had also demonstrated that Europe need not be entirely united to beat the Turks: an ad hoc coalition of just a few southern Mediterranean states was enough to check a cumbersome Ottoman state based on theocracy and despotism. The East-West imbalance would only grow worse, as population and economic activity increased at far greater rates under European free markets, Protestantism, and global trade. In contrast, the military culture of the Ottomans, originating in the steppes of eastern Asia Minor and having reached the limits of its easiest extension, found itself for the first time up against states more formidable than the enervated Byzantines and other isolated kingdoms in the Balkans— nations whose continual improvements in gunpowder weapons, advanced fortifications, superior ships, and sophisticated military tactics could easily outweigh the martial prowess of individual Turkish warriors.

There is also an irony in the galley fighting on the Mediterranean between cross and crescent, inasmuch as the North Atlantic states of England, France, and Holland by 1571 possessed better and more numerous ships than the archaic galleys that collided at Lepanto. Even as the Ottomans and the southern European states fought for what they thought was world military supremacy, the oceangoing navies to the north cemented their hold on New World and Asiatic colonies and trading routes, proving that the real strategic prizes were no longer to be found in the Mediterranean. In the new era of guns and sails it made no sense to put between two hundred and four hundred men on an oared vessel that could easily be blown apart at a distance by a man-of-war that had half a galley's crew. By 1571 the Spanish were the most sophisticated sailors on the Mediterranean, and yet in less than twenty years the galleons and cannon of its armada would prove in all ways inferior to a British fleet that had uniformly superior guns, crews, officers, and sails.

Finally, Don Juan had proved at Lepanto that the southern Europeans no longer need fear the dreaded Turks, whose century-long advance through the Balkans had so terrified Christendom. With the reconquest of Spain (1492) and the victory at Lepanto, the future of military dynamism was no longer with horsemen, nomads, or corsairs, but returned to the old paradigm of classical antiquity: superior technology, capital-creating economies, and civic militias. The Ottomans had fashioned a brilliant military empire based on the courage of nomadic warriors, the purchase of European firearms and military expertise, and the great schisms in Christendom between Catholic, Orthodox, and Protestant. At last, however, there was to be a reckoning once the easy source of Ottoman capital dried up with the collapse of Byzantium and the European opening of maritime commerce with Asia. The sultans would find imported technology increasingly expensive to buy or emulate, and they would learn in the process that European military science was not static, but evolving even as it was sold abroad. "All the world learned," wrote Cervantes of Lepanto in *Don Quixote*, "how mistaken it had been in believing the Turks were invincible."

CAPITALISM, THE OTTOMAN ECONOMY, AND ISLAM

Why was the Ottoman fleet at Lepanto the product of booty, raiding, tariffs on trade with the West, and tribute, while the ships of Venice and the Papal States were more the dividends of the capital found in banking, industry, colonization, and exploration? Why as a rule did the Ottomans and other Islamic states trade raw materials for manufactured goods with the Europeans? Why were there renegade European fabricators, munitions and ship designers, and mercenary commanders in Istanbul, but relatively few Turkish counterparts employed in the West? Why did Europe not learn of the mass fabrication of cannon and galleys from the Ottomans? And why were not the novel galleasses in the Turkish rather than the Christian fleet?

True market economies never fully developed in the Muslim world because they were in jeopardy without freedom and antithetical to the Koran, which made no distinction between political, cultural, economic, and religious life, and therefore discouraged unfettered economic rationalism. Scholarly controversy still rages about the nebulous relationship between Islam and free markets, as historians and economists for centuries have attempted to explain why Europe in the past was able to project its power into the heart of the Islamic world, and why today the economies of Islamic states are so much smaller than their Western counterparts—why, for instance, the gross national product of a tiny Israel exceeds the aggregate economic output of all Islamic nations along the northern coast of Africa.

The debate makes strange bedfellows. Progressive Western scholars have tried their best to suggest that Arab economies are merely "different" from, rather than less efficient than, their Western counterparts, since European and American observers do not factor into the equation the salutary benefits of Islamic culture—reduced crime, stronger families, less gratuitous consumerism, and more charitable giving. They add that for centuries Muslim states found ingenious ways to circumvent formal religious strictures against compound interest—forgetting that such stealth and cumbersome procedures in themselves harmed easy capital creation. Oddly, Islamic economists have sometimes taken a much different—and more honest—approach in acknowledging the moral impediments to capital formation inherent in Islamic religion. Many take pride that in Muslim countries today there are religious and ethical checks to materialism and sheer economic rationalism.

If the Ottoman fleet at Lepanto was less advanced than its European counterpart, and if a single European state had the ability to construct and finance a near equal number of ships as the sultan's empire, so today the entire Islamic world of well over 1 billion people—albeit hardly monolithic—finds itself at a clear military disadvantage against individual Western militaries, despite the enormous wealth created by oil production and exportation. Just as Venice might match the Ottomans in galleys, so now a France, England, or America singly possesses air forces, ships, and nuclear weapons beyond the aggregate strength of the entire Islamic world. Twenty-four hundred years after Cyrus the Younger hired the Ten Thousand to win his kingdom, and five hundred years after the Ottoman emulation of the Arsenal at Venice, Saddam Hussein was buying all his arms from Western merchants with the profits from oil revenue, an industry created and maintained by hired Western technological expertise.

Free capital is the key to war making on any large scale, what Cicero called "the sinews of war," without which an army cannot muster, be fed, or fight. Capital is the wellspring of technological innovation, which is inextricably tied to freedom, often the expression of individualism, and thus critical to military success throughout the ages. That capitalism was born in the West, expanded through Europe, survived the alternate Western-inspired paradigms of socialism and communism, and found itself inextricably tied with personal freedom and democracy in its latest global manifestation explains in no small part Western military dominance from the age of Salamis to the Gulf War. There is past and present a vast difference between Western and Islamic approaches to capitalist economies:

> Whereas democratic capitalism is a development of human experience, the basis of the economic doctrine of Islam is divinely inspired. Therefore, the economic life of a Muslim is not entirely a materialistic or this-worldly vocation. Its stimulus is derived both from the individual's drive to gain wealth and from his wish to be an obedient servant of God. Thus intent counts, and the type of economic activity a Muslim engages in must be legitimate (M. Abdul-Rauf, *A Muslim's Reflections on Democratic Capitalism*, 60).

The purpose of capitalism, even sixteenth-century Mediterranean capitalism, was not social justice or "intent" or the desire to be "legitimate," but, as it has always been, the acknowledgment of the eternal greed of man—critical in crafting a system that recognizes natural self-interest. What made seventeenth-century Cypriots and Greeks despise the Turks was not merely ethnic and religious hatred but the gradual destruction of their own economic and material life under Ottoman rule. As absentee landowners Venetians in the eastern Mediterranean had been every bit as merciless to their Greek-speaking sharecroppers and peasants as their later Ottoman successors—the rich palaces still seen today in Venice are proof enough of their eastern Mediterranean extortion—but their knowledge of export trade, their ability to sell agricultural produce at the highest prices in Mediterranean ports, and their propensity to set up some industries all resulted in a trickle-down prosperity.

For oppressed peasants to be better off in the long run under Ottoman rule, taxes would have to be markedly lower than under the Europeans, since the latter created far more capital, some of which eventually enhanced the population at large. The great hatred of capitalism in the hearts of the oppressed, ancient and modern, I think, stems not merely from the ensuing vast inequality in wealth, and the often unfair and arbitrary nature of who profits and who suffers, but from the silent acknowledgment that under a free market economy the many victims of the greed of the few are still better off than those under the utopian socialism of the well-intended. It is a hard thing for the poor to acknowledge benefits from their rich moral inferiors who never so intended it.

> For a capitalist system to work, the state had to protect, not regulate or in-terfere with, free markets. Both for political and religious reasons, this the sultan could not do: The Ottomans had then no idea of the balance of trade. . . . Originated from an age-old tradition in the Middle East, the Ottoman trade policy was that the state had to be concerned above all that the people and craftsmen in the cities in particular would not suffer a shortage of necessities and raw material. Consequently, the imports were always welcomed and encouraged, and exports discouraged. (H. Inalcik, in K. Karpat, ed., *The Ottoman State and Its Place in World History,* 57)

Capitalism is not merely commerce, but brings with it a sophisticated infrastructure of insurance, corporations, bookkeeping, dividends, inter-est, freely accessed information, and official government protection of property and profit. Without free prices and free markets that best judge what people need and want, efficient production is impossible, since the appetites and requirements of millions are not immediately known, but only poorly guessed at and then often ignored by a coercive central state.

Lepanto bought time for a beleaguered Mediterranean West to re-place its lost power of classical political unity with the much stronger force of a transoceanic market. If the Middle Ages (A.D. 500–1500) had seen a holding action in Europe, as small squabbling monarchies kept out a series of Arabs, Vikings, Mongols, and Ottomans from central Europe and conducted the Crusades and *Reconquista,* so the new nation-states of the West would move to the offensive against not merely the Islamic world but indigenous peoples in Africa, Australia, and the New World as well. It was not that there was not innate, even superior genius at Istanbul: the Turkish lighthouse on the Bosphorus with its leaded-glass windows and lanterns fueled by wicks floating in oil was far superior to European mod-els. There were a number of brilliant Ottoman mathematicians, medical writers, and engineers. But all such thinkers usually worked in isolation from contemporary research in Europe. None enjoyed broad domestic in-stitutionalized support—ever wary about possible counterreaction from Islamic fundamentalists.

Absent was a holistic system that might translate individual brilliance into mass-produced items that would benefit and enrich the population without regard to state, religious, or cultural interests. The result was that while the sultan could hire a Venetian ship designer and set up dockyards patterned after the Arsenal of Venice, there was no indigenous theory or practice to advance Ottoman ship construction or to ensure continual nautical innovation apart from Western emulation. To do so would require competitive bidding, unrestricted profits, a monetized economy integrated with the Mediterranean, and a publishing, banking, and university presence in Asia Minor. Anything less meant that the sultan had to employ his enormous capital from conquest, taxation, and raiding to buy what he could not fabricate himself—a strategy that guaranteed his soldiers would never have as many or quite as effective weapons as their Western enemies. Thousands would die at Lepanto for those very reasons.

WAR AND THE MARKET

Capitalism in its most basic form was born in ancient Greece; that heritage helps to explain why the postclassical Europeans in their centuries of religious and political cannibalism nevertheless protected their autonomy from non-Westerners and were as wealthy as their more unified Islamic rivals. The word for profit, *kerdos,* is ubiquitous in the Greek language. Although classical scholars are still divided between "modernists" and "primitivists" who disagree about the extent of unfettered markets and an abstract appreciation of capitalist theory, there is a growing consensus that by the fifth century B.C. Greek economic activity—especially at imperial Athens—was decentralized, governed by supply and demand, and characterized by sophisticated notions of markets, profit, banking, and insurance, with government assurance of the sanctity of private property and rights of inheritance.

By the mid-fifth century B.C. the Greeks themselves were sensitive to the role that money and markets were beginning to play in warfare. Subsequent conservatives like Plato and Aristotle lamented that battle was no longer a contest of courage waged by hoplite phalanxes, but had become an unfettered enterprise on land and sea where money allowed armies to travel far from home, to be paid and maintained in the field, and to be augmented by mercenaries and sophisticated weaponry such as fleets, siege engines, and artillery. Capital, not courage, would determine who lived and who died. In the West during the fifth and fourth centuries B.C. ethical restraints on war making and economic activity seem to have been abandoned about the same time, ending for good the nascent idea of limited wars fought according to protocol, martial hierarchies, and moral economies that operated on principles other than the purely commercial. The impetus was largely capitalistic and democratic: designers were free to profit by building better weapons than their competitors, while rulers sought to arm as many of their subjects as cheaply and lethally as possible.

In the first book of Thucydides' history the great democratic statesman Pericles reminds his fellow Athenians about the innate military advantages their own market economy offered in a war against the more parochial agrarian states of the Peloponnese. Pericles concluded:

> Those who are yeomen farmers are more likely to risk their own lives than their property, for they believe that while they might survive the fighting, they are not sure that their capital will. Thus, although the states of the Peloponnese could defeat all of Greece in a single pitched battle, they would have no luck against a military organization so vastly different from their own. (Thucydides 1.143.2–3)

The sentiment that war was a question of money was grudgingly acknowledged even at Sparta, where King Archidamus at about the same time (431 B.C.) warned his blinkered comrades that "war was no longer a matter of hoplite arms, but of money" (Thucydides 1.83.2).

During the subsequent Hellenistic age, this novel notion that money won wars became unquestioned. The looting of the Achaemenid treasuries by Alexander the Great spurred a military renaissance in the eastern Mediterranean for more than two centuries as relatively small cadres of Greek-speaking dynasts ruled vast Asiatic populations in Seleucid Asia and Ptolemaic Egypt because of their ability to establish sophisticated trading regimes, corporate agriculture, and vast mercenary armies equipped with elaborate siege engines, catapults, and ships—all based on the conversion of the old Achaemenid treasuries to minted coinage. Rome was the capitalist war machine par excellence of the ancient world, as military activity was first gauged in terms of economic feasibility—illustrated by the rich record of imperial papyri and inscriptions that attest to the intricate system of logistical supply contracted out to private businessmen. The classical cultures, unlike their adversaries in the eastern Mediterranean and to the north, predicated their military success in part on the ability to coin money, respect private property, and operate free markets.

In the twilight of the empire, observers were quick to point out that Roman military impotence was a result of a debased currency, exorbitant taxation, and the manipulation of the market by inefficient government price controls, corrupt governmental traders, and unchecked tax farmers—the wonderful system of raising capital operating in reverse as it devoured savings and emptied the countryside of once-productive yeomen. But even during the collapse of the empire and the subsequent Dark and Middle Ages, Europeans were adept in fabricating a variety of superior military goods in great numbers, from plate armor to matchless double-edged swords, crossbows, and Greek fire, prompting many states to publish decrees forbidding their merchants from exporting such arms to potential enemies.

The alternative to capitalist-financed warfare was either simple coercion—the forced impressment of warriors without pay—or tribal musters fueled by promises of booty. Both systems could result in enormous and spirited armies: Vercingetorix's quarter-million-man Gallic army that nearly defeated Caesar at Alesia (52 B.C.) and the nomadic invasions of Genghis Khan (1206–27) and Tamerlane (1381–1405), who overran much of Asia, are the most notable examples. Cetshwayo, as we shall see, mustered 20,000 Zulus, who massacred the British at Isandhlwana (1879). But even the most murderous hordes could not really sustain—feed, clothe, and pay—a military force with sophisticated weaponry for a lengthy period of time. At some point farmers, traders, and merchants do not work if they are not paid, and standing armies are nearly impossible to maintain without regular salaries and contracts for supply.

For those states, ancient and modern, that failed to adopt the tenets of capitalism and private enterprise, if they were to war long enough, they would eventually encounter Western armies that were supplied by an amoral and unfettered market. In such cases, the numbers, brilliant leadership, and battlefield courage of the Other could be nullified by smaller, even poorly led armies that were better fed, equipped, and armed by those who saw profit in war. Ali Pasha's failure at Lepanto was not his tactical folly; nor was it an absence of courage on the part of the Janissaries, or even a dearth of Turkish bullion. The tragic loss of thousands of Ottoman faithful in the waters off Aetolia was due rather to the Christians' more or less godless system of market capitalism that produced in plenitude galleasses, harquebuses, cannon, boarding nets, mass-produced galleys—and risk-taking commanders who had no hesitation in sawing off their ships' prows at a moment's notice.

PART THREE

❦

Control

EIGHT

Discipline—or Warriors Are Not Always Soldiers

Rorke's Drift, January 22–23, 1879

Free though they are, they are not entirely free—for law is their master, whom they fear far more than your men fear you. Whatever their law commands, that they do; and it commands them always the same: they are not allowed to flee in battle from any foe, however great the numbers, but rather they are to stay in their ranks and there conquer or perish.

—HERODOTUS, *The Histories* (7.104)

KILLING FIELDS

"Each Man in His Place"

THE LAST MOMENTS at the battle of Isandhlwana were ghastly. Colonel Anthony Durnford's Natal Native Horse—250 horsemen and 300 foot soldiers from the Ngwane and Basuto tribes—after minutes of firing murderous volleys that had mowed down the attacking waves of Zulus, ran out of ammunition. Unfortunately for Durnford, his native contingent was not formed up in a square. It had spread itself thinly along the ridge on foot, in a loose line of some six hundred to eight hundred yards, firing carbines without bayonets. Durnford, like every British commander at the camp on the ridges of Isandhlwana, had vastly underestimated the size of the Zulu *impis* (regiments). Consequently, for most of the late morning he had unnecessarily exposed his men to attack in sorties well beyond camp, failing utterly as the senior officer in command at Isandhlwana to form up the garrison into some type of the standard British defensive perimeter. Durnford would pay for his tactical imbecility with his life and those of his men. Thousands of Zulus easily poured through their thinned ranks, stabbed and routed them, and were soon among the wagons—and at the backs of the regular army itself! Almost everywhere along the British lines, soldiers were firing far more slowly as they searched desperately for additional ammunition.

For the first time, after almost an hour of being butchered by systematic British volleys, the Zulus could at last use their deadly assegais (spears) at will. The close-quarter fighting with the European camp attendants ensured them freedom from the deadly rifle fire that had broken their initial charges across the open ground. Once in the confines of the camp, the barefoot, lightly clad warriors, armed with razor-sharp spears, enjoyed an actual advantage over their heavily laden British enemies, who for the most part wielded awkward single-shot Martini-Henry rifles designed to kill at a thousand yards, not five. *"Gwas Unhlongo! Gwas Inglubi!"*—"Stab the white men! Stab the pigs!" the Zulus yelled, as any British or native cavalryman still lucky enough to have a mount desperately rode out to attempt to cut a way through the throng.

Meanwhile, the British infantry front some six hundred yards to the northeast—about four hundred imperial riflemen of the veteran 24th Regiment were still alive there—began to break up into small isolated squares, islands of fifty or sixty men who methodically blasted away at the waves of Zulus that lapped around them on all sides. A few dozen, when their ammunition was exhausted, shook hands and then charged with their bayonets. Some used knives and captured assegais to take as many Zulus with them as they could. Zulus reported after the battle that some unarmed British soldiers finally died swinging their empty rifles and pounding the enemy with their fists. All were overwhelmed once they ran out of bullets for their guns, giving the Zulus the opportunity to attack them at a distance with thrown spears and their own sporadic rifle fire.

The bravery of the 24th came as no surprise. The regiment had been described by contemporaries as "no boy recruits but war-worn matured men, mostly with beards. Possessed of splendid discipline and sure of success, they lay on their position making every round tell" (M. Barthorp, *The Zulu War,* 61). But after Lord Chelmsford had divided his forces, the remaining men of the 24th, too few and too short of easily accessible ammunition, were never formed into one large defensible square and were thus destined to be annihilated in pockets and small groups. It was as if their officers—like the Roman generals at Cannae—had done everything to ignore their intrinsic advantages of Western discipline and superior offensive power.

Nearly 20,000 Zulu warriors roamed freely inside the extended British lines that had once ranged as far as 2,500 yards in a vast and haphazard semicircle around the slopes of the hill of Isandhlwana. Such a deployment, as the British commanders, Lieutenant Colonels Henry Pulleine and Anthony W. Durnford, at last realized in the moments before they were butchered, was no way to fight the Zulu nation. Methlagazulu, a Zulu veteran of the battle, later told the British of Colonel Durnford's last minutes:

> They made a desperate resistance, some firing with pistols and others using swords. I repeatedly heard the word "fire" given by someone, but we proved too many for them, and killed them all where they stood. When all was over I had a look at these men, and saw an officer with his arm in a sling, and with a big moustache, surrounded by carbineers, soldiers, and other men I didn't know. (*Narrative of Field Operations Connected with the Zulu War of 1879*, 38)

By 2:00 in the afternoon of January 22, 1879, it was all over, a little less than two hours after the Zulu *impis* had first surrounded the camp. Of the six companies of the 24th Regiment, fewer than a dozen men escaped. Twenty-one officers were killed on the spot. Almost all of the original 1,800 troops at Isandhlwana died—950 regular British troops, colonial volunteers, and camp and wagon attendants, along with 850 native Africans in various Natal regiments. Only a few scattered survivors managed to ride to safety in the general confusion. Several hours later the troops of Lord Chelmsford's center column of relief returned to the site of the slaughter:

> The dead lay everywhere, in windrows. Every body was mutilated, with the stomach slashed open, in order, the Zulus believed, to release the spirit of the dead. Here, a ghastly circle of soldiers' heads was laid out; there, a drummer boy hanging from a wagon by his feet, with his throat cut. A Natal mounted policeman and a Zulu lay dead, locked together as they had fallen, the policeman uppermost. Two other combatants lay close together, the Zulu with a bayonet thrust through his skull and the white man with an *assegai* plunged into his chest. A soldier of the 24th lay speared through

the back, with two other *assegais* by him, the blades bent double. It was the same all over the field. (D. Clammer, *The Zulu War*, 96–97)

In fact, the British army never again put underage boys on active service—they had found at Isandhlwana five youths with their genitals cut off and placed in their mouths. Many Zulu warriors cut out the bearded jaws of the British dead as victory trophies. Others had stomped the intestines of the corpses to jelly and further desecrated the truncated torsos. Some heads were arranged in a circle. In turn, the grotesque blasts from the enormous .45-caliber slugs of the British Martini-Henry rifles—limbs blown away, cheeks and faces blasted apart, chests and stomachs shredded with gaping holes—marked the far more numerous Zulu dead and would identify the surviving wounded from Isandhlwana for a generation to come. Later European observers noted aging warriors still in agony decades after the battle, legs and arms missing and their bodies disfigured with hideous bullet scars.

A century of fighting in South Africa had taught the Boer settlers that vastly outnumbered Europeans, even equipped with slow-firing and inaccurate flintlock muzzle-loaders, could defeat Zulu forces fifty to a hundred times their number—*if* a series of careful protocols was followed. Discipline was the key. A secure camp had to be established in the bush, with the clumsy supply wagons circled and then chained together into a fortified laager—a bothersome task requiring hours of strenuous labor to unhitch, maneuver, and interlock the wagons into an impenetrable wall. Scouts and patrols were to be sent at regular hourly intervals, given the Zulu propensity to crawl stealthily through the range grass in great numbers without being seen. Ammunition had to be stockpiled in the center and freely distributed among the wagons in the circle to ensure a continuous volley of fire from single-shot rifles that would keep the much faster Zulus away from the ramparts. Ideally, shooters would be placed shoulder-to-shoulder to provide a carpet of fire and to prevent Zulus from leaping between the defenders and pouring through gaps—as well as reinforcing group morale and facilitating talking to one another as soldiers fired.

If there was time, the ground around the laager should be first cleared of major obstacles, allowing an open field of fire for riflemen—and then limbs of thornbushes and broken bottles scattered, or better yet, ditches and ramparts readied to slow down the rush of barefoot and exposed warriors. Field artillery—and primitive Gatling machine guns if available—should be anchored at vulnerable points of the laager to divert waves of the attackers toward rifle fire on the sides. All this was necessary to overcome the intrinsic advantages of enormous numerical superiority, speed, and surprise enjoyed by the Zulus. The vastly outnumbered Europeans, to be successful, had to kill Zulus yards distant, before the running warriors leaped into their lines. Yet at Isandhlwana the British followed none of their own carefully established protocols. Why?

Isandhlwana was the first major encounter of the Zulu War, and the British officers in their initial arrogance had not appreciated how adept the Zulus were in moving thousands of their warriors long distances only to remain undetected within yards of British camps. While the Martini-Henry rifle was sighted to 1,500 yards, and fired a deadly .45-caliber bullet weighing 480 grains that lost little of its accuracy even at great distances, it was nevertheless a single-shot, not a repeating, weapon. True, experienced riflemen with the standard seventy cartridges in their pouches for a time could fire off up to twelve rounds a minute. But the need to load each bullet individually meant that dispersed lines of British soldiers, apart from fortifications or reinforced squares, might be overwhelmed by waves of sprinting Zulus, as dozens of the attackers swarmed individual riflemen fumbling for cartridges. Even the best riflemen might take five seconds to eject a cartridge, load a new one, aim, and fire—a mostly unsustainable rate over hours of shooting. If there were even slight interruptions in supplying cartridges—and there were several at Isandhlwana—then the ensuing hiatus of regular volleys might allow a fast-moving *impi* to close the critical distance through the killing zone to break into and obliterate British lines. Even with full pouches, a rapid-firing rifleman might exhaust his personal supply of cartridges within five or six minutes and then find himself outnumbered in hand-to-hand stabbing contests.

In America, repeating Spencer and Henry rifles had been used in the last years of the Civil War; Union troops under Sherman had employed both on their marches through Georgia and the Carolinas in autumn 1864 and early 1865. The model 1873 Winchester lever-action repeating .32-caliber rifle was ubiquitous on the American plains and could fire three times more rapidly than the Martini-Henry—well over thirty bullets a minute compared to the Martini's ten or twelve. But innate British military conservatism (the earlier so-called Brown Bess flintlock musket had been retained as the standard infantry weapon for decades), the arrogance that repeating weapons were not critical in colonial wars against spear-carrying natives, shortsighted financial economies, and the desire for a heavy, powerful rifle that could shoot an enormous slug at great ranges—all these factors prevented the adoption of much more rapid-firing, smaller-caliber guns in the English army. The Anglo-Zulu War was about the last occasion in which European troops used single-shot rifles against native forces, and at Isandhlwana there were no Gatling guns to provide repeating fire for the garrison.

Among the British officer corps on the morning of January 22 there was no awareness of the need for caution. Isandhlwana was to be the battle that the English commander in Zululand, Lord Chelmsford, had wanted and got: a chance to pit British riflemen, supported by cavalry and artillery, against the aggregate military strength of the Zulu nation. That desire for open battle may explain why Chelmsford ignored the stream of messages that reached him from his beleaguered camp during the late morning and early afternoon of the twenty-second. In his mind the presence of the Zulu army on a clear plain was something to be welcomed, not feared. The British had sought a decisive battle to end what they envisioned as a short and inexpensive campaign. They now had the high ground.

Their real fear was a protracted guerrilla war of constant skirmishing and ambush, not a European-style collision of arms in broad daylight. Chelmsford also had artillery and more than 500,000 rounds of rifle ammunition in the camp at Isandhlwana. Moreover, there were crack battalions present, like the 24th Regiment, which were long experienced in putting down sustained volleys of gunfire that could kill any advancing native enemy en masse at 1,000 yards and annihilate him at 300. Or so it was thought.

The main Zulu *impi* of some 20,000 warriors had been on the move for days, and had more than five miles to run before it reached the camp at Isandhlwana. Zulus, who like the Aztecs had evolved their war making from ritualized warfare, still preferred to fight during the day and in swarms—and always to approach openly to attempt their famed outflanking movement: perfect targets for disciplined ranks of British riflemen. Lord Chelmsford knew this and so had few ostensible worries. Four decades earlier in December 1838, had not Andres Pretorius with fewer than 500 Boer ranchers defeated 12,000 Zulus at the Ncome River (thereafter known as Blood River), killing more than 3,000 outright and wounding thousands more? Unlike the English, the Boers had used slow-firing, less accurate, and clumsy flintlock muskets, methodically shooting from their protected wagon laager at the masses of oncoming Zulus for more than two hours before sending out horsemen to ride down hundreds more of the wounded and fleeing.

Other than naïveté and haughtiness, then, what precisely had gone wrong four decades later at Isandhlwana? The British had invaded Zululand in January 1879 with three unwieldy columns, whose total strength was around 17,000 men. A lengthy supply train of 725 wagons and 7,600 oxen carried rations, tents, artillery batteries, and some 2 million rounds of ammunition for an envisioned brief two- to three-month campaign—enough bullets to shoot every Zulu man, woman, and child nearly ten times over. Although the mixed force of British infantry, native auxiliaries, and colonial settlers was itself hardly a third the strength of the Zulu army—there were little more than 5,400 regular British infantrymen under his entire command—Chelmsford's plan was to separate his forces still further to advance on the Zulu stronghold at Ulundi with three columns that would cross the two-hundred-mile border at seventy- to forty-mile intervals. That way he might systematically flush the Zulus into committing to a decisive battle, thereby precluding either a guerrilla war or a sudden major invasion into British-governed Natal.

The absence of good roads in Zululand made it nearly impossible anyway to drive all 725 wagons of the invasion force in a single file. From the experience of various wars against other tribes in southern Africa, and a recent raid on Zulu kraals a few days earlier, the British were convinced that no native charge in Africa could withstand sustained European rifle fire. They were eventually to be proved right, but such confidence rested on a modicum of disciplined precaution.

Chelmsford himself was attached to the center column that camped out at Isandhlwana. But then he further diluted his center force's strength by marching out the morning of the attack with 2,500 men—far more than the number left behind at the camp—in search of rumored *impis* of some 20,000 Zulus. Although warned at 9:30 while he was still only twelve miles away that the British were under attack back at Isandhlwana, Chelmsford believed that Pulleine, Durnford, and their troops were merely being tested by enemy probes and in no real danger. So for the rest of the morning and early afternoon, a British force larger than that left to be annihilated at Isandhlwana would camp less than a four-hour march away and yet send no aid—despite receiving a series of messages that his men were surrounded and desperate. Apparently, Chelmsford believed that he, not Pulleine at Isandhlwana, was closer to the real Zulu main force and that the camp could deal with this sideshow on its own. He was to be proved wrong on every count. Had he marched immediately when the first message arrived from Pulleine, Chelmsford would have perhaps arrived at Isandhlwana during the heat of the battle, thus restoring the camp's original strength—and thereby still overcoming the flawed tactics of his subordinates.

Lieutenant Colonel Henry Pulleine, along with the reckless Durnford, deserves much of the responsibility for the subsequent catastrophe. After Chelmsford had marched out, Pulleine, who had never been in combat, much less in command of such a large battle force, made no arrangements to bring his forces into a square during the first attack. Instead, fewer than six hundred British troops were arranged to cover more than a mile of camp frontage—far too great a distance to achieve any solid line of defense. Pulleine actually ordered his scattered companies to *advance* toward the Zulus to form a line that might connect with Durnford's mounted troops. The latter had foolishly ridden well beyond camp and then in retreat had posted his thin line of natives far too distant from the regular British rifle companies.

There was also to be no reserve; the left flank was not defended but left open. From the onset the British never offered a complete circle of resistance at all, leaving the wagons and tents completely undefended. Some men had rushed from their tents without bayonets or extra cartridges. The Zulus could not have wished for a better scenario under which to attack. After an initial respite of some fifteen minutes in the fighting—the Zulus were bewildered that hundreds of their bravest warriors were blown apart at nearly 1,000 yards by the initial British volleys—Pulleine still had a second opportunity to withdraw all his units to the camp, where they could have re-formed into a square around some of the wagons, food, and ammunition boxes. Instead, due to panic, inexperience, or an inadequate appreciation of the peril his troops were in, he ordered no change in formation.

The wagons the prior night had not been pulled into a laager and thus the camp itself extended well over three-quarters of a mile. Chelmsford, after issuing orders at the onset of the campaign that laagers were mandatory and trenches desirable, himself chose to insist on neither at Isandhlwana. He claimed that he had planned to move out from the temporary encampment at Isandhlwana the next day. He later stated that his inexperienced teamsters would have taken all night to accomplish the wagon fortifications, that the ground had been too hard to dig and entrench, and that the natural rise had ensured the high ground and thus a sure field of fire anyway in case of attack. Almost all the colonial officers in the camp who had experience with the Zulus were alarmed about the lack of preparations; only those who left the next morning with Chelmsford survived.

Chelmsford's own official written declarations—calling for the need for stout laagers each night, constant communications between columns, frequent cavalry patrols, and high readiness against Zulu surprise attacks—were documents of record only. In practice he operated on the erroneous belief that columns of 1,000 to 2,000 Europeans with Martini-Henry rifles could do as they pleased. And although there were a half million rounds of .45 cartridges in the camp, almost all the defenders ran out of bullets well before the final slaughter. Ammunition was stored in a central depot, in heavy wooden boxes, fastened by copper bands held down by screws in the lids, and had not been liberally distributed among the various companies. Indeed, Durnford's native troops were soon unable to reach the arms depot. Other colonial and native companies may have been refused resupply by a quibbling quartermaster, on the grounds that they were wrongly opening boxes belonging to the 24th Regiment! Survivors' accounts relate the confusion of desperate men trying to break open the heavy containers with their bayonets, scoop up bullets, and then frantically run off to their distant lines to resume firing. Those supply parties who found accessible cartridges often had to travel nearly half a mile to resupply the more distant riflemen. Even after the disastrous decision not to laager the camp, to send out more than half the force on a wild-goose chase on the morning of the battle, and to scatter the remaining defenders in an indefensible position, the British nevertheless might well have withstood the Zulu onslaught had plentiful ammunition been dispersed throughout the defense.

After the individual companies of the 24th Regiment were overwhelmed, a few retreated back to the wagons to search for shelter and cartridges. Captain Younghusband, according to Zulu oral accounts, was among the last to die, firing from the bed of the wagon until he was shot down by the horde around him. Zulu narratives stressed the discipline of the last moments of the British defenders: "Ah, those red soldiers at Isandhlwana, how few there were, and how they fought! They fell like stones—each man in his place" (D. Clammer, *The Zulu War*, 86). Various witnesses attest that Durnford collected together a small circle of riflemen, yelling "Fire" at precise intervals as their limited ammunition ran out. In the last horrific minutes of spearing and shooting, no battalion of regular British riflemen broke and ran, despite being outnumbered by more than forty to one.

So ended the slaughter at the hill of Isandhlwana, the most heralded, though not the most costly, disaster in colonial British history. While the London press would soon make much of the general incompetence that had led to the calamity, it was scarcely mentioned that 2,000 Zulus were killed outright, and another 2,000 crawled away to die or were so disabled by wounds as to be incapable of fighting. Thus, the one clear-cut British defeat of the Zulu War also took the greatest toll on the Zulu nation during the entire war. In each minute of the battle the doomed defenders had killed or wounded more than thirty Zulus! Since not more than six hundred troops in the camp were actually firing with Martini-Henry rifles, we should assume that each British infantryman killed or wounded on average between five and seven Zulus before perishing.

King Cetshwayo, when told the news of his "victory," remarked in sorrow, "An *assegai* has been thrust into the belly of the nation. There are not enough tears to mourn the dead." The price of destroying a small British garrison was the killing or wounding of nearly a tenth of his army. Cornelius Vign, who was visiting the Zulus at the time, reported of the mass mourning among women and children that took place in the kraal of one Msundusi who was killed at Isandhlwana, a scene that must have been repeated thousands of times over for the Zulu dead in the weeks after the battle: "When they came into or close to the *kraal,* they kept on wailing in front of the *kraals,* rolling themselves on the ground and never quieting down; nay, in the night they wailed so as to cut through the heart of anyone" (C. Vign, *Cetshwayo's Dutchman,* 28). In the Zulu way of war the British defeat suggested an end to hostilities altogether. After all, in an open battle, an opposing tribe had been wiped out and thus should logically cease fighting. "The King was glad when he heard that his people had gained the victory over the Whites," wrote Vign, who served as a Dutch translator for Cetshwayo, "and thought that the war would now be at an end, supposing that the Whites had no more soldiers" (*Cetshwayo's Dutchman,* 30).

Another Zulu *impi* of fresh, mostly middle-aged reserves, more than 4,000 strong, was now heading toward Rorke's Drift six miles away, against a tiny contingent of little more than a hundred British soldiers who were quietly garrisoning a supply station and hospital. Once these stragglers were finished off, the rest of the British would surely see the futility of their assault and retreat back into Natal. It would prove one of the great ironies of the British-Zulu wars that at the first notice of the attack two "unexceptional" lieutenants in command at Rorke's Drift immediately began to fortify their position, form up into a close-knit line, distribute ammunition freely, and so in the next sixteen hours utilize the discipline of the British army to offset the vast numerical superiority and great bravery of an entirely fresh Zulu army.

"A Worse Position Could Hardly Be Imagined"

Unlike the high ground at Isandhlwana, everything at Rorke's Drift favored the Zulus. The two tiny stone houses, about forty yards apart, former farmsteads turned into a missionary station, were nearly indefensible. One structure was employed by the British as a hospital. In it were thirty-five wounded or sick soldiers who somehow had to be incorporated into a makeshift defense of the camp. Thatched roofs meant that the storehouse and hospital could be torched. Worse still, the high ground on three sides of the post was soon to be held by the Zulus. There were a number of encumbrances—orchards, walls, ditches, buildings—surrounding the outpost that might impede fire and allow the running warriors to seek cover.

The hill of Oskarberg to the south of the camp allowed enemy snipers to shoot freely at defenders all along the north rampart. Moreover, hundreds of Europe's most modern rifles were in the hands of the Zulus, who hours earlier at Isandhlwana had also looted more than 250,000 rounds of .45-caliber ammunition. When the attack began a little past 5:00 P.M., it was getting dark, giving cover to the Zulus as they began to surround the outpost. "A worse position could hardly be imagined," an officer remarked of the British defenses at Rorke's Drift. The British found themselves with a contingent only 5 percent of the size of the force that had just perished at Isandhlwana—and there the high ground and terrain had favored the doomed.

There was no experienced senior officer to be found at the compound. The tiny garrison's commander, Brevet Major Henry Spalding, had shortly before noon ridden from Rorke's Drift to Helpmakaar ten miles away to seek reinforcements, leaving the post in the hands of two junior officers. As he left he called to his subordinate John Chard to remind him that he was now in command—but added that there was almost no likelihood of any action during his brief absence. Most men of the garrison were disgruntled that the real chance for action and glory lay a few miles to the north in Zululand proper at Isandhlwana, where the center column was trying to flush out the Zulu *impis*—not at a border supply depot in Natal far behind the purported front lines.

Lieutenant John Chard had only a few weeks earlier arrived in South Africa and was attached to the Royal Engineers; he was supervising the construction of a ferry a few hundred feet below at the drift. His cocommander was Lieutenant Gonville Bromhead, in charge of B Company, 2nd Battalion of the 24th Regiment, whose other companies were being annihilated at Isandhlwana. Neither Chard nor Bromhead, who was essentially deaf, had much battlefield experience. They certainly were not considered stellar officers by their superiors—"hopeless," a superior of Bromhead once wrote of him. Nothing in the record of either presaged the great heroism and leadership that both would display in the desperate ten hours of continuous shooting to come. But a former master sergeant, James Dalton—over six two in height, barrel-chested, fifty years of age—in charge of the commissary had seen plenty of fighting, and he seems to have been involved in many of the key initial decisions involving the defense of the outpost.

Besides the absence of good natural fortifications and senior experienced command, the post was vastly outnumbered. There were only 139 British soldiers, and 35 were bedridden. Excluding cooks, orderlies, and teamsters, only 80 were actual riflemen. In the minutes after the news arrived that the regiment at Isandhlwana was wiped out, and fresh *impis* of more than 4,000 Zulus were on their way, a disturbing number of fleeing Europeans and terrified native auxiliaries, who might have aided the trapped garrison, peeled off and rode to safety farther west into Natal. While British accounts suggest that the Zulu attack was haphazard and spontaneous, it was far more likely that tribal leaders realized that most of Chelmsford's supplies were at Rorke's Drift. The capture of the outpost would feed thousands of hungry Zulus and essentially wipe out the stores of the center column.

The idea that 80 riflemen could do what nearly 2,000 could not seemed absurd. Westerners usually fought outnumbered—sometimes vastly so at Salamis, Gaugamela, Tenochtitlán, Lepanto, and Midway—but nonetheless they had armies of a few thousand with which to offer a resistance. Even Cortés in his final assault on Mexico City had hundreds, not dozens, of Europeans. Numerical inferiority, as we have seen, can be offset by superior technology, spirited troops, good infantry, plentiful supplies, and discipline, but Europeans needed the cohesiveness or firepower of hundreds to offer a semblance of resistance to thousands. Alexander the Great's 50,000 could defeat a quarter million Persian troops; but had he only 10,000 on the morning of October 1, 331 B.C., Mazaeus would have overwhelmed Parmenio, and the Macedonians might well have been slaughtered to the man.

A couple of British soldiers were dispatched to the nearby post at Helpmakaar to bring reinforcements. Then the occasional refugees that had escaped Isandhlwana—mostly remnants of the colonial Natal carbineers and mounted police—rode on by the outpost and refused to join in its defense. About one hundred colonial cavalrymen under the command of Lieutenant Vause, who had earlier ridden up from Isandhlwana and taken positions at Rorke's Drift, suddenly bolted when they saw the size of the Zulu attacking army. Their departure took one hundred potential Martini-Henry rifles from the garrison's meager defenses. When they fled, Captain Stephenson's company of native African riflemen also soon fled, along with Stephenson himself and a few noncommissioned European officers. Chard's men shot one sergeant as he galloped away.

Besides the obvious effect on morale—in the two to three hours between the confirmation of the disaster of Isandhlwana and the attack on the garrison at Rorke's Drift, the British defenders had witnessed a series of colonial and native troops ride in, spread tales of horror, then flee in terror—the reduction in the number of men for the perimeter defenses changed the entire plan of resistance. If Chard and Bromhead might have had 450 or so troops to man the tiny wall when the news of the impending attack reached them, they were lucky to have even a hundred men either skilled or well enough to fire a rifle—only about one shooter per every twelve feet of the makeshift rampart. Chard quickly determined that the fortifications would need additional interior walls, to serve as an inner sanctum when the thinly manned, mealie-bag outer redoubt was inevitably overwhelmed.

The enemy was especially formidable. An army was approaching of more than 4,000 Zulus under the command of King Cetshwayo's brother, Prince Dabulamanzi. The latter had broken his brother's orders on two counts: he was not to enter British-ruled Natal from Zululand—Rorke's Drift was right across the border—and he was to avoid an assault on any British troops behind ramparts. Although Dabulamanzi found himself in command of two of the older divisions of Cetshwayo's army—the some 3,000 to 3,500 warriors of the *uThulwana* and *uDloko* regiments were mostly married men between forty-one and fifty years of age—he had 1,000 younger unmarried men in their early thirties of the *inDlu-yengwe*. All had served in the reserve at Isandhlwana. Before the attack on Rorke's Drift, they had spent the past few hours killing fugitives and the wounded who were crisscrossing the plain in their desperate efforts at escape. After his Zulus were safely across the Buffalo River into Natal, Dabulamanzi quickly united the three divisions and began preparations to have the entire force assault the British outpost. A few of the warriors had had some experience in intertribal fighting of the last decade. Most important, they were relatively fresh and had not seen much action in the slaughter at Isandhlwana, in which a tenth of the Zulu nation's manhood was wounded or killed in a single afternoon.

All felt they had to dip their spears before returning home, especially given the startling success of their peers at Isandhlwana in breaking the British lines. Finally, a number had their own muskets, and a smaller group had looted some of the nearly eight hundred Martini-Henry rifles and hundreds of thousands of rounds of ammunition found at Isandhlwana. If sharpshooters could be positioned on Oskarberg hill above the compound to provide covering fire, while the entire mass charged head-on against the weaker parts of the north wall, then the Zulus might take the compound with the first charge.

The unknown problem facing the Zulus, however, was the nature of the troops in B Company of the 24th Regiment holed up at Rorke's Drift. Like Leonidas's Spartans at Thermopylae, there was scarcely any chance that they would flee, despite the odds and the macabre battle to come. At least eighty were regular British riflemen and crack shots who could usually hit an individual Zulu warrior at some three hundred yards and knock down a dense mass of swarming fighters at a thousand yards. All were determined to win or die on the spot, and dying was the far more likely scenario, given the overwhelming numbers of the enemy. Why did the British choose to fight under such hopeless conditions? Theirs was a discipline that grew out of the training and regulation of the British army, the fear of and respect for their officers, and the camaraderie and loyalty to one another. Because they were behind makeshift fortifications, the Zulus could not count on outflanking movements and infiltration that had proved so successful at Isandhlwana. To take the compound, the Zulus would have to brave rifle fire and bayonet thrusts, jump over the makeshift walls, and kill all the men in the compound.

The shooting itself would go on steadily for ten hours—British redcoats methodically blasting apart Zulu bodies at close range with .45-caliber rifle fire and slicing through exposed arms, legs, and bellies with razor-sharp bayonet jabs, the Zulus less successfully trying to stab the shoulders or necks of the riflemen on the ramparts with assegai thrusts and hoping that their own snipers might somehow hit the bright redcoats from the slopes above. During the afternoon of the twenty-second and early morning of the twenty-third, Chard and Bromhead would turn their tiny garrison into a veritable firestorm that would pour lead into the bodies of hundreds of Zulu warriors, such killing all predicated on a strict adherence to formal British military practice and discipline that would keep men at the ramparts shooting continuously without respite, their shoulders, arms, and hands blue and bloody from powder burns and the enormous kick of the Martini-Henry rifles.

Sixteen Hours at Rorke's Drift

2:30 P.M., January 22, 1879. In the minutes after receiving the news of the slaughter at Isandhlwana, Chard, Bromhead, and Dalton agreed that flight from Rorke's Drift in slow-moving, ox-drawn wagons with the wounded was impossible. Instead, they ordered all the tents dismantled, but abandoned outside the compound as impediments to the attackers. Next, they surveyed the circumference and quickly planned a wall of defense. The depot's plentiful supply of heavy biscuit boxes and mealie bags might allow the garrison limited protection—if they could somehow in the next hour or so be stacked chest-high into some type of rampart. Here Chard's expertise as a Royal Engineer proved invaluable. Immediately, he, Bromhead, and Dalton organized work parties and began building a parapet to connect the two stone buildings, parked wagons, and stone kraal into an oblong circle of defense. Soldiers and the native troopers, who had not yet fled, stacked the boxes (one hundred pounds) and the mealie bags (two hundred pounds) four to five feet high to allow riflemen some protection while aiming and reloading.

The bags were a godsend, since their weight and density meant that bullets could not penetrate the British wall, while it was almost impossible to knock the heavy sacks over. Holes were gouged in the hospital's outside wall to allow the patients to shoot at the *impis* approaching from the south. In a stunning feat of improvised labor, officers, native soldiers, the sick, and British enlisted men in little more than an hour constructed a barricade of some four hundred yards—all under the threat of imminent annihilation. Fortunately, there was a slight rise on the north side of the compound, and the mealie-bag rampart there incorporated this natural advantage, resulting in a breastwork whose outer face was often over six feet high. No Zulu could vault such a height, but would have to hoist himself over in the face of British bullets and bayonets.

3:30, January 22, 1879. Chard, who, given his marginal seniority over Bromhead, was exercising command of the defense, returned to the river, collected his small engineering detail that was working on the ferry, brought up the water carriage and tools, and evacuated the landing. While he was now assured by a variety of messengers that thousands of Zulus, who had just massacred a force twenty times larger than his own, were headed his way, neither he nor his men showed any visible signs of panic. Instead, he and Bromhead carefully walked along the circumference of the small makeshift fort, ensuring that the wall was four feet high throughout. Then they ordered work ceased to ensure that the exhausted men could rest before the general assault.

Riflemen of the 24th Regiment were stationed at proper intervals, ammunition pouches filled and piles of additional cartridges heaped at their feet. Bayonets were fixed. The two junior officers, with hardly any experience of Africa, much less of the Zulus, in less than two hours and under the threat of sure destruction, had done the opposite of their senior and more experienced commanders at Isandhlwana—and thus given their vastly outnumbered fighters a chance of survival that the doomed at Isandhlwana never had.

4:30, January 22, 1879. With the arrival of the Zulus and the first scattered fire, the native and colonial contingents abruptly fled, leaving behind B Company, 2nd Battalion, 24th Regiment, with its skeleton force of fewer than a hundred regular British soldiers, who then had to rearrange themselves on the weakened rampart. Chard realized that the original fortification might soon prove too large a perimeter to hold with vastly reduced forces—he had little more than a hundred able-bodied men, no longer 450—so he constructed a second wall of biscuit boxes, running north and south to connect the storehouse with the north wall, in effect providing a vastly smaller circuit should the northwestern wall be overrun.

5:30, January 22, 1879. Firing in earnest began on the north mealie-bag wall. Here the British lines were stretched the thinnest, and there was an unfortunate series of natural obstacles—the orchard, fence, a ditch a mere thirty yards away, and some brush and the six-foot wall immediately outside the British defenses—which gave the waves of running Zulus places of cover to coordinate their attack. Meanwhile, from the slopes of Oskarberg to the south, some Zulus with the captured Martini-Henry rifles were shooting at the backs of the British defenders on the north wall and occasionally scoring hits. Crying *"Usuthu! Usuthu!,"* the thousand strong of the *inDlu-yengwe* sprinted against the south wall. Within minutes the entire outpost was under attack—by sniper fire from Oskarberg hill, by repeated human wave attacks against the ramparts by spearmen, and from sporadic shooting by Zulus hidden in the ditch and behind the fence, buildings, and trees right outside the British wall.

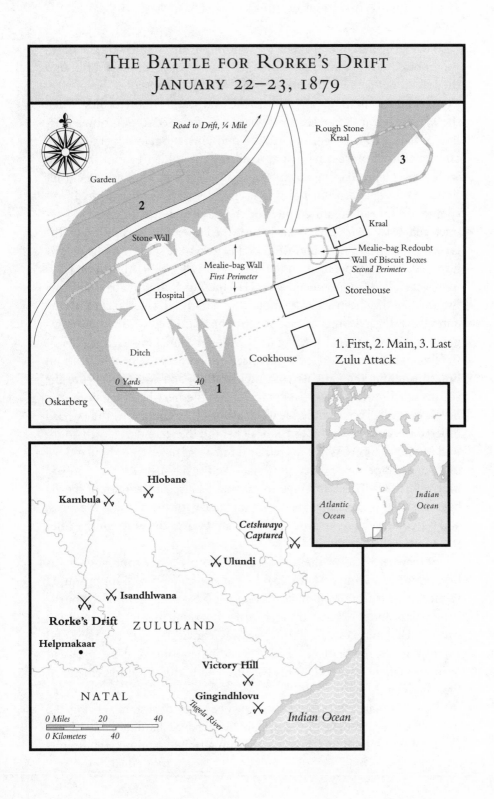

THE BATTLE FOR RORKE'S DRIFT
JANUARY 22–23, 1879

Road to Drift, ¼ Mile

Rough Stone
Kraal

3

Garden

2

Kraal

Stone Wall

Mealie-bag Redoubt

Wall of Biscuit Boxes
Second Perimeter

Mealie-bag Wall
First Perimeter

Hospital

Storehouse

Ditch

Cookhouse

1. First, 2. Main, 3. Last
Zulu Attack

0 Yards   40

1

Oskarberg

Hlobane

Kambula

*Cetshwayo
Captured*

Ulundi

Isandhlwana

Rorke's Drift   ZULULAND

Helpmakaar

Victory Hill

Gingindhlovu

NATAL

Tugela River

Indian Ocean

0 Miles   20   40

0 Kilometers   40

Atlantic
Ocean

Indian
Ocean

For the next hour and a half, a few dozen British soldiers on the north wall mowed down wave after wave of Zulus, most of whom soon found they could not get over the mealie bags without being shot or bayoneted. The chief problem for the British was the overheating of their rifles. When the Martini-Henry's barrels slowly began to glow red, the soft brass casings of the cartridges began to expand upon insertion, fouling the breech and sometimes preventing firing, requiring the soldier to ram them out with a cleaning rod—thereby allowing small groups of Zulus to cluster under the bags and begin hoisting each other over the barricade. In response, Bromhead organized interior charges of selected riflemen to bayonet and blast apart Zulus that had leaped over the bags. Most of the growing number of dead and wounded British were shot from the rear by hundreds of Zulus perched on the heights of Oskarberg. Almost no riflemen were killed from Zulu assegais. Had the Zulus coordinated their rifle fire and had they been accurate shots, they could easily have picked off the entire British garrison, inasmuch as they had hundreds of shooters compared to the paltry British firing force of fewer than a hundred.

7:00, January 22, 1879. At the onset of darkness the hospital was on fire, threatening the patients with incineration, and with its capture the collapse of the entire western rampart. For the next hour or more in a heroic escape, all but eight made it out alive—at just about the time Chard ordered the entire garrison to fall back behind the secondary north-south wall of biscuit boxes. While his reduced force was defending about a third of its original perimeter, an additional—and final—fallback position was hastily fortified. This last refuge consisted of a circular redoubt of mealie bags stacked nine feet high, allowing sanctuary for the hospital evacuees, and a secondary rampart from which to shoot over the heads of the riflemen on the shrinking wall.

Somewhere out on the plain—perhaps only a few thousands yards beyond the Zulu ring—Major Spalding at last rode up with his promised reinforcements from Helpmakaar. But once he saw the glow of the burning hospital and the Zulu throng, he turned around and took his reserves back to Helpmakaar. Apparently, he was convinced that his men and camp were already obliterated. Had Spalding continued, there is a good chance he might have fought his way in to add critical reinforcements at the climax of the battle.

10:00, January 22, 1879. After nearly five hours of sustained firing, the battle slowly began to favor the British. Lieutenant Chard noted in his official report, "A desultory fire was kept up all night, and several assaults

were attempted and repulsed, the vigor of the attack continuing until after midnight. Our men, firing with the greatest coolness, did not waste a
single shot, the light afforded by the burning hospital being of great help
to us" (*Narrative of Field Operations Connected with the Zulu War of 1879*,
46–47).

With the onset of darkness the Zulu snipers on Oskarberg had gradually lost their targets and then joined the general fray. The new reduced
perimeter had incorporated the sturdy storehouse as its south wall, in
essence eliminating the chance that soldiers on the ramparts could any
longer be fired upon freely from the rear. The burning hospital, as Chard
noted, had the unintended effect of illuminating the immediate area
around the camp and thus highlighting the Zulus as they ran toward the
British defenses. Although there were numerous dead and wounded
British, the reduced circuit meant that riflemen were also firing much
closer together in their final stand, giving a greater concentration of rifle
fire than before and making the supply of ammunition more efficient. If
the British were bone-tired since their scramble to fortify the compound
more than seven hours earlier, the Zulus were in even worse shape—having essentially no food for nearly two days and marching or fighting nonstop for twelve hours.

11:30, January 22, 1879. The British abandoned the stone kraal that
had formed the northeastern hinge of their rampart, and now were down
to a tiny circuit of less than 150 yards in extent. Many of their bayonets—
horrific weapons of triangular steel some twenty-one inches long—were
bent or twisted. Their gun barrels burned their hands and routinely
jammed. Most expected that a final rush of the 3,000 or so Zulus up in the
hills would at last overwhelm the garrison. The beleaguered troops in the
tiny circuit could have had no idea of the toll their rifles was taking on
the enemy, nor of the enormous hunger and weariness that overcame the
attackers as midnight approached.

Still, the Zulus continued to test the British fire, in vain efforts to vault
the walls. Most often they were shot or bayoneted as they struggled to
wrestle the barrels of the British rifles away—the red-hot steel also often
scorching hands and arms in the melee. But after midnight the attacks became sporadic, as Chard and Bromhead dispatched half the defenders to
repair the mealie-bag wall, distribute ammunition, and bring the water
cart inside the perimeter to prepare for the expected final battle at dawn.

4:00 A.M., January 23, 1879. At first light, Chard surveyed the debris of
the battlefield and ordered parties to begin once more to strengthen the

wall, to collect Zulu weapons from the killing ground, and cautiously to explore the plain beyond the outpost. The Zulus were mysteriously gone from the killing field, but nevertheless, soldiers were kept on the barricades in expectation of a renewal of a general attack.

7:00, January 23, 1879. An enormous line of Zulus suddenly appeared along the surrounding crests, but then seemed to drift wearily away, abandoning the siege at the moment a final charge surely would have overwhelmed the garrison. They were either too exhausted and hungry to continue or had spied Lord Chelmsford's relief column in the distance. Reconnaissance parties discovered 351 enemy dead; the number of wounded who crawled away and eventually died may have added another 200 to the fatality total. Later accounts suggest that the total Zulu dead ranged somewhere from 400 to 800 as bodies were found for miles beyond Rorke's Drift for the next several weeks. It was generally true of the entire Zulu War that the British vastly underestimated the number of Zulu dead, since in the immediate aftermath of their battles they rarely went out beyond a half mile to count bodies, and had no idea that the majority of Zulus they shot, without medical care or food and water, crawled away to die. The British lost just fifteen dead and twelve wounded. Colonel Harford, who arrived with Chelmsford's relief column the next day, remarked that the wreckage of the fort "gave the appearance and feeling of devastation after a hurricane, with the dead bodies thrown in, the only thing that remained whole being a circular miniature fortress constructed of bags of mealies in the centre" (D. Child, ed., *The Zulu War Journal of Colonel Henry Harford, C.B.,* 37).

After the battle, the British counted more than 20,000 cartridges expended, a phenomenal number for a mere hundred or so soldiers who were doing the actual firing. In over eight hours of continuous shooting, the garrison had fired some two hundred .45 cartridges per man. On average each British soldier had killed or wounded five or so Zulus. For every redcoat killed, more than thirty Zulus fell, in what was a complete reversal of Isandhlwana:

In both actions, the Zulus employed the same simple encircling stratagem, attacking *en masse* with no great sophistication but extraordinary courage. Rorke's Drift proved that a company of steady, rifle-armed infantry could repel 4,000 Zulus—with a number of basic provisos: 1) a compact fighting formation; 2) a rudimentary breastwork, or *laager,* to fight behind; 3) a ready supply of ammunition. The first two of these conditions had been underlined repeatedly by the Boers; the third was elementary. The conclusion was inescapable. The difference between the greater disaster at Isandhlwana and the lesser triumph at Rorke's Drift was that a couple of not particularly brilliant lieutenants had taken the fundamental precautions neglected by their superiors. (A. Lloyd, *The Zulu War, 1879,* 103)

In a twenty-four-hour period comprising the greatest victory in Zulu history, King Cetshwayo nevertheless had lost at Isandhlwana and Rorke's Drift well over 4,000 warriors of his 20,000-man army. There were still two enemy columns in his homeland; and an aroused Britain was scrambling to send thousands of fresh recruits to avenge a massacre. The Zulu nation had no experience with a modern force of disciplined riflemen who would aim, fire, and reload modern firearms on command, and when shooting individually do so according to strict protocols concerning the range and nature of the target.

Why did the British at Rorke's Drift triumph against such odds? They were clearly better supplied with food, medical treatment, and ammunition; their soldiers were far better-trained shots. Most important, their system of institutionalized discipline ensured a steady curtain of fire unlike anything previously experienced in the native wars of Africa. Britain's industrialized, fully capitalist economy had the wherewithal to transport and supply thousands of such men miles from home. European science was responsible for the Martini-Henry rifle—a terrible gun whose enormous bullet and uncanny accuracy helped to destroy Zulu manhood outright.

All during the campaign, British officers had sought out decisive battles to win or lose the war through open engagements. During the sixteen hours on the ramparts at Rorke's Drift, dozens of British soldiers—Acting Assistant Commissariat Officer Dalton (Victoria Cross), who was the real stalwart in the organization of the defenders, Surgeon Reynolds (Victoria Cross), who created the ad hoc station for the wounded, and Private Hook (Victoria Cross), who rescued the sick from the hospital—took the initiative and acted in independent fashion to improve the defenses. All the shooters on the wall had entered the army with a clear sense of rights and responsibilities, with abject loyalty to peers of their regiment. Such regimental discipline mandated that the men would continue to shoot until exhaustion and death—and strict British firearms training guaranteed that they would usually hit what they aimed at. On January 22, 1879, the garrison at Rorke's Drift proved to be the most dangerous hundred men in the world.

THE IMPERIAL WAY

Why Fight the Zulus?

Most conflicts do and yet do not begin over disputed borders. So it was with the Anglo-Zulu War of 1879, which ostensibly started from disagreement over the exact boundaries between Zululand and the European provinces of Natal and the Transvaal, but in truth was inevitable, given the colonials' desire for more land, labor, and security. Other than the pretext of a preemptory attack, the British had no ostensible reason for invading Zululand. Even most of the state ministries in London wanted nothing to do with a war in southern Africa at a time when the empire's more critical interests in India, Afghanistan, and Egypt required its full resources. No observer on either side ever made the case that a Zulu army had crossed into either Natal or the Transvaal to prompt hostilities. King Cetshwayo's repeated orders were to avoid sending his *impis* across the borders of Zululand.

Although other parts of South Africa were relatively uninhabited when land-hungry Dutch and English ranchers and farmers first settled there during the seventeenth through nineteenth centuries, Zululand was the ancestral home of a number of tribes and had been relatively ignored by Europeans. But by the outbreak of the war in 1879 a general division of lands in southwest Africa had been well established, one that marked clear boundaries for King Cetshwayo's autonomous and densely inhabited Zulu kingdom. Yet in early January 1879 Lord Chelmsford crossed the Buffalo-Tugela River with a combined force of more than 17,000 men and invaded the Zulu nation on orders from the high commissioner of South Africa, Sir Bartle Frere. Whereas Chelmsford was ostensibly "protecting" Natal, his real mission was to find the Zulu *impis*, destroy them in pitched battle, capture Cetshwayo, and thereby dismantle the autonomous Zulu nation itself. The Anglo-Zulu War from the beginning was a war of aggression against the Zulu people, fought to eliminate forever the threat of a huge indigenous army mustered across the border from relatively sparsely populated British and Boer settlements. The administrator of the Transvaal, Lord Shepstone, candidly outlined the British concern over the presence of Zulu *impis:* "Had Cetshwayo's thirty thousand warriors been in time changed to labourers working for wages, Zululand would have been a prosperous peaceful country instead of what it now is, a source of perpetual danger to itself and its neighbours" (J. Guy, *The Destruction of the Zulu Kingdom,* 47).

After years of border disputes with the Boers of neighboring Transvaal, the question of Zululand's territorial integrity had earlier been put to a British-sponsored boundary inquiry commission, which promptly reported to Frere that the disputed lands in question probably belonged to the Zulus! Boer aggression, accompanied by British acquiescence, not Zulu imperial expansion, the commissioners found, had prompted the border crisis. Because of the nature of European—and especially Boer—methods of cattle ranching, literally thousands of acres were needed for each autonomous family, creating an absurd paradox of the local landscape: a colonial population that demanded enormous amounts of formerly tribal land, but lacked the population density on its own to defend the very range it had expropriated. In neighboring Natal province over 80 percent of the land—some 10 million acres—was owned by just 20,000 Europeans, leaving 2 million acres of the least desirable countryside to be fought over by 300,000 African natives. The European colonials alone did not have the wherewithal to protect what they had so boldly taken.

Because the British government had no real interest in annexing Zululand—there was little natural wealth there, plenty of disease, and a proud, hard-to-rule population—and since there was no evidence of Zulu aggression toward either Natal or the Transvaal, the exact reasons why the British army invaded in 1879 still remain a mystery. Immediate motives are probably to be found in the wide latitude given the unpredictable Frere, who was determined to prompt a war at all costs in the belief that the tide of history was inevitably against the peculiar brand of Zulu militarism—and that with the conquest of Zululand he might be recognized as the imperial proconsul of a new and huge confederated South Africa.

Specifically, Frere and his staff were mostly concerned with the Zulu army of some 40,000 warriors, an extraordinary muster from a people that probably numbered fewer than 250,000. To Frere's way of thinking, the existence of such a powerful native military on the borders of European colonies was a disaster waiting to happen, especially given the Zulus' warlike record of conquest during the past century and the white colonials' constant demand for grazing range. Frere apparently glossed over the fact that the Zulu army had been mobilized and yet at peace with the British for some thirty-seven years and that the disruption of the prevailing and peaceful status quo would have to start with the Europeans. The complaints of the more levelheaded Sir Henry Bulwer, the governor of Natal, that the British should honor the results of their own board of inquiry, were swept aside. Frere instead sought to extend the protection of his government to the aggressive Boer settlers, who were eager for the imperial army of England to settle scores with their old nemesis, the Zulus.

Desperate to precipitate hostilities, Frere seized on three incidents that he proclaimed made war unavoidable. A Zulu chief, Sihayo, had dragged back two of his adulterous wives from Natal, a British protectorate, and then executed them in Zululand—a deed shocking to Frere's own sense of British imperial territorial sanctity and purported English nineteenth-century morality in general. King Cetshwayo then refused to hand over Sihayo. In response, the British, like Greek princes who pledged to sail to Troy over a perceived abduction, felt that a question of honor demanded a prompt rejoinder to the kidnapping. Next, an imperial surveying party along the Tugela River between Zululand and Natal was detained—though not harmed—by some Zulu hunting parties, who rightly suspected that such a mapping expedition was a prelude to formal annexation of some of their borderlands. Finally, to Frere's further chagrin, some missionaries had recently fled Zululand, claiming that their Christian Zulu converts were often treated poorly and sometimes killed by Cetshwayo.

Largely on such secondhand information, and apparently on grounds that Zulus did not conduct themselves in their own country as English gentlemen, Frere believed that he had legal cause for a full-scale invasion of a sovereign Zululand. His final ultimatum demanded that Cetshwayo abandon his remarkable system of military organization and with it his enormous army altogether. The reply of the Zulu king, variously translated and sometimes erroneously reported in a variety of sources, was striking for its candor and pride:

> Did I ever tell Somtseu [Shepstone, the British representative to Zululand] I would not kill? Did he tell the white people I made such an arrangement? Because if he did so he deceived them. I do kill; but do not consider that I have done anything yet in the way of killing. Why do the white people start at nothing. I have not yet begun to kill; it is the custom of our nation and I shall not depart from it. Why does the Governor of Natal speak to me about my laws? Do I go to Natal and dictate to him about his laws. . . . (Cf. D. Morris, *The Washing of the Spears,* 280)

Both Boer and English colonial settlers—slavery had been outlawed in southern Africa for decades—wanted cheap manual labor to develop their farms and the infrastructure of colonies in Transvaal and Natal. They obviously resented the idea that 40,000 adult male Zulus were subject to military service and hardly likely to cross the border unarmed and needy as cheap migrant laborers. Sir Garnet Wolseley, who replaced Chelmsford as commander in chief of British forces at the conclusion of the war, also jotted down in his diary the British view of an ideal postbellum Zululand:

> Our dispute with Cetshwayo who had been guilty of cruelties to his people: that he took life without trial & that under his rule neither life nor property were even safe. That by the military system he maintained, he prevented the men from marrying & from working & so kept them poor. . . . In future all men should be allowed to marry & to come & go when they liked & to work for whom they liked, so that they might become rich & and prosperous as we wished them to be. (A. Preston, ed., *The South African Journal of Sir Garnet Wolseley, 1879–1880,* 59)

In addition, local entrepreneurs relished the idea of a sizable British military commitment to the colony—the crown would eventually spend some £5.25 million during the Zulu wars—and so lined up to supply the army. The horse and stock owners, wagonmakers, and teamsters of Natal welcomed the opportunity to hike prices to astronomical levels, as did colonial residents who appreciated the infusion of capital and manpower into southern Africa. Chelmsford and the British officer corps in Natal also were eager for the chance for a cheap, quick, and glorious victory that could only advance their careers. There was keen competition among officers to win assignments for the envisioned invasion—a military adventure anxiously anticipated as short, relatively safe, and full of opportunities to win glory against an admittedly brave but technologically backward foe.

Europeans and the Other

In a wider sense, the war was also a result of a more insidious British, and characteristically European, attitude toward indigenous peoples, predicated on a strange blend of chauvinism, violent imperialism, and often misguided goodwill. To the British, Cetshwayo's army was an impediment to the chance of "civilization" for his people, who logically should gladly embrace the religion and culture of a "superior" race. Christianity might bring to the Zulus an end of polygamy, random murder and execution, occasional cannibalism, mutilation of the dead, degrading nudity, sodomy, and what the missionaries considered a bizarre array of ritu-

alistic sexual practices that surrounded the purification of warriors—
uku-hlobonga, or intercrural (between the legs) sex without phallic penetration for the unmarried warriors, and *sula izembe,* full sexual
intercourse for the married after the fighting to "wipe the ax." English law
would also prevent the random killing of Cetshwayo's subjects and lead to
a fixed rather than nomadic citizenry, thus providing the necessary foundation for an efficient capitalist economy that would respect private property and foster a higher standard of living—or else.

In 1856, the British pointed out, in a vicious civil war Cetshwayo had
butchered more than 7,000 of his brother's warriors, along with another
20,000 of his own tribal family, including the aged, women, and children.
That killing field on the Tugela River was thereafter known as Mathambo,
"the Place of the Bones." Earlier, Shaka had killed ten times the number of
Cetshwayo's victims. Zulu kings, like the Aztec monarchy, had killed far
more indigenous people in their own tribal wars and random murder
sprees than did the Europeans on the battlefields of their conquest. On the
eve of his succession, Cetshwayo had murdered nearly every brother, half
brother, cousin, and remote relative in Zululand who could conceivably
contest his claim to the throne.

The power of the British army was felt to be proof enough of the general superiority of the European way of life—or so it was thought on the
eve of what Frere and Chelmsford assumed would be a rapid conquest. In
any case, the British crossed the border on January 11, and Frere proudly
wrote, "I hope that by God's helping a very few weeks will now enable us
to get rid of the incubus which has so long strangled nearly all life in these
Colonies" (C. Goodfellow, *Great Britain and South African Confederation,
1870–1881,* 165).

Like the Spanish experience in Mexico and the American westward
expansion, the British conquest of Zululand followed an often predictable
sequence of events that over some four centuries characterized European
entry into Asia, the Americas, Australia, and Africa. By 1800 Europe accounted for only 180 million of the world's nearly 900 million residents,
but occupied or controlled in some form or another almost 85 percent of
the world's land surface. By 1890 two-thirds of all oceangoing ships were
British, and half the maritime commerce of the world was facilitated by
British-built vessels—most of the transport across the seas in some way
facilitated or profited British imperialism. The productive capacity of
British factories and the skill of the imperial fleet and merchant marine
meant that troops and supplies could be landed at any place on the globe
in a matter of weeks—an ability shared by no other country outside

Europe and few within. In some sense, Britain was in Asia, Africa, Australia, and the Americas simply because it alone of the peoples of the world easily could be.

Initial European maritime exploration of the sixteenth century had led to sporadic colonization of foreign lands, followed by eventual full-scale invasion and conquest. Small numbers of Europeans—the French in Southeast Asia, the Spanish in the Americas, the Germans in central Africa, the British almost everywhere—usually provoked hostilities by either annexing land outright or trespassing on indigenous hunting or grazing territory in search of minerals, gold, ports, or water. Colonists and traders often followed, intent on permanent settlement. Legal documents—whether fiats of the Spanish crown or wordy proclamations of British bureaucrats—were hurriedly crafted and read to illiterate native royalty to provide the necessary Western pretext for annexation. It was an odd but characteristic Western custom to read out a list of grievances before a European army slaughtered its native and illiterate foes. Lord Frere, like Cortés before, was careful to predicate his destruction of an entire nation on the published premise of legal and moral right: he issued a thirteen-point statement of demands, which an illiterate Cetshwayo could not read or whose logic he could not fully fathom even when translated.

Often initial and tiny expeditionary forces, due to European arrogance in command, overreliance on mere technology, and ignorance about the enormous size of indigenous armies, were slaughtered—the *Noche Triste* and Isandhlwana could be matched by countless other debacles in Indochina, America, central Africa, and India. The later sale of European firearms at times during the nineteenth century gave native peoples some respite, such as the slaughter of American cavalrymen at Little Big Horn (1876), the British debacle at Maiwand in Afghanistan (1880), and the Ethiopian victory over the Italians at Adwa (1896). But such European setbacks—the great majority confined to the latter nineteenth century when easily operated repeating rifles and plentiful cartridges were traded freely with indigenous peoples—were almost immediately followed by renewed attacks of wiser, better-equipped, and better-led Western armies that sought not merely more land but, as purported vengeance, the entire conquest and at times destruction of a people.

Throughout colonial fighting, the desecration of European dead after an initial defeat—the sacrificed Spaniards on the pyramids of Mexico City, the disemboweled at Isandhlwana, the decapitated British at Khartoum—was felt to be cause enough later to give no quarter and to annihilate, as long as the Europeans slaughtered in pitched battle according to their ideas of fair rules of engagement. Almost always, Europeans were outraged when they discovered the decapitated, scalped, or disemboweled corpses from their small overrun garrisons. They felt that such mutilation—outside of battle, committed against the dead, inclusive of women and children—was a far more depraved act than their blasting apart the bodies of indigenous warriors with cannon and rifle fire—acts committed in battle against the living warrior class.

Tribal leaders such as Montezuma, Crazy Horse, and Cetshwayo occasionally appear as sympathetic figures in European chronicles. Native written accounts do not exist other than in oral interviews collated by Christian missionaries and explorers. Indigenous leaders often naïvely announced that the repulse of European interlopers might mean an end to hostilities, clueless that their own temporary victory over an advance European force sealed their fate against a second wave of Westerners who welcomed the pretext of revenge to cement their plans of conquest.

Cannibalism and human sacrifice, the mutilation of the dead, murdering prisoners, idol worship, polygamy, and the absence of written law were typically cited as pretexts for European annexation of territory during their four centuries of colonialism in the Americas, Asia, and Africa. Unlike their adversaries, the French, Spanish, and British announced that they killed thousands reluctantly and as an unavoidable precursor for improving the lot of indigenous peoples through the difficult process of Westernization. Missionaries, high church officials, and intellectuals in Britain objected to the rapacity of empire building, but sought remedy through amelioration or assimilation rather than withdrawal: Zulus should be Westernized, made into civilized British subjects, and thus protected under the law from both imperial oppression and their own indigenous savagery. Few, if any, of the most liberal critics counseled that the Europeans should go home and leave the Zulus in peace—or as the case might be, free to murder and to continue tribal war among their own.

Usually, a Cortés or Chelmsford found plenty of indigenous allies to help his cause, as Europeans sought to target first the most numerous and warlike tribes of the region to be conquered, on the theory that the fall of an Aztec or a Zulu nation would end native unrest in the environs and find sympathetic allies among those who had previously been brutalized by just such warlike regimes. Providing firearms or European material goods to natives also ensured that there were always plentiful tribal contingents in the Americas or Africa who would join in on European expeditions, eager for plunder, safety from their enemies, and a continuous supply of other sundries from Western traders. Nor should we forget that many natives, victims of decades of tribal slaughter, hated the Aztecs and Zulus far more than they did the Europeans.

The fighting itself, at least in these first-generation colonial struggles, had a typical scenario which pitted technology and discipline against courage and numbers. Thus, the Zulus, like the Aztecs, did not manufacture their own firearms and did not understand Western decisive battle in which lines of soldiers sought to charge or fire in careful unison, and to do so in order and on command before, during, and after the melee. The Zulus had captured or traded for guns for decades, but the British idea of sustained and regular mass volleys—itself a result of careful training and a comprehensive system of discipline—was entirely alien to the African manner of war. Even with the use of some eight hundred modern Martini-Henry rifles and hundreds of thousands of rounds of ammunition taken after Isandhlwana, Zulu marksmanship remained sporadic, inaccurate, and nearly always ineffective.

In theory the Zulu nation after Isandhlwana was as well armed as the remnants of the British center column and twenty times more numerous. But just as the Ottoman harquebusiers at Lepanto never mastered the European practice of massed musketry formation and firing in unison, so Zulu sharpshooters saw firearms as simply a more effective indigenous weapon—a knobkerrie with better penetrating power or an assegai with superior range—to enhance the traditional emphasis of individual battle prowess. Zulus nearly always aimed high, on the logic that like a javelin cast, the gun's projectile would otherwise quickly lose momentum and fall. Although they captured a number of field guns at Isandhlwana, and even dragged caissons and supply wagons off, the *impis* never employed such artillery against the British—lacking not merely the experience and knowledge of heavy gunnery but also the discipline to load, sight, and fire heavy weapons at regular intervals, not to mention the skilled teamsters to hitch draft oxen to caissons.

Ports and oceangoing ships were central to European power, bringing in an almost endless stream of manufactured firearms and supplies to the conflict. In the Zulu War, men, guns, food, and ammunition were continually shipped in from Cape Town and Durban. After the disaster at Isandhlwana, an entirely new British army—nearly 10,000 additional enlisted men and more than 400 officers—in less than fifty days began arriving in Natal from England. Usually, native armies had no conception that a Vera Cruz or Durban was a mere transit station that allowed

Spanish or British conquistadors to tap whatever manpower they needed in a matter of weeks from an overcrowded and restless Europe thousands of miles—but only weeks—away.

Aztec, Islamic, or Zulu forces almost always depended on rapid envelopment and outflanking movements, which had worked so well against neighboring indigenous tribes. Without much improvisation they relied on highly trained, far more mobile, numerically superior, and courageous warriors to ambush or surprise smaller, plodding European contingents—successful enterprises in local landscapes of dense brush, forest, or jungle. Traditional battle rituals, even in the final battles with Europeans, were usually not altogether jettisoned, meaning that indigenous people were less likely to fight at night, rarely followed up their occasional military victories with unchecked pursuit, and sometimes allowed cultural (e.g., religious festivals, pre-battle dancing and eating festivities, annual fertility rites) or natural (e.g., seasonal considerations, unusual astronomical observations) phenomena to override sheer battle efficacy. After Lord Chelmsford invaded, Cetshwayo mustered his army and then had his witch doctors induce vomiting among some 20,000 frontline troops. It took three days to administer the tonic, parade each warrior before a massive vomiting pit, and have them wait fasting until the entire army was "cleansed," severely weakening the critical stamina of the *impis*.

Westerners, from the Greeks onward, also had an array of war-making rituals: pre-battle sacrifices, harangues, and music; sacred days of truce; ceremonial dress and drill. But these traditional practices were sometimes rigged, often postponed, or even abandoned altogether should military necessity determine otherwise. Predictably, most European armies did not practice pre-battle rituals of fasting, vomiting, purging, or self-mutilation that might impede the effectiveness of soldiers on the battlefield. More likely, as preparation for the fighting, European troops were to receive a rum ration, a stern exhortation, or a last-minute reminder of firing protocol. Since Greek times pre-battle sacrifices and rituals had been faked, since they served more as morale boosters than as real communication with the gods.

The Europeans were willing to fight 365 days a year, day or night, regardless of the exigencies of either their Christian faith or the natural year. Bad weather, disease, and difficult geography were seen as simple obstacles to be conquered by the appropriate technology, military discipline, and capital, rarely as expressions of divine ill will or the hostility of all-powerful spirits. Europeans often looked at temporary setbacks differently from their adversaries in Asia, America, or Africa. Defeat signaled no angry god or adverse fate, but rather a rational flaw in either tactics, logistics, or technology, one to be easily remedied on the next occasion—and there was almost always a next occasion until conquest—through careful audit and analysis. The British in Zululand, like all Western armies, and as Clausewitz saw, did envision battle as a continuation of politics by other means. Unlike the Zulus, the British army did not see war largely as an occasion for individual warriors to garner booty, women, or prestige.

Indigenous peoples more often fought alongside Europeans than did individual Europeans with natives. Cortés found help in the hundreds of thousands of Tlaxcalans in Mexico, as did the British with the so-called Kaffirs in Africa. Both the Aztecs and the Zulus found essentially no Europeans willing to fight alongside them against other white invaders. Narváez wished to destroy Cortés, not the Spanish cause, and thus after his defeat most of his men joined in to march on Tenochtitlán. John Dunn at times helped the Zulus, but in the Anglo-Zulu War of 1879 he quickly rejoined the British. Not a single European fought in Cetshwayo's ranks against the British, although nearly all Boers despised English government in Africa. In contrast, thousands of Africans joined various colonial regiments.

Trouble for Europeans occurred most often only against their own colonials; the Boers in Africa and the Americans both fought costly wars of independence against the British, employing weapons, discipline, and tactics that were in many cases the equal of or superior to those of their British overseers. The Boers, for example, killed far more Englishmen in a single week of the Boer War—nearly 1,800 at Magersfontein, Stormberg, and Colenso alone from December 11 to 16, 1899—than did the Zulus during the entire fighting of 1879!

Many scholars have been reluctant to discuss the question of European military superiority because either they confuse it with larger issues of intelligence or morality or they focus on occasional European setbacks as if they are typical and so negate the general rule of Western dominance. In fact, the European ability to conquer non-Europeans—usually far from Europe, despite enormous problems in logistics, with relatively few numbers of combatants, and in often unfamiliar and hostile terrain and climate—has nothing to do with questions of intelligence, innate morality, or religious superiority, but again illustrates the continuum of a peculiar cultural tradition, beginning with the Greeks, that brought unusual dividends to Western armies on the battlefield.

Zulu Postmortem

The aftermath of Rorke's Drift is a fair enough representation of the typical colonial war that was waged in the latter nineteenth century, one repeatedly acted out in the Congo, Egypt, the Sudan, Afghanistan, and the Punjab. After the victory of the garrison at Rorke's Drift, Lord Chelmsford, with a vastly augmented army, renewed his invasion of Zululand. Besides the earlier bloody standoffs that year at Ineyzane (January 22), the River Intombi (March 11), the siege of the small garrison at Eshowe (February 6–April 3), and Hlobane (March 27–28), the British then fought three decisive battles at Kambula (March 29), Gingindhlovu (April 2), and Ulundi (July 4). In the first two of these final three engagements, British and colonial troops, in fortified camps, would have utterly annihilated the attacking Zulus had the latter pressed their near suicidal charges and human wave attacks to the bloody end.

In the last battle of the war at Ulundi, fought near King Cetshwayo's headquarters, a British square—replete with artillery and Gatling guns—deliberately abandoned its fortified camp to march out in open challenge, thereby prompting an attack by the Zulus, who had learned of the futility of charging fortifications, but not the equal stupidity of trying to break a solid formation of European riflemen in an unobstructed plain of fire. In less than forty minutes, the British square of some 4,165 Europeans and 1,152 Africans repulsed 20,000 Zulus, killing at least 1,500 in the process and wounding twice that number, many of whom wandered off to die in hiding.

When it was all over, the British and Zulu dead were buried on the field of Ulundi; in typical Western fashion the British erected a plaque over those they had wiped out: "In Memory of the Brave Warriors who fell here in 1879 in defence of the Old Zulu Order." The British, like the Spanish in Mexico and the Americans in the West, had not merely defeated their more numerous enemies but destroyed their autonomy and culture in the process. Books continue to be written about the handful of British redcoats who heroically held firm at Rorke's Drift, but not more than a few dozen names remain of the several thousand courageous Zulus who were blasted apart by Martini-Henry rifles. In that regard, they tragically joined the thousands of anonymous Persians, Aztecs, and Turks who were killed en masse and remain forgotten as individuals, as real persons apart from the historian's bloodless figures of "40,000" killed or "20,000" lost. In contrast, the engine of Western historiography—itself the dividend of the free and rationalist tradition—commemorates in detail their far fewer killers. Without a Herodotus, Bernal Díaz del Castillo, or Gianpietro Contarini, men's bravery in battle fades with the rot of their corpses.

When the Zulu War broke out in January 1879, Cetshwayo could count on somewhere between 30,000 and 40,000 available troops. Six months later the British had shot down at least 10,000 on the various battlefields of Zululand, and no doubt nearly as many later succumbed to wounds. No accurate record of Zulu dead was ever made; but the absence of medical care and the nature of the Martini-Henry .45-caliber slug suggest that thousands of wounded throughout the war died of shock or infection, or simply bled to death. The heavy, soft projectile of a Martini-Henry rifle, not to mention the ordnance of the Gatling gun and artillery piece, made a horrific hole in the human body, as the crippled and ugly scarred bodies of the few surviving Zulu veterans attested. Indeed, on one of the worst days in English colonial history, January 22, 1879, the British army nevertheless may well have killed more than 5,000 Zulus at Isandhlwana, Rorke's Drift, and Ineyzane, or between 12 and 16 percent of the entire Zulu army.

By war's end most of the Zulu nation's cattle were killed, scattered, or stolen. Its system of imperial regimentation was shattered, as the British imposed an unworkable peace, by dividing up Cetshwayo's kingdom into thirteen warring states—a solution that by design precluded prosperity in Zululand and further war against its neighboring European colonies. The "victory" of 1879 was achieved at the cost of only 1,007 British soldiers killed in battle, along with 76 officers. A small, undetermined number of additional troops succumbed to tropical disease and wounds. For the six months of the war the British soldier had on average killed ten or more Zulus for every trooper lost, despite being generally outnumbered at various battles by magnitudes of between five and forty to one. The legacy of the British invasion, battlefield conquest, and rather shameful settlement that divided the Zulu people into impotent warring factions was the end of an independent state and the virtual destruction of an entire way of life.

ZULU POWER AND IMPOTENCE

Shaka

Africa produced no more warlike tribe than the Zulus. Of the hundreds of tribal armies of the continent, none were as sophisticated as Zulu *impis* in either their organization or their command structure. In native wars on the continent no other tribe could match Zulu discipline. Alone of native armies, the Zulus had largely abandoned missile weapons, in favor of a short spear in order to fight at close ranges. Yet a minuscule British force obliterated Africa's most feared military in a matter of months. How was that possible?

Like the Aztec empire before the Spanish invasion, the Zulu nation was a relatively new creation when the Europeans arrived in Natal in real numbers during the nineteenth century. For nearly three hundred years prior to 1800, the Zulus were but one of dozens of nomadic Bantu-speaking tribes who slowly migrated into what is now Natal and Zululand. But at the beginning of the nineteenth century, Dingiswayo, a chief of the Mthethwa, one of many Nguni tribes, radically departed from the traditional Bantu practice of local raiding and skirmishing by seeking to incorporate defeated tribes into a national army.

In his effort to build a federated system through the creation of a professional military, Dingiswayo curtailed the past practice of ritualistic wars fought mostly with missile weapons over grazing rights, in which casualties remained relatively light and noncombatants were largely untouched. In the eight years of his reign (1808–16) Dingiswayo laid the foundations for the Zulu empire by overturning the ancestral protocols of Bantu culture in southwest Africa, incorporating rather than exterminating or enslaving defeated tribes, seeking commerce with the Portuguese along the coast, and making civilian life itself subservient to military training. One of his most successful lieutenants, the revolutionary leader Shaka of the tiny Zulu tribe, eventually assumed control of the empire (1816–28) and transformed it to serve an enormous standing army, in ways unimagined even by old Dingiswayo himself. Shaka's revolutionary changes in military practice mark the real rise of Zulu power, a warring kingdom that would exist for the next sixty years (1816–76) until the British conquest. Before being murdered by his siblings in 1828, Shaka had entirely altered the African manner of war, resisted white encroachment, slaughtered 50,000 of his enemies in battle, and gratuitously murdered thousands more of his own citizens in increasingly frequent bouts of imperial dementia. The legacy of Shaka's twelve-year reign was a loose imperial coalition of some half million subjects and a national army of nearly 50,000 warriors. During the decade of formation of the new Zulu empire perhaps as many as 1 million native Africans had been killed or starved to death as a direct result of Shaka's imperial dreams. South Africa thus illustrates a mostly unrecognized characteristic of the European colonial military experience: in Africa, Asia, and the Americas, both indigenous tribes and Europeans usually killed more of their own people in battle than they did one another. Between 1820 and 1902, for example, Shaka and his successors killed vastly more Zulus than did Lord Chelmsford, and the Boers slaughtered far more British than did Cetshwayo.

A Garrison State

Much myth and romance surround the Zulu military, but we can dispense with the popular idea that its warriors fought so well because of enforced sexual celibacy or the use of stimulant drugs—or even that they learned their regimental system and terrifying tactics of envelopment from British or Dutch tradesmen. Zulu men had plenty of sexual outlets before marriage, carried mostly snuff on campaign, only occasionally smoked cannabis, drank a mild beer, and created their method of battle advance entirely from their own experience from decades of defeating tribal warriors. The general idea of military regimentation, perhaps even the knowledge of casting high-quality metal spearheads, may have been derived from observation of early European colonial armies, but the refined system of age-class regiments and attacking in the manner of the buffalo were entirely indigenous developments.

The undeniable Zulu preponderance of power derived from three traditional sources of military efficacy: manpower, mobilization, and tactics. All three were at odds with almost all native African methods of fighting. The conquest of Bantu tribes in southeast Africa under Shaka's leadership meant that for most of the nineteenth century until the British conquest—during the subsequent reigns of Kings Dingane (1828–40), Mpande (1840–72), and Cetshwayo (1872–79)—the Zulus controlled a population ranging between 250,000 and 500,000 and could muster an army of some 40,000 to 50,000 in some thirty-five *impis*, many times larger than any force, black or white, that Africa might field.

Unlike most other tribal armies of the bush, the Zulus were no mere horde that fought as an ad hoc throng. They did not stage ritual fights in which customary protocols and missile warfare discouraged lethality. Rather, Zulu *impis* were reflections of fundamental social mores of the Zulu nation itself, which was a society designed in almost every facet for the continuous acquisition of booty and the need for individual subjects to taste killing firsthand. If the Aztec warrior sought a record of captive-taking to advance his standing, then a Zulu could find little status or the chance to create his own household until he had "washed his spear" in the blood of an enemy.

The entire nation was regimented—as in the manner of classical Sparta—by age-class systems that might supersede even tribal affiliations. Boys were to undergo formal military training and serve as baggage carriers at fourteen or fifteen. By late adolescence most Zulu males were expected to be full-fledged warriors who could run fifty miles a day without shoes as they entered the *impis*. Cohorts of bachelors were arranged into lifelong regiments, and men were not allowed to marry officially until their late thirties without special compensation; thus the ability to establish an independent family served as a great social dividing line within the army. Under Shaka's system as many as 20,000 males under the age of thirty-five were to remain unmarried and subject to constant military service. Even the older warriors, who could take legal wives and establish their own kraals, or autonomous households, often found themselves instead on lengthy campaigns.

Yet a notion of enforced "celibacy" among warriors is exaggerated, since Zulu males routinely engaged in a variety of sexual activities short of full penetration with women. Rather, "celibacy" meant that warriors were not allowed to pair off with permanent mates to form autonomous households or to have intercourse with virgins until their late thirties. Since the delay in childbearing among young women meant a reduction in Zulu fertility itself, such age-class rites may in fact have been intended by Shaka to control the population of Zululand—and the unsustainable exploitation of grazing land by cattle ranching in an already overpopulated landscape.

Whatever the exact cause of the peculiar practice of age-class regimentation, the result was an unusual esprit de corps among troops, as *impis*—marked by distinctive names, particular headdresses, jewelry, feathers, and shield insignia—usually fought as separate units for the entire life span of their warrior age-cohorts. Tactically, the Zulu mode of attack was simple but efficient. Battle deployment was named after the Cape buffalo, as each *impi* was divided into four groups, comprising the flanks or "horns" of two younger regiments. These wings quickly spread out around both sides of the enemy, hoping to encircle the opposing force and drive it back against the "chest" or veteran regiment of the *impis*, while the "loins" or aged reserves would then come up when the hostile force was fully engaged. While predictable, the standardization of attack proved successful against rival tribes of the plains, given the Zulus' uncanny ability to sneak undetected through the grass and brush, sprint to surround and enclose a surprised enemy, and then finish him off in close combat with stabbing spears and billy clubs.

Under Shaka's reign, the army had largely abandoned the throwing spear for the short stabbing assegai—now to be called the *iKlwa* from the sucking noise it made when being pulled from the chest or belly of an enemy—and tall cowhide shield. The new assegai had a much larger and heavier iron blade than its throwing counterpart, and a far shorter shaft, inasmuch as it was to be used most often as an underhand stabbing weapon in concert with the larger shield. Like a Roman legionary, who likewise closed with his enemy to battle face-to-face, the Zulu warrior could bang or catch his shield on the enemy as he came up quickly with a sharp upward thrust from his assegai, whose relatively small size and sharp edge made it more similar to a *gladius* than to a Greek spear. Each warrior also brandished a knobkerrie, or hardwood club with a knob on the end. Unlike nearly every other tribal force in Africa, the Zulus waged war hand-to-hand, without missiles, and expected to meet the enemy head-on and defeat him through greater courage, weapons skill, and muscular strength. Bright uniforms—including feathers of various kinds, cow-tail tassels, and leather necklaces and headdresses—war shouts, the beating of spear against shield, and pre-battle dances were aimed at striking fear into the enemy before the initial onslaught.

Typically, a Zulu *impi* might cover as much as one hundred to two hundred miles in a campaign in a matter of three days, as it brought along little food or supplies, but was expected to live off the captured cattle of its enemy. Young boys, or *uDibi*, carried along sleeping mats and what food they could manage to pack and still keep up with the *impis*. Once the enemy was targeted, leaders of the *impis* met to assign respective regiments to the horns, chest, and loins. The army approached the enemy at a run, intending to surround and crush it in a matter of minutes, followed by plundering the defeated's territory before striking for home. In battle itself, the lifelong training with the assegai and knobkerrie, together with the tough conditioning of the *impis* and the expertise at rapid envelopment, resulted in a marked fighting edge for Zulu warriors during the hand-to-hand fighting. Yet both past and present panegyrists of Zulu courage have largely forgotten the inherent military weakness of the entire system, inherent flaws that made it extremely vulnerable not only to formal European armies such as the British but even to vastly outnumbered, less well trained colonial militias of Boers and English settlers.

First, while Zulu warriors endured a tough course of military training, and then submitted to a lifelong and often brutal regimentation in their *impis,* their resulting courage and ferocity did not result in anything comparable to the European notion of military discipline, which emphasized drill, close-order formation of line and column, synchronized group volleys, a strict chain of command, abstract notions of tactics and strategy, and a written code of military justice. Instead, rival *impis* were likely to brawl and even fight to the death in internecine disputes, far exceeding any of the typical fistfights in the British army between regiments.

Nor was there a true system of command, as individual *impis* often disobeyed direct orders from their king—the *uThulwana, uDloko,* and *inDlu-yengwe* regiments at Rorke's Drift ignored Cetshwayo's orders not to attack the fortified position or venture into Natal—fighting as independent units without synchronized command. Thus, the *uThulwana* and *uDloko* met the *inDlu-yengwe* regiment largely by chance, as the younger *inDlu-yengwe* dared Prince Dabulamanzi to join his two older *impis* for an ad hoc assault on Rorke's Drift. Other than a loose, formulaic plan of attack, there was no systematic approach to drill and close-order marching, resulting in a general chaos during the actual fighting and little chance that retreats would not turn into simple routs or that attacks would follow in ordered waves. While the Zulus fought face-to-face, they did so as individuals; the *impis* did not rely on serried ranks and simultaneous spear thrusting to achieve a shock effect at the first collision. Against Rorke's Drift, a series of uncoordinated assaults resulted in dissipation of Zulu strength. In contrast, a sudden mass assault designed to put thousands of warriors at a concentrated point of the barricade within a few minutes would have overwhelmed the tiny garrison.

The Zulu warrior lived in a world of spirits and witchcraft that was antithetical to the rather godless European emphasis on sheer military efficacy governed by abstract rules, regulations, and the technology of brutal rifles, Gatling guns, and artillery. Before battle, witch doctors concocted potions of sacrificial bull's intestines, herbs, and water to give warriors strength for the ordeal to come. Zulus were put on strict diets and given emetics—which could only have weakened their stamina—and pieces of ceremonial human flesh. After slaying a foe, the corpse was disemboweled to allow the spirit to escape and to prevent retribution against the killer. Sorcerers sought to hex rival clans through voodoolike curses and incantations. The mysterious ability of British soldiers to slaughter thousands of attacking Zulus with rifle fire while losing very few was likewise explicable only through magic, not the logic of training, science, and discipline. Thus, after each terrible slaughter, Zulu tactics changed not at all, as superstition was invoked to explain the miraculous curtain of lead that met the *impis* as they neared the British lines.

In the Zulu mind witchcraft explained why the British killed hundreds with their rifles, whereas Zulus, with the same captured weapons, invariably hit a small percentage of their targets—in every case, almost always firing far too high (to give the bullet "power") and never in coordinated volleys. After the terrible Zulu defeat at Kambula, the surviving warriors were convinced of the intervention of supernatural creatures on the British side, and so quizzed Cornelius Vign as to why "so many white birds, such as they had never seen before, came flying over them from the side of the Whites? And why were they attacked also by dogs and apes, clothed and carrying fire-arms on their shoulders? One of them even told me he had even seen four lions in the *laager*. They said, 'The Whites don't fight fairly; they bring animals to draw down destruction upon us' " (C. Vign, *Cetshwayo's Dutchman*, 38). In later attacks against Europeans tribal attackers shot their rifles at artillery explosions, believing that shells contained little white men who burst out to kill everyone in their midst. In the aftermath of the war, veterans were convinced they had been beaten by a protective curtain of steel that the British had hung over their army, perhaps a divine explanation for either the wall of lead put down by the redcoats or the reflections from British bayonets.

Brave and Weak

Zulu tactics were static and thus predictable to Europeans. A fortified camp or British square could expect a double-envelopment movement from the outset as a prelude to the advance of the main "chest." While in theory the "loins" were a mobile reserve, they were not under central command and thus were not directed to precise points of resistance or weakness in the enemy line. Often they played no role in the fighting at all and were just as likely to flee as to reinforce in cases of initial failure of the chest and horns.

Much is made of the impressive Zulu mobility, but two key factors are often ignored. The army could carry few firearms—though nearly 20,000 muskets and rifles had been entering Zululand for decades before the

British invasion—due to the absence of any wheeled transport to bring along sizable reserves of cartridges. And because food was not carried in any quantity, Zulu armies required immediate victory before exhaustion and hunger set in. At Rorke's Drift a final concerted effort at daybreak might have broken the British defenses, but by morning the Zulu besiegers had had essentially nothing to eat for over two days and were famished to the point of physical weakness.

It is easy for modern scholars to ridicule the ponderous supply trains and immobility of Chelmsford's lugubrious columns. But the British army, not the Zulus, came to each battle well fed, well supplied, and in possession of nearly limitless ammunition and firearms. British wagons may have looked near comical—eighteen feet long, six feet wide, and more than five feet high—and required anywhere from ten to nineteen chained oxen to pull them even five miles a day in the rough terrain of Zululand. Yet they could carry an amazing 8,000 pounds of guns and ammunition, as well as plenty of fodder, food, and water. In later battles any Zulus who made their way into British camps immediately broke open captured provisions in the heat of battle—as the partly eaten food in the mouths of their corpses later attested.

The fully laden, ponderous, and sunburned British soldier in Africa has become a caricature of impracticality, ignorance, and addiction to material comfort. In fact, he was a far more lethal warrior than his lightly clad, nimble Zulu opponent. The latter has recently been nearly deified on American campuses—tragically so, in the case of the genocidal Shaka— as some sort of irresistible and deadly freedom fighter. He was neither fearsome nor freedom loving. In reality, the most deadly man in Africa was typically a pale British soldier, not much over five feet six inches in height, 150 pounds in weight, slightly malnourished, most often enrolled from the industrial ghettos of England, vastly overburdened with a ten-pound rifle and some sixty pounds of food, water, and ammunition on his belt and in his pack. Such an apparently unimpressive warrior, in fact, would himself typically shoot down three or more Zulus in almost every engagement of the war.

Most *impis* did not hit the enemy as one cohesive unit, and the absence of body armor had always ensured that Zulu spearmen had never been able to crash headlong even into the lines of their tribal enemies. Shields were used for individual defense and as weapons, not to form a vast wall of protection. Zulus practiced only a swarming method of warfare, in this regard similar to the Aztec manner of running into enemy lines to stab and hack away in small groups. If the attacker was vastly outnumbered, terrified, or in loose formation, then the Zulu charge and envelopment were inevitably successful. But against a fortified position or a defensible square of British riflemen, the entire line of assault would break and then disperse in the face of sustained volleys or subsequent bayonet charges.

Even the acquisition of firearms did not alter static Zulu tactics, as shooters on their own attempted to fire sporadically at the enemy while other warriors engaged with spears. No Zulus were taught either to charge in line or to shoot on orders. Cetshwayo never sought a comprehensive method of firearms loading and firing, despite the availability of guns in Zululand for some fifty years before the Anglo-Zulu War of 1879. Although horses had been introduced more than two centuries earlier in southern Africa, the Zulus rode only sporadically, and neither bred them in great numbers nor adopted any methodical approach to creating mounted patrols—ensuring that the British had more mobile scouts and deadly pursuers in the aftermath of battle.

The result was often a haphazard method of Zulu attack with both traditional and European weaponry, in which thousands of men more or less ran at will straight at the enemy, while others shot at random from a distance, hoping that sheer numbers, noise, and their own speed would panic or collapse the adversary. At Isandhlwana the thin British lines, gaps in the formations, and poor distribution of ammunition allowed such attackers success. In nearly all other subsequent engagements—the night fiasco at Hlobane is the notable exception—the tactics of uncoordinated charges turned out to be suicidal. When such assaults failed, there were never ordered calls for retreat, much less a fighting withdrawal or organized covering sorties. Rather, entire *impis,* as tribal Germans on the Roman frontier, collapsed and ran headlong from the enemy. Thousands in the Zulu wars were ridden down by British horsemen who lanced, shot, and hacked at will once the *impis'* charge was broken and panic set in.

British accounts record hundreds of incidents of unmatched Zulu bravery—men in their forties and fifties who charged headlong into the barrels of blazing Gatling guns, and hundreds of fighters who trampled over their own dead to wrestle with the bayonets of British riflemen at Rorke's Drift before Martini-Henry rifles discharged their enormous bullets into their necks and faces. During the preliminary fighting before the final battle of Ulundi, Frances Colenso records, "a single warrior, chased by several Lancers, found himself run down and escape impossible. He turned and faced his enemies; spreading his arms abroad he presented his bare breast unflinchingly to the steel, and fell, face to the foe, as a brave soldier should" (*History of the Zulu War and Its Origin*, 438). In tribal war-fare of southern Africa the Zulus found that for nearly a century their un-matched courage, physical prowess, speed, and enormous numbers brought decisive victory and often the slaughter of their enemies. But in a fight against disciplined ranks of trained British riflemen their prior method of success spelled national self-destruction.

Whereas the Zulus had discarded much of the traditional military rit-uals of southern Africa—missile warfare, staged contests, and the taking of captives for ransom—Cetshwayo still apparently envisioned the im-pending war with the British as a single staged event of military prowess. In his mind his army would fight "on one day only" and then come to terms with the British. If the Zulu leadership had examined both the vic-tories and the defeats at Isandhlwana and Rorke's Drift, they would have jettisoned the entire traditional method of attack and instigated a guer-rilla war to ambush British wagon trains on the move—and, at all costs, to avoid charging entrenched positions and squares of British infantry. When the war broke out, Cetshwayo himself seemed to have sensed that the odds were all in favor of the Zulus—if they avoided entrenched British riflemen and fought the European only through surprise, during transit, or at night.

The Zulus had a much larger army, knew the terrain intimately, and had clear warning of the advance of the three British columns. Moreover, Zululand—without roads, largely unmapped, laced with rivers and streams, hilly and full of gullies and canyons—was nearly impossible to traverse by wagons full of tons of equipment that could scarcely travel more than five miles on a good day. Constant Zulu attacks on such columns might have stranded British regiments deep in Zululand without recourse to resupply, thereby dragging out a war that had no real support from either the general staff or the prime minister back in London. Instead, ritual, custom, and tradition ensured that the horns, chest, and loins of the Zulu *impis* would attack as usual—and so were to be slaugh-tered as usual by British riflemen.

Whereas the Zulus were famous for their obedience to royal edicts, since the reign of Shaka—who had routinely strangled those who sneezed, laughed, or simply looked at him in his presence—there was an arbitrariness surrounding punishment that tended in the long run to un-dermine Zulu cohesion and central command. Nearly every major Zulu leader from Dingiswayo and Shaka to Cetshwayo—who was probably poisoned after the British conquest—was murdered. Mpande, Cetshwayo's father, reigned for more than thirty years (1840–72) and died alone in his sleep, but only by abrogating most of his power to local *impis* and in his later years to his son.

In contrast, the British army, which routinely flogged and jailed its felons, had a written code of punishment and laws. Individual troopers more or less knew what was expected of them, assumed a relatively uniform and predictable application of justice throughout the ranks, and considered their own persons sacrosanct from arbitrary execution. For the most part, they followed orders from a sense of justice rather than mere fear. No British officer or magistrate had absolute power over an underling in the manner of a Zulu or an Aztec king. The small professional army of England was far more representative of civic militarism than the thousands mustered in Cetshwayo's *impis:* the former fought with the understanding that military life was a reflection of civilian customs and values, the latter that the society mirrored the army. In a nation of millions the British army was tiny, but even the queen could not execute a single soldier without at least a hearing or trial.

COURAGE IS NOT NECESSARILY DISCIPLINE

The Traditions of the British Army

By 1879 there were larger and better-organized European militaries—the French and the German especially—than the British colonial army. The murderous American Civil War (1861–65) and the short but violent Franco-Persian War (1870–71) had put an end to the common use of massed cavalry and the tactics of slow marching through ordered lines. The machine gun, new repeating rifles, and artillery shells destroyed the last aristocratic pretensions of mounted grandees and ushered in the dawn of modern industrial warfare. In contrast, the British after Waterloo (1815), with few exceptions (the disastrous Crimean War of 1854–56 is the oddity that proves the rule), fought colonial wars, against enemies that had neither modern weapons, elaborate fortifications, nor sophisticated tactics. The result was the maintenance of a peculiarly reactionary army, which increasingly found itself outside the modern Western evolution toward enormous levies of well-armed conscripts. The Victorian army—more so than the navy—mirrored the class divisions of British society. Since it was largely unchallenged by other more modern European and American forces, it saw no need until the eleventh hour either to dismantle the tactics of a bygone age or to substitute merit for birth as the chief criterion for career advancement.

Only in the decade before the Zulu War had the British undersecretary of war, Edward Cardwell, at last made any meaningful attempt at reform by eliminating purchased commissions, improving conditions for enlisted men, and urging the adoption of modern rifles, artillery, and Gatling guns. Nevertheless, by 1879 there were still only 180,000 British soldiers—far smaller than the quarter-million-man army of the Roman Empire—to defend an empire that spanned Asia, Africa, Australia, and North America and that was frequently in turmoil throughout India, Afghanistan, and southern and western Africa. Insufficient numbers and class bias were not the only problems. The army was also plagued by chronic budgetary crises—the navy still received the bulk of British defense expenditures—which led to poor pay and weapons that were often outmoded. Far too many officers in the latter nineteenth century, even after the abolition of the purchase system in which aristocrats literally bought commissions, were still ingrained with a conservative mentality that looked suspiciously upon science and the accompanying mechanical expertise that fueled an industrial society. What saved the British army and made it a deadly constabulary force in the colonial wars of the nineteenth century, despite poor generalship and inadequate funding, was its legendary discipline and training. British redcoats for the most part were better drilled and motivated than almost any other troops in the world. When formed up in their infamous squares, they were the best soldiers both in and outside Europe in laying down a continuously accurate and sustained deadly volley of rifle fire.

In the minutes before the attack on Rorke's Drift, not a single regular British soldier fled to join the hundreds of colonials and native troops that took off before the approach of thousands of Zulus. Instead, fewer than one hundred able-bodied men continuously fired more than 20,000 rifle rounds and were at the ramparts for some sixteen hours. At the bloodbath at Isandhlwana hours earlier, nearly all the regular companies of the 24th Regiment of the British regular army were overwhelmed in situ rather than dispersed in flight. Uguku, a Zulu veteran of the slaughter, later recalled of that British final stand:

They were completely surrounded on all sides, and stood back to back, and surrounding some men who were in the centre. Their ammunition was now done, except that they had some revolvers which they fired at us at close quarters. We were quite unable to break their square until we had killed a great many of them, by throwing our *assegais* at short distances. We eventually overcame them in this way. (F. Colenso, *History of the Zulu War and Its Origin,* 413)

At Rorke's Drift in the moments before the Zulu arrival, Lieutenant Chard's men shot a European sergeant who fled with Captain Stephenson's Natal Native Contingent. Chard felt no need to mention the shooting in his report, and the British officer corps undertook no investigation into the apparently justified killing of a colonial noncommissioned officer who left his post. Sir Garnet Wolseley later even criticized Lieutenants Melville and Coghill, the valiant duo who tried to save the queen's color at Isandhlwana. In Wolseley's view under no circumstances were British officers *ever* to ride out of camp while their beleaguered men were alive and still fighting—despite the sanctity of the regimental banner. The few mounted troops who got away from Isandhlwana after the collapse of the infantry's resistance naturally came under later suspicion.

After the minor disaster at the Intombi River, Lieutenant Harward was court-marshaled for riding off for help while his soldiers were still surrounded by Zulus. Although Harward was acquitted by a military court of justice, General Wolseley insisted that his own dissent be read at the head of every regiment in the army. Wolseley's disgust at the idea of a British officer leaving his men framed his apology to the rank and file and illustrated the trust that lay at the heart of the army's legendary discipline:

The more helpless the position in which an officer finds his men, the more it is his bound duty to stay and share their fortune, whether for good or ill. It is because the British officer has always done so that he occupies the position in which he is held in the estimation of the world, and that he possesses the influence he does in the ranks of our army. The soldier has learned to feel that, come what may, he can in the direst moment of danger look with implicit faith to his officer, knowing that he will never desert him under any possible circumstances. It is to this faith of the British soldier in his officers that we owe most of the gallant deeds recorded in our military annals; and it is because the verdict of this Court-Martial strikes at the root of this faith, that I feel it necessary to mark officially my emphatic dissent from the theory upon which the verdict has been founded. (D. Clammer, *The Zulu War,* 143)

The great strength of the British army was to form in lines and squares. In the former formation each row of three or four lines of sol-

diers—often prone, kneeling, and standing—fired on command, reloaded, and then again shot five to ten seconds later. The exact sequence
of shots from the entire company ensured a near steady curtain of fire
even from single-shot Martini-Henry rifles. In a box four right angles ensured a safe center for baggage, refuge for the wounded, and reserves—the
integrity of the entire square predicated on the idea that no British soldier
would give way at any point along the perimeter. Often to ensure fire control, stakes were placed at one-hundred-yard intervals in the killing field
to allow gunnery sergeants to hone the sequence of firing and individual
riflemen to calibrate their aim.

The onslaught of a British lancer attack against the Zulus was equally
frightening in its carefully disciplined stages:

> The 17th Lancers—the Duke of Cambridge's Own—were a proud regi-
> ment. "Death or Glory" was their motto, and Balaclava was amongst their
> battle honours. Drury-Lowe [colonel of the regiment] drew them up
> meticulously, as if on parade.... Watching the troopers on their big
> English horses, with their blue uniforms and white facings, they appeared
> a machine, so precise was their dressing. Drury-Lowe advanced his regi-
> ment at the walk in a column of troops, and, as the ground leveled, gave the
> orders: "Trot—Form squadrons—Form Line!" then, with the men drawn
> up two deep, "Gallop!" the horses leapt forward, and as the line of steel-
> lipped lances came to the rest, pennons streaming, "Charge!" and a cheer
> broke from the square. The regiment rapidly overtook the retreating Zulus,
> and the lances, as unsparing as the assegais, rose and fell as the troopers im-
> paled warrior after warrior, and flicked the bodies from the points. (D.
> Clammer, *The Zulu War,* 214)

What Is Western Discipline?

The display of courage while under attack is a human trait common to
fighters everywhere. All warriors can exhibit extraordinary bravery. Nor is
the ancillary of courage, obedience to command, a peculiarly Western
characteristic. Both tribal and civilized militaries find success from the
fear, even terror, that fighters hold for their leader, general, king, or autocrat. Individual Zulus who grasped the red-hot barrels of Martini-Henry
rifles on the north rampart at Rorke's Drift were as brave as the
Englishmen who calmly blew them to pieces seconds later with .45-caliber
rifle slugs. They were nearly as obedient to their particular generals as

well, charging on command in human wave attacks against fortified positions.

But in the end the Zulus—who could be executed on a nod from their king—not the British, ran away from Rorke's Drift:

> It seems paradoxical to us that men who were so brave in their attacks would run away in panic when their attacks eventually failed. It did not seem paradoxical to the Zulus. They expected to run away if their attacks eventually failed. . . . Once a body of men began to run away, the effect on other men was contagious, as it is in most armies. Shaka's regiments sometimes ran away like this too. It was the traditional end to a Zulu battle. They either destroyed their enemies or ran away. (R. Edgerton, *Like Lions They Fought*, 188)

Hours earlier, after the moment of their greatest victory at Isandhlwana, most of the *impis* dispersed home with booty—far different were they in triumph from the murderous British lancers who six months later after the slaughter at Ulundi still rode down the defeated Zulus for hours on end. Why did brave and obedient Zulus in both victory and defeat lack the discipline of brave and obedient British soldiers?

From the Greeks onward, Westerners have sought to distinguish moments of individual courage and obedience to leaders from a broader, more institutionalized bravery that derives from the harmony of discipline, training, and egalitarian values among men and officers. Beginning with the Hellenic tradition, Europeans were careful to organize types of purported courage into a hierarchy, from the singular rashness of bold individual acts to the cohesive shared bravery along a battle line—insisting that the former was only occasionally critical to victory, the latter always.

Herodotus, for example, after the battle at Plataea (479 B.C.) noted that the Spartans did not bestow the award of valor to Aristodemus, who rushed out from the formation in near suicidal charges to stab away at the Persians. Instead, the Spartans gave the prize to one Posidonius, who fought alongside his fellow hoplites in the phalanx bravely but "without any wish to be killed" (9.71). Herodotus goes on to imply that Aristodemus had not fought with reason, but as a berserker to redeem his sullied reputation incurred from missing out on the glorious last stand at Thermopylae the summer before.

The Greek standard of courage is inextricably tied to training and discipline: the hoplite is to fight with cold reason, not from frenzy. He holds his own life dear, not cheap, and yet is willing to offer it for the polis. His success in battle is gauged not entirely on how many men he kills or how much personal valor he displays, but to the degree his own battleworthiness aids the advance of his comrades, the maintenance of order in defeat, or the preservation of the formation under attack.

This emphasis on the sanctity of the group was not just a Spartan ethos, but a generally held code throughout the Greek city-states. Frequently in Greek literature we hear that same theme of group cohesion among average soldiers—all citizens can be good fighters if they dedicate themselves to the defense of their peers and culture at large. In Thucydides' second book the Athenian general Pericles reminds the Assembly during his funeral oration that truly brave men are not those berserkers who are in "evil circumstances and thus have the best excuse to be unsparing of their lives." Such men, he says, "have no hope of better days." Rather, the truly courageous are those "to whom it makes an enormous difference if they suffer disaster" (Thucydides 2.43.6).

We hear throughout Greek literature of the necessity of staying in rank, of rote and discipline as more important than mere strength and bravado. Men carry their shields, Plutarch wrote, "for the sake of the entire line" (*Moralia* 220A). Real strength and bravery were for carrying a shield in formation, not for killing dozens of the enemy in individual combat, which was properly the stuff of epic and mythology. Xenophon reminds us that from freeholding property owners comes such group cohesion and discipline: "In fighting, just as in working the soil, it is necessary to have the help of other people" (*Oeconomicus* 5.14). Punishments were given only to those who threw down their shields, broke rank, or caused panic, never to those who failed to kill enough of the enemy.

Similarly, there is nothing but disdain for gaudy tribal fighters, loud yelling, or terrifying noise if such show is not accompanied by the discipline to march and stay in rank. "Images don't inflict wounds," Aeschylus says (*Seven Against Thebes*, 397–99). Thucydides has the Spartan general Brasidas, in his attack against Illyrian villagers, sum up the early Western contempt for tribal warfare:

> They hold terror in the onset of their attack for those who have no experience with them. They are indeed dreadful looking due to their sheer numbers; the very din of their yelling is intolerable; and they create an image of terror even in their empty brandishing of their weapons. But they are not what they seem when it comes time to fighting hand-to-hand with those who can endure such threats. Since they have no regular battle order, they

are not ashamed to abandon any position once they are hard pressed; and since both fleeing and attacking are thought to be equally honorable, their courage cannot ever really be tested. . . . Such mobs as these, if one will only withstand their first charge, will only make a boast of courage from afar with threats. But for those who give in to them, they pursue right on their heels, eager to display courage when the situation appears safe. (4.126.5–7)

The Zulus were far more prone than the Illyrians to press home the attack against solid ranks; nevertheless, Thucydides' general contrast between yelling and spectacle versus holding firm in a line—"regular battle order"—is relevant to the Anglo-Zulu War. Those soldiers in both wars who could drill in formation, accept and pass on orders, and recognize a central chain of command were more likely to advance, stay put, and retreat in unison and formation. Across time and space such a systematic rather than haphazard movement of men proves the more effective in killing the enemy.

The Classical Paradigm

Aristotle, typically so, was the most systematic of Greek thinkers in dissecting the nature of courage and its relationship to self-interest, obedience, and discipline. He reaches almost the same conclusions as other Greek thinkers in explaining why certain types of bravery are preferable and lasting than others—and inseparable from the notion of the state and a trust in its government. In his careful analysis of five types of military bravery, Aristotle gives precedence to civic courage, which amateur citizen soldiers alone possess, due to their fear of cowardice before their commonwealth and fellow citizens and their desire for recognition of virtue that such public bodies offer to selfless men. "A man," Aristotle notes in echoing Pericles, "should not be brave because he is forced to be, but because courage is itself a noble thing" (*Nicomachean Ethics* 3.8.5).

Aristotle also recognizes a second apparent courage, that of better-trained or superior-equipped soldiers who can afford to be brave because they hold material advantages. But he warns us that such purportedly courageous men are not really so: once their transitory advantages cease, they are the likely to flee. Aristotle also acknowledges a third type of apparent bravery often mistaken for true courage, that of the berserker, who due either to pain, frenzy, or anger fights without reason and without regard for death—or the welfare of his peers. This, too, is a transitory courage that can flee when the spirit of audacity resides.

Nor do Aristotle's fourth and fifth categories, those respectively of the blind optimist and of the ignorant, meet the criteria of courageousness. Their war spirit can be based on erroneous perceptions and is thus ephemeral. Some men are brave because they have carefully gauged the odds to be in their favor; but such fighters can be either mistaken in their assessment of the battlefield or unaware that advantage is fickle and prone to change in seconds. In either case their courage is not rooted in values and character, much less is it a product of a system, and thus neither lasting nor always dependable in the heat of battle.

By the same token the ignorant fight well only because they are under the mistaken impression that the advantage is with them; they flee when they gain knowledge of their real danger. Like the optimist, the unaware reflect a relative courage, not an absolute value. Plato in his dialogue *Laches* makes the same point when Socrates argues that true courage is the ability of a soldier to fight and stay in rank, even when he knows the odds are against him—in contrast to the apparent hero who battles bravely only when all the advantages are on his side.

Very early on in Western culture the notion of discipline was institutionalized as staying in rank and obeying the orders of superior officers, who gained their authority from constitutional prerogative. The annual oath of the Athenian ephebes—the young military recruits who for two years were to guard the port of Piraeus and hinterland of Attica—contained the following promise: "And I will not desert the man at my side wherever I am positioned in line . . . I will offer my ready obedience at any time to those who are exercising their authority prudently, and to the established laws and to those laws which will be judiciously in force in the future" (M. Tod, *Greek Historical Inscriptions,* [Oxford 1948] vol. 2, #204). Authors such as Xenophon and Polybius talked of armies as walls, each course an individual company, each brick a soldier—the mortar of discipline keeping men and companies in their exact places and ensuring the integrity of the bulwark. The alternative, in Xenophon's words, was chaos "like a crowd leaving a theater" (*Cavalry Commander* 7.2). Classical culture accepted that militiamen were to be neither terrified of their rulers nor recklessly brave. Rather, they were predictable in battle, both in the placement and movement of their own bodies and in their mental and spiritual readiness to accept commands. In the heat of combat all men are likely to lose their fear of a king before death. Bravery, as Aristotle saw, also can be a fickle emotion. Cossacks, as modern military historians have noted of all such nomad warriors, were reckless in pursuit, but often abjectly cowardly when roles were reversed and they found themselves in shock battle against enemy columns.

The Roman army sought further to bureaucratize civic courage through training and close adherence to close-order formation, regimental élan, and the recognition that bravery was not individual prowess. Josephus, the Jewish Roman historian of the early first century A.D., in a famous and often quoted observation, remarked of Roman battlefield superiority:

> If one looks at the Roman military, it is seen that the Empire came into their hands as the result of their valour, not as a gift of fortune. For they do not wait for the outbreak of war to practise with weapons nor do they sit idle in peace mobilizing themselves only in time of need. Instead, they seem to have been born with weapons in their hands; never do they take a break from training or wait for emergencies to arise. . . . One would not be incorrect in saying that their maneuvers are like bloodless battles, and their battles bloody maneuvers. (*Jewish War* 3.102–7)

Nearly four hundred years later Vegetius, the fourth-century-A.D. author of a manual on Roman military institutions, could once more see such training and organization at the root of Roman battle success: "Victory was granted not by mere numbers and innate courage, but by skill and training. We see that the Roman people owed the conquest of the world to no other cause than military training, discipline in their camps, and practice in warfare" (Vegetius *Epitoma rei militaris* 1.1). Vegetius's popularity with the Franks and other Germanic monarchies that evolved in western Europe during the Middle Ages arose from his emphasis on creating disciplined lines and columns. In their eyes, he showed how Teutonic furor might be properly channeled into creating spirited but disciplined foot soldiers.

Drill, Rank, Order, and Command

Discipline as it emerged in Europe is the attempt at the institutionalization of a particular type of courage through training and rote, and is manifested in the preservation of rank and order. This Western obsession with close-order drill is hinged on the fact that whereas all men are prone to bolt and run when the situation becomes hopeless, training and belief can alter such behavior. The key is not to make every man a hero, but to create men who by and large are braver than their untrained allies in withstanding an enemy charge, and in the heat of battle follow the orders of superiors to protect the men at their sides. Their obedience is given to a timeless and enduring civic system, not to a tribe, family, or friends of the moment.

How is discipline achieved and sustained over centuries? Greek, Roman, and later European armies found the answer through drill and a clear-cut written contract between soldier and state. Seventeenth-century commanders like William Louis of Nassau connected their preference for mass firepower directly to Greek and Roman writers of tactics who stressed the need for phalangites and legionaries to stay in close formation. The ability to march in order and line up in rank has immediate and more abstract advantages. Troops can be deployed and be given orders more quickly and efficiently when they march in close formations. Close-order columns and lines are the fountainheads of collective fire and make sequential volleys by rifle companies possible. But drill itself in a larger sense reinforces the soldier's attention to commands. The willingness to march in step with his peers is at the source of a Western soldier's readiness to do exactly what his commanding officer orders. A man who can find his spot in formation, march in cadence with his fellows, and keep rank is more likely to obey other more key orders, to use his weapons on command, and ultimately to defeat the enemy.

Westerners especially put a much greater emphasis on just this strange notion of keeping together in time:

> But in fact close-order drill is conspicuous by its absence in most armies and military traditions. From a world perspective, indeed, the way Greeks and Romans and then modern Europeans exploited the psychological effect of keeping together in time was an oddity, not the norm of military history. Why should Europeans have specialized in exploiting the extraordinary possibilities of close-order drill? (W. McNeill, *Keeping Together in Time*, 4)

McNeill goes on to give a variety of answers to his own question, but central to his entire discussion is the notion of civic community, or the idea that freemen enter a consensual contract with their military and thereby expect rights and accept responsibilities. In such an environment, drill is not seen necessarily as oppressive even to highly individualistic Westerners, but as an obvious manifestation of egalitarianism that brings all soldiers from widely varying backgrounds into a uniformly clothed, identical-appearing, and fluid-moving single body, where private identity and individual status is for a time shed. Drill, McNeill believes, was quite at home in "active, participatory citizenship that was the hallmark of the Greek and Roman concepts of freedom" (112). We might add that the close order of the Greek phalanx, where each man occupied a slot equidistant from another, was a reflection of the assembly hall, in which every male citizen held the same right as another—and both egalitarian bodies were ultimately fueled by the Greek countryside, where a checkerboard of farms, not vast estates, was the norm.

Adolescents who enter the freshman class at, for example, Virginia Military Institute are immediately shorn of their hair, deprived of their civilian clothes, and taught to drill and march in step—as prior class, race, or political loyalties fade into the columns of identically appearing, moving, and chanting cadets. Take the most vicious street or motorcycle gang, replete with Uzi machine guns and years of experience in shooting rival thugs, and it would not stand a chance in battle against a regiment of armed VMI classmates—none of whom have a single serious misdemeanor record of arrest or have fired a shot in anger their entire lives. Yet VMI cadets, unlike well-disciplined Nazis or Stalinist goose-stepping infantrymen, are fully apprised of the conditions of their service and are largely protected through a system of military justice from capricious punishment—and accept that gratuitous violence on their own part will be severely punished. Such is the power of drill and the discipline it spawns in creating civic loyalty from tribal and familial obligations.

Fighting in rank and formation is in some sense the ultimate manifestation of Western egalitarianism, as all hierarchy outside the battlefield fades before the anonymity of a phalanx of like-minded and trained peers. Presumably, the Carthaginians hired the Spartan drillmaster Xanthippus in the First Punic War for the same reason the Japanese enlisted French and German field instructors during the latter nineteenth century: to create soldiers, whether phalangites or riflemen, who could drill and march in rank and therefore fight in the deadly manner of Westerners—as both the Romans and the Americans were shortly to learn. Vegetius, some two millennia ago, outlined this peculiar Western emphasis on drill:

Right at the beginning of their training, recruits must be taught the military step. For on the march and in the battle line nothing should be kept safeguarded more diligently than that all the troops should keep in step. This can only be achieved through repeated practice by which they learn how to march quickly and in formation. An army which is split up and not in order is always in serious danger from the enemy. (*Epitoma rei militaris* 1.1.9)

Central to the European tradition of military discipline is the emphasis on defense, or the belief, as we have seen from Herodotus, that it is better not to run than to be an accomplished killer. Aristotle in the *Politics* (7.1324b15ff) relates the strange customs of nonpolis peoples who put unusual emphasis on killing the enemy—Scythians cannot drink from a ceremonial cup until they have killed a man, Iberians put spits around warriors' graves to mark the number of men they had slain in battle, Macedonians must wear a halter, not a belt, until they cut down a man in battle—as in sharp contrast with the mores of the city-state. The Zulu army also belonged to this long tribal tradition, as its warriors received necklaces of willow sticks signifying the number of "kills" each had confirmed.

As Aristotle also pointed out, the Western emphasis on defensive cohesion, closely associated with drill and order, puts the highest premium on maintaining the integrity of a position or formation. All codes of military justice in the West clearly define cowardice first as running from formation or abandoning rank, regardless of the situation, not as a failure to kill particular numbers of the enemy. If an Aztec warrior found prestige in overwhelming and capturing a string of noble prisoners, a Spanish harquebusier or pikeman was heralded for keeping his place in line and supporting the cohesion of the line or column as it rather anonymously mowed down the enemy. In the context of the Zulu wars the British, like the Zulus, possessed a method of attack and a predictable manner of fighting. But the British system accentuated formation, drill, and order, and called courageous those who upheld those very values. In an abstract sense, soldiers who fight as one—shoot in volleys, charge on order as a group, retire when ordered, and do not pursue rashly, prematurely, or for too long—defeat their enemies.

The Anglo-Zulu War of 1879 provides stunning examples of Zulu bravery pitted against British discipline. But whereas the Zulu military was often as brave as the British, no one would claim it was as disciplined:

The key invention is that of the state, that is, civil in contrast with kin-based social control. Civil government is the dividing line, the threshold, the horizon between that which is civilized and that which is not. Only the state can raise large armies. It alone can discipline and train men into soldiers rather than warriors. Only government can command, not request, and can punish those who do not feel like fighting that day. . . . The primitive warrior was without the backing of an organized, structured government. He was unwilling to submit to discipline, and incapable or impatient of obeying definite command. He discovered only the tactical principles inherent in animal hunting. . . . He was too immediately concerned with the engagement just ahead to plan campaigns instead of battles. (H. Turney-High, *Primitive War*, 258)

There were eleven Victoria Crosses awarded at Rorke's Drift—one for almost every ten soldiers who fought. None were awarded on the basis of "kills," though we have several eye-witness accounts of individual British marksmen shooting dozens of Zulus at great ranges. Modern critics suggest such lavishness in commendation was designed to assuage the disaster at Isandhlwana and to reassure a skeptical Victorian public that the fighting ability of the British soldier remained unquestioned. Maybe, maybe not. But in the long annals of military history, it is difficult to find anything quite like Rorke's Drift, where a beleaguered force, outnumbered forty to one, survived and killed twenty men for every defender lost. But then it is also rare to find warriors as well trained as European soldiers, and rarer still to find any Europeans as disciplined as the British redcoats of the late nineteenth century.

NINE

Individualism

Midway, June 4–8, 1942

Now where men are not their own masters and independent, but are ruled by despots, they are not really militarily capable, but only appear to be warlike. . . . For men's souls are enslaved and they refuse to run risks readily and recklessly to increase the power of somebody else. But independent people, taking risks on their own behalf and not on behalf of others, are willing and eager to go into danger, for they themselves enjoy the prize of victory. So institutions contribute a great deal to military valor.
—HIPPOCRATES, *Airs, Waters, Places* (16, 23)

FLOATING INFERNOS

THERE WERE TWO deadly places to be on the morning of June 4, 1942, during the first day of the battle of Midway—at that point the greatest aircraft carrier battle in the history of naval warfare. The first was on four Japanese aircraft carriers under aerial attack from American dive-bombers. All had their planes parked on their decks being refueled and rearmed when they were unexpectedly attacked. Gasoline tanks, high explosives, and ammunition were recklessly exposed to a shower of American 500- and 1,000-pound bombs. The hangar decks below were also littered promiscuously with munitions and torpedoes. Frantic crews tried in vain to switch their armaments from a planned land attack on Midway to a sudden impromptu assault on the newly located American carrier fleet a little less than two hundred miles to the east.

Under those rare circumstances of carrier vulnerability, a single 1,000-pound bomb that hit the targeted deck full of gassed and armed planes might trigger a series of explosions that could incinerate the entire ship and send it to the bottom in minutes—1,000 pounds of explosives ruining in a minute or two what five years of labor and 60 million pounds of steel had created. During the battle of Midway, three of the imperial Japanese prized fleet carriers—the *Akagi, Kaga,* and *Soryu,* all veterans of an unbroken string of Japanese successes during the prior six months— were precisely in that rare state of absolute defenselessness when American dive-bombers began their headlong plunges from as high as 20,000 feet, entirely unseen from below. In less than six minutes—from 10:22 to 10:28 A.M. on June 4, 1942—the pride of the Japanese carrier fleet was set aflame and the course of World War II in the Pacific radically altered. Unlike the great naval battles of the past—Artemisium (480 B.C.), Salamis (480 B.C.), Actium (31 B.C.), Lepanto (1571), Trafalgar (1805), and Jutland (1916)—Midway was fought in the open seas: once sailors lost their platform of safety, unscathed and burned orphaned crewmen alike would find neither shore nor small boats to pick them up.

The 33,000-ton *Kaga* ("Increased Joy"), with its arsenal of seventy-two bombers and fighters, was probably attacked first by twenty-five American SBD Dauntless dive-bombers of squadrons VB-6 and VS-6, led by the skilled pilot Wade McClusky from the American carrier *Enterprise.* Nine of McClusky's planes made it through the horrendous antiaircraft defenses. All dived toward the carrier at more than 250 mph. Four bombs hit their target. Within seconds Japanese planes, gassed, armed, and ready for takeoff, instead began exploding, causing gaping holes in the flight deck and killing almost anyone in their general vicinity. Anything metal on deck—wrenches, pipes, fittings—simply became deadly shrapnel that shredded all flesh in its path. Two subsequent American bombs ripped apart the ship's elevator and ignited all the armed planes waiting below on the hangar deck. One bomb blew apart the carrier's island, killing all the officers on the bridge, including the captain of the *Kaga.*

Almost immediately, power went out. The *Kaga* stopped dead in the water and began exploding. Carriers seldom broke in two and sank quickly. They were not often caught and targeted by the huge shells of battleships and were among the most seaworthy of capital ships even when torpedoed—which was rare, given their protective net of cruisers and destroyers. Nevertheless, in minutes eight hundred of the *Kaga's* crew were burned alive, dismembered, or vaporized into nothingness. Ship-to-ship air warfare, with its lethal combination of bomb, torpedo, machine-gun fire, and aviation fuel, even without the horrific shelling of sixteen-inch naval guns, could be an ungodly experience. Whereas the Japanese had done precisely the same thing to American battleships half a year earlier at Pearl Harbor, their own blazing carriers now were not at dock, but on the high seas, hundreds of miles from Japanese-held territory. Their slight hope of rescue and medical attention lay only with other Japanese ships, themselves under aerial attack and thus wary of approaching too close to the exploding and flaming carriers. A few officers chose to go down with their vessels, out of shame of disappointing their emperor.

At nearly the same time the *Kaga* was struck, her sister ship the 34,000-ton *Akagi* ("Red Castle")—Admiral Nagumo's flagship—with most of its sixty-three planes, was caught in exactly the same manner by Dick Best and at least five SBD dive-bombers of the 1st Division of Bombing Squadron VB-6, also from the carrier *Enterprise*. While this smaller group of airborne attackers had only 5,000 pounds of ordnance among them, the *Akagi* was likewise in the midst of launching at least forty fully gassed and armed planes heading out to demolish the *Yorktown*. At least two and maybe three of the Americans' bombs hit the carrier. The explosions incinerated the Japanese planes as they were taking off and blasted holes throughout the deck before reaching the volatile fuel tanks and magazines below. Rear Admiral Kusaka recorded that

> the deck was on fire and anti-aircraft and machine guns were firing automatically, having been set off by the fire aboard ship. Bodies were all over the place, and it was not possible to tell what would be shot up next. . . . I had my hands and feet burned—a pretty serious burn on one foot. That is eventually the way we abandoned the *Akagi*—helter-skelter, no order of any kind. (W. Smith, *Midway*, 111)

Unlike those who are attacked in land warfare, men shelled and bombed on carriers at sea have little avenue of flight, their escape limited by the small perimeter of the flight deck. An infantryman subject to the hellish shelling on Guadalcanal might run, dig, or find shelter; a Japanese sailor on an exploding carrier at Midway had to choose from among being burned alive, suffocating inside the ship, being strafed and engulfed on a red-hot flight deck, or jumping overboard to drown, be burned on the high seas, or on occasion be attacked by sharks in the warm waters of the Pacific. The best hope of a Japanese man in the water was to be rescued by American ships, which meant life and safety in a prisoner-of-war camp in the United States. The worst nightmare of an American sailor or airman in the seas of Midway was capture by the Japanese navy, which spelled a quick interrogation, followed by either beheading or being thrown overboard bound with weights.

As for the attackers, unlike high-altitude "precision" bombing by multiengine aircraft at 20,000 feet and above, naval dive-bombers were far more likely to hit the target—if the pilots were not themselves engulfed by their own explosions, shot down, or simply unable to pull out of a dive that brought them within feet of the enemy deck. At Midway a single Dauntless dive-bomber closing to a thousand feet above the target with a 500-pound bomb would prove more lethal than an entire squadron of fifteen B-17s three or four miles above, despite each dropping 8,500 pounds of explosives.

One such bomb from one of the American dive-bombers plowed into the hangar and ignited the *Akagi's* stored torpedoes, which immediately began to rip the ship open from the inside out. Unlike British aircraft carriers, neither the faster and more agile Japanese nor the American flattops had armored decks. Their wooden runways offered poor protection for the fuel, planes, and bombs in storage below—and themselves were easily ignited along with the planes preparing for takeoff. More than two hundred men from the *Akagi* were either killed or lost in seconds. A Japanese naval officer and celebrated pilot, Mitsuo Fuchida, on the *Akagi* recalled the general calamity inside the carrier:

> I staggered down a ladder and into the ready room. It was already jammed with badly burned victims from the hangar deck. A new explosion was followed quickly by several more, each causing the bridge structure to tremble. Smoke from the burning hangar gushed through passageways and into the bridge and ready room, forcing us to seek other refuge. Climbing back to the bridge I could see that *Kaga* and *Soryu* had also been hit and were giving off heavy columns of black smoke. The scene was horrible to behold. (M. Fuchida and M. Okimiya, *Midway, the Battle That Doomed Japan*, 179)

The best naval pilots of the imperial fleet were being slaughtered in a matter of minutes. Just as important was the loss of the most skilled flight crews in the Japanese navy, the rare and irreplaceable experts who had mastered with long experience the difficult arts of rapidly arming, maintaining, and fueling aircraft on a bobbing carrier.

In this incredible six-minute period a third Japanese carrier, the 18,000-ton *Soryu* ("Green Dragon"), was about to experience the same inferno inflicted on her two sister ships. This time the damage was done by

Max Leslie and his Bombing Squadron 3 from the American aircraft carrier *Yorktown*, itself now little more than a hundred miles away. Of *Soryu's* crew, 718 were soon incinerated. None of the ordnance from the American dive-bombers were effective armor-piercing weapons, which under most circumstances was a clear drawback, as such ordnance were often unable to smash unimpeded through even the wooden flight decks to explode among the interior magazines, engines, and fuel tanks below. Given the absolute failure of forty-one American torpedo planes minutes earlier, there seemed little chance to reach the vulnerable insides to sink the carriers through the Dauntlesses' small bombs alone. But, as in the case of the *Akagi* and *Kaga*, for once the lighter American bombs had an unexpected windfall: since all three carriers were caught preparing planes for takeoff, the most vulnerable targets on the Japanese carriers at 10:22 A.M. were in fact their wooden decks. The explosions of the exposed and loaded Japanese bombers and fighters would send the blasts from their own fiery gasoline and bombs downward right into their own ships. One American bomb under these rare conditions might set off dozens more on deck.

When hit, *Soryu* was about ten to twelve miles north and east of two other burning carriers, likewise about to launch planes for a massive air strike against the three American fleet carriers. Leslie's thirteen dive-bombers came in from more than 14,000 feet unnoticed—the Japanese fighters were too busy at sea level finishing their slaughter of Lem Massey's last few lumbering American torpedo bombers to patrol the clouds above. At least three bombs from the *Yorktown's* pilots hit the *Soryu*—1,000-pound ordnance released from little more than 1,500 feet—quickly turning the smaller carrier into an inferno, as the blasts from the bombs themselves, exploding Japanese planes, gas lines, and ammunition tore the ship to pieces. Within seconds she lost power entirely. After thirty minutes the call went out to abandon ship. The captain of the *Soryu*, Admiral Yanagimoto, was last seen yelling *"Banzai"* on the engulfed bridge. The last four planes in Leslie's attack squadron felt that further bombing of the wrecked *Soryu* was redundant and so altered their dives to focus on a battleship and destroyer. Belowdecks Tatsuya Otawa, one of the *Soryu* pilots, saw that "everything was blowing up—planes, bombs, gas tanks" (W. Lord, *Incredible Victory*, 174)—before he, too, was blasted over the side of the ship into the sea.

The fourth and last Japanese carrier, the more modern 20,000-ton *Hiryu* ("Flying Dragon"), which had gradually drifted to the southeast during the morning attacks from army and marine bombers based on Midway, largely escaped the first morning wave of American carrier dive-

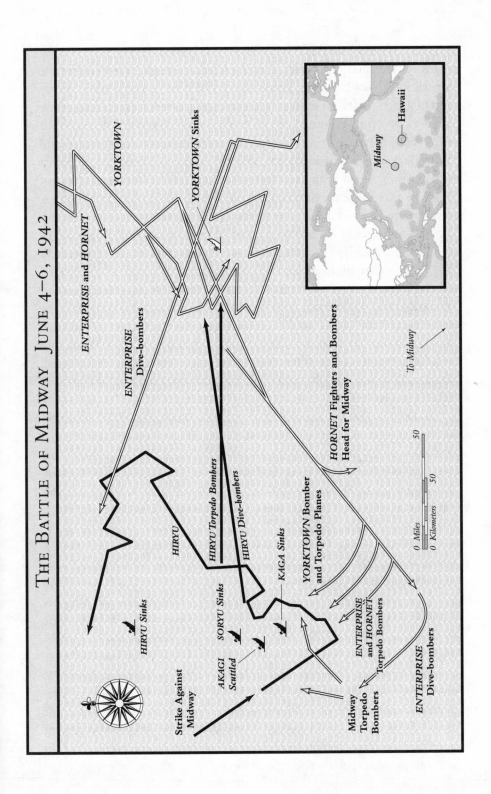

The Battle of Midway June 4–6, 1942

bombers. Within minutes *Hiryu* was able to launch her own devastating attack on the *Yorktown,* which contributed to the eventual sinking of the American carrier. However, late in the day of June 4, a returning formation of American dive-bombers without fighter escort from the *Enterprise* and *Yorktown* finally found her too. At a little before 4:00 P.M. twenty-four SBDs from the *Enterprise,* ten of them orphaned from the disabled and listing *Yorktown,* led by Lieutenants Earl Gallagher, Dick Best, and Dewitt W. Shumway, dived unnoticed from the clouds. Four bombs were direct hits, and once more the Americans ignited Japanese fighters and bombers that were ready for takeoff. The *Hiryu*'s plane elevator was blown out of the deck and against the bridge. Almost all of the dead were caught below the deck and engulfed in raging fires—more than four hundred perished. The *Hiryu*'s captain, Rear Admiral Tamon Yamaguchi, one of the brightest and most aggressive commanders in the Japanese navy, remained on the bridge and went down with his ship—an irreplaceable loss, since he was believed by many to be groomed as the successor to Admiral Yamamoto himself, Commander in Chief of the imperial fleet. When told by an aide that there was still money in the ship's safe that might be saved, Yamaguchi ordered it left alone. "We'll need money for a square meal in hell," he murmured (W. Lord, *Incredible Victory,* 251).

In less than twelve hours 2,155 Japanese seamen were dead, four fleet aircraft carriers were wrecked and soon to sink, and more than 332 aircraft, along with their most skilled pilots, were gone. Before the battle was over, a heavy cruiser was sunk, and another heavily damaged. The *Akagi, Kaga, Hiryu,* and *Soryu,* the pride of the imperial fleet, veterans of campaigning against the Chinese, British, and Americans, were resting at the bottom of the Pacific Ocean. In six minutes the momentum in the Pacific naval war had swung for good to the Americans as the worst fears of the Japanese admiralty of massive American retaliation were realized after only six months of fighting.

In strictly military terms the number of dead at Midway was not large—fewer than 4,000 in the two fleets. The losses were a mere fraction of what the Romans suffered at Cannae, or the Persians at Gaugamela, and much less costly than the bloodbaths of the great sea battles of Salamis, Lepanto, Trafalgar, and Jutland—or the Japanese slaughter to come at Leyte Gulf. But the sinking of the carriers represented an irreplaceable investment of millions of days of precious skilled labor, and even scarcer capital—and the only capability of the Japanese to destroy both the American fleet and Pacific bases. More than one hundred of the best carrier pilots perished in one day, equal to the entire graduating class of naval aviators that Japan could turn out in a single year. Never had the Japanese military lost so dramatically when technology, matériel, experience, and manpower were so decidedly in its favor. Back in Washington, D.C., Admiral Ernest J. King, chief of all U.S. naval operations, concluded of the action of June 4 that the battle of Midway had been the first decisive defeat of the Japanese navy in 350 years and had restored the balance of naval power in the Pacific.

Again, the carriers themselves were irreplaceable. During the entire course of World War II the Japanese launched only seven more of such enormous ships; the Americans in contrast would commission more than one hundred fleet, light, and escort carriers by war's end. The Americans would also build or repair twenty-four battleships—despite losing nearly the entire fleet of the latter at Pearl Harbor—and a countless number of heavy and light cruisers, destroyers, submarines, and support ships. During the four years of the war the Americans constructed sixteen major warships for every one the Japanese built.

Worse still for the Japanese, the highest monthly production of all models of Japanese navy and army aircraft rarely exceeded 1,000 planes, and by summer 1945 the sum was scarcely half that due to American bombing, the need for factory dispersal, and matériel and manpower shortages. In contrast, the Americans soon turned out a sophisticated B-24 heavy bomber of some 100,000 parts every sixty-three minutes; American aircraft workers, who vastly outnumbered the Japanese, were also four times more productive than their individual enemy counterparts. By August 1945, in less than four years after the war had begun, the United States had produced nearly 300,000 aircraft and 87,620 warships. Even as early as mid-1944, American industry was building entire new fleets every six months, replete with naval aircraft comparable in size to the entire American force at Midway. After 1943, both American ships and airplanes—sixteen new *Essex*-class carriers outfitted with Helldiver dive-bombers, Corsair and Hellcat fighters, and Avenger torpedo bombers— were qualitatively and quantitatively superior to anything in the Japanese military. The modern *Iowa*-class battleships that appeared in the latter half of the war were better in speed, armament, range, and defensive protection than anything commissioned in the Japanese navy and were far more effective warships than even the monstrous *Yamato* and *Mushasi*. Within a few months after Midway, not only had the United States naval and air armies made up all the losses from Midway, but its entire armed forces were growing at geometric rates, while the Japanese navy actually began to shrink as outmoded and often bombed-out factories could not even replace obsolete ships and planes lost to American guns, let alone manufacture additional ones. This was the Arsenal of Venice and Cannae's aftermath all over again.

Still, the American bombing on the morning of June 4 had been costly. The *Hornet* had lost eleven of her twelve Wildcat fighters, the *Yorktown* five dive-bombers and fighters, and the *Enterprise* fourteen dive-bombers and a fighter. But these losses were tolerable compared to the near complete massacre of the American torpedo bombers minutes earlier.

THE ANNIHILATION OF THE DEVASTATORS

The battle of Midway can be understood by two inextricably connected events: the destruction of an entire American air arm by Japanese fighter pilots which moments later led directly to the demise of Japan's own carriers. Just as deadly a predicament as being on the Japanese carriers at the battle of Midway was the piloting of lumbering obsolete TBD Devastator torpedo bombers, which early in the morning of June 4 had inaugurated the American carrier attack. In some sense, their annihilation by the Japanese Zero fighters, together with the dogfighting of a few American Wildcat fighters, allowed their unseen dive-bombing comrades the opportunity to attack unmolested. All the American torpedo bombers would make gallant approaches against the Japanese fleet; none would hit their targets; and almost all, with their two-man crews, would be shot down. Out of the eighty-two men who headed for the Japanese carriers in the TBDs, *only thirteen survived*. Yet one of the two Japanese air commanders at Midway, Mitsuo Fuchida, scoffed in his official report on the eve of the battle that the Americans lacked the will to fight.

Commissioned in the mid-1930s, the TBD Devastators were by the outbreak of the war incapable of devastating anything; in reality, they were little more than flying coffins for both pilot and rear gunner. When loaded with their sole 1,000-pound obsolete torpedo—itself unreliable and as likely to plow harmlessly beneath the target as to fail to explode even when it did hit—the planes themselves could barely manage a hundred mph. Fully loaded, they had a combat range of only 175 miles. When attacking ships that were headed in the opposite direction at thirty knots, the TBDs were forced to hug the sea to ensure a proper launching approach as they narrowed the gap at real speeds of less than sixty mph—if there were no head winds. The loaded planes could scarcely climb. Such agonizingly long and exposed runs made them easy targets for Japanese Zero fighters, which sometimes at Midway were swarming in masses of forty or more and diving from far above at three hundred miles an hour. In contrast to the Americans' obsolete craft, Japanese torpedo planes by 1941 could dive at nearly three hundred mph and carry a far heavier and more effective torpedo at greater range.

Thirty-five of forty-one Devastators on June 4 were shot down attacking the Japanese carriers—a fact today scarcely comprehensible under the protocols of contemporary American military practice, in which troops enjoying overwhelming technological, material, and numerical superiority are sometimes not committed to battle out of fear of losing a handful of combatants. Most of the Devastator crews had never taken off armed with a torpedo from the deck of an aircraft carrier—and now they were sent on a mission in their decrepit aircraft, with scarcely enough fuel to return home, against a mostly unknown and unlocated target. The American military was later aghast over the use of Japanese kamikaze planes in the last year of the war; but the orders for the Devastator attacks at Midway were themselves little more than suicidal.

Midway was the last major battle in which the obsolete torpedo bombers were used; on Midway itself a few marine pilots were already flying a small number of the new replacement Grumman TBF Avengers, which, armed with new torpedoes, by war's end would compile a formidable record of low-level attacks on the Japanese fleet. The Avengers could nearly double the speed of the Devastators, carried twice as much armament, and could take far more punishment. But none had yet replaced the ancient TBDs on any of the carriers at Midway—indeed, nineteen of the replacement Avengers arrived from Norfolk, Virginia, at Pearl Harbor on May 29, one day *after* the *Hornet* had sailed out to Midway. Only six were ferried to the marines at Midway. Had the Avengers replaced the Devastators on all three carriers, the American tally of sunken ships might have been even greater, and the loss of pilots surely less—although, as we shall see, the ultimate decision of Midway, in some sense, rested with the sheer vulnerability of the obsolete planes, which drew in the greedy Zeros in droves, when the real danger to the Japanese fleet was high, not low, in the skies. In any case, the naval historian Samuel Eliot Morison, in remarks reminiscent of Livy's summation of Cannae, entitled an entire section of his narrative "The Slaughter of the Torpedo-Bombers." Abject slaughter it was.

On the morning of June 5 Lieutenant Commander John C. "Jack"

Waldron, commander of the VT-8 torpedo squadron on the *Hornet*, distributed copies of his final message to his crews shortly before takeoff. The mimeographed papers ended on a melancholy note:

> MY GREATEST HOPE IS THAT WE ENCOUNTER A FAVORABLE TACTICAL SITUATION, BUT IF WE DON'T AND WORST COMES TO WORST, I WANT EACH ONE OF US TO DO HIS UTMOST TO DESTROY OUR ENEMIES. IF THERE IS ONLY ONE PLANE LEFT TO MAKE A FINAL RUN-IN, I WANT THAT MAN TO GO IN AND GET A HIT. MAY GOD BE WITH US ALL. GOOD LUCK, HAPPY LANDINGS, AND GIVE 'EM HELL! (G. Prange, *Miracle at Midway*, 240)

Jack Waldron took off for the last flight of his life from the *Hornet* at 8:06 A.M. to lead fifteen Devastators against the Japanese fleet. Problems arose almost immediately after launching. The *Hornet*'s accompanying thirty-five dive-bombers and ten Wildcat fighters, obscured by cloud cover, quickly overflew the lumbering Devastators. Waldron was left to find and attack the carriers himself—an almost impossible task, since there would be neither Wildcats to ward off the attacking Zeros nor high-flying Dauntless dive-bombers to divert the antiaircraft fire of the imperial fleet. Instead, the entire air and sea defenses of the Japanese ships would be trained on Waldron's slow planes coming in over the water at one hundred mph. The *Hornet*'s dive-bombers fared even worse, never finding the Japanese fleet at all and thus not dropping a single bomb. The failure of the *Hornet*'s fighters and dive-bombers to find their targets was perhaps not as baffling an event as some historians note, when we remember that the individual planes had neither effective radar nor advanced navigation instruments and were mostly piloted by inexperienced airmen—none of the *Hornet*'s pilots had ever seen action—who flew over a nondescript endless Pacific looking for tiny dots below.

Because of the numerous diversionary maneuvers to avoid early morning air attacks from Midway, the Japanese carriers under Admiral Nagumo were not exactly cruising where the American staff had calculated their position to be when the American fleet's bombers and fighters were scheduled to arrive. Instinctively, Waldron anticipated the enemy's change in course; he immediately veered to the north and so commanded the first American naval air squadron to find the Japanese fleet.

Without fighter cover or friendly bombers above, realizing that he was the first American carrier pilot to attack, and reconciled that after torpedoing the Japanese fleet his planes would not have enough gasoline to reach their home carrier even if they survived their bombing runs,

Waldron radioed his intention to the *Hornet* that he was pressing ahead anyway. Captain Marc Mitscher recalled that Waldron "promised he would press through against all obstacles, well knowing his squadron was doomed to destruction with no chance whatever of returning safely to the carrier" (S. Morison, *Coral Sea, Midway, and Submarine Actions, May 1942–August 1942*, 117).

The first incoming Zero shot down one of Waldron's TBDs, and for the next few minutes fourteen planes of Torpedo 8 in succession were also riddled with machine-gun and cannon bursts. The few planes that closed to drop their torpedoes missed the *Akagi* and the *Soryu* entirely. Those crippled Devastators that did not explode through machine-gun fire disintegrated when they hit the sea, clipping the waves and cartwheeling at one hundred mph. Waldron himself was last seen standing upright in his blazing cockpit. His intuition and navigational skill had at last led Torpedo 8 directly to the Japanese carriers, but unfortunately the *Hornet*'s supporting bombers and fighters were still behind him, mostly lost, and spread far distant above—and he was flying a TBD Devastator.

Infantry battle in modern warfare is brutal and terrifying, but the wounds of naval pilots are often even more savage and the chances of survival virtually nil. Usually, we imagine that the aircraft's metal skin, glass canopy, and armored seat below the pilot deflected gun bursts and gave the targeted occupant a modicum of protection. In fact, since planes often hit a spray of bullets at high speed, the combined force of bullet and streaking target at the point of entry more often literally tore the pilot apart. Moreover, the naval airman in World War II sat atop thousands of pounds of fuel and high explosives inches from his feet, ready to vaporize him the instant enemy cannon fire and tracers ignited the lethal mixture.

Flying a loaded Devastator at Midway would be similar to driving a Ford Pinto in the slow lane, with its trunk and seats loaded with dynamite, as other, far faster drivers shot at it with machine guns as they passed by. Unlike the care of the wounded in land warfare, even ostensibly nonfatal injuries could not be quickly treated, as the pilot could not be evacuated to the rear. Being shot was the beginning, not the end, of the misery—the same gunfire that drew blood also damaged or destroyed the plane itself, promising in a few seconds an even worse crash and ensuing fireball of exploded gasoline. Even in peacetime the site of a downed passenger plane at sea is littered with tiny scraps of aircraft metal—the far more fragile bodies of the occupants often pulverized or burned beyond recognition by the force of impact and ensuing fire.

In an ideal carrier attack, the Devastators were to come in last, after the SBD Dauntless dive-bombers first screamed down from 15,000 feet, with their faster Wildcat fighters descending from even higher above to cover their assault. Then once the enemy ships and planes were occupied, the lumbering torpedo planes in theory might sneak into the melee unmolested at sea level to launch their torpedoes. But given the American mix-up in navigation, all of Waldron's Devastators bore the full brunt of the Japanese antiaircraft and air attack. Not a single plane of Torpedo 8 survived. Of thirty crewmen who left the *Hornet* at eight that morning, only Ensign George H. Gay outlived the massacre; though wounded, he somehow crawled free once his Devastator hit the sea, and then floated unnoticed by the Japanese ships until picked up in the water by an American rescue plane the next afternoon. The fate of Torpedo 8 was only the first of the three slaughters of the torpedo squadrons on June 4, but we have only Gay's later account to learn what transpired in the last minutes of the lives of his twenty-nine squadron members.

As the deadly Zeros returned periodically to the carriers to refuel and rearm during the morning turkey shoot, an observer on the *Akagi* noted that the "service crews cheered the returning pilots, patted them on the shoulder, and shouted words of encouragement. As soon as a plane was ready again the pilot nodded, pushed forward the throttle, and roared back into the sky. This scene was repeated time and again as the desperate air struggle continued" (M. Fuchida and M. Okimiya, *Midway, the Battle That Doomed Japan,* 176). American pilots would find little chance of recovery even if they survived being shot down by these Zeros; most who climbed out of their sinking bombers were strafed in the water. The two naval pilots known to be taken prisoner at Midway were interrogated, then shortly afterward bound, weighted, and thrown overboard. Standard orders for Japanese patrolling ships were to question prisoners to learn of the enemy's situation and then "dispose of them suitably."

General morale on the Japanese carriers was sky-high and bordered on arrogance. And why not? As of yet the fleet had not suffered a real defeat and had nothing but contempt for the fighting potential of American sailors, infantrymen, and pilots. From the outbreak of the war on December 7, 1941, the Japanese carrier forces alone had sunk or disabled eight battleships and two cruisers (Pearl Harbor, December 7) and bombed and sunk the British battleships *Repulse* and *Prince of Wales* (off Kuantan, December 10), the cruisers *Houston* and *Marblehead* (north of Java, February 4, 1942), the British cruisers *Exeter, Cornwall,* and *Dorsetshire* (February 27 off Tjilatjap and April 5 near Colombo). They sent to the bottom or severely damaged three allied aircraft carriers (HMS

Hermes near Trincomalee on April 9 and the *Lexington* and *Yorktown* [damaged] at the battle of Coral Sea, May 8)—all at a cost of a few destroyers and a single light aircraft carrier. For the preparations for Midway, the United States had one battleship and only three carriers in its entire Pacific fleet. The Americans had not yet sunk a single Japanese capital ship. Former pilot Masatake Okumiya and aeronautical engineer Jiro Horikoshi summed up this remarkable record of Japanese naval-air victories in the first half-year of the war:

> The tally of enemy and Japanese ships lost in the first six months of the war was a literal realization of the Navy's concept of "ideal combat conditions," to "wage a decisive sea battle only under air control." For the ten years prior to the Pacific War we had trained our airmen implicitly to believe that sea battles fought under our command of the air could result only in our victories. The initial phases of the Pacific War dramatically upheld this belief. (M. Okumiya and J. Horikoshi, *Zero!*, 153)

This confidence often accounted for the gratuitous cruelty shown toward captured soldiers, who were considered cowardly for surrendering. During the earlier Wake Island campaign immediately following Pearl Harbor, Japanese sailors had brutalized captured American marines and routinely clubbed them before shipping them off to camps in Japan and China. At least five Americans were ceremoniously beheaded on one transport's deck, then their bodies mutilated to cheers from Japanese sailors before being dumped overboard. From the beginning of the Pacific War there was a savagery—arising partly from innate racial animosity, partly out of the perversion of the ancient Bushido code of military protocol by Japanese militarists in the 1930s, partly from pent-up anger over the long European colonial presence in Asia—in the Japanese approach to battle that would soon draw retaliation from the Anglo-American forces. That mutual hatred explains much of the tension and spirit of the combatants at Midway.

Almost as a general rule, Japanese soldiers, well after the killing on the battlefield had ceased, would go on to butcher and torture surrendering and unarmed captives—in China, the Philippines, and the Pacific—with far more frequency than either the British or the Americans. The Allies had nothing comparable to Japanese concentration camps, where macabre medical experiments and routine shootings were not unusual. True, the Americans would eventually engage in brutality on a far greater scale, as the firebombing of the Japanese cities and the nuclear attacks on

Hiroshima and Nagasaki attest. But in American eyes—and this was entirely characteristic of the Western way of war that had originated on the daylight killing fields of ancient Greece and evolved into the Roman, medieval, and Christian concept of a just war *(ius in bello)*—its indiscriminate carpet bombing was far different from murdering prisoners.

The Allies killed on a massive scale, but almost exclusively through open and direct assault, with veritable notification of intent, often in reprisal, and under hostile fire—*not* customarily in camps or after the firing had stopped. Japanese antiaircraft and fighters attempted to shoot down parachuting bombing crews, who were usually executed upon forced landing in enemy territory. To Americans, the Japanese were "free" in open combat to prevent bomber attacks on their urban and industrial sites. They knew the American planes were coming, and they should expect retaliation for starting the war and waging it in China and the Pacific in a most beastly and cruel manner. The Americans further reasoned that as long as they were killing during the actual exchange of gunfire, and doing so as part of an effort to wreck the military-industrial base of imperial Japan, all was more or less fair in pitched battle. In contrast, the Japanese simply counted the dead, and figured that hundreds of thousands more of their own innocent civilians had died from American bombs than American captives tortured and executed by their camp interrogators and guards.

This dichotomy was true enough of all East-West engagements in the history of warfare: Westerners decried summary executions and torture of their captured defenseless combatants, while their own far better-armed and -equipped forces openly and "fairly" butchered thousands during the fighting. Non-Westerners saw such machine-gunning, artillery barrages, and carpet bombing against their own relatively ill equipped soldiers and even more vulnerable civilians as barbaric—even as they often mutilated and executed prisoners of war. In that sense, for example, Hernán Cortés and Lord Chelmsford were outraged when Aztecs and Zulus tortured and killed captives, but themselves thought nothing of riding down and spearing from the rear thousands of poorly protected Native Americans and Zulus in the heat of battle. The British were horrified over the beheading and desecration of their dead at Isandhlwana, but assumed that the machine-gunning of hundreds of spear-carrying Zulu warriors at the battle of Ulundi was fair play. To the Americans, firebombing and the incineration of nearly 200,000 Japanese soldiers, workers, and civilians in a single week over Tokyo during March 1945, while sending Japanese captives to relatively humane prisoner-of-war camps in the American heartland, made perfect military sense; to the Japanese, the murder of downed B-29 pilots, often by summary beheading, was small recompense for the cremation of hundreds of thousands of their kin.

At about the same time that Waldron's Torpedo 8 was being annihilated in its doomed attack on the *Soryu,* another group of Devastators— Lieutenant Commander Eugene E. Lindsey's fourteen torpedo planes from Torpedo 6 of the carrier *Enterprise*—flew over the *Akagi* and headed for the *Kaga.* Although the *Enterprise's* torpedo planes had more experience than Waldron's Devastators—some had fought during the recent Marshall and Wake Islands campaigns—like the *Hornet* planes, Lindsey's TBDs came in without fighter escort and unaided by dive-bombers, which were still high in the clouds. The original miscalculations in finding the Japanese fleet, the cloud cover, and great variance in altitudes between torpedo bombers, fighters, and dive-bombers meant that this batch of Devastators also lost contact early on with the other *Enterprise* fighter escorts. The latter never did find its carrier's torpedo or dive-bombers and returned to their carrier without firing a shot.

This complete absence of supporting aircraft ensured that the slaughter of Torpedo 6 was inevitable. But the ease with which the Japanese brought down this second wave of torpedo planes gave a false sense of security to the naval gunners of the imperial fleet—some officers felt that they could shoot down the entire American naval force itself, without even attacking their home carriers by air. Air Commander Genda on the *Akagi* rightly likened the Devastators to tired mules. After a few hours of knocking down the land-based bombers and the carrier torpedo planes, the crewmen of the imperial fleet found the Americans surprisingly brave, but amateurish and inexperienced, with antiquated planes and substandard torpedoes. Their assessment was generally right on nearly all counts.

Twenty-five Zeros from the targeted carriers screeched down from their high-flying air patrol to blast apart Torpedo 6, miles from the Japanese fleet. For fifteen minutes antiaircraft and fighters shredded the lumbering Devastators, which split off to form an attack from both sides of the *Kaga.* Lindsey's plane was one of the first to be hit and quickly incinerated. Finally, at 9:58 A.M., almost two hours after they had taken off from the *Enterprise,* four surviving TBDs got close enough to launch their torpedoes at the *Kaga.* None found their mark. These were the only planes of the fourteen of this second attack to return. Another twenty crewmen from the Americans' torpedo planes had disappeared into the sea. The slaughter of the TBDs continued.

Three American carriers were launching air squadrons against the

Japanese fleet at Midway at about 8:00 A.M. on June 4, and now the final torpedo plane attack—Lem Massey's twelve Devastators from Torpedo 3 of the *Yorktown*—reached the *Soryu* just about the time the *Hornet* and *Enterprise* TBDs were falling into the sea. Like the other fated torpedo planes, Massey's came in without fighter escort, drawing the full attention of the Japanese antiaircraft and aerial defense. Only five TBDs even got close enough to launch torpedoes against the *Hiryu*. Three of these were shot down far short of the target. From six to ten Zeros followed the remnants of Torpedo 3 all the way to the carrier, forcing the plodding American planes down to little more than 150 feet above the sea.

Massey, like Waldron and Lindsey earlier, did not survive the morning. Neither skill nor courage meant anything when piloting an obsolete Devastator. The few crewmen of Torpedo 3 who made it back reported that Massey was one of the first to be hit and was last seen standing on the wing of his plane, after crawling out of a flaming cockpit. The *Yorktown*'s tiny and outmanned fighter escort under Jimmy Thatch was valiantly fighting off still more Zeros miles above Massey and could offer no help to his Torpedo 3. Again, through an unfortunate mixture of bad luck, general incompetence, and faulty staff procedure, the entire dive-bombing and fighter arm of the third American carrier, *Hornet*, played absolutely no role in the initial attacks on the Japanese fleet. All of *Hornet*'s Wildcats and Dauntlesses either turned back to the carrier, made emergency landings at Midway itself, or crashed into the sea out of fuel. Only Waldron's torpedo planes found the enemy, and without exception they were shot down.

By the time the Japanese had beaten off the third American torpedo attack, the protective cover of the fleet's Zeros was in disarray and near sea level, not at the required height far above the fleet, in formation scouting for dive-bombers. Many Japanese fighters after the morning shooting were landing to refuel and rearm, and the entire attention of the fleet's antiaircraft arsenal was focused on blasting away at sea level the last of the doomed torpedo planes. Miraculously, at nearly the exact time as the third and final TBD attack was repulsed, dozens of the high-flying Dauntless bombers from the *Enterprise* and *Yorktown* finally arrived as if on cue. The first 102 American carrier planes had either been shot down or become lost, but there were still 50 dive-bombers left—less than a third of the original force—to begin the attack. Now to their utter amazement they dived untouched from 15,000 feet to ignite the *Akagi, Kaga,* and *Soryu*.

To the modern American at the millennium, these carrier pilots of more than a half century ago—Massey, Waldron, and Lindsey last seen fighting to free themselves in a sea of flames as their planes were blasted apart by Zeros—now appear as superhuman exemplars of what constituted heroism in the bleak months after World War II. Even their names seem almost caricatures of an earlier stalwart American manhood—Max Leslie, Lem Massey, Wade McClusky, Jack Waldron—doomed fighters who were not all young eighteen-year-old conscripts, but often married and with children, enthusiastic rather than merely willing to fly their decrepit planes into a fiery end above the Japanese fleet, in a few seconds to orphan their families if need be to defend all that they held dear. One wonders if an America of suburban, video-playing Nicoles, Ashleys, and Jasons shall ever see their like again.

THE IMPERIAL FLEET MOVES OUT

Midway was one of the largest sea battles of World War II and, like the battle of Leyte Gulf two years later, one of the most complex and decisive engagements in the history of naval warfare. Fought over three days across the international date line, it involved a theater more than 1,000 miles wide. The battle saw Japanese carrier attacks against Midway, carrier-to-carrier torpedo and dive-bombing, aerial dogfights between Zeros and both land- and carrier-based American fighters, submarine torpedoing and destroyer counter-depth-charging, sorties by American army high-altitude and marine dive and torpedo bombers based on Midway, and futile efforts by Japanese battleships and heavy cruisers to engage the American carriers and cruisers in naval gunfire. Men above, on, and under the vast Pacific the first week of June 1942 were fervently trying to blow each other up.

Admiral Yamamoto, the architect of the successful Japanese surprise attack on Pearl Harbor, assembled for the Midway-Aleutian offensive nearly two hundred warships—carriers, battleships, cruisers, destroyers, submarines, and troop carriers—whose combined displacement exceeded 1.5 million tons, manned by more than 100,000 sailors and pilots, and commanded by 20 admirals. Eighty-six of the ships would be engaged in the Midway theater alone. The scale of the clash with the American fleet would thus approximate the enormous numbers of combatants present at the gargantuan East-West sea battles of the past at Salamis (150,000 to 250,000) or Lepanto (180,000 to 200,000). The Japanese fleet that steamed out to Midway was the largest and most powerful flotilla in the history of naval warfare—until the Americans themselves collected an even larger and more deadly armada a little over two years later at the battle of Leyte Gulf.

The fliers on the carriers *Akagi, Kagi, Hiryu,* and *Soryu* were among Japan's best airmen and had far more years of experience than their green counterparts in the American fleet. The entire armada boasted a potential air arm of nearly seven hundred naval and land-based planes on carriers and transports, and more than three hundred near Midway alone. So confident were the Japanese of victory at Midway—"the sentry of Hawaii"—that they envisioned the campaign as a prelude to even more vast operations that would ideally send their undefeated carrier forces against New Caledonia and Fiji in early July 1942, then later that month on to bomb Sydney and Allied bases in southern Australia, before assembling the entire fleet for a knockout blow against Hawaii in early August.

By early fall 1942 Yamamoto's dream of a lightning-fast offensive against the bewildered and unprepared Americans would be complete with the occupation of Midway. After the loss of all its Pacific bases, supply lines to Australia cut, and the Pacific fleet sunk, the United States would surely ask for a negotiated peace—one that ratified Japanese control of Asia and demarcated in the Pacific clear limits to American influence. The April 18 surprise bombing attack on Tokyo by carrier-based B-25 medium bombers had only convinced the Japanese high command to hasten its summer final plans to rid the Pacific of the American nuisance.

Scholars have often faulted the various components of Yamamoto's plan, which would prove to be overly sophisticated, poorly coordinated, and possessed of too many aims: the conquest of Midway, occupation of some of the western Aleutian islands, and destruction of the American carrier fleet were difficult to obtain in unison and at times even antithetical objectives. The Japanese fleet was therefore fragmented into a series of disconnected striking forces—five at least with their own various subgroups—that were so dispersed and often without communication that the Japanese were never able to focus their vast numerical superiority at any one place.

Ideally, Yamamoto's ships would inaugurate hostilities by dispatching more than fifteen submarines east of Midway to detect the early approach of the American fleet from either Hawaii or the West Coast. The submarines could fuel marine search planes, as well as send advance notice to the main fleet concerning the size and number of the approaching enemy before torpedoing the capital ships in transit. But because of superb American intelligence concerning the entire Japanese mode of attack,

nearly all the submarines arrived too late. They gave Yamamoto no information about the Americans' progress. For most of the early battle they
lagged far behind most of the U.S. fleet, without a clue that the Americans
were in fact already off Midway and waiting for the Japanese carriers.

Next, a northern force under Vice Admiral Moshiro Hosogaya would
lead two light carriers, six heavy and light cruisers, twelve destroyers, six
submarines, and other assorted ships, along with 2,500 troops to occupy
the Aleutians—an assault that would turn out tactically successful, but
without any strategic advantage to the Japanese. Whereas the occupation
of Midway could lead to attacks on Hawaii and the headquarters of the
American fleet, no one in the Japanese admiralty could ever explain
the long-term significance of occupying one or two frigid islands in the
Bering Sea, the site of few American troops and no industry—and far
from both Hawaii and the West Coast of the United States.

Against Midway itself, the Japanese would send Admiral Nagumo's
1st Carrier Striking Force, with the *Akagi, Kaga, Hiryu,* and *Soryu,* supported by subgroups of two battleships, three cruisers, and eleven destroyers. After the carriers' planes softened up the island through repeated
bombing sorties, Rear Admiral Raizo Tanaka would arrive with twelve
transports and three destroyer transports carrying 5,000 troops to occupy
Midway. If the occupation force needed cover, or should the American
fleet take the bait and attempt to contest the invasion, Vice Admiral Takeo
Kurita would then provide further firepower for the assault with four
heavy cruisers and two destroyers—to be joined with Admiral Kondo's
even larger force of two battleships, four heavy cruisers, a light cruiser,
eight destroyers, and a light carrier. The Japanese envisioned a late-arriv-
ing, crippled, and naïve American navy, desperate to attack a succession of
decoy ships, to be pounced on in turn by ever larger and more deadly imperial carriers and battleships in waiting.

Rear Admiral Ruitaro Fujita would follow up with two seaplane carriers and two small ships to occupy nearby tiny Kure Island, in hopes of
establishing a land-based air force to aid in reconnaissance over Midway
and attacks on the American fleet. In a surface engagement the Americans
had nothing comparable to match the Japanese heavy guns, and should
the carriers lose their protective air screen or find themselves too near the
quick Japanese fleet, there was nothing in their arsenal to prevent the battleships from blasting the American ships out of the sea.

The heart of the Japanese armada was elsewhere. Four battleships,
two light cruisers, and twelve destroyers were far to the north of Midway
under Vice Admiral Takasu, in conjunction with Admiral Yamamoto's

main force of three battleships—including the monstrous 64,000-ton *Yamato*, whose 18.1-inch guns could throw enormous shells over twenty-five miles—a light cruiser, nine destroyers, and three light carriers. This northern force would cover the flanks of the Aleutian assaults, and in theory be positioned to return southwest to Midway should the Americans contest the invasion there. In Yamamoto's thinking he had created an iron chain of interlocking naval forces, spanning a thousand-mile gap from the Aleutians to Midway, which would bar all westward movement to the Americans, ensuring that there would never again be an American bombing attack on the Japanese mainland. For all its complexity, there was a certain simple logic to the Japanese plan: by blockading the northern Pacific between the Aleutians and Midway itself, Yamamoto guaranteed that either his northern or his southern forces would flush out the vastly outnumbered and bewildered Americans. The latter would either have to fight or see their islands both north and south lost. How odd that the sacrifice of fewer than a hundred green American torpedo pilots would ruin all of Yamamoto's elaborate ideas of annihilating the American Pacific fleet.

The vast distance between the two groups also meant that the numerically inferior Americans could not simultaneously protect both. Yamamoto's battleships and the carriers would act as a sort of roving reserve that would rush to the point of American counterattack, while the Aleutian and Midway assault forces and accompanying battleship and cruiser fleets completed their invasions. It was unlikely that the timid Americans would show up until the Aleutians and Midway were occupied—and then they would be met by land-based bombers from those newly acquired bases and naval planes freed from protecting vulnerable troop transports. Since the Japanese fleet was hitherto undefeated and qualitatively superior, it should not require its combined strength anyway to blast away a weak and inexperienced American challenge.

The only ostensible problem for the Japanese was that they assumed the vastly outnumbered Americans would be complacent and surprised, rather than tipped-off and waiting. Admiral Nagumo's intelligence report concluded on the eve of the battle: "Although the enemy lacks the will to fight, it is likely that he will counterattack if our occupation operations progress satisfactorily." Yamamoto apparently could not conceive that the previously beaten Americans might anticipate the landings at Midway— much less that they might arrive there first with three carriers to concentrate on the Japanese carrier force under Nagumo. But the Americans had radar on their ships and on Midway itself, which in effect would serve as an unsinkable aircraft carrier.

In the American scenario of a carrier war deliberately waged in close proximity to Midway, the match was about even—four Japanese to the American three flattops, the latter aided by auxiliary air support from the island. In Napoleonic fashion Admiral Chester Nimitz would deal with segments of Yamamoto's chain, destroying links in isolation until the odds were more even: first sink the carriers, the heart of the Japanese fleet, then prevent the more strategically important Midway landings, and finally turn to an airborne assault on Yamamoto's battleships and cruisers if need be.

Just assembling the colossal fleet had meant that the Japanese ships left ports 1,800 miles apart, and even when arriving at their destinations some ships would remain a thousand miles distant. If radio silence were to be maintained, there was little likelihood that all the components of the armada could preserve communications—critical, when a key element of the cumbersome plan was to draw out the American outnumbered fleet, to be swarmed on cue by superior forces converging from the north and south.

To oppose these forces, the Americans could scarcely scrape up three carriers—including the heavily damaged *Yorktown,* which had just limped in nearly wrecked from the battle of Coral Sea. A tiny contingent under Rear Admiral Robert Theobald was sent to the Aleutians with two heavy cruisers, three light cruisers, and ten destroyers, but was poorly deployed and played no role in preventing the Japanese from landing or attacking enemy ships. There were no American battleships in Hawaii to deploy to Midway. Instead, Admiral Nimitz hastily gathered what he had—a mere eight cruisers and fifteen destroyers. Nineteen submarines were patrolling from Midway to Pearl Harbor.

The Japanese plan was unwieldy but not in itself doomed to failure, given the imperial fleet's vast numerical superiority in every category of ship and its far more experienced crews. But as we shall see, at critical stages during the planning, fighting, and aftermath of the battle, American military personnel at all ranks were unusually innovative, even eccentric, and always unpredictable. Most were unafraid to take the initiative to craft policy when orders from superiors were either vague or nonexistent—in a fashion completely antithetical to the protocols of operations in the imperial fleet, which in turn mirrored much of the prevailing values and attitudes inherent in Japanese society. The result was that Americans improvised when plans went awry, resorted to new and innovative methods of attack when orthodoxy was unproductive—not unlike the Christians' sawing off their galley prows at Lepanto to increase cannon accuracy or Cortés sending his men into a volcano to replenish their stores of gunpowder.

WESTERN AND NON-WESTERN JAPAN

At Midway the Americans enjoyed a technological edge only in radar and communications. Their frontline carrier planes—Wildcat fighters, Devastator torpedo planes, and Dauntless dive-bombers—were uniformly inferior to Japanese models, which possessed superior speed, maneuverability, and more reliable ordnance. By 1942 Japanese torpedoes were the best in the world, American arguably the worst. The Zero fighter—light, fast, and easy to construct—was a product of engineering genius. There was nothing like it in the U.S. Army Air Corps in 1941. The four Japanese carriers themselves were every bit as modern as British and American models. Japan had built battleships that were the largest on the seas: the *Yamato* and soon-to-be-launched *Musashi,* whose gross tonnages and armaments were far superior to any surface ship in either the British or the American navy at the outbreak of the war.

Clearly, the American victory at Midway was not due—as alleged by some postbellum Japanese observers—to the superiority of Western technology. Indeed, for well over half a century Japan had adopted many of the tenets of European military organization and methods of armament, as part of a massive revolution in Japanese society to embrace Western science and industrial production. By the beginning of the twentieth century, a state with few natural resources had become a veritable world power largely through its embrace of the Western way of warfare. Japanese ships at Midway were the embodiment of Western, not Asian, military science.

Japan had never been colonized or conquered by Westerners until 1945. Its distance from Europe, proximity to an isolationist and inward-looking nineteenth-century America, absence of inviting land and plentiful resources, and enormous hungry population made it unattractive to would-be Western conquistadors. Yet in its initial, belated encounters with the West, nineteenth-century Japan had consciously decided to emulate and improve on, rather than reject, Western methods of industrial production and technological research. Whereas the airplane was invented in America, the self-propelled ironclad battleship and aircraft carrier in Britain and America, and the entire notion of a seagoing, oil-burning navy entirely a European development, the Japanese by 1941 had matched, and in some cases outpaced, both the British and the Americans in naval and aerial designs. Unlike other Asian countries—China especially stands out—Japan in the latter nineteenth century had gradually begun to ignore its innate cultural inhibitions to adapting wholesale Western ideas of capitalism, industrial development, and military operations. Even its cultural conservatives conceded that Western barbarians and devils could never be resisted simply by superior courage and samurai vigor. Japan's survival would be found through the adoption of European weapons and methods of mass production—with Japanese ingenuity at each step of the way ready to improve where warranted.

After the first contact in the mid-sixteenth century with the Portuguese, from whom they learned to fabricate firearms, the Japanese within a few decades were equipping entire armies with improved cannon and muskets—and in the process threatened the samurai hierarchy, whose martial capital hinged on a spiritual, antitechnological, xenophobic, and antimodern foundation. In reaction to such new technology, feudal lords gradually disarmed the population and prevented the further importation of arms as part of a general ban against all foreign influence. The result was that by the early seventeenth century nearly all trade outside of Japan was outlawed. Oceangoing vessels were prohibited. Christianity was made illegal and most foreigners deported. By 1635 Japan was once again closed off from any contact whatsoever with "big-nosed, smelly" barbarians, a situation that was to remain static until Admiral Matthew Perry sailed into Tokyo Bay in 1853 with an armada of formidable American warships. By then Japanese technological progress had all but stagnated, and there remained only a few antiquated gunpowder weapons in the entire national arsenal with which to oppose the Americans.

Perry's cannon and explosive shells, his steam-powered fleet, and his rifle-carrying marines convinced the Japanese to admit foreign ships. By 1854 when Perry returned to Japan from China, the Japanese formally signed treaties allowing American ships access to their waters and free sailing in the surrounding seas. Several European nations followed suit and began trading with Japan and interfering throughout the entire Asian subcontinent. But from such humiliation came radical change. In contrast to Eastern resentment in China and Southeast Asia, the Japanese reaction against foreign encroachment was to get even rather than merely angry, as they recognized the folly of an imperial power's rejection of Western science. After a few futile efforts at resistance, Japanese culture in a sweeping and unprecedented revolution, in both the ideological and the material sense, began to adopt Western manufacturing and banking practices at full scale.

By the last quarter of the nineteenth century the power of the Japanese warlords was at an end. In 1877 in Satsuma a last-ditch uprising of samurai warriors, armed with traditional swords and matchlock muskets, was soundly defeated by a conscripted army, outfitted and drilled in the European style, proving to the Japanese that the Western way of war trumped class, tradition, and national heritage and was insidiously effective in its allegiance solely to battlefield utility. The samurai clans were now mere curiosities, and the population united behind an emperor and the new effort to emulate the modern European nation-state:

> Orders for rifles and cannon went to France. . . . When Germany defeated France in 1871, the Japanese quickly switched to the victors. Soon Japanese soldiers were goose-stepping and following Prussian infantry tactics. Japanese naval officers, most of whom were *samurai* from the once rebellious Satsuma clan, learned from the British Royal Navy, often after years at sea aboard British ships. Japan's new ships would be built in England, too, for Britain ruled the sea and the Japanese wished to learn from the best. Japan's Westernization was not confined to military matters. Western arts, literature, science, music, and fashion also flourished. University students feasted on anything Western . . . as *samurai* became industrialists, railroad magnates, and bankers. (R. Edgerton, *Warriors of the Rising Sun,* 44)

The result was that by 1894 the Japanese had driven China out of Korea—thanks to a completely Westernized military that was better organized and armed than any force in Asia. Whereas the Chinese had only haphazardly imported European guns and ships, and then generally resisted the infrastructure necessary to fabricate their own modern arms industry, the Japanese army and navy were employing the fruits of Japan's own nascent but burgeoning arms production and adopting the latest European tactical doctrine, with their own innovative efforts such as night attacks and mass assaults at perceived weak points.

During the Boxer Rebellion of 1900, Japanese expeditionary forces proved to be among the best armed, disciplined, and organized of all the European-led contingents that marched in relief to Peking. And when the Russo-Japanese War broke out in 1904, the Japanese, although vastly outnumbered, quickly proved not only that their naval and land forces were better structured and disciplined than the much larger Russian contingents but that their guns, ships, ammunition, and modern methods of supply were vastly superior as well. Their naval gunfire was especially deadly, and applied with far better accuracy and rates of fire and at greater distances than the Russians'.

In one of the most remarkable revolutions in the history of arms, Japan found herself in more than a quarter century (1870–1904) the near military equal of the best of European powers. Although lacking the population and natural resources of its immediate neighbors Russia and China, Japan had proved that with a topflight Westernized military it could defeat forces far greater in number. Japan is thus the classic refutation of the now popular idea that topography, resources such as iron and coal deposits, or genetic susceptibility to disease and other natural factors largely determine cultural dynamism and military prowess. The Japanese mainland was unchanging—before, during, and after its miraculous century-long military ascendancy—but what was not static was its radical nineteenth-century emulation of elements of the Western tradition completely foreign to its native heritage.

Not only were Japanese admirals and generals dressed and titled like their European counterparts, their ships and guns were nearly identical as well. Unfortunately for their Asian adversaries, the Westernized Japanese military was not a mere passing phase. Japan envisioned Western arms and tactics not as an auxiliary to centuries-long Japanese military doctrines or as a veneer of ostentation, but as a radical, fundamental, and permanent restructuring of Japan's armed forces that would lead to hegemony in Asia.

Yet the Japanese wide-scale adoption of Western technology was also not always what it seemed at first glance. There remained stubborn Japanese cultural traditions that would resurface to hamper a truly unblinkered Western approach to scientific research and weapons development. The Japanese had always entertained an ambiguous attitude about their own breakneck efforts at Westernization:

> After the visit of Perry, the Japanese had to admit that Western technology, if not all other aspects of Western culture, was also far superior to her own. Admissions like these would be unsettling for any people, and they were especially galling for the Japanese because, more than most peoples on earth, they were imbued with a sense of the greatness, the inherent superiority, even the divinity of their own "Yamato" race. The ambivalence of the Japanese about their worthiness was palpably painful. Because many felt

inferior, they came to fear and hate Westerners as they had earlier feared and hated the Chinese. When Westerners later proved to be vulnerable, the temptation to destroy them grew. (R. Edgerton, *Warriors of the Rising Sun*, 306)

Most unfortunate was the official stance of the Japanese government that slowly sought to form a systematic apology for the admitted incongruity of a country adopting wholesale the technology and industrial processes of an entirely different—and purportedly corrupt and barbaric—culture. The eventual answer that emerged was framed in mostly racist and chauvinist terms: Europeans were derided not merely as decadent, ugly, smelly, and self-centered but also as innately spoiled, pampered, and soft—lazy men who triumphed only through clever inventions and machines rather than the inherent courage of their manhood.

Already by the early twentieth century, a sophisticated Japanese exegesis was crystallizing about the entire relationship between European technology and Japanese culture: Japan's was a superior warrior race that had merely grafted ideas from abroad to allow its more heroic fighters to compete on a level playing field. Thus, while industrialists and research scientists would proceed with modernizing the Japanese economy and military along European lines, the populace at large would remain a largely hierarchical, autocratic, and Asian society—notions of Western liberalism were to be rejected as vehemently as European science was to be emulated.

Japan would continue to be governed by arcane notions of shame that dictated every aspect of public behavior, delineating how the average Japanese might express emotion, act in public, and spend money on housing and material goods. Devotion to the emperor would be absolute. Individualism in the decadent Western sense would not follow on the heels of the importation of European technology. The military would enjoy almost total control of the government. Thus, the classic paradox immediately arose: could modern and rapidly evolving Western arms and military organization be integrated into a static Japanese culture *without* the accompanying political and cultural baggage of individualism, consensual government, laissez-faire capitalism, and free expression? It is one argument of this book that the Western way of war is grounded not merely in technological supremacy but in an entire array of political, social, and cultural institutions that are responsible for military advantages well beyond the possession of sophisticated weapons. Superior technology cannot merely be imported; if it is not to become immediately static and therefore obsolete, the accompanying practices of free inquiry, the scientific method, unfettered research, and capitalist production must be adopted as well.

The absence of large reservoirs of natural resources inside Japan, the rise of fascism in Europe during the 1920s and 1930s, the history of racism by European colonists, and the discrimination against Asian immigrants to America helped to solidify the position of Japanese nationalists and right-wing militarists before World War II. For a small country like Japan, without either land or material reserves, but strapped with a large population, surrounded by a European colonial presence in Hong Kong, Singapore, Macao, the Philippines, and Southeast Asia, and confronted with a strong American military in the Pacific, it was natural that ancestral veins of samurai bravery should be reworked for new ore. The old chivalric code of Bushido, the Shinto idea of a chosen Japanese people, and the traditional exultation of the warrior might be transmogrified into a harsh and patently racist idea in the industrial age that foreigners were weak and cowardly and therefore fair game for the worst sort of atrocities when the inevitable war broke out.

There were at least two primary foundations of prewar Japanese military thought. The first was the state religion of Shinto—unbroken imperial sovereignty of the living god, the emperor, the divine origin of the Japanese race, and the manifest destiny of Japan. In this regard, the blending of political and religious authority was not unlike that of the Achaemenids, Arabs, Aztecs, and Ottomans and entirely antithetical to their respective Western adversaries. Second was the ancestral and feudal samurai code that was reinterpreted and refashioned as Bushido by nineteenth-century militarists—the idea that the warrior values of a medieval elite could be superimposed upon the entire new nation-state of modern Japan.

This other strain in Japanese culture—the lingering suspicion of things foreign—and the outbreak of hostilities with China in 1931 made the importation of the most recent technological innovations from abroad more difficult. The more a bellicose Japan sought a nationalist but Westernized military, the less likely America and Britain were to extend it easy financial credits, the latest technology, and imported resources. At home the more Japan sought the most recent designs in foreign military hardware, the more its own hypocrisy would become apparent. After all, it was again borrowing superior science from a society it ostensibly dismissed as corrupt and inferior, and yet it refused to undergo the radical political and cultural restructuring along Western lines that would ensure sustainable technological parity. The same paradox would plague much of the Third World for the rest of the twentieth century: buying Western technology is not the same as maintaining it, adapting it, fabricating it, and training a citizenry to use and improve upon it. Japan, for example, had even better planes than the Americans at Midway, but notions of individualism, freedom, and politics quite different from Western cultures. The rise of Japanese military governments, with their insistence on emperor worship, continued to stifle free debate, individualism, and popular dissent—at the moment when such an enlightened approach to research and industrial policy was most critical for the continued growth and innovation of Japan's arms industry. This combination of Western hostility toward Japanese militarism, and Japan's own reluctance to embrace an open and free society, resulted in a general stagnation of technological innovation—and an occasional inability to make use of even native genius.

While the Japanese navy was technologically the equal of, or perhaps superior to, the Americans at Midway in June 1942, such parity could not last once the American government, private industry, and the citizenry at large mobilized for war. In fact, within a mere year and a half after Pearl Harbor, not only were Japanese forces numerically inferior to the American military, but in key areas such as aeronautical design, artillery, tanks, radar, nuclear research, medicine, food supply, base construction, and the mass production of matériel, they were far behind as well. By 1944 the Japanese air force, army, and navy were more or less using the same equipment with which they had started the war, while their American counterparts were producing planes, ships, and vehicles scarcely imaginable in 1941.

About the only reason for American weapons inferiority at Midway was a general complacence following World War I, fueled by the country's utopian ideas of world peace, by its isolationism, and by an economic depression. By late 1941 the Americans were still awakening from nearly two decades of abject neglect of military preparedness and were not free from sluggish economic growth and high unemployment. In contrast, the Japanese for nearly ten years had devoted a much larger percentage of their much smaller national product to defense expenditure, and had amassed far more firsthand empirical research from the battlefields of China. At Midway—for perhaps the last moment in the war—the Japanese had both better and more numerous planes and ships.

There is also no real evidence that the Westernized Japanese military was reluctant to engage in decisive battle in the fashion of head-on Western practice. Ostensibly, the Japanese navy was every bit as aggressive as the American. Its nineteenth-century adaptation of German tactics of frontal charges and mass assault would prove disastrous against American army machine guns, automatic rifles, and field artillery. Its huge battleships were proof that its navy envisioned using superior firepower to blast enemy surface ships to pieces in set artillery duels, as had happened against the Russians in 1904. While it is true that the indigenous military traditions of samurai warfare had strong ritual elements that could elevate form over function—firearms although known since the sixteenth century were more or less outlawed for the next two hundred years—by 1941 the Japanese navy was aggressive and often as willing as the Americans to enter in a head-to-head battle to the death. Along with the importation of Western arms had come the Western idea of frontal assault.

Where the Japanese were at a distinct disadvantage in their approach to Western battle practice was in the failure to use such decisive tactical engagements to wage a relentless war of total annihilation—a ghastly practice that was mostly outside their samurai traditions. The Japanese were not comfortable with the rather different Western notion of seeking out the enemy without deception, to engage in bitter shock collision, one whose deadliness would prove decisive for the side with the greater firepower, discipline, and numbers.

Instead, against the Russians in 1904–5, and the Chinese from 1931 to 1937, the Japanese military fought a succession of brilliant battles, but such victories in themselves were often left incomplete and not necessarily seen as part of an overall strategic plan of destroying the enemy outright until he lost the ability to wage war. The Japanese knew plenty about killing thousands of combatants on the battlefield, and they were willing to sacrifice even more of their own in suicidal and heroic frontal assaults against entrenched positions, but such martial ferocity was not the same as the Western desire for continual and sustained shock encounters until one side was victorious or annihilated. In the Japanese as in the Islamic way of war, surprise, sudden attack, battlefield calamity, and disgrace should force an opponent to the bargaining table to discuss concessions.

In the case of the Pacific War the Japanese preference for diversion and surprise at the expense of a series of frontal actions meant that often key opportunities were lost. After a brilliant unexpected attack on Pearl Harbor that left the Americans defenseless, there was no follow-up plan to keep bombing the island into submission, followed perhaps by raiding the West Coast ports to destroy the last home of the Pacific carrier fleet. Instead, Admiral Nagumo's carriers immediately sailed away from Hawaii after the initial Sunday morning attacks of December 7, leaving the critical American fuel tanks that supplied the entire Pacific fleet unscathed—and the American carriers undiscovered and untouched. At the battle of Coral Sea in the weeks before Midway, a tactical Japanese victory led to a strategic defeat when the Japanese, stunned by the fierce American resistance and the loss of dozens of their best carrier pilots, postponed the invasion of Port Moresby. Both the battle of Midway and the later monumental engagement of Leyte Gulf saw Japanese tactics fail largely through the dispersion of their forces in the naïve belief that the enemy could be deceived rather than encountered and blasted apart:

> They overvalued surprise, which had worked so well at the beginning and always assumed they could get it. They loved diversionary tactics—forces popping up at odd places to confuse the enemy and pull him off base. They believed that the pattern for decisive battle was the same at sea as on the land—lure the enemy into an unfavorable tactical situation, cut off his retreat, drive into the flanks, and then concentrate for the kill. (S. Morison, *Coral Sea, Midway, and Submarine Actions, May 1942–August 1942*, 78)

Japanese mobility and ruse were reflected not just in Admiral Yamamoto's famous dictum about the relative industrial capacity of the two belligerents—that he could raise hell in the Pacific for six months but could promise nothing after that. Rather, almost all serious strategists in the Japanese military also acknowledged their discomfort with a quite novel situation of all-out warfare with the Americans and British that would require continual head-on confrontations with the Anglo-American fleet. In 1941 no one in the Japanese high command seemed aware that a surprise attack on the Americans would in Western eyes lead to total war, in which the United States would either destroy its adversary or face annihilation in the attempt. But, then, it was a historic error of non-Westerners, beginning with Xerxes' invasion of Greece, to assume that democracies were somehow weak and timid. Although slow to anger, Western constitutional governments usually preferred wars of annihilation—wiping the Melians off the map of the Aegean, sowing the ground of Carthage with salt, turning Ireland into a near wasteland, wasting Jerusalem before reoccupying it, driving an entire culture of Native Americans onto reservations, atomizing Japanese cities—and were far more deadly adversaries than military dynasts and autocrats. Despite occasional brilliant adaptation of trickery and surprise, and the clear record of success in "the indirect approach" to war—Epaminondas's great raid into Messenia (369 B.C.) and Sherman's March to the Sea (1864) are notable examples—Western militaries continued to believe that the most economic way of waging war was to find the enemy, collect sufficient forces to overwhelm him, and then advance directly and openly to annihilate him on the battlefield—all part of a cultural tradition to end hostilities quickly, decisively, and utterly. To read of American naval operations in World War II is to catalog a series of continual efforts to advance westward toward Japan, discover and devastate the Japanese fleet, and physically wrest away all territory belonging to the Japanese government until reaching the homeland itself. The American sailors at Midway were also the first wave of an enormous draft that would mobilize more than 12 million citizens into the armed forces. In the manner of the Romans after Cannae or the democracies in World War I, American political representatives had voted for war with Japan. Polls revealed near unanimous public approval for a ghastly conflict of annihilation against the perpetrators of Pearl Harbor. The United States would also continue to hold elections throughout the conflict as the elected government crafted one of the most radical industrial and cultural revolutions in the history of the Republic in turning the country into a huge arms-producing camp.

The Japanese, in contrast, had only sporadically adopted nineteenth-century European ideas of constitutional government and civic militarism—and both had been discredited by military regimes of the 1930s. Japanese military thinkers believed that a far superior method of fielding large and spirited armies—and one more in line with their own cultural traditions—lay in inculcating the entire population with a fanatical devotion to the emperor and a shared belief in the inevitable rule of the Japanese people. A few wise and all-knowing military officers alone could appreciate the Japanese warrior spirit, and most of them saw little need for the public to debate the wisdom of attacking the largest industrial power in the world:

> What Westerners did not realize was that underneath the veneer of modernity and westernization, Japan was still Oriental and that her plunge from feudalism to imperialism had come so precipitously that her leaders, who were interested solely in Western methods, not Western values, had neither the time nor inclination to develop liberalism and humanitarianism. (J. Toland, *The Rising Sun,* vol. 1, 74)

After the battle of Midway, the magnitude of the disaster was kept from the Japanese people—even the wounded were kept in isolation—

who were told only of a great "victory" in the Aleutians. In sharp contrast, the American electorate not only received intimate details of the battle but could actually read in a major newspaper the vital information that Japanese codes had been cracked before the shooting even began. Individualism was subsumed in Japanese group consensus:

> Because it [the Japanese leadership] was imbued with the national ideology it was difficult if not impossible for it to analyze the military situation in a coldly realistic, scientific manner. Japanese military training emphasized "spiritual mobilization"—*Seishin Kyoiku*—as the most important aspect of preparing troops for battle. Essentially, this was indoctrination in the spirit and principles of the Japanese national ideology: the identification of the individual with the nation and his subordination to the will of the Emperor. It was the continuation of a process which had begun much earlier in the schools. One reason for conscription in Japan was the opportunity presented for the military to train virtually the entire male population in the ideals of *Bushido* and the *Kodo* (the Imperial Way). (S. Huntington, *The Soldier and the State*, 128)

The result was that for most of the war Japan deployed large forces and highly motivated troops—at Midway there were far more Japanese men under arms than American, and they were clearly as spirited and eager for battle. But the absence of civic militarism—the idea of a free citizenry voting to craft the conditions of its own military service through consensual government—would also mean a different kind of warrior: the often-stereotyped fanaticism rather than contractual obligation, spirit rather than cold reason, uniformity over individuality, the embrace of suicide in addition to sacrifice, and official praise of anonymous national spirit in lieu of individual citation and personal honorific decree. These more subtle cultural differences would clearly be manifest at Midway—and they would also help explain why a numerically superior foe was so soundly defeated.

Much is made of Japan's seemingly marked disadvantage in natural resources, its smaller population, and its tiny landmass. But at Midway, Japan had access from its newly acquired empire to plenty of oil for its ships and food for its sailors, who vastly outnumbered the Americans. We should remember that Japan's population was nearly half that of the United States. Its burgeoning empire in the Pacific brought it a rich supply of strategic metals, rubber, and oil, and it had a good decade head start in equipping its military. For all practical purposes, with the Russian border almost silent by

1941, and large parts of occupied Manchuria relatively dormant for most of 1941–42, Japan was fighting a single adversary in the Anglo-American Pacific military—quite unlike the United States, which was devoting the majority of its equipment and most of its armed forces to defeating the Germans and Italians and supplying the British, Chinese, and Soviets thousands of miles away. America, *not* Japan, was in the unenviable and unwise predicament of fighting a two-front war with deadly adversaries and poorer allies. Whereas America clearly adopted a policy of defeating the Nazis first, nearly all of Japan's resources were devoted to attacking the Anglo-Americans in Asia and the Pacific. The Japanese for well over a half century had made critical transferences of Western economic and military practices in creating a modern navy and a sophisticated industrial economy. At least for a brief period of a year or two, this long-standing adaptation of European technology had allowed it to compete with any Western military power, as its stunning naval victories in the first six months of World War II attested. Once the conflict began, Japan had secure sources of raw products and an entire energized military nursed on the religion of Japanese racial superiority, martial values, and imperial destiny.

Religious fervor, Bushido, hari-kari, going down with the ship, and the kamikazes lent the Japanese a sense of arrogance in victory—and fanaticism and fatalism in defeat. But such practices often had negative ramifications in the mundane practice of war itself and would prove no substitute for the freewheeling individualism of a "decadent" foe. Brilliant admirals are still needed after their ships blow up. Seasoned pilots are more valuable as instructors than as suicide bombers. Junior officers who are vocal rather than silent are critical assets; assessing rather than accepting blame may be shameful, but it is often indispensable in war; and the expertise of skilled generals is lost when they disembowel themselves. By the same token, ingenious Japanese sailors have hands-on experience that admirals should freely hear about. War planners need to fear an informed and aroused electorate; and arguing with an emperor over strategy is often a more fruitful exercise than bowing in his presence.

Despite claims of creating a Greater East Asian Co-Prosperity Sphere among conquered fellow Orientals in Korea, Southeast Asia, China, and the Pacific islands, Japan possessed no sustained tradition of a free voting citizenry or the idea that non-Japanese Asians would wish to join the Japanese army in the hopes of someday receiving the same constitutional guarantees and freedoms as the Japanese themselves. Japan would live and die by the race card—defining (and demonizing) America as "white" and thus Japan as a kindred but clearly superior "yellow" people. Inside Japan itself during the battle of Midway, there were no free press, no elections, and a military dictatorship that functioned ostensibly at the beck and call of an emperor-king. The result was the fascinating anomaly that whereas the Asian countries surrounding Japan had been subjected to decades of onerous French, Dutch, German, British, and American racism and imperialism, indigenous populations, after initial celebrations greeting their Asian liberators, were more likely to aid the "white" Americans than their brethren Asian Japanese. After all, the elected government of the former might at some distant time extend independence to its subjects and satellites; the dictatorship of the latter—self-defined as a race rather than an idea—spelled only economic exploitation with no chance of parity at any future date. The hearts of men in a democracy are more likely to change and evolve than the will of the emperor.

Whereas in theory the Americans could be a culture rather than a race (although blacks, for example, were still shamefully denied the vote in many American states and fought in the Pacific in segregated roles, and often as cooks and orderlies), the entire creed of Japanese militarism rested on the implicit assumption of innate Japanese racial superiority over its "inferior" Asian subject peoples. Had Japan embraced a Western democratic tradition and a cultural shift to individualism and self-expression, it might well have been able to galvanize the entire Asian subcontinent against the grasping Europeans—but, then, under that scenario there might well have been no need for World War II.

If the absence of such liberal institutions hampered the overall Japanese war effort on June 4, 1942, it was the regimentation of the Japanese military culture itself, seen mostly in the sheer absence of individuality, that would prove so critical in such a fast-moving and far-ranging battle like Midway. Close examination of the battle suggests that the Americans' intrinsic faith in individualism, a product itself of a long tradition of consensual government and free expression, at every turn of the encounter proved decisive. Far better than luck, surprise, or accident, the power of the individual himself explains the Americans' incredible victory.

SPONTANEITY AND INDIVIDUAL INITIATIVE AT MIDWAY

It would be a caricature of the complex relationship of soldier to state to suggest that Americans at Midway were individualists whereas Japanese sailors and pilots were unthinking automatons. Obedience is the nature of military life in nearly every culture. Without a chain of command, orders and military discipline cannot exist. The American navy was highly disciplined at Midway, and there were thousands of imaginative and brilliant Japanese soldiers who did give their best ad hoc efforts to remedy the disaster on June 4.

That being said, individualism was a different notion in the traditional culture of Japan, whose citizenry for centuries had seen little need to elect representatives, freely to write and say what they wished, or to demonstrate spontaneously for a redress of grievances:

> A willingness to subordinate the individual to the group, to sacrifice individual interests for the good of the family, for the good of the village, and for the good of the nation (it being understood that in the case of incompatibility of these goods, the good of the larger group must come first), combined with a stress on harmony in the family, in the village, and in the nation which held that any threat to unity was morally wrong, and he who created conflict by a challenge to the status quo was necessarily the wrongdoer. (R. Dore, *Land Reform in Japan*, 393)

Even those scholars who resent the stereotypical and Eurocentric view that the Japanese put little premium on individualism—and thus consensual government itself—have conceded that the Japanese notion of the individual evolved differently from the practice in the West:

> To the Western reader, even to one who lived through the 1930s in Germany, the Japanese military's authoritarian pyramid of support, based on these stratified hamlets, must seem suffocating and restrictive. How many of us would have been willing to subordinate our individuality completely to family, village, and nation? And yet there is no reason to conclude that Japanese who did not belong to the prominent stratum of this organic society believed that they were being suffocated, or dictated to, or if they did, minded it. (R. Smethurst, *A Social Basis for Prewar Japanese Militarism*, 182)

We do not wish to suggest that highly motivated and disciplined Japanese troops, who were uniformly courageous and without exception willing to die for their emperor, were therein less capable warriors than the Americans. Rather, in a complex and drawn-out battle like Midway, and even more so during the Pacific War in general, there were numerous opportunities lost to the imperial fleet due to a lack of initiative endemic within the Japanese military—and this was typical rather than exceptional of Japanese society at large. Mitsuo Fuchida and Masatake Okumiya, high-ranking veterans of the Japanese navy, offer a near Thucydidean analysis of their imperial navy's defeat at Midway:

> In the final analysis, the root cause of Japan's defeat, not alone in the Battle of Midway but in the entire war, lies deep in the Japanese national character. There is an irrationality and impulsiveness about our people which results in actions that are haphazard and often contradictory. A tradition of provincialism makes us narrow-minded and dogmatic, reluctant to discard prejudices and slow to adopt even necessary improvements if they require a new concept. Indecisive and vacillating, we succumb readily to conceit, which in turn makes us disdainful of others. Opportunistic but lacking in a spirit of daring and independence, we are wont to place reliance on others and to truckle to superiors. (M. Fuchida and M. Okumiya, *Midway, the Battle That Doomed Japan*, 247)

In at least four critical ways—the breaking of the Japanese naval codes, the repair of the carrier *Yorktown*, the nature of the U.S. naval command, and the behavior of American pilots—the American faith in individuality rather than group consensus, spontaneity rather than rote, and informality rather than hierarchy proved decisive at Midway.

The Code Breakers

The most obvious contrast was in the critical sphere of intelligence gathering, which may have decided the battle before it had begun. The deciphering of constantly altered encoded messages, as opposed to behind-the-lines espionage and covert intelligence gathering in general, is a fine art. It combines complex mathematical skills, a sophisticated knowledge of linguistics, a social and historical awareness of the context in which secret messages are transmitted, familiarity with the mechanics of radio transmission, and a commonsense appraisal of what is likely rather than what is absolutely proved to be transmitted. The example of the brilliant British efforts at cracking top-secret German codes—the Bletchley Park decrypts of Wehrmacht telegraphed messages collectively known as UL-TRA—illustrates that the best code breakers are individualistic, often eccentric thinkers, from all walks of life, though often overrepresented by those formerly ensconced in university mathematics and language departments.

Such highly creative minds function best when given autonomy and a general relaxation from protocols of military discipline. The persona of the decipherer is often not merely ill suited but antithetical to military regimentation. The American navy's cryptanalysts, in their informality and nonconformity, seem similar to the unorthodox renegades who created the computer revolution forty years later in the Silicon Valley of California. It is surely no accident that of all the belligerents in World War II, the British and the Americans, with formal military branches of cryptanalysis dating back to World War I and completely autonomous universities, were the most accomplished code breakers—and the Japanese the most dismal.

Before the Japanese fleet arrived anywhere near Midway, the American high command knew approximately the general location, direction, timetable, and objectives of Yamamoto's armada. The frantic American efforts to fortify and equip the once mostly neglected Midway with planes, artillery, and troops; the rapid mustering of the American naval counterresponse; the failure of the Japanese submarines to find, much less attack, the American fleet; and the safe transit of the American carriers to a strategic point to lie in wait for the arriving Japanese ships were all due to the American navy's breaking of Japanese encoded telegraphed messages. By mid-May 1942 Midway was suddenly bristling with guns, planes, and defenders, and it is hard to imagine that the Japanese invasion force could have easily taken the main island, even had their fleet knocked out the American carriers.

The men generally credited with pioneering the American navy's effort at cracking the critical top Japanese naval code—known as JN-25 of some 45,000 five-digit numbers—were Commanders Joseph J. Rochefort and Laurence Safford. "I didn't keep very good files," Rochefort confessed of his work. "I carried it all in my head" (G. Prange, *Miracle at Midway*, 20). In slippers and smoking jacket, Rochefort ran an unusually autonomous Pacific Fleet Combat Intelligence Unit (known as HYPO), which was more or less given free rein by Safford in a windowless basement office at Pearl Harbor to decipher Japanese transmissions as it saw best:

> It is difficult to determine which of the two was the more eccentric. Safford, who graduated from the Naval Academy at Annapolis in 1916, was one of those people who are the despair of uniform tailors as well as orderly or-

ganizations. He wore his hair in the "mad-professor" style and talked disjointedly because his mouth could not keep up with his mind; his forte was pure mathematics. Rochefort was mild-mannered, dedicated, and serious but also persistent, energetic, and impatient of hierarchies and bureaucracy, his mind unfettered by orthodox officer training. (D. van der Vat, *The Pacific Campaign, World War II,* 88–89)

Rochefort's tight-knit group received the full support of the traditional Admiral Nimitz, who was not in the least fazed by his men's appearance or the manner in which HYPO was run. True, the freethinking, strange-looking assortment of unmilitary types raised eyebrows elsewhere in the American high command—Admiral King was unimpressed with their operation. But it is impossible to imagine their counterparts in the Japanese navy, in which such informality, neglect of protocol, queer dress and appearance, failure to keep meticulous records, and a general disdain for military life could not be excused on the premise that a collection of intellectuals and assorted oddballs needed such freedom and exemption to further the war effort.

Most serious students of Midway have no hesitation in attributing much of the American victory to Rochefort's effort. Samuel Eliot Morison concluded that Midway "was a victory of intelligence, bravely and wisely applied" (*Coral Sea, Midway, and Submarine Actions, May 1942–August 1942,* 158). The Japanese veterans and historians Fuchida and Okumiya concur in their analysis of the first major naval defeat of the Japanese in modern times:

[I]t is beyond the slightest possibility of doubt that the advance discovery of the Japanese plan to attack was the foremost single and immediate cause of Japan's defeat. Viewed from the Japanese side, this success of the enemy's intelligence translated itself into a failure on our part—a failure to take adequate precautions for guarding the secrecy of our plans. . . . But it was a victory of American intelligence in a much broader sense than this. Equally as important as the positive achievements of the enemy's intelligence on this occasion was the negatively bad and ineffective functioning of Japanese intelligence. (*Midway, the Battle That Doomed Japan,* 232)

The individualism of Rochefort and his group—and their ability and freedom to function successfully within the American military—were representative of a long Western emphasis on self-expression and initiative that were dividends of constitutional government, market capitalism, and personal freedom. Hundreds of brave Japanese sailors would be cremated at Midway because an officer working in his slippers knew they were coming.

The Repair of the Yorktown

If intelligence gave the Americans prior warning of the Japanese plan of attack, the amazing restoration of the damaged aircraft carrier *Yorktown* ensured that there would be three, not two, American carriers to meet Admiral Nagumo's four. Without the vital role of the *Yorktown*'s air squadrons in sinking the Japanese carriers, and the carrier's drawing the entire Japanese counteroffensive away from the *Enterprise* and *Hornet,* the battle could easily have been lost. The constant dogfighting of Jimmy Thatch's Wildcat fighters, the superb dive-bombing of Max Leslie's SBDs, and the sacrifice of Lem Massey's Devastators would not have been possible were it not for the innovative repair work on their mother ship done a few days earlier at Pearl Harbor.

The *Yorktown* had suffered major damage less than a month before Midway, receiving at least one direct bomb hit and numerous near misses on May 8 during the battle of Coral Sea. Japanese naval bombers had ruined the flight deck, destroyed galleries and bulkheads deep inside the ship, lowered her speed to twenty-five knots, and cracked her armor belt. Several near misses had acted like depth charges and cracked apart her fuel lines, resulting in massive oil slicks. She limped back into Pearl Harbor on May 27, with interior electrical cables and fuel tanks ruined. Her air squadrons were decimated from losses to Japanese planes and antiaircraft fire. The Japanese at any rate were convinced that *Yorktown* had sunk in the Coral Sea. Most professional American estimates forecast that a thorough repair job would require at least three months, and possibly six to make her perfectly seaworthy.

Instead, work began minutes after *Yorktown* had reached the Pearl Harbor dry dock. Before the water had even drained completely from the yard, engineers, maintenance technicians, and assorted fabricators, accompanied by Admiral Nimitz himself, were walking around the huge ship in hip boots, inspecting the damage and jotting down needed materials. Thousands of individual agendas were immediately set into motion:

Over 1,400 men—shipfitters, shipwrights, machinists, welders, electricians—poured in, over and under the ship; they and the yard shopmen worked in shifts the rest of that day and the next and during the whole of two nights, making the bulkhead stanchions and deck plates necessary to restore the ship's structural strength, and replacing the wiring, instruments and fixtures damaged in the blast. (S. Morison, *Coral Sea, Midway, and Submarine Actions, May 1942–August 1942*, 81)

Local residents complained of power outages as hundreds of electric arc welders drained the island's power grid. Much of the work was done ad hoc without blueprints or formal instruction:

There was no time for plans or sketches. The men worked directly with the steel beams and bars brought on the ship. Coming to a damaged frame, burners would take out the worst of it; fitters would line up a new section, cut it to match the contour of the damage; riggers and welders would move in, "tacking" the new piece in place. Then on to the next job. . . . (W. Lord, *Incredible Victory*, 36–37)

The result was that less than sixty-eight hours after she had arrived, on Saturday morning, May 30, *Yorktown*, with electricians and mechanics still on board, outfitted with new planes and replacement pilots, left dry dock. The last repairmen left by motor launch as the carrier headed out of port to meet Admiral Nagumo's carriers. In celebration of the amazing feat, the band of the carrier that was heading farther west, not back east as once promised, ironically played "California, Here I Come" on the patched-together flight deck.

Far different was the Japanese reaction to damage done to and loss of pilots of their two newest and most deadly carriers, *Shokaku* and *Zuikaku*, when the latter returned from the same battle of Coral Sea. Of the *Shokaku*, which sailed into the Kure naval base (ten days *earlier* than *Yorktown* arrived at Pearl Harbor, and with far less structural damage), the fleet's air commander, Captain Yoshitake Miwa, concluded that its damage was not serious but nevertheless might require three months of repair work. Her sister carrier, the *Zuikaku*, although utterly untouched by the Americans, had lost 40 percent of her aircrews at Coral Sea; thus, she sat in port in excellent condition during the entire battle of Midway waiting for replacement planes and pilots. The contrast between the American and Japanese responses to repairing the respective damage from the Coral Sea engagement was undeniable:

He [Nimitz] must have every available flattop, hence the drive and urgency behind his pressure to put the crippled *Yorktown* in fighting trim. This was a tremendous performance and a dramatic preliminary victory. In contrast, the Japanese dawdled over the repair of *Shokaku* and in replenishing *Zuikaku,* secure in their confidence that they could lick the hell out of the U.S. Pacific Fleet without the help of those two Pearl Harbor veterans. (G. Prange, *Miracle at Midway,* 384)

Had the roles been reversed—innovative command and repair crews being turned loose at Kure, not Pearl Harbor—then Admiral Nagumo would have faced two, not three, American carriers with *six* flattops, not four. In that scenario it is difficult to see how the *Enterprise* and *Hornet* could have escaped sinking.

We know of the brilliance of the American command that insisted on the *Yorktown*'s sudden repair. But what is mostly lost to the historical record are the hundreds of individual decisions and impromptu ingenuity of American welders, riveters, electricians, carpenters, and supply officers who on their own and without written orders turned a nearly ruined ship into a floating arsenal that would help sink the 1st Mobile Carrier Striking Force of Admiral Nagumo.

Flexibility in Command

Admiral Yamamoto's grand tactical plan at Midway was inflexible. Few, if any, of his more astute subordinates made any sustained effort to convince their admiral that the imperial fleet's assets would be far too widely dispersed, that precious planes and ships would be wasted in the Aleutian operations, and that the entire contradictory strategy of destroying the American fleet while taking islands a thousand miles distant was absurd. A long tradition of deference to superiors, coupled with Yamamoto's reputation after Pearl Harbor, precluded any serious give-and-take that might have resulted in at least some alterations. Admiral Nagumo's chief of staff, Rear Admiral Kusaka, noted of many senior officers' private reservations about Yamamoto's formula, "The fact was that the plan had already been decided by the Combined Fleet headquarters and we were forced to accept it as it had been planned" (G. Prange, *Miracle at Midway,* 28).

Yamamoto's intractable strategic framework nearly ensured tactical problems, which similarly reflected an institutional hierarchy within the Japanese imperial command that discouraged initiative and independent thinking. Critics of the Japanese leadership at Midway usually focus on Admiral Nagumo's key decisions on the morning of June 4: (1) his orders to send most of the fleet's protective cover of fighter planes along with the bombers to attack Midway; (2) his decision also to send all four carriers' bombers at once against Midway, without keeping a reserve in case of the sudden appearance of American carriers; and (3) his critical determination not to launch his planes immediately when he learned of the presence of the American carriers, but instead ordering them to be refitted from bombs to naval torpedoes. In all three instances Nagumo—who committed suicide in an underground bunker on Saipan in June 1944—simply followed the standard procedure of the Japanese navy, without realizing how different the fight with the Americans might be from the past experience of easy victories over surprised, outnumbered, and inexperienced adversaries.

As for the attacks against Midway itself, it was traditional Japanese fleet protocol that all bombing sorties were to be accompanied by massive fighter escorts. But two conditions in the skies over Midway immediately made that doctrinaire approach subject to alteration on June 4: the Midway fighter defenses were not effective, meaning the bombers could hit their targets well enough with only minimal fighter cover; and second, the Japanese inability to locate the American fleet suggested that it was critical to retain a massive fighter reserve over Nagumo's carriers against possible American naval attack. Yet neither Nagumo nor his officers saw the need to alter long-held beliefs to fit the circumstances at hand.

Nagumo devoted nearly his entire air arm to a target that was not mobile and did not have a fighter or bomber force capable of seriously endangering the Japanese fleet or its planes. The immovable Midway could not become lost to Nagumo's intelligence, nor, as the morning's continuously unsuccessful bombing sorties proved, could it ruin his carriers. In contrast, the mobile and undetected *Enterprise, Hornet,* and *Yorktown* could surely do both.

It would have been an innovative and unorthodox move for Nagumo to keep back half his bomber strength, ready to attack at a minute's notice the American fleet, while retaining fighters at full strength over the carriers. That way he could still always send in much smaller, regular sorties against Midway, as he probed for the American naval presence. Launching everything at once in naval warfare was sometimes a sound strategy—the American admirals would do just that against Nagumo in the minutes to come—but only as a preventative against fast-moving carriers, whose dive-bombers were deadly; it made little sense against islands whose aircraft was obsolete and demonstrably unable to hit a ship at sea.

Nagumo—and here Admiral Yamamoto's grand plan deserves much of the blame—was concentrating on the wrong objective that could do him little harm, while neglecting the very target that could send his ships to the bottom.

Even more critical was the decision to rearm his bombers before sending them off instantaneously against the newly discovered American carriers. The undeniable advantage the planes would reap from carrying torpedoes rather than bombs was immediately offset by having all four Japanese carriers at once exposed with a scrambled mess of gasoline, armed planes, and bombs on their flight decks. Nagumo was also worried about sending off his bombers immediately without fighter escort—the latter pilots were exhausted from the Midway raid, involved in air cover, and also refueling. Yet his unescorted dive-bombers would have at least sighted the American fleet; some would have made it through the defenses and inflicted damage. It was the desire to destroy the enemy at all costs, and to keep planes away from a targeted flight deck, that made Admiral Spruance later in the afternoon launch every available dive-bomber of the *Enterprise* and *Yorktown* against the *Hiryu*. Despite having no fighter support, the Americans blasted the Japanese carrier to pieces.

It was good policy to attack land facilities with bombs, and ships with excellent Japanese torpedoes; but battle rarely gives allowance for good policy and instead demands instantaneous adaptation. In carrier war a fleet's planes should be up in the air defending the ships and far away hunting down the enemy. As Fuchida and Okumiya point out, "Nagumo chose what seemed to him the orthodox and safe course, and from that moment his carriers were doomed" (*Midway, the Battle That Doomed Japan*, 237). Even Admiral Kusaka later admitted that it was a wise insurance policy to hold back substantial numbers of planes ready and armed to take off immediately once enemy carriers were sighted, but conceded that caution seemed needless at Midway: "It was almost intolerable for the commander at the front to keep its half strength in readiness indefinitely only for an enemy force which might not be in the area after all" (G. Prange, *Miracle at Midway*, 215).

Finally, there was an institutional, indeed fossilized approach to the Japanese use of carriers and battleships that did not adapt to the highly volatile and constantly changing battle realities of the Pacific theater. Battleships in the war against the Americans were no longer vehicles of national prestige whose primary mission was to fire away at other battleships and atomize cruisers and destroyers. Rather, they were most effective in screening far more valuable aircraft carriers—adding their enormous antiaircraft arsenal to the protection of the irreplaceable flattops, ringing the carriers to ensure that submarines and approaching planes might first dilute their attack (battleships in general were enticing to pilots, but harder to hit from the air, better armored, and less vulnerable to torpedoes), while protecting troop transports as they softened up shore targets with their enormous sixteen- and eighteen-inch guns.

Had all Yamamoto's battleships ringed Nagumo's carriers and then at night sailed off to blast away the runways at Midway itself, there is a good likelihood that more American bombers would have been shot down, that many more of both land- and sea-based planes would have diverted their attacks from the Japanese carriers to these impressive capital ships, and that there would not have been the dire necessity to launch naval planes against Midway once it was under constant naval shelling by the bulk of Yamamoto's battleships. Instead, the battleships saw no action. For most of the war, Japan's massive *Yamato* and *Musashi,* and other battleships like them, were completely wasted assets, which were rarely properly deployed in any of Japan's engagements in the Pacific. The Americans, in contrast, after the disaster at Pearl Harbor and the later sinking of the British *Prince of Wales* and *Repulse* and numerous heavy cruisers by Japanese naval bombers, quickly crafted an entirely new role for battleships. From now on, the navy's behemoths would be attached whenever possible to carriers, as at Okinawa, where they could protect and draw off fire, or, as in the Philippines or at Normandy Beach, shell enemy ground forces.

Ideally, carrier groups should also steam in staggered formations to disperse airborne attack. Unfortunately, the Japanese approached Midway in just the opposite fashion: they clustered their four carriers in close proximity even as their critical battleships were far distant. Far better it would have been for them to form two, or even three, carrier task forces, all within fifty miles of each other to coordinate aerial attacks from the four dispersed flattops. That way they could dilute incoming bombers, such as the American practice of the dual Task Forces 16 and 17 that resulted in the previously damaged *Yorktown* absorbing all the Japanese bombs, freeing the distant *Enterprise* and *Hornet* from any attack at all. One can only imagine what would have transpired at Midway had the fiery and singularly combative Admiral Yamaguchi been posted fifty miles distant from the *Kaga* and *Akagi,* with direct control of the air resources of the *Hiryu* and *Soryu*—a dozen or so Japanese battleships ringing both carrier task forces. But, then, that tactic would have required real decentralization and a lateral, elastic supreme command, rather than an enormously layered hierarchy under the absolute power of an admiral who was virtually incommunicado.

The American system of command was far more flexible and the fleet's orders inherently broad enough to allow for alteration as the battle for Midway unfolded. Nimitz essentially directed Admiral Frank J. Fletcher and Admiral Spruance to make use of American intelligence by cruising in at the flank of the superior Japanese fleet, to hit it hard with everything they had, and then to withdraw when Japanese surface ships rushed to the rescue. The details of the American proposed attack—indeed, the nature of the deployment of the ships themselves—were left up to the commanders, Fletcher and Spruance. Nimitz's orders directed both "to inflict maximum damage on the enemy by employing strong attrition tactics." Their attacks were to "be governed by the principle of calculated risk, which you shall interpret to mean the avoidance of exposure of your force to attack by superior enemy forces without good prospect of inflicting, as a result of such exposure, greater damage on the enemy" (G. Prange, *Miracle at Midway,* 99–100).

In contrast, Admiral Nagumo felt duty-bound to launch an attack in the "right" way, as Admirals Spruance and Fletcher, entirely on their own, sent almost the entire American air arm after the Japanese at the first opportunity. Such actions by Spruance and Fletcher may have been precipitous, but they were grounded in the wisdom that in carrier war the first strike is often the most critical, since it can wipe out the enemy's ability to retaliate and can obliterate the platform itself for hundreds of planes in the air.

When there were rare disagreements among the high echelons of the Japanese admiralty, such tension often manifested itself in counterproductive and strangely formalistic ways: offers to resign or even commit suicide, rival efforts to accept rather than allot blame, determination to go down with the ship to atone for tactical blunders—even an earlier wrestling match during the Pearl Harbor campaign between Admirals Nagumo and Yamaguchi over deployment of the latter's carriers. How different was the informal and relaxed American system. Admiral Fletcher on the damaged *Yorktown* transferred to Admiral Spruance key decisions for launching the fleet's planes—without rancor or worry about the honor of command:

He [Fletcher] knew well that the admiral who led his ships to the major American sea victory of World War II would be a popular hero, assured of his place in history. Yet, when he realized that he could no longer command his air striking units at top efficiency, he turned the reins over to Spruance. This was an act of selfless integrity and patriotism in action. The reputations of Nimitz and Spruance have overshadowed Fletcher, but he was the link between the two, a man of talent who had the brains and character to give a free hand to a man of genius. (G. Prange, *Miracle at Midway,* 386)

Both the Japanese and the American military traditions prized supreme command from the field—a hallmark of Western military practice since the culture of hoplite generals fighting in the front rank of the Greek phalanx—but the Americans were far more ready to abandon form for function in a complex battle theater of the magnitude of Midway. Admiral Yamamoto, who had dreamed up the entire unworkable plan, was on the *Yamato* itself. But since the Japanese were observing radio silence, and the admiral's flagship was sailing far from the scene of the carrier war, there was almost no chance of direct and instant communications between officers in battle and the Japanese high command. Yamamoto was about as in control of Midway as Xerxes was on his imperial throne perched on the hills above Salamis—but the former with far less firsthand information of the battle's progress.

In comparison, Admiral Nimitz at Pearl Harbor had an almost instantaneous appreciation of the events of June 1942 as they transpired and so kept up a constant advisory dialogue with his admirals. In fact, Nimitz in his office at Pearl Harbor was closer to the action at Midway, both concretely and electronically, than Yamamoto was in his battleship at sea. The Japanese tradition of the supreme commander being in the foremost ship in the fleet (and in a battleship during a carrier war!), the readiness for an experienced carrier commander to go down with his vessel, and the unquestioning acceptance of a tactical blueprint from on high were disciplined and soldierly, but not necessarily militarily efficacious, practices. Like some exalted warlord, Yamamoto drew up his formal plan, ordered his subordinates to follow it, and then in relative isolation and silence cruised out to battle in the huge, ostentatious—and mostly irrelevant—*Yamato.*

Unfortunately, his adversaries paid little heed to the samurai tradition, but were in constant electronic communication and ad hoc consultations as they drew up new contingency plans and on occasion traded command. American admirals preferred to supervise the complete abandonment of their sinking ships—and characteristically thereby lost fewer of their men when their vessels sank. They were more eager to obtain a new warship than go down with the old, learning from, rather than being consumed in, defeat. When thousands of their sailors were trying to find salvation in a sinking ship's last moments, they cared little whether President Roosevelt's photograph might soon rest at the bottom of the Pacific.

Not all naval battles call for imagination and adaptation. Eccentric, pugnacious, and independent American admirals like Halsey and Fletcher could at times—as during the battles of Coral Sea, the engagements off Guadalcanal, and the victory in Leyte Gulf—nearly endanger their fleets through their very aggressiveness. But in general, it is a truism of carrier war and of battle itself that there is a fog in armed conflict, that set plans are often obsolete the minute the shooting starts, and that reaction, innovation, and initiative more often than not outweigh the merits of method, consensus, and adherence to hierarchy and protocol. In that regard, it is advantageous on the battlefield to have soldiers more independent than predictable, with officers who look to what works at the moment, rather than adhere to what is accepted as conventional.

The Initiative of the Pilots

The Americans had outdated airplanes, often unskilled pilots, and little experience in carrier war. They did, however, launch repeated aerial attacks, in which highly individualistic aircrews employed unpredictable sorties and unorthodox methods of attack that had the effect of disrupting the Japanese carrier fleet and making possible its final destruction. Japanese observers on the carriers shook their heads over the amateurishness of the first eight futile shore and naval American air attacks—and then were aghast when the ninth wave of dive-bombers came out of nowhere to destroy their fleet.

Scholars often remark that the Midway-based army bombers and marine pilots—flying obsolete Brewster Buffaloes, Vaught Vindicators, new Avenger torpedo bombers, outclassed navy SBD dive-bombers, Wildcat fighters, B-26 Marauder light bombers, and B-17 Flying Fortresses— failed to do any real damage to the Japanese fleet. Yet their repeated attacks, if uncoordinated, spontaneous, and unskilled, were nearly constant and so had the effect of keeping the Japanese off guard, and their critical fighters engaged, soon worn out, and often in need of fuel and ammunition. Before the carriers were finally set ablaze, no fewer than five sorties flew out from Midway itself, often on the initiative of the pilots themselves.

Before the day of the decisive battle, at a little after noon on June 3, nine army B-17s left Midway to attack the incoming Japanese fleet when it was still six hundred miles away. The pilots had no combat experience and carried less than eleven tons of bombs between them. They scored no hits. As the B-17s returned to Midway hours later, a motley group of PBY scout planes—scarcely able to reach speeds of one hundred mph—took off. Each was jury-rigged to carry a single torpedo and headed out for the Japanese fleet and another surprise nighttime attack. Other than some slight damage to a tanker, this second and even more bizarre sortie had little success.

The next morning at 7:00 as the Japanese carrier planes were off hitting Midway, American torpedo bombers and B-26s from the islands once more zoomed toward Admiral Nagumo's carrier fleet. There was no real flight plan, much less any integrated tactics between the squadrons. Lieutenant Ogawa on the *Akagi* thought the entire morning attack inept—a judgment confirmed when the imperial fleet's Zeros shot down most of the Avengers and one of the four B-26s. The Americans again scored no hits.

A little more than an hour later, fifteen B-17s arrived again over the Japanese fleet to begin a fourth American bombing attack. Dropping their ordnance from nearly 20,000 feet, the Fortresses got close with only a few bombs—they would later make fantastic claims of damage—but again they scored no hits. A few minutes later eleven decrepit marine Vindicators arrived and began old-fashioned glide-bombing attacks from as low as 500 feet. They scored no hits either.

All five attacks from Midway were spontaneous, involving marine, army, and navy pilots, in a strange assortment of at least five different types of bombers, attacking from 500 to 20,000 feet, with inadequate preparation, defective torpedoes, and bombs that could not seriously damage modern armored ships. When they were done, all the Japanese ships were intact, half of Midway's planes were gone, but the fleet was left frazzled and tired from hours of constant vigilance and shooting—just as the three doomed waves of Devastators from the *Enterprise, Hornet,* and *Yorktown* now appeared on the horizon to begin their own equally unproductive torpedo runs. Captain Fuchida and Commander Okumiya summed up the Midway attacks, with special emphasis on how busy the Japanese were repelling the first five American aerial sorties:

> It was our general conclusion that we had little to fear from the enemy's offensive tactics. But, paradoxically, the very ineffectiveness of the enemy at-

tacks up to this time contributed in no small measure to the ultimate American triumph. We neglected certain obvious precautions, which had they been taken, might have prevented the fiasco that followed a few hours later. The apparently futile sacrifices made by the enemy's shore-based planes were, after all, not in vain. (*Midway, the Battle That Doomed Japan,* 163)

The torpedo pilots from the three American carriers, as we have seen, were just as innovative, if soon subject to much of the same fate, given their inferior equipment and lack of experience. But by any fair measure, few naval pilots should have located the Japanese fleet at all. The *Hornet*'s fighters and dive-bombers did not; 45 planes, or almost one-third of the initial 152 planes of the first American strike, never even saw the enemy. Radio contact with Midway was difficult, and no updated reports were forwarded to the pilots after takeoff to indicate that the Japanese had radically altered course away from Midway and were headed in the near-opposite direction. In the hour or more it took the Americans to reach the Japanese, the enemy carriers would be thirty or forty miles to the north from their last reported position, and thus in theory safe from the incoming bombers, which were at their limit of operations, low on fuel, and headed in the wrong direction.

A number of American air commanders ignored standard operational orders and thereby found the Japanese through their own initiative. Jack Waldron, *Hornet* air commander of the Devastators, told his squadron, "Just follow me. I'll take you to 'em" (W. Smith, *Midway,* 102). And he did, and to their deaths—rightly surmising that Nagumo would change course once he got reports of the American carriers. Waldron's ingenuity ensured that he found the Japanese, that all his planes would therefore be shot down, and that the Japanese fighter cover would, in the process of the American slaughter, be ignorant of the dive-bomber peril far above. Had Waldron not changed course, he would never have found the enemy fleet, and thus it was likely that the Japanese would have much more easily beat off the other attacks and have been waiting for the SBDs.

Similarly, when Wade McClusky, leading the dive-bombers of the *Enterprise,* arrived at the anticipated interception point 155 miles distant, his planes likewise found no Japanese fleet. Instinctively, he, too, made an instantaneous judgment that Nagumo's carriers had changed course (he was helped by the wake of the Japanese destroyer *Arashi,* which was steaming to catch up to Nagumo's force) and thus began making a long sweeping search north to the Japanese carriers, which he found at the limit of his bombers' fuel reserves. Had McClusky not guessed, and guessed rightly—or had he circled while trying to radio for orders—*Enterprise*'s bombers, like *Hornet*'s, would have played no role in the fighting. Both the *Akagi* and *Kaga* would have escaped, and surely either the *Enterprise* or the *Hornet* would have quickly felt their wrath. No wonder that the captain of the *Enterprise*, George Murray, called McClusky's initiative "the most important decision of the entire action" (G. Prange, *Miracle at Midway*, 260).

During the actual bombing runs, individual American pilots made snap decisions to redirect their attacks contrary to their last orders, when they saw that crippled ships needed more attention or felt that their bombs might be better dropped on fresh targets. Improvisation ensured that the *Hiryu* was sunk and the heavy cruiser *Mogami* seriously damaged, both suffering devastating hits from American bombers that had been ordered elsewhere.

Such freethinking American pilots in their recklessness and infectious enthusiasm could often be ineffective, if not downright dangerous, as we have seen in the failed shore-based attacks from Midway. A number of impromptu B-17 sorties were foolhardy, and one even attacked an American submarine. An unwise effort of B-24s on June 6 to fly at night to bomb Wake Island resulted in abject failure—the planes did not find the island and the mission's commander, Major General Clarence Tinker, was never heard from again. Nevertheless, comparison between the Japanese and American scouting, fighter, and bomber pilots reveals far more capacity for initiative and adaptation among the Americans. At Midway, as would be true throughout the Pacific War, that autonomy paid off.

INDIVIDUALISM IN WESTERN WARFARE

The Americans would lose dozens of carriers, battleships, and cruisers in the three years following Midway to brave and brilliant Japanese sailors and pilots, as the United States sought to ruin Japan, rather than remove the threat of the Japanese military. On Guadalcanal, Tarawa, Peleliu, Iwo Jima, Okinawa, and in a number of naval actions off the Solomon Islands, thousands of Americans of all services would be slaughtered by well-planned and organized Japanese assaults. Yet the astounding fact remains: in less than four years, after being surprised and caught in a state of virtual unpreparedness, the United States—while devoting the majority of its forces to the European theater of operations, and without banzai charges, kamikaze attacks, or ritual suicides—not only defeated an enormous and seasoned Japanese military but destroyed the Japanese nation itself, ending its half-century existence as a formidable military power and indeed a modern industrial state. Japan's navy, army, and air force had not merely lost the Pacific War but ceased to exist in the process.

The result was that by August 1945 the Japanese nation was in far worse shape than it had been a century earlier in 1853 when Commander Perry arrived in Tokyo Bay and helped spur the original Westernization of Japan. A century of Westernization without liberalization had brought Japan not parity with, but destruction by, Western powers. Critical to that unprecedented and brutal American military achievement of some forty-five months was a long tradition of reliance on individual initiative, which was in sharp contrast to a venerable Eastern emphasis on group consensus, obeisance to imperial or divine authority, and the subjugation of the individual to society. The beginning of the end for the Japanese was Midway, where they lost their best airmen and irreplaceable aircrews and the core of their carrier fleet—and, most important, in a mere three days had their confidence shattered to such a degree that they would now fear, rather than look eagerly to, engaging American ships on the horizon.

Individualism had long played a role in Western military efficacy and usually manifested itself on the battlefield at three levels: from supreme command to the soldiers themselves to the larger society that fielded and armed its combatants. All cultures are capable of creating brilliant and highly idiosyncratic military leaders who exercise independence and intuition. Rome met a number of such gifted tribal commanders and Eastern monarchs—Jugurtha, Vercingetorix, Boudicca, Mithradates—whose skill often led to battlefield victories. But their individualism, and that of others to follow like them, was not characteristic of their cultures at large, but prominent only to the degree that they enjoyed absolute power. Thus, after their deaths—and all enemies of Rome usually died in battle or committed suicide—their wars of liberation collapsed, suggesting that their brand of monarchy, theocracy, or tyranny could rarely produce a succession of gifted military leaders, much less a nation of followers who could rely on their own initiative and autonomy to wage war.

The same holds true of dynasts such as the pharaohs, the New World potentates in Mexico and Peru, and the Chinese emperors and Ottoman sultans, who likewise centralized military authority into their own hands and discouraged initiative on the part of their subjects, ensuring that the chance of victory lay not in military improvisation, but only in their own—often flawed—judgment. In contrast, generals like Themistocles, the Spartan genius Lysander, Scipio Africanus, the brilliant Byzantine Belisarius, Cortés, and moderns like George Patton and Curtis LeMay were at odds with their own state, surrounded by equally independent-thinking subordinates, and keen to exploit the initiative rather than merely the discipline of their own troops.

Soldiers in the ranks of Western armies often exercised an independence of judgment not found in other societies. Here one thinks of the "old man" at the battle of Mantinea (418 B.C.) who stopped the battle to warn the Spartan high command of its unwise deployment; the brutal give-and-take among Xenophon's Ten Thousand in Asia Minor (401 B.C.), who were as much a mobile democracy-in-arms as a hired band of killers; the various eccentric bands of Frankish aristocracy who bickered as much as they fought the enemy during the Crusades; the fractious admirals before Lepanto or career British soldiers in India and Africa during the nineteenth century, whose skill and imagination brought success despite mediocre higher command.

All people at times act as individuals, and as humans prize their freedom and independence. But the formal and often legal recognition of a person's sovereign sphere of individual action—social, political, and cultural—is a uniquely Western concept, one that frightens, sometimes rightly so, most of the non-Western world. Individualism, unlike consensual government and constitutional recognition of political freedom, is a cultural, rather than political, entity. It is the dividend of Western politics and economics, which give freedom in the abstract and concrete sense to individuals and in the process foster personal curiosity and initiative unknown among societies where there are no true citizens and neither government nor markets are free.

As we have seen in the case of Salamis and Cannae, an insidious individualism grows out of the larger Western traditions of freedom, constitutional government, property rights, and civic miliarism. The Athenian *ekklēsia* voted for the disastrous expedition to Sicily (415–413 B.C.) and then adopted decisive and heroic measures to keep Athens in the war for another nine years—in much the same way as the British Parliament in the nineteenth century or the American Congress during the twentieth authorized all sorts of political and economic policies that turned the war effort over to thousands of autonomous and freethinking citizens. From the assertion of the fifth-century sophist Protagoras that "man is the measure of all things" to the Universal Declaration of Human Rights adopted by the United Nations in 1948 and drafted by Western jurists ("the peoples of the United Nations have in the Charter reaffirmed their faith in fundamental human rights, in the dignity and worth of the human person and in the equal rights of men and women . . ."), there is a 2,500-year tradition of personal liberty and innate trust in the individual, rather than the political or religious collective, unparalleled in the non-West. For good or evil, few Westerners believe that a sacred cow is more important than a human, that the emperor is superior to the individual person, that a religious pilgrimage is the fulfillment of a human's life, that in war a suicidal charge is often required for an individual's excellency, or that a combatant must risk his or her life to save the emperor's picture.

In contrast, Japan, in lieu of independent supreme commanders, innovative soldiers, and a sovereign legislature, relied on ironclad obedience, as have most Western adversaries of the past two and a half millennia. Rigid hierarchy and complete submission of the individual to the divinity of the Japanese emperor meant that the wisdom of a small cadre of militarists shaped policy largely without ratification or even knowledge of the Japanese people, who were never envisioned as free persons with unique rights that were natural at birth and protected by the state. Like the enormous armies of the ancient imperial East, all that centralized control and mass ideology led to a wonderfully trained, large, and spirited military, but one vulnerable to the counterattacks of a nation-in-arms, drawing on the collective wisdom of thousands of freethinking individuals.

With the end of the Pacific War, the ruin of Japanese society, and the disgrace of the militarists, the final century-old roadblock to full implementation of Western-style parliamentary democracy and all that accompanied it was removed. The postwar introduction of constitutional government brought land redistribution. Freedom of the press and dissent, the emancipation of women, and the creation of a middling consumer class were also dividends of the American occupation. The result—if not a radical Japanese reinterpretation of the role of the individual and society—was at least that at the millennium Japan has one of the most well led, innovative, and technologically advanced militaries in the world—under the complete control of an elected legislature and chief executive and subject to civilian audit.

If its past partial embrace of Western military research and development brought Japan near technological parity with European and American military forces at the turn of the century, its current far more comprehensive adaptation of Western political and social institutions has ensured it a military that is, at least tactically, the near equal of any in

Europe today. In the next century Japan's scientific progress in arms will not hinge entirely on foreign emulation, but be powered by the engine of its own free and liberal society—if it continues to encourage individual talent and initiative to a degree unknown at any time in its long and war-like past.

TEN

Dissent and Self-Critique

Tet, January 31–April 6, 1968

The expedition to Sicily was not so much a mistake in judgement, considering the enemy they went against, as much as a case of mismanagement on the part of the planners, who did not afterwards take the necessary measures to support those first troops they sent out. Instead, they turned to personal rivalries over the leadership of the people, and consequently not only conducted the war in the field half-heartedly, but also brought civil discord for the first time to the home front. . . . And yet they did not fail until they at last turned on each other and fell into private quarrels that brought their ruin.

—THUCYDIDES, *The Peloponnesian War* (2.65.12–13)

BATTLES AGAINST THE CITIES

American Embassy, Saigon

SAIGON WAS QUIET, as it should be during the holidays. There was a thirty-six-hour truce in effect for the Tet Nguyen Dan celebration and various festivals commemorating the lunar new year. In any case, the Vietcong rarely came into the southern urban centers of Vietnam to attack openly with sizable forces. All that changed suddenly and without warning in the early morning of January 31, 1968. The entire country of South Vietnam, or so it seemed from panicky reports that flashed into American headquarters in Saigon, had come under fire in a matter of minutes from enemy infiltrators. Cities, villages, even rural hamlets—

more than one hundred in all—were being overrun. Such a scenario at first seemed preposterous to American commanders. They were convinced that the enemy would never attack en masse, and especially not after heavy bombing attacks during 1967 that had gradually turned the tide against North Vietnam.

The center of American power in South Vietnam was the capital city of Saigon, supposedly a sacrosanct fortress. The bastion for this vast network of military and civilian support, MACV (Military Assistance Command Vietnam), was the American embassy, its walls of ugly concrete the consummate image of the strength and commitment of the United States to stop the communist incursion from the North and thereby allow for the eventual creation of a democratic, capitalist nation in the South. After the riveting success of World War II, two decades earlier, and the salvation of a capitalist, "free" South Korea in 1953, the American military during the first few years in Vietnam still operated with a sense of invincibility. In their eyes, the problem in Southeast Asia was not defeating the enemy, but finding him and then coaxing him to come out and fight, where he would then be promptly destroyed through overwhelming American firepower.

But city streets were as inimical to the Western way of war as dense jungle. If the Americans wished to bomb and shoot openly and thereby incinerate thousands of communists, then the North Vietnamese would attack stealthily and at night, and not always with even the pretext of shooting exclusively at combatants. Indeed, the embassy, too, was a target—in fact, the first objective of the entire massive enemy offensive that began nationwide at about 3:00 in the morning on January 31. Some 4,000 Vietcong guerrillas, many in civilian clothes and soon aided by infiltration units from the regular army of North Vietnam, attacked nearly all the main South Vietnamese and American government installations in Saigon. Hundreds of small cadres attempted to storm the military headquarters of the Army of the Republic of Vietnam (ARVN), the state radio and television stations, police compounds, government agencies, and individual homes of army, police, and American officials in a madcap plan to raise general insurrection among the population and thereby inaugurate the long-promised war of national liberation.

Nineteen Vietcong commandos planned to force their way through the sealed American embassy grounds and overpower a skeleton detail of surprised and sleepy guards. Pulling up in a truck and taxicab, they blasted a hole in the compound wall, killed five American marines, and then began to fire grenades and automatic weapons against the heavy doors of the main chancery in a vain attempt to enter the offices of the embassy proper. What would the American public think, when in just a few hours television broadcasts sent the nation images of Vietcong peering from the windows of Ambassador Ellsworth Bunker's own office?

It was not to be so. Within five hours helicopters had landed American airborne troops onto the grounds. The Americans killed all nineteen enemy infiltrators and secured the embassy. The enemy assault, like dozens more that morning against President Nguyen Van Thieu's palace and other Vietnamese and American buildings, was a complete surprise and yet failure at the same time. As they urged on their troops, planners in North Vietnam boasted that the raids would signal a general uprising against the Americans and their "puppet" Vietnamese hosts:

> Move forward aggressively to carry out decisive and repeated attacks in order to annihilate as many American, Satellite and Puppet troops as possible in conjunction with political struggle and military proselytizing activities.... Display to the utmost your revolutionary heroism by surmounting all the hardships and difficulties and making sacrifices to be able to fight continually and aggressively. Be prepared to smash all enemy counter attacks and maintain your revolutionary standpoint under all circumstances. (L. Berman, "Tet Offensive," in M. Gilbert and W. Head, eds., *The Tet Offensive*, 21)

Most residents of Saigon, however, were far more concerned about the lack of security and the random shooting in their streets. Worried American and Vietnamese officers and bureaucrats barricaded themselves in thousands of private residences and began firing at anyone suspicious.

Few Vietnamese had any desire to turn on their own government, much less on the Americans, and the majority of the local population watched from the sidelines. Almost no one joined the communist "uprising." Most were keen to monitor closely the degree of Vietcong success— weighing the odds that the communists and not the Americans might soon be in control of their lives. Like the Tlaxcalans who followed Cortés to slaughter other indigenous Mexicas, or the tribal irregulars who were attached to Chelmsford in Zululand, the South Vietnamese were ready to fight with the murderous Westerners against the hated communists—but only if the Americans could guarantee military success and bring permanent relief to Vietnam. Now their very embassy was under attack!

By midmorning the Americans were cleaning up the mess on the grounds, as Ambassador Bunker arrived for work, accompanied by dozens of television cameras and reporters, many of whom sent back fantastic cables that the Vietcong had for a time taken over the American embassy and were in possession of the main chancery. The misinformation came not only from the press. Back home President Lyndon B. Johnson scurried to assure the nation that the raid was more like a riot in a Detroit ghetto than a major military operation. General William Westmoreland, in charge of the American command in Vietnam, would insist to the nation that the systematic attacks were mere diversionary probes to draw resources away from the ongoing siege at Khesanh far to the north. He nevertheless welcomed such enemy concentrations, since they made much easier targets for overwhelming American firepower; while politicians fretted over the offensive, Westmoreland saw a chance for decisive victory.

The next month would prove wrong Westmoreland's initial guess that Tet was some enormous ruse, but he was accurate in his belief that thousands of enemy Vietnamese were now more likely to be in the open, vulnerable, and shortly to be annihilated. The entire effort of Westmoreland's previous three years in Vietnam had been to create the conditions of traditional Western decisive battle, in which the American military might draw on its wonderfully trained and disciplined shock infantry and enormous technological and material superiority to blast apart the enemy and then go home. The problem for the Americans in Vietnam, as for Westerners overseas in general, had always been the reluctance of the enemy to engage in set battle pieces, instead turning war into one of infiltration, jungle fighting, terror bombing, and house-to-house raiding. In retreat, not battle, Darius III had found safety from Alexander; Abd ar-Rahman had far more success looting Narbonne than meeting Charles Martel at Poitiers; the Aztecs sometimes won when they attacked the Spanish at night, in surprise, or in mountain passes. Cetshwayo would have been far better off ambushing wagons than charging British squares.

Sixty million Americans back home during the next week of fighting saw a somewhat different picture of the first night's attack. Cameras flashed back images of a few dead Americans on the compound grounds. Tanks and howitzers rushed through the streets of Saigon. Headlines flashed "War Hits Saigon." An especially disturbing picture was shown for days on television: General Nguyen Ngoc Loan blowing the brains out of a captured Vietcong infiltrator. That the prisoner had been part of infiltration units which just earlier had gunned down many of Loan's security forces, including one officer at home with his wife and children, or that enemy agents out of uniform and in civilian dress were not accorded the same treatment as captured soldiers, was lost in the journalistic frenzy. Eddie Adams, the Associated Press photographer who snapped the picture for *Life* magazine, won the Pulitzer Prize for photography.

The image of those scattered brains apparently summed up the entire mess of Tet—dying Americans unable to protect the nerve center of their massive expeditionary force while their corrupt South Vietnamese allies shot the unarmed and innocent—at a time when the public was assured that "the light is at the end of the tunnel." As they watched their television sets, Americans wondered if victory really was at hand and were troubled over what and whom to believe:

> It says something about this war that the great picture of the Tet Offensive was Eddie Adam's photograph of a South Vietnamese general shooting a man with his arms tied behind his back, that the most memorable quotation was Peter Arnett's damning epigram from Ben Tre, "It became necessary to destroy the town to save it" and that the only Pulitzer Prize awarded specifically for reporting an event of the Tet offensive was given two years later to Seymour M. Hersh, who never set foot in Vietnam, for exposing the U.S. Army massacre of more than a hundred civilians at My Lai. (D. Oberdorfer, *Tet!*, 332)

Outside the embassy a vicious battle erupted at the Phu Tho racetrack that the Vietcong had occupied as the main element of their attack, a traffic hub for several main boulevards with enough open spaces to coordinate an entire army. Homes surrounding the track were stuffed with hundreds of snipers. It took a week of house-to-house fighting for American army troops and ARVN forces to locate and expel the Vietcong, who rarely surrendered and had to be killed almost to the last man. Yet on television Americans were being blamed for blasting apart residences, as if no one noticed that urban snipers were shooting marines in the middle of a holiday truce.

It took almost three weeks for the last organized infiltrators to be killed or expelled from Saigon. A company of marines from the 3rd Battalion, 7th Infantry Division, tried to storm the Phu Tho racetrack and locate a Vietcong battalion in brutal fighting typical of the urban firefight:

> Recoilless rifles blasted holes through walls, grenade launchers were fired through the jagged cavities, and then soldiers clambered into the smoking entrances. Hundreds of panic-stricken civilians fled past the armored carriers as the battle raged on. The column continued to contest the Viet Cong

in fierce house-to-house fighting as it pressed closer to the racetrack. Gunships swooped down to blast apart structures with minigun and rocket salvos. By one o'clock that afternoon [January 31] the company had advanced two more city blocks. Then the Viet Cong withdrew to positions dug in behind the concrete park benches, backed up by heavy weapons located in concrete towers on the spectator stands inside the racetrack itself. (S. Stanton, *The Rise and Fall of an American Army*, 225)

Bloodbath at Hué

Even worse city fighting was far to the north, near the Demilitarized Zone (DMZ), in the provincial capital of Hué—a picturesque former imperial city of the once-unified Vietnam, containing about 140,000 residents. Although it was South Vietnam's third largest city, and near the North Vietnamese border, Hué was still relatively untouched by war. That was soon to change. At about the same time the American embassy was attacked, three columns of North Vietnamese forces, including two full regiments and two Vietcong battalions—their numbers eventually to rise to nearly 12,000 troops—stormed the city. They soon met up with infiltrators that had mixed in with the Tet holiday crowds, quickly brushed aside the small ARVN garrisons, and then occupied the "Citadel," a massive fortress overlooking the old city amid ancient palaces and temples.

Once the North Vietnamese were in control, agents systematically fanned out, searching for South Vietnamese soldiers, government officials, American sympathizers, and foreigners in general. Somewhere between 4,000 and 6,000 were rounded up. Most of those were clubbed or shot to death. Doctors, priests, and teachers were especially targeted. Three thousand bodies were eventually found in mass graves. The others were written off as "missing." Although Western reporters were soon ubiquitous in Hué, few commented on the executions; those who did often denied they even occurred.

The American counterattack spearheaded by U.S. marines was ferocious, leading to twenty-six days of nonstop fighting, tank attacks, reinforcements, and air strikes to recapture the nearly demolished Citadel. As in Saigon, marines often had no idea where or who the enemy was until they were fired upon from private houses:

I finally began to understand why we had experienced such difficulty getting across the street. Many of these houses were one-story homes, but a couple were two-story affairs, providing excellent and advantageous firing positions for the waiting NVA [North Vietnamese Army]. From these positions, the NVA could shoot right down on us, point-blank as we tried to run across the street. This was obvious and we understood the situation clearly, so we had directed our return fire at the windows and doorways of the houses across the street, which were the likely enemy firing positions. What we had not realized was that the NVA were also shooting at us from well-connected, dug-in positions *between* the houses, at street level. (N. Warr, *Phase Line Green*, 159–60)

The Americans had been trained to fight a war of maneuver and annihilation, in which they roamed wetlands and the jungle to engage in sharp but brief firefights before calling in artillery and air strikes and then heading back to fortified and relatively secure compounds. Like hoplite soldiers or Lord Chelmsford's redcoats, the point of war was to find the enemy and then defeat him through greater Western firepower, itself the product of superior discipline, technology, and supply. But whereas General Westmoreland claimed that Tet was an enemy blunder in allowing his forces the rare opportunity to fight the North Vietnamese in the open, few of the enemy offensives during Tet resulted in traditional Western collisions of shock battle. More often, to gain advantage from the American edge in firepower meant to call in artillery and air strikes on urban residences that housed Vietcong snipers—and whose destruction only alienated their South Vietnamese owners and incited hostile media attention back in America.

At Hué the Vietcong and North Vietnamese infiltrated in small independent units, at night, and often out of uniform. They fired automatic weapons, mortars, and grenade launchers from house windows, behind walls, and in crowds, forcing the marines to fight a counterattack reminiscent of Stalingrad, in which the enemy had to be expelled block by block, destroying hundreds of residences in the process. Often the Americans' choice was either to be picked off at random by well-ensconced snipers or to blast apart entire—and often historic—buildings by using howitzers and aerial bombardment:

They were unshaven, grimy, and covered with dust from the shattered brick and stone buildings. Sweat and bloodstains covered their fatigues. Elbows and knees stuck out of holes in their uniforms, the same ones they had worn for two weeks. . . . The Marines, who were trained to be a mobile, amphibious reaction force, had become moles. They had become a static, immobile collection of rats, hunkered down in a junk pile of crumbled

MAJOR BATTLES OF THE TET OFFENSIVE
JANUARY 31, 1968

NORTH VIETNAM

DMZ

Khesanh ✗ ✗ Quangtri

✗ Lang Vei ✗ Hué

✗ Ashau

THAILAND

✗ Da Nang
✗ Hoi An

LAOS

✗ Kham Duc

✗ Quangngai

✗ Dakto

✗ Kontum

✗ Pleiku

CAMBODIA

SOUTH
VIETNAM

✗ Quinhon

✗ Banmethuot

0 Miles   100   150
0 Kilometers   150

✗ Nha Trang

✗ Dafat

✗ Bien Hoa

✗ Chau Doc   Saigon ✗

CHINA

Pacific
Ocean

Vinh Long ✗   ✗ My Tho
✗ Ben Tre

✗ Can Tho

Camau
✗

South
China Sea

houses, surrounded by shell-pocked courtyard walls, burned-out automobiles, and downed trees and power lines. Death was waiting to tap them on the shoulder at any time, and many would never know where it came from. (G. Smith, *The Siege of Hue,* 158)

Yet in less than a month the enemy was expelled from Hué. The final tally of the dead was dramatically lopsided. Americans and their South Vietnamese allies—the Elite Black Panther company (Hac Bao) was given the privilege of storming the imperial palace and slaughtering the last enemy holdouts—had killed 5,113 of the enemy. Only 147 Americans were lost in action, with 857 wounded—fatality figures that in their own right would have signaled a landmark victory in both world wars. Yet reporters who freely roamed Hué ignored the respective sacrifices and were uninterested in the larger tactical situation. Instead, they mostly interviewed American soldiers in the midst of the dirty street fighting. Often they sent back mini-interviews like the following with a marine taking a minute's break from firing:

What's the hardest part of it?

Not knowing where they are—that's the worst thing. Riding around, running in sewers, the gutter, anywhere. Could be anywhere. Just hope you can stay alive, day to day. Everybody just wants to go back home and go to school. That's about it.

Have you lost any friends?

Quite a few. We lost one the other day. The whole thing stinks, really. (S. Karnow, *Vietnam,* 533)

For the first time in the history of Western warfare—in fact, of any conflict anywhere at any time—soldiers in the heat of battle could be seen instantly by millions of their parents, siblings, and friends in the safety of their living rooms. Images of the wounded and dead were flashed home in gruesome detail—and in color—by reporters of any nation, who were mostly free to go, see, and send back what they wished, with the likelihood it would be heard, read, or seen by the American voting public within hours, if not minutes. When such technological breakthroughs in instant video communications, often in abbreviated snippets and without context, were married to the traditional Western emphasis on unlimited freedom, the result was soon a level of civilian vehemence against the war rarely seen in the past, even among the voices of dissent against the Athenian expedition to Sicily, the European conquest of the Americas, or the British conduct during the Zulu and Boer Wars.

While Americans saw pictures of atrocious killing on television and interviews with disgusted marines, who found their South Vietnamese allies as reluctant to charge fixed positions alongside them as their North Vietnamese enemies were deadly, almost no reports were issued about the North Vietnamese massacres of the innocent. Much less was there any appreciation of the astounding ability of surprised and outnumbered U.S. marines to expel 10,000 from a fortified urban center in just over three weeks at the cost of fewer than 150 dead. Hué, brutal as it turned out to be, was yet another impressive American military victory, perhaps a feat of arms rivaling any bravery shown in either World War I or II. And the Americans were not done.

Khesanh

When the North Vietnamese and Vietcong broke the thirty-six-hour Tet truce on January 31, they systematically attacked the main cities of Saigon, Quangtri, Hué, Da Nang, Nha Trang, Quinhon, Kontum, Banmethuot, My Tho, Can Tho, and Ben Tre with more than 80,000 troops. Altogether thirty-six of forty-four provincial capitals were invaded at a time when 50 percent of the South Vietnamese army was on leave for the holidays. Yet in most places, except for Saigon and Hué, enemy infiltrators were expelled within a week. That counterattack was an amazing feat in and of itself, because the Americans were caught off guard—intelligence warnings of the size and date of the invasion were issued weeks prior, but largely ignored by the squabbling MACV high command.

Even though relatively small numbers of troops had infiltrated key installations in the hearts of major cities like Saigon and Hué, the North Vietnamese initially achieved a psychological dividend far out of proportion to the actual damage inflicted on the Americans and their allies. They were learning quickly that they need not win the offensive, but only overrun for a few days purportedly secure areas in order to cause a firestorm of recrimination and unrest in America. Moreover, at first the American command was confused over enemy intent. General Westmoreland himself felt that the Tet offensives were diversionary tactics to draw American forces away from the siege at Khesanh. Yet the opposite was more likely true: the early siege at Khesanh was designed to divert attention from the urban attacks to come in the following week.

At a little after 5:00 in the morning on January 21, ten days before the formal start of the Tet Offensive, thousands of North Vietnamese troops unleashed an artillery barrage as part of a general assault on an American base at Khesanh. The latter was a forward-area garrison near the DMZ that was intended to cut the supply of troops and matériel from North Vietnam. During the last week of January, news of the beleaguered base ran around the world. Many newspapers dubbed the siege another Dien Bien Phu, where a French garrison in 1954 was nearly annihilated before surrendering its 16,000 survivors.

Yet at Khesanh daily air strikes, hourly resupply, relatively safe evacuation of Lao and Vietnamese refugees, and constant communications kept the besieged 6,000 troops in relatively good shape. Was there much strategic value in hanging on to the surrounded Khesanh? It was hard to ascertain any. The Americans chose to hold the isolated outpost as bait, apparently as a deliberate plan to draw whole North Vietnamese divisions into an open firefight, or they were worried that withdrawal would signal a critical weakness in an American election year, when antiwar protests were on the rise. Whatever the rationale for the decision to stay, far from being another Dien Bien Phu, Khesanh was yet another devastating American demonstration of firepower. While the French had been cut off, outnumbered, without much air support, and isolated in North Vietnam near the Chinese border, the Americans were supplied daily, reinforced, south of the DMZ, in constant and easy communications, and able to drop tons of ordnance on the enemy. Nonetheless, the surrounded marines were also in a sea of seasoned North Vietnamese troops and themselves somewhat unsure of their exact mission. What was the eventual American plan for Khesanh? Was it, as professed by Westmoreland, a key to the defense of the DMZ and possible future operations in Laos, or simply a killing zone to incur enemy body counts and thus to be abandoned once the siege was lifted?

Veteran North Vietnamese troops had surprised and overrun the Lao and Vietnamese garrison at Lang Vei nearby, along with their American advisers, thus giving them full control of land routes into Khesanh. Soon the base was being shelled almost hourly—on some days as many as a thousand incoming artillery, rocket, and mortar rounds—in an effort to wear down the marines and destroy the airstrip. The North Vietnamese were equipped with some of the latest Soviet and Chinese weaponry, such as the 122mm heavy mortar, surface-to-surface missiles, flame-throwers, tanks, and 130mm heavy artillery, most of it adapted from basic designs dating back to World War II and based on original German, French, and American models. Thousands of Chinese and Soviet advisers worked stealthily but feverishly in the North to unload the artillery batteries and train the Vietnamese in their use.

Despite the new lethal armament, the American counterresponse was frightening and constituted one of the most deadly artillery and air assaults in the history of infantry battle. During the nearly three-month-long siege—from January 20 to mid-April 1968—110,022 tons of bombs were dropped and 142,081 rounds of artillery fired. Some estimated that the true American total was in excess of 200,000 cannon shells. Such astonishing firepower demanded constant rearmament; and eventually more than 14,000 tons of supplies were flown into Khesanh, all under continuous fire. Thousands of North Vietnamese were incinerated in the jungle surrounding the camp. Most estimates put the enemy dead and severely wounded around 10,000—half the 20,000 believed to be involved in the original siege.

Khesanh was to become an abject communist slaughter. If back home Americans in and out of government protested that there were needless marine deaths in defending a frontier outpost, North Vietnamese were publicly silent about their own logic of sacrificing thousands of their young men in a failed effort to storm a tiny airstrip. An American air force pilot remarked of the obliteration:

In mid-February, the area looked like the rest of Vietnam, mountainous and heavily jungled with very little visibility through the jungle canopy. Five weeks later, the jungle had become literally a desert—vast stretches of scarred, bare earth with hardly a tree standing, a landscape of splinters and bomb craters. (T. Hoopes, *The Limits of Intervention,* 213)

Fewer than 200 Americans were killed, with 1,600 wounded, 845 of which were evacuated. No doubt the real figures were somewhat higher when one considers the fighting in and around Khesanh at Lang Vei, the overland rescue effort in April (Operation Pegasus), and the loss of transport and combat pilots. Still, for every one American killed at Khesanh, fifty North Vietnamese lost their lives—lopsided figures approaching the horrendous slaughter ratios between Spaniards and Aztecs in Mexico or British and Zulus in southern Africa.

Instead of amazement at the carnage, the American media throughout the siege forecast a terrible defeat. After the beginning of the Tet offensives, and the near simultaneous capture of the intelligence ship *Pueblo* in Korean waters, *Life* magazine warned its readers against global American reversals culminating in "the looming bloodbath at Khe Sanh." After a month into the siege, when the level of American counterfire was well established, on March 22 Arthur Schlesinger, Jr., wrote in the *Washington Post,* "Whatever we do, we must not re-enact Dien Bien Phu." He went on to warn Americans, "Let us not sacrifice our brave men to the folly of generals and the obstinance of Presidents." Oliver E. Chub, Jr., echoed the general hysteria in the *New Republic:* Khesanh, he said, recalling Bismarck's remark about the relative value of German soldiers versus intervention in the Balkans, "was not worth the life of a single Marine." He concluded that the siege "could easily end in a military disaster unprecedented in the Vietnam war" (B. Nalty, *Air Power and the Fight for Khe Sanh,* 39–40). Meanwhile, within three weeks of the beginning of the siege, wings of B-52s—in a preview of the Gulf War bombing tactics years later—had worked out a grid system around the besieged base, in which three bombers blanketed a one-by-two-kilometer box every ninety minutes, around the clock, with explosives and napalm. The air force methodically began to destroy nearly every living thing within one kilometer of the marine ramparts.

The siege ended on April 6, and with it a close to the last of the fighting that had lingered after the culmination of the Tet Offensive. But then in late June, convinced that the resistance had been an overwhelming American success, the MACV ordered the base dismantled. On July 5 Khesanh was razed! The Americans destroyed in hours what the North Vietnamese communists could not in months. All the bridges on nearby Route 9, which weeks earlier had been so laboriously repaired to enable land convoys to reach the trapped marines, were systematically blown up. In the aftermath of the Tet Offensive and subsequent bombing halts, the Americans had apparently determined to abandon their previous idea of walling off the DMZ and stationing troops in forward defense areas near the North Vietnamese border. The marines who had braved constant fire for nearly three months were furious and in near revolt at the news; they felt that possession of the base, not the number of enemy killed, had signified that their lost friends had at least died for something tangible.

By April 1968 both sides in the upcoming American presidential election were talking of winding down the American military presence, either through Robert Kennedy's promise of negotiated withdrawal, Hubert Humphrey's hints of bombing halts, or Richard Nixon's alternative of gradual "Vietnamization." As Admiral Ulysses Grant Sharp, American naval commander of the Pacific fleet, put it after the amazing American victory at Khesanh, "They got so damned hysterical back in Washington over the Tet offensive that they sort of went off the deep end and decided to get the war over with even if we weren't going to win it" (B. Nalty, *Air Power and the Fight for Khe Sanh*, 104). The gallant defense of the compound, terrible damage to the North Vietnamese, and abrupt abandonment of Khesanh were all emblematic of what Vietnam had become by late spring 1968, a quagmire where military operations did not necessarily have anything to do with perceptions about the value or course of the war. Khesanh, better even than Hué, revealed the incompetence of the high command, the bravery and discipline of the marines, the astonishing technological superiority of the air force—and the complete hysteria of much of the American media, which during the war habitually downplayed America's ability to hurt the enemy, only in the aftermath of the conflict to exaggerate communist losses and suffering. The South Vietnamese ambassador to the United States, Bui Diem, perhaps best summed up the paradox of winning yet losing Tet:

> Not long after, it became clear to me that the complete withdrawal of U.S. forces from Vietnam would be only a matter of time and modalities. In that sense, the Tet attacks of 1968 could well be considered a prelude to the end of the war five years later. Thus, Tet was the climax of the Second Indochina War. Indeed, to me, Tet was the time when U.S. public opinion and misconception snatched defeat from the jaws of potential victory. ("My Recollections of the Tet Offensive," in M. Gilbert and W. Head, eds., *The Tet Offensive*, 133)

VICTORY AS DEFEAT

Quagmire

After Tet the American military often boasted that they had not suffered a single major defeat by enemy forces during the entire fighting in Vietnam. That brag, even for the entire decade of United States involvement, is largely valid, except for a few small compounds staffed by American advisers that were sometimes surprised and for a time occasionally overrun. Although there would be various phases of the Tet Offensive that would go on for months, the first stage of the fighting was essentially over in little less than a month. By the end of February 1968

Hué was free, and Khesanh was relieved in early April; smaller cities were liberated and secure by the end of the first week of the assaults.

Despite the sensational media coverage of the offensive, public opinion polls continued to show that a majority of American citizens supported United States involvement all through Tet—some surveys reported that 70 percent of the citizenry wished military victory rather than withdrawal. Walter Cronkite may have returned from Vietnam to announce to millions of Americans that their military was mired in stalemate and that "the only rational way out . . . would be to negotiate, not as victors, but as an honorable people" (N. Graeber, "The Scholar's View of Vietnam," in D. Showalter and J. Albert, *An American Dilemma,* 29), but most Americans were still willing to support a war they thought could be won outright. The military's problem in Vietnam, at least in the short term, was not an absence of an approving majority back home, but the growth of a vocal, influential, and highly sophisticated minority of critics—activists who cared much more deeply about abruptly ending American involvement than did the majority of supporters in maintaining it.

In the strictly military sense the tragedy of Tet was hardly found in defeat. The calamity was that in the wake of victory the Americans failed to capitalize on the communist disarray, halted the bombing, and gave the enemy the impression of weakness, rather than exultation in its success. Indeed, the decisive victory of Tet in 1968 marked a beginning of radical American retrenchment. The great buildup of 1965–67 was soon to peak at 543,000 total troops on April 4, 1968, and would then abruptly decline so that there were fewer than 30,000 soldiers on December 1, 1972, and essentially none after the cease-fire of 1973. President Johnson seemed to grasp the nature of his own dilemma of winning battles and losing the public relations war in America when he addressed his cabinet on February 28, 1968, a month after the beginning of Tet:

We have to be careful about statements like Westmoreland's when he came back and said that he saw "light at the end of the tunnel." Now we have the shock of this Tet Offensive. Ho Chi Minh never got elected to anything. . . . He is like Hitler in many ways. . . . But we, the President and the Cabinet, are called murderers and they never say anything about Mr. Ho. The signs are all over here. They all say "Stop the War," but you never see any of them over there. Then he launches the Tet attack, breaks the truce and escalates by firing on 44 cities, all at the time that we are offering a bombing pause. It is like the country lawyer who made the greatest speech of his life but they electrocuted the client. We are like that now. (L. Berman, "Tet Offensive," in M. Gilbert and W. Head, eds., *The Tet Offensive*, 43)

Even the North Vietnamese admitted that they had suffered a terrible defeat. Somewhere around 40,000 Vietcong and NVA regular troops had been killed in a few weeks. More of the enemy died during the single year of 1968 than all the Americans lost during the entire involvement of the United States for more than a decade. The communist strategy of bringing local cadres into the streets proved an unmitigated disaster. Far from causing a general insurrection, it only ended up in a bloodbath, destroying the Vietcong infrastructure in the South for at least two years. After Tet there was essentially no effective military arm of the National Liberation Front (NLF) left. It had to be rebuilt from scratch without its most veteran organizers. Such were the costs of the North Vietnamese's complete misunderstanding of the lethality of American airpower, the discipline of its troops, and the overwhelming superiority of its supply train—factors that on the battlefield could trump for a while longer the disadvantages of surprise, poor generalship, and social unrest back home.

A variety of top-ranking communists came to admit the terrible price of Tet. Colonel General Tran Van Tra, in typical doublespeak, nevertheless confessed of the losses caused by the disastrous mistake to engage the Americans directly:

> We did not base ourselves on scientific calculation or a careful weighing of all factors, but in part on an illusion based on our subjective desires. For that reason, although that decision was wise, ingenious, and timely, and although its implementation was well organized and bold, there was excellent coordination on all battlefields, everyone acted very bravely, sacrificed their lives, and there was created a significant strategic turning point in Vietnam and Indochina, we suffered large sacrifices and losses with regard to manpower and material, especially cadres at the various echelons, which clearly weakened us. (R. Ford, *Tet 1968*, 139)

If the North Vietnamese knew they had lost the Tet Offensive, why did it seem to most Western observers that the enemy had in fact won?

Much of the problems in perception grew out of raised expectations immediately prior to the offensive. The beleaguered American military, stung by the antiwar movement, had prematurely assured the public at the beginning of 1968 that the war was winding down in an American victory. As part of the overly optimistic appraisal, it compounded the error by acknowledging that it was no longer enough for the Americans to defeat the enemy outright on the battlefield. By 1968 it was equally crucial for the military to achieve at least four other objectives if opposition at home were to cease and public support were to continue: proof that after four years of intense ground fighting, the North Vietnamese were close to capitulation; hard evidence that the South Vietnamese were at last ready to shoulder the majority of their defense obligations; assurance that America could achieve rapid withdrawal with a minimum of casualties; and confidence that South Vietnam was a liberal and humane democracy.

Tet, a clear American victory, dashed those pretensions. It showed that all these goals were now problematic; in a paradoxical way, the defeat ultimately proved the North Vietnamese long-term strategy prescient, if unconcerned with the human costs of such a sacrificial policy. As long as they were willing to suffer literally thousands of dead for a chance to engage the Americans, time was on the communists' side. So an American intelligence officer summed up General Vo Nguyen Giap's brutal strategy of attrition: "His is not an army that sends coffins north; it is by the traffic of homebound American coffins that Giap measures his success" (G. Lewy, *America in Vietnam,* 68).

As long as the Soviets and Chinese supplied top-notch weaponry, as long as the Vietcong could pose to influential American journalists, academics, and pacifists as liberationists and patriots, rather than truce breakers and terrorist killers, and as long as the American military tried to fight a conventional war under absurd rules of engagement and over corpses counted and not ground taken and held, the North Vietnamese would recruit ample fresh manpower on the promise of a free nation to come—and always kill some Americans in the terrible arithmetic of relative body counts. An Aztec herald once warned Cortés that the Mexicas could lose 250 to every one Castilian and still win. In the modern context such an admonition had a profound effect on General Westmoreland—not because there were too few Americans or too many enemy on the battlefield, but because politically there really was a set limit to the number of American fatalities to be incurred. The American political establishment may have believed that Vietnam was a proxy war in an ongoing global twenty-five-year struggle against communist tyranny; but the American people increasingly doubted the need to give up their treasure and sons so far away, when the Chinese and Russians were unlikely to reach the shores of the United States via Vietnam. Had Westmoreland been Cortés at Tenochtitlán in 1520, he would have reported the Aztec threat back to King Philip, asked for instructions, and demanded more conquistadors before advancing. In actuality, Cortés agreed with the Aztec herald's prognosis of numerical disparity and so planned to kill 250 Aztecs for every conquistador he lost!

During the Tet Offensive a total of 800,000 refugees left their villages, many of them flocking to Saigon, which was soon to swell to nearly 4 million persons. The American-sponsored rural pacification program known as Civil Operations and Revolutionary Development Support (CORDS) was near shambles, as hope faded that the countryside would ever be completely secure. The attack on Hué, the massacres there, and the penetration of the embassy grounds shocked many South Vietnamese. If American bureaucrats in downtown Saigon were not immune from attack, how safe were rural Vietnamese? Khesanh, heroically saved as a key base near the DMZ, was abandoned and razed—with no consideration of the symbolism involved therein in a war replete with symbolism. Undersecretary of the Air Force Townsend Hoopes summed up the American depression:

> One thing was clear to us all: the Tet offensive was the eloquent counterpoint to the effusive optimism of November. It showed conclusively that the U.S. did not in fact control the situation, that it was not in fact winning, that the enemy retained enormous strength and vitality—certainly enough to extinguish the notion of a clear-cut allied victory in the minds of all objective men. . . . Even the staunch and conservative *Wall Street Journal* was saying in mid-February, "We think the American people should be getting ready to accept, if they haven't already, the prospect that the whole Vietnam effort may be doomed, that it may be falling apart beneath our feet." (*The Limits of Intervention*, 146–47)

After the victory of Tet the American military requested another 206,000 troops and a quarter million additional reserves—hardly a display to the American people that its armed forces were winning the war on the ground. Hoopes called that request a "stunner." Without new battle tactics or long-term strategy, the MACV leadership envisioned an even larger American presence, exceeding the supposed 525,000-man limit. Yet the American people wondered: had not the United States a little more than twenty years earlier in Normandy defeated the German Wehrmacht with fewer troops in less time? The requests for more men were ignored.

The record-keeping of the U.S. military in Vietnam was notoriously inexact in assessing enemy dead, but by necessity it was mostly accurate in reporting American fatalities. Thus, most observers believed that Tet cost somewhere between 1,000 and 2,000 American dead. The American people cared little that their boys were killing the enemy at unheard-of ratios of thirty and forty for each GI lost. They, like the military, looked instead to body counts—but, like General Giap, to American rather than North Vietnamese—and saw them soar to intolerable rates of more than three hundred or four hundred dead a week.

How odd that at the pinnacle of a lethal 2,500-year-old military tradition, American planners completely ignored the tenets of the entire Western military heritage. Cortés—also outnumbered, far from home, in a strange climate, faced with near insurrection among his own troops and threats of recall from home, fighting a fanatical enemy that gave no quarter, with fickle allies—at least knew that his own soldiers and the Spanish crown cared little how many actual bodies of the enemy he might count, but a great deal whether he took and held Tenochtitlán and so ended resistance with his army largely alive. Lord Chelmsford—likewise surrounded by critics in and out of the army, under threat of dismissal, ignorant of the exact size, nature, and location of his enemy, suspicious of Boer colonialists, English idealists, and tribal allies—at least realized that until he overran Zululand, destroyed the nucleus of the royal kraals, and captured the king, the war would go on despite the thousands of Zulus who fell to his deadly Martini-Henry rifles.

American generals never fully grasped, or never successfully transmitted to the political leadership in Washington, that simple lesson: that the number of enemy killed meant little in and of itself if the land of South Vietnam was not secured and held and the antagonist North Vietnam not invaded, humiliated, or rendered impotent. Few, if any, of the top American brass resigned out of principle over the disastrous rules of engagement that ensured their brave soldiers would be killed without a real chance of decisive military victory. It was as if thousands of graduates from America's top military academies had not a clue about their own lethal heritage of the Western way of war.

Analogies, True and False

In the sixth and seventh books of his history of the Peloponnesian War (431–404 B.C.), Thucydides chronicles a litany of errors on the part of the Athenian leadership and its citizenry during and after their armada's voyage to Sicily (415–413 B.C.). He tells us that there was sharp debate over the decision to send the fleet in the first place and that the allies of Athens on Sicily, who requested help from Syracusan aggression, proved to be corrupt, duplicitous, weak, and in the end worthless in battle. The chief Athenian architect of the expedition, Alcibiades, was recalled by a volatile Assembly back home before he even entered battle. He ended up giving aid to the enemy and residing in Sparta—the chief antagonist of Athens during the entire twenty-seven-year Peloponnesian War.

The other commanders, Lamachus and Nicias, were irresolute, blinkered, and paranoid about the political consequences of becoming bogged down in an unwinnable war, despite the overwhelming force they brought along from Athens. Indeed, the old conservative Nicias's reluctance to attack Syracuse decisively, coupled with his request for massive reinforcements, seemed driven more by worry about his own political future than by strategic wisdom. While Thucydides laments that the campaign could have been won had the Athenians just supported their troops, his own history at times seems to belie those very conclusions. The Athenians, he tells us, sent not one armada, but two—men, ships, and supplies in excess of even the amount requested by their own generals.

In the end, his account of Sicily reads as Sophoclean tragedy, or, as General Omar Bradley remarked of the possibility of fighting the Chinese in the early 1950s, "the wrong war, at the wrong place, at the wrong time, and with the wrong enemy." Sicily, after all, was an entirely new theater of operations, eight hundred miles by sea from Athens, against a power that had not directly attacked Athens, and at a time when the Spartan army at home was free to march up to the walls of Athens.

No wonder, Thucydides tells us, that the Athenian public quickly lost heart with the continual news of deadlock overseas and the need for ever more men and matériel. In a consensual society, ancient or modern, voices are raised when overseas military operations prove expensive, costly in lives, and without promise of eventual victory. In that sense the rise of American antiwar sentiment was predictable. Dissent at home was in line with the entire history of Western opposition to its own military practice on those rare occasions when victory proves elusive—often with results that are not necessarily negative to the long-term interests of the state, although admittedly abjectly harmful to the unfortunate soldiers in the field.

The Americans' objectives, both local and geopolitical, were more or less clear from the start: the security of an independent noncommunist Vietnamese state in the South, and with it an end to general communist aggression in Southeast Asia. But the methods of achieving those seemingly moral goals were far less apparent. The formula for victory was never fully thought out. The eventual costs were never seriously computed. Ideally, it was believed in the early 1960s, the Americans would train a sophisticated democratic army of resistance. In two to three years this reconstituted Army of the Republic of Vietnam could perhaps defend itself, albeit, as in the Korean instance, requiring a near permanent American presence of 30,000 or so GIs along a demilitarized zone to preserve the peace. A grateful Vietnamese populace would then support this newly democratic government and willingly enlist in its army to save the country from communism, which in the past had led to so many civilian deaths and dislocations. Or so it was all thought.

Yet by 1964 the communists proved tougher, the South Vietnamese weaker, and the American people more skeptical than imagined. At that point—somewhere between late 1964 and mid-1965—President Johnson undertook a disastrous strategy of steady escalation, without changing the ground rules under which previously small American contingents had operated. The president knew nothing about military affairs. He showed no awareness that such a tremendous commitment of sending hundreds of thousands of American soldiers to Vietnam to defeat Third World communists—more than half a million troops, 1.2 million bombs a year, thousands of enemy killed each month, three hundred to four hundred dead Americans per week—raised the geopolitical and domestic stakes among friends and enemies. Failure to win with such a sizable force could only invite further Soviet adventurism in the wake of perceived American weakness, increase domestic unrest, and highlight the incompetence of the South Vietnamese government. Once empires commit such resources to military adventures, time becomes an enemy rather than an ally, as the inability to achieve immediate success sends ripples of doubt—fatal to any hegemon—beyond the battlefield to lap at uneasy allies and citizens at home.

Yet the Americans for nearly a decade went on to fight a conventional war in unconventional terrain without the presence of clearly demarcated battle lines or even a home front. Since the overall strategy was the promise to stop communism's spread in Asia while at all costs avoiding even indirect or accidental confrontations with either the Soviets or the Chinese, a number of paradoxes arose that thwarted planners every time a change in American strategy was debated. Generally, the policy that coalesced was a reluctance to mine harbors—which was not allowed until 1972—or to wipe out key government installations in Hanoi and Haiphong in fear of killing communist foreign suppliers and consultants. There was an absolute and unquestioned prohibition on invading North Vietnam. Urban power plants and supply depots that provided the energy to unload war supplies were off limits for years. For most of the war, no allowance was given for entering Cambodia, Thailand, or Laos in force, the sites of vast enemy supply dumps and sanctuaries. Airpower and artillery strikes, along with fortified defensive bases, were emphasized, rather than ambitious guerrilla offensives and sustained counterinsurgency efforts to rid the cities and villages of Vietcong.

The irony was that in their misguided efforts to restrain the war according to murky and poorly thought-out parameters, the American administration ensured that the killing would go on for nearly a decade. In the topsy-turvy world of Vietnam, indiscriminate bombing of jungles would be seen as acceptable military practice, when the far more humane precision attacks on factories and dockyards in Hanoi would not be—and thus as a result thousands of American lives would be sacrificed in defeat. Visitors to Hanoi after the war were startled that the city seemed to have suffered little damage from bombing—despite assertions from antiwar activists that the American military had killed thousands in the streets and nearly leveled the capital.

The Johnson and Nixon administrations thought that they could achieve another Korea—a victory of sorts that had been won despite a South Korean government that was corrupt, a huge Chinese army that had entered the war, nearly 50,000 American lives that had been lost, and strict political parameters on the way that the Korean conflict had been waged. Yet they often misread the entire Korean analogy. In relative terms the Soviets and Chinese were both much weaker than the United States in 1950 than they were in 1965. In the prior war neither had posed a credible nuclear threat to American shores. But the government of the United States further underestimated the traditional Chinese fear of conventional American military power, failing to remember that the communists had lost 800,000 dead in Korea to massive American air and artillery strikes and largely had no wish to repeat that debacle in Vietnam. While it was true that precautions were needed in order not to provoke the communist nuclear powers, in most cases an inordinate concern with the Russians and Chinese unduly curtailed the range of American responses.

By 1965, as long as the Americans were convinced of the potential for wider and possibly nuclear involvement, they avoided hitting Soviet ships in North Vietnamese waters, pursuing fighter aircraft across national borders, and threatening Hanoi to such a degree that direct Soviet or Chinese intervention would be necessary to save the regime. It was seen as preferable by the Johnson administration to lose American lives to Chinese and Russian volunteers quietly than to have them killed in battle openly. In addition, American pilots had quickly dominated the skies over North Korea, but by 1972 in Vietnam there were sophisticated Soviet and Chinese air defenses—8,000 antiaircraft guns, 250 surface-to-air missile batteries, between two hundred and three hundred modern jet fighters, and thousands of foreign advisers—that meant the toll of lost American aircraft would continue to rise in any sustained bombing campaign. The terrain of Vietnam was much more heavily forested than Korea's, making bombing accuracy more difficult as canopies of brush hid the exact location of enemy troops.

Far more important, the South Korean president, Syngman Rhee, had garnered more domestic support than any of the South Vietnamese leaders. Rhee had been able to pose as a protector of Korean autonomy against the northern puppets of Chinese Stalinists—in a manner that Ho Chi Minh had done in Vietnam by reminding the population that the Americans were merely the latest imperialists in a long line of Japanese and French aggressors who were all eventually evicted from Vietnamese ground. In Korea the Americans were convinced that their persistence had stopped a communist tidal wave headed toward Japan. Few, in contrast, believed the loss of Vietnam would result in a communist sphere of influence much larger than Southeast Asia—and few American citizens or soldiers cared about Southeast Asia. Americans in 1964 were also a different people than during the immediate postwar years of the 1950s at the beginning of the Cold War—more affluent, reform-minded, and often tired of two decades of costly and constant deterrence to worldwide communism.

Finally, in Korea the United States faced a real threat of a united communist bloc; but by 1965 many Americans sensed—no doubt often naïvely—that China and Russia were near-enemies, that Vietnam was a traditional foe of China, and that the Cambodian, Laotian, and Thai communists were never completely unified, themselves sharing a long history of antagonism toward each other and against the Vietnamese. So it became far more difficult in Vietnam to convince America's allies or its own people that communist aggression in Vietnam endangered either Europe or America:

> Vietnamese Communism, obnoxious though it might seem, presented no clear threat to American national security. Had Vietnam been in Africa or west Asia rather than on the border of China, a communist take-over from the colonial French or from a local anti-Communist regime would have occasioned only passing concern. (D. Oberdorfer, *Tet!*, 334)

All these considerations would have been moot had the United States won the war decisively and quickly. But that envisioned victory was impossible under the conditions in which the military conducted the war—and millions of Americans would become angry and eager to apprise their own military and political leaders of just that ignorance and incompetence.

Fault Lines

As early as 1965, three years before Tet, vast fault lines over the conduct of the war had developed inside the American military and political establishment, as the media and popular culture reached a consensus that war was not merely wrong but increasingly amoral. On the radical left, an old coalition of communists, socialists, and pacifists, teamed with assorted newer dissidents and anarchists—the entire gamut from Tom Hayden, Jane Fonda, and Abbie Hoffman to Susan Sontag, Mary McCarthy, Ramsey Clark, and the Berrigan brothers—openly advocated an American exit. They accepted, if not welcomed, defeat and saw the American role as predictably imperialist, racist, and exploitative—in character, in their view, with much of American history. Indeed, many wished to conduct war crimes tribunals to indict American generals and politicians.

Less extreme, but perhaps as naïve, were many traditional liberals who increasingly became radicalized as the war progressed. They envisioned the North Vietnamese more as European socialists and the Vietnam conflict solely as a "civil war"—despite evidence of North Vietnamese atrocities dating back to the early 1950s, direct Soviet and Chinese involvement, and almost no groundswell of support among South Vietnamese for communism. Both these factions called for immediate U.S. withdrawal and either openly advocated or were indifferent to a North Vietnamese military victory.

Middle-of-the-road Democrats still believed in the Cold War idea of containment. But after Tet, dissidents and ex-members of the Johnson administration, such as Robert McNamara, felt that the cost of victory in Vietnam was perhaps too high and too divisive in its effect on American society. Many reasoned that American troops were better deployed elsewhere, especially as bulwarks against Soviet and Chinese aggression in Europe and Korea. In general, by 1970 such moderates called for a negotiated settlement, and, barring that, a gradual but irrevocable U.S. withdrawal to save the country from tearing itself apart.

Conservatives were equally split. Those on the extreme right like Barry Goldwater and George Wallace, whose 1968 running mate was Curtis LeMay, saw no reason why the war could not be ended quickly and victoriously, through any means possible—including an invasion of the North and perhaps the use of tactical nuclear weapons. They were confident of American tactical military superiority over the North Vietnamese and the nation's strategic edge over Russia and China. What was lacking, in their eyes, was not American power, but will.

Many more-mainstream Republicans were equally furious at the military's rules of engagement, but believed a vigorous conventional war could bring results rather quickly without the need for full-scale invasion of the North or a declaration of war. Thus, they advocated wider bombing of North Vietnam, raids into Laos, Cambodia, and Thailand, hot aerial pursuit into purportedly neutral countries, mining of enemy harbors, and a blockade of Vietnamese waters. By 1970 Vietnamization under Richard Nixon was their creed, hoping that sustained American bombing would bolster the South Vietnamese's own resistance.

Finally, some mainstream populists and conservative isolationists, ranging from senators such as Wayne Morse and Mike Mansfield to the editors at the *Wall Street Journal,* argued that Vietnam was outside the American sphere of interest altogether and not worth any American dead. Their calls for withdrawal, however, centered on the terrible waste of American lives and capital in Asia—quite unlike their counterparts on the radical Left, who seemed to worry more about Vietnamese than American dead.

Other fault lines were not so ideological. Southerners, for example, put a high premium on American "honor" and generally supported escalation if it led to victory, while those in New England and on the West Coast were more likely to advocate immediate retreat. Black and Hispanic leaders, even if sizable percentages of their constituencies were committed to serving and dying in Vietnam, saw resistance to the war as integral to larger civil rights issues and alliances with liberal whites, and so generally approved of an immediate end at any cost. Women tended to value peace more highly than victory. The educated favored reassessment, if not acknowledgment of defeat, while those without college degrees were more likely to support official U.S. policy.

In the context of identifying support for the war, the traditional rubrics "Republican" and "Democrat" began to mean little. Even the more rigid binaries "hawks" and "doves" often evolved to "fascists" and "communists," and ultimately "war criminals" and "traitors"—all reminiscent of Thucydides' gripping portrait of the stasis at Corcyra (Corfu; 427 B.C.) in the third book of his history. Consensual societies, Thucydides relates, when confronted with debilitating wars, steadily rip away the thin veneer of hard-won culture—civility, moderation, and honesty in expression becoming the predictable first casualties of extremism. All of these divides were to be expected in a free society at odds over the conduct and expense of a seemingly unwinnable and unpopular war. The plays of Aristophanes, tragedies of Euripides, and history of Thucydides during the Peloponnesian War offer ample precedent of antiwar dissent at the beginning of Western civilization. But what made the issue of protest much different in Vietnam from the long tradition of Western opposition to military operations were perhaps three new factors in Western culture.

First, the electronic age ensured that killing would be televised instantaneously. Few American military leaders, who allowed free rein to television reporters and photojournalists, realized the ramifications of this media revolution. World War I or II might have ended differently had Europeans watched the charge at the Somme firsthand, or had citizens of the United States seen the carnage at Omaha Beach while reporters editorialized on the air about the insanity of Americans charging fixed positions from a stormy sea. Film strips of the Somme, in fact, shocked the British public; and had there been more such movies, and had they been broadcast live, England may well have lost public support for the war entirely. Belatedly, the American high command finally appreciated the full extent of the revolutionary changes in media coverage of the war in Vietnam:

> The picture of a few flaming Saigon houses, presented by a gloomy-voiced telecaster as an instance of the destruction caused in the capital, created the inevitable impression that this was the way it was in all or most of Saigon. This human tendency to generalize from a single fact to universal conclusion has always been a prime cause for the distorted views regarding Vietnam and certainly contributed to the pessimism in the United States after the Tet offensive in 1968. (M. Taylor, *Swords and Plowshares*, 215)

This sheer spontaneity of visual images, with the accompanying requirement for split-second editing and commentary, also now put a much higher premium on journalistic integrity and competence—at a time when reporters were in demand and sent to Vietnam without much experience or guidance. Millions might see an American GI torch a rural village, but be given no immediate commentary as to why. The bombing of Hué was broadcast worldwide, creating a crescendo of anti-Americanism, while the mass graves of thousands of innocents slain by the communists in the same city were not simultaneously seen on American TV screens.

Second, Vietnam was conducted during the greatest period of cultural and political upheaval in American history—civil rights, women's liberation, rock music, drugs, and the sexual revolution—ensuring that the war would serve as a general catalyst for antiestablishment activity of all sorts and as a rallying point for a wide variety of dissidents. Photojournalists and television teams adapted to the new media culture in their contrarian approach, and thus differed from the old print reporters of past wars. If would-be Pattons of the American military wished for brief assignments in Vietnam solely to garner combat experience and headlines for future promotions, so equally careerist journalists and reporters might find immediate fame and celebrity status should they hype an especially egregious example of American ignominy or incompetence. That so many high military officers and reporters—at odds over the war, yet so similar in the nature of their own respective careerist conduct—habitually lied to the American people was regrettable but predictable, given the nature of the American involvement.

Third, America in the early 1960s was at the peak of economic prosperity, achieving a general level of affluence never before witnessed by any civilization. The result was literally millions of dissident Americans—students, intellectuals, journalists—who had access to travel, leisure, and money without the confines of the past drudgery of constant rote labor. A lifestyle of freedom, mobility, and affluence that had once been confined to a small aristocracy was now available to millions. Whereas in the past, campus-bound poor students worked long hours and worried about grades and future employment, while professors rarely left their campuses and often taught enormous course loads, in America of the early 1960s millions of activists had the time and freedom to travel—and money to expend energy in protest and general activism.

Television had large budgets for roving correspondents, satellite transmissions, air travel, and investigative reporting. Universities offered free tuition, draft deferments, and liberal scholarships. Grants, sabbaticals, fellowships, and subsidized presses offered a formerly impoverished class of academic new opportunities to publish and disseminate criticism of the war. The antiwar movement became a multimillion-dollar industry, whose existence, like the vast expenditures in Vietnam, was entirely predicated on the enormous productivity of the American capitalist economy. The result was that often the level of protest crossed traditional boundaries of dissent and directly aided the enemy, as the North Vietnamese later confessed:

> Every day our leadership would listen to world news over the radio at 9 A.M. to follow the growth of the American antiwar movement. Visits to Hanoi by people like Jane Fonda and former Attorney General Ramsey Clark and ministers gave us confidence that we should hold on in the face of battlefield reverses. We were elated when Jane Fonda, wearing a red Vietnamese dress, said at a press conference that she was ashamed of American actions in the war and that she would struggle along with us. (L. Sorley, *A Better War*, 93)

In the long history of Western warfare it is hard to imagine a more difficult conflict than Vietnam, in which the American soldier had a host of enemies undreamed of by earlier combatants: citizens of his own country who often condemned his service and gave aid to the enemy, Vietnamese civilians who at any time and at any place might reveal themselves to be Vietcong terrorists and infiltrators, and his own government, which on grounds other than military logic restricted where and how he might retaliate against the enemy.

The Mythologies of Vietnam

The American press and media had it mostly right relatively quickly about Vietnam: the military and administration in Washington often misled and occasionally lied about the course of the war. American tactics—especially carpet bombing of jungles and forests—were ineffectual, if not occasionally inhumane and counterproductive. The method of exemption to the draft was not equitable. The South Vietnamese government was often dishonest. The rules of engagement were comic.

So the journalists and reporters were absolutely correct that the American high command was inept in its prosecution of this strange war. Only 15 percent of some 536,000 troops in Vietnam were combat soldiers. While it was true that there were no absolutely safe areas in Vietnam due to terrorists and infiltrators, the vast majority of veterans did not have much contact with the enemy. After a year's service, when those rare frontline GIs were at last acculturated to the rigors of war, they were abruptly sent home. Officers often saw no more than six months of combat; and some rear-echelon bases were replete with swimming pools, movie theaters, and nightclubs.

Such critical problems needed and got public exposure. Dissent was invaluable and helped to draw needed reexamination about the purpose, conduct, and very morality of the undeclared war so far from America's borders. Military reform, needed legislation concerning the abuse of presidential power, and scrutiny over the wisdom of America's overseas interventions all followed from the antiwar movement. After 1968 the American military fought smarter, was leaner, and under General Creighton W. Abrams eliminated many of the abuses highlighted by the media. In the end, as in the case of ancient Athens's disastrous Sicilian expedition, there was a good case to be made that it was not in America's interest to commit such a huge investment of treasure and lives so far from home, in a war that could not be won outright under the accepted Cold War rules of engagement, which made it nearly impossible either to cut completely the lines of communist supplies or to invade the North.

Yet within that general critique of American policy, there often arose a hysteria—the predictable license of a free, affluent Western society that so bothered critics of democracy from Plato to Hegel—which shrouded truth and left mythology in its wake. The result is that today few know whether an independent, noncommunist South Vietnam was viable either after the American victory in Tet or during the punishing bombing of the North in 1973—had the facts concerning the progress of the war or the sordid history and conduct of the North Vietnamese communists been accurately and soberly reported to the American people. Despite the media coverage, however, we can speculate that far fewer Vietnamese would have died or been exiled had the communists not conquered the entire country in 1975.

Nearly everything that was reported by the Western press about Tet was just as misleading as either the North Vietnamese claims of a great military victory or the American military's assurance that the communist offensive had no long-term lasting political consequences that might lead to a change in U.S. policy. In *Big Story* the veteran reporter Peter Braestrup devoted a massive two-volume work to exposing the deception and sometimes outright lies that were promulgated by the Western media about the Tet Offensive. In his view the story of a hard-fought American victory, characterized by remarkable American bravery, did not fit well with either the sensationalism that built journalistic careers or the general antiwar sentiments of the reporters themselves.

While the South Vietnamese government was hardly Jeffersonian, it was not true that either the National Liberation Front or the North Vietnamese enjoyed massive popular support among the South Vietnamese. Before Tet the communists boasted—and it was so reported—that 10 million of 14 million South Vietnamese lived in sectors under their direct control and would thus logically welcome the Tet "liberation." In truth, the vast majority of the South Vietnamese were living within ARVN and American security zones. Almost no one joined in the general uprising. Most felt more, not less, terrified of the communists after the failed Tet Offensive. Hué was not left completely in ruins. Far from being desolate and nearly abandoned, the city received tons of U.S. aid for reconstruction. By the end of the year, most refugees had returned and the city was pretty much functioning as it was before the fighting. Nevertheless, the media reported otherwise: "the only way Hué could be won was by destroying it."

That erroneous remark was an echo of Peter Arnett's famous reporting of an American officer's summation of the fighting at Ben Tre, a village in the Mekong Delta: "It became necessary to destroy the town to save it" (D. Oberdorfer, *Tet!,* 184). Yet there was little evidence—other than from Arnett himself—that any American officer said anything of the sort. It was reported as such to an astonished and outraged American public, proof as it were of the deliberate and mindless manner in which the military had responded during the Tet Offensive. Arnett never identified by name the officer who was his purported source. Nor did he produce anyone—civilian or military—who could corroborate the statement. A military investigation to ferret out the guilty officer turned up nothing. In fact, U.S. advisers at Ben Tre, who were overrun by Vietcong, may well have called in air strikes to prevent their own annihilation; and such bombing probably resulted in civilian casualties. But there was no evidence that the Americans deliberately, or as an act of official policy, destroyed Ben Tre.

Nor was the bombing of the South or North aimed at innocent civilians. The greater slaughter of innocents was accomplished through indiscriminate North Vietnamese and Vietcong artillery and guerrilla attacks. The Vietnamese landscape was not rendered barren by either American bombing or the use of herbicides. Only 10 percent of the countryside was subjected to defoliants during the spraying program between 1962 and 1971, where less than 3 percent of the population lived. During the year of Tet, new strains of imported rice were planted on 40,000 hectares. By 1969 rice production reached 5.5 million metric tons, higher than any year since World War II. By 1971 such miracle strains of American rice had resulted in the highest recorded crop in the history of South Vietnam, at some 6.1 million metric tons. By 1972, under American pressure, the South Vietnamese government was at last granting title of more than 2 million acres to nearly 400,000 farmers—at a time when there was essentially no private property in the North, where in the 1950s thousands had been branded as capitalists and either exiled or killed, often for owning as little as two acres. What ruined the Vietnamese rural economy was Vietcong infiltration of the countryside and collectivization of farmland—confirmed after 1975, when during the peace, farm production of all kinds collapsed. By the late 1970s Vietnam was one of the poorest countries in the world, near starvation in an area of Asia surrounded by the affluence of Japan, Indonesia, and South Korea. The degree that the economy improved at all in the 1980s and 1990s was predicated entirely on the introduction of modest market reforms.

Nor were all critics of the American presence in Vietnam principled dissidents. Even long after the war, many openly confessed to welcoming a communist victory and so gave a romantic view of Tet that revealed more about their own ideology than any truthful account of what transpired on the battlefield:

> More generally, the Tet Offensive made a powerful contribution to the rebuilding of some sort of socialist presence in the United States. . . . As the insurgents burst into view, "shouting their slogans and fighting with nerve-shattering fury," we realized that they were not just noble victims, but that they were going to win the war. Carried along by the momentum of their endeavor, we wanted to be associated with the Vietnamese revolutionaries (Tet made the NLF flag an emblem) and to figure out how our newly discovered vision of "power to the people" might be realized here in the United States. . . . The Offensive demonstrated that socialism was not just a moral stance or an academic persuasion, but a real possibility embodied in collective action of real people. (D. Hunt, "Remembering the Tet Offensive," in M. Gettleman et al., eds., *Vietnam and America*, 376)

Completely ignored were the massacres at Hué, the general defeat of the North Vietnamese during Tet, and the distaste for communism in both South Vietnam and America. Instead, the murderous North Vietnamese attack and executions during a holiday truce were dubbed "swift and peaceful" (366).

Although the South Vietnamese were corrupt and sometimes brutal, they never engaged in wholesale massacre on the scale of the North. Well before the killings at Hué, the communists had compiled a sordid record of executions and persecution that was forgotten or went ignored by critics of the war. There was never any intent on the part of the North Vietnamese to participate honestly in a national election of 1956 that would have allowed all Vietnamese to vote freely and without coercion; in 1976 such "free" elections resulted in communists winning 99 percent of the vote. When the country was originally partitioned (1954), nine out of ten refugees headed south rather than north—the total number of refugees voting with their feet eventually reaching almost a million. Well over 10,000 Vietnamese were executed during the communist land collectivization of the early 1950s; indeed, the figure may have approached 100,000—a prelude to the Cambodian holocaust of 1977–78 to come. Yet later, prominent antiwar critics pleaded:

> Did we who were in Vietnam, and opposed the U.S. effort there, expect the instant eclipse of the Provisionary Revolutionary Government and the imposition of rule by the North? I didn't. Did we anticipate reconciliation, as happened in Hungary after the revolution? That is what I hoped for. Did we foresee a whole chain of reeducation camps in which tens of thousands of people would be incarcerated without trial for indefinite periods? Did we expect the liberators to be condemned a few years later by Amnesty International as violators of human rights? Did we expect hundreds of thousands of boat people to take to the sea and leave the ancestral lands that they valued so highly? (W. Shawcross, "The Consequence of the War for Indochina," in H. Salisbury, ed., Vietnam Reconsidered, 244)

The answers were "of course"—and plain to any sensible observer of either the atrocious civil rights record of the North Vietnamese in the decades before the war or the systematic slaughters in the Soviet Union and China by Communist Party bosses. Perhaps the greatest moral crime of the American dissidents was their later near unanimous silence about the Cambodian holocaust—truly one of the most horrible and inhumane events of the twentieth century. The few who wrote about the killing often blamed America for the Khmer Rouge—as if those who fought communism had caused a communist victory that led to a communist holocaust.

But not all criticism of the American war was mere coffeehouse academic posturing. Hundreds of Americans visited Hanoi to aid the North

Vietnamese. Tom Hayden and Jane Fonda broadcast propaganda hostile to U.S. troops in the field, and purportedly named their son Troi (later changed to Troy) after a North Vietnamese hero. In the midst of the war, David Halberstam wrote a mostly favorable biography of Ho Chi Minh (*Ho* [New York, 1971]). Prominent liberals such as Martin Luther King falsely claimed that the North Vietnamese were influenced by the ideals of the American Constitution and that our bombing resembled Nazi atrocities during World War II. Communists such as Herbert Aptheker and Michael Myerson assured Americans that the POWs were well treated. Both men met with ranking enemy officials, were interviewed on North Vietnamese radio, and then gave lectures on the nobility of the communist cause.

In general, American visitors to North Vietnam saw the communists as "heroes," and American prisoners as war criminals. David Dillinger, who questioned American POWs in Hanoi, called their torture the "prisoner of war hoax," claiming that the Nixon administration had fabricated reports of tortured and innocent American prisoners. "The only verified torture associated with the American prisoners held by the North Vietnamese," pontificated Dillinger, "is the torture of prisoners' families by the State Department, Pentagon, and the White House" (G. Lewy, *America in Vietnam*, 336). Anne Weills summed up best the activists' feelings in a much later reflection: "You should understand that it was considered a great honor to be able to go to Vietnam, for us in the antiwar movement, and to meet Mm. Binh in Paris [head of the National Liberation Front delegation]. These were our heroines and heroes" (J. Clinton, *The Loyal Opposition*, 124). Allen Ginsberg wrote a poem: "Let the Viet Cong win over the American army! . . . and if it were my wish, we'd lose & our will/be broken/& our armies scattered" (*Collected Poems, 1947–80*, New York, 1984, 478).

Noam Chomsky, who visited Hanoi in 1970, years after the war was over, best summed up the antiwar activists' persistent view of America:

> We attack a country, we kill several million people, we wipe the place out, we carry out chemical warfare, we leave the place littered with bombs from which people are still dying, we carry out extensive chemical warfare with hundreds of thousands of victims, and after all of this, the one humanitarian issue is whether they are forthcoming about information about American fliers who were shot down bombing them. That's the only humanitarian issue left. You'd have to go to Nazi Germany to find that level of cowardice and viciousness. (J. Clinton, *The Loyal Opposition*, 195)

To the chagrin of reporters and antiwar activists, the French journalist Jean Lacouture, whose 1968 laudatory book *Ho Chi Minh* was a source of Halberstam's biography, later admitted in an interview that ideology, not truth, drove much of the reporting of the war:

> My behavior was sometimes more that of a militant than that of a journalist. I dissimulated certain defects of North Vietnam at war against the Americans, because I believed that the cause of the North Vietnamese was good and just enough so that I should expose their errors. I believed it was not opportune to expose the Stalinist nature of the North Vietnamese regime, right at the time Nixon was bombing Hanoi. (G. Sevy, ed., *The American Experience in Vietnam*, 262)

A veteran American reporter of Asia, Keyes Beech, put the coverage of the war in some perspective a decade after the American defeat:

> The media helped lose the war. Oh yes, they did, not because of any massive conspiracy but because of the way the war was reported. What often seems to be forgotten is that the war was lost in the U.S., not in Vietnam. American troops never lost a battle; but they never won the war.... Visitors to that miserable, impoverished capital [Hanoi] often hear their Vietnamese hosts complain about the hostile press treatment they now receive in comparison to the good old days. ("How to Lose a War: A Response from an 'Old Asia Hand,' " in H. Salisbury, ed., *Vietnam Reconsidered*, 152)

The media likewise created an entire mythology around the American GI and the returning Vietnam veteran. Far from being driven insane by the experience, suffering from PTSD (post-traumatic stress disorder), or reduced to an alcoholic or drug stupor, veterans adjusted about as well as past war returnees and showed no higher incidence of mental illness than found in the general population:

> The portrayal of the Vietnam vet as well-adjusted and untroubled by the war would have undermined [the] antiwar agenda, and hence evidence that Vietnam veterans were readjusting or had readjusted well to American society tended to be drowned out by excited and strident recriminations leveled against the U.S. government. (E. Dean, *Shook Over Hell*, 183)

Drug usage was no higher in Vietnam than among those of similar age groups in the general civilian population. Instead, most veterans later expressed remorse over the senseless loss of close friends and also over their inability to win the war, the subsequent communist takeover, relocation camps, boat people, and the Cambodian holocaust. Ninety-one percent of those who served in Vietnam later stated that they were glad to have done so.

Nor did blacks and Hispanics die in Vietnam disproportionate to their numbers in the general population, in some sort of racist plot by the American government. Thomas Thayer's exhaustive statistical profile concluded that "Blacks did not bear an unfair burden in the Vietnam war in terms of combat deaths despite allegations to the contrary. . . . The typical American killed in combat was a white, regular, enlisted man serving in an army or marine corps unit. He was 21 years old or younger" (*War Without Fronts*, 114). Eighty-six percent of all dead were listed as Caucasian.

If there were generalizations to be made, it was largely a question of class. The vast majority of those who fought in Vietnam as frontline combat troops—two-thirds of whom were not drafted but volunteered—were disproportionately lower-class whites from southern and rural states. These were young men of a vastly different socioeconomic cosmos from the largely middle- and upper-class journalists who misrepresented them, the antiwar activists and academics who castigated them, and the generals of the military high command who led them so poorly. Class was the third rail that antiwar activists did not concern themselves with. Perhaps that unease explains why popular films like *The Deer Hunter* (which the leftist war correspondent Peter Arnett called "fascist trash"), the music of Creedence Clearwater Revival (e.g., "Fortunate Son"), and the early songs of Bruce Springsteen (e.g., "Shut Out the Light," "Born in the U.S.A.")—which all dealt with either ethnic or lower-class attitudes toward the inequities in the conduct of the war—were either ignored or criticized by the more elitist critics of Vietnam. Yet far from being either crazy, mutinous, or disillusioned, most of such soldiers who fought bravely in Vietnam had volunteered, and later confirmed that they were unabashedly proud of their service. Ninety-seven percent of those Americans who saw tours in Vietnam were granted honorable discharges from the military.

Such attitudes and conduct on the part of American soldiers were especially surprising in an undeclared war that lasted for more than a decade and was fought under horrific conditions. It was also rarely reported that Vietnam was a much more brutal war for those who served than was World War II—again proof of the superb record of the

American soldier. Infantrymen in the Pacific, for example, on average saw forty days of combat in four years; combat soldiers in the field in Vietnam averaged more than two hundred days of contact with the enemy in a single year-long tour of duty.

Most American books about the Vietnam War published between 1968 and 1973 are not accurate. Unlike contemporary accounts of the Zulu War or Midway, they consistently garnered selective data and provided exegesis designed either to galvanize contemporary domestic public opinion or to defend past opinions, positions, and conduct of dubious accuracy or ethics. Most narratives devoted entire sections to the one hundred or so innocent civilians slaughtered by the Americans at My Lai, but almost nothing concerning the nearly 3,000 graves of those executed in cold blood by the communists at Hué. The great, unsung tragedy of the antiwar movement was that its own lack of credibility, fairness, and fondness for hyperbole did as much to tarnish the hallowed Western tradition of open dissent and careful audit of military operations as did the worst excesses of the American military in Vietnam.

AFTERMATH

A Unified Vietnam

The Americans' war lasted another five years after Tet. With the withdrawal of American ground troops and air support from Vietnam during 1973–74, the eventual defeat of South Vietnam was assured. Soviet and Chinese support escalated without worry of American bombing. Immediately after the negotiated peace accords of 1973, the North Vietnamese sent four times as much military supplies into the South than during the war year of 1972—so confident were they of immunity from American air strikes. Unlike the situation in Korea, where the United States left thousands of troops to ensure the armistice, nearly all American soldiers were gone by March 1973. Saigon fell to a massive communist offensive on April 30, 1975. Yet the North Vietnamese had paid a terrible price for victory—at least a million combat dead, and perhaps just as many missing and wounded. In the end, the communists had four times as many war dead as did the South Vietnamese army alone.

Many charges were leveled that the Americans in more than a decade of bombing may have inadvertently killed 50,000 civilians. If true, that was a terrible and tragic consequence of the war, and reflects poorly on the air force's often indiscriminate bombing of rural trails, jungles, and hamlets in order to interdict the flow of supplies. But as a percentage of the total North Vietnamese population, that unfortunate figure still represented a far smaller civilian toll than what occurred over Germany and Japan during World War II—and a fraction of the some 400,000 civilians that were believed killed by indiscriminate communist shelling and rocketing of cities, as well as terrorist attacks. In defeat, the United States lost 58,000 total dead and spent more than $150 billion, aside from the social and cultural costs back home.

A communist victory brought more death and even greater dislocation to the Vietnamese than did decades of war—more often slowly by starvation, incarceration, and flight, rather than by outright mass murder. The occupation by the Japanese and French had led to moderate exoduses from Vietnam in the past, but nothing in the history of the country was comparable to mass departures from South Vietnam after the communist takeover in 1975. Exact numbers are in dispute, but most scholars accept that well over 1 million left by boat; and hundreds of thousands of others crossed by land into neighboring Thailand and even China. Aggregate numbers of fleeing Vietnamese vastly exceeded the original trek south during the partition of the country in 1954 that had numbered more than a million. America alone eventually took in 750,000 Vietnamese and Southeast Asians, other Western countries another million. Those who died in leaky boats or in storms numbered between 50,000 and 100,000; to leave, most bribed communist officials—only to be robbed on the high seas by the Vietnamese navy. It should be noted as well that by 1980 the Vietnamese communists had also exiled thousands of ethnic Chinese in a countrywide campaign of ethnic cleansing.

In the first two years after the fall of Saigon (1975–77), there were almost twice as many total civilian fatalities in Southeast Asia—from the Cambodian holocaust, outright executions, horrendous conditions in concentration camps, and failed escapes by refugees—as all those incurred during ten years of major American involvement (1965–74). When asked about the thousands of doctors, engineers, and professionals sent to concentration camps, a North Vietnamese official said, "We must get rid of the bourgeois rubbish." Yet in private, the communist chief of press relations in Ho Chi Minh City remarked of emigration to America, "Open the doors and everyone would leave overnight" (S. Karnow, *Vietnam*, 32, 36).

No figures exist on the numbers who died in reeducation camps—forty established in South Vietnam alone—but they are believed to have been in the thousands. The elite of the Communist Party quickly selected the most lavish of American and South Vietnamese homes for their own residences. The American Left made a good case that South Vietnam was run by a corrupt aristocracy; but such theft paled in comparison to the communist government that took over in 1975, under which even Chinese and Soviet ships had to pay bribes to unload their cargoes in Haiphong, and local officials made fortunes by providing exemptions to any who wished to leave the country or evade the camps. Most media accounts of postwar Vietnam did not suggest that the peace was more costly to Southeast Asia than was war against the Americans, that communist officials killed or drove out far more of their own countrymen in twenty-four months of armistice than had the Americans in a decade of fighting.

In the short term the scenario of the domino theory, so ridiculed by critics of the Cold War, turned out to be largely true. With the fall of Vietnam, Cambodia and Laos came under communist domination; Thailand was for a time marginalized and forced to sever most ties with Americans. After 1975 the Soviet Union showed a greater, rather than reduced, tendency to intervene abroad, as fighting broke out in Afghanistan, Central America, and eastern Africa. The communist Vietnamese army grew, rather than shrank, after the war. It soon ranked as the third largest land force in the world after China and Russia—its frontline soldiers and paramilitary troops numbered 3 million—and subsequently fought both Cambodia and China. Few American activists of the past antiwar movement protested the hundreds of thousands of Asians who killed each other from 1975 to 1980. But, then, all those who died on both sides were communists.

The Vietnam experience stands as the worst-case scenario imaginable in a free society at war—a test of the institution of free criticism fundamentally distorted, in which many of the dissidents were ignorant, their tools of communication instantaneous and enormously powerful, and their sympathies more with the enemy than with their own soldiers. Yet the allowance of such a critique, even under such singular conditions, did not undermine the power of the United States in the long run. The loss of Vietnam to communism was not a harbinger of things to come, given the apparently inevitable march of democratic capitalism during the 1980s and 1990s—a tide that finally even washed away Vietnam's former patron, the Soviet Union, and eroded orthodoxy in communist China. Today, 179 of the 192 autonomous countries in the world have some sort of genuine legislature, with elected representatives. Vietnam, like Castro's Cuba, was, and is, on the wrong side of history.

Determinists will argue that Vietnam, sooner or later, will be free and that the American war was mostly a peripheral theater of needless American losses that did not affect the major containment of Soviet communism or the inevitable global onslaught of democratic consumer capitalism. There were dominoes, but they were too small to be of global importance. On the other hand, supporters of the war might still counter that the fighting in Vietnam did weaken communism and helped to protect the Philippines, Malaysia, and Singapore—and that the final American defeat ensured that thousands of Southeast Asians were killed or doomed to suffer in poverty and tyranny until the supposedly inevitable wave of Western-style freedom reaches them in the twenty-first century. For the millions who died in Southeast Asia immediately after the American withdrawal, and for the thousands of now rotting Americans and Vietnamese who were killed in Vietnam in a misguided crusade to prevent just those later atrocities, such "what-ifs" about the long-term future of Vietnam mean nothing.

Vietnam and the Western Way of War

The American military in Vietnam, far from being incompetent, in its daily operations reflected all the lethal elements of the traditional Western paradigm. Despite exaggerated reports of rampant drug use and sedition, the American soldier remained disciplined and well trained, even when it was clear that the war was not being fought to win, and even with a sizable number of vocal critics at home. Whatever the inequalities of the draft, civic militarism was very much still alive in America. With eventual changes in the voting age, all GIs eighteen years and older could voice their views in the national elections and express freely to journalists opinions about the conditions of their own military service. The opposite was not true of the Vietcong and North Vietnamese. Most American soldiers, it was believed, voted for leaders who advocated continued military involvement in Vietnam. When they fought in Vietnam, it was generally true that a majority of Americans wanted them there; when they began to leave, most Americans preferred that they did so. Again, voting and free speech were not characteristic of either the Vietcong or the North Vietnamese army. Ultimately, that key difference was recognized even by the communists who won. Former Vietcong general Pham Xuan An later remarked in disgust: "All that talk about 'liberation' twenty, thirty years ago, all the plotting, all the bodies, produced this, this impoverished, broken-down country led by a gang of cruel and paternalistic half-educated theorists" (L. Sorley, *A Better War*, 384).

Freedom the Americans fought for, and free they were who fought. But paradoxically, while enjoying almost no freedom during the conflict, its promise drove on many Vietnamese who joined a communist cause disguised as a war for independence. The Vietnamese peasant was assured a war of "liberation"—*libertas* being a very Roman republican idea, rather than one of indigenous Vietnamese heritage. But since the communists had fought continually against the Japanese, French, and Americans for some thirty years, they never had occasion to govern in peace—and thus had never been held accountable for the fulfillment of promises offered. That illusion vanished with victory in 1975, when at last a true accounting came due for three decades of democratic rhetoric. Duang Van Toai, a former supporter of the Vietcong, explained the paradox of why he and others aided a movement that was so hostile to freedom:

> Like others of the opposition movement in Vietnam and in the United States, I was hypnotized by the political programs advocated by the National Liberation Front, which included the famous and correct policy of national reconciliation without reprisals and a policy of non-alignment with and independence from the Americans, the Russians, and the Chinese. . . . Under the domination of the Japanese, there were almost two million Vietnamese dying of hunger, but no one fled Vietnam. Under the Saigon governments during the war, hundreds of thousands of prisoners were arrested and jailed, but no one fled the country. Yet those who are pro-Hanoi or are hypnotized by the propaganda of Hanoi claim that the boat people are economic refugees . . . [but] among the refugees . . . were also the Vietcong, the former opposition leaders, and even the former justice minister of the Vietcong. You can imagine the situation of justice in a country if the justice minister of that country had to flee. ("Freedom and the Vietnamese," in H. Salisbury, ed., *Vietnam Reconsidered,* 225)

It was *not* by assurances of no free elections, no private property, and no free speech to come that the Vietcong and North Vietnamese had galvanized their army, but by the very Western notions of creating a "republic" of elected officials and a free press. The result was that Vietnamese soldiers in service to communism (itself a nineteenth-century European offshoot of Western utopian thinking that went back to Plato) fought as nationalists against foreigners in the mistaken hope of just that Western ideal of personal freedom and national autonomy. Instead, they found that in 1975, on the first occasion of real peace in three decades of war, their own government was not really a republic and they were hardly free at all. It was also another unnoted irony of the entire Vietnamese war that those who resisted the Americans did so by incorporating the promises—but never the reality—of America: empty dreams that fooled not only their own soldiers but much of the American academic and journalistic establishment as well. The Democratic Republic of Vietnam, which was the official name of communist North Vietnam, did not draw its nomenclature from the hallowed traditions of Southeast Asia or the perversions of Stalinism, but from the language of freedom of Greece and Rome. Yet there was never to be either a democracy or a republic in Vietnam.

The American economy produced a surfeit of arms, war supplies, and consumer goods in Vietnam that had the effect of drawing more than a million peasants from the countryside into an already overcrowded Saigon of 3 million persons and creating a booming economy in the process. In general, the American capitalist economy found it much easier to ship and airlift matériel thousands of miles across the seas than did China or Russia to their clients on their own front doorstep. American weapons were as a rule also better than the enemy's, especially in areas of communications, aircraft, radar, ships, and armor. In cases where the Vietcong and North Vietnamese achieved parity—mostly in automatic rifles, mortars, antitank guns, mines, and grenades—it was solely as a result of imported Chinese and Russian arms, themselves ultimately patterned after European designs or a result of the Western tradition of research. The history of Soviet arms production and development is the story of American aid during World War II, the copying and capturing of German arms on the eastern front (1941–45), the recruiting of German scientists after the war, the constant emulation of Western designs through espionage and defection, and ultimately the eighteenth- and nineteenth-century importation of British, French, and German consultants to modernize the czarist military.

The Vietnamese drew on no indigenous scientific tradition—except for a few cases of ingenious antipersonnel bamboo and wooden traps—to craft their tools of killing. Without Western-style arms, the communists would have been annihilated. The same is true of Vietnamese military organization and discipline. North Vietnamese equivalents to terms like "division" and "general," coupled with training in automatic arms and infantry tactics, were ultimately patterned after Soviet and Chinese exemplars—themselves borrowed from Western militaries. While the North Vietnamese made undeniable changes in battle operations to reflect native realities, it was a great irony of the war that Americans were killed by automatic rifles that looked hauntingly similar to M-14s and M-16s, and by privates, lieutenants, companies, and regiments that at the most basic organization level mirror-imaged their own. It would take a near expert to distinguish an American 81mm mortar from its North Vietnamese 82mm counterpart.

Despite the wholesale importation of Western arms and organization by the North Vietnamese, the Americans quickly learned that their own military—free, individualistic, superbly supplied, expertly equipped, eager for decisive battles of shock—was not static. Rather, the American armed forces evolved throughout the war and proved superior to the North Vietnamese, despite horrendous supply lines, the absence of clear-cut fronts and battle lines, restrictive rules of engagement that nullified traditional Western preferences for decisive battle, and domestic opposition.

No American army in 1944 would have fought the Germans in France without permission to cross the Rhine or to bomb Berlin at will. Japan would have won World War II had the United States simply fought in the jungles and occupied towns of the Japanese empire, promising not to bomb Tokyo, mine its harbors, attack its sanctuaries, or invade its native possessions, while journalists and critics visited Tokyo and broadcast to American troops from Japanese radio stations. Neither Truman nor Roosevelt would have offered to negotiate with Hitler or Stalin after the successful Normandy landings or the devastating bombing campaign over Tokyo in March 1945. GIs in World War II were killed in pursuit of victory, not in order to avoid defeat or to pressure totalitarian governments to discuss an armistice. In war it is insane not to employ the full extent of one's military power or to guarantee to the enemy that there are sanctuaries for retreat, targets that are off limits, and a willingness to cease operations anytime even the pretext of negotiations is offered.

The American military itself did not react well to these Orwellian impositions on operations. The number of rear-echelon troops soared— somewhere between 80 and 90 percent of all soldiers who went to Vietnam never saw real combat. One-year tours of duty ensured that many green recruits would be killed in the first months of combat only to have the survivors sent home when they were battle-wise and more likely to be effective leaders in teaching others the nature of staying alive in the field. The military often turned Vietnam into an American bureaucratic nightmare: "The Military Assistance Command staff directory was more than fifty pages long. It included a chief of staff, two deputy commanders and their staffs, a deputy chief of staff for economic affairs, two deputy affairs, a staff secretariat, and three complete 'staff groups,' a general staff, a 'special staff,' and a 'personal staff' " (R. Spector, *After Tet*, 215).

Sometimes the insistence to fight openly and directly in battle still only took on the semblance of the traditional Western war—shock battle, direct assault, overwhelming firepower—without the accompanying corollary of seizing and holding property. Blasting apart the enemy with superior fire and advancing with disciplined landed infantry was entirely in the European military tradition of Alexander the Great and Charles Martel. Taking and then abandoning real estate that was captured at great cost was not. On May 10, 1969, for example, General Melvin Zais, commander of the 101st Airborne, unleashed his troops against the infamous "Hamburger Hill" (Hill 937). In a horrendous firefight, involving direct assault on the ridge, his men suffered fifty-six dead while killing more than five hundred of the enemy. When responding to vociferous attacks at home from politicians over the apparent waste of American lives in that ten-to-one exchange—the hill was abruptly abandoned after capture— Zais inadvertently summed up the entire Western way of war and why it did not necessarily always lead to strategic victory in Vietnam:

> That hill was in my area of operations, that was where the enemy was, that's where I attacked him. . . . If I find him in another hill . . . I assure you I will attack him. . . . It is true that hill 937, as a particular piece of terrain, was of no particular significance. However, the fact that the enemy force was located there was of prime significance. (G. Lewy, *America in Vietnam*, 144)

A limited war that ignored the capture and protection of land, and in essence sought to avoid the defeat of an often corrupt South Vietnam, rather than to achieve victory over a battle-hardened communist army of North Vietnam—whether wisely for necessary reasons of avoiding a larger conflict, or in error due to trumped-up fears of Soviet and Chinese intervention—was a referendum on American political wisdom, not a true litmus of Western military power. Few, then and now, doubt whether America could have won the Vietnam War; many remain unsure whether it should have.

Who Lost the War?

Despite recent arguments to the contrary, the media in themselves did not lose the Vietnam War. Journalists did not snatch political defeat from military victory. Rather, they only contributed to the collapse of American power and resistance, by accentuating frequent American blunders and South Vietnamese corruption, without commensurate attention paid to North Vietnamese atrocities, the brutal history of communism in Asia, and the geopolitical stakes involved. Their ability to sensationalize relatively minor American setbacks and exaggerate modest communist victories often helped to turn public opinion and thus give them undue influence with American politicians who directed the course of the war.

Yet ultimately, the American military command itself forfeited the war, despite brave soldiers, good equipment, and plentiful supplies. The top echelon lost the conflict because they accommodated themselves without imagination to the conditions of political audit and scrutiny that made it difficult, but not impossible, to win. Conservatives and principled liberals were correct in their assessment of the absurdity of the prevailing American strategy: the former demanding Americans fight to win any war they undertake, the latter insisting America could not fight to win, given the political situation, and so should not fight. Once the nation understood the conditions under which the war was deemed necessary to be fought, and the cost required to fight it that way, it determined it was not in their interest to pay it. The military could have easily won the war it wanted to fight, but did not know how to fight the war that it was asked to win—a war that was nevertheless winnable with daring and ingenuity. So instead, they bombed incessantly and unwisely—seventy tons for every square mile in Vietnam, five hundred pounds of explosives for every man, woman, and child in the country—without ever learning why hundreds of thousands of Vietnamese were fighting on behalf of a murderous communist dictatorship that would soon enslave their country and ruin its economy. A realist of the Bismarck school, without regard to human suffering or the misery of the Vietnamese under communism, would argue that it was not in the geopolitical interest of the United States to expend such vast amounts of its manhood and capital on a relatively insignificant country, which, left to its own as a communist dictatorship, would probably become as likely a nuisance to its communist neighbors as it was to America—when the real shift in the Cold War meant the struggle was no longer over mere land, but about global economics, technology, and mass consumer culture.

If it was not the intention of the media and press people who sent home their biased and often one-sided reports to apprise America of the inconsistency of its own politicians and military command, the result was nevertheless sometimes just that. The long-held Western tradition of free speech and self-critique ultimately did not ruin America despite the ruination of its cause in Vietnam. The communists won the war and lost the peace, massacring their people and destroying their economy—all in a closed and censored society. America, despite its propensity for self-loathing, lost the war and won the peace, its model of democracy and capitalism winning adherents as never before, with its reformist military emerging stronger, not weaker, after the ordeal.

The record of Vietnam—books, motion pictures, official documents—remains a nearly exclusive Western phenomenon. Antiwar activists criticized this monopoly of information even as they themselves published and lectured in a free society and thus contributed to that very dominance of Western publication. The communist version of the war, when it did appear in print or video, was immediately subject to skepticism. Few doubted that publication of such information was not free, and the government that controlled the dissemination of knowledge was not credible. In contrast, at various times the American government and its critics were duplicitous, but rarely at the same time on the same issue. In that marketplace of conflicting accounts, most observers sensed that freedom was the guarantor of the truth, and so looked for veracity anywhere but in North Vietnamese, Chinese, or Russian accounts. The American experience in the Vietnam War—whether noble or shameful—remains an almost exclusively Western story.

WAR AMID AUDIT, SCRUTINY, AND SELF-CRITIQUE

While the manner of civilian audit, dissent, and self-critique during the Vietnam War was different from Western past practice, it was nevertheless hardly new in spirit. Pericles ("Squill-Head") was ridiculed on the Athenian stage in the same manner that General Westmoreland ("Waste-More-Land") was pilloried on American campuses. Pericles, not Westmoreland, branded the foreheads of his captives and was attacked by Athenian critics for doing so. Jane Fonda dallied with her nation's enemies, precisely as did Athenian rightists who fawned over Sparta in the closing months of the Peloponnesian War. Plato, remember, in a near treasonous outburst, called the great victory at Salamis a mistake that had made the Athenians worse as a people.

To Aeschylus, war was but "the food of Ares." Sophocles saw it as "the father of our sorrows." Even the imperialist Pericles could dub it "an utter folly." "They make it a wasteland and call it peace," said Tacitus of the Roman army's conduct in colonial wars. The stuff of Western history, drama, oratory, poetry, and art—Brueghel, Goya, and Picasso—has always been frank criticism of contemporary conflict and often of the absurdity of war in general. Euripides' dramas, staged before nearly 20,000 voting Athenian citizens, reflect the evolving understanding of the human and material costs of battle during the Peloponnesian War. Three decades of plagues, coups, destruction of neutral states, and disaster at Sicily were far more similar to Vietnam than to World War II. Euripides' *Trojan Women*, presented not long after the Athenian slaughter of the Melians (415 B.C.), chronicles how the innocent wives, mothers, and children of the Trojans, not just soldiers, suffer the consequences of war. The comic playwright Aristophanes also wrote several plays—*Acharnians, Peace,* and *Lysistrata*—that ridicule the endless traffic in war charges that the profiteer and the megalomaniac are more interested in themselves than in the citizens. While a Spartan army marched through the countryside of Athens, the Athenian populace watched its own citizens denigrate the policy of forced evacuation and continued war with Sparta.

The conduct of Jane Fonda, Tom Hayden, and the Berrigan brothers may have been treasonous, but not to such an extent as the medizing Greeks, who in 480 B.C. joined the Persians at Salamis. Press conferences in Saigon—known as the Five O'Clock Follies—may have been acrimonious and characterized by endless charges and countercharges, but they were no less vehement than the near physical altercations that took place between Themistocles and his coadmirals on the eve before Salamis, or the hangings and near open war between the Spanish and Italians hours before the fight at Lepanto. The media may have destroyed the reputation of General Westmoreland, but no more so than the gossipy Athenian Assembly did to the hero Themistocles, who was exiled and died abroad, shunned at home. The criticism of the Vietnam War ruined Lyndon Johnson, but the storm of dissent in the Peloponnesian War led to Pericles being fined—and eventually worn out, sick, and dead before the third year of the twenty-seven-year-old conflict was over.

Just as there were no North Vietnamese dissidents in Washington protesting their own soldiers' slaughter at Hué, so Xerxes, like the Politburo in Hanoi, brooked neither dissident nor audit. Again, remember the fate of the dismembered Phoenician admirals at Salamis or poor Pythius the Lydian, who all mistakenly believed that they could reason with the Great King. It remained a truism that a Greek at Salamis, a Roman at Cannae, a Venetian at Lepanto, an Englishman at Rorke's Drift, and Americans at Midway and Vietnam all could vote and speak as they pleased—and this was not true of Persians, Carthaginians, Ottomans,

Zulus, Japanese, and Vietnamese. Even autocrats like Alexander or Cortés commonly responded to critics among their staff and soldiers in a way that Aztec and Persian emperors were not accustomed.

Lyndon Johnson may have been destroyed by his domestic critics, but millennia earlier even the autocrat Alexander the Great did not escape the scrutiny of Western contrarians. The philosopher Diogenes, when asked by Alexander what he wished, purportedly replied that the king move out of his sunlight. Alexander was no doubt a thug and a dangerous man, who for a time derailed Western freedom, but he was an amateur autocrat compared to the Persian Achaemenids. He was far more likely to be arguing with his Macedonian generals than was Xerxes with his satraps, far more likely to be attacked in the Assembly Hall by a Demosthenes—and far more likely to be told to move out of the way on a street corner by a philosopher than was Darius at the court in Persepolis. Hernán Cortés, who gave his king a subcontinent and ships of precious metals, was nevertheless largely shunned and ostracized in his old age, his past daring and killing more an object of vituperation from clerics, censure from bureaucrats, and lawsuits from former colleagues than cause for lasting praise and commemoration from the Spanish crown.

Throughout the ordeal of Vietnam, the Congress and the president were at odds over the conduct of the war, as various generals were paraded before Congress to testify, even as congressional representatives and senators were ordered to the White House to give an account of their "disloyal" votes. But unlike Roman republicans, few American generals had their own separate military commands. American senators were rarely interfering on the field of battle. Squabbling and running to the press in Vietnam paled before the confrontation between the consuls the night before Cannae. L. Aemilius Paulus and the reckless C. Terentius Varro, elected officials both, despised each other, and so their plans for their shared army worked at cross-purposes. Fabius Maximus, whose strategy finally turned the tide of the Second Punic War, for a time was the most unpopular man at Rome, dubbed a coward for his tactics of delay. The achievement of Charles Martel at Poitiers was often ignored by later chroniclers largely because he was demonized by the church as a confiscator of ecclesiastical lands.

In the midst of his conquest, Cortés was branded a criminal by Diego Velázquez, governor of Cuba. His sojourn in Mexico City itself was interrupted when Pánfilo de Narváez arrived in Vera Cruz with a writ for his arrest. Father Bernardino de Sahagún had little good to say about his own countryman, Hernán Cortés, but wrote with empathy about the natives whom the conquistador slaughtered. For all of Cortés's "official" letters to Charles V, we receive a somewhat different story from his contemporaries. Bartolomé de Las Casas thought the Spanish treatment of the Indians abominable, and so wrote in detail about the sins of the conquest. By the time of his death, Cortés was largely ignored, unappreciated, severely criticized in print, and in need of money. In contrast, what little we know of the critics of Montezuma come from Spanish, not Mexican, written sources. While Spaniards criticized Cortés in his success for his hubris and cruelty, Aztec lords turned on Montezuma only for his failure to eject the Spanish from Tenochtitlán. No Aztec wrote or criticized the decision to kill thousands of innocents on the Great Pyramid.

John Colenso, bishop of Natal, and his daughters devoted their lives to apprising the British public of their government's cruelty toward the Zulus. In turn, the British press issued sensational and often inaccurate news about Isandhlwana, convincing the public to muster unnecessarily large relief contingents, but also to question whether it had all been necessary in the first place. Few careers—not Chelmsford's or that of his successor, Sir Garnet Wolseley—were enhanced by the fighting. The Colensos were about as active on the Zulu behalf during the war and as critical of British inhumanity as American antiwar activists were sympathetic to the North Vietnamese.

The Japanese read of Midway as a great victory; wounded sailors were confined to hospitals to ensure the news of the disaster never reached the public. Admiral Yamamoto alone created the flawed plan and felt no need for much discussion and brooked no dissent. All this was in contrast to a wild American public discourse in which sensitive details of the intelligence of the battle were leaked to newspapers before the fighting had even begun. American strategy was debated in open meetings called by Admiral Nimitz, and the results sent to Washington to be ratified or rejected by an elected government. Ho Chi Minh, though a professed communist, was far more kindred to the Japanese militarists than he was to the Americans.

Vietnamese often turned to American academics, religious figures, and intellectuals in attempts to nullify American power that their own army could not. When the communist campaign to denigrate the Americans and sanctify the North Vietnamese reached the world stage, it was no accident it did so largely through Western, rather than communist or Third World, media. "American puppets" and "running dog capitalist warmongers" may have sounded neat on American campuses, but they were not the vocabulary of truth, and so were not what convinced the

American public to call an end to their war in Vietnam. The *New York Times* and *60 Minutes* alone could do what *Pravda* and the *Daily Worker* could not: prevail on the American people that the war was unwinnable and unjust. To the North Vietnamese, the loud-speaking, confusing, and fractious Americans—William F. Buckleys and Jane Fondas alike—were not so much evil or good as they were insidious.

What, then, are we to make of this final tenet of Western military practice, this strange 2,500-year-old habit of subjecting military operations to constant and often self-destructive political audit and public scrutiny? Can anything good come of a volatile Western citizenry that dictates when, where, and how its soldiers are to fight, even as it permits its writers, artists, and journalists freely and sometimes wildly to criticize the conduct of their own troops? Surely in the case of reporting the Tet Offensive and the Vietnam War—whose vehemence and absurdity make it a pivotal case study of the entire wisdom of allowing dissent and open attacks on the military—cannot the argument be made that the public license lost a war that America could have won?

If the conduct of an unbridled media and constant public scrutiny of even the most minute military operations harmed the American effort in Vietnam, it is equally true that the institutions and process of that self-recrimination helped to correct serious flaws in American tactics and strategy. The United States military in Vietnam under General Abrams from 1968 to 1971 fought a far more effective war than it had between 1965 and 1967, largely as a result of dissent in and out of the military. The bombing of 1973, far from being ineffective and indiscriminate, brought the communists back to the peace table through its destruction of just a few key installations in North Vietnam. Nixon's so-called Linebacker II campaign was far more lethal to the war machine of Hanoi than the much-criticized indiscriminate Rolling Thunder campaign years earlier. If in 1965 the Johnson administration had no idea what was at stake in Vietnam, or what would evolve as the ultimate rules of engagement, by 1971 the Nixon government understood precisely the American dilemma. As a result of the antiwar sentiment and the freedom of dissent, Nixon knew only too well the nature of the quagmire that he was in.

More important still, Tet was not a single battle, nor was Vietnam in and of itself an isolated war. Both occurred on a worldwide canvas of the Cold War, a much larger global struggle of values and cultures. In this context, the license of the West, while it was detrimental to the poor soldiers who were asked to repel the Tet Offensive, had the long-term effect of winning, rather than forfeiting, American credibility. To defeat the West, it is often necessary not merely to repel its armies but to extinguish its singular monopoly over the dissemination of information, to annihilate not merely its soldiers but its emissaries of free expression.

This more insidious component of Western military practice, the supposedly astute and tenacious communists of North Vietnam never understood. Instead, they were confused about America in Vietnam, condemning its administration but careful to avoid blanket criticism of its people; damning its military but praising its intelligentsia; ecstatic over the slanted reporting of the news but occasionally baffled and hurt when an honest story emerged about the nature of their own thuggish regime; smug in American television's broadcast of the "liberation" of Saigon, furious at the later coverage of the boat people. If the perplexed North Vietnamese were gladdened that the *Washington Post* could say worse things about its own military than they did communists, and if they were curious why an American movie star could pose in Hanoi on an artillery battery rather than put on a patriotic play at Carnegie Hall—and still come home without a prison sentence—they were equally furious when asked about the nature of the 1976 "free" elections, and surprised at the few brave reporters who finally told the world of the communist holocaust in Cambodia.

This strange propensity for self-critique, civilian audit, and popular criticism of military operations—itself part of the larger Western tradition of personal freedom, consensual government, and individualism—thus poses a paradox. The encouragement of open assessment and the acknowledgment of error within the military eventually bring forth superior planning and a more flexible response to adversity. The knowledge that military conduct is to be questioned by soldiers themselves, to be audited and scrutinized by those outside the armed forces altogether, and to be interpreted, editorialized, and often mischaracterized by reporters to the public can ensure accountability and provide for a wide exchange of views.

At the same time, this freedom to distort can often hamper military operations of the moment, as Thucydides himself saw and Plato feared in the *Republic*—and as was the case of the Tet Offensive in Vietnam. In Vietnam due to frankness and hysteria in place of reasoned and positive assessment, America may have prolonged its agony and lost battles in the field, but surely not the war against communism. Had America been as closed a society as was Vietnam, then it may well have won the battle but lost the war, much like the Soviet Union, which imploded after its involvement in Afghanistan—a military intervention similar to America's in Vietnam in terms of tactical ineptitude, political denseness, and strategic imbecility, but a world apart in the Russians' denial of free criticism, public debate, and uncensored reporting about their error. How odd that the institutions that can thwart the daily battle progress of Western arms can also ensure the ultimate triumph of its cause. If the Western commitment to self-critique in part caused American defeat in Vietnam, then that institution was also paramount in the explosion of Western global influence in the decades after the war—even as the enormous and often bellicose Vietnamese army fought for a regime increasingly despised at home, shunned abroad, and bankrupt economically and morally.

In the next few decades it shall come to pass that Vietnam will resemble the West far more than the West Vietnam. The freedom to speak out, the titillating headline, the flashy exposé, and the idea that a man in tie and suit, not one sporting sunglasses, epaulets, and a revolver, is commander in chief are more likely in the end to win than lose wars, on and off the battlefield. Thucydides, who deplored the Athenian stupidity surrounding the Sicilian expedition and had hardly a good word to say for the Athenian Assembly and its unchecked rhetoricians, was nevertheless impressed by the Athenians' amazing propensity to correct past blunders and to persevere against unimagined adversity.

If we began this chapter with that historian's sharp criticism of Athenian fickleness and absence of support for its own expedition, we should end by noting Thucydides' other, less well known observation concerning such an open culture's conduct of war. It turned out that the Syracusans fought so well against Athens, Thucydides believed, because they, too, were a free society and "democratic just as the Athenians" (*The Peloponnesian War* 7.55.2). He concluded that free societies are the most resilient in war: "The Syracusans proved this point well. For precisely because they were the most similar in character to the Athenians, they made war upon them so successfully" (8.96.5).

EPILOGUE

Western Warfare—
Past and Future

For every state war is always incessant and lifelong against every
other state. . . . For what most men call "peace," this is really only a
name—in truth, all states by their very nature are always engaged in
an informal war against all other states.
—PLATO, *Laws* (1.626A)

THE HELLENIC LEGACY

FROM THE FIGHTING of early Greece to the wars of the entire twentieth century, there is a certain continuity of European military practice. As
the chapter epigraphs suggest, this heritage of the Western war is not
found in its entirety elsewhere, nor does it begin earlier than the Greeks.
There is no Egyptian idea of personal freedom in the ranks; no Persian
conception of civic militarism or civilian audit of the Great King's army;
no Thracian embrace of the scientific tradition; no disciplined files of
shock phalangites in Phoenicia; and no landed infantry of small property
owners in ancient Scythia—and thus no military in the ancient
Mediterranean like the Greeks at Thermopylae, Salamis, or Plataea.

This 2,500-year tradition explains not only why Western forces have
overcome great odds to defeat their adversaries but also their uncanny

ability to project power well beyond the shores of Europe and America. Numbers, location, food, health, weather, religion—the usual factors that govern the success or failure of wars—have ultimately done little to impede Western armies, whose larger culture has allowed them to trump man and nature alike. Even the tactical brilliance of a Hannibal has been to no avail.

That is not to say that throughout three millennia all Western forces have shared an exact blueprint in their approach to war making through periods of upheaval, tyranny, and decay. Phalangites are a long way from GIs, and the victory at Tenochtitlán is distant from Salamis. Nor should we forget that the non-West has also fielded deadly armies, such as the Mongols, Ottomans, and communist Vietnamese, that have defeated all opposition in Asia for centuries and kept Europe at bay. But the military affinities in Western war making across time and space from the Greeks to the present are uncanny, enduring, and too often ignored—which suggests that historians of the present age have not appreciated the classical legacy that is at the core of Western military energy throughout the ages. There is a sense of déjà vu as these chapters unfold, an eerie feeling that phalangites, legionaries, mailed foot soldiers, conquistadors, redcoats, GIs, and marines all shared certain recurring core ideas about how to wage and win wars.

In battles against the peoples of Asia, Africa, and the New World, tribal and imperial alike, there is a shared legacy over centuries that allowed Europeans and Americans to win in a consistent and deadly manner—or to be defeated on rare occasions only when the enemy embraced their own military organization, borrowed their weapons, or trapped them far from home. Notice that nowhere in these case studies were Western victories a product of innately superior intelligence, Christian morality, or any notion of religious or genetic exceptionalism. While Persians, Carthaginians, Muslims, Aztecs, Ottomans, Zulus, and Japanese all battled in a wide variety of ways, they do share two affinities throughout the ages: none fought exactly as Westerners—or across the oceans as well. Xerxes, Darius III, Abd ar-Rahman, Montezuma, Ali Pasha, and Cetshwayo all envisioned war as a theocratic, tribal, or dynastic crusade, in which speed, deception, numbers, or courage might negate the discipline of Western infantry or the technology and capital of Europe. Montezuma could not envision fighting in the Mediterranean, just as Ali Pasha would never see the Americas.

In just the few episodes we have examined, the similarities are clear. Greek sailors in 480 B.C., in the way that they created and manned their

fleet, discussed and voted on strategy before battle, and chose and audited
their leadership, were far more similar to Venetians at Lepanto two millennia later than they were to the sultan's men, who by law were slaves like
Xerxes' seamen at Salamis. By the same token, the rows and files of
Alexander's small army of expeditionary phalangites were in spirit replicated at Cannae, as well as Rorke's Drift and the other battles of the Zulu
War. Outnumbered British redcoats fired on orders, sought to form rank,
and charged on command and in unison. The close-ordered ranks and
files of the phalanx, whether of Macedonian pikemen or British shooters,
are not known outside of the European experience. The manner in which
Rome reconstituted its armies after the defeat at Cannae was not all that
unlike the American restoration after Pearl Harbor in the months before
Midway. Both cultures in the aftermath of defeat drew on common republican traditions of drafting their free voting citizenry into nations-in-
arms.

It is a general rule that the Macedonian phalanx, like the army of
Hernán Cortés, the Christian fleet at Lepanto, and the British company at
Rorke's Drift, fought with weaponry far superior to that of their adversaries. There was little chance that the Aztecs, for all their rich local natural resources, on their own accord could make harquebuses, gunpowder,
or crossbows, the Ottomans topflight bronze cannon, and the Zulus
Martini-Henry rifles—and little doubt that a harquebus was deadlier than
a javelin, a Venetian 5,000-pound cannon more lethal than its Ottoman
clone, and a .45-caliber slug far superior to an assegai. Japan learned to its
advantage in the nineteenth century that Europe alone could design battleships—and that battleships were superior to anything that floated in
the Sea of Japan. The North Vietnamese did not fight with the tribal
spears of their past.

Western military power, however, is more than superior technology.
Just as the peace movement and the constant political audit of the military in Vietnam conditioned the behavior of American armies in
Southeast Asia, so Bishop Colenso and his family published critiques
against the British invasion of Zululand. Bernardino de Sahagún's narra-
tive of the Spanish conquest of Mexico sought to criticize the morality of
his countrymen's army—in a way unthinkable in Aztec, Vietnamese, or
Zulu society. It is no accident that Themistocles, like both the victorious
Cortés and Lord Chelmsford, did not die a hero in a homeland grateful to
him for the slaughter of its enemies. Did such dissent weaken consistently
Westerners' ability to wage war? Not always, at least not in the long term.
The tradition of Western critique and audit has not only established

European credibility and so served to ensure that the written and published story of war was largely Western; it has also shown that minds outside the battlefield ultimately had a say in how their nation's treasure and manhood were spent, sometimes saving the military from itself.

OTHER BATTLES?

The battles of this study are offered as representative examples of general traits rather than absolute laws of military. They are episodes that reflect recurring themes, not chapters in a comprehensive history of Western warfare. That being said, however, I am not certain that the conclusions would have been very different if we had examined other randomly chosen encounters from roughly the same periods and places with similar outcomes—say, Plataea (479 B.C.), Granicus (334 B.C.), Trasimene (217 B.C.), Covadonga (718), the conquest of Peru (1532–39), the siege of Malta (1565), Coral Sea (1942), and Inchon (1950). In nearly all those engagements the same paradigms of freedom, decisive shock battle, civic militarism, technology, capitalism, individualism, and civilian audit and open dissent loom large. In the flesh it is a long way from Greek fire to napalm, from ostracism to impeachment, but in the abstract, not so distant after all.

Even a random catalog of exclusively abject Western defeats—Thermopylae (480 B.C.), Carrhae (A.D. 53), Adrianople (A.D. 378), Manzikert (1071), Constantinople (1453), Adwa (1896), Pearl Harbor (1941), and Dien Bien Phu (1953–54)—would not lead to radically different conclusions. In most of these cases, vastly outnumbered Western armies (Romans under Crassus, Byzantines under Romanos, Italians in Ethiopia, French in Vietnam) were unwisely deployed or poorly prepared—and again far outside of Europe. Even these catastrophes did not always endanger in their immediate aftermaths Greece, Rome, Italy, America, or France. Defeats that had more lasting historical impact—Adrianople, Constantinople, or Dien Bien Phu—came at the borders of European territory and near the end of collapsing regimes or empires. And the victorious Other had either Western-inspired arms or Western-trained consultants among the ranks.

The Western military heritage, itself a dividend of a much larger and peculiar cultural foundation, did not determine in some preordained fashion the outcome of every encounter between West and non-West. Rorke's Drift, but for Chard, Bromhead, and Dalton, could have easily been lost. Salamis, Lepanto, and Midway also involved brilliance in tactical command. Wars are fought by men who are fickle and in real conditions that are wholly unpredictable—heat, ice, and rain, in tropical and near arctic conditions, close and far from home. Western armies in Africa, Asia, and the Americas, as soldiers everywhere, were often annihilated— often led by fools and placed in the wrong war at the wrong place at the wrong time. But their armies, for the cultural reasons this book has outlined, fought with a much greater margin of error than did their adversaries.

Themistocles, Alexander the Great, Cortés, and the British and American officers of the last two centuries enjoyed innate advantages that over the long duration could offset the terrible effects of imbecilic generalship, flawed tactics, strained supply lines, difficult terrain, and inferior numbers—or a simple "bad day." These advantages were immediate and entirely cultural, and they were not the product of the genes, germs, or geography of a distant past. The Zulu empire was doomed to be conquered once the British decided to invade its borders, regardless of its victory at Isandhlwana, despite the tactical lapses of Lord Chelmsford, and irrespective of courageous *impis*.

In examining many of these worst-case scenarios of the Western approach to war making, such as Cannae or Tet, the resilience and lethality of the West seems even more remarkable. If the tradition of dissent can survive Vietnam, then its place in Western military practice will remain unquestioned. If Western infantry was prevalent during the so-called Dark Ages of the mounted knight, then its intrinsic advantages at Poitiers seem even more evident both earlier and later. Mustering legions of free citizens at Cannae, only to lose to a mercenary army of Hannibal, requires careful consideration of the entire value of civic militarism. The war against the Zulus, Africa's most disciplined and organized army, is an unlikely but valuable lesson in understanding the unmatched worth of Western order, rank, and file.

THE SINGULARITY OF WESTERN MILITARY CULTURE

Discussion of Western military prowess demands a precision in nomenclature often lacking in most accounts of the history of warfare. Political freedom—an idea found nowhere outside the West—is *not* a universal characteristic of humankind. Western elections and constitutions are not the same as tribal freedom, in which much land and few people occasionally give individuals opportunity to find solitude and independence. The desire to fight as freemen is also different from the simple élan of defenders who expel tyrants and foreign powers from their homeland. Persians, Aztecs, Zulus, and North Vietnamese all wished to be free of foreign troops on their native soil, but they fought for the autonomy of their culture—not as free voting citizens with rights protected by written and ratified constitutions. A Zulu could roam relatively free on the plains of southern Africa, enjoying a somewhat more "free" lifestyle than a British redcoat in a stuffy barracks; but the Zulu, not the Englishman, was subject to execution by a nod of his king. Shaka proved this tens of thousands of times over. North Vietnamese communists duplicitously promised to their troops a Western-style "democratic republic"—not an Asian dynasty, communist police state, or feudal society—the reward for conducting a nationalist war against foreign intruders.

All armies engage in mass confrontations at times; few prefer to do so in horrendous collisions of shock and eschew fighting at a distance or through stealth when there is at least the opportunity for decisive battle. Likewise, armies from the Persians to the Ottomans often developed sophisticated methods of mustering troops; none outside the West drafted fighters with the implicit understanding that their military service was part and parcel of their status as free citizens who were to determine when, how, and why they were to go to war. Foot soldiers are common in every culture, but infantrymen, fighting en masse, who take and hold ground and fight face-to-face, are a uniquely Western specialty—the product of a long tradition of a middling landholding citizenry who expresses unease with both landless peasants and mounted aristocrats.

The ability to use a weapon, even to improve its effectiveness with practice, is not comparable to inventing and fabricating arms in mass quantities. Africans and American Indians could employ European rifles, become crack shots, and occasionally repair broken stocks and barrels. Yet they could not produce guns in any great number, if at all, much less craft improved models or find in a written literature the abstract principles of ballistics and munitions to conduct advanced research.

Buying and selling is a human trait, but the abstract protection of private property, the institutionalization of interest and investment, and the understanding of markets are not. Capitalism is more than the sale of goods, more than the existence of money, and more than the presence of the bazaar. Rather, it is a peculiar Western practice that acknowledges the self-interest of man and channels that greed to the production of vast amounts of goods and services through free markets and institutionalized guarantees of personal profit, free exchange, deposited capital, and private property.

Warriors are not necessarily soldiers. Both types of killers can be brave, but disciplined troops value the group over the single hero and can be taught to march in order, to stab, thrust, or shoot en masse and on command, and to advance and retreat in unison—something impossible for the bravest of Aztecs, Zulus, or Persians. Every army possesses men of daring, but few encourage initiative throughout the ranks, and welcome rather than fear innovation, so apprehensive are they that an army of independent-thinking soldiers in war just might prove the same as citizens in peace. Bickering among soldiers and disagreement among a small cadre of generals—whether Hitler's captains or Aztec lords—are universal traits of armed forces. But the institutionalization of critique in the military—soldiers' subservience to political leaders, existence of law courts, uniform codes of discipline subject to review, appeal, and ratification—is unknown outside the West. The freedom among citizens to criticize wars and warriors openly and profligately has no pedigree outside the European tradition.

THE CONTINUITY OF WESTERN LETHALITY

What of the present and future? Will—and should—this lethal heritage of Western warfare continue? In a series of border wars during the years 1947–48, 1956, 1967, 1973, and 1982, the tiny nation of Israel fought and decisively defeated a loose coalition of its Arab neighbors, who were supplied with sophisticated weapons by the Soviet Union, China, and France. The population of Israel during those decades never exceeded 5 million citizens, whereas its surrounding antagonists—at various times including Syria, Egypt, Lebanon, Jordan, Iraq, and the Gulf states—numbered well over 100 million. Despite having nearly indefensible borders and a tiny population base, and often being surprised, the outnumbered Israeli army—itself the creation of a brilliant generation of European émigrés—consistently fielded better-organized, -supplied, and -disciplined armies of superbly trained and individualistic soldiers. Israel itself was a democratic society of free markets, free elections, and free speech. Its enemies simply were not.

In less than three months—April 2–June 14, 1982—a British expeditionary force crossed some 8,000 miles of rough seas and expelled a well-entrenched Argentine army on the Falklands, which was easily supported by ships and planes from the Patagonian coast a mere two hundred miles away. At a cost of some 255 British lives—mostly seamen who perished from missile attacks on Royal Navy cruisers—the government of

Margaret Thatcher won back the small islands in the South Atlantic at little cost, despite enormous logistical problems, the excellent imported weapons of its adversary, and the complete surprise of the initial Argentine invasion. Again, the democratic and capitalist society of the United Kingdom sent out better-trained and more disciplined combatants in this strange little war, soldiers far different from those fielded by the Argentine dictatorship.

On January 17, 1991, a coalition of U.S. allies defeated the veteran army of Iraq—1.2 million ground troops, 3,850 artillery pieces, 5,800 tanks, 5,100 other armored vehicles—*in four days,* at a loss of fewer than 150 American servicemen and -women, most of whom were killed by random missile attack, friendly fire, or other accidents. Saddam Hussein's military, like the Argentines', had purchased excellent equipment. Many of his soldiers were seasoned veterans of a brutal war with Iran. They were entrenched on or adjacent to their native soil. Their earlier invasion of Kuwait, like the takeover of the Falklands and the Yom Kippur War, was a complete surprise. The Iraqi army could be easily supplied by highway from Baghdad.

The Iraqi soldiers were not merely poorly disciplined and organized. None of them were in any sense of the word free individuals. The Republican Guard turned out to be about as effective against Westerners as had been Xerxes' Immortals. Not a single soldier who was incinerated by American jets voted to invade Kuwait or fight the United States. Saddam's own military plans were not subject to review; his economy was an extension of an in-house family business. His military hardware—from poison gas to tanks and mines—was all imported. Any Iraqi journalist who questioned the wisdom of invading Kuwait was likely to end up like Pythius the Lydian on the eve of Xerxes' invasion of Greece. The Iraqi military—itself having no ability to invade Europe or the United States—was nearly annihilated not far from the battlefields of Cunaxa and Gaugamela, where Xenophon's Ten Thousand and Alexander the Great had likewise routed indigenous Asian imperial armies so long ago.

Analysis of most other recent wars suggests that even the direct importation of Western tanks, planes, and guns, or the adoption of Western-designed weaponry from other sources, does not always guarantee the success of the Other. That Arab and Argentine officers were trained abroad meant little. Nor did it matter much that their armies were organized and modeled after those in Europe. Israel, Britain, and the United States and its major European partners in the Gulf War, often despite difficult logistics, all found victory relatively easy, after short, violent fighting, drawing on a combination of practices common to Europe alone during the last 2,500 years of Western warfare.

Quite simply, the Israeli, British, and American military shared a common cultural approach to war making—a holistic tradition that transcended howitzers, and jets and one quite different from their respective and sometimes courageous adversaries. Nothing that has transpired in the last decades of the twentieth century suggests an end to Western military dominance, much less to war itself. Had the United States unleashed its full arsenal of brutal military power and fought without political restrictions, the war in Vietnam would have been over in a year or two and may well have resembled the lopsided affair in the Gulf War.

There are three often discussed military scenarios for the future: no wars, occasional wars, or a single, world-ending war. I think we can dismiss the first fantasy without much discussion. War, as the Greeks teach us, seems innate to the human species, the "father of us all," as Heraclitus says. Both idealists on the left and pessimists on the right—whether Kantian utopians or gloomy Hegelians worried over the end of history—have at times prognosticated a cessation to civilized warfare. The former have hoped for global peace under the aegis of international judicial bodies, most recently incarnated by the United Nations and the World Court; the latter lament a spreading global atrophy as a result of depressing uniformity of worldwide capitalism and entitlement democracy, under which the unheroic and enervated citizens of the planet shall risk nothing if it might endanger their comfort.

Yet an often idealistic and self-proclaimed pacifistic Clinton administration (1992–2000) called out the American military for more separate foreign deployments than any presidency of the twentieth century. Contemporary wars are not merely frequent but often brutal beyond anything in the nineteenth century. The Rwandan and Balkan holocausts were tribal bloodletting of the precivilized variety, mostly immune to international stricture and denunciation. The Gulf War of 1991 drew down the might of the United States to its National Guard reserves, a state of mobilization rarely reached even during the worst crises of the Cold War. A not insignificant percentage of the world's oil supply was for a time either embargoed, aflame, or in peril at sea. Belgrade was bombed and the Danube blocked; and there was unchecked mass murder for six years in Bosnia and Kosovo, only hours away from Rome, Athens, and Berlin. Nations, clans, and tribes, it seems, will continue to fight despite international threats, sanctions, and the lessons of history, regardless of the intervention of the world's sole superpower, oblivious to the economic absurdity inherent in modern military arithmetic. The conduct of a war can be rational, but often its origins are not.

By the same token, despite a growing uniformity in the world's militaries—their automatic weapons, chain of command, and the appearance of their uniforms are becoming Western to the core—there is little solace that some new global culture has ushered in a period of perpetual peace. Those consumers of different races, religions, languages, and nations, who all wear Adidas, buy Microsoft computer programs, and drink Coke, are just as likely to kill each other as before—and still watch *Gilligan's Island* reruns on their international television screens afterward.

Gifted intellectuals of vision and character, products of this new Westernized intellectual culture, could only sigh when during the spring of 1982 in the isolated harsh seas of the South Atlantic, British seamen blew up Argentines and vice versa. The European-educated, Argentine Nobel Prize winner Jorge Luis Borges remarked of the idiotic stakes involved in the Falklands War that the two civilized nations were "like two bald men fighting over a comb." But fight they did, and neither seemed like Nietzschean "men without chests" who might think a few thousand windy hills of scrub in the middle of nowhere were not worth any disturbance to their Sunday afternoon televised football games. Thucydides, who claimed he wrote history as "a possession for all time," reminds us that states fight for "fear, self-interest, and honor"—not always out of reason, economic need, or survival. Honor, even in this age of decadence, despite the gloomy predictions of Plato, Hegel, Nietzsche, and Spengler, still exists and will, I think, still get people killed for some time to come.

True, some key ingredients of traditional Western warfare appear to be all but gone. Mercenary armies in America and Europe are the norm. They are not necessarily entirely professional militaries, but outlets for the disaffected of society who seek economic opportunity alone in serving, with the realization that those of a far different social class will determine where, when, and how they will fight and die. Fewer Americans—soldier and civilian alike—are voting than ever before. Most have not a clue about the nature of their own military or its historic relationship with its government and citizenry. The rise of a huge federal government and global corporations has reduced the number of Americans who work as autonomous individuals, either as family farmers, small businesspeople, or owners of local shops. Freedom for many means an absence of responsibility, while the culture of the mall, video, and Internet seem to breed uniformity and complacence, rather than rationalism, individualism, and initiative. Will the West always, then, possess persons of the type who fought at Midway, or citizens who rowed for their freedom at Salamis, or young men who rushed to reform their battered legions in the aftermath of Cannae?

Pessimists see in the lethargic teenagers of the affluent American suburbs seeds of decay. But I am not so sure we are yet at the point of collapse. As long as Europe and America retain their adherence to the structures of constitutional government, capitalism, freedom of religious and political association, free speech, and intellectual tolerance, then history teaches us that Westerners can still field in their hour of need brave, disciplined, and well-equipped soldiers who shall kill like none other on the planet. Our institutions, I think, if they do not erode entirely and are not overthrown, can survive periods of decadence brought on by our material success, eras when the entire critical notion of civic militarism seems bothersome to the enjoyment of material surfeit, and an age in which free speech is used to focus on our own imperfections without concern for the ghastly nature of our enemies. Not all elements of the Western approach to warfare were always present in Europe. The fumes of Roman republicanism kept the empire going long after the ideal of a citizen soldier sometimes gave way to a mercenary army.

Nor is a second scenario likely either, that of a total war brought on by a nuclear America, Europe, Russia, China, or a warlike Islamic world that would incinerate the planet. Two colossal enemies—the Soviet Union and America—did not employ their huge nuclear arsenals for some fifty years of the Cold War. There is no reason to think that either is more rather than less bellicose after the fall of communism. Their legacy to others is nuclear restraint, not recklessness. Strategic arsenals, both nuclear and biological, are shrinking, not growing. If the history of military conflict is any guide, there is also no assurance to believe that possession of nuclear weapons will always be tantamount to mutually assured destruction. Defensive systems in the cosmos are already on the verge of being deployed. The ability to shield blows is a law of military history, forgotten though it has been in the last half century during the threat of a nuclear Armageddon. The swing is once more toward the defensive, as vast sums are allocated to missile protection, to counterinsurgency, and even to body armor to deflect bullet, shrapnel, and flame.

Any nation in this new century that threatens the use of the atomic bomb realizes that it is faced with two unpleasant alternatives: massive reprisal in kind, and soon the possibility that its use will be deflected or destroyed before harming its adversary. Prudence in the use of strategic nuclear weapons, not profligacy, remains the protocol in hot and cold wars. Plague, nerve gas, and new viruses not yet imagined, we are told, will kill us all in the future. But military historians will answer that the forces of vigilance, keen border defense, technologies of prevention and vaccination, and counterintelligence are also never static. The specter of deterrence draws on a human, not a culturally specific, phenomenon, inasmuch as all nations—even democracies—engage in brinkmanship to protect their self-interests. A rogue state that sponsors a terrorist with a vial in Manhattan is still cognizant that its own continued existence is measured by little more than a fifteen-minute missile trajectory.

If we are to have neither perpetual peace nor a single conflagration to end the species, the third option, that of random and even deadlier conventional wars (more men and women have died in battle since World War II than perished in that conflict), seems to be a certainty in the thousand years to come. We in the West still shudder at the carnage of World War II largely because it took the lives of so many Westerners. We forget that far more Koreans, Chinese, Africans, Indians, and Southeast Asians have died in mostly forgotten tribal wars, at the hands of their own government and during hot spots of the Cold War in the half century after the end of Hitler's Germany.

In this regard, the future of Western warfare seems somewhat more disturbing since so many have perished since 1945 due to the diffusion of Western arms and tactics to the non-West. The most obvious worry is the continual spread of Western notions of military discipline, technology, decisive battle, and capitalism *without* the accompanying womb of freedom, civic militarism, civilian audit, and dissent. Such semi-Western autocracies on the horizon—a nuclear China, North Korea, or Iran—may soon, through the purchase or the promotion of a Western-trained scientific and military elite, gain the capability nearly to match European and American research and development of weaponry and organization without simple importation or sale—and without any sense of affinity with, but abject hostility to, their original mentors. Just as deadly as satellite guidance systems in China is a Chinese chain of command with a flexibility and initiative modeled after that in Europe and America, or a private rather than state munitions industry.

In these new flash points to come, can the non-West import our weaponry and military organization and doctrine apart from the cargo of their birth? Can a capitalist China, Iran, Vietnam, or Pakistan, with a scientific elite, for any sustained period really equip and organize a sophisticated army, superior to any Western military, without free citizens, individualism in command hierarchy, constant audit, and oversight of its strategy and tactics? Or do such would-be antagonists merely pick the fruit of the West which soon withers without the deep taproots of intellectual, religious, and political tolerance? Will they merely win occasional battles but not wars, or perhaps threaten us endlessly with the specter of a half dozen nuclear-tipped missiles over Los Angeles?

A military command may steal secrets daily over the Internet, but if it cannot discuss those ideas openly with its civilian and military leadership, then there is no guarantee that such information will find its optimum application to ensure parity with the West. Even should our present adversaries adopt consensual government, free speech, and market economies, would they then really remain our adversaries? Would the embrace of Western culture gradually smother centuries of religious, ethnic, cultural, and racial hostility to the West itself? Perhaps, perhaps not. But the question is not the only one of relevance, for there is no guarantee now, nor was there in the past, that the West itself is monolithic, always stable, or not prone to turn its vast arsenal upon itself. States that become thoroughly Western are less likely to attack the traditional West, but not less likely *enough* to ensure that they will *never* attack the traditional West—and each other. The horror of organized warfare throughout history has *not* been the constant fighting outside of Europe between tribal societies, or even between the West and the Other, but the far deadlier explosions inside Europe *between Westerners.* The more the world becomes thoroughly Western, it seems to me, the larger the Europeanized battlefield shall become.

We should thus take note of another general truth from these studies. Usually, the story of Westerners fighting others is a narrative of battle outside Europe and America. Except for moments of Asian, African, and Islamic intrusion into the periphery of Europe—Xerxes, Hannibal, the Mongols, Moors, and Ottomans—the core of Western culture itself has not been in danger since the breakup of the Roman Empire. Nothing on the horizon suggests that non-Westerners will fight major wars inside Europe or the United States. When battle has ravaged the interior of the West, it is the result of civil war or struggle for hegemony between Western powers. I see no reason why such a scenario will not be more likely in the century to come than invasions and attacks from those outside the Western paradigm.

THE WEST VERSUS THE WEST

With the worldwide spread of shared ideas of democracy, capitalism, free speech, individualism, and a globally connected economy, it may be that world-encompassing wars will be less likely. Yet it will also be true that when wars do break out, they will be far more lethal and draw on the full resources of a deadly military tradition. We see glimpses of that today— tribal fights in which hideous Western weapons are used by those who have not a clue how to create them.

The peril to come, however, is not just the spread of atomic weapons and F-16 fighter jets but much more so the dissemination of knowledge, rationalism, the creation of free universities, perhaps even the growth of democracy, capitalism, and individualism themselves throughout the world—the real ingredients, as we have seen in these case studies, of a most murderous brand of battle. Most see in the advance of rationalism, capitalism, democracy, and their ancillary values the seeds of perpetual peace and prosperity. Maybe, but we must remember that these ideas are also the foundations that have created the world's deadliest armies of the past.

The real hazard for the future, as it has always been in the past, is not Western moral decline or the threat of the Other now polished with the veneer of sophisticated arms, but the age-old specter of a horrendous war inside the West itself, the old Europe and America with its full menu of Western economic, military, and political dynamism. Gettysburg in a single day took more Americans than did all the Indian wars of the nineteenth century. A small Boer force killed more British troops in six days than the Zulus did in a year. Most of the crises that have plagued the world in the twentieth century grew out of Europe's two world wars—the status of Germany, the division and unification of Europe, the rise and collapse of the Russian empire, the spread of communism after the defeat of fascism, the mess in the Balkans, and the entry of America into the affairs of the world.

Many have accepted the truism that democracies do not fight democracies. Statistics seem to support this encouraging belief. But in the Western context, given the lethality of Western arms, there is little margin of error, since even a single intramural European war can bring carnage and cultural chaos in its wake. Consensual governments, in fact, have often fought other Western consensual governments. Athens wrecked its culture by invading democratic Sicily (415 B.C.). Democratic Boeotia fought democratic Athens at Mantinea (362 B.C.). Republican Rome ended the Achaean federated states of Greece and leveled Corinth (146 B.C.). Italian republics of the Renaissance were constantly at each other's throat. Revolutionary France and parliamentary England were deadly enemies; a democratic United States fought twice against the consensual government of Britain. There was a Union and Confederate president and Senate. The Boers and the British in southern Africa each had elected representatives. Both elected prime ministers in India and Pakistan have at times threatened each other. The presence of a Palestinian parliament has not brought peace to the Middle East; and there is no assurance that should its autonomy grow, that elected body would be any less likely than Mr. Arafat to war with Israel. There was also a parliament of sorts under the kaiser. Hitler first came to power through election, not a coup. The Russian entry into Chechnya received parliamentary approval.

Democracies are more likely *not* to war against each other; but when they do—and they have—the ensuing conflict from both sides draws on the entire terrible menu of Western warfare itself. For every Nicias, there can be a democratic counterpart Hermocrates of Syracuse; for each assembly-line Venetian Arsenal, an efficient Genovese dockworks; for every citizen soldier Grant, there may well be a Lee; for each ingenious Mauser, a Colt; for every eccentric and highly trained German rocket scientist, a British radar genius. Western civil war inside Europe or America will not necessarily be such a catastrophic event simply because it shall take more lives than those lost in Mao's China or in the fifty years of bloodletting in Africa—although such fighting might well exceed those totals. Rather, Western fratricide, as it has in the past, threatens an entire civilization, which for good or evil has given the world its present standard of living and is the source of its industrialization, technological advance, popular culture, and blueprints for political organization.

We should be apprehensive that there are once again fundamental upheavals transpiring in Europe, more so that at any time since the 1930s. The growth in influence of a unified Germany has scarcely begun. The specter of a pan-European state highlights the increasing ambiguous position of Great Britain and seems to create unity among its members by collective antagonism toward and envy of the United States. The insecurity of eastern Europe is part of a larger dilemma facing a Russia neither quite European nor Asian. The pride and fears of a Westernized Japan remain—accentuated by the rise of a capitalist China and the unpredictability of two Koreas, who themselves promise a new unified nationalist identity, perhaps fueled by South Korean capitalism and North Korean nuclear arms. Resurgent isolationism in America grows when its own intervention is at an all-time high and yet support for it is at a historic low. Waterloo, the Somme, Verdun, Dresden, and Normandy seem the far deadlier ghosts that may well haunt the world in the future.

I am not so worried about constant warring in the millennium to come between the West and non-West—more flare-ups, for example, in the Middle East and its environs, or murderous insurrections in Africa and South America—if such theaters, despite the deadly gadgetry, remain outside the Western tradition and embrace different indigenous approaches to fighting. Rather, if history is any guide to the future, has not instead the real danger to the world's progress and civilization always arisen when a Western army turns its deadly arsenal upon itself? If so, let us pray for another half century of aberrant European and American peace, for a few more decades of rare Western behavior so at odds with its own past. Let us remember as well that the more Western the world becomes, the more likely that all its wars will be ever more Western in nature and thus ever more deadly. We may well be all Westerners in the millennium to come, and that could be a very dangerous thing indeed. Culture is not a mere construct, but when it comes to war, a very deadly reality that often determines whether thousands of mostly innocent young men and women live or die.

Western civilization has given mankind the only economic system that works, a rationalist tradition that alone allows us material and technological progress, the sole political structure that ensures the freedom of the individual, a system of ethics and a religion that brings out the best in humankind—and the most lethal practice of arms conceivable. Let us hope that we at last understand this legacy. It is a weighty and sometimes ominous heritage that we must neither deny nor feel ashamed about—but insist that our deadly manner of war serves, rather than buries, our civilization.

Glossary

Achaemenid: The royal ruling house of the Persian Empire between 557 and 323 B.C.

anabasis: Greek for "march up-country"; also the title of works by the historians Xenophon and Arrian, chronicling the respective marches into Asia by the Ten Thousand and Alexander the Great.

ARVN: Army of the Republic of Vietnam—the military of the South Vietnamese government.

assegai: The short Zulu spear, equipped with a large metal head, and to be used for thrusting rather than throwing.

Attica: The hinterland and civic territory surrounding the city of Athens.

Aztecs: The people who lived in Aztlán ("white place of the herons"), located around Tenochtitlán; used as a synonym for the more generic term "Mexicas," the residents of the Aztec empire in central Mexico.

Boers: European colonists in South Africa, originally of Dutch descent.

boulē: Usually the upper body of legislative government of most Greek city-states.

Bushido: "The way of the warrior"—the purported code of the samurai, an amalgam of values championed by the Japanese military shortly before World War II, and drawing on elements of Zen Buddhism, Japanese feudalism, and the fascism of the 1930s.

Byzantine: Generally, the civilization of the Eastern Roman Empire that gradually developed an exclusively Greek culture after the foundation of Constantinople in A.D. 330; the Byzantines kept the traditions of the Roman Empire alive in a Greek context for a thousand years until their destruction in 1453.

caudillo: Spanish for "leader"; used often in the context of the sixteenth-century Caribbean and Mexico, where for a generation or two Spanish conquistadors and governors exercised near absolute power.

centurions: The chief professional officers of the Roman legion, who each managed a century of about a hundred soldiers. Under the reforms of the early republic, there remained sixty centurions per legion, but six were assigned to each of the ten cohorts, the new principal tactical units of the Roman army.

Companion Cavalry: The veteran heavy cavalrymen who anchored the wings of Alexander the Great's army and served as the aristocracy of Macedonian society.

consuls: The two annually elected executive officers of the Roman Republic, entrusted with enforcing the decrees of the Senate and leading large armies into battle.

Dark Ages: A chronological term referring to the period in western Europe between A.D.

500 and 1000, in which the collapse of institutions after the fall of the Roman Empire led to a dearth of information about the subsequent five hundred years of European history.

devshirme: The Ottoman inspection every four years of conquered Christian provinces to select suitable Christian youths for forced conversion to Islam and eventual entry into Ottoman public service.

DMZ: Demilitarized Zone, the official border between North and South Vietnam established by the peace accords of 1954; purportedly to be immune from military operations by either side; in fact, the scene of some of the most violent fighting in the Vietnam War.

ekklēsia: The assembly of all voting citizens in most Greek city-states.

eleutheria: The ancient Greek word for political freedom.

galleass: A large hybrid galley of three sails, high sides, and plentiful cannon; used haphazardly as a Mediterranean warship in the sixteenth and seventeenth centuries.

galleon: A large sailing vessel with multiple sails and three or four decks, used for both commerce and war on the high seas between the fifteenth and seventeenth centuries.

galley: A large oared vessel of a single sail with unusually low sides, used on the Mediterranean as a warship from Roman times to the end of the sixteenth century.

galliot: A small, fast galley, which often had two sails and relied on both oars and wind.

Gatling gun: An early machine gun that achieved high rates of fire through rotating barrels on a central axis turned by a crank.

gladius: The short Roman sword of the legionary, over two inches wide and two feet long, used for both cutting and thrusting, and thought to have been adapted from an earlier Spanish weapon.

grapeshot: Clusters of small iron balls shot out of cannon as antipersonnel projectiles.

harquebus: An early matchlock musket, often requiring a barrel rest to support its great weight.

Hellenic: Literally "Greek"; often used to describe the period of Greek history between 700 and 323 B.C.

Hellenistic: An era of eastern Mediterranean history between the death of Alexander the Great (323 B.C.) and the Roman victory at the battle of Actium (31 B.C.).

hidalgos: Minor impoverished Spanish nobility, mostly Castilians, Andalusians, and Extremeños, who as conquistadors sailed to the New World to find fortune, celebrity, and renewed social status.

hoplite: A Greek heavy infantryman, who fought with body armor, large shield, and spear in mass formation. The term originally denoted the agrarian class of the Greek city-states, who could afford the necessary panoply, but eventually referred to any soldier who fought in the phalanx.

hypaspists: "Shield bearers," infantrymen of the Macedonian army, with large shields and short spears, who provided flexible defense between the Companion Cavalry and the phalanx proper.

Immortals: Select infantrymen who comprised the imperial guard of the Achaemenid empire and whose numbers remained constant at 10,000.

impi: A generic term for the assembled Zulu army, but more regularly an individual Zulu regiment.

jihad: A religious war of Muslims against perceived enemies of Islam.

kraal: A small Zulu hamlet surrounded by a rough stockade; also used of a cattle enclosure and, in a more generic sense, a Zulu household.

laager: An Afrikaner camp, usually ringed by interlocking wagons.

legionaries: Roman foot soldiers between 300 B.C. and A.D. 500, equipped with a javelin *(pilum)*, short sword *(gladius)*, and large oblong shield *(scutum)*, who fought in a legion of about 6,000 men.

MACV: Military Assistance Command Vietnam—the title of the American military presence in South Vietnam.

Malinche: Cortés's Indian name, derived from the Aztec *Mainulli* or *Malinali* (the twelfth Mexican month); originally the name of Doña Marina, the companion and translator of Cortés, and then by association to Cortés himself.

Mamluks: A servile caste of warriors who eventually came to dominate Egypt from the thirteenth through seventeenth centuries.

maniple: A unit of the Roman army, numbering at full strength about 200 legionaries; thirty maniples made up a legion of 6,000 soldiers. For most of the early republic, maniples were the chief tactical units of the army.

medieval: An adjective referring to the culture of the Middle Ages, from the Latin *medius* ("middle") + *aevum* ("age").

metic: A resident alien of the Greek city-state; most numerous in Athens.

Middle Ages: A chronological term roughly describing some 1,000 years of European history between the collapse of Rome (A.D. ca. 450) and the beginning of the Renaissance (ca. 1450); used most often in association with western Europe.

Natal: A British colony in southwestern Africa, located to the immediate south and west of Zululand, with its capital at Durban.

Panhellenic: Literally "all Greek"; often used in association with the loose alliance of Greek city-states that fought Persia.

phalangites: Pike-bearing Macedonian infantrymen who fought in the phalanx of the Hellenistic age.

phalanx: A formation of heavy-armed hoplites or phalangites, consisting of columns of spearmen from eight to sixteen men deep.

pike: A long pole with sharp metal tip; pikes, as distinguished from spears, were over ten feet in length and required both hands for use. Most commonly associated with the Macedonians and medieval Swiss infantry.

polis: A politically autonomous Greek city-state, including the urban center and surrounding rural territory; plural: poleis.

proskynēsis: The act of prostrating oneself before a lord and/or kissing his feet; a normal practice in Persia, but considered repugnant to Hellenic culture when Alexander attempted to introduce it among his troops.

Punic Wars: Three wars (264–241 B.C.; 218–201 B.C.; 149–146 B.C.) fought between Rome and Carthage, which eventually led to the destruction of Carthage itself.

res publica: Roman form of consensual government under which popular representatives, more often than the people themselves, voted for both executive officers and general legislation.

samurai: Feudal Japanese warriors, whose mythical military code of conduct and values the Japanese military attempted to resurrect and instill in its soldiers in the 1930s and early 1940s.

sarissa: The long pike of some fourteen to twenty feet, carried by Macedonian infantrymen with both hands.

Ten Thousand: Greek mercenaries hired by Cyrus the Younger in 401 B.C. to anchor his Persian army in its quest to capture the Persian crown.

timariot: An Ottoman lord who was given conquered land and control of rural serfs in exchange for promises to provide soldiers during war.

tribunes: The six senior military officers of a legion; in a political sense, magistrates of the state entrusted to watch over the interests of the plebs.

trireme: A Greek warship with three banks of oarsmen, consisting of about 170 rowers.

Victoria Cross: The British military's highest award for bravery—a bronze medal in the shape of a Maltese cross.

Vietcong: Purportedly, an independent communist insurgency group in South Vietnam; in fact, an army dependent on the guidance and supply of the communist government of North Vietnam.

Western: Generic adjective for European civilization that grew up in and west of Greece, and shared core values that originated in classical antiquity, including but not limited to constitutional government, civil liberties, free exchange of ideas, self-critique, private property, capitalism, and separation between religious and political/scientific thought.

For Further Reading

Chapter One: Why the West Has Won

There is an entire genre of scholarship devoted to various explanations of Western military dominance, mostly from the sixteenth century onward. See most prominently C. Cipolla, *Guns, Sails and Empires: Technological Innovation and the Early Phases of European Expansionism* (Cambridge, 1965); M. Roberts, *The Military Revolution, 1560–1660* (Belfast, 1956); G. Parker, *The Military Revolution: Military Innovation and the Rise of the West, 1500–1800*, 2nd ed. (Cambridge, 1996); J. Black, *A Military Revolution? Military Change and European Society, 1550–1800* (Basingstoke, England, 1991); P. Curtin, *The World and the West: The European Challenge and the Overseas Response in the Age of Empire* (Cambridge, 2000); D. Eltis, *The Military Revolution in Sixteenth-Century Europe* (New York, 1995); and C. Rodgers, ed., *The Military Revolution Debate: Readings on the Military Transformation of Early Modern Europe* (Boulder, Colo., 1995). For the argument of an even earlier military revolution, see A. Ayton and J. L. Price, eds., *The Medieval Military Revolution: State, Society, and Military Change in Medieval and Early Modern Europe* (New York, 1995).

For East-West contacts and exchanges of technology, see D. Ralston, *Importing the European Army: The Introduction of European Military Techniques and Institutions into the Extra-European World, 1600–1914* (Chicago, 1990); R. MacAdams, *Paths of Fire: An Anthropologist's Inquiry into Western Technology* (Princeton, N.J., 1996); L. White, *Machina Ex Deo: Essays in the Dynamism of Western Culture* (Cambridge, Mass., 1968); and especially, D. Headrick, *Tools of Empire: Technology and European Imperialism in the Nineteenth Century* (New York, 1981). The wider question of European cultural dynamism is covered brilliantly in two books: D. Landes, *The Wealth and Poverty of Nations: Why Some Are So Rich and Some So Poor* (New York, 1998), and E. L. Jones, *The European Miracle: Environments, Economies, and Geopolitics in the History of Europe and Asia* (Cambridge, 1987). See also the essays in L. Harrison and S. Huntington, eds., *Culture Matters: How Values Shape Human Progress* (New York, 2000).

A good discussion of the nature of Western culture and its critics in the university is found in three engaging works: K. Windshuttle, *The Killing of History: How Literary Critics and Social Theorists Are Murdering Our Past* (New York, 1996); A.

Herman, *The Idea of Decline in Western History* (New York, 1997); and D. Gress, *From Plato to NATO: The Idea of the West and Its Opponents* (New York, 1998). See also T. Sowell, *Conquests and Cultures: An International History* (New York, 1998).

In contrast, the bibliography of anti-Western criticism is huge, but a good introduction to the nature and methodology of the scholarship is K. Sale, *The Conquest of Paradise: Christopher Columbus and the Columbian Legacy* (New York, 1990); D. Peers, ed., *Warfare and Empires: Contact and Conflict Between European and Non-European Military and Maritime Forces and Cultures* (Brookfield, Vt., 1997); F. Fernandez-Armesto, *Millennium: A History of the Last Thousand Years* (New York, 1995); M. Adas, *Machines as the Measure of Men: Science, Technology, and Ideologies of Western Dominance* (New York, 1989); T. Todorov, *The Conquest of America: The Question of the Other* (New York, 1984); and F. Jameson and M. Miyoshi, eds., *The Cultures of Globalization* (Durham and London, 1998).

Postmodern approaches to Western dominance characterize M. Foucault, *The Archaeology of Knowledge* (New York, 1972); M. de Certeau, *The Writing of History* (New York, 1988); E. Said, *Culture and Imperialism* (London, 1993); *Orientalism* (London, 1978); F. Jameson, *Postmodernism, or, The Cultural Logic of Late Capitalism* (London, 1991). For a sampling of the traditionalists' defense of Western civilization, see S. Clough, *Basic Values of Western Civilization* (New York, 1960), and C. N. Parkinson, *East and West* (London, 1963). N. Douglas has an amusing polemic on the West in *Good-Bye to Western Culture* (New York, 1930).

Representative works of the biological and geographical explanations for the rise of the West are J. Diamond, *Guns, Germs, and Steel: The Fates of Human Societies* (New York, 1997); A. Crosby, *Ecological Imperialism: The Biological Expansion of Europe, 900–1900* (Cambridge, 1986); and M. Harris, *Cannibals and Kings: The Origins of Cultures* (New York, 1978). An effort to balance natural determinism with human agency and culture is found in W. McNeill, *The Rise of the West* (Chicago, 1991), and *The Pursuit of Power: Technology, Armed Force, and Society Since A.D. 1000* (Chicago, 1982).

A masterful survey of the role between culture and war is J. Keegan's *A History of Warfare* (New York, 1993). See, too, K. Raaflaub and N. Rosenstein, eds., *War and Society in the Ancient and Medieval Worlds* (Cambridge, Mass., 1998). Surveys of the "Great Battles" are best begun with E. Creasy, *The Fifteen Decisive Battles of the World: From Marathon to Waterloo* (New York, 1908); T. Knox, *Decisive Battles Since Waterloo* (New York, 1887); J. F. C. Fuller, *A Military History of the Western World* (New York, 1954); A. Jones, *The Art of War in the Western World* (New York, 1987); and R. Gabriel and D. Boose, *The Great Battles of Antiquity: A Strategic and Tactical Guide to Great Battles That Shaped the Development of War* (Westport, Conn., 1994).

Chapter Two: Freedom—or "To Live as You Please"
Salamis, September 28, 480 b.c.

The chief problems associated with the battle surround the exact date of the fighting, the size of the Persian fleet, the purported ruse of Themistocles, and the identification of particular islands in the Salamis strait. These issues are discussed in a number of fine histories in English of the Persian Wars. See, for example, J. Lazenby, *The Defence of Greece 490–479 B.C.* (Warminster, England, 1993); P. Green, *The Greco-Persian Wars* (Berkeley, Calif., 1994); and C. Hignett, *Xerxes' Invasion of Greece* (Oxford, 1963). Still valuable is G. B. Grundy, *The Great Persian War and Its Preliminaries* (London, 1901). In some ways, George Grote's masterful chronicle of Salamis in the fifth volume of his *History of Greece,* 2nd ed. (New York, 1899) remains unmatched; a new edition with an Introduction by Paul Cartledge is now available from Routledge (London 2000).

A number of scholars have attempted to sort out the baffling topography and conflicting ancient accounts of the battle. See G. Roux, "Éschyle, Hérodote, Diodore, Plutarque racontent la bataille de Salamine," *Bulletin de Correspondance Hellénique 98* (1974), 51–94, and the relevant sections in H. Delbrück, *Warfare in Antiquity,* vol. 1 of *The History of the Art of War* (Westport, Conn., 1975); N. G. L. Hammond, *Studies in Greek History* (Oxford, 1973); and W. K. Pritchett, *Studies in Ancient Greek Topography I* (Berkeley and Los Angeles, 1965). For comments on the pertinent Greek passages in Herodotus and Plutarch, see W. W. How and J. Wells, eds., *A Commentary on Herodotus* (Oxford, 1912), vol. 2, 378–87, and F. J. Frost, *Plutarch's Themistocles: A Historical Commentary* (Princeton, N.J., 1980).

The idea of freedom in the Greek world is discussed in a number of books. Begin with A. Momigliano, "The Persian Empire and Greek Freedom," in A. Ryan, ed., *The Idea of Freedom: Essays in Honour of Isaiah Berlin* (Oxford, 1979), 139–51; and O. Patterson, *Freedom in the Making of Western Culture* (New York, 1991). See also the essays in M. I. Finley, *Economy and Society in Ancient Greece* (New York, 1982). For the later symbolism of Salamis in popular Athenian ideology, see C. Meier, *Athens: A Portrait of the City in Its Golden Age* (New York, 1998), and N. Loraux, *The Invention of Athens: The Funeral Oration in the Classical City* (Cambridge, Mass., 1986).

There are a number of fine studies of the Achaemenids that draw on Persian sources in addition to Greek literature. See H. Sancisi-Weerdenburg and A. Kuhrt, *Achaemenid History I: Sources, Structures and Synthesis* (Leiden, 1987); J. Boardman et al., eds., *The Cambridge Ancient History,* 2nd ed., *Persia, Greece and the Western Mediterranean c. 525 to 479* (Cambridge, 1988); J. M. Cook, *The Persian Empire* (New York, 1983); M. Dandamaev, *A Political History of the Achaemenid Empire* (Leiden, 1989); and A. T. Olmstead, *History of the Persian Empire, Achaemenid Period* (Chicago, 1948). On the history of Iran, see the chapter on the Achaemenids in R. Frye, *The History of Ancient Iran* (Munich, 1984). And for the letter of Darius to Gadatas, see R. Meiggs and D. Lewis, eds., *A Selection of Greek Historical Inscriptions to the End of the Fifth Century B.C.* (Oxford, repr. ed., 1989).

More specific accounts of Greek-Persian cultural relations are covered in D. Lewis, *Sparta and Persia: Lectures Delivered at the University of Cincinnati, Autumn 1976, in Memory of Donald W. Bradeen* (Leiden, 1977), and *Selected Papers in Greek and Near Eastern History* (Cambridge, 1997); A. R. Burn, *Persia and the Greeks: The Defence of the West, c. 546–478 B.C.* (New York, repr. ed., 1984); M. Miller, *Athens and Persia in the Fifth Century B.C.* (Cambridge, 1997); and especially the article by S. Averintsev, "Ancient Greek 'Literature' and Near Eastern 'Writings': The Opposition and Encounter of Two Creative Principles, Part One: The Opposition," *Arion* 7.1 (Spring/Summer 1999), 1–39. For an accessible synopsis of the Persian army, see A. Ferrill, *The Origins of War: From the Stone Age to Alexander the Great* (New York, 1985).

On Greek navies and sea power in general, see C. Starr, *The Influence of Sea-Power on Ancient History* (New York, 1989); L. Casson, *The Ancient Mariners: Seafarers and Sea Fighters of the Mediterranean in Ancient Times* (London, 1959), and *Ships and Seamanship in the Ancient World* (Princeton, N.J., 1971); and J. S. Morrison and R. T. Williams, *Greek Oared Ships 900–322 B.C.* (London, 1968). For reconstructions of the ancient trireme, consult J. S. Morrison, J. F. Coates, and N. B. Ranov, *The Athenian Trireme: The History and Reconstruction of an Ancient Greek Warship* (Cambridge, 2000), and *An Athenian Trireme Reconstructed: The British Sea Trials of 'Olympias,'* British Archaeological Series 486 (Oxford, 1987).

There is also a growing academic industry that chronicles the Greeks' purported prejudicial perceptions of Persia; cf. E. Hall, *Inventing the Barbarian: Greek Self-Definition Through Tragedy* (Oxford, 1989); F. Hartog, *The Mirror of Herodotus* (Berkeley and Los Angeles, 1988); and P. Georges, *Barbarian Asia and the Greek Experience: From the Archaic Period to the Age of Xenophon* (Baltimore, Md., 1994). An extreme example is P. Springborg, *Western Republicanism and the Oriental Prince* (Austin, Tex., 1992).

Chapter Three: Decisive Battle
Gaugamela, October 1, 331 B.C.

Gaugamela is amply treated in a variety of academic genres, most of them narrow journal articles in academic publications. For the general reader, it is best to begin with purely military histories of Alexander's reign. There exists a fine, though brief monograph on the battle by E. W. Marsden, *The Campaign of Gaugamela* (Liverpool 1964). Gaugamela also forms a key part of the discussion in J. F. C. Fuller, *The Generalship of Alexander the Great* (London, 1958); is reviewed competently by H. Delbrück, *Warfare in Antiquity,* vol. 1 of *The History of the Art of War* (Westport, Conn., 1975), and J. F. C. Fuller, *A Military History of the Western World,* vol. 1 (London, 1954); and is found as well in E. Creasy, *The Fifteen Decisive Battles of the World: From Marathon to Waterloo* (New York, 1908).

For purely military matters, see also J. Ashley, *The Macedonian Empire: The Era of Warfare Under Philip II and Alexander the Great, 359–323 B.C.* (Jefferson, N.C., 1998), and D. Engels, *Alexander the Great and the Logistics of the Macedonian Army* (Berkeley, Calif., 1978). N. G. L. Hammond is brilliant on Alexander's army but far less so on any historical assessment of his reign and achievements: e.g., *Alexander the Great: King, Commander, and Statesman* (Park Ridge, N.J., 1989); *Three Historians of Alexander the Great: The So-Called Vulgate Authors, Diodorus, Justin, and Curtius* (Cambridge, 1983); and, with G. T. Griffith, *A History of Macedonia,* vol. 2 (Oxford, 1979).

The complex ancient sources of information about Gaugamela—mostly reconciliation of the contrary accounts of Plutarch, Diodorus, Arrian, and Curtius—are best discussed in J. R. Hamilton, *Plutarch's Alexander: A Commentary* (Oxford, 1969); N. G. L. Hammond, *Sources for Alexander the Great: An Analysis of Plutarch's Life and Arrian's Anabasis Alexandros* (Cambridge, 1993); A. B. Bosworth, *A Historical Commentary on Arrian's History of Alexander,* vol. 1 (Oxford, 1980); J. C. Yardley, *Justin: Epitome of the Philippic History of Pompeius Trogus, Books 11–12: Alexander the Great* (Oxford, 1997); J. Atkinson, *A Commentary on Q. Curtius Rufus' Historiae Alexandri Magni, Books 3 & 4* (London, 1980); and L. Pearson, *The Lost Histories of Alexander the Great* (New York, 1960).

There are countless biographies of Alexander the Great that discuss the campaign of Gaugamela. The most accessible in English are R. Lane Fox, *Alexander the Great* (London, 1973); W. W. Tarn, *Alexander the Great,* vols. 1–2 (Chicago, 1981); P. Green, *Alexander of Macedon* (Berkeley and Los Angeles, 1974); U. Wilcken, *Alexander the Great* (New York, 1967); and especially the excellent and sober portrayal by A. B. Bosworth, *Conquest and Empire: The Reign of Alexander the Great* (Cambridge, 1988). Despite the work of Bosworth, Green, and important journal articles by E. Badian, the romance of Alexander the Great as a philosopher king and advocate of universal brotherhood has again regained credence both in America and elsewhere in the current age of multiculturalism and renewed ethnic tension in the Balkans.

For the Western origins and traditions of decisive battle, see V. D. Hanson, *The Western Way of War: Infantry Battle in Classical Greece* (Berkeley, 2000); and *The Other Greeks: The Family Farm and the Agrarian Roots of Western Civilization* (Berkeley, 1999); D. Dawson, *The Origins of Western Warfare: Militarism and Morality in the Ancient World* (Boulder, Colo., 1996); R. Weigley, *The Age of Battles: The Quest for Decisive Warfare from Breitenfeld to Waterloo* (Bloomington, Ind., 1991); R. Preston and S. Wise, *Men in Arms: A History of Warfare and Its Interrelationships with Western Society* (New York, 1970); and G. Craig and F. Gilbert, eds., *Makers of Modern Strategy: Military Thought from Machiavelli to Hitler* (Princeton, N.J., 1943). For the difference in primitive skirmishing and shock "civilized" collisions, see H. H. Turney-High, *Primitive War: Its Practice and Concepts* (Columbia, S.C., 1971).

General Persian sources are discussed under the prior chapter devoted to Salamis, but there are a few works specific to the later Achaemenid era, and especially to Darius III. See, for example, E. Herzfeld, *The Persian Empire* (Wiesbaden, 1968); A. Stein, *Old Routes of Western Iran: Narrative of an Archaeological Journey* (New York, 1969); and for a revisionist view, P. Briant, *Histoire de l'empire perse* (Paris, 1996).

Chapter Four: Citizen Soldiers
Cannae, August 2, 216 B.C.

Primary sources for Cannae are the historians Polybius (3.110–118) and Livy (22.44–50), with anecdotal information found in Appian, Plutarch's *Fabius,* and Cassius Dio. The main problems of the battle lie in reconciling Polybius's much larger figures for both the size of (86,000) and number killed in (70,000) the Roman army with the usually more suspect Livy's smaller—and more believable—figures (48,000 killed). In addition, scholars still argue over Hannibal's wisdom in not marching on Rome and besieging the city in the shocking aftermath of the slaughter. Less critical controversies surround the exact armament and tactics of Hannibal's African and European allies—were they swordsmen or pikemen or both?—and the positioning of the Roman encampments.

Graphic accounts of the battle itself are available in M. Samuels, "The Reality of Cannae," *Militärgeschichtliche Mitteilungen* 47 (1990), 7–29; P. Sabin, "The Mechanics of Battle in the Second Punic War," *Bulletin of the Institute of Classical Studies* 67 (1996), 59–79; and V. Hanson, "Cannae," in R. Cowley, ed., *The Experience of War* (New York, 1992).

For the larger topographical, tactical, and strategic questions that surround Cannae, see F. W. Walbank, *A Historical Commentary on Polybius*, vol. 1 (Oxford, 1957), 435–49; J. Kromayer and G. Veith, *Antike Schlachtfelder in Italien und Afrika* (Berlin, 1912), vol. 1, 341–46; and H. Delbrück, *Warfare in Antiquity*, vol. 1 of *The History of the Art of War* (Westport, Conn., 1975), (Berlin, 1920), vol. 1, 315–35.

The most balanced and researched account of the Second Punic War and the battle of Cannae is J. F. Lazenby's excellent *Hannibal's War: A Military History of the Second Punic War* (Norman, Okla., 1998), which provides a narrative closely supported by ancient sources. For a more general study, see B. Craven, *The Punic Wars* (New York, 1980), and N. Bagnall, *The Punic Wars* (London, 1990).

For military biographies of Hannibal for the general reader, consult K. Christ, *Hannibal* (Darmstadt, Germany, 1974); S. Lanul, *Hannibal* (Paris, 1995); J. Peddie, *Hannibal's War* (Gloucestershire, England, 1997); and T. Bath, *Hannibal's Campaigns* (Cambridge, 1981). Questions of manpower and the potential of Roman military mobilization are surveyed in A. Toynbee, *Hannibal's Legacy*, 2 vols. (London, 1965), and especially P. Brunt, *Italian Manpower 225 B.C.–A.D. 14* (London, 1971).

There are good, accessible accounts of the history and institutions of ancient Carthage in D. Soren, A. Ben Khader, and H. Slim, *Carthage: Uncovering the Mysteries and Splendors of Ancient Tunisia* (New York, 1990); J. Pedley, ed., *New Light on Ancient Carthage* (Ann Arbor, Mich., 1980); and G. and C. Picard, *The Life and Death of Carthage* (New York, 1968). S. Lancel, *Carthage: A History* (Oxford, 1995), has a lively narrative of Roman-Carthaginian interaction. The larger strategic canvas of Roman imperialism and the Punic Wars is discussed in W. V. Harris, *War and Imperialism in Republican Rome 327–70 B.C.* (Oxford, 2nd ed., 1984), and J. S. Richardson, *Hispaniae, Spain, and the Development of Roman Imperialism, 218–82 B.C.* (New York, 1986).

The traditions of civic militarism and constitutional government as they relate to military efficacy are thematic in D. Dawson, *The Origins of Western Warfare* (Boulder, Colo., 1996), and discussed in detail by P. Rahe, *Republics, Ancient and Modern* (Chapel Hill, N.C., 1992). In a series of articles and books, B. Bachrach has made the argument for a military continuum in western and northern Europe without much interruption from imperial Roman times to the Middle Ages; see especially his *Merovingian Military Organization (481–751)* (Minneapolis, Minn., 1972).

The bibliography of the Roman army is vast; a good introduction to the legions of the republic is F. E. Adcock, *The Roman Art of War Under the Republic* (Cambridge, Mass., 1940); H. M. D. Parker, *The Roman Legions,* 2nd ed. (Oxford, 1971); B. Campbell, *The Roman Army, 31 B.C.–A.D. 37: a sourcebook* (London 1994); and L. Keppie, *The Making of the Roman Army* (Totowa, N.J., 1984). For the influence of Cannae on later Western military thought, see J. Kersétz, "Die Schlacht bei Cannae und ihr Einfluss auf die Entwicklung der Kriegskunst," *Beiträge der Martin-Luther Universität* (1980), 29–43; A. von Schlieffen, *Cannae* (Fort Leavenworth, Kans., 1931); and A. du Picq, *Battle Studies* (Harrisburg, Pa., 1987).

Chapter Five: Landed Infantry
Poitiers, October 11, 732

We have almost no full contemporary account of the battle of Poitiers, since a number of the standard sources for late antiquity and the early Dark Ages end before 732. Gregory of Tours stopped his *Historia Francorum* in 594. The anonymous *Liber Historiae Francorum* was completed at 727. Venerable Bede's history leaves off at 731, a year before the battle.

Although the *Chronicle of Fredegar* ends at 642, a continuator left a brief account of the fighting in 732 (J. M. Wallace-Hadrill, *The Four Books of the Chronicle of Fredegar with its Continuations* [London, 1960]), as did the anonymous continuator of the *Chronicle of Isidore* (T. Mommsen, *Isidori Continuatio Hispana, Monumenta Germaniae Historica, Auctores Antiquissimi,* vol. 11 [Berlin, 1961]). The absence of good firsthand accounts of the battle have led to widely contrasting appraisals of its conduct and importance. It is common to read in major surveys of the age—before 1950 almost exclusively in German and French—that Poitiers marked the rise of feudalism, the dominance of heavy knights in stirrups, and the salvation of Western civilization, even as more sober accounts deny that horsemen played much, if any role, at Poitiers, that feudalism as it later emerged was years in the future, and that Abd ar-Rahman's invasion was merely one of a series of small raids that gradually waned in the eighth century, as the Muslim bickering in Spain and Frankish consolidation in Europe inevitably conspired to weaken Islamic expansion from the Pyrenees. Most likely, Poitiers was an understandable victory of spirited infantrymen on the defensive, rather than the result of a monumental technological or military breakthrough, a reflection of increasing Arab weakness in extended operations to the north, rather than in itself the salvation of the Christian West.

For the battle of Poitiers itself, see the monograph of M. Mercier and A. Seguin, *Charles Martel et la bataille de Poitiers* (Paris, 1944). Consult especially the work of B. S. Bachrach, "Charles Martel, Mounted Shock Combat, the Stirrup, and Feudalism," in his *Armies and Politics in the Early Medieval West* (Aldershot, England, 1993). This volume of essays serves as a collection of Bachrach's most compelling arguments about the relative importance of cavalry, horsemen, and fortifications during the Merovingian and Carolingian periods. See also his *Merovingian Military Organization* (Minneapolis, Minn., 1972), and "Early Medieval Europe," in K. Raaflaub and N.

Rosenstein, eds., *War and Society in the Ancient and Medieval Worlds* (Washington, D.C., 1999).

On the Franks, the latter Merovingians, and the early Carolingians, there are good surveys in K. Scherman, *The Birth of France* (New York, 1987); P. Riché, *The Carolingians: A Family Who Forged Europe* (Philadelphia, 1993); E. James, *The Origins of France: From Clovis to the Capetians, 500–1000* (London, 1982); and H. Delbrück, *The Barbarian Invasions,* vol. 2 of *The History of the Art of War* (Westport, Conn., 1980).

For the life of Charles Martel, see R. Gerberding, *The Rise of the Carolingians and the Liber Historiae Francorum* (Oxford, 1987). For two famous narratives of the battle, consult J. F. C. Fuller, *A Military History of the Western World, vol. 1, From the Earliest Times to the Battle of Lepanto* (London, 1954), 339–50, and E. Creasy, *The Fifteen Decisive Battles of the World: From Marathon to Waterloo* (New York, 1908), 157–69.

European war making between A.D. 500 and 1000 is outlined in D. Nicolle, *Medieval Warfare: Source Book, vol. 2, Christian Europe and Its Neighbors* (New York, 1996), which has much comparative material. Perhaps the most accessible and analytical account is J. Beeler, *Warfare in Feudal Europe, 730–1200* (Ithaca, N.Y., 1971). General detail about arms and military service—albeit mostly after 1000—is easily accessed in a variety of standard handbooks, especially P. Contamine, *War in the Middle Ages* (London, 1984), and F. Lot, *L'Art militaire et les armées au moyen age en Europe et dans le proche orient,* 2 vols. (Paris, 1946), which has a list of German and French secondary sources that concern the battle. Cf. random mention also in M. Keen, ed., *Medieval Warfare* (Oxford, 1999); T. Wise, *Medieval Warfare* (New York, 1976); and A. V. B. Norman, *The Medieval Soldier* (New York, 1971). For the later warfare of the Franks and western Europeans, consult J. France, *Western Warfare in the Age of the Crusades, 1000–1300* (Ithaca, N.Y., 1999), and *Victory in the East: A Military History of the First Crusade* (Cambridge, 1994).

Valuable essays on the cultural aspects of medieval warfare are collected in D. Kagay and L. Andrew Villalon, eds., *The Circle of War in the Middle Ages: Essays on Medieval Military and Naval History* (Suffolk, England, 1999). There are a number of excellent illustrations in T. Newark, *The Barbarians: Warriors and Wars of the Dark Ages* (London, 1988).

Provocative ideas about the larger culture and history of Europe during the so-called Dark Ages are found in H. Pirenne, *Mohammed and Charlemagne* (London, 1939), and R. Hodges and D. Whitehouse, *Mohammed, Charlemagne, and the Origins of Europe: Archaeology and the Pirenne Thesis* (Ithaca, N.Y., 1983). For standard surveys of the intellectual cosmos of the Middle Ages in the West, begin with R. Dales, *The Intellectual Life of Western Europe in the Middle Ages* (Washington, D.C., 1980), and W. C. Bark, *Origins of the Medieval World* (Stanford, Calif., 1958). For more literary emphasis, see M. Golish, *Medieval Foundations of the Western Intellectual Tradition, 400–1400* (New Haven, Conn., 1997). See also the classic survey and standard view of the Dark Ages by C. Oman, *The Dark Ages, 476–918* (London, 1928).

The early history of Islam and the creation of an expansive Arab military culture are surveyed by P. Crone in *Slaves on Horses: The Evolution of the Islamic Polity*

(Cambridge, 1980), and *Meccan Trade and the Rise of Islam* (Princeton, N.J., 1987); cf. M. A. Shaban, *Islamic History, A.D. 600–750 (A.H. 132)* (Cambridge, 1971).

For the long-term significance of Poitiers, see the counterfactual speculations of B. Strauss, "The Dark Ages Made Lighter," in R. Cowley, ed., *What If?* (New York, 1998), 71–92.

Chapter Six: Technology and the Wages of Reason
Tenochtitlán, June 24, 1520–August 13, 1521

The conquest of Mexico has taken center stage in the contemporary academic cultural wars, especially concerning the use of evidence that is drawn mostly from either Spanish eyewitnesses or Spanish collections of Aztec oral narratives. Often scholars accept Spanish descriptions of the magnificence of Tenochtitlán and the beauty of its gardens, zoos, and markets, but reject outright the same authors' more gruesome accounts of cannibalism and systematic human immolation, sacrifice, and torture. European "constructs" and "paradigms" are considered inappropriate contexts in which to understand Aztec culture, even as Mexican art, architecture, and astronomical knowledge are praised in more or less classical aesthetic and scientific terms. Yet, our interests here are not in relative moral judgments, but in military efficacy, not so much the amorality of the conquistadors as the methods of their conquest.

We should remember also that our present argument for military dynamism based on technological preeminence is not always shared by Spanish accounts of the times, which quite wrongly emphasize the conquistadors' moral "superiority," innate intelligence, and Christian virtue.

There are a number of justifiably renowned narratives of the Spanish conquest. Perhaps unrivaled in its sheer power of description is still W. H. Prescott, *History of the Conquest of Mexico* (New York, 1843). For modern English readers, H. Thomas, *Conquest: Montezuma, Cortés, and the Fall of Old Mexico* (New York, 1993) is invaluable. See also R. C. Padden, *The Hummingbird and the Hawk: Conquest and Sovereignty in the Valley of Mexico, 1503–1541* (Columbus, Ohio, 1967). For some good comparative discussion, see also A. B. Bosworth, *Alexander and the East* (Oxford, 1996).

A plethora of contemporary and near contemporary accounts surrounds the conquest. Begin with the masterful narrative of Bernal Díaz del Castillo, *The Discovery and Conquest of Mexico, 1517–1521*, trans. A. P. Maudslay, (New York, 1956); the letters of Hernán Cortés, whose reliability has often been questioned (*Letters from Mexico*, trans. A. Pagden [New York, 1971]); and P. de Fuentes, *The Conquistadors: First-Person Accounts of the Conquest of Mexico* (New York, 1963).

For Aztec narratives and harsh criticism of the Spanish conquest, see Bernardino de Sahagún, *General History of the Things of New Spain: Florentine Codex, Book 12— The Conquest of Mexico,* trans. H. Cline (Salt Lake City, Utah, 1975), and the anthology edited by Miguel Leon-Portilla, *The Broken Spears: The Aztec Account of the Conquest of Mexico,* 2nd ed. (Boston, 1992). Cf. also Fernando de Alva Ixtlilxochitl, *Ally of Cortés* (El Paso, Tex., 1969).

Biographies of Cortés are innumerable; the most accessible are S. Madariaga, *Hernán Cortés: Conqueror of Mexico* (Garden City, N.Y., 1969), and J. M. White, *Cortés and the Downfall of the Aztec Empire: A Study in a Conflict of Cultures* (New York, 1971). The near contemporary hagiography by Francisco López de Gómara, *Cortés: The Life of the Conqueror by His Secretary* (Berkeley, Calif., 1964), contains much information not found elsewhere.

A specialized study of Spanish military practice of the sixteenth century can be found in G. Parker, *The Army of Flanders and the Spanish Road, 1567–1659: The Logistics of Spanish Victory and Defeat in the Low Countries' Wars* (Cambridge, 1972), and R. Martínez and T. Barker, eds., *Armed Forces in Spain Past and Present* (Boulder, Colo., 1988). On the general status of sixteenth- and seventeenth-century European warfare, see C. M. Cipolla, *Guns, Sails, and Empires: Technological Innovation and the Early Phases of European Expansion 1400–1700* (New York, 1965); J. Black, *European Warfare 1160–1815* (New Haven, Conn., 1994); and F. Tallett, *War and Society in Early-Modern Europe, 1495–1715* (London and New York, 1992). For the political and military position of Spain in the sixteenth century and the effect of its empire on its influence in Europe, see J. H. Elliott, *Spain and Its World, 1500–1700: Selected Essays* (New Haven, Conn., 1989), and R. Kagan and G. Parker, eds., *Spain, Europe and the Atlantic World: Essays in Honour of John H. Elliot* (Cambridge, 1995).

Ross Hassig has written a series of seminal books on Aztec warfare that seeks to explain the conquest from a Native American perspective: *Mexico and the Spanish Conquest* (London and New York, 1994); *Aztec Warfare: Political Expansion and Imperial Control* (Norman, Okla., 1988); and *War and Society in Ancient Mesoamerica* (Berkeley and Los Angeles, 1992). For larger questions of Aztec culture and society, consult P. Carasco, *The Tenocha Empire of Ancient Mexico: The Triple Alliance of Tenochtitlan, Tetzcoco, and Tlacopan* (Norman, Okla., 1999), and G. Collier, R. Rosaldo, and J. Wirth, *The Inca and Aztec States, 1400–1800: Anthropology and History* (New York, 1982).

The key role of the Spanish brigantines on Lake Texcoco is covered in C. H. Gardiner, *Naval Power in the Conquest of Mexico* (Austin, Tex., 1956), and his *Martín López: Conquistador Citizen of Mexico* (Lexington, Ky., 1958).

For cultural explanations that downplay the role of European tactics and technology in the conquest, see the article by G. Raudzens, "So Why Were the Aztecs Conquered, and What Were the Wider Implications? Testing Military Superiority as a Cause of Europe's Preindustrial Colonial Conquests," *War in History* 2.1 (1995), 87–104. Also see T. Todorov, *The Conquest of America: The Question of the Other* (New York, 1984); I. Clendinnen, *Ambivalent Conquests: Maya and Spaniard in Yucatan, 1517–1570* (Cambridge, 1987); and I. Clendinnen, *Aztecs: An Interpretation* (Cambridge, 1991). And for a critique of all such approaches, see K. Windschuttle, *The Killing of History: How Literary Critics and Social Theorists Are Murdering Our Past* (New York, 1997).

Chapter Seven: The Market—or Capitalism Kills
Lepanto, October 7, 1571

For centuries, accounts of Lepanto were cloaked in Christian triumphalism that emphasized the great relief in the West that the Turk was finally checked in his expansion across the Mediterranean. More recent study of the battle has been remarkably free of ideological bias. There still is absent, however, a single up-to-date scholarly monograph in English devoted entirely to the engagement itself. As a consequence, we often forget that aside from Salamis and Cannae, Lepanto may have been the single deadliest one-day slaughter in European history. Surely, in no other conflict have Westerners butchered more prisoners than did the Spanish and Italians in the aftermath of the battle, when most of the thousands of Turkish seamen lost their lives. The battle of Lepanto takes its place alongside the Somme and Cannae as a testament to man's ability to overcome the constraints of time and space in killing literally thousands of human beings in a few hours.

For complete accounts of the battle that discuss primary sources in Italian, Spanish, and Turkish, see G. Parker, *Spain and the Netherlands, 1559–1659* (Short Hills, N.J., 1979); D. Cantemir, *The History of the Growth and Decay of the Ottoman Empire,* trans. N. Tinda (London, 1734); A. Wiel, *The Navy of Venice* (London, 1910); and especially K. M. Setton, *The Papacy and the Levant (1204–1571), vol. 4, The Sixteenth Century from Julius III to Pius V* (Philadelphia, 1984). W. H. Prescott, *History of the Reign of Philip the Second,* vol. 4 (Philadelphia, 1904), has an engaging narrative of the battle. Other than disagreements over casualty numbers, the actual position of a few ships in the vicinity of the Greek coast, and the long-term strategic consequences of the victory, there is little major scholarly controversy concerning the actual events of the battle.

For more specialized assessments see A. C. Hess, "The Battle of Lepanto and Its Place in Mediterranean History," *Past and Present 57* (1972), 53–73, and especially M. Lesure, *Lépante: La crise de l'empire Ottomane* (Paris, 1971). There are also invaluable discussions of the strategy and tactics of Lepanto in the surveys of C. Oman, *A History of the Art of War in the Sixteenth Century* (New York, 1937); J. F. C. Fuller, *A Military History of the Western World, vol. 1, From the Earliest Times to the Battle of Lepanto* (London, 1954); and R. C. Anderson, *Naval Wars in the Levant, 1559–1853* (Princeton, N. J., 1952).

Lepanto and the primary sources for the battle are also the subjects of chapters in scholarly accounts of sixteenth-century warfare; see, for example, G. Hanlon, *The Twilight of a Military Tradition: Italian Aristocrats and European Conflicts, 1560–1800* (New York, 1998); J. F. Guilmartin, Jr., *Gunpowder and Galleys: Changing Technology and Mediterranean Warfare at Sea in the Sixteenth Century* (Cambridge, 1974); and W. L. Rodgers, *Naval Warfare Under Oars, 4th to 16th Centuries* (Annapolis, Md., 1967). There are good illustrations in R. Gardiner and J. Morrison, eds., *The Age of the Galley: Mediterranean Oared Vessels Since Pre-Classical Times* (Annapolis, Md., 1995).

See also F. C. Lane, *Venetian Ships and Shipbuilders of the Renaissance* (Westport, Conn., 1975).

A number of accessible narratives of the battle exists for the general reader, with good contemporary illustrations. See, for example, R. Marx, *The Battle of Lepanto, 1571* (Cleveland, Ohio, 1966), and J. Beeching, *The Galleys of Lepanto* (London, 1982). Valuable information about Lepanto can be found in biographies of Don Juan of Austria, especially the classic by W. Stirling-Maxwell, *Don John of Austria* (London, 1883), with its collation of contemporary sources; and see, too, the moving narrative of C. Petrie, *Don John of Austria* (New York, 1967). For the spectacular commemoration of the Christian victory in art and literature, see L. von Pastor, *The History of the Popes, from the Close of the Middle Ages* (London, 1923). An anthology, G. Benzoni, ed., *Il Mediterraneo nella Seconda Metà del '500 alla Luce di Lepanto* (Florence, 1974), has a perceptive article in English for the general reader on Ottoman sources of the conflict: H. Inalcik, "Lepanto in Ottoman Sources," 185–92.

For conditions of the Mediterranean economy and society in the sixteenth century, see D. Vaughan, *Europe and the Turk: A Pattern of Alliances* (New York, 1976); K. Karpat, ed., *The Ottoman State and Its Place in World History* (Leiden, 1974); and H. Koenigsberger and G. Mosse, *Europe in the Sixteenth Century* (New York, 1968). On questions of geography and capitalism, see especially the works of F. Braudel, *Civilization and Capitalism, 15th–18th Century: The Perspective of the World* (New York, 1979), and *The Mediterranean and the Mediterranean World in the Age of Philip II*, vol. 1 (New York, 1972). Cf., too, E. L. Jones, *The European Miracle: Environments, Economies, and Geopolitics in the History of Europe and Asia* (Cambridge, 1987).

For earlier Western military practice, see J. France, *Western Warfare in the Age of the Crusades, 1000–1300* (Ithaca, N.Y., 1999). More detailed accounts of the Turkish army and navy are found in R. Murphey, *Ottoman Warfare, 1500–1700* (New Brunswick, N.J., 1999). On the economy of Venice, see W. H. McNeill, *Venice: The Hinge of Europe, 1081–1797* (Chicago, 1974), and A. Tenenti, *Piracy and the Decline of Venice 1580–1615* (Berkeley and Los Angeles, 1967).

Ottoman military, social, and economic life is a vast field, but good introductions to the structure of the empire and its approach to finance and military expenditure are found in the sympathetic studies of H. Inalcik, *The Ottoman Empire: The Classical Age 1300–1600* (London, 1973); W. E. D. Allen, *Problems of Turkish Power in the Sixteenth Century* (London, 1963); S. Shaw, *History of the Ottoman Empire and Modern Turkey, vol. 1, Empire of the Gazas: The Rise and Decline of the Ottoman Empire, 1280–1808* (Cambridge, 1976). More recent general surveys are A. Wheatcroft, *The Ottomans* (New York, 1993), and J. McCarthy, *The Ottoman Turks: An Introductory History to 1923* (London, 1997).

The relationship between Islam and capitalism is a minefield of controversy, as Western critics on occasion emphasize the inherent restrictions on the market found under Muslim rule, even as Muslim scholars themselves often argue that there is nothing incompatible with free markets in the Islamic faith. For a review of the problems, see H. Islamoglu-Inan, ed., *The Ottoman Empire and the World-Economy* (Cambridge, 1987); M. Choudhury, *Contributions to Islamic Economic Theory* (London, 1986); and M. Abdul-Rauf, *A Muslim's Reflections on Democratic Capitalism*

(Washington, D.C., 1984). David Landes has written two excellent appraisals on the role of capitalism in East-West relations: *The Rise of Capitalism* (New York, 1966), and *The Unbound Prometheus: Technological Change and Industrial Development in Western Europe from 1750 to the Present* (Cambridge, 1969).

Chapter Eight: Discipline—or Warriors Are Not Always Soldiers
Rorke's Drift, January 22–23, 1879

There is a heavily footnoted official British history of the war that is a model of nine-teenth-century scholarship: *Narrative of Field Operations Connected with the Zulu War of 1879* (London, 1881). A number of fascinating memoirs were also published in connection with the war. The Zulu-speaking Henry Harford was attached to the Natal Native Contingent and was involved in the thick of the fighting of the center column; see D. Child, ed., *The Zulu War Journal of Colonel Henry Harford, C.B.,* (Hamden, Conn., 1980). A defense of Colonel Durnford, whose misguided deploy-ments may have lost Isandhlwana, together with a contemporary sympathetic ac-count of the Zulus, is found in F. E. Colenso (daughter of the bishop of Natal), *History of the Zulu War and Its Origin* (Westport, Conn., 1970). For an account written shortly after Isandhlwana and Rorke's Drift by a veteran of tribal wars in South Africa, see also T. Lucas, *The Zulus and the British Frontiers* (London, 1879). There is a small amount of information about the end of the Zulu War in the diaries of Sir Garnet Wolseley: A. Preston, ed., *The South African Journal of Sir Garnet Wolseley, 1879–1880* (Cape Town, 1973). More valuable is a memoir of a Boer translator employed by the Zulus, Cornelius Vign, whose diary was translated from the Dutch by Bishop J. W. Colenso: C. Vign, *Cetshwayo's Dutchman: Being the Private Journal of a White Trader in Zululand During the British Invasion* (New York, 1969).

J. Guy has written a sympathetic portrait of the fall and aftermath of the Zulu kingdom that makes much of the economic foundations of the war, specifically the exploitative nature of British and Boer colonial life: *The Destruction of the Zulu Kingdom: The Civil War in Zululand, 1879–1884* (Cape Town, 1979). See also C. F. Goodfellow, *Great Britain and South African Confederation, 1870–1881* (London, 1966), and especially J. P. C. Laband and P. S. Thompson, *Field Guide to the War in Zululand and the Defence of Natal 1879* (Pietermaritzburg, South Africa, 1983).

For a classic narrative of the rise of the Zulus and the Anglo-Zulu War of 1879, see D. Morris, *The Washing of the Spears: A History of the Rise of the Zulu Nation Under Shaka and Its Fall in the Zulu War of 1879* (New York, 1965). The major campaigns of the war are covered well by D. Clammer, *The Zulu War* (New York, 1973); M. Barthorp, *The Zulu War* (Poole, England, 1980), which contains invaluable illustra-tions; and A. Lloyd, *The Zulu War, 1879* (London, 1974). The most up-to-date ac-counts of the war is R. Edgerton, *Like Lions They Fought: The Zulu War and the Last Black Empire in South Africa* (New York, 1988), which has graphic accounts of the ac-tual fighting, and S. Clarke, ed., *Zululand at War: The Conduct of the Anglo-Zulu War* (Johannesburg, 1984).

There are a number of monographs devoted entirely to Rorke's Drift. Perhaps the best known is M. Glover, *Rorke's Drift: A Victorian Epic* (London, 1975), but there are also fascinating illustrations and photographs in J. W. Bancroft, *Terrible Night at Rorke's Drift* (London, 1988). See, too, R. Furneux, *The Zulu War: Isandhlwana and Rorke's Drift* (London, 1963).

The bibliography on Zulu culture and the brief existence of its empire is huge, but besides comprehensive accounts, there are accessible introductions in English to the main issues and problems. See the various surveys in J. Selby, *Shaka's Heirs* (London, 1971); A. T. Bryant's classic, *The Zulu People: As They Were Before the White Men Came* (New York, 1970); and J. Y. Gibson, *The Story of the Zulus* (New York, 1970). An American missionary, Josiah Tyler, has left a vivid narrative of Zulu life and customs in *Forty Years Among the Zulus* (Boston, 1891). Perhaps the best account of the Zulu army is I. Knight, *The Anatomy of the Zulu Army: From Shaka to Cetshwayo, 1818–1879* (London, 1995).

For a small sampling of the myriad of publications on the nineteenth-century British army, see G. Harries-Jenkins, *The Army in Victorian Society* (London, 1977); G. St. J. Barclay, *The Empire Is Marching* (London, 1976); T. Pakenham, *The Boer War* (New York, 1979); M. Carver, *The Seven Ages of the British Army* (New York, 1984); and J. Haswell, *The British Army: A Concise History* (London, 1975). For the importance of drill, see W. H. McNeill, *Keeping Together in Time: Dance and Drill in Human History* (Cambridge, Mass., 1995); and for the relationship of drill, bravery, and the nature of courage, see W. Miller, *The Mystery of Courage* (Cambridge, Mass., 2000).

For general accounts of the nature of tribal warfare, see B. Ferguson and N. L. Whitehead, eds., *War in the Tribal Zone: Expanding States and Indigenous Warfare* (Santa Fe, N.M., 1992); J. Haas, ed., *The Anthropology of War* (Cambridge, 1990); and especially H. H. Turney-High's classic, *Primitive War: Its Practice and Concepts* (Columbia, S.C., 1971).

Chapter Nine: Individualism
Midway, June 4–8, 1942

The battle of Midway has been the subject of several books, and often marks the "midway" chapter in comprehensive treatments of the Pacific theater of operations during World War II. For monographs on the battle itself, one should begin with G. Prange (assisted by D. Goldstein and K. Dillion), *Miracle at Midway* (New York, 1982), which covers the main problems. P. Frank and J. Harrington, *Rendezvous at Midway: U.S.S. Yorktown and the Japanese Carrier Fleet* (New York, 1967), has an analysis of the repair, return, and sinking of the *Yorktown* in the battle. Walter Lord's *Incredible Victory* (New York, 1967) is a well-written popular account that draws on firsthand oral and written interviews with both Japanese and American veterans of the battle. In addition, there are at least four general studies that largely describe the battle from the American side: A. Barker, *Midway: The Turning Point* (New York, 1971); R. Hough, *The Battle of Midway* (New York, 1970); W. W. Smith, *Midway: Turning Point of the Pacific* (New York, 1966); and I. Werstein, *The Battle of Midway* (New York, 1961).

For chapter treatments of Midway in general histories of the Pacific theater, still invaluable is Samuel Eliot Morison's *Coral Sea, Midway, and Submarine Actions, May 1942–August 1942*, vol. 4 of *History of United States Naval Operations in World War II* (New York, 1949); to be complemented by J. Costello, *The Pacific War, 1941–1945* (New York, 1981); and H. Willmott, *The Barrier and the Javelin: Japanese and Allied Pacific Strategies, February to June 1942* (Annapolis, Md., 1983). D. van der Vat, *The Pacific Campaign, World War II: The U.S.-Japanese Naval War, 1941–45*, has a good general review of the battle with invaluable observations from the Japanese side. In John Keegan's *The Price of Admiralty: The Evolution of Naval Warfare* (New York, 1989), Midway is discussed as representative of the gradual diminution of the battleship in favor of the aircraft carrier. R. Overy, *Why the Allies Won* (New York, 1996), also has some astute pages devoted to the battle that emphasize Japanese advantages in weapons and experience. The importance of American intelligence operations is discussed in D. Kahn, *The Codebreakers: The Story of Secret Writing* (New York, 1996), and R. Lewin, *The American Magic: Codes, Cyphers and the Defeat of Japan* (New York, 1982).

There are a number of helpful photographs, drawings, charts, tables, and statistics that concern the Japanese navy in A. Watts and B. Gordon, *The Imperial Japanese Navy* (Garden City, N.Y., 1971), and J. Dunnigan and A. Nofi, *Victory at Sea: World War II in the Pacific* (New York, 1995).

Two veterans of the Midway-Aleutian campaign, M. Fuchida and M. Okumiya, in *Midway, the Battle That Doomed Japan: The Japanese Navy's Story* (Annapolis, Md., 1955), wrote a riveting memoir from the Japanese side, which is balanced and reflective throughout. M. Okumiya and J. Horikoshi, along with M. Caidin (*Zero!* [New York, 1956]), discuss Midway in the context of the Pacific naval air war. Equally interesting is the diary of M. Ugaki, *Fading Victory: The Diary of Admiral Matome Ugaki, 1941–45* (Pittsburgh, Pa., 1991). There is an anthology of Japanese eye-witness accounts on the major naval encounters of the Pacific theater in D. Evans, ed., *The Japanese Navy in World War II in the Words of Former Naval Officers* (Annapolis, Md., 1986).

There are also fine chapters from the Japanese point of view in R. O'Connor, *The Imperial Japanese Navy in World War II* (Annapolis, Md., 1969); P. Dull, *A Battle History of the Imperial Japanese Navy* (Annapolis, Md., 1978); E. Andrie, *Death of a Navy: Japanese Naval Action in World War II* (New York, 1957); and J. Toland, *The Rising Sun: The Decline and Fall of the Japanese Empire, 1936–1945*, 2 vols. (New York, 1970).

Much of the battle can be learned from biographies of the opposing supreme commanders. See H. Agawa, *The Reluctant Admiral: Yamamoto and the Imperial Navy* (Annapolis, Md., 1979); J. Potter, *Yamamoto: The Man Who Menaced America* (New York, 1965); T. Buell, *The Quiet Warrior: A Biography of Admiral Raymond A. Spruance* (Boston, 1974); and E. Hoyt, *How They Won the War in the Pacific: Nimitz and His Admirals* (New York, 1970).

A number of books discuss the process of Westernization in Japan. See, in general, S. Eisenstadt, *Japanese Civilization: A Comparative View* (Chicago, 1995); and M. and S. Harries, *Soldiers of the Sun: The Rise and Fall of the Imperial Japanese Army, 1868–1945* (New York, 1991). A more academic and detailed appraisal is found in J.

Arnason, *Social Theory and Japanese Experience: The Dual Civilization* (London and New York, 1997). The specifics of Japan's adaptation of Western military practice and European technology during the nineteenth century are found in E. L. Presseisen, *Before Aggression: Europeans Prepare the Japanese Army* (Tucson, Ariz., 1965); R. P. Dore, *Land Reform in Japan* (London, 1959); and especially S. P. Huntington, *The Soldier and the State: The Theory and Politics of Civil-Military Relations* (Cambridge, Mass., 1957).

On the history of the Japanese military and Japan's cultural assumptions in the organization and practice of war, see T. Cleary, *The Japanese Art of War: Understanding the Culture of Strategy* (Boston, 1991), and R. J. Smethurst, *A Social Basis for Prewar Japanese Militarism: The Army and the Rural Community* (Berkeley and Los Angeles, 1974). Robert Edgerton, *Warriors of the Rising Sun: A History of the Japanese Military* (New York, 1997), provides a good discussion of Japanese behavior toward conquered peoples and captives, and suggests that the 1930–45 period of brutality may have been an aberration in the long history of Japanese military practice.

Chapter Ten: Dissent and Self-Critique
Tet, January 31–April 6, 1968

More has been written on Vietnam than perhaps on all the other battles of this volume combined, no doubt reflecting the wealth and influence of American media and publishing, and the somewhat self-absorption of the present generation of Americans who grew up in the aftermath of World War II. Obvious differences exist over the conduct of the Vietnam War, but increasingly they seem predicated more on chronology than ideology. Much of what was published between 1965 and 1978 is hostile to the American presence and strategy, either the work of leftist critics who emphasize the inhumanity of the United States' presence, or of more conservative scholars who cite military ineptitude coupled with weak political leadership.

But by the early 1980s—after the absence of free elections in a unified Vietnam, the mass exodus from Vietnam by the boat people, the Cambodian holocaust, the Soviet invasion of Afghanistan, and the Iran hostage crisis—there was a gradual but unmistakable shift in perceptions about Vietnam. While most Americans still agreed that the war had been fought wrongly, and perhaps unnecessarily, a good many argued that nevertheless the cause was more right than wrong, and the war could have been won with the right decisive military strategy. There was a confident air among revisionists who felt history had somehow proved them right, and a worried, if sometimes apologetic, stance by most earlier vehement critics, some of whom had visited North Vietnam, praised the communist regimes of Southeast Asia, and broadcast on radio propaganda against U.S. soldiers in the field.

For a synopsis on various topics of research, see J. S. Olson, *The Vietnam War: Handbook of the Literature and Research* (Westport, Conn., 1993), and R. D. Burns and M. Leitenberg, *The Wars in Vietnam, Cambodia, and Laos, 1945–1982* (Santa Barbara, Calif., 1983). For Tet itself, begin with the somewhat dated but still invaluable monograph by D. Oberdorfer, *Tet!* (New York, 1971). There are some insightful essays on the offensive collected in M. J. Gilbert and W. Head, eds., *The Tet Offensive* (Westport, Conn., 1996). See also W. Pearson, *Vietnam Studies: The War in the Northern Provinces, 1966–8* (Washington, D.C., 1975). There are also good chapters on the Tet Offensive in standard histories of the battle, e.g., S. Stanton, *The Rise and Fall of an American Army: U.S. Ground Forces in Vietnam, 1965–1973* (Novato, Calif., 1985). P. Braestrup's massive two-volume study of the coverage of Tet remains a damning portrait of the American media: P. Braestrup, *Big Story: How the American Press and Television Reported and Interpreted the Crisis of Tet 1968 in Vietnam and Washington* (Boulder, Colo., 1977). Some interesting maps and illustrations of the Tet Offensive are found in J. Arnold, *Tet Offensive 1968: Turning Point in Vietnam* (London, 1990).

For the failures of United States intelligence to give an accurate prediction of the Tet surprise, see R. F. Ford, *Tet 1968: Understanding the Surprise* (London, 1995), who blames the political infighting among intelligence agencies that resulted in failure to make proper use of the excellent raw data that were gathered. There are some invaluable essays on the war and especially the role of airpower during Tet in D. Showalter and J. G. Albert, *An American Dilemma: Vietnam, 1964–1973* (Chicago, 1993); for military operations in the aftermath of Tet, see R. Spector, *After Tet: The Bloodiest Year in Vietnam* (New York, 1993).

For statistics about the soldiers who fought in Vietnam—age, economic background, type of service, race, casualty ratios, etc.—see T. Thayer, *War Without Fronts: The American Experience in Vietnam* (Boulder, Colo., 1985); and for misconceptions about Vietnam veterans: E. T. Dean, *Shook Over Hell: Post-Traumatic Stress, Vietnam, and the Civil War* (Norman, Okla., 1989). Some of the political intrigue in Washington that surrounded Tet is discussed in T. Hoopes, *The Limits of Intervention: An Inside Account of How the Johnson Policy of Escalation in Vietnam Was Reversed* (New York, 1973), who devotes a chapter to the offensive.

Reasons for the American loss in Vietnam are examined carefully by J. Record, *The Wrong War: Why We Lost in Vietnam* (Annapolis, Md., 1998)—mostly military ineptitude and the absence of political and strategic reasons for being there in the first place. G. Lewy, *America in Vietnam* (New York, 1978); L. Sorley, *A Better War: The Unexamined Victories and Final Tragedy of America's Last Years in Vietnam* (New York, 1999); and M. Lind, *Vietnam, the Necessary War: A Reinterpretation of America's Most Disastrous Military Conflict* (New York, 1999), all mention the misrepresentations of Tet as part of larger efforts to correct the standard wisdom that Vietnam was not winnable and was morally wrong—as represented perhaps best by the popular accounts of S. Karnow, *Vietnam: A History* (New York, 1983), and N. Sheehan, *A Bright Shining Lie: John Paul Vann and America in Vietnam* (New York, 1988).

Tet looms large in various collections of primary documents, speeches, and articles that are designed as readers for university courses; the editors of such anthologies adopt a critical approach to America's intervention and the military's conduct in general in Vietnam. See J. Werner and D. Hunt, eds., *The American War in Vietnam* (Ithaca, N.Y., 1993); G. Sevy, ed., *The American Experience in Vietnam: A Reader* (Norman, Okla., 1989); M. Gettleman et al., eds., *Vietnam and America: A Documented History* (New York, 1995); and J. Rowe and R. Berg, eds., *The American*

War and American Culture (New York, 1991). More balanced collections of documents are found (through 1965) in M. Raskin and B. Fall, eds., *The Vietnam Reader: Articles and Documents on American Foreign Policy and the Viet-Nam Crisis* (New York, 1965), and H. Salisbury, ed., *Vietnam Reconsidered: Lessons from a War* (New York, 1994). For favorable accounts of those protesters who went to North Vietnam, see M. Hershberger, *Traveling to Vietnam: American Peace Activists and the War* (Syracuse, N.Y., 1998), and J. Clinton, *The Loyal Opposition: Americans in North Vietnam, 1965–1972* (Boulder, Colo., 1995).

There are also numerous recent narratives of the twenty-six-day, house-to-house fighting at Hué, many of them memoirs by veterans of the ordeal. See N. Warr, *Phase Line Green: The Battle for Hue, 1968* (Annapolis, Md., 1997); K. Nolan, *Battle for Hue, Tet, 1968* (Novato, Calif., 1983); G. Smith, *The Siege of Hue* (Boulder, Colo., 1999); and E. Hammel, *Fire in the Streets: The Battle for Hue, Tet 1968* (Chicago, 1991). On Khesanh, see the moving narrative of J. Prados and R. Stubbe, *Valley of Decision: The Siege of Khe Sanh* (New York, 1991), and cf. R. Pisor, *The Siege of Khe Sanh* (New York, 1982). The role of airpower in the siege is well chronicled in B. Nalty, *Air Power and the Fight for Khe Sanh* (Washington, D.C., 1973), published by the Office of Air Force History.

There are good revisionist, strongly opinionated memoirs written shortly after the war by some of the principal American military figures involved. Start with W. C. Westmoreland, *A Soldier Reports* (New York, 1976); M. Taylor, *Swords and Plowshares* (New York, 1972); and U. S. Sharp, *Strategy for Defeat: Vietnam in Retrospect* (New York, 1978).

Index